CASES IN STRATEGIC MARKETING

DAVID ROSENTHAL
Miami University

LEW G. BROWN
University of North Carolina at Greensboro

Prentice Hall
Upper Saddle River, NJ 07458

Acquisitions Editor: Whitney Blake
Editorial Assistant: Anthony Palmiotto
Editor-in-Chief: James Boyd
Marketing Manager: Shannon Moore
Production Editor: Lynne Breitfeller
Managing Editor: Bruce Kaplan
Manufacturing Buyer: Lynne Breitfeller
Production Manager: Gail Steier de Acevedo
Manufacturing Manager: Vincent Scelta
Design Manager: Patricia Smythe
Illustrator: D. K. Kohn Design
Composition: Omegatype Typography, Inc.

ISBN: 0-13-086359-9

Prentice-Hall International (UK) Limited, London
Prentice-Hall of Australia Pty. Limited, Sydney
Prentice-Hall Canada, Inc., Toronto
Prentice-Hall Hispanoamericana, S.A., Mexico
Prentice-Hall of India Private Limited, New Delhi
Prentice-Hall of Japan, Inc., Tokyo
Simon & Schuster Asia Pte. Ltd., Singapore
Editoria Prentice-Hall do Brasil, Ltda., Rio de Janeiro

Printed in the United States of America

10 9 8 7 6 5 4 3 2 1

To my wife Addie and my children Neal and Lauren thanks for your love and support.

To Joyce, Dana, and Lauren Brown with thanks for your love and support.

We would like to express our appreciation to the numerous companies that have cooperated in developing these cases and to the colleagues who have worked with us as co-authors, reviewers, and advisors.

Contents

Part I Segmentation and Buyer Behavior

1. West Point Market 1
2. Trap-Ease America 11
3. The Cottages Resort and Conference Center 15
4. Polaroid and the Family Imaging Market 37
5. Multicon, Inc. 61
6. Smith's Home Foods 77
7. The Greensboro Housing Authority 83

Part II Industry Structure and Competitive Analysis

8. Sidethrusters 97
9. Gillette and the Men's Shaving Market 109
10. Enterprise Rent-A-Car: Selling the Dream 135
11. Scotia Aqua-Farms 141
12. Anheuser-Busch Dominates in the 1990's 157
13. American Greetings Faces New Challenges in the 1990's 185
14. Shades of Black 201
15. Supportive HomeCare: Positioning for the 1990's 215
16. Lowe's Companies, Battling Home Depot 231

Part III International

17. Kodak versus Fuji 239
18. Ito-Yokado Company 255

Part IV Product

19. Verbatim Challenges 3M for Market Leadership 281
20. Broderbund Software 297
21. Baxter: Scientific Products Division 323

Part V Price

22. Alma Products, Inc. 341
23. Southwestern Ohio Steel 345

Part VI Promotion

24. Jefferson-Pilot Corporation 357

25. Replacements Limited 381

26. Miami University: The Redskins Name Controversy 403

27. The O'Henry Hotel 413

Part VII Supply Chain and Distribution

28. FieldPro Manufacturing Company 429

29. Johnson & Quin: The Carling Printing and Graphics Decision 437

30. The David J. Joseph Company: The Henderson Shredder Project 455

31. Icon Acoustics: Bypassing Tradition 469

32. Chemical Additives Corporation—Specialty Products Group 473

33. Thai Chempest 487

Part VIII Ethics and Social Responsibility

34. Southwestern Ohio Steel, LP: The Matworks Decision 497

35. Starbucks Coffee Company: The Dorosin Issue 503

36. Hoechst-Roussel Pharmaceuticals, Inc.: RU486 513

Part IX Comprehensive Cases

37. Intermark: Designing UNICEF's Oral Rehydration Program in Zambia 529

38. Chateau des Charmes Wines, LTD 547

39. Schweppes Raspberry Ginger Ale 563

Appendices

Appendix A: Analyzing Strategic Marketing Cases 575

Appendix B: Financial Analysis for Marketing Strategists 589

Appendix C: Presenting Marketing Cases Orally 601

Preface

Strategic marketing creates competitive advantage. Those organizations that understand the role and practice the processes of strategic marketing gain an advantage over those organizations that do not. Strategic marketing is the central activity of a modern enterprise. Strategic marketing requires an articulation of the organization's vision, mission, objectives, and culture. More than any other organizational activity, strategic marketing defines and maintains the desired relationship between the organization and its environment. Strategic marketing specifies the customer base, develops an understanding of customer needs and behaviors, accounts for the activities and initiatives of competition, and evaluates the economic, social and cultural, international, legal and political, and technological environments. In response to the conditions external to the organization, strategic marketing molds the organization, determines product and production specifications, pricing, promotional activity, and distribution, indicates financial requirements, and dictates needed human skills. Strategic marketing defines the role of the organization.

Fitting the organization to the needs of the environment has never been more critical. The rate of change in the environment has accelerated. At no previous time have organizations faced a more turbulent, confusing, and threatening set of conditions. Impetus for significant change will come from many sources, including government, international and domestic economic and market forces, demographic shifts and lifestyle changes, and structural evolution of many industries. Marketers will have to anticipate and understand the complex interactions of these changes if they are to develop effective programs to position their organizations in the most advantageous manner.

A course in marketing strategy must be directed toward preparing students to enter this complex decision-making environment. Much of the coursework in the business curriculum is devoted to exposing students to the concepts, definitions, and models that comprise "best practice" in the business world, but at a theoretical level. It is the role of a course in marketing strategy to bring together the tools and processes described in other classes and forge them into a unified and systematic approach to problem solving and decision making. To accomplish this task, students are required to develop a comprehensive framework that enables them to apply independent critical intelligence and to make judgments in a complex world of different and competing points of view.

The use of cases encourages students to practice their analytical and decision-making skills and to develop a practical, comprehensive framework. The case approach provides a practice arena in which students may integrate and apply their marketing knowledge to gain experience. Students are called upon to apply their knowledge to many different types of organizations in many situations, thereby providing them exposure and wisdom beyond their current level of personal experience. Therefore, this edition of *Cases in Strategic Marketing* includes case studies that provide a variety of strategic marketing situations that cover the spectra of large and small, public and private, product and service, domestic and international companies. It also includes appendices covering case analysis, financial analysis, and oral presentations. Following this preface is a table containing the companies featured in the cases.

THE CASE APPROACH

In order to effectively use cases, it is essential that both students and instructors understand the nature of case studies and the teaching objectives of cases. A case typically is an accurate, historical record of a business situation that actually has been faced by business executives. It is, to the best abilities of the case researchers and writers, a reflection of the sum of the information available to the executive(s) who had to make the decision, including the surrounding facts, opinions, and prejudices on which executive decisions frequently have to depend.

A case study attempts to vicariously place students into a managerial position in which they will have to "size up" the situation and suggest some action for the organization. The action is typically a plan (set of decisions) that addresses the key issues of the case. Therefore, the case most often provides some degree or focus for the student, as well as some discussion of the environment, in order to develop the decision-making situation.

The objective of the case approach is not for students to develop "right" solutions, or rote knowledge, that they will be able to apply in a future situation. Rather, the case approach provides students with a perspective concerning the complexity of the issues that organizations face, practice in discerning the critical issues, application of theory, an understanding of the interrelated complexity of business functions, and discussion concerning important issues faced by modern enterprises. Case studies provide students with an in-depth learning experience in a given business situation that is difficult to obtain elsewhere.

THE CASEBOOK

This casebook is designed to be used in upper-level marketing strategy and marketing management courses. Marketing strategy or marketing management is usually the capstone course in marketing and is typically required for all marketing majors and minors. The general objective of the capstone course is to pull together marketing theory and practice into a broad understanding of marketing and its application. Other courses in marketing provide an overview of marketing, as in the principles of marketing course, or an in-depth study of various functional areas, such as sales management, advertising, pricing, channels, and so on. The marketing strategy or marketing management course asks students to solve problems and develop comprehensive marketing strategies in situations that are not clearly predetermined as promotional, segmentation, or channels of distribution. Utilizing a top-management perspective, students must consider all of an organization's systems and their interrelationships in developing marketing recommendations.

The Cases

The marketing case studies developed and chosen for this casebook offer students a broad exposure to a cross section of strategic marketing solutions. Each of the 39 cases included in this casebook has been extensively classroom tested. They were chosen for inclusion to be pedagogically sound, appealing to students, stimulating to teach, and on target with respect to the leading problems and issues in strategic marketing.

All of the cases included in this book are concerned with real companies, although a few are disguised at the company's request. They are supported with extensive industry information to provide the background material necessary to understand and assess an organization's competitors and markets. All of the cases are decision focused.

Among the 39 cases, 17 deal with well-known national organizations, eight with moderately sized regional companies, 11 are small businesses, and 11 involve international firms. The cases are all multidimensional and comprehensive in that all of the marketing functional areas, as well as the target market, must be considered in the analysis of each case. More than 30 of the cases require significant financial analysis, 14 deal with some form of entrepreneurship, and 10 cases involve significant consideration of ethical issues.

The Appendices

In an effort to assist students in the development of their frameworks, three appendices are included. The first appendix provides an orientation to case analysis and presents a practical analytical framework for addressing strategic marketing issues (Appendix A—Analyzing Strategic Marketing Cases). The second appendix presents the fundamentals for financial analysis (Appendix B—Financial Analysis for Marketing Strategists). The third appendix (Appendix C—Presenting Marketing Cases Orally) assists the student in developing and making oral presentations. These appendices are designed to help students when initially approaching case analysis and to lend some structure to the process of marketing analysis. Because some instructors prefer a different format for case analysis, these sections have been placed after the cases. Therefore, the instructor can assign those appendices considered appropriate to his or her personal teaching style. In addition, with this approach, instructors have the flexibility of using the case-only approach or supplementing the casebook with their own materials, a collection of strategic marketing readings, or a traditional textbook.

ACKNOWLEDGMENTS

We are deeply indebted to many individuals for their assistance and encouragement in the preparation of this casebook. First, we would like to thank Linda Swayne and Peter Ginter, who were instrumental in developing the structure of the book, and in providing several of the cases included. We also wish to thank the appendix contributors—W. Jack Duncan (Appendix A), Bennie H. Nunnally, Jr. (Appendix B), Gary F. Kohut and Carol M. Baxter (Appendix C). Their work provides practical structure and supporting content to students in their search for a well-crafted framework, as well as guidance in effective communication. We would also like to thank our reviewers—Henry C. K. Chen, University of West Florida, and Kathleen Krentler, San Diego State University.

Finally, this book would not have been possible without the case writers and the organizations about which they have written. Typically, the organizations have given a great deal of time to contribute to the education of tomorrow's business leaders. Case writing is a difficult art requiring many hours of library research, personal interviews, and detailed analysis. The case contributors listed in this text represent some of the finest case researchers anywhere. Many of the case writers are members of the North American Case Research Association (NACRA) and/or the Society for Case Research

(SCR). Both organizations contribute extensively to the quality of the cases developed by their members and we recognize that without them, many of the cases in this book would not have been written, or not nearly so well.

David W. Rosenthal and Lew G. Brown

BIOGRAPHIES

David W. Rosenthal is Associate Professor of Marketing at the Richard T. Farmer School of Business Administration, Miami University, Oxford, Ohio. He holds a BS in Economics from the Wharton School at the University of Pennsylvania, an MBA from Southern Illinois University, Edwardsville, and a DBA from the Darden School at the University of Virginia. Dr. Rosenthal teaches and consults in the areas of strategic marketing and sales management, and he conducts focus group research across a broad variety of topics. He has been recognized as an outstanding teacher and has been awarded Miami's Effective Educator Award, and is the sole recipient of the university's prestigious Philip R. Shriver Award for Sustained Excellence in Teaching.

Dr. Rosenthal is a member of the North American Case Research Association (NACRA) where he served as President in 1995. He has published four cases in the association's *Case Research Journal* and has three times been runner up for the Curtis E. Tate, Jr. Award for the Outstanding Case presented at NACRA's annual meetings. Dr. Rosenthal serves on the Editorial Review Board for the *Case Research Journal*. He is also a member of the Society for Case Research (SCR) and serves on its board of directors. He has published three cases in the association's *Annual Advances in Business Cases*. His cases have appeared in numerous textbooks and electronic case databases.

Lew G. Brown is Associate Professor of Marketing in the Department of Business Administration, Joseph M. Bryan School of Business and Economics, University of North Carolina at Greensboro. He holds a BA in Political Science, a Masters of Public Administration, a Masters of Business Administration, and a Ph.D. in Marketing, all from the University of North Carolina at Chapel Hill. Dr. Brown teaches and consults in the areas of marketing management and strategic marketing, and he conducts research on the subject of convenience as a strategic and tactical marketing variable. Students and colleagues have recognized his outstanding teaching by awarding him UNCG's Alumni Teaching Excellence Award and the Bryan School's Outstanding Faculty Award. He also serves as the Bryan School's Director of Undergraduate Programs.

Dr. Brown is a member of the North American Case Research Association (NACRA) and serves as its Vice President for Programs. He has published eight cases in the association's *Case Research Journal* and has twice won the prestigious Curtis E. Tate, Jr., Award for the Outstanding Case presented at NACRA's annual meetings. Dr. Brown serves on the Editorial Review Board for the *Case Research Journal*, and received the Journal's Outstanding Reviewer Award for 1999. He also writes the company cases for Philip Kotler and Gary Armstrong's *Principles of Marketing* textbooks. His cases have appeared in numerous textbooks and electronic case databases.

COMPANIES FEATURED IN THE CASES

	domestic	entrepeneur	government organizaton	international	large company	local company	new product	private	product	public	service	small company	technology
1. West Point Market	x								x			x	
2. Trap-Ease America	x								x			x	
3. The Cottages Resort and Conference Center	x										x	x	
4. Polaroid and the Family Imaging Market	x				x		x			x			
5. Multicon, Inc.		x										x	x
6. Smith's Home Foods						x		x	x				
7. The Greensboro Housing Authority	x		x								x		
8. Sidethrusters		x							x			x	
9. Gillette and the Wet–Men's Shaving Market					x		x						
10. Enterprise Rent-A-Car: Selling the Dream	x				x						x		
11. Scotia Aqua-Farms	x								x			x	
12. Anheuser-Busch Dominates in the 1990's				x	x				x	x			
13. American Greetings Faces New Challenges in the 1990's				x	x				x	x			
14. Shades of Black	x								x	x		x	
15. Supportive HomeCare: Positioning for the 1990's						x					x		
16. Lowe's Companies: Battling Home Depot	x				x				x				
17. Kodak versus Fuji				x	x				x				
18. Ito-Yokado Company				x	x				x	x			
19. Verbatim Challenges 3M for Market Leadership					x				x	x			
20. Broderbund Software				x					x	x			x
21. Baxter: Scientific Products Division				x					x	x			
22. Alma Products, Inc.		x								x		x	
23. Southwestern Ohio Steel						x					x		
24. Jefferson-Pilot Corporation	x				x					x	x		
25. Replacements Ltd.	x				x				x				
26. Miami University: The Redskins Name Controversy	x									x	x		
27. The O'Henry Hotel	x					x					x		

(Continued on next page)

(Continued)

	domestic	entrepeneur	government organizaton	international	large company	local company	new product	private	product	public	service	small company	technology
28. FieldPro Manufacturing Company	x								x	x			
29. Johnson & Quin: The Carling Printing and Graphics Decision									x	x	x	x	
30. The David J. Joseph Company: The Henderson Shredder Project	x								x				x
31. Icon Acoustics: Bypassing Tradition	x	x										x	x
32. Chemical Additives Corporation—Specialty Products Group					x		x			x			
33. Thai Chempest				x	x				x				
34. Southwestern Ohio Steel, LP: The Matworks Decision										x	x		
35. Starbucks Coffee Company: The Dorosin Issue					x					x	x		
36. Hoechst-Roussel Pharmaceuticals, Inc.: RU486				x			x		x				
37. Intermark: Designing UNICEF's Oral Rehydration Program in Zambia				x						x			
38. Chateau des Charmes Wines, LTD				x							x		
39. Schweppes Raspberry Ginger Ale				x	x		x						

West Point Market: The Potential for Expansion

J. B. Wilkinson and Gary B. Frank

As Russ Vernon, owner/manager of West Point Market, pushed open the door to his store, he could hear the Sunday morning cleaning crew hard at work. The mechanical drone of their sweepers and buffers moving to the beat of rock-a-billy music was a sharp contrast to West Point's normal business day sounds of classical music, customer chatter, and the rolling rattle of grocery shopping carts. As usual, Russ stopped to greet several of the crew before stepping down to his basement office, but on this particular day he cut the chit-chat short because he could hardly wait to look at the proposed plan for a new and expanded West Point Market. Jackie Long from Peterson/Raeder Architects had dropped the plans off the previous day. However, Russ had been too busy managing the typical "Saturday in West Point" problem to even glance at them. He now wanted to spread them out and carefully consider the project as a whole—cost, design concepts, merchandise plan, employees, customers, and risk.

BACKGROUND

West Point Market was founded in 1936 by Russ Vernon's father and two other partners. It had been a neighborhood meat market that also sold cheese. The original store had only 3,000 square feet of floor space and was located in a congested urban area. In 1941 the store doubled its size by moving to its present location, 1711 West Market Street, which borders a very affluent neighborhood in Akron, Ohio. Between 1941 and 1960, the store developed into a "quality food store" serving higher-income shoppers who wanted premium brands and high-quality meats and produce.

Russ Vernon entered the business in 1960 as a stock clerk and "learned the business from the bottom up!" By 1978 Russ had become sole shareholder and president, a status that enabled him to embark on an ambitious program of expansion and innovation designed to change the strategic direction of West Point Market.

Throughout the 1970s, Russ had experimented with gourmet merchandising in several product categories, such as wine, cheese, crackers, candy, coffee, and condiments. Customers had responded enthusiastically to items like raspberry vinegar, Canadian Black Diamond Cheddar, Fox's Mustard from upstate New York, and David

This case was prepared by Professor J. B. Wilkinson of Youngstown State University and Professor Gary B. Frank of The University of Akron, as a basis for class discussion. It is not intended to illustrate either effective or ineffective handling of an administrative situation.

Copyright © 1992 by the Case Research Journal and J. B. Wilkinson. ISBN 0-13-017095-X.

Berg hotdogs. The financial impact was also favorable—gourmet items had higher markups, which translated into higher gross and net profit margins.

By the late 1970s, Russ was convinced that West Point Market needed to position itself as an upscale, gourmet food store. Food retailing in Akron, Ohio, had become intensely competitive. Competitive survival would depend on West Point's ability to build and retain a loyal customer base that would be relatively insensitive to the low-price appeals of conventional supermarket chains. To do this, West Point Market would have to offer a greater variety of specialty products throughout the store and provide gourmet-to-go food. West Point's customer base was heavily dominated by two-income families and professionals who demanded convenience, quality, and service. A number of customers had asked for greater selection and better quality in the deli and bread departments. The small number of prepared foods available in the deli area were very popular, and requests for more items were a daily occurrence.

In 1980 Russ expanded the store to 13,800 square feet (10,500 square feet selling space). The additional space created by the expansion was used to establish a prepared foods department called "The Movable Feast," to house heavy-duty ovens for baking a few European specialty breads, and to enlarge the cheese and wine departments. The Movable Feast was an overwhelming success. Offering items such as asparagus lasagna, cheese-filled tortellini with ham in mustard vinaigrette, and white-meat chicken dressed in tarragon-flavored mayonnaise, it earned national recognition in 1985 when Russ was awarded the Silver Spoon Award from the National Association for the Specialty Food Trade. Also, with more than 350 cheese selections and 2,220 different wines, West Point Market became the premier place in Akron to shop for party food.

After the 1980 expansion, Russ began to experiment with special promotions, especially those that could increase visibility and enhance the image of West Point as an exciting, upscale store. Russ wanted to make West Point a *destination* for shoppers—perhaps even an entertainment—rather than a stop on the way to somewhere else. To this end, weekly sampling of cheeses, wines, and coffee were augmented by promotional events such as a high tea, complete with bagpipers, for a British products promotion or a brass band playing Sousa marches during a "United Tastes of America" event. Russ also developed a six-page newsletter that is mailed quarterly to more than 5,000 local West Point customers. The newsletter highlights upcoming West Point events and features columns on wine and cheese, menus and recipes using gourmet products, and in-depth articles on food (i.e., the nuances of olive oil). Also, to appeal to value-conscious shoppers, Russ started a weekly bag stuffer promoting special price reductions on pricey products like 98-cent "killer" brownies or deep-dish seafood quiche for $3.98 a slice.

By 1986, West Point Market had gained a reputation throughout the Akron area as a specialty food store. Annual sales had increased from $3 million to $5.4 million over a five-year period. Moreover, such spectacular growth was achieved in the midst of a vicious price war among Akron grocery chains early in 1986 that caused several national chain stores to exit the Akron market.

THE COMPETITIVE ENVIRONMENT

The competitive structure for food retailing in Akron was highly concentrated and price-oriented. The recent price war between major supermarket chains in Akron had forced most supermarkets to lower prices and operate on lower margins. Gross profit margins and weekly sales per square foot of selling space were only now beginning to approach national supermarket norms (21 percent to 22 percent and $7.48, respectively). However, industry observers were optimistic about the future. Reductions in store capacity (square footage) and number of competitors appeared to have eased competitive pressures; triple couponing, predatory pricing tactics, and excessive promotional gimmicks looked to be a thing of the past. Competitive rivalry seemed to be more predictable and less nasty.

In terms of market concentration, the Acme/Click chain held a 32 percent market share in the Akron Primary Statistical Area (PMSA) (Exhibit 1). Acme/Click stores followed a combination store format (food and general merchandise) and offered buyers a wide variety of food products, including private labels, generics, ethnic specialties, and upscale produce, meats, seafood, deli, and bakery items at reasonable prices. The largest and newest Acme/Click was only a few blocks down the street from West Point Market. It was a large facility (more than 75,000 square feet) that also leased space to noncompeting services such as postal, banking, travel, floral, photo, health/beauty, cleaning, and tailoring. Giant Eagle, Apples, and Finast accounted for another 32 percent of Akron area sales and competed on the basis of a superstore format (more than 30,000 square feet of typical grocery items). Twin Value had just entered the Akron market as a hypermarket (food, pharmacy, general merchandise, hardware, appliances, and home repair). IGA, Sparkle, and Carl's were relatively small, conventional supermarkets (less than 20,000 square feet) with a "neighborhood clientele."

EXHIBIT 1   Competitive Profile for Food Retailing, Akron PMSA[a]

| | Counties | | |
	Summit	Portage	Total
Population			
Households	186,144	50,315	236,456
Adults	376,050	105,294	481,344
Food Stores[b]			
Number	367	92	459
Sales ($1000s/year)	$699,955	$136,377	$836,332
Square Feet/Selling Area	1,790,000	348,000	2,138,000
Market Shares[c]			
Acme/Click (12)[d]	—	—	32%
Giant Eagle (5)	—	—	15%
Apple's (3)	—	—	11%
Twin Value (1)	—	—	6%
IGA (4)	—	—	4%
Finast (2)	—	—	6%
Sparkle (13)	—	—	5%
Carl's (3)	—	—	7%

[a]The Akron Primary Statistical Area (PMSA) encompasses Summit and Portage counties.
[b]U.S. Department of Commerce, Bureau of the Census, *1987 Census of Retail Trade*, Geographic Area Series, Ohio.
[c]Estimated for the PMSA as a whole. *Akron Beacon Journal*, 1987 Akron Market Area Grocery Study. Unpublished Report.
[d]Store/Chain and Number of Stores in the Akron PMSA.

To Akron food shoppers, West Point Market was perceived to be a small, very expensive food store that stocked a large selection of cheese and wine, premium brands, prime meats, and gourmet products. West Point's closest competitor in terms of merchandise and clientele was Bissons, a small, independent supermarket (15,000 square feet) that stocked quality products and specialized in kosher foods. Bissons was located only half a mile down the street from West Point, but Bissons was an ailing business, suffering from a heavy debt burden caused by overexpansion. Between 1969 and 1979, Bissons had built four additional stores in the Akron area. By 1986 Bissons had had to scale back to its main store near West Point and was barely able to pay its suppliers.

With an average gross profit margin of 33.4 percent and a guest registry of shoppers from a 50-mile radius, West Point Market seemed to occupy a secure niche in the competitive arena for food stores in northeast Ohio. Yet Russ was somewhat uneasy. Several supermarkets in Akron had changed their store formats to reflect the current trends in food retailing toward larger stores and greater variety, including upscale merchandise. For example, the nearby Acme/Click had an on-premise bakery, a large wine selection, a prime meat counter, fresh seafood, and gourmet frozen foods. Throughout the entire store, attempts to increase variety through stocking higher-quality brands and specialty items were being made on a daily basis. Russ was a little concerned that complacency and failure to evolve might cause West Point Market to lose its competitive advantage in upscale merchandise selection or that the store's point of difference might become "fuzzy" to food shoppers.

Well-known upscale supermarkets such as Byerly's in Minnesota, Dierberg's in St. Louis, Gelson's in Los Angeles, and J. Bildner & Sons in Boston offered high-quality food in a service-oriented environment and catered to a discriminating shopper. Upscale food shoppers had high expectations. They demanded unique, high-quality products and exceptional service in a "plush" shopping environment.

AN OPPORTUNITY FOR EXPANSION

The opportunity for further expansion surfaced six months ago. The property next door to West Point Market unexpectedly came on the market for an asking price of $225,000. Russ bought it immediately even though he had no definite plan for its use. However, acquisition of the additional property stimulated Russ to think about enlarging the store further, improving the store's exterior appearance, and redesigning its interior space, shelving/display, and decor. Initially, Russ made up a list of "ideal" store characteristics based on his knowledge of the specialty food trade and his previous visits to upscale food stores in other parts of the country. Peterson/Raeder Architects then put these ideas into operation in a set of preliminary plans and prepared initial cost estimates.

According to the preliminary plans, the new store would have 25,000 square feet on the main floor, with an additional 6,000 square feet of backroom and office space in the basement. Approximately 20,000 square feet of selling space was allocated among 15 major areas in a boutique-type layout (Exhibit 2). Exhibit 2 describes each area in terms of proposed square footage, sales, and gross profit margin.

As shown in Exhibit 2, the store's layout was designed to lead shoppers from the entrance through the gift-basket and wine departments, to the cheese and produce departments, the Movable Feast deli, the cafe, the bakery, seafood, meat, dairy, frozen foods, and chocolate shop. Last, along the perimeter of the store, were the fruit gift basket and floral areas. The grocery area was divided into two sections by the produce

EXHIBIT 2   Proposed Store Areas

GIFT BASKET SHOP

Area of 480 sq. ft. selling handcrafted baskets, silk fruit and vegetables, dried flowers, and candles. Gross profit margin is 50 percent. Current sales are $48,600 a year.

WINE SHOP

A 2,100 sq. ft. area for over 3,000 imported and domestic wine labels. Wines average a gross profit margin of 32 percent. Wine sales account for 10.3 percent of current sales.

CHEESE SHOP

Housing 350 imported and domestic cheeses, the cheese shop would occupy a space of 600 sq. ft. and carry an average profit margin of 40 percent. Bries and Cheddars are top sellers and can sell for up to $20 per lb. Current cheese sales, including store-prepared cheese spreads, specialty products (e.g., Brie filled with brandy-soaked apricots), and cheese trays, account for 6.5 percent of store sales.

GROCERY

The grocery department accounts for 24.4 percent of store sales and gross profit margins range from 20 percent on staples (flour, sugar, soft drinks, and paper goods) and national brands to 40 percent on specialty items such as blue corn chips in the snack aisle and oatmeal stout in the imported beer section. Although average gross margin for grocery products is low (28 percent), grocery shelving would take up 6,500 of the 20,000 sq. ft. proposed selling space.

PRODUCE

The produce department would occupy 2,300 sq. ft. and feature a variety of exotic and upscale items such as shiitake mushrooms, glazed fruits, fresh Russian tarragon, and celery root as well as standard fare such as iceberg lettuce and white onions. Produce accounts for 10.6 percent of current store sales. Gross margins average 35 percent.

MOVABLE FEAST DELI

Established in 1978, this department at 1,200 sq. ft. would be five times its original size. It accounts for 8 percent of current sales. The deli features both cooked and prepared entrees, pates, deli meats and cheeses, salads, soups, and other specialty items that carry profit margins of 54 percent. A new corporate catering and box lunch business would also operate out of this area. Adjoining the deli would be a casual sitdown cafe called "Beside the Point," which would seat 23. The cafe area would be a customer enhancement—not a profit center.

BAKERY

The 1,000 sq. ft. bakery department would represent a substantial addition to the current store. It would be a scratch/bake-off operation that would also be supplied by some outside sources. The bakery would feature loaf breads such as Cheddar bread, French breads, and specialty breads (European Rye, pumpernickel, sourdough. etc.), rolls and bagels, croissants, and pastry items such as West Point's famous "killer brownies." Gross profit margins are expected to average 54 percent. Because the current store does not have the production capacity to bake breads in high volume, nor the necessary equipment for baking specialty breads and rolls (e.g., croissants), current sales ($297,000) and gross margins primarily reflect goods purchased from suppliers.

SEAFOOD

The seafood department would be doubled to 500 sq. ft. and seafood selections expanded to include 12 varieties of fresh fish, shellfish, and oven-ready dishes such as seafood kabobs and stuffed swordfish. The department would also feature a variety of seafood salads and chilled ready-to-eat seafood (shelled shrimp, snow crab legs, etc.). Seafood currently accounts for 5.1 percent of store sales and has a gross margin of 30 percent.

MEAT

The meat department would occupy 1,200 sq. ft. and carry prime beef, pork, lamb, veal, and poultry. Some prepared items would be offered, e.g., stuffed pork chops, storemade sausage, kabobs, and so on. A self-service frozen meat and seafood case would adjoin the area. The meat department currently accounts for 19.2 percent of store sales and has gross margins of 27 percent.

(Continued on next page)

Exhibit 2   *(Continued)*

DAIRY

This department would be doubled to 800 sq. ft., which would allow for additional juice and milk selections. Other products in this area include cheese, eggs, fresh pasta, and other refrigerated products such as salad dressings and English muffins. The dairy department currently does 3.7 percent of store sales and has gross margins of 25 percent.

FROZEN FOODS

Frozen foods currently constitute 3.1 percent of total sales and the area would be expanded to 750 sq. ft. The freezer cases would house approximately 200 items with a 25 percent gross profit margin.

CHOCOLATE SHOP

This would represent a new department in the store plan and would require 250 sq. ft. of space. The department would feature boxed and bulk candy, imported as well as locally produced hand-dipped chocolates. Chocolates currently account for less than 1 percent of sales but they carry gross margins of 50 percent.

FRUIT BASKET SHOP

Fruit baskets are currently housed in the basement so this 140 sq. ft. would represent a new selling area in the store. However, fruit baskets have been popular gift items and account for 2.7 percent of current sales. Gross profit margins on fruit baskets average 40 percent.

FLOWER SHOP

The flower shop would represent a new business for West Point Market. The current plan calls for it to occupy 180 sq. ft. Floral arrangements, potted plants, and stems have gross profit margins of 50 percent in most food stores.

FRONT END

This 2,000 sq. ft. area would have five checkout lanes and would not be a profit center.

department display tables, with the first four aisles located near the entrance/exit. The divided grocery section, shortened gondolas, and "widened boulevards" were used to create interest and encourage free flow customer movement through the store.

Other design elements included innovative use of color, wood and brass fixtures, angled grocery aisles, lowered ceiling heights in a number of departments and dramatic lighting effects. For example, the ceiling above the fruit and vegetable area would be lowered to nine feet, and California redwood grid soffit drops with low voltage spotlights and experimental SPX35 General Electric lighting hung over the produce tables. Also, the exterior of the store would have an impressive entry—a substantial glass foyer, flanked by tall columns, which overlooked a bricked plaza landscaped with flower/shrub areas. The parking lot would be expanded from 60 to 140 customer parking spaces.

Overall, the proposed store expansion and design represented Russ' conception of an "ideal" store format for West Point Market. Moreover, several elements of the proposal would solve problems that acted as serious constraints to the profitability potential of the current store. Certain departments and service areas in the store were woefully inadequate to serve the demands of a high-income clientele. For example, food preparation for "The Movable Feast" was currently on two levels. The heavy-duty bread ovens were located on the main floor, and the prepared-foods kitchen was split into two areas in the basement: the "hot" kitchen, which had roasting ovens and range tops, and the "cold" kitchen, which served as a general preparation or assembly area for salads, dips, etc. In order to prepare potato salad, potatoes would be boiled in the "hot" kitchen and moved by conveyer belt to the "cold" kitchen where other ingredients would be added. As a result, labor productivity was low, and the basement kitchen was a potential fire hazard.

West Point's bread-baking capability was a sore point with customers. Only French bread and hard rolls were baked on-premise, and current production capacity could not keep up with demand, especially on Fridays, Saturdays, and holidays. Chronic bread shortages angered customers who had counted on buying West Point's French bread or hard rolls for a special occasion. Most of what West Point had in the way of loaf breads, rolls, and baked goods was purchased from outside suppliers. Every effort was made to find suppliers who could offer exceptional quality; in fact, some of the suppliers were actually "homemakers" who baked their specialties (e.g., pies, cakes, etc.) for West Point in their own homes. However, buying breads and baked goods from outside suppliers constituted an image problem for West Point—customers "expected" an on-premise, scratch bakery in a high-priced, specialty food store.

Other problem areas included produce, seafood, and dairy. Inability to provide the variety demanded by food hobbyists and gourmets and to carry adequate inventory in these areas combined to create severe stocking problems and mild customer dissatisfaction. Finally, the store itself simply did not look like an upscale food store. Most well-known upscale food stores across the country had exciting, theatrical shopping environments that had been designed to have high visual appeal. West Point's facade was plain, and, though the interior was kept spotlessly clean, it lacked aesthetic appeal.

The estimated cost for the proposed project, including construction cost and additional capital for inventory expansion, was $2 million, which would have to be financed through a bank loan. Recent discussions with bank officials indicated that the loan would carry a 10 percent interest rate and be amortized over a 20-year period. Sales revenue would have to increase to cover the required loan payment and interest plus any increase in annual operating costs. The major increase in operating cost would be for labor—at least $250,000 annually. Although West Point Market currently employed more than 75 workers, approximately 25 additional cashiers, clerks, cooks, and stockers would be needed to guarantee West Point's strategy of high levels of customer service. Also, several new managers would be required: director of food service, flower designer, and business manager (CPA). Other anticipated increases in annual operating costs included higher energy costs ($30,000), greater inventory carrying costs ($5,000), and additional repairs and maintenance ($30,000).

Whether the Akron area could support a larger West Point Market was a major concern to Russ. On the basis of NASFT (National Association for the Specialty Food Trade, Inc.) membership opinion and data, it was widely believed by industry experts that upscale food shoppers were more likely to be from households with above-average income, with fewer than average household members, and with a higher incidence of working women. Compared to local population norms, the greatest distinguishing characteristic of upscale food shoppers was higher-than-average income, followed by the greater incidence of working women. The demographic characteristic against which upscale shoppers conformed most closely to the local population norm was age. Finally, four out of ten upscale shoppers were men.

West Point customers tended to be between 45 and 60 years old with high disposable income ($60,000+ annual family income). Many were from two-income families with professional occupations. Ninety percent of West Point's customers lived in the Akron area. The average customer transaction was $23. Russ had gathered data on population characteristics of the Akron PMSA (Exhibit 3) to determine market potential for an upscale supermarket. However, the implications of the data were not "crystal" clear.

Other considerations involved customer satisfaction and West Point's competitive niche in Akron. West Point Market was currently and very successfully positioned as a specialty food store. Under the proposed expansion plan, it would become an upscale

EXHIBIT 3   Population, Occupation, and Income Characteristics of the Akron PMSA, 1980

Age

Total Persons	660,328
Under 5 years	45,127
5 to 9 years	47,693
10 to 14 years	53,426
15 to 19 years	63,704
20 to 24 years	65,105
25 to 34 years	107,049
35 to 44 years	72,305
45 to 54 years	70,419
55 to 64 years	66,883
65 to 74 years	41,074
75 years and over	27,543

Years of School Completed

Persons 25 years old and over		385,379
Elementary:	0 to 4 years	6,718
	5 to 7 years	16,874
	8 years	26,672
High School:	1 to 3 years	67,210
	4 years	154,223
College:	1 to 3 years	54,327
	4 or more years	59,355
Percent High School Graduates		69.5

Labor Force Status

Persons 16 years and over	502,093
Labor Force	309,851
Percent 16 years and over	61.7
Civilian Labor Force	309,580
Employed	284,477
Unemployed	25,103
Percent of Civilian Labor Force Unemployed	8.1
Female, 16 years and over	263,888
Labor Force	126,902
Percent Female 16 years and over	48.1

Civilian Labor Force	126,873
Employed	117,620
Unemployed	9,253
Percent of Civilian Labor Force Unemployed	7.3
With Own Children Under 6 years	38,427
in Labor Force	15,722
Married, Husband Present	147,221
in Labor Force	66,722

Occupation

Employed Persons 16 years and over	284,477
Managerial and Professional Specialty	64,516
Technical, Sales, and Administrative	85,810
Service Occupations	37,722
Farming, Forestry, and Fishing	2,383
Precision Production, Craft, and Repair	37,859
Operators, Fabricators, and Laborers	56,187

Income in 1979

Households	234,197
Less than $5,000	26,563
$5,000 to $7,499	15,674
$7,500 to $9,999	17,117
$10,000 to $14,999	33,506
$15,000 to $19,999	34,393
$20,000 to $24,999	32,638
$25,000 to $34,999	42,545
$35,000 to $49,999	22,242
$50,000 or more	9,519
Median	$18,466
Mean	$21,035

Source: U.S. Department of Commerce. Bureau of the Census. *1980 Census of Population and Housing. Census Tracts,* Akron, Ohio.

supermarket with several new departments (chocolate and flower shop). Managing these departments would require new competencies.

On the plus side, Russ had seen a recent study by Frost & Sullivan that projected gourmet food retail sales to grow from $8.5 billion in 1986 to $13 billion by 1990. In 1986, total grocery store sales were $305 billion and growing very slowly (4.4 percent in 1986 and expected to increase only 2.6 percent in 1987). Thus, gourmet food retail sales were a small fraction of total grocery store sales, but growing faster than total grocery store sales.

Finally, Russ was concerned that as a larger store, West Point might lose its intimate atmosphere, its commitment to customer service, and its close personal relationship with customers. In the minds of many customers, West Point Market had a warm, folksy personality that seemed a lot like Russ himself. For most customers, Russ and West Point Market were one and the same. Russ typically greeted each and every customer throughout most of the day. He could be seen examining merchandise, wiping dust off the shelves, talking with employees, sampling the food, and "running" the store. In a larger, more sophisticated store, Russ wondered if he would still be able to say, "I know who I am and who my customers are?" Would West Point's customers feel "at home?"

DECISION SITUATION

Russ needed to make a firm decision soon. The bank was waiting for him to submit a formal loan application. Although loan approval was virtually certain, Russ felt nervous. In his mind, the strategic benefits of repositioning were uncertain, and the expansion entailed substantial financial risks. If he went through with this plan for expanding and restructuring his store operation, it would be analogous to turning Tugboat Annie into the Queen Mary! As a larger store with higher overhead, West Point Market would have to generate significantly greater sales revenue simply to break even. Russ was also worried about the space allocated to some of the departments. He questioned whether each of the departments under the proposed plan would be able to earn its allocated space.

Trap-Ease America: The Big Cheese of Mousetraps

Lew G. Brown

On a spring morning in April, Martha House, president of Trap-Ease America, entered her office in Costa Mesa, California. She paused for a moment to contemplate the Ralph Waldo Emerson quote that she had framed and hung near her desk.

> If a man [can]…make a better mousetrap than his neighbor…the world will make a beaten path to his door.

Perhaps, she mused, Emerson knew something that she didn't. She *had* the better mouse trap—Trap-Ease—but the world didn't seem all that excited about it.

Martha had just returned from the National Hardware Show in Chicago. Standing in the trade show display booth for long hours and answering the same questions hundreds of times had been tiring. Yet, this show had excited her. Each year, National Hardware Show officials hold a contest to select the best new product introduced at the show. Of the more than 300 new products introduced at that year's show, her mousetrap had won first place. Such notoriety was not new for the Trap-Ease mousetrap. It had been featured in *People* magazine and had been the subject of numerous talk shows and articles in various popular press and trade publications. Despite all of this attention, however, the expected demand for the trap had not materialized. Martha hoped that this award might stimulate increased interest and sales.

Trap-Ease America had been formed in January by a group of investors who had obtained worldwide rights to market the innovative mousetrap. In return for marketing rights, the group agreed to pay the inventor and patent holder, a retired rancher, a royalty fee for each trap sold. The group then hired Martha to serve as president and to develop and manage the Trap-Ease America organization.

The Trap-Ease, a simple yet clever device, was manufactured by a plastics firm under contract with Trap-Ease America. It consisted of a square, plastic tube measuring about 6 inches long and 1½ inches square. The tube was bent in the middle at a 30-degree angle, so that when the front part of the tube rested on a flat surface, the other end was elevated. The elevated end held a removable cap into which the user placed bait (cheese, dog food, or some other tidbit). A hinged door was attached to the front end of the tube. When the trap was "open," this door rested on two narrow "stilts" attached to the two bottom corners of the door (see Exhibit 1).

This case was prepared by Professor Lew G. Brown of the University of North Carolina at Greensboro, as a basis for classroom discussion. It is not intended to illustrate either effective or ineffective handling of an administrative situation.

EXHIBIT 1

The trap worked with simple efficiency. A mouse, smelling the bait, entered the tube through the open end. As it walked up the angled bottom toward the bait, its weight made the elevated end of the trap drop downward. This elevated the open end, allowing the hinged door to swing closed, trapping the mouse. Small teeth on the ends of the stilts caught in a groove on the bottom of the trap, locking the door closed. The mouse could be disposed of live, or it could be left alone for a few hours to suffocate in the trap.

Martha felt the trap had many advantages for the consumer when compared with traditional spring-loaded traps or poisons. Consumers could use it safely and easily with no risk of catching their fingers while loading it. It posed no injury or poisoning threat to children or pets. Further, with Trap-Ease, consumers could avoid the unpleasant "mess" they encountered with the violent spring-loaded traps—it created no "clean-up" problem. Finally, the trap could be reused or simply thrown away.

Martha's early research suggested that women were the best target market for the Trap-Ease. Men, it seemed, were more willing to buy and use the traditional, spring-loaded trap. The targeted women, however, did not like the traditional trap. They often stayed at home and took care of their children. Thus, they wanted a means of dealing with the mouse problem that avoided the unpleasantness and risks that the standard trap created in the home.

To reach this target market, Martha decided to distribute Trap-Ease through national grocery, hardware, and drug chains such as Safeway, K mart, Hechingers, and

CB Drug. She sold the trap directly to these large retailers, avoiding any wholesalers or other middlemen.

The traps sold in packages of two, with a suggested retail price of $2.49. Although this price made the Trap-Ease about five to ten times more expensive than smaller, standard traps, consumers appeared to offer little initial price resistance. The manufacturing cost for the Trap-Ease, including freight and packaging costs, was about $.31 per unit. The company paid an additional 8.2 cents per unit in royalty fees. Martha priced the traps to retailers at $.99 per unit and estimated that after sales and volume discounts, Trap-Ease would realize net revenues from retailers of 75 cents per unit.

To promote the product, Martha had budgeted approximately $60,000 for the first year. She planned to use $50,000 of this amount for travel costs to visit trade shows and to make sales calls on retailers. She would use the remaining $10,000 for advertising. So far, however, because the mousetrap had generated so much publicity, she had not felt that she needed to do much advertising. Still, she had placed some advertising in *Good Housekeeping* and in other "home and shelter" magazines. Martha currently was the company's only "salesperson," but she intended to hire more salespeople soon.

Martha had initially forecasted Trap-Ease's first-year sales at five million units. Through April, however, the company had sold only several hundred thousand units.

QUESTIONS

1. Martha and the Trap-Ease America investors feel they face a "once-in-a-lifetime" opportunity. What information do they need to evaluate this opportunity? How do you think the group would write its mission statement? How would *you* write it?

2. Has Martha identified the best target market for Trap-Ease? What other market segments might the firm target?

3. How has the company positioned the Trap-Ease relative to the chosen target market? Could it position the product in other ways?

4. Describe the current marketing mix for Trap-Ease. Do you see any problems with this mix?

5. Who is Trap-Ease America's competition?

6. How would you change Trap-Ease's marketing strategy? What kinds of control procedures would you establish for this strategy?

The Cottages Resort and Conference Center, Hilton Head Island

David Rosenthal

INTRODUCTION AND CASE BACKGROUND

Bud Briggs, sales and marketing manager for The Cottages Resort and Conference Center, was preparing the annual marketing plan for the resort. He was having difficulty deciding what recommendations he should make regarding advertising, sales, and additions to property facilities. He pushed himself away from the stack of papers in front of him and watched out the window as another foursome approached the green located just a few yards from the offices. The weather was perfect: bright, sunny and warm, typical for an August morning on Hilton Head Island, South Carolina.

Bud, an avid golfer himself, thought enviously that he would much rather be on the course than drafting the marketing plan for fiscal year 1988. In the eight weeks that Briggs had been in the position of sales and marketing manager, he had developed a thorough understanding of the operations of the property, but putting it all down on paper was difficult.

It was clear that the occupancy rates for The Cottages, at only about half the Hilton Head Island average, would have to be improved during the coming year. Briggs was confident that the executives of Benchmark, the management company that operated the property on a daily basis, would support his recommendations with the necessary funding if he presented his case well. It was imperative that he prove himself with this first marketing plan, but he knew that his resources would certainly be limited.

Briggs had been reviewing the sales records in an attempt to draw some conclusions regarding The Cottages' current customer base. The Cottages catered both to businesses as a meeting facility and to individual recreational travelers as a resort. On the business side, although the largest number of group reservations had come from Georgia and North Carolina, many had originated as far away as Texas, Illinois, and Massachusetts. The content of their meetings was as diverse as their points of origin. On the recreational side, there were even fewer patterns that Briggs could discern.

Briggs was convinced that the property had only scratched the surface of the market. Everyone who had actually seen the property had quickly fallen in love with the quiet surroundings and the individual-villa concept. The key appeared to be attracting more visits, but how? The current sales team was doing all that could be expected. Would an additional salesperson add enough short term business to cover the new position? The advertising and promotional program certainly needed improvement. Even the operations of the property could benefit from more attention in Briggs' opinion.

As he gazed out the window, one of the golfers, sporting a pair of outlandishly green pants, sank a 50-foot putt. Bud shook his head and returned to his work, only to be interrupted by his secretary. "Bud, it's the Consolidated Southeastern group. They want to talk to you about the lack of a restaurant here on the property." As Briggs reached for the phone he made a mental note to highlight the prospect of adding a restaurant when writing the marketing plan. It seemed to be a major stumbling block in negotiating with some meeting planners.

THE COTTAGE PROPERTY

The Cottages Resort and Conference Center opened in 1985 to serve the needs of businesses for convention and meeting facilities in a relaxing atmosphere and the needs of vacationers seeking a recreational resort.

The actual facilities included 72 individual townhome villas providing a maximum of 160 available rooms. The villas were situated among southern oaks, palmetto, and jack pines shrouded with Spanish moss and were within easy walking distance of the conference facility. Villas were configured in a one-, two-, or three-bedroom design. Included in each villa were bedroom(s) with attached bath, a living room, a completely equipped kitchen, dining room, and front and back porch. The layout of the villas typically provided a view of the adjacent golf course, a small pond or waterway (frequently under the "management" of an alligator or two), and wooded "wild" areas. The entire property gave the impression of a well-cared-for, quiet residential area, rather than that of a fast-paced resort.

The conference center itself provided more than 10,000 square feet of meeting space. The facilities offered a broad range of scale and meeting atmosphere. The "Board Room" was luxuriously appointed with leather chairs and a mahogany table that would seat 20 people. The ballroom could be divided into three smaller rooms or could accommodate a meeting of 300 people.

The latest "meeting technology" was employed in the design of the conference center. The most advanced audiovisual equipment was available. Most rooms were equipped with electronically operated drop-down front and rearview screen projectors, variable lighting controls, and complete sound systems. In order to provide the best meeting atmosphere, the rooms were designed with maximum ceiling height (17 feet), recessed lighting, including fluorescent, incandescent, and natural sources, and ergonomically designed "18 hour" chairs. Outside each of the meeting rooms larger decks and screened porches provided activity areas and a view of the golf course and its environs.

On-site, The Cottages offered a variety of recreational activities in addition to lodging and meeting facilities. The conference center also housed a weight room, saunas, locker room facilities with showers, two racquetball courts, and an indoor/outdoor heated pool. A fleet of bicycles was also available for guest use. A "general store" had recently been opened providing amenities and travel necessities, and a lounge adjoined the check-in area.

Off-site, The Cottages maintained relationships with the Shipyard Golf Course and Shipyard Racquet Club, as well as with Oyster Reef Golf Course and Hilton Head Country Club. Guests were able to play at reduced prices at these facilities and were able to gain preferential treatment in scheduling and support.

Although The Cottages property was not actually on the beach, it was within comfortable walking distance. Guests had access to the private beach and the use of a beach house for private functions.

In addition to the recreational activities provided directly by the resort, there were numerous opportunities available from the surrounding Hilton Head Island area, from fishing to paragliding. The Cottages maintained a fleet of chauffeured vans to provide ground transportation for guests.

HILTON HEAD ISLAND

In 1663 Captain William Hilton, an English ship captain, observed a high bluff on his nautical charts. Over the years Captain Hilton's headland became known as Hilton Head Island. The island was actually a small, foot-shaped barrier island just off the coast of South Carolina. It was approximately 30 miles north of Savannah, Georgia, and roughly 90 miles south of Charleston, South Carolina. The island was 12 miles long and 5 miles wide. It encompassed 42 square miles of semitropical marshland and woods. It had 12 miles of white sand beaches.

Hilton Head Island's average annual temperature was 65 degrees (F). In the summer the high temperatures were in the 90s and the lows in the 70s. In the winter months the days were generally in the high 50s to 60s and the nights were in the 40s. In 1956 the first bridge to the mainland was completed, beginning the modern development of the island. In 1987 the island had approximately 2,000 hotel rooms, and 4,000 villas to accommodate the nearly 900,000 annual visitors. The island had a 1987 permanent population of about 18,000. There were 324 holes of championship golf, 211 tennis courts, 478 shops and restaurants, and 8 marinas. Six national airlines served Savannah airport, roughly 40 miles from the island. Two commuter airlines served Hilton Head Island airport.

Although the island was considerably developed, it still offered sanctuary to many species of wildlife. More than 140 species of birds had been spotted on the island. Alligators were common, as were porpoises. Fishing and shelling were excellent.

The island was divided into "plantations," or planned communities. In 1987 there were nine such plantations, with two more under development. The Cottages was centrally located on the Shipyard Plantation. (Exhibits 1 and 2 show the location and configuration of Hilton Head Island.)

MARKET AND COMPETITION

Economic conditions for Hilton Head Island had been consistently favorable during the 1980s and were expected to continue to be positive. Briggs had gathered some specific data from the local Chamber of Commerce, and from trade publications:

- Island permanent population had increased by 6,637 over the previous five years and was expected to increase by an additional 4,750 by 1990.
- Of the $412,576,284 gross sales reported for the island in 1986, 64% or $265,000,000 was hospitality related, up $120,000,000 over 1980.
- Occupancy had improved over last year by 6.9% for the period January to June. Room nights available increased by 861, and room nights sold increased by 5,132.

EXHIBIT 1: Eastern U.S.—Hilton Head Island

- For the first half of 1987, Southeastern and Middle Atlantic states experienced an occupancy rate of 64.8%, an increase of .8% over the first half of 1986. The average room rate was up 3.3% to $59.55 over the same period.
- The inventory of rooms available on Hilton Head Island was expected to increase only marginally in 1988.

The meetings and convention business had grown on Hilton Head over the past seven years, resulting in estimated revenues of $42,000,000 in 1986. (Historical data on meetings and conventions is shown in Exhibit 3.) The total number of resort visitors, including group, individual business, and pleasure travelers had been on the rise since 1972 (Exhibit 4).

Briggs believed that the competition for The Cottages Resort and Conference Center had to be divided into two basic classifications, business/group competition, and resort vacation competition. The markets for each were considerably different, and the key factors on which properties competed differed from one classification to the other as well.

On the business side, the major competitors to The Cottages were four major convention hotels located on the island—Hyatt, Inter-Continental, Marriott, and Mariner's Inn. Each of these hotels was located on beach-front property, had extensive meeting facilities, and large sales staffs. Several other hotels on the island were considered to be secondary competitors, including Radisson, Palmetto Dunes, Hilton Head Beach and Tennis, and Holiday Inn. Off the island, Seabrook, Kiawah, Wild Dunes, Amelia Island, Pinehurst, Cloister, Callaway, and Pine Isle competed regionally for convention business. (A detailed description of the competition is presented in Exhibit 5.)

EXHIBIT 2: Hilton Head Island

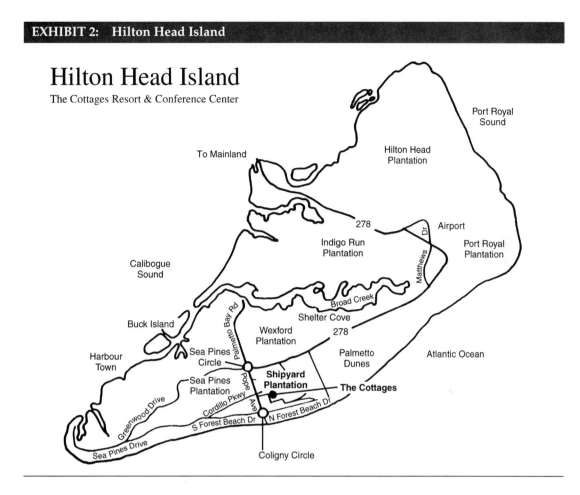

Hilton Head Island
The Cottages Resort & Conference Center

EXHIBIT 3   Hilton Head Island Meeting and Convention Attendance, 1980–1986

Year	Est. # of Groups	Est. # of Attendees	Est. $ Expended
1980	964	118,500	30,000,000
1981	1,250	104,500	24,000,000
1982	1,060	136,500	29,000,000
1983[a]	1,639	192,300	31,500,000
1984	1,900	160,000	28,771,000
1985[b]	1,945	172,000	36,000,000
1986	2,300	200,000	42,000,000

[a]Figures include Mariner's Inn from its opening in March 1983.
[b]Figures include Inter-Continental, which opened in fall 1985.

EXHIBIT 4　　Hilton Head Island Annual Resort Visitors, 1972–1986

Year	Annual Visitors	Year	Annual Visitors
1986	980,000	1978	550,000
1985	875,000	1977	428,718
1984	825,000	1976	391,725
1983	750,000	1975	265,893
1982	680,000	1974	194,361
1981	700,000	1973	112,068
1980	648,000	1972	72,233

THE DECISION PROCESS

Liz Kiley, sales manager for The Cottages, described the decision process in selecting a meeting site, "When a company is looking at Hilton Head, they usually look for the best location, and the top four have the best locations on the island. Three of them are chain hotels, and, therefore, have the benefits of chain affiliation, including advertising, referrals, and huge financial reserves. They have all of the amenities…and the beach. Whenever we speak with a potential group, we know that they are talking to at least one of the four in addition to The Cottages. Economics play a part in the decision, but really it comes down to the "personality" of the property. The big hotels are all the same—elevators, long hallways, lots of hustle and bustle. The Cottages' quiet "home away from home" atmosphere is a big difference."

The process of planning a meeting was complex and varied widely from company to company. Although the trade press suggested that there was a trend toward companies employing professional meeting planners, many companies simply handed over the responsibility for planning a meeting to a secretary. Frequently, a secretary was told to "make a few calls and get some information together about a few places on Hilton Head"—and nothing else. It was often left to the secretary to decide which places to call and what information should be sought. Larger groups tended to be managed by well-informed meeting planners, while smaller meetings generally were planned by secretaries.

Industry sources estimated that about 25 percent of travelers used travel agents to book their trips, and for frequent business travelers, the proportion increased to 40 percent. Similarly, 40 percent of all travelers asked their travel agents to make a recommendation about where to stay.

Because the country's 30,000 travel agents were so influential in the decision making process, they were heavily targeted by leisure-industry marketers. Travel agents were commonly inundated by direct-mail advertising pieces, specialty advertising of all sorts, from alligators to zinc-oxide, and even free trips. A variety of travel magazines and directories were also targeted specifically toward travel agents.

On the tourist/vacation side of The Cottages trade, the competition was even more fragmented than on the business side. In addition to the major hotels on the island, which provided about 2,000 rooms, there were about 4,000 villas available. Some of the villas were configured as a resort (The Cottages), while others were rented privately. Competition for the vacationers was, therefore, more difficult to pinpoint.

EXHIBIT 5   Competitor Analysis

PROPERTY	WILD DUNES	AMELIA ISLAND	PINE HURST
Group			
Social			
Catering			
Location (Geographic)	Outside Chas.	Amelia Island	North Carolina
No. Guest Rms./Suites	345 Vill/1000 rms	1200 rms/125 ste	310 rms/23 ste
Estimated Bus. Mix:	68 Group	70 Group	
Group/Social%	32 Social	30 Social	
Dist. from Airport	24 mi/45 min	29 mi/35 min	70 mi/45 min
Airport Trans. Avail.	Pvt. Comp.	Yes/$15	Yes
Golf on Property	36 Holes	27 Holes	Yes
Tennis No. Indoor	N/A	N/A	No
No. Outdoor	19/1 Ctr. Ct.	25	28
Pool Inside	N/A	1 Heated	1 Heated
Outside	2 lg./1 sm.	1 Heated	4
Health Club/Spa	Plan next yr.	Yes	Yes
No. of Mtg. Rooms	13 in/3 cabanas	18	18
Total Sq. Feet	12,000	20,000	13,000
Lgst. Mtg./Bqt. Rms.	4,224	5,439	5,000
Extensive A/V	Off Prop.	Yes	Yes
No. of Restaurants	4/2	5	5
Gourmet Restaurants	1	1	1
No. of Lounges	2	2	2
Entertainment	Bar/Beach	Nightly	Yes
Room Services Y/N	N/A	Yes	Yes
24 Hr. Rm. Service	No	No	N/A
Guest Room Rate EP			
FAP			
Social Rate	$85–$266	$99–$270	$74
Date Opened or Refurbished	1982	1977	N/A
Cond. of Property	Good	Excellent	Very Good
Previous Year Occupancy/Avg. Rate			

PROPERTY	CLOISTER	CALLAWAY	PINE ISLE
Group			
Social			
Catering			
Location (Geographic)	Sea Island		Lake Lanier
No. Guest Rms./Suites	264 rms	800 rm/10 ste	250 rm/4 ste
Estimated Bus. Mix:		55 Group	8 Group
Group/Social%		45 Social	20 Social
Dist. from Airport	60 mi/75 min	1 hr/$25 pp/ pway	47 mi/1 hr
Airport Trans. Avail.	$20 pp		Contract Out
Golf on Property	54 Holes	63 Holes	18 Holes

(Continued on next page)

Exhibit 5 *(Continued)*

PROPERTY *(continued)*		CLOISTER	CALLAWAY	PINE ISLE
Group				
Social				
Catering				
Location (Geographic)		Sea Island		Lake Lanier
Tennis	No. Indoor	No	No	3
	No. Outdoor	18	19	4
Pool	Inside	No	1	1 Heated
	Outside	2	1	1 Heated
Health Club/Spa		No	Yes	Yes
No. of Mtg. Rooms		6	12	19
Total Sq. Feet		15,000	36,000	18,000
Lgst. Mtg./Bqt. Rms.		6,975	10,800	4,356
Extensive A/V		Yes	Yes	Yes
No. of Restaurants		5	9	4
Gourmet Restaurants		2	2	1
No. of Lounges		3	2	1
Entertainment		Nightly	Nightly	Nightly
Room Services Y/N			Yes	Yes
24 Hr. Rm. Service			No	Yes
Guest Room Rate	EP			
	FAP	$94–$274		
Social Rate				
Date Opened or Refurbished		1983		1974
Cond. of Property		Good	Good	Good
Previous Year Occupancy/Avg. Rate				

PROPERTY		HH BEACH & TENNIS	HOLIDAY INN	SEABROOK
Group				
Social				
Catering				
Location (Geographic)		Folly Field	S. Forest Bch.	Outside Chas.
No. Guest Rms./Suites		280/1, 2, vill.	200 rms	420/1, 2, 3, vill
Estimated Bus. Mix:		15 Group		40 Group
Group/Social%		27 Social		60 Social
Dist. from Airport		40 min	45 min	37 mi/50 min
Airport Trans. Avail.		Yes	Yes	Yes
Golf on Property			No	2–18 Holes
Tennis	No. Indoor			N/A
	No. Outdoor	10	Available	20
Pool	Inside			N/A
	Outside	2	1	2
Health Club/Spa		No	No	N/A
No. of Mtg. Rooms		7	3	5
Total Sq. Feet		12,500	4,500	4,500
Lgst. Mtg./Bqt. Rms.		90	12,000	2,080
Extensive A/V		No	No	Yes
No. of Restaurants		1	1	4

(Continued on next page)

Exhibit 5 *(Continued)*

PROPERTY *(continued)*	HH BEACH & TENNIS	HOLIDAY INN	SEABROOK
Group			
Social			
Catering			
Location (Geographic)	Folly Field	S. Forest Bch.	Outside Chas.
Gourmet Restaurants			1
No. of Lounges	1	1	2
Entertainment	No	Nightly	Nightly
Room Services Y/N	No	Yes	No
24 Hr. Rm. Service		No	No
Guest Room Rate EP			
FAP			
Social Rate	$119–$169	$50–$129	$100–$283
Date Opened or Refurbished	1982	1973	1970
Cond. of Property	Good	Fair	Good
Previous Year Occupancy/Avg. Rate			

PROPERTY	KIAWAH	PALMETTO DUNES	THE COTTAGES
Group			
Social			
Catering			
Location (Geographic)	Outside Chas.	Palm. Dunes Pl.	Shipyard Pl.
No. Guest Rms./Suites	150 rm/300 vill	540/ 1, 2, 3, vill.	145/1, 2, 3, vill.
Estimated Bus. Mix:	55 Group	30 Group	57 Group
Group/Social%	45 Social	70 Social	43 Social
Dist. from Airport	36 mi/50 min		45 min
Airport Trans. Avail.	Pvt. Comp/$30		Yes
Golf on Property	3 Courses	27 Holes	27 Holes
Tenni No. Indoor	N/A		2 Rac. Ball
No. Outdoor	30	25	20
Pool Inside	N/A		1
Outside	4	24	1
Health Club/Spa	N/A	No	Yes
No. of Mtg. Rooms	24	6	8
Total Sq. Feet	12,000	4,800	10,000
Lst. Mtg./Bqt. Rms.	4,096	90	3,557
Extensive A/V	Yes	Yes	Yes
No. of Restaurants	5	14	*
Gourmet Restaurants	1	3	
No. of Lounges	4	5	1
Entertainment	Nightly	Yes	No
Room Services Y/N	Yes	N/A	No
24 Hr. Rm. Service	No		N/A
Guest Room Rate EP		N/A	$95–$270
FAP			
Social Rate	$145–$325		$65–$195

(Continued on next page)

David Rosenthal

Exhibit 5   *(Continued)*

PROPERTY (continued)	KIAWAH	PALMETTO DUNES	THE COTTAGES
Group Social Catering Location (Geographic)	Outside Chas.	Palm. Dunes Pl.	Shipyard Pl.
Date Opened or Refurbished	1976	1976	1985
Cond. of Property	Good	Very Good	Excellent
Previous Year Occupancy/Avg. Rate			35%/$65

PROPERTY	THE MARINERS INN	MARRIOTT	INTER-CONTINENTAL
Group Social Catering Location (Geographic)	Palametto Dunes	Shipyard	Port Royal Pl.
No. Guest Rms./Suites	324/20 sts.	338/8 sts.	418/rooms
Estimated Bus. Mix: Group/Social%	60 Group 40 Social	60 Group 40 Social	60 Group 40 Social
Dist. from Airport	45 min	45 min	45 min
Airport Trans. Avail.	Yes	Yes	$16 PP
Golf on Property	No	27 holes	3 courses
Tennis No. Indoor	No	N/A	N/A
No. Outdoor		20	16
Pool Inside	1	1	1
Outside	1	1	3
Health Club/Spa	Yes	Yes	Yes
No. of Mtg. Rooms	13	13	15
Total Sq. Feet	13,000	13,320	23,000
Lst. Mtg./Bqt. Rms.	4,000	10,000	14,000
Extensive A/V	Yes	Yes	
No. of Restaurants	3	2	2
Gourmet Restaurants	1	1	1
No. of Lounges	1	1	1
Entertainment	Nightly	Yes	Nightly
Room Services Y/N	Yes	Yes	Yes
24 Hr. Rm. Service	No		Yes
Guest Room Rate EP			
FAP			
Social Rate	$105–$165	$105–$155	$145–$195
Date Opened or Refurbished	1983	1981	1985
Cond. of Property	Excellent	Very Good	Excellent
Previous Year Occupancy/Avg. Rate	60%		

(Continued on next page)

Exhibit 5   *(Continued)*

PROPERTY	HYATT	SEA PINES	RADISSON
Group			
Social			
Catering			
Location (Geographic)	Palm Dunes	Sea Pines Pl.	Hwy. 278
No. Guest Rms./Suites	500 rm/35 ste	500/1, 2, 3, vill.	156/suites
Estimated Bus. Mix:	50 Group	40 Group	65 Group
Group/Social%	50 Social	60 Social	35 Social
Dist. from Airport	45 min	47 mi/1 hr	45 min
Airport Trans. Avail.	Yes	Pvt. Comp. $18 pp	Comp.
Golf on Property	3 courses	6½ courses	No
Tennis No. Indoor	N/A	N/A	No
No. Outdoor	26	90	2
Pool Inside	2	1	No
Outside	—	5	1
Health Club/Spa	Yes	N/A	1
No. of Mtg. Rooms	19	13	3
Total Sq. Feet	18,000	10,000	2700
Lgst. Mtg./Bqt. Rms.		220 dinner	2700
Extensive A/V	Contract out	Pvt. Comp.	Contract
No. of Restaurants	3	3	None
Gourmet Restaurants	1	1	None
No. of Lounges	2	3	None
Entertainment	Nightly	Nightly	None
Room Services Y/N	Yes	No	Yes
24 Hr. Rm. Service	—	No	Yes
Guest Room Rate EP			$49
FAP			
Social Rate	$115–$205		
Date Opened or Refurbished	1976	1958	1987
Cond. of Property	Very Good	Good	New
Previous Year Occupancy/Avg. Rate			

"I guess that our vacationers come to us in four or five different ways," Kiley commented. "Some are return visitors. They have been here for a meeting or convention and enjoyed it, so they came back with their families or their friends. That sort of relates to the second group. They have heard about us from friends and relatives, word of mouth. We do a fair amount of promotion with travel agencies, and they recommend us to their clients, so that is another way. Occasionally, one of the other hotels has overbooked and sent us some business. They usually stay with us after that. The other Benchmark properties work with us to refer clients back and forth, as well. We don't get much walk-in trade, that's for sure, not with our location and the regulations around here about signs and such."

THE COTTAGES' ORGANIZATION

The ownership and management of The Cottages consisted of a complex set of relationships. The overall property, including the conference center, the recreation facilities, and several of the villas, belonged to American Service Corporation of Greenville, S. C. (Amserve). Amserve was a banking and investment company that had originally developed the property, and it was to it that the Benchmark Management Company reported.

Benchmark was responsible for the management of the property on a day-to-day basis. All of the normal activities of the property, including sales and marketing, engineering, housekeeping, reservations, conference services, catering, front desk, and accounting, were the responsibility of Benchmark. Benchmark received a management fee based on the profitability of the property. Benchmark also operated several other resorts: The Woodlands Inn (Houston, Texas), Seabrook Island Resort (Charleston, South Carolina), Chaminade (Santa Cruz, California), and Cheyenne Mountain Inn (Colorado Springs, Colorado).

Most of the 72 villas were owned by about 25 to 35 investors. Benchmark paid the individual owners a percentage of the room revenues generated by the rentals of the villas. In addition, the owners of the villas could reserve the use of the villas, more or less at their discretion, thereby making the inventory of rooms variable. In some instances the private use of the villas had come into conflict with the efforts of the sales group to schedule large meetings.

Although there was no restaurant on the premises, Benchmark maintained a contract with a local caterer and restauranteur to provide meals for Cottages guests. The caterer offered a complete selection of gourmet meals, wines, and beverages. The meals, snacks, and special events were determined by the meeting planner from Cottages menus and were delivered to a staging area in the conference center in time for set up and serving. The actual serving was done at tables set in the meeting rooms. Although the atmosphere was pleasant, the ambiance that an actual restaurant could provide was missing. A "typical menu" offered by the caterer for a meeting day is shown in Exhibit 6. The caterer's contract was to continue through September 1988. The Cottages was also willing to arrange group or individual dining at island restaurants if requested. Hilton Head Island was home to a wide variety of restaurants of all types, from fast food chains to regional gourmet specialties. The nearest restaurants were within walking distance or a short ride in one of the Cottages' complimentary vans.

THE COTTAGES' MEETINGS AND PACKAGES

Benchmark's philosophy was to combine "Living, Learning, and Leisure" in each of their properties. Thus, they provided the highest-quality accommodations, the best-engineered meeting facilities, and the broadest range of recreation possible at each of their resorts.

The typical business meeting held at The Cottages generated roughly 200 room nights. The average group consisted of about 60 people, mostly male, between the ages of 35 and 60. Meetings generally lasted 3½ days, one day being spent entirely in business sessions, one afternoon of golf sponsored by the organization (which provided no revenues to The Cottages), and the remainder split between business and individual leisure activities. On an average day, the groups spent $30–$40 per person on food, and $10–$15 per person on beverages. A typical round of golf cost $40 per person. Most groups held one special event, such as a luau or barbecue.

For the vacationer, The Cottages also offered a number of package plans. The "Island Golf Package," for example, included accommodations, maid service, 18 holes of golf each day (including golf cart), one bucket of practice balls per day, activities for

EXHIBIT 6   Sample Menus

BREAKFAST

Chilled juices	Chilled juices	Hot apple juice with
Strawberry and blueberry crêpes	Fluffy scrambled eggs	cinnamon stick
with sauce	Bacon or sausage links	Broiled grapefruit
Crisp bacon	Hash brown potatoes	Choice of French toast or pancakes
Fresh grape cluster	Hot biscuits	with honey and maple syrup
Croissants and muffins with	Beverage	Bacon, sausage, or ham
assorted jams	*$6.25*	Hash brown potatoes
Beverage		Beverage
$6.00		*$8.75*

Melon balls in champagne	Chilled seasonal melon
Egg au vanneau	Country-style scrambled eggs
Lyonnaise potatoes	Broiled breakfast steak
Cinnamon baked apple	Baked cinnamon apple
Croissants, assorted breads	Hash brown potatoes
with jams	Breakfast breads and pastries
Beverage	Beverage
$9.00	*$11.75*

LUNCHEONS

THE FRENCH CONNECTION	**THE CARVERY**	**CROISSANT CREATIONS**
Seasonal green salad	Soup du jour	Soup du jour
Quiche du jour	Open face prime rib (hot or cold)	Shrimp and crab croissant
Seasonal vegetables	Potato salad, dill pickle	Curry chicken pecan croissant
Rolls with butter	Fruit garnish	Marinated vegetable salad
Sherbet	Ice cream sundae	Chocolate mousse
Beverage	Beverage	Beverage
$8.75	*$13.50*	*$10.50*

SEA & SHORE SALAD BAR	**DELI PLATTER**
Soup du jour	Soup du jour
Potato salad, shrimp salad, Belgian	Ham, Genoa salami, roast beef,
cucumber salad, pasta salad,	turkey breast,
Marinated vegetable salad,	Swiss and American cheese,
cole slaw, fruit salad	potato salad,
Assorted seasonal greens	Sliced egg, dill pickle
with toppings	Deli garnishes
Choice of dressings, assorted	Fruit tarts
breads and butter	Beverage
Pecan or apple pie	*$10.50*
Beverage	
$9.95	

(Continued on next page)

Exhibit 6 *(Continued)*

LUNCHEON BUFFET
Minimum 30 people
Sliced, chilled seasonal fruit
Tomato and onion vinaigrette,
cole slaw, potato salad
Select any three: Chicken cacciatore,
seafood newburg, broiled grouper, sliced roast
sirloin of beef au jus, beef bourguignonne,
or chicken mandarin
Rice pilaf, fresh vegetable du jour
Assorted cakes and pastries
Beverage
$14.50

NEW YORK STYLE DELI BUFFET
Minimum 25 people
Carved meats and cheese
Ham, beef, turkey, salami, pepper loaf, liverwurst,
olive loaf, American and Swiss cheese
Salad Bar
Lettuce greens, tomato slices, sliced cucumbers,
carrot sticks, flowerettes of broccoli and cauliflower,
mushrooms, celery, bean sprouts, bacon bits, egg, red
onions, dill pickles, relishes, grated cheese, potato
salad, mayonnaise, mustard, hot sauce
Assorted breads and rolls with butter
Assorted pastry tray
Beverage
$10.95

SPECIALTY DINNERS

Brochette of seafood
Tossed seasonal greens
Medallions of tenderloin
Sauce Charon, périgourdine,
béarnaise
Seasonal vegetable
Rissole potatoes
White chocolate macadamia nut
mousse
Beverage
$28.00

Shrimp bisque
Spinach salad with hot
bacon dressing
Individual beef Wellington
Sauce périgourdine
Fresh seasonal vegetables
in cornucopia
Strawberry cheesecake
Beverage
$30.00

Fettuccine carbonara
Salad Maurice jardin
N. Y. strip sirloin steak
Marchand de vin
Seasonal vegetable
Twice-baked potato
White chocolate macadamia nut
mousse
Beverage
$32.00

Seafood Chowder
Salad Maurice jardin
Whole Maine lobster
Parsleyed boiled potatoes
Seasonal vegetables
Strawberry flan
Beverage
Market Price

Salad Maurice jardin
Petite filet mignon and lobster tail
with drawn butter
Croquette potato
Seasonal vegetable
Piña Colada mousse
Beverage
$31.00

She Crab soup
Hearts of bibb lettuce salad
with walnut vinaigrette
Trio of game medallions:
Pheasant, duck, quail
Potatoes Anna
Vegetable du jour
Strawberry tartlet
Beverage
$36.00

Delice of Fruit au Port
Tomato and avocado vinaigrette
Tournedos Oscar
Twin medallions of beef with crabmeat
and asparagus with sauce béarnaise
Seasonal vegetable
Rissole potatoes
Petite apricot flan
Beverage
$28.95

children, use of the fitness center, swimming pool, etc. In the "high season" a couple would pay $70 per person for a one-bedroom townhome per night. The typical vacationers were a couple, ages 35 to 60, staying 3 to 5 nights, usually on one of the package plans.

PRICING AND PROMOTION

For transients, the prices varied according to a complex formula that took into account the number of people per room or villa, the type of villa, the season of the year, and the recreational "package." Comparisons with competing resorts on Hilton Head had convinced Briggs that The Cottages pricing was about average. On average for 1987, the social room rate was $52.73 per person per night.

The pricing for groups was dependent upon the size of the group, the amenities requested, and the season of the year. More importantly, as was the common practice in the industry, the sales staff was free to offer a lower-than-standard rate if it became necessary to attract a group's business. The average for 1987 was roughly $74 per person per night.

The Cottages' promotional efforts in 1987 had taken a variety of forms. Regionally, major feeder cities such as Atlanta, Georgia; Columbia, South Carolina; and Charlotte, North Carolina; had been targeted with newspaper advertisements and billboards promoting golf and beach packages. The travel section of *Southern Living Magazine* had been used monthly to promote the overall services of the resort and conference center. The travel agent market had been targeted throughout the year through advertisements in *HIT, Travel Agents Market Place,* and the *Official Airline Guide Travel Planner.* The Cottages also had participated in the placement of a cooperative advertisement with the other resort represented by Benchmark. In addition, collateral materials including about 75,000 award-winning brochures had been distributed in 1987.

Promotional activities included attendance at local, regional, and national trade shows for specific industries, delivery of promotional pamphlets and collateral materials, presentation of specialty advertising merchandise such as chocolate alligators, and invitations to special "FAM" (familiarization) visits. A "FAM" consisted of an all-expenses-paid trip to the resort, which generally cost about $500 per person. The 1987 advertising and promotional budget is presented in Exhibit 7.

THE COTTAGES' SALES ORGANIZATION

The sales organization for The Cottages consisted of three segments: the on-site sales team, the sales rep organizations, and the national sales organization at Benchmark. The on-site team consisted of Bud Briggs, Tina Burdette, and Liz Kiley. The three of them accounted for roughly 90 percent of the group business and virtually all of the vacation business in 1987. The two sales rep organizations, one located in Atlanta and the other in New York City, contributed roughly 10 percent of the group business in 1987, whereas the national sales organization had only succeeded in booking one group over that period. The sales rep organizations were paid on a retainer-plus-commission basis.

On-site sales people were paid salary plus bonuses for "plus business." Tina Burdette had been with The Cottages from its inception, had worked for the previous management company and had stayed on with Benchmark. Burdette had extensive contacts in the industry and was well connected to the "grapevine" on the island.

EXHIBIT 7   1987 Promotional Budget

Advertising and Promotional Cost History,
January 1, 1987–December 31, 1987

		J	F	M	A	M
Payroll	Act	12,565	9,823	13,521	13,832	11,785
	Bud	12,634	12,085	12,340	12,508	12,340
Advertising	Act	27,267	37,230	53,305	21,067	21,651
	Bud	47,222	30,599	34,783	22,539	20,898
Merchandising	Act	1,792	3,792	2,992	2,492	2,492
	Bud	2,792	2,792	2,992	2,992	2,992
Operating Exp. (Other)	Act	2,363	3,839	3,394	2,456	3,123
	Bud	2,050	2,050	2,150	1,650	1,650
Public Relations	Act	622	1,743	2,162	2,893	600
	Bud	600	1,600	1,600	1,100	1,100
Representation and Trade Shows	Act	3,600	9,570	9,939	9,415	6,916
	Bud	6,100	8,100	10,900	11,500	7,400
Telephones	Act	626	1,522	1,250	947	1,237
	Bud	1,550	1,550	1,400	1,400	1,400
Entertainment and Travel	Act	2,590	3,034	2,930	5,044	4,957
	Bud	1,200	1,750	2,950	3,900	3,900
Total	Act	51,424	70,552	89,493	58,144	52,760
	Bud	74,148	60,526	69,115	57,589	51,680

Whenever a group was planning to come to Hilton Head, it seemed that Burdette knew immediately. Liz Kiley had been with The Cottages for only about a year. She had started in conference services, but had quickly moved over into sales as well. Nearly all of the Cottages employees "pitched in" to help in areas other than their primary job responsibilities.

THE COTTAGES' RECENT PERFORMANCE

Benchmark had only been responsible for the management of the property for the past 18 months. A previous management company had been fired by Amserve. Currently,

J	J	A	S	O	N	D	TOTAL	
9,593	10,897						82,016	**YTD**
12,255	12,789	12,145	12,554	12,279	12,356	12,785	86,951	**YTD**
							149,070	**YEND**
15,845	18,788						195,153	**YTD**
15,695	16,710	15,237	16,650	16,594	5,415	4,553	188,446	**YTD**
							246,895	**YEND**
2,492	1,792						17,844	**YTD**
2,992	2,992	2,992	2,992	2,992	2,992	2,992	20,544	**YTD**
							35,504	**YEND**
1,774	1,690						18,639	**YTD**
1,650	1,700	2,400	2,100	2,100	2,200	2,100	12,900	**YTD**
							23,800	**YEND**
500	750						9,270	**YTD**
1,100	600	1,100	2,000	600	1,600	1,600	7,700	**YTD**
							14,600	**YEND**
6,865	7,243						53,518	**YTD**
11,000	7,900	9,700	11,800	9,500	11,100	7,000	62,900	**YTD**
							112,000	**YEND**
892	1,088						7,562	**YTD**
1,400	1,400	1,400	1,400	1,400	1,400	1,400	8,500	**YTD**
							12,100	**YEND**
3,626	5,928						21,650	**YTD**
3,750	4,200	3,200	5,250	3,150	4,250	4,500	28,109	**YTD**
							42,000	**YEND**
41,587	48,146						412,106	**YTD**
49,842	48,291	48,174	54,746	48,615	41,313	36,930	411,191	**YTD**
							640,969	**YEND**

there were rumors that Amserve was looking for a buyer for the property. If a sale were to take place, the contract between Amserve and Benchmark would be unlikely to survive and would have to be renegotiated with the new owners. Briggs believed that a strong showing in 1988 could influence Amserve to continue with the property.

The Cottages had not been performing up to the expectations of Benchmark over their 18-month management. Briggs had been installed as director of marketing and sales specifically to improve The Cottages' financial condition. The latest figures available for fiscal year 1987 indicated that The Cottages was running at an occupancy figure of only 31.7 percent whereas the average for their four major competitors was nearly 60 percent. (Exhibits 8 and 9 show the current room revenue and occupancy rates for The Cottages and their top four competitors for fiscal year 1987.)

David Rosenthal

EXHIBIT 8   Room Revenue Performance

MARKET SHARE ANALYSIS (ROOM REVENUE)
OCTOBER 1986 TO JULY 1987 (304 DAYS)

A Hotel	B Number of Guest Rooms	C % of Occupancy for Period	D Actual Avg. Rate for Period	E Potential Room Sales (B × D × 304 days)	F Actual Room Sales (B × C × D)	G Dollar Share of Total Market (E ÷ Total of E)	H Market Share Percentage (F ÷ Total of F)
Marriott	350	66.8	80.91	8,608.824	5,748.331	17.9%	20.4
Mariners Inn	324	61.7	94.47	9,304.917	5,741.131	19.4%	20.3
Hyatt	520	57.0	91.47	14,459.577	8,790.724	30.1%	31.2
Intercontinental	416	54.0	104.50	13,215.488	7,136.305	27.5%	25.3
The Cottages	85–160	31.7	55.16	2,426.378[a]	769.651	5.1%	2.8
Total	1,695–1,770	57.0	92.65	48,015.184	28,186.142	100%	100

*Based on 43.988 available as indicated on the Occupancy Market Share Analysis.

EXHIBIT 9   Occupancy Analysis

THE COTTAGES RESORT AND CONFERENCE CENTER
MARKET SHARE ANALYSIS (OCCUPANCY)
OCTOBER 1986 TO JULY 1987 (304 DAYS)

A Hotel	B Number of Guest Rooms	C Total Number of Room Nights Available to Sell This Year (B × Days in Yr)	D Total Number of Room Nights Sold This Year	E Percent of Occupancy for the Year (D ÷ C)	F Room Share of Total Market Percent (C ÷ Total of C)	H Market Share Percent (D ÷ Total of D)
Marriott	350	106,400	71,075	66.8	19.9	23.4
Mariners Inn	324	98,496	60,772	61.7	18.5	20.0
Hyatt	520	158,080	90,105	57.0	29.6	29.6
Intercontinental	416	126,464	68,290	54.0	23.7	22.4
The Cottages	85–160	43,988	13,952	31.7	8.3	4.6
Total	1,695–1,770	533,428	304,194	57.0	100	100

Sea Pines and Palmetto Dunes conference centers are direct competitors of The Cottages. However, due to certain extenuating circumstances, the figures identifying these two facilities are not available. It is the opinion of management that Sea Pines and Palmetto Dunes both exceeded figures of The Cottages.

Briggs commented on the recent performance of The Cottages. "At the current activity level, we are just about breaking even, or perhaps generating a small profit. About half the room revenue goes to cover variable costs, the rest is contribution. We should be able to improve that by increasing the average room rates actually charged. It seems that we are having to give deeper concessions to the groups than we ought to. The major task facing us, though, is simply to increase occupancy. I see no reason that we can't increase to 30,000 room nights this year. Our current mix is about 60–40 business to social, but I'd like to see it shift to about 70 percent business, and 30 percent social. I think Benchmark and American Services would be happy with those numbers. It surely would help if the national sales office were to come through with the 5,000 room nights they are forecasting.

THE COTTAGES' PERSONAL TOUCH

"Whenever a meeting is held here, the participants leave raving about the quality of their experience. They like the accommodations, the recreation, the personal service that they have received in running their meetings, and particularly the villa concept. Having a small home all to oneself lets people 'get away from it all,' even in a big meeting setting. People really appreciate that.

"The villa concept is hard to conceptualize, though. I don't really think that most of the meeting planners understand what it looks like, and the advantages that it provides. We keep hearing that meeting planners want to have all their participants in the same building...one of the big hotels. Once they have seen the property, though, that all changes. Somehow, we've got to do a better job of conveying the villas concept, but, at $500 out-of-pocket cost, we can't afford to give every meeting planner and travel agent a free trip.

"Our people are our biggest asset. We really knock people out with our service. Everybody in the whole organization participates when a group is here—the salespeople, the secretaries, everybody. We do whatever it takes to make our visitors' stay the best experience they've ever had. One of our major problems is our location. It has its good points. We are right on the golf course. Shipyard Plantation is right in the middle of the island. It is quiet and peaceful. The problem is that we aren't on the beach. It's about a fifteen-minute walk to get there. When people hear that we aren't on the beach, it becomes a real obstacle to the sale. You just can't convince them that a few minutes' walk, or a bike ride, or stepping into one of our vans is an acceptable alternative."

THE OPTIONS FOR 1988—ADDITION OF A SALESPERSON

Briggs was considering the addition of another on-site salesperson. Both Kiley and Burdette were at their limits in terms of number of group clients they could handle. The time spent servicing current groups and dealing with inquiries left too little time available for prospecting. There was no question that coverage of potential accounts would improve, and that the goal of increasing the meetings side of The Cottages' business would be supported by the addition of a new salesperson. Further, Briggs believed that the nature of the sale almost required a personal contact to handle objections and to negotiate for the property.

The cost involved in such a move concerned Briggs. About $20,000 to $25,000 salary would be required to attract the caliber of person needed. Further, the benefits package provided by Benchmark would add a similar amount to the overall expense.

Beyond the costs, Briggs was concerned about his ability to justify the need for an additional person. Adding a person was a long-run commitment, not just a one-time expenditure. He himself had only been at The Cottages for eight weeks, so how would Benchmark view a request for additional staffing? Further, Briggs was wary of applying a long-term solution to a short-term problem. It would take time to recruit and select a new salesperson, to train that person, and to oversee the work. That time investment would put a real drain on the current staff and take away from the important task of gaining new business. Because of the complexity of the sale and of the interactions with the rest of the organization, it would take some time before the new salesperson could make a positive contribution on his own. Given that Amserve was thinking of selling The Cottages, Briggs was fearful that he could not even offer the security that the position would be there after a few months.

OPTION TWO—INCREASING THE PROMOTIONAL BUDGET

A second option that appealed to Briggs was simply increasing the promotional budget by a sizable margin. The budget for 1987 had been approximately $325,000. Media advertising, direct mail, collateral materials, and merchandising were all accounted for in that figure.

Briggs explained, "Awareness is the key. We simply have to make people aware that The Cottages exists, and that it is the premier resort and conference center in the Southeast. Our past advertising has done a good job, but it hasn't gone far enough. When the salespeople call a potential client, if that meeting planner hasn't even heard of The Cottages, the sale is almost impossible. Besides, when people have seen the property, they are hooked. If we can increase the number of people that we can bring here on 'FAM' trips, we can increase the business."

The difficulty with raising the promotional budget was the uncertainty and difficulty of measuring results. Briggs was at a loss about how to prove the worth of advertising versus direct sales contacts. He also knew that the meeting planners and travel agents received many of the travel industry magazines, all of them full of enticing pictures and exotic resorts. At what level of expenditure did an advertisement "break through" into meaningful awareness? (Exhibit 10 lists media costs for some major travel industry magazines.)

OPTION THREE—AN ON-PREMISE RESTAURANT

A third option was to build an on-premise restaurant. Briggs was convinced that the lack of a restaurant on-site was a major drawback. "The meeting planners are very concerned over the lack of a restaurant. They simply can't believe that we can serve quality meals in a quality fashion without a facility on-site. It seems to be a problem every time we talk to a group. I'm certain that it has cost us business.

"The caterer that we deal with is really excellent. The food is well prepared, and they offer us a good selection. Still, we have had some problems. A few weeks ago we had a group in, and they were having steak for dinner. One of the men wanted his steak rare. We do have a microwave, so we could cook it some more, but we couldn't give

EXHIBIT 10   Media Cases—Selected Travel Magazines

	Full Page B & W 1×	Circulation	Target Audience
Best's Insurance Convention Guide	$1,155	7,764	Insurance Meeting Planners
Business Travel News	4,125	42,617	Planners & Travel Agents
Corporate Meetings & Incentives	3,385	40,252	Corporate Executives and Travel Agents
Corporate Travel	4,125	40,523	Corporate Travel Decision Makers
Medical Meetings	1,795	13,249	Meeting Planners in Health Care
Meeting News	6,125	70,658	Meeting Planners
Meetings & Conventions	7,410	79,166	Meeting Planners
Official Meeting Facilities Guide	4,290	17,089	Association Corporate Travel Agents
Successful Meetings	5,815	77,457	Executive Meeting Planners
OAG Travel Planner & Hotel Motel Guide	2,140	63,128	Travel Agents
Official Hotel & Resort Guide	7,040	21,500	Travel Agents
Travel Agent	2,400	34,724	Travel Agents

Note: Four-color advertising added 20 percent to 40 percent to the B & W costs. Multiple insertions (6×) brought per-issue costs down by roughly 25 percent.

him a rarer steak. When something like that happens, it takes about 20 minutes to get something delivered from the caterer. Occasionally, we have the problem of having too few meals, or too many meals, or someone wanting to change from one selection to another. We can't do the repair jobs. We also cannot provide traditional room service, although the kitchens in the villas alleviate that problem somewhat.

"Sometimes it just doesn't seem that the caterer is really giving us his complete attention. He runs two restaurants on the island and does a lot of other catering."

Estimates for the cost of building an addition to the conference center to house complete kitchen facilities ranged from $350,000 to $500,000 for a turnkey operation. These figures did not include the costs of dining rooms, furnishings, or other expenses normally associated with a restaurant. Briggs had intended to use the existing facilities, the meeting rooms and furnishings, for dining areas. If remodeling and furnishings were to be included, an additional $350,000 would be required. In 1987, Briggs estimated that The Cottages had sold approximately $300,000 in food, on which they had received a 10 percent commission. If the restaurant operated according to industry norms, Briggs could expect to receive the same 10 percent of gross food revenues as contribution. Briggs also estimated that sales of alcoholic beverages had roughly a 50 percent contribution and that level would also hold if they were to open the restaurant. For planning purposes Briggs estimated that the life of the facility would be approximately 10 years, but that furnishings would have to be replaced at least every five years. He also thought that the company's cost of capital was in the 12 percent range.

Briggs was concerned about how the restaurant would fit in, given the legal environment on the island. The necessary zoning and permits were often difficult and sometimes impossible to obtain for any sort of building or improvement. A new restaurant would require at least several months of legal maneuvering with no guarantee that the necessary permits would be forthcoming. Briggs recalled the difficulty that The Cottages had run into in placing a sign at the entrance to the property. After months of argument, they were still prohibited from displaying a sign. With no guarantee of permits, Briggs feared that Benchmark and Amserve would deny any request for capital expenditures for 1988. Further, once the caterer learned of the restaurant project, would there be an effect on the quality of food and service until the opening?

CONCLUSION

All of the options were complicated by the breadth of the market that The Cottages had been serving. Analysis of the past customers had yielded no consistent patterns. It seemed logical that they should focus their efforts because they could apply only limited resources toward gaining new business. Liz Kiley had argued for targeting specific cities and concentrating promotional efforts on them. Tina Burdette seemed to favor more local efforts, saying, "Once someone has decided to come to Hilton Head, it's a lot easier to convince them that The Cottages is the best place than to try to argue someone into coming to Hilton Head at all."

Briggs rose from his desk, stretched, and watched out the window as another foursome prepared to hit their approach shots to the green. As he observed, the first of the group hit an errant shot that rattled into a palm tree to the right of the green and dropped with a splash into the pond between the golf course and the conference center. As he went back to his work he thought, "Maybe working on the marketing plan isn't so bad after all."

Polaroid and the Family-Imaging Market

Lew G. Brown and David R. Vestal

"Don't do anything that someone else can do. Don't undertake a project unless it is manifestly important and nearly impossible."

—Edwin Land
Founder
Polaroid Corporation

INTRODUCTION

At precisely 7:30 A.M. on a cold, blustery, New England day in January 1992, Roger Clapp, project manager for the Joshua Project, walked into the conference room near his office in Polaroid's Cambridge, Massachusetts, office complex known as Technology Square. The Joshua team leaders were already present: Vicki Thomas and Nick Ward from marketing; Rick Kirkendall, division vice president for Consumer Imaging; Roy Baessler, camera engineering; Howard Fortner, camera manufacturing; Ron Klay, film assembly manufacturing; Roger Borghesani, film assembly engineering; John Sturgis, film systems; Louise Reimenschneider, photographic systems; Bob Ruckstuhl, film programs; Harry Korotkin, finance; and Bob McCune, who served as the group's organizational development/team building facilitator. The group had been meeting every Tuesday morning since 1988 when Roger had assumed leadership of the Joshua Project, the code name for Polaroid's newest camera for the instant photography market.

Roger and Hal Page, the Joshua leader before Roger, used the meetings as a way to coordinate the many disparate efforts that went into any high-technology product's development. At each meeting, group members discussed what was going on in their areas and what problems they were encountering. Roger believed that if everyone had lots of information about all project areas and the project's overall direction, they would align their area's activities with that direction. The meetings would produce a self-aligning process.

As Roger said good morning, he glanced around the room. He could tell the group members were tired. They had been working hard on Joshua for a long time and they had learned that he expected a lot from them. Five-day, 55-hour weeks were not enough.

This case was prepared by Professor Lew G. Brown and Undergraduate Research Assistant David Vestal of the University of North Carolina at Greensboro, as a basis for class discussion. It is not intended to illustrate either effective or ineffective handling of an administrative situation. The authors express their appreciation to Polaroid, the Photo Marketing Association, and Morgan Stanley for their cooperation in developing this case.

Most team members worked six-day weeks, often working into the night. Roger was always there, too. He didn't ask them to do anything he didn't do.

From his previous work with project teams, Roger had realized that groups went through three stages. Initially, the group felt excited as it kicked off a multimillion-dollar development project and faced the technological, marketing, and business challenges. Toward completion of the project, the group would experience the exhilaration of seeing its work come to fruition. However, the middle stage was the hardest. The group would go through an emotional "dip" when it seemed that every problem or delay brought more problems and delays. They would feel that they would never complete the project. There would be much frustration.

Roger realized that he and Bob McCune faced the challenge of keeping the group moving through this middle stage, but he had to admit that even he sometimes felt the project was impossible. He knew, however, that the project was manifestly important to revitalizing Polaroid's instant camera sales.

"Well, let's get started," Roger began as he glanced at the Countdown Clock. During 1990, Roger realized that he needed to create a sense of urgency in the team. The team had decided to have the camera ready for introduction in late 1992, but Roger worried that it was easy for team members to feel that they had plenty of time or that deadlines were flexible.

Therefore, he had ordered the construction of a "countdown clock." The clock counted down the number of days and hours to "zero day"—the target day when everything had to be ready to meet the market introduction schedule. The clock ran on electricity and had a battery backup. The clock started with a key, but after it had been started, no one could stop it. Roger wanted to make it clear to the group that there would be no on-again, off-again deadlines.

The group had agreed to start the clock in late 1990. Now it hung on the wall in the conference room, looming over their meetings and reminding them that time did not stand still.

"Besides our usual reports from each area, we have a meeting in three weeks with the corporate officers," Roger said. "We need to make a presentation on Joshua's status, so we need to begin to prepare for that today. However, most importantly, we need to begin to develop our marketing strategy for the U.S. market. Therefore, we'll conclude today's meeting with a presentation from the marketing folks that will serve as background for their recommended strategy, which they will present also in three weeks. First, however, let's start with reports of good news."

POLAROID'S HISTORY

Edwin Land started Polaroid Corporation in 1937 in a Cambridge garage and developed the polarization process. In 1943, while on vacation with his family in Santa Fe, New Mexico, his three-year-old daughter asked why she could not see right away the picture of her he had just taken. Within an hour, Land had developed a mental picture of the camera, the film, and the chemistry that would allow him to solve the puzzle his daughter had presented.

In 1948, Land introduced the first Polaroid instant camera. By the time he stepped down as the company's chief executive officer in 1980, at age 70, he had built Polaroid into a $1.4 billion company. When he died in 1991, he left behind 537 patents, second only to Thomas A. Edison. (See Exhibits 1 and 2 for Polaroid's financial data.)

Land's single-minded pursuit of technology led to many successes but also to his career's major failure. Convinced that he needed to take his instant photography concept from the portrait camera to the movie camera, Land and his engineers developed the Polavision instant movie system, launching it in 1977. Although Polavision met Land's criteria of being "nearly impossible," it was not quite "manifestly important." Polavision was too late—other companies had already invented videotape recording. Within two years, Polaroid had to write off the project at a cost of $68.5 million.

William McCune, Jr., Polaroid's president, felt that the company needed to move away from its dependence on amateur instant photography. Rather than stand in the way, Land resigned in 1980, and McCune became chairman.

McCune led Polaroid's diversification efforts, moving into disk drives, fiber optics, video recorders, inkjet printers, and floppy disks. By the mid-1980s, however, some observers argued that the diversification effort was not paying off.

EXHIBIT 1   Consolidated Statements of Earnings and Balance Sheets

(In millions, except per share data)	1991	1990	1989
		Years Ended December 31,	
Net sales			
United States	$1,113.6	$1,058.3	$1,091.8
International	957.0	913.4	812.9
Total net sales	2,070.6	1,971.7	1,904.7
Cost of goods sold	1,082.5	1,011.8	966.0
Marketing, research, engineering, and administrative expenses	741.5	675.6	634.5
Restructuring and other expense	—	—	40.5
Total costs	1,824.0	1,687.4	1,641.0
Profit from operations	246.6	284.3	263.7
Other income/(expense)			
Litigation settlement, net of employee incentives	871.6	—	—
Interest income	25.6	19.7	37.2
Other	(2.2)	(4.7)	(2.1)
Total other income	895.0	15.0	35.1
Interest expense	58.4	81.3	86.2
Earnings before income taxes	1,083.2	218.0	212.6
Federal, state, and foreign income taxes	399.5	67.0	67.6
Net earnings	$ 683.7	$ 151.0	$ 145.0
Primary earnings per common share	$ 12.54	$ 2.20	$ 1.96
Fully diluted earnings per common share	$ 10.88	—	—
Cash dividends per common share	$ .60	$ .60	.60
Weighted Average Common Shares Outstanding (000's)	$ 49,943	$ 51,519	$ 57,568
Stock price			
High	$ 28⅛	$ 48⅛	$ 50⅜
Low	$ 19⅝	$ 20¼	$ 27⅞

(Continued on next page)

Exhibit 1   *(Continued)*

Polaroid Corporation and Subsidiary Companies

(In millions)	Years ended December 31,		
	1991	**1990**	**1989**
Assets			
Current assets			
Cash and cash equivalents	$ 162.9	$ 83.8	$ 131.2
Short-term investments	82.3	114.2	148.1
Receivables, less allowances	476.1	441.6	459.5
Inventories	524.3	519.0	529.9
Other assets	94.3	81.7	77.1
Total current assets	1,339.9	1,240.3	1,345.8
Property, plant, and equipment			
Total property, plant, and equipment	1,598.9	1,440.0	1,326.7
Less accumulated depreciation	1,049.5	979.0	895.8
Net property, plant, and equipment	549.4	461.0	430.9
Total assets	1,889.3	1,701.3	1,776.7
Liabilities and Stockholders' Equity			
Current liabilities			
Short-term debt	$ 145.9	$ 168.6	$ 299.0
Current portion of long-term debt	$ 26.7	79.4	70.4
Payables and accruals	237.4	218.4	216.2
Compensation and benefits	131.8	123.8	143.9
Federal, state, and foreign income taxes	102.8	41.0	44.7
Total current liabilities	644.6	631.2	774.2
Long-term debt	471.8	513.8	531.8
Redeemable preferred stock equity	—	348.6	321.9
Preferred stock	—	—	—
Common stockholders' equity			
Common stock, $1 par value, authorized 150,000,000 shares	75.4	75.4	75.4
Additional paid-in capital	379.5	379.5	379.5
Retained earnings	1,609.9	1,038.3	955.8
Less: Treasury stock, at cost	1,083.7	1,053.1	997.5
Deferred compensation—ESOP	208.2	232.4	264.4
Total common stockholders' equity	772.9	207.7	148.8
Total liabilities and stockholders' equity	1,889.3	1,701.3	1,776.7

Source: *Polaroid Corporation 1991 Annual Report*

EXHIBIT 2   Income and Assets by Geographic Area

(In millions)	Years ended December 31,		
	1991	**1990**	**1989**
Sales			
United States			
Customers	$1,113.6	$1,058.3	$1,091.8
Intercompany	438.5	421.4	407.7
	1,552.1	1,479.7	1,499.5
Europe			
Customers	624.6	598.5	504.5
Intercompany	287.3	159.6	167.4
	911.9	758.1	671.9
Asia/Pacific and Western Hemisphere			
Customers	332.4	314.9	308.4
Intercompany	51.0	11.0	9.1
	383.4	325.9	317.5
Eliminations	(776.8)	(592.0)	(584.2)
Net Sales	$2,070.6	$1,971.7	$1,904.7
Profits			
United States	$ 120.9	$ 179.9	$ 150.2
Europe	94.4	97.7	115.0
Asia/Pacific and Western Hemisphere	40.3	23.8	31.5
General corporate expense	(18.0)	(13.4)	(13.0)
Eliminations	9.0	(3.7)	(20.0)
Profit from operations	246.6	284.3	263.7
Other income less interest expense	836.6	(66.3)	(51.1)
Earnings before income taxes	$1,083.2	$ 218.0	$ 212.6
Assets			
United States	$1,153.9	$1,055.0	$1,054.2
Europe	548.7	507.3	475.7
Asia/Pacific and Western Hemisphere	165.8	160.2	168.1
Corporate assets (cash, cash equivalents, and short-term investments)	245.2	198.0	279.3
Eliminations	(224.2)	(219.2)	(200.6)
Total Assets	$1,889.4	$1,701.3	$1,776.7

Source: *Polaroid Corporation 1991 Annual Report*

In contrast, sales to amateur photographers and sales of instant cameras for business use were going strong. By 1986, these sales accounted for 55 percent of Polaroid's revenues. Consumers were still interested in instant cameras. To stimulate that demand, Polaroid introduced the Spectra camera in 1986, its first major new camera since the SX-70 in 1972. Some observers predicted that Spectra, priced at $150 to $225, was too expensive and would not sell. It sold anyway.

Edwin Land probably felt vindicated that Polaroid was refocusing on its core business, amateur instant photography. Polaroid had no direct competition in the U.S. instant photography market. The company had won a patent infringement suit against Kodak in 1985. The court ruling required Kodak to exit the instant photography business and pay Polaroid approximately $1 billion.

However, Land and Polaroid knew that the company faced severe competition in the larger photography market. Video camcorders, easy-to-use 35mm point-and-shoot cameras (often called 35mm rangefinders), and one-hour film developing were cutting deeply into Polaroid's market. Worldwide sales of instant cameras had fallen from a peak of 13 million units in 1978 to about 4 million in 1991. The new 35mm cameras were outselling instant cameras five to one. Polaroid realized that it had to do something to reinvigorate the amateur photography market and to expand its base.

HOW INSTANT CAMERAS WORK

In black-and-white instant photography's early days, the camera user had to pull the exposed instant picture from the camera, wait about one minute, peel off a piece of paper, and use a small sponge to apply a chemical coating to the picture to stop its development. Then the picture had to dry before someone could safely handle it.

When Polaroid introduced color instant photography in 1963, the technology had advanced so that the user still had to time the picture's development and remove the print from the film sheet but did not have to apply any chemicals. The film was still "sticky" for several minutes.

In 1972, Polaroid introduced the SX-70 instant camera, which used what the company called "integral film." As the name implied, the new film was an integrated structure that did not require the user to do any timing or other treatment. There were no excess pieces of the film or paper to discard. The one-piece unit contained all the chemicals necessary for development of the picture. The user still had to wait several minutes for the exposed picture to develop fully.

With integral film, within four-tenths of a second after the user pushed the shutter release button and exposed the film, the camera partially ejected the exposed film unit. A battery contained in the film cartridge powered the camera and the motor that ejected the film. As the camera ejected the picture, the film passed between two metal rollers. These rollers squeezed the film, bursting a small pod at the leading edge of the film. This pod contained chemical reagents that spread between the film unit's receiving and negative layers. The chemicals reacted with the negative layers based on the nature of the layer and the amount of each layer's exposure to light during the exposure process. (See Exhibit 3.) These reactions determined the lightness, darkness, and color of each area of the final picture. This chemical process was what the users saw as they watched the film develop from the plain, grayish-green initial film color to the finished picture. All of this development took place outside the camera in full light. Opacifying dyes in the reagent layer blocked additional light from entering the light-sensitive layers once the film exited the camera.

Because the users did not have to peel anything from the integral film unit or apply any chemical, they were technically able to take another picture immediately. However, because the camera only partially ejected the picture, the users had to take the exposed picture from the camera and find a place to put it, usually a pocket or nearby table. If the users took a second picture before removing the first, the second film unit

EXHIBIT 3: How Polaroid Instant Film Works

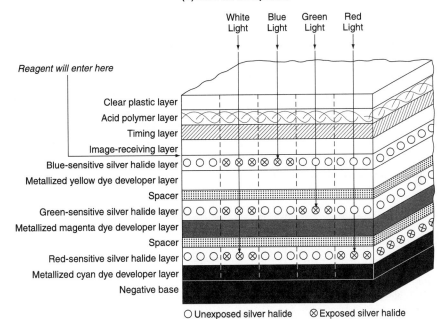

(A) The Film at Exposure

White Light   Blue Light   Green Light   Red Light

Reagent will enter here

Clear plastic layer
Acid polymer layer
Timing layer
Image-receiving layer
Blue-sensitive silver halide layer
Metallized yellow dye developer layer
Spacer
Green-sensitive silver halide layer
Metallized magenta dye developer layer
Spacer
Red-sensitive silver halide layer
Metallized cyan dye developer layer
Negative base

○ Unexposed silver halide   ⊗ Exposed silver halide

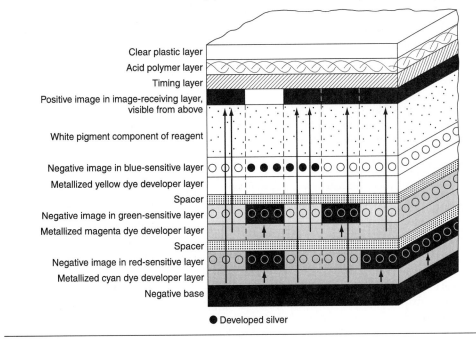

(B) The Developed Picture

Clear plastic layer
Acid polymer layer
Timing layer
Positive image in image-receiving layer, visible from above
White pigment component of reagent
Negative image in blue-sensitive layer
Metallized yellow dye developer layer
Spacer
Negative image in green-sensitive layer
Metallized magenta dye developer layer
Spacer
Negative image in red-sensitive layer
Metallized cyan dye developer layer
Negative base

● Developed silver

Source: Neblette's Handbook of Photography and Reprography

would simply push the first out of the camera, causing it to fall to the floor. (See Exhibit 4 for a description of Polaroid's camera line.)

NEW-PRODUCT DEVELOPMENT AT POLAROID

In the 1940s and 1950s, a product-development process called "skunkworks" sprung to life at Polaroid. This process allowed maverick individuals or groups to pursue new-product design ideas unofficially. These individuals or groups frequently generated technology-driven new-product designs, giving little, if any, consideration to marketing or business strategy. Further, operating managers often had only limited influence over the design of machinery. Film and camera development followed parallel paths. Development of the film pack occurred after development of the film components. This development process invariably resulted in major problems when managers tried to get all the parts to work together.

EXHIBIT 4   Guide to Polaroid Instant Cameras

OneStep Flash Camera
   Built-in electronic flash folds down when not in use.
   Flash range 4 to 10 feet.
   Autofocus. Range 4 feet to infinity.
   Used 600 PLUS film.
   Easy to use, just point and shoot.
   Suggested retail $27 to $33. Dealer price $27.

Cool Cam Camera
   Built-in electronic flash folds down when not in use.
   Flash range 4 to 10 feet.
   Autofocus. Range 4 feet to infinity.
   Uses 600 PLUS film.
   Easy to use, just point and shoot.
   Free, matching camera bag with return of camera registration card.
   Suggested retail $30 to $35. Dealer price $27.

Impulse Cameras
   Impulse
      Focus range 2 feet to infinity.
      Manual dual lens for close-up shots 2 to 4 feet.
      Pop-up flash, range 4 to 10 feet.
      Uses 600 PLUS instant film.
      Easy to use, just point and shoot.
      Suggested retail $40 to $45. Dealer price $36.

   Impulse AF
      Has same features as Impulse plus:
      Autofocus.
      Self-timer.
      Flash range 2 to 14 feet.
      Suggested retail $80 to $85. Dealer price $71.50.

Spectra Cameras
   Spectra 2 AF Camera
      Autofocus, range 2 feet to infinity.
      Auto exposure, flash range 2 to 15 feet.
      Uses Spectra instant color film.
      Pictures guaranteed for one full year after camera purchase (up to a limit of 10 packs of film).
      Camera folds to fit neatly in a briefcase.
      Easy to use, just point and shoot.
      Suggested retail $79 to $85. Dealer price $74.
   Spectra AF Camera
      Has same features as Spectra 2 AF plus:
      Self-timer.
      Control panel allows user to turn off automatic features.
      Viewfinder displays symbols to help get best pictures.
      Suggested retail $100 to $110. Dealer price $85.

Source: Polaroid Corporation

BIRTH OF A NEW PROCESS

In 1984, a skunkworks team from camera engineering began discussing Polaroid's next camera, and a team from film research began to work on possibilities for a new film. The two groups met unofficially to share ideas. These "blue sky" meetings focused on the problems of picture quality, film cost, and camera size. The groups soon narrowed their discussions to a film that would fit a smaller camera.

Unlike some skunkworks groups, these two groups sought marketing's participation. In 1984 and 1985, Polaroid's internal market research group conducted focus groups to get consumer reactions to small, medium, and standard-sized instant cameras with picture-storage features. The results from these focus groups suggested that some consumers would be interested in the smaller camera and its smaller pictures. Polaroid President I. MacAllister Booth asked his assistant, Roger Clapp, to develop the idea.

THE JOSHUA STORY

Enter Joshua. Even as Polaroid introduced the Spectra camera in 1986, Booth, who had just assumed the CEO's position, realized that the company had to continue work on its next new camera. He appointed Peter Kliem as director of research and engineering, combining two departments that had traditionally had separate new-product development responsibilities. Clapp took responsibility for camera engineering. Booth also asked Hal Page, Polaroid's vice president for quality, to become program manager for the next consumer camera. For the first time, Polaroid had a single, high-level program manager responsible for all aspects of new-product development—for film as well as camera, for manufacturing as well as marketing.

Page began a yearlong process of reexamination to generate ideas for a new camera. He started brainstorming sessions by showing a training film that featured a cartoon character named Joshua. In the film, Joshua finds himself trapped in a box and tries all the obvious ways to escape. Finally, in frustration, Joshua gently taps his finger against a wall and unexpectedly finds that his finger has poked a hole. He struggles to make the hole bigger and escapes.

Joshua sent a message to the hundreds of people from many functional groups who attended Page's brainstorming sessions. To generate truly innovative ideas for a new camera, the employees would have to attack new problems with new ways of thinking—"out-of-the-box" approaches. To create something other than an extension of Polaroid's existing cameras, people would have to think creatively and give up old prejudices, including, perhaps, their prejudice against smaller cameras. The brainstorming sessions also helped participants face the tension-filled question of whether new products should be "technology driven" or "marketing driven." Participants soon learned the answer: They had to be both.

Hal Page also showed the groups a film that dramatically illustrated the value of internal picture storage for the new camera. The film showed tourists at Disney World using 35mm automatic cameras to take picture after picture. Other tourists, however, stood around watching their one Polaroid picture develop and searching for a place to put it. Page and others thought consumers would take more pictures if they did not have to stop after each one to find a place to put it while it developed. Furthermore, consumers would damage and lose fewer pictures.

This storage feature, however, required that the camera's film bend around a chute after exposure to enter the storage compartment. Engineers told Larry Swensen, a member of the marketing department, that Polaroid's standard film would not bend without breaking or coming apart. Swensen, however, refused to accept this conventional wisdom. He made a working model of a camera that allowed standard film to make a 180-degree U-turn during processing. The camera released the photographs into a built-in storage chamber, where the user could view them as they developed. No longer would the user need to interrupt picture taking to find a safe place for each picture. Out-of-the-box thinking had begun to work.

Page also used outside marketing consultants. Based on studies of small cameras that Polaroid had conducted between 1984 and 1986, the consultants concluded that there would be a market for a smaller instant camera and that the camera would not cannibalize Polaroid's existing lines. Additional outside studies in 1987 and 1988 examined consumer preferences regarding camera size, camera price, and film price. Another study estimated the sales volume that Polaroid could expect from various feature combinations.

Polaroid had based these studies on the assumption that it would set the retail price of the new camera at $150. As the studies progressed, however, management concluded that the market at the $150 retail price would be too small and that it should price the camera so that its retail price would be about $100. This change required more market studies.

In 1988, Hal Page left Polaroid, and Roger Clapp took over what employees had dubbed the "Joshua Program." Roger had been with Polaroid 22 years, having earned a bachelor's degree in chemical engineering at Northeastern University and an MBA from Harvard. Although Page and his groups had made much progress, many technical and marketing hurdles remained. Design engineers faced tradeoffs between size and other features, such as performance and cost. As a result, the planned camera had become too large. Roger Clapp remarked that it looked like a "brick." Clapp stopped the design process and ordered the developers to reconsider all tradeoffs. This planned four-week pause, however, turned into an eight-month interruption, as it opened the door for reconsideration of all the lingering issues.

As Clapp's managers reviewed the Joshua project, they realized that they needed to clarify the camera's market potential at a $100 price and to conduct new research to bring marketing fully behind the program. The managers agreed that the last market research hurdle would be an Assessor Test conducted by Professor Glenn Urban of MIT's Sloan School of Management.

The Assessor Test involved setting up mock stores at six geographically diverse sites in the United States. These "stores" offered 25 different cameras (both Polaroid's and competing models), with prices ranging from inexpensive to expensive. Each store had a real counter, a film rack, feature cards, and sales clerks to answer questions. As a part of the interview process, Polaroid's advertising agency created full-color sheets of print advertising for the new camera. Polaroid also developed realistic Joshua camera models. Over a one-month period, 2,400 people participated in market interviews and testing at the six "stores." Researchers carefully screened participants on factors such as age, sex, race, and economic status to make sure the group represented demographics of the U.S. population as a whole.

During this time, another camera design emerged from a one-man skunkworks. Although the Joshua project was well under way, Larry Douglas had continued to work on his idea. Douglas' camera offered an ingenious design for a camera that popped open to take a picture, then closed automatically. Polaroid ordered market research on Douglas' camera.

The two studies provided convincing evidence that there was a market for a smaller instant camera and that Joshua would be the preferred product. Polaroid's board of directors gave Joshua the go-ahead in late 1989.

VISION TO REALITY

Although Polaroid had devoted an extraordinary amount of time and energy to the Joshua project before its final approval, the camera and the film were still in the development stage. Polaroid employees throughout the company still had to solve many problems.

Manufacturing had to install a new computer-aided-design system and to select a new material and design for the camera's mainframe. The camera would employ through-the-lens viewing, the same viewing system found on millions of 35mm cameras. The picture storage compartment would have to hold up to all 10 of the pictures in a film package, and the camera would have to pass Polaroid's four-foot drop test and meet other aggressive quality goals.

Polaroid created a cross-functional steering committee to manage the film manufacturing process. This team addressed issues such as how to include the battery in the smaller film pack and how to design the film manufacturing process itself. Like Polaroid's other instant film, Joshua's film would come in a package of 10 exposures and would cost the consumer about $1 per picture, as compared with about $.40 for a conventional 35mm picture. The picture would be about 2⅛ by 2⅞ inches, a pocket-sized format that was smaller than conventional 35mm prints.

Electronics engineers designed a new microcontroller to be the heart of the Joshua camera. The new controller solved many longstanding technical and manufacturing problems. Using software, it provided "track and hold," "trim and speed," and "wink" features to measure the light available for the picture, set the exposure, and find the distance from the camera to the subject. In other words, like many 35mm cameras on the market, Joshua would have "automatic everything." In all these processes, managers insisted on meeting the highest quality and reliability standards.

By Labor Day 1991, the Joshua team had produced 24 Joshua prototype cameras for testing by Polaroid employees over the holiday weekend. Twenty-three cameras worked. The team continued to produce cameras for weekend tests and made a concentrated assault on any problems the tests identified. For Christmas 1991, the team produced 300 Joshua cameras for non-Polaroid employees from coast to coast to test. This test represented the earliest time in a product's development that Polaroid had ever placed cameras with outside users. Managers believed that they were making a new camera that met real customer needs, but they wanted to base their decisions on market research, not on instincts.

Analysis of the pictures taken in the field tests suggested that Joshua users took more vertical pictures and more close-ups than did users of other Polaroid cameras. Based on these reactions, engineers adjusted the camera's exposure systems to perform optimally in vertical format or close-up situations. Polaroid also conducted market tests in foreign countries. Polaroid calculated that by the time it announced the camera, more than 2,000 Polaroid and non-Polaroid consumers would have made more than 55,000 images for picture analysis.

BACK AT THE MEETING: THE U.S. FAMILY-IMAGING MARKET

After the team members had made their initial status reports, Roger turned to Vicki Thomas, senior marketing manager. Vicki had recently joined Polaroid from GTE. She had an undergraduate degree in political science from the University of Vermont and an MBA from the American Graduate School of International Management.

"As you know, we have been focusing on camera and film manufacturing and on market research," Roger said. "It is now time for us to begin to develop our marketing strategy for the U.S. consumer market. At our last meeting we asked Vicki to prepare an overview of the market so we would have a background for the marketing plans she, Nick, and Rick will present later. Vicki."

"Thanks, Roger. I have prepared a series of overheads that summarize the U.S. market that I want to share with you now. This first overhead (Exhibit 5) presents a U.S. economic overview. We feel that the recession is over and that economic conditions will improve slowly during 1992 and into 1993. Disposable income will increase about 2 percent over 1991, and the prime rate and inflation will remain relatively low. We also believe the unemployment rate will continue in the low 7 percent range and that consumer confidence will remain relatively unchanged at about 65 on a 0-to-100 scale. There may be some higher taxes on individuals and corporations due to the federal government's budgetary problems. In summary, we feel that consumers remain cautious and that they are increasingly searching for value in the products and services they purchase.

EXHIBIT 5:   U.S. Economic Overview

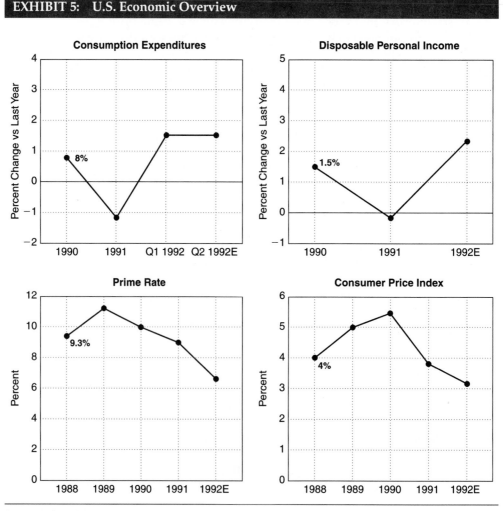

Source: Polaroid Corporation

This concern with value puts pressure on instant photography because many consumers feel that instant film's price is very high compared with standard 35mm film.

"This overhead (Exhibit 6) provides a societal overview and shows that we believe that the United States is becoming increasingly fragmented. Minority populations are becoming more significant, as is the mature population. Further, we are also seeing an explosion of specialized media and communication channels. The United States is becoming a 'salad bowl' instead of a 'melting pot.'

"We now turn to the U.S. camera market itself (Exhibit 7). This overhead uses Photo Marketing Association data and Morgan Stanley data to show that, although the total still-camera market (not including camcorders) is flat, 35mm rangefinder camera sales (the so-called point-and-shoot 35mm camera without interchangeable lenses) are growing rapidly. The 35mm rangefinder has taken share from other camera types in the last six years. The

EXHIBIT 6   Societal Overview

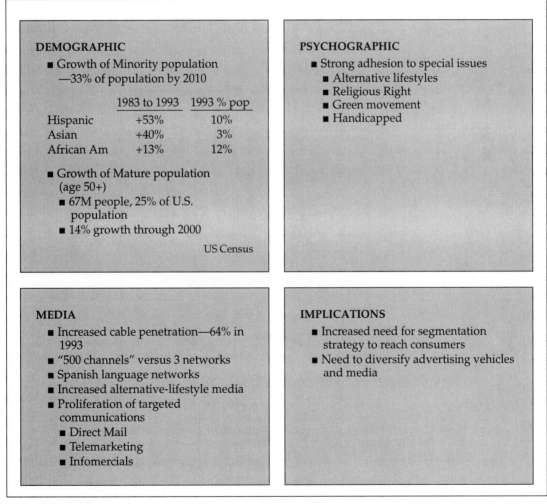

DEMOGRAPHIC
- Growth of Minority population
  —33% of population by 2010

	1983 to 1993	1993 % pop
Hispanic	+53%	10%
Asian	+40%	3%
African Am	+13%	12%

- Growth of Mature population (age 50+)
  - 67M people, 25% of U.S. population
  - 14% growth through 2000

US Census

PSYCHOGRAPHIC
- Strong adhesion to special issues
  - Alternative lifestyles
  - Religious Right
  - Green movement
  - Handicapped

MEDIA
- Increased cable penetration—64% in 1993
- "500 channels" versus 3 networks
- Spanish language networks
- Increased alternative-lifestyle media
- Proliferation of targeted communications
  - Direct Mail
  - Telemarketing
  - Infomercials

IMPLICATIONS
- Increased need for segmentation strategy to reach consumers
- Need to diversify advertising vehicles and media

Source: Polaroid Corporation

EXHIBIT 7:   U.S. Camera Market Overview

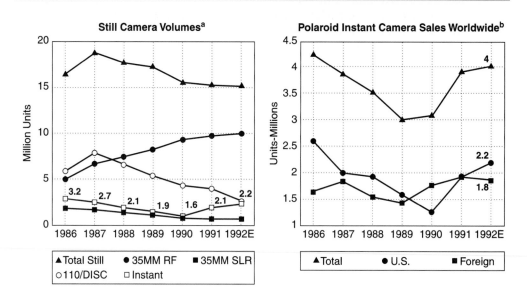

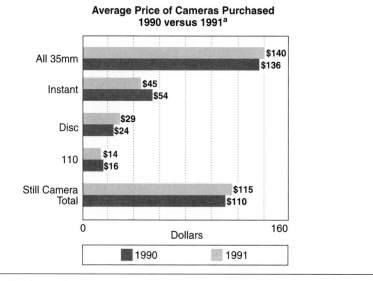

[a]Source: Photo Marketing Association
[b]This data provided by Morgan Stanley & Co., not Polaroid. Its use here is for case purposes only.

rangefinders offer excellent photo quality, automated functions, ease of use versus traditional 35mm Single Lens Reflex cameras, compact size, built-in zoom lenses in some cases, and relatively low prices (as low as $19.95 for some simple versions). Vivitar, Olympus, and Polaroid have seen their total shares of the camera market grow in the past four years, whereas Kodak's has fallen. Many major players are introducing new models.

   "We estimate that about 90 percent of households own a still camera of some kind and about 20 percent own an instant camera. As you know, although our U.S. consumer business is reasonably healthy, our sales revenue has been flat since 1986, even though our shipments and market share are up. Average 35mm rangefinder camera prices have been in the $95 range for the past five years, but average instant-camera prices are falling into the low $40 range. The average price for 35mm SLR cameras is $333 today, compared with about $195 in 1986.

"I thought you would also be interested in camera distribution and prices, so I included these next two overheads (Exhibits 8 and 9) based on Photo Marketing Association data. The major change since 1986 has been the almost one-third increase in our percentage distribution through discount stores, including stores such as Wal-Mart and Kmart. The Photo Marketing Association's research indicates that consumers purchase 58.1 percent of 110/125/disc/instant cameras in discount department stores and another 23.7 percent in other mass retail stores."

"Exhibit 8 reflects the importance of mass retailers (including discount stores) in the camera market. Camera sales through these outlets dwarf average sales in other outlets; but, as you can see, the average prices are much lower."

EXHIBIT 8   Camera Distribution and Prices 1991

| | AVERAGE NUMBER OF CAMERAS SOLD PER FIRM[a] | | | | |
Camera Type	All Specialty Retailers Combined	Camera Store No Mini Lab	Camera Store with Mini Lab	Stand Alone Mini Lab	All Mass Retailers Combined
35MM SLR	122	84	174	42	22
35MM RF	359	253	665	90	2,662
110/DISC	194	12	324	13	165
Instant:					
Spectra	24	11	32	12	N/A
Impulse	35	22	43	15	12
Cool Cam	68	12	105	11	N/A
Other	37	13	50	13	2,050
Total Inst.	82	32	118	23	1,371
Total Still Cameras	401	241	770	91	2,916
	AVERAGE PRICE PER CAMERA				
35MM SLR	$373	$413	$364	$391	$387
35MM RF	$205	$258	$200	$168	$37
110	$18	$25	$18	$22	$15
Instant:					
Spectra	$122	$143	$118	$136	N/A
Impulse	$68	$72	$67	$86	$39
Cool Cam	$35	$40	$34	$54	N/A
Other	$117	$62	$56	$75	$30
Total Inst.	$82	$108	$67	$97	$30

[a]Numbers sold are per firm, not per outlet. A firm that sells a particular camera format may not do so in all its outlets.
Source: Photo Marketing Association

EXHIBIT 9:   Still Cameras Purchased: Format Mix (by outlet type)

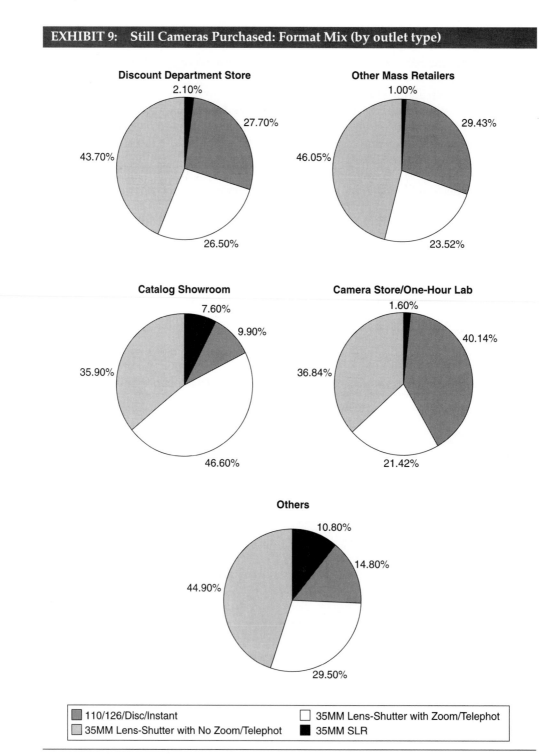

Note: Other mass retailers include combination/hypermarket, supermarket, drug store, department store (not discount).
Base: Total still cameras purchased, except single-use cameras.
Source: Photo Marketing Association

"Exhibit 9 shows that these cameras account for about 28 percent of the cameras sold in discount stores and about 29 percent in other mass retailers. Our top ten accounts generated about 60 percent of our sales in 1991 versus about 45 percent in 1986."

"Exhibit 10 uses data from the Photo Marketing Association and Morgan Stanley to describe the U.S. film market. As you can see, total exposures are flat, as are our film shipments. However, 35mm film is taking a growing market share while our sales are

EXHIBIT 10: Film Market

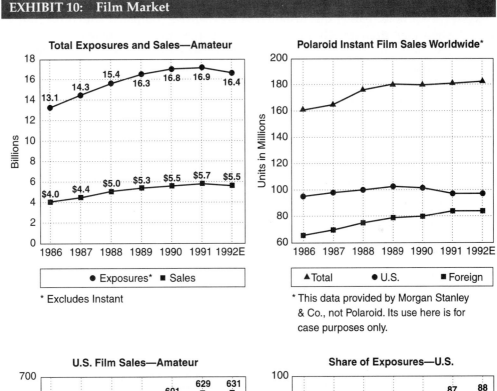

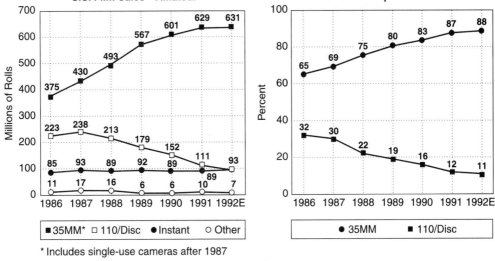

aSource: Photo Marketing Association

53

relatively flat. As you know, film purchasing accounts for 18 percent of the $12 billion amateur camera/film market and film processing accounts for 45.5 percent. Still cameras themselves account for 13.3 percent of annual sales.

"This overhead (Exhibit 11) again uses Photo Marketing Association data to show that our dollar volume of film sales to the amateur market has been relatively flat since 1988, although the dollar volume will increase slightly this year. Unit volume, however, has been declining since 1988. Instant film captures only a 1.5 percent share of the total film exposures and only 3.7 percent of the rolls or packages of film sold. Only about 2.8 percent of households purchase instant film in a three-month period, buying about three packs. This compares with 43 percent who purchase 35mm film, buying almost five rolls.

"I noted earlier that instant film is expensive compared with other film. Exhibit 11 shows this dramatically. In fact, the price gap between instant and 35mm film *per developed image* has been widening over the past six years. The cost per developed image for instant film will be about $.97 this year versus about $.39 for 35mm film. I analyzed some Photo Marketing Association data that indicated that consumers pay an average *premium* of almost 31 percent when they select "fast" processing versus regular processing at photo-processing outlets.

"While I'm discussing processing, this overhead (Exhibit 12) shows that the growth in minilab, 1-hour processing seems to have peaked and that discount and grocery store processing is actually growing faster than minilab. Most grocery/discount stores offer one-day turnaround. This is where we feel the growth is."

"Vicki, while you are on the subject of film, do you have any data on where consumers are buying film?" John Sturgis asked. "You folks are always asking me about making the film, but we haven't really discussed consumer buying habits."

"Good question, John," Vicki responded. "Let me see, I believe I have an overhead here on that. Yes, here it is (Exhibit 13). As I noted earlier, we have seen a significant increase in our camera sales in discount department stores. This chart based on Photo Marketing Association data shows that consumers purchased almost 37 percent of film in these stores, easily outdistancing drugstores and supermarkets. As in camera sales, our top 10 customers now account for about half of our film shipments, up from about one-third in 1986."

"How are we doing on consumer awareness?" Howard Fortner asked. "Like John, I worry about making the cameras rather than selling them. But I notice that when I meet people and tell them I work for Polaroid, often they really don't know much about us or our cameras."

"Another good question, and right on cue, Howard," Vicki responded. "I'll ask Nick to show you some overheads he prepared."

Nick Ward had only recently joined Polaroid as senior marketing research analyst. He had previously been with Kraft/General Foods and had a Ph.D. in experimental psychology from the University of Kansas and an undergraduate degree from UCLA in mathematical psychology.

"Howard, this overhead (Exhibit 14) shows some results from the Photo Marketing Association's most recent consumer-tracking studies. As you can see, Kodak has tremendous consumer awareness in both cameras and film, whereas we hover in the 40 percent to 50 percent range. Our camera awareness is significantly below 50 percent in terms of top-of-mind awareness. As you know, our research shows that most Polaroid owners also have at least one other camera in their home. Our advertising tracking studies show that about one-third of consumers see instant cameras fitting their lifestyle. However, consumers' perceptions of our cameras' quality have fallen somewhat,

EXHIBIT 11:   Sales Data

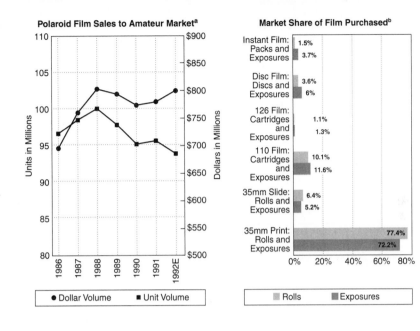

Polaroid Film Sales to Amateur Market[a]

Legend: ● Dollar Volume   ■ Unit Volume

Market Share of Film Purchased[b]

Film Type	Rolls	Exposures
Instant Film: Packs and Exposures	1.5%	3.7%
Disc Film: Discs and Exposures	3.6%	6%
126 Film: Cartridges and Exposures	1.1%	1.3%
110 Film: Cartridges and Exposures	10.1%	11.6%
35mm Slide: Rolls and Exposures	6.4%	5.2%
35mm Print: Rolls and Exposures	77.4%	72.2%

Legend: ▨ Rolls   ▨ Exposures

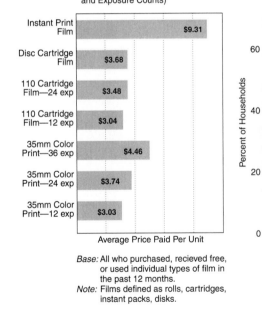

Price Paid Per Unit of Film[b]
(By Users of Individual Film Types and Exposure Counts)

Film Type	Average Price Paid Per Unit
Instant Print Film	$9.31
Disc Cartridge Film	$3.68
110 Cartridge Film—24 exp	$3.48
110 Cartridge Film—12 exp	$3.04
35mm Color Print—36 exp	$4.46
35mm Color Print—24 exp	$3.74
35mm Color Print—12 exp	$3.03

Base: All who purchased, recieved free, or used individual types of film in the past 12 months.
Note: Films defined as rolls, cartridges, instant packs, disks.

Percent of Households that Purchased Film, and Average Number of Rolls Per Household Per Quarter—Total U.S. by Film Type[b]

Percent of Households: Total 54.2%, 35mm Print 43.4%, 35mm Slide 2.6%, 110 9.4%, 126 1.3%, Disc 3.2%, Instant 2.8%

Average # of Rolls Bought per Quarter: 4.87, 4.63, 4.53, 2.81, 2.31, 3.16, 3.21

[a]Source: Morgan Stanley Research Estimates
[b]Source: Photo Marketing Association

55

EXHIBIT 12:   Minilab Processing

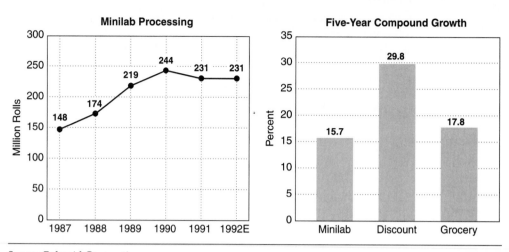

Source: Polaroid Corporation

EXHIBIT 13:   Percentage Breakdown of Household Film Purchased in the Past 12 Months (By Outlet Type)

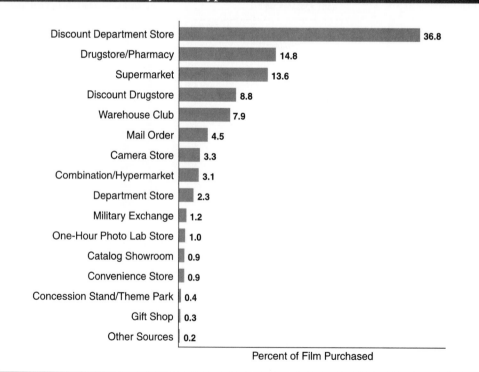

Source: Photo Marketing Association

EXHIBIT 14:   Advertising and Promotion

Which Photo Products/Brands Do You Recall Seeing or Hearing Advertised in the Past 12 Months?[a]

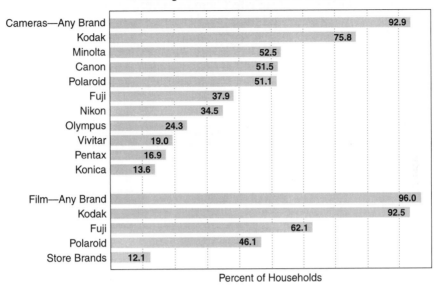

Brand	Value
Cameras—Any Brand	92.9
Kodak	75.8
Minolta	52.5
Canon	51.5
Polaroid	51.1
Fuji	37.9
Nikon	34.5
Olympus	24.3
Vivitar	19.0
Pentax	16.9
Konica	13.6
Film—Any Brand	96.0
Kodak	92.5
Fuji	62.1
Polaroid	46.1
Store Brands	12.1

Percent of Households

U.S. Advertising Awareness[b]

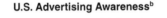

■ Spending ($)*   ● Awareness (%)
■ Share of Voice (%)

Advertising and Promoting Expenses as a Percent of Sales Worldwide[c]

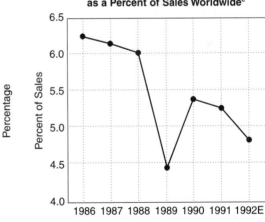

*Specific data points are not disclosed on the graphs. Graphs represents relative magnitudes of spending, awareness, and share of voice.

**Data for graph provided by Morgan Stanley & Co., not by Polaroid. Use is for case purposes only.

[a]Source: Photo Marketing Association
[b]Source: Polaroid Corporation
[c]Source: Morgan Stanley Research**

probably due to our advertising our OneStep and Cool Cam cameras at less than $30, the "under 30 clams" ads.

"I guess the next logical question relates to our advertising spending. So, this overhead also compares our U.S. advertising spending and share of voice with our awareness. There is some lag effect here from year to year. I've also included a graph showing our advertising and promotion expenses as a percent of worldwide sales.

"Exhibits 15 and 16 summarize some Photo Marketing Association information I've gathered about the knowledge and use of cameras. The first chart on Exhibit 15 indicates that 53 percent of the survey's respondents felt they knew almost nothing or just a little about photography. The second chart compares consumers' views of picture

EXHIBIT 15

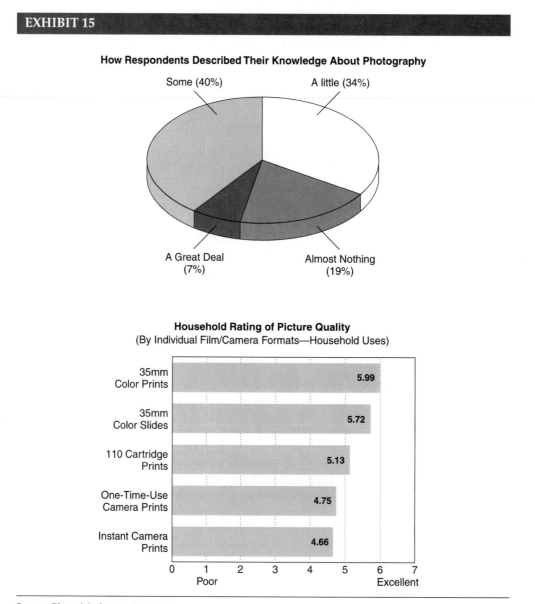

How Respondents Described Their Knowledge About Photography

Some (40%)
A little (34%)
A Great Deal (7%)
Almost Nothing (19%)

Household Rating of Picture Quality
(By Individual Film/Camera Formats—Household Uses)

Format	Rating
35mm Color Prints	5.99
35mm Color Slides	5.72
110 Cartridge Prints	5.13
One-Time-Use Camera Prints	4.75
Instant Camera Prints	4.66

0 (Poor) — 7 (Excellent)

Source: Photo Marketing Association

EXHIBIT 16: Camera Usage

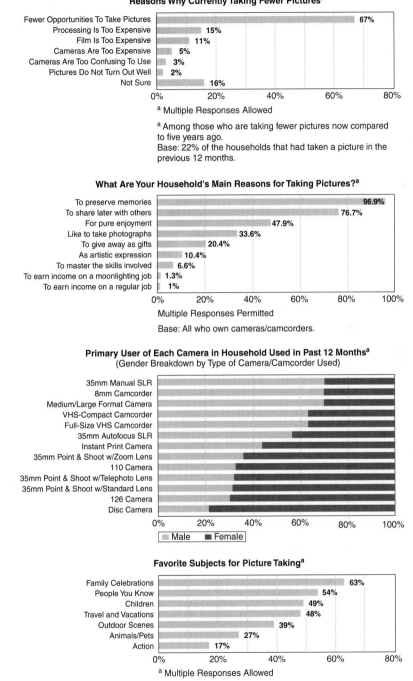

Reasons Why Currently Taking Fewer Pictures[a]

Fewer Opportunities To Take Pictures	67%
Processing Is Too Expensive	15%
Film Is Too Expensive	11%
Cameras Are Too Expensive	5%
Cameras Are Too Confusing To Use	3%
Pictures Do Not Turn Out Well	2%
Not Sure	16%

[a] Multiple Responses Allowed

[a] Among those who are taking fewer pictures now compared to five years ago.
Base: 22% of the households that had taken a picture in the previous 12 months.

What Are Your Household's Main Reasons for Taking Pictures?[a]

To preserve memories	96.9%
To share later with others	76.7%
For pure enjoyment	47.9%
Like to take photographs	33.6%
To give away as gifts	20.4%
As artistic expression	10.4%
To master the skills involved	6.6%
To earn income on a moonlighting job	1.3%
To earn income on a regular job	1%

Multiple Responses Permitted

Base: All who own cameras/camcorders.

Primary User of Each Camera in Household Used in Past 12 Months[a]
(Gender Breakdown by Type of Camera/Camcorder Used)

35mm Manual SLR
8mm Camcorder
Medium/Large Format Camera
VHS-Compact Camcorder
Full-Size VHS Camcorder
35mm Autofocus SLR
Instant Print Camera
35mm Point & Shoot w/Zoom Lens
110 Camera
35mm Point & Shoot w/Telephoto Lens
35mm Point & Shoot w/Standard Lens
126 Camera
Disc Camera

■ Male ■ Female

Favorite Subjects for Picture Taking[a]

Family Celebrations	63%
People You Know	54%
Children	49%
Travel and Vacations	48%
Outdoor Scenes	39%
Animals/Pets	27%
Action	17%

[a] Multiple Responses Allowed

[a]Source: Photo Marketing Association

quality. Respondents gave instant prints the lowest rating. Our tracking studies also show that consumers see instant cameras as being more expensive and less flexible and compact than other camera types.

"Exhibit 16 again uses Photo Marketing Association data to reflect that consumers are taking fewer pictures because they feel they have fewer opportunities much more than because of their concern over the cost of film and processing. People cited their desire to preserve memories and share those memories later with others as their main reasons for taking pictures. Notice also that instant cameras' primary users are females. We also know that the average instant camera user is somewhat older than the average users of other cameras. For example, our average user is about 46 years old versus about 41 years old for users of 35mm rangefinders. The favorite subjects for picture taking are family celebrations and people. I should also add that we estimate that there are approximately 9.5 million households that have and use a Polaroid camera, about an equal number that have a Polaroid camera but don't use it, and about 75 million households that don't own a Polaroid.

"Finally, our research also shows that the Joshua camera has good product imagery; that is, compared to our other cameras, consumers see it as similar to a 35mm camera and as having a stylish appearance and contemporary design. Consumers also found it easier to handle, more full-featured, and more fully-automatic than our other cameras. Consumers also felt they would be more likely to use the camera for vacations, weekend and day trips, and sporting events than our other cameras. Research also shows that consumers want a better camera that is easier to operate and that they can carry on trips in the U.S."

"Nick, did you find any commonalities among the consumers who liked the Joshua camera in your research?" asked Roy Baessler.

"Yes, Roy. At this time, we can say that the camera appeals to younger, upscale, career-minded people who are intelligent, stylish, adventurous, and friendly," Nick responded. "I know those terms sound very general to an engineer, but those are the adjectives we've used to describe people who like the new camera design.

"Roger, that's all the background information we wanted to present today."

THE ASSIGNMENT

"Thanks, Vicki and Nick. As I said, we need to spend the time in these meetings over the next two weeks to prepare for our meeting with the corporate officers. I'd like to ask Vicki, Nick, and Rick to be prepared to present an outline of a U.S. marketing strategy for Joshua at our meeting in three weeks. Meanwhile, if any of you have suggestions for them, please feel free to share them. I'm sure they'll appreciate your ideas."

As the meeting adjourned, Vicki gathered her overheads. She glanced at the countdown clock and then at Nick. "I'm starting to hate that clock," she announced. "We've lost seven days since our last meeting! There's just too much to do and too little time."

Multicon, Incorporated

David W. Rosenthal

John E. Clark, executive vice president of Multicon, shook his head and smiled as he walked off the second tee. His ball had hooked badly into the trees and high rough on the left side of the second hole, and his next shot would be a difficult one. "There's no doubt about it," he said, "As little as I have played, I can't just come out and put the ball in the fairway. This is only the second time I've been out this year, but I guess that I can't complain…. Business has been so hectic since the 'split' that I just haven't had time to work on my game."

Clark referred to the split that had removed Multicon from divisional status as part of Murphy Controls Company more than a year before. "We're still completing the move to become an independent company now," he said, eyeing his golfball and measuring the approach to the green with a harsh stare. "As a matter of fact, there are some shifts in ownership and organization that are going to take place shortly, and they will really put us in a position to move!" Falling silent, Clark hesitated, momentarily considering which club to use for his next swing. His hand paused briefly on his pitching wedge, the correct club for simply playing his ball back to the fairway, but quickly settled on his two-iron. Undaunted by the brow of the hill over which his ball would have to rise or the trees it would have to negotiate on its way to the green about 200 yards distant, Clark slashed at the ball.

"Our biggest difficulty, other than financing, of course, is a strategic issue. It is an extremely complex situation," commented Clark as he walked greenward. "Multicon has made a good name for itself as a 'systems house' putting together 'turnkey' robotics installations for manufacturing concerns. But, we are good at both general-purpose robotics and vision systems." Clark's second shot had rattled into the trees to the right of the green, and he now had an almost impossible shot just to put his ball on the green and keep it there. "The question facing us now is, should we continue in robotics or should we specialize in vision systems?" Clark's third shot rolled quickly down the sloping green, past the hole and off into the fringe about 25 feet away.

As he lined up his lengthy putt, Clark noted, "The big advantage of staying with robotics is that we have developed some great expertise in a variety of applications. That's 'money in the bank.' At the same time, vision systems are really state-of-the-art, and there are only a few companies in the country that have our knowledge and proven abilities in that area. We'd be awfully hard to touch in a couple of years." Clark settled himself over his putt, stroked the ball, and watched motionless as it broke to his right and settled about 18 inches from the hole. After his tap-in for a bogey five, Clark commented, "Guess I'll have to settle for bogey…. My practice time is unlikely to get any better for the foreseeable future."

This case was prepared by Professor David Rosenthal of Miami University as a basis for class discussion. It is not intended to illustrate either effective or ineffective handling of an administrative situation.

Copyright © 2000 Prentice-Hall, Inc. ISBN 0-13-017118-2.

COMPANY DEVELOPMENT

Multicon had begun in mid-1982 as a division of Murphy Controls Company. Murphy Controls Company was a small, Cincinnati-based distributor of industrial control devices. At that time, it was apparent that the programmable controls distributed by the company lent themselves to networking with industrial microcomputers, and that an increasing need for appropriate software was developing. The Multicon Division was formed to improve Murphy's position in this business.

Clark, then a regional manager with Automatix, a Boston-based firm in robotics and machine vision, was hired to manage the new division with help from Roscoe C. Forche, a member of the Murphy Controls engineering staff.

"I won't say that those were the 'good old days,' because they weren't," said Forche. "Business was tight; the economy was lousy. We were right in the depths of the recession, and capital expenditures on machinery were at a low point. Start-up problems were the rule rather than the exception. Still, we had a good base to work from, and we knew for certain that the market would improve."

In the twelve-month period ended December 31, 1983, the division had achieved sales of $929,000 and an after-tax profit of $71,000. Multicon was created as of January 1, 1984, to take over the operations of the division. In calendar year 1984, Multicon generated sales of $1,903,000 and an after-tax profit of $58,000. Additional financial information may be found in Exhibits 1, 2, and 3.

EXHIBIT 1   Comparative Income Statement

	1983	1984
Sales	$928,921	$1,903,349
Cost of sales:		
Materials	$626,015	N/A
Program development	81,332	N/A
	$707,347	$1,513,768
Gross profit on sales	$221,574	$ 389,581
Operating expenses:		
Wages and benefits	$ 62,175	$ 152,402
Travel and sales promotion	23,173	72,323
Shop expense	8,755	N/A
Depreciation, rent, insurance	12,511	20,968
Utilities and telephone	6,918	11,343
Supplies	N/A	13,782
Interest	N/A	21,754
Other	14,195	32,547
	$127,727	$ 324,119
Income before provision for federal income taxes	$ 93,847	$ 65,462
Provision for federal income taxes	$ 23,289	$ 7,200
Net Income	$ 70,558	$ 58,262

EXHIBIT 2   Balance Sheet—Calendar Year 1984

Assets
Current assets:

Cash	$ 746
Accounts receivable, net	253,102
Receivables from affiliate	49,668
Inventories	192,741
Costs & profits in excess of billings on uncompleted contracts	263,692
Other	346
Total current assets	$760,295

Property and equipment:

Furniture and fixtures	$ 47,652
Shop equipment	4,928
Leasehold improvements	3,725
Automobile	8,865
	$ 65,170
Less—Accumulated depreciation	8,770
	$ 56,400
Deferred organization costs, net	$ 8,989
Total assets	$825,684

Liabilities and Shareholders' Equity
Current liabilities:

Note payable	$110,000
Trade accounts payable	364,944
Accrued payroll and other	30,625
Advance payments from customers	62,822
Deferred income taxes	12,600
Total current liabilities	$580,991

Shareholders' equity:

Common stock, no par value, 100,000 shares authorized, 60,000 shares issued and outstanding, stated at	$ 500
Paid-in capital	186,231
Retained earnings	57,962
	$244,693
Total liabilities and shareholders' equity	$825,684

The executives of Multicon expected the company to generate billings of $3.21 million in calendar year 1985, based on existing bookings and as a result of an evaluation of outstanding proposals. The company currently held a $450,000 line of credit with local banks and anticipated additional capital requirements of $150,000 plus an increase in bank debt to cover up to a total of $850,000 in working capital. The company was expected to generate a pretax profit of $287,000 for 1985 if sufficient working capital could be secured, but despite the excellent record of growth, local banks were not enthusiastic about increasing the company's debt position.

EXHIBIT 3 Statement of Changes in Financial Position for the Year Ended December 31, 1984

Sources of Cash:	
Operations	
Net income	$ 58,262
Expenses not requiring an outlay of cash-deferred	
income taxes	12,600
Depreciation and amortization	8,169
Cash provided by operations	$ 79,031
Increase in	
Note payable	$ 85,000
Trade accounts payable	262,293
Accrued payroll and other	30,625
Advance payments from customers	62,822
Total sources of cash	$519,771
Uses of Cash:	
Additions to property and equipment	$ 53,046
Deferred organizational costs	6,754
Dividends paid	300
Increase in	
Trade accounts receivable	156,281
Receivables from affiliate	72,957
Inventories	254,341
Other	346
Total uses of cash	$544,025
Decrease in cash	$ (24,254)
Cash, beginning of period	25,000
Cash, end of period	$ 746

ORGANIZATION

By June 1985 the Multicon organization had grown to include eighteen people. Ronald P. Barker, 44, was the president and chief executive officer of both Murphy Controls Company and Multicon. At Multicon his duties principally related to overall supervision and increasingly to finances. Clark, 31, was executive vice president and was responsible for all marketing, engineering, manufacturing, and administrative activities. Increasingly, Clark found himself in the role of CEO as Barker retreated to managing the parent company, Murphy Controls Company.

    The engineering functions of the business were overseen as a whole by Forche, 31, from his position as vice president of engineering. Forche controlled all technical matters in all functional areas of the firm, reporting to Clark in a staff relationship. Also reporting to Clark were Terrell Zielesnick, manager of applications engineering, and Geoff D. Plum, manager of project engineering. Generally, Zielesnick was responsible for the sales development engineering, whereas Plum was responsible for the design and actual building of the systems. An organization chart and brief biographies of the officers are shown in Exhibits 4 and 5.

PRODUCTS

Multicon operated in computer-aided manufacturing in two principal markets, machine vision and industrial robots. The company acted as a "systems house," connecting a variety of manufacturers with end users. The term "value added reseller" was also used to describe the types of activities conducted by Multicon.

Clark described Multicon's business as being similar to that of a good stereo salesperson. "When a customer visits a good stereo salesperson, they are asked about their

---

EXHIBIT 4: Organization Chart, June 1985

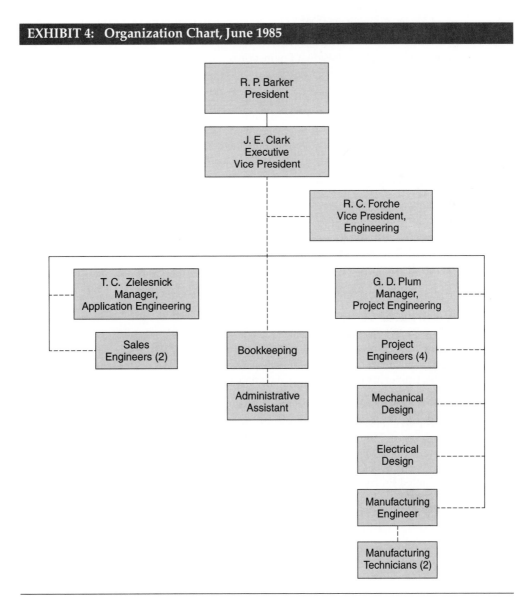

EXHIBIT 5   Executive Biographies

John E. Clark

Cofounder and Executive Vice President

Age 32

BBA Marketing, University of Cincinnati, Cincinnati, Ohio, 1976

1976–1980 Sales engineering positions with Honeywell and Texas Instruments

1980–1982 Regional Manager, Automatix, Inc., a Boston-based start-up company in the field of machine vision and robotics

1982–1983 Manager, Multicon division of Murphy Controls Company

1984–present Executive Vice President, Multicon, Inc.

Charter member of Robotics International and the Machine Vision Association of Society of Manager Engineers (SME).

Roscoe C. Forche

Cofounder, and Vice President Engineering

Age 31

BS and MS, University of Cincinnati, Cincinnati, Ohio, 1975 and 1977

1978–1982 Sales Engineer and Manager Technical Services, Murphy Controls Company

1982–1983 Chief Engineer, Multicon Division of Murphy Controls Company

1984–present Vice President Engineering, Multicon, Inc.

Charter member of Robotics International and Machine Vision Association of SME.

Geoff D. Plum

Manager, Project Engineering

Age 35

BSC and MBA, University of Louisville, Louisville, Kentucky, 1973 and 1980

1968–1980 General Electric Company, various positions including manufacturing engineer, production supervisor, and advanced manufacturing engineer

1980–1985 Cincinnati Milacron, Industrial Robot Division, Supervisor of Application Development

1985–present Multicon, Inc., Manager, Project Engineering

Charter member of Robotics International of SME.

Terrell Zielesnick

Manager, Applications Engineering

Age 35

BSEE, Ohio State University, Columbus, Ohio, 1977

MBA, University of Cincinnati, Cincinnati, Ohio, 1985

1976–1980 Goodyear Atomic Corporation, Electrical and Project Engineer

1980–1981 Ziel-Blossom and Associates, Electrical Engineer

1981–1984 Crouse Hinds Company, Supervisor, Applications Engineering

1984–present Multicon, Inc., Manager, Applications Engineering

Member of the Institute of Electrical and Electronic Engineers

Member of Robotics International of SME

Registered Professional Engineer, Ohio.

needs, the amount of money they wish to spend, the types of music they listen to, and how they wish to listen. Perhaps even the type of furniture and housing they have can play a role. Having gained an understanding of the client's needs, the salesperson, using his knowledge of the available equipment in the market, can help to pick out the most appropriate kind of speakers, a turntable from another manufacturer, an amplifier from a third company, and so forth."

"A systems house brings together the best robotic or vision components for a particular job, writes programming to enable the assembled components to do the work, develops instructions and training for the users, installs the equipment, and troubleshoots the whole thing until it is running smoothly. In short, a manufacturer who wishes to install a robotic assembly would make use of a systems house to hand over an operational set of equipment, a turnkey system."

The Multicon company provided one-, two-, and three-dimensional vision systems for machine guidance, part sorting, inspection, and gauging. Integrating hardware from the major vision systems manufacturers with application engineering, software, optics, lighting, and peripheral devices, the company offered operational systems for industrial users. As of June 1985, the company had successfully installed more than 25 vision systems. Primary suppliers of vision systems to Multicon were Automatix Autovision Systems and Opcon 20/20 Systems.

In the industrial robot area, Multicon had focused efforts on assembly, sophisticated parts handling, and special processes. The company offered turnkey robot cells, including hardware, software, and peripherals such as end-of-arm tooling, sensor integration, parts delivery systems, and controls. Multicon was a designated Systems Application Center for Hitachi America and a Systems Integrator Reseller for Cincinnati Milacron.

The company had designed and installed a number of systems for a broad spectrum of applications, including a vision system for the high-speed inspection of consumer products packaging, labeling, and content; a machine vision system with custom optics and lighting to inspect for casting flaws in the bores of machined parts; a machine vision system for the detection of weld seams in rolled steel; and robot cells for the loading of lead fittings into the die cavity of injection-molding machines.

OPERATIONS

Multicon sales took place on a project basis. Sales leads came from direct contact, trade-show activities, presentations to industry associations, and referrals from manufacturers and customers. John Clark oversaw the sales activities of the two individuals who called on prospective customers, and he made sales calls himself as well.

Once a customer contact had been established, the Multicon executives and engineers took great pains to determine that the prospective customer had a definite and viable need for a robotic or machine vision system, and that Multicon possessed the expertise to deliver an operational solution. It was often required that samples of the customer's product be made available and that engineering documentation be provided.

As Terrell Zielesnick, who provided presale engineering support, noted, "The worst thing that can happen is for a customer to have a misconception about his needs and our capabilities. If a clear problem is not defined, we won't attempt to develop a proposal. It is not uncommon to find 'customers' who are simply looking for a free education or who have heard about this newfangled robotics stuff and figure that it is about time to jump into it. It takes us a long time and a lot of effort to develop a well-reasoned proposal to solve a specific problem. We can't afford to waste our energies on too many unaccepted proposals. Besides, the well-defined projects are difficult enough!"

Generally, a Multicon sales engineer visited the prospective customer's site and attempted to further qualify the project by reviewing its technical and commercial content. He attempted to determine whether it was a project Multicon was competent to do, whether the project was funded, who the competition might be, and why the customer wanted to do the project. The particulars were then reviewed by Clark and Zielesnick, who authorized further development and a feasibility study, possibly including a customer-funded demonstration.

Pricing was the responsibility of the marketing group, headed by John Clark. Once a proposal was written, it was submitted for review to a committee composed of Clark, Forche, Zielesnick, and Plum. Proposals were not submitted to a customer before approval by that group. Once a proposal was accepted, the project was transferred to the engineering and production departments. Typically, a project manager was appointed who shepherded the project through engineering, design, and production. The final step in the process consisted of a demonstration and acceptance by the customer at the Multicon facility. Multicon employees then followed the project into the customer's location for installation, start-up, testing, and training.

As a value-added remarketer, Multicon marked up the price of the hardware that it sold as part of its systems. Although the actual markups varied from supplier to supplier and even from product to product, the company set 30 percent as a target markup. Increasingly, however, robotics hardware was being marked up only an average of about 15 percent, whereas vision systems hardware continued to average roughly 30 percent. Considerable downward pressure appeared to be building on robotics equipment prices. In the installation of most systems, testing, software development controls, training and setup costs added from half to twice the cost of the hardware alone. These labor-intensive functions were difficult to estimate and added considerable risk to the pricing process. Should a particular job be quoted at too large a price, the customer would be unlikely to contract for the system, but if the price were too low, difficulties in the engineering or applications process could actually result in a loss for Multicon.

THE ROBOTICS INDUSTRY

In 1985 the robotics industry was in a state of rapid change. Technological advances during the previous 10 years and growing capability to apply the benefits brought by robotic automation had brought the industry to a new level of sophistication. Even the definition of an industrial robot had changed dramatically in just a few years. Whereas old definitions had focused on the ability of a robot to accomplish "3-D tasks" (Dumb, Dirty, and Dangerous) to the advantage of human workers, the new definition focused on flexibility. In 1985, the Robotic Industries Association defined an industrial robot as "a reprogrammable, multifunctional manipulator designed to move material, parts, tools or specialized devices through variable programmed motions for the performance of a variety of tasks."

Industrial robots had been invented about 25 years before, but the real growth in installation and use of robots in industry had only begun in the early 1980s. At that time, industry analysts eagerly developed forecasts for market growth reaching yearly sales of $2 billion by 1990. Individual companies predicted their own sales to be as high as $1 billion by 1990 and loudly proclaimed their projections to the press.

By 1985, however, it had become obvious that the industry had not grown at the pace predicted earlier. A variety of reasons were commonly cited as constraints to the adoption of robots, primary among them: the economic recession of the early 1980s, unrealistic expectations about the capabilities of robots brought on by popular movies such as *Star Wars*, lack of government support in the form of tax incentives for installation, and labor demands for maintaining employment levels. Actual installations and sales figures for the industry are shown in Exhibits 6 and 7.

The purchase and installation of a robotic manufacturing cell was often an emotional one, stemming from a variety of fears. Industry sources countered these fears by referring to the following points: (1) Most current robot installations involved the selection of a robot over another form of equipment, not to replace a person; (2) robots in factories generally performed the hazardous, boring, demoralizing, and repetitive tasks

EXHIBIT 6: Shipments by U.S.-based Robot Suppliers

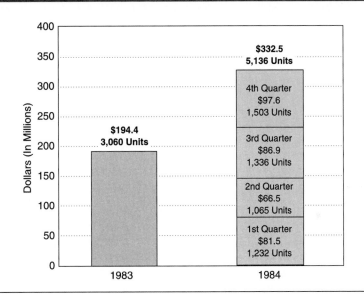

EXHIBIT 7: U.S. Robot Population (Installed Base)

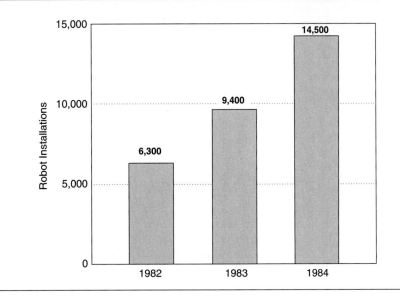

that allowed workers to be removed from dangerous environments; (3) the increased productivity offered by robots could pave the way to a shorter work week, higher pay, and better working conditions; and (4) higher productivity could mean fewer jobs lost to overseas manufacturers in competitive industries.

Industry analysts and participants had anticipated that after the economic recession ended, there would be an industry shakeout reducing the number of competitors in the market. The shakeout had not yet occurred in June 1985, but there were indications that many companies were on the brink of insolvency. Clark described the situation: "We're also starting to see, not the demise of the industry, but that the industry troubles are starting to have an effect. Only three years ago, everybody forecasted the industry as being just absolutely successful, with high growth rates, good profitability—and every major company wanted in. GE got into it; Westinghouse got into it; and Caterpillar bought into Advanced Robotics. GM bought into GM-Fanuc (GMF). Just this year, Ford bought into American Robotics. Everybody thought it was just nirvana."

But now, in 1985, the headaches are starting to show. Outside of GMF, whose numbers are suspect because they're part of GM and you can't get a handle on them, everybody's losing money. *Everybody's* losing money. I think that's starting to have its toll. People look at GE, you know, as an illustration of the problems in the industry. They had huge corporate resources, a lot of commitment, big hoopla, and they have not been a major factor in the market.... And they've been in it for four or five years.

One of the main problems with the industry today is that in 1980 everybody believed the forecasts. In 1980, numbers were banging around like you wouldn't believe. The problem is that because everyone believed the forecasts, they built to capacity and staffed to meet that inflated view of demand. Now the industry is plagued by overcapacity. Many companies went so far as to buy inventory, almost on speculation. Now they have literally hundreds of robots stuck in warehouses. They have to sell them off cheap, and I think that generates a lot of pressure. A guy is running a profit center, and he's getting killed by having this inventory tie up his capital. I think that's part of the crash coming, the reductions in pricing, just to correct the initial forecast errors.

The shakeout's started. I think the economy's as good as it's going to get for a couple more years. And I think that, if anything, from a capital-equipment standpoint, it may even be on the downside. GMF's market presence in automotive goods, which is the biggest user of robotics to date, is being felt by the rest of the robot community. And I think, if you put those two things together, people've been living on high hopes for a little bit too long and the reality is starting to close them down. Some people are just plain running out of money.

The robotics industry was characterized in two ways, by the applications for which robots were purchased and by the companies who manufactured (or assembled) the robots. The major industry applications had been in the automotive industry, primarily in the area of spot welding. Estimates ranged as high as 60 percent of industry sales going to automotive spot-welding applications. Other automotive applications included: arc welding, materials handling, painting, stamping, and metal working. Automotive applications as a whole were estimated to account for as much as 80 percent of robot sales. Other applications included parts manufacturing, injection molding, and materials handling. A list of major U.S. robotics firms and their estimated market shares for 1983 and 1984 is shown in Exhibit 8.

EXHIBIT 8   U.S. Robot Manufacturers: Estimated Share of Market, 1983–1984

	Share of Market	
Manufacturer	**1983**	**1984**
Cincinnati Milacron	17%	17–20%
Westinghouse/Unimation	15%	6–7%
GMF Robotics	9%	30–35%
DeVilbiss	9%	4%
Automatix	7%	7%
Others	43%	27–36%

THE MACHINE VISION INDUSTRY

Machine visions systems ranged in complexity from simple television camera–computer hookups to sophisticated laser-based, three-dimensional robotic controls. The basic concept of a vision system was to "digitalize" an image, providing a source of data for a computer software package to interpret. In simple terms, a television camera would take a digital picture of a brightly lit scene, breaking the image into thousands of individual points or cells called pixels. Each pixel would be assigned a numeric value between 0 and 63, according to the pixel's level of brightness or darkness. A microcomputer attached to the system would then be capable of interpreting the numeric data from the image, according to a set of programmed instructions.

A simple illustration of an application might be a vision system to determine whether an assembly line had a part on it at a given location. The vision system would "view" the location, registering a constant level of brightness when no part was present. As a part was delivered to that point, the level of brightness would change, causing a change in the numeric value of the pixels in the image, allowing the computer to recognize that a part had arrived.

Similar to the early predictions regarding the robotics industry, estimations of market size and growth in the machine vision area varied widely during 1985. Estimates of the 1984 machine vision market ranged from $40 million to $80 million and from 50 to 120 companies participating. Estimates for market growth ranged from 50 percent per year to an optimistic doubling each year, yielding market size projections of $1 billion by 1990. The range of market projections is illustrated in Exhibit 9.

The machine vision market in 1985 was dominated by a group of five companies controlling up to 80 percent of the sales in the area. The remainder of the market was divided among many smaller firms. The market was characterized by many small, start-up companies with limited product lines and capabilities. The five major companies and their estimated 1985 market shares are shown in Exhibit 10.

John Clark described the market. "There is no barrier to entry. None. Any halfway bright person could go to Digital Equipment Company and buy an O. E. M. computer, say, for about $5,000 and from any number of companies buy an interface board that lets a camera "talk" to the computer, and go to any video store and buy an off-the-shelf camera that's used for security surveillance or something, put it all in a cabinet that

---

EXHIBIT 9   Machine Vision Industry Market Estimates, 1985

	Market Estimate	
Year	Companies	Dollars
1980	30	N/A
1981	N/A	N/A
1982	N/A	N/A
1983	N/A	$35M–$84M
1984	50–120	$75M–$80M
1985	150	$150M
**		
1987		$480M
**		
1989		$455M
1990		$800M–$1B

N/A: Not available. M = million, B = billion

EXHIBIT 10   Machine Vision Industry: Estimated Market Shares by Company, 1985

Company	Estimated Share
Auromatix	20–22%
View Engineering	20–22%
Machine Vision International (MVI)	14–15%
General Electric	5–10%
Diffracto	8–10%
Others	21–33%

---

costs a couple hundred bucks, and he's got a vision system. It doesn't do much, and it's not very sophisticated, but he's a player in the market! That is what is happening right now. The market is just full of "mom and pop" companies, little guys with a garage. It's a mess."

The purchase of a vision system was often less emotional than the purchase of a robot. Although considerable publicity had surrounded the issue of job displacement with robots, little pressure had been felt by the vision industry. Vision systems purchase decisions tended to be made at lower levels of management than were robot purchase decisions, because plant managers apparently did not require the same reassurance of upper management support as they did with robot installations.

Zielesnick suggested that purchasers of vision systems were less sensitive because the systems often did the job better than the currently used processes. "A good example is label inspection. Picture dishwashing-liquid bottles coming by. You are sitting in a chair in front of a conveyor, and the bottles are coming by at the rate of five a second, 300 a minute. On the other side of the conveyor is a mirror, and your job is to look both at the front of the bottle, and in the mirror, at the back of the bottle. You are supposed to identify those bottles that have torn labels or labels that are misplaced by more than a sixteenth of an inch. That's a lousy job, and you probably aren't doing it very well."

Competition in the vision systems market focused on product characteristics, particularly computing speed and power, developing software packages and decision logic, and developing expertise in on-site engineering elements such as lighting, lenses, and so forth. Increasingly, manufacturers of vision systems were relying on systems houses for programming and on-site engineering functions in the channel of distribution.

THE CURRENT DECISION: INTERVIEW WITH JOHN CLARK

The thing that makes our strategic decision so difficult is that we have some compelling reasons to stay with robotics, and at the same time, we have strong reasons to go with vision systems. With our resources, I'm not sure that we can afford to do both…at least, not well.

Robotics

Currently our sales are roughly 60 percent robotics and 40 percent vision. A robot system is worth anywhere from $60,000 to $120,000 in sales to us on the average. A vision system can go anywhere from $20,000 to $200,000, with an average installed price of about $75,000. When we started the year, we were shooting for 40 percent robotics and 60 percent vision, but it just hasn't worked out that way. With a small company like ours, a single large order can make a dramatic shift.

Our position in the robotics industry is at once a problem and an advantage. We are one of a number, probably less than 100, of systems houses in the country. In terms of skills and experience, that number falls to about 50. But, that number is growing, and the robot manufacturers are encouraging it. We are software and controls oriented, but other systems houses are positioned at the metal-fabricating end of the business. They can actually design a system and build the conveyors to actually create a production line. Our stated policy is that we don't want to get into metalworking. We have a good skill set, and we have good people, but we will be competing with companies that can provide the metal side, too.

Another problem with the robotics business is the margins. The robot manufacturers aren't giving us the margins that we need right now. Fifteen percent is typical. If you look at a robot cell that cost $100,000 installed, there is probably a $60,000 robot in there. At 15 percent, that generates a nice volume, but it is actually a cash burden. We actually have to go out and buy that piece of equipment. If we have to carry it for 90 or 120 days while we put all the pieces together, program it, put it into the customer's plant, and start it up…all before we get paid: that 15-percent margin almost doesn't cut it. That may change. We are trying to force the robot manufacturers to change, but I just don't know.

Robotics is very, very service oriented. There is nothing wrong with that, but the big leverage comes from having a product to sell. Our role in the robotics business is strictly service; design engineering, drafting, mechanical engineering, electrical engineering, training, and start-up. There is no proprietary product that Multicon will own. When you place a robot cell, sure you gain the expertise and knowledge of that application, but the next placement, even for the same application, will require a completely new set of services. You can't just plug it in.... There's no "product" opportunity there.

On the positive side, the robot market is growing at 50 or 60 percent per year, and it will continue for a lot of years. We are in a very, very good start-up service. The market is more mature than the vision market, so we think that a robot is easier to sell than a vision system right now. The industry has already gone through the pains of education and establishing its worth. Our overall marketing costs are lower in robots than in vision. Further, we have a good name in the business, and we have great expertise.

A key to success for us has been our people. We've got good access to robotics engineers, and there is a shortage of robotics and machine vision engineers in the marketplace. Still, we have been able to hire key people, and we will be able to attract more, particularly in robotics.

Machine Vision

We are early, early in the machine vision cycle or phase of development. We are one of a very, very select few machine vision systems houses in the country. There may be three or four people like us, but I've only identified one. I'm sure that there are others, but there aren't many. Because of that, we can establish a very strong market identity, and that is very important.

We have established some good relationships, probably stronger relationships with our machine vision vendors than we have with our robot vendors. They are embracing us just a little bit tighter for a whole variety of reasons, but that is a definite plus.

Probably the major advantage for vision is that it gives us the opportunity to become product driven. There are real opportunities to develop proprietary packages based around a piece of machine vision hardware that becomes "a product" out in the market. Our first is a label-inspection package. The consumer-products packaging community doesn't want to buy a vision system for label inspection. They want to buy something to inspect labels, and they want the vision system to be 'transparent.' They don't want to have to fool with it. Their product comes through the test space; a good product is passed through, and a bad product is kicked out. We have a standard system that will do that with standard design, standard manufacture, standard software, and standard lighting. We'll still have to customize it a little, but we can tell a customer that we can or cannot do the job in about an hour.

Machine vision is a higher risk going in than robotics for every project. The initial contact on a new application is riskier from our standpoint. We may look at it; we may evaluate it and say that we can do it. Our assumptions and evaluations may not be as accurate in vision. Its easier to be off, and at that point, we are pumping a lot of unforeseen resources to finish a commitment made to the customer. That is a risk.

A big problem in machine vision is that it is difficult for us to find people to work on it. It is a skill that is not in the market, so you kind of have to "home grow" it. There is a significant cost in finding people and in training them to contribute. We should be hiring people six months to a year before we really need them. We need to invest the $50,000 to $70,000 per head in educational costs to get them up the learning curve. Right now, that is a problem for us.

Another major concern is that the machine vision manufacturers won't always be willing to rely on service groups like us. As they get more sophisticated in their applications software, it will become much easier to tell the vision system to do something. Users won't need a systems house to design, program, and install a system. It is the old "user friendly" issue. The more the manufacturers invest in research, the less important our role as just an applier will become.

CONCLUSION

Clark smiled as he stood over his golf ball on the right side of the fairway on the par-five eleventh hole. For one of the few times today, he had driven the ball straight and long. Looking toward the green, he reached for his three-wood. Despite the long distance to the green and the pond guarding the approach, Clark intended to take the risky shot rather than "laying up" with an iron. After taking a practice swing, he addressed the ball and smoothly stroked what had to be his best shot of the day.

"Well, we'll see," laughed Clark, replacing his club in his bag. The result of the shot was not visible as the pond was out of sight over a ridge in the fairway and the green was too far to see a ball clearly. "There are only so many opportunities, and you have to do the best with them that you can!"

Smith's Home Foods: Bringing Home the Bacon

Lew G. Brown

Ronald Smith, president of Smith's Country Hams[1] in Ashton, North Carolina, walked into his daughter's office and plopped down in one of the chairs across from her desk. "Christy," he said, "I've just been looking at last month's numbers, and they are pretty discouraging. We've got to find a way to get the home foods business moving. I'm not sure what's wrong, but I think we've somehow got the cart before the horse. I'm convinced that if we could just find the right button, and push it, everything would work well."

Christy Smith looked across the desk at her casually dressed father. "Dad, I am just as frustrated as you are," she replied. "Nothing we try seems to work right. Even when we do attract new customers, they are the wrong kind."

Christy was a very busy person. In addition to her duties at Smith's, she commuted daily to a major university located in a neighboring city, where she was a senior business major. Although she had worked in the family business for as long as she could remember, she had been pleased and surprised when her father had asked her to take over the newly formed Smith's Home Foods operation. Glancing at the calendar on her desk, she noted the date—April 4, 1997. She could hardly believe that five months had passed since taking on the assignment. Although pleased with her father's confidence in her, she knew that he felt frustrated about the slow development of the Smith's Home Foods business.

As Christy and her father talked, Sonny Jones, one of Home Foods' two full-time salespeople, entered the office and joined the conversation. He seemed upset. "We just got two more turndowns from the finance company," he grumbled. "They rejected both of the families I sold plans to last night. We just can't seem to get onto the right side of the street."

"What do you mean?" Ronald asked.

"It's the same old story," Sonny replied. "Both families I called on last night live in Dogwood Acres—they're nice people and all, but they don't have very high incomes. We have to find a way to attract the higher-income folks who live across the road in Ashton Estates."

Ronald Smith rose to leave. "Whatever the problem is, I'm depending on the two of you to figure it out and tell me what we need to do. And you need to get moving quickly."

This case was prepared by Professor Lew G. Brown of the University of North Carolina at Greensboro, as a basis for class discussion. It is not intended to illustrate either effective or ineffective handling of an administrative situation.

[1]Name of company and location are disguised.

BACKGROUND

Smith's Country Hams, a 25-year-old family business that focuses on wholesale meat products such as ham, bacon, and other pork products, sells to restaurants and fast-food operations in eastern North Carolina. In July 1996, seeking growth opportunities, Ronald Smith started a new division—Smith's Home Foods. He got the idea from an employee who had previously worked for another home-delivered foods company. Ronald, who was always looking for new ways to make money, believed the idea had potential. He knew that people were seeking more convenience. Therefore, a service that provided home-delivered meats, vegetables, and fruits should be in considerable demand. He also realized that he could use his own meat products in the business, thereby providing new sales for Smith's Country Hams.

Ronald reconditioned an old production facility that had been idle and set up offices there for Smith's Home Foods. He put the employee who had the idea in charge of the business. However, by October 1996, the employee had failed to meet Ronald's expectations and had resigned. Ronald then asked Christy to take over. He knew this would be a challenging assignment for her. She was still a full-time university student. As a result, she could devote only afternoons and whatever time she could squeeze from her evenings to manage Smith's Home Foods.

THE HOME FOODS BUSINESS

The home-delivered foods business centers on providing families with prearranged assortments of foods that are delivered to their homes. Smith's Home Foods offers 11 standard packages, containing various combinations of frozen meats, vegetables, and fruits. The packages differ in size and cost, but each provides a four-month food supply. Exhibit 1 shows the items in a typical package. Exhibit 2 summarizes the characteristics of each of the 11 packages.

When Christy first assumed management of the operation, she wondered why everything was sold in four-month packages. According to Sonny Jones, who had once worked with a competing food service, most competitors offer similar four-month packages. As a result, the quantity of food delivered with each package requires that customers own a freezer or purchase one. Therefore, Smith's Home Foods, like other home-foods companies, also sells a 21-cubic-foot freezer on an installment payment plan. In general, the requirement of having a freezer does not appear to be a barrier to food-package sales.

Christy believes that customers gain many benefits from the home delivery of food. First, it's convenient—customers can make fewer trips to the store because Smith's Home Foods packages make a large variety of foods readily available in the home. Therefore the person who does the cooking has fewer worries about whether enough food is available. Second, Christy believes that Smith's offers superior quality products, especially meats, compared with those consumers typically find at grocery stores. She and her father carefully select the meat offered in the packages. Of course, they supply their own high-quality Smith's Country Ham products. All other meats are purchased from other quality wholesalers, either in individually wrapped portions, such as eight-ounce T-bone steaks, or in "family portions," such as five-pound rib roasts. The wholesalers vacuum pack the meats with plastic shrink wrap to protect their freshness and flavor. Meats packed this way and frozen will maintain their freshness indefinitely. Smith's Home Foods packages feature brand-name meats, such as Morrell,

EXHIBIT 1   Contents of a Typical Smith's Home Foods Package

```
107 Pounds Net Weight Beef
     6 Chuck Roasts (2 lb avg.)
     4 Shoulder Roasts (2 lb avg.)
     1 Sirloin Tip Roast (3 lb avg.)
     1 Eye of Round Roast (3 lb avg.)
     1 Bottom Round Roast (3 lb avg.)
    20 Ribeye Steaks (8 oz)
    12 T-Bone Steaks (12 oz)
       Cube Steak (8 lb)
       BLS Stew Beef (10 lb)
    18 Chopped Beef Steaks (8 oz; 9 lb case)
       Ground Beef (32 lb; 1 lb rolls or 4 oz patties)
       Pork Chops (6 lb)
       BLS Pork Chops (6 lb)
       Dinner Ham (5 lb)
    30 Misc. Meats
    20 Fryers
     1 Seafood
    60 Vegetables (16 oz)
    12 Fruits
    32 Juices (12 oz)
       Cheese (6 lb)
       Margarine (6 lb)
```

Bank	$1,094.38
Tax	54.71
	1,149.09
Deposit	35.00
Amount Financed	1,114.09
Finance Charge	56.23
Deferred Payment	1,170.32
Total Price	1,205.32

Four Payments at $292.58
$68.04 per Week

Armour, Jimmy Dean, and Fishery products. The packages also include brand-name fruits and vegetables, such as Dulany and McKenzie, which are purchased from wholesalers. Smith's guarantees the quality of its food, stating that it will replace any food that fails to completely satisfy the customer.

Finally, Christy argues, purchasing food through a home food service saves consumers money. Because customers buy in large quantities, they receive lower prices. And they escape any price increases that occur during the four-month period covered by their food packages. Making fewer trips to the store also helps customers avoid expensive impulse purchases.

EXHIBIT 2   **Characteristics of Smith's Home Foods Packages**

Food Package Number	Pounds of Meat per Week	Minimum Freezer Size	Family Size	Package Price[a]
1	14	21 cu ft	3–4	$1,205
2	12	18	3–4	1,088
3	12	18	3	1,070
4	10	15	2–3	940
5	17	21	4–5	1,532
6	6.5	12	2	655
7	8	15	2–3	1,093
8	9.5	12	2–3	825
9	11	15	2–3	809
10	11	15	2–3	834
11	13	21	4–5	958

[a]Price for four-month package, including tax and finance charges.

SMITH'S HOME FOODS' MARKETING PROGRAM

Smith's prices its food packages at $655 to $1,532, including tax and finance charges, with an average price of $1,000. Smith's cost of goods sold averages 48 percent for the 11 packages, not including a variable cost of $30 per package for delivery. Customers can pay cash, or they can charge or finance their purchases. Although Smith's accepts Visa and MasterCard, customers seldom use these cards to purchase the food packages. Another option allows customers to pay one half in cash on signing the contract and the final half within 30 days without an interest charge.

Smith's provides credit to qualified customers through the Fair Finance Company of Akron, Ohio, one of the few finance companies that finances food purchases. Customers who opt for financing make a $35 down payment and fill out a credit application. If Fair approves the application, the customer makes the first payment—one-fourth of the amount financed—30 days after the delivery of the food. Thus, on a $1,200 food package financed by Fair, the customer makes four $300 payments. Because the first payment is not due until a month after delivery, the financing plan allows the customer to save $75 a week for food in each of the four weeks leading up to the first payment, and so forth for the remaining three payments. Although the finance company absorbs the risks of the purchase, Smith's assumes the risk until the first payment is made. That is, if a customer receives the food but does not make the first payment, Smith's accepts responsibility for the entire amount financed and must take whatever action it can to obtain payment or reclaim the food.

When a salesperson submits an order for a food package, if the customer wants to finance it, Smith's faxes a copy of the order to Fair Finance Company. Typically, the finance company approves or rejects the application within one business day. If credit is approved, a clerk completes a "pull sheet," which tells warehouse employees which package the customer purchased and what items are included. Typically, the warehouse manager holds orders until five or six are ready to be pulled and then sets a delivery date with the customer.

For customers who want to purchase freezers, Smith's sells a 21-cubic-foot freezer for approximately $800, with a cost of goods sold at $435. This freezer can also be financed through a separate finance company—consumers pay $12.95 down and make 24 monthly payments of about $33. When a customer orders a freezer and credit is approved, Smith's calls a local appliance store that delivers the freezer to the customer and installs it. Once installed, the freezer must run for about three days before it reaches the appropriate temperature to receive the food. Therefore, Smith's must coordinate food delivery with delivery of the freezer.

Smith's stores its inventory in the Smith's Country Hams warehousing and cold-storage facilities. It has a one-ton pickup truck equipped with a freezer box to make the delivery to customers. Two Smith's Country Hams employees make the deliveries, personally placing the food in the customer's freezer.

Smith's Home Foods uses both personal and mass-selling techniques to promote its service. Its two full-time salespeople, Sonny Jones and Barbara Johnson, both earn salaries plus commission on their own sales. Sonny and Barbara have also recruited four other part-time, commission-only salespeople. Smith's pays its salespeople a $100 commission on each package sold. It also pays an additional $25 commission to both Sonny and Barbara for each sale made by the part-time salespeople. The same commissions are paid on each freezer sold.

When the salespeople make a call, they must often meet with the customers in the evening, spending as long as two hours discussing the service and completing the applications. Each salesperson carries a three-ring binder that contains all the information needed for a sales presentation. The binder includes 12 pages of beef and pork product pictures, six pages of poultry and fish product pictures, three pages of vegetable and fruit product pictures, and one page of dessert pictures. Additional pages describe the costs and terms for each of the 11 packages. The binder also contains pictures of freezers and lists substitutions allowed in the packages.

To generate leads for the sales force, Smith's uses several mass-selling techniques. First, it has advertised three times recently in the local Ashton paper, which also serves the small adjoining community of Wolfsburg and the surrounding county with a total population of about 100,000. Each insert costs about $.04. The inserts stress the money-saving features of the service and include a detachable postcard that consumers can mail, postage paid, to the company.

More recently, the company has contracted with the local Welcome Wagon to distribute a $10-off coupon for Smith's products along with the other promotions that it gives to newlyweds, families who have just had babies, and new arrivals to the community. Finally, Christy also prepared a flyer that outlines the service. Salespeople place these flyers in various locations around the community, such as beauty parlors.

Christy does not feel that Smith's Home Foods faces any direct competition in the Ashton area. Another large, well-established company, Southern Foods of Greensboro, North Carolina, operates a home foods service very similar to Smith's. However, although Southern Foods also operates in some other states and has customers throughout North Carolina, it does not directly target the Ashton area. In fact, Christy feels that Southern Foods has probably helped her business—it has developed the market generally and acquainted potential customers with the kinds of services that Smith's offers.

When Christy took over, she made a number of immediate changes in an effort to improve performance. She redesigned the food packages to make them more attractive and developed the newspaper insert, flyer, and sales book. Despite these efforts, however, the business has developed very slowly.

Although only about eight families had contracted for the service when Christy took over, Smith's now has 60 customers. However, many of the families who signed up since she arrived will soon be finishing their first package. Christy is concerned about how many of these customers will reorder. She is also worried about how long her father's patience will last. He had told her that he would invest as much as $250,000 to get this business going. He had already invested $25,000 in inventory. Furthermore, he estimated that Smith's Home Foods annual fixed costs amounted to $57,000, including salaries, rent and utilities, and other overhead. Christy wondered about the business's profitability and about how many customers she needed to reach to break even.

The Greensboro
Housing Authority

Lew G. Brown, William M. Kawashima,
Diana H. Carlin, and Margaret K. Craig

LIFE IN THE PUBLIC SECTOR

Elaine Ostrowski, executive director of the Greensboro Housing Authority (GHA), closed her front door and walked to the end of her driveway to pick up the morning newspaper. She noticed that the North Carolina air had a touch of fall about it this morning, but she knew that September still held more summerlike days. "You have to get used to the heat in this job," she mused as she slipped the paper out of its plastic bag. Elaine glanced quickly at the front page. "Well, at least we're not on the front page," she thought. "I think I'll wait until I get to the office to tackle the letters to the editor."

In April 1992, the authority announced that it was seeking a 10- to 12-acre site on which to build a 50-unit public housing community. Responding to a request from the Greensboro City Council, the Authority said that it would focus its search on areas in the city's western sections. The City Council had previously encouraged the GHA to locate public housing communities in city areas where there were fewer such developments.

In August, the GHA announced that it had selected a site near the Adams Farm community, a predominantly white, upper-middle-class neighborhood in southwest Greensboro. Area residents quickly voiced their opposition. Several hundred residents attended a community meeting where Elaine and other GHA officials presented their development plans. Elaine showed slides of the city's newer public housing developments. One area resident, however, had responded by saying, "Who cares what they look like? We are worried about the people you are going to put there." Two days later at a GHA Board of Commissioners' meeting, residents voiced their concerns over the proposed site's cost and topography, the development's effect on their property values, and the site's lack of convenient access to shopping and public transportation. The board, however, voted to approve the plan and to forward it to the U.S. Department of Housing and Urban Development for approval.

Elaine arrived at her office early, hoping to get some things done before the day became hectic. She sat at her desk and opened the newspaper to the editorial page. As

This case was prepared by Professors Lew G. Brown, William M. Kawashima, and MBA students Diana H. Carlin, and Margaret Craig of the University of North Carolina at Greensboro, as a basis for class discussion. It is not intended to illustrate either effective or ineffective handling of an administrative situation. The authors express their appreciation to the Greensboro Housing Authority for its cooperation in developing this case.

she expected, she quickly spotted a letter to the editor that carried the headline "Public housing would ruin property values." Three paragraphs from the letter read:

> To make matters worse, when Ostrowski was asked did she think the surrounding property values would be affected, she said she didn't know. This is not the kind of answer one would expect from a person who has been on the job for over 10 years.

> What she was really saying is that the GHA couldn't care less about the value of homes located around public housing. The presentation the GHA made was a complete sham and insulted the intelligence of all those in attendance.

> The homeowners are not going to stand idly by and let some city employee spend our tax dollars to devalue our property. We have all worked very hard to build our homes for ourselves and our families and we will all work twice as hard to ensure that the value is maintained.

Elaine slumped in her chair and gazed out the window. Every public official knew what it was like to have members of the public attack their program or to attack them personally. It still hurt, especially when the attack was wrong. She had not said that she didn't know. She had said that the authority did not have any information that suggested that property values around scattered-site housing declined. She had stated that, in fact, the GHA had done studies that indicated that property values continued to increase. She and the authority did care, and they understood property owners' concerns. However, the letter reminded her that perceptions are reality and that the public's perceptions were often clouded by preconceived ideas.

When Elaine accepted her position, she had made a conscious effort to keep the authority out of the news because a scandal involving her predecessor had created unfavorable publicity. Now, a decade later, she realized that she had made a mistake in maintaining a silent presence.

On one hand, Elaine knew that GHA had been very successful. The authority had won regional and national recognition for some of its innovative programs, such as the Police Neighborhood Resource Centers (PNRC) and its youth programs. Many civic and business leaders admired GHA's effective management. Yet, despite these accomplishments, Elaine felt that many members of the public still held a largely negative opinion of public housing and its residents, or they did not know anything about the authority and its programs.

MEANWHILE...

Several blocks away, Jerry Lawson, a member of the GHA's Board of Commissioners, sat at his desk in a well-appointed office. Although he was president of Baron Financial, Inc., Jerry's mind this morning was on his other career. Jerry worked in two very different worlds, financial services for the upwardly mobile and public housing for low-income families. His business colleagues were often puzzled by his dual role.

Lately, Jerry had been thinking about people's attitudes toward public housing. Every time business colleagues made comments such as, "It must be awful working with all those welfare people," it reminded him of some of the misconceptions he had about public housing before joining the board. He wished more people could have a chance to meet the many hardworking, decent, public housing residents.

Jerry read the same letter to the editor that Elaine had seen. He recalled that a week ago the Guilford County Board of Commissioners, which had no formal relationship with GHA, had voted 6–1 to ask the authority to hold another public hearing on the new site. One commissioner's statement was representative: "I've never seen a housing project yet, I don't care how new and how well planned, that ended up in six months' time looking like anything but a damned housing project." He then added, "Those places invariably become slums and everybody knows it."

To Jerry, this was all too familiar. A little more than two years ago, GHA had proposed building a 50-unit development in a northeast Greensboro community. This development represented the first new public housing community in more than seven years. The city desperately needed the housing to help the more than 800 families on the waiting list. Then, too, area residents had raised similar objections to the project. But the City Council had approved rezoning the site, and HUD had approved the project. That development, Laurel Hill, had just opened.

"We've got to do a better job," Jerry thought. "We can't keep fighting the same battles. We need to educate the community about public housing. GHA needs a marketing strategy just like any other business."

HISTORY

The City of Greensboro (1992 population 190,000) established the Greensboro Housing Authority in 1941, shortly after Congress passed the National Housing Act, which provided communities with federal funding for public housing. The 1930s depression had left many cities with inadequate housing for low-income citizens. For example, Greensboro's civic leaders then estimated that one-third of the city's housing was substandard and that 45 percent lacked sanitary facilities. As a result, the mayor appointed GHA's first board of commissioners, and the board made plans to build 2,500 housing units over the following 10 years.

World War II intervened, and GHA did not complete the first two 400-unit community developments until 1952. By 1992, the authority had constructed a total of 2,435 housing units in sixteen public-housing communities that served approximately 6,500 residents. The total number of residents served at any one time could vary due to vacancies and units that were out of service for renovation.

Congress had passed the National Housing Act with the goal of providing *temporary* housing for low-income families. It was expected that these families would eventually move out of public housing as their financial situations improved. Indeed, many of GHA's public housing residents did succeed in moving into the private-sector housing market.

However, socioeconomic changes over the last several decades had made it difficult for many families to make the transition from public to private housing. In the 1950s and 1960s, many low-income families migrated from rural areas into the cities. Simultaneously, urban renewal projects depleted the supply of affordable low-income housing. As a result, some low-income families and individuals became permanent public housing residents. Either they lacked the education, skills, or training to improve their financial status, or there were simply no adequate houses that they could afford.

Before the 1970s, GHA, like other housing authorities, built large public housing communities. The authority located these densely populated 200- to 400-unit complexes in southeast Greensboro. Most citizens, when they thought of public housing, thought of these communities.

In the late 1970s, GHA adopted the scattered-site concept and built smaller, 50-unit housing complexes in locations throughout the city. GHA purposely designed scattered-site communities to blend in with the surrounding neighborhood, and the public often did not identify these communities as public housing projects.

During the 1980s, the federal government severely reduced public housing funding. The cutbacks halted new construction for almost a decade. However, approval of new capital funding in the late 1980s allowed GHA to develop the Laurel Hill community. Because the authority expected very little funding for new housing construction, it was renovating many older, large complexes to improve the public's image of these neighborhoods and to help preserve the existing housing stock.

In 1992, the authority's mission statement provided that:

It is the mission of the Greensboro Housing Authority to provide decent, safe, and sanitary housing for the low-income residents of the City of Greensboro. To fulfill this mission, the Greensboro Housing Authority has adopted the following objectives:

1. Provide for the responsible management of Greensboro Housing Authority's programs.
2. Improve the public perception of Greensboro Housing Authority's public housing communities.
3. Assist Greensboro Housing Authority families to attain self-sufficiency.
4. Seek opportunities to increase the supply of affordable rental units.

ORGANIZATIONAL STRUCTURE

As a public corporation (much like an airport authority), GHA administered low-income housing programs, including public housing and rental assistance. GHA had a contractual agreement with the federal government through the Department of Housing and Urban Development (HUD) to deliver these services. HUD provided the subsidies needed to offset the deficits resulting from the below-market rent that residents of public housing paid. HUD subsidies provided approximately two-thirds of GHA's operating budget, and rental income accounted for one-third. City, county, and state governments had, in the past, provided limited funds for capital improvements. Exhibit 1 presents GHA's 1990, 1991, and 1992 operating budgets. These budgets do not include special grant monies HUD provided for specific programs, such as the Drug Elimination Program.

Greensboro's mayor appointed the seven-member board of commissioners that governed the housing authority. However, the housing authority operated as an independent agency and was not part of city government. Its employees were not city employees. Each commissioner served a five-year term without pay. At least one public housing resident served on the board. The board met monthly to review the agency's operations, such as its new construction plans, operating budgets, and policies.

The board of commissioners also hired the executive director, who managed the authority's daily operations and its 123 employees. The executive director's immediate staff consisted of the deputy executive director, the director of administration, the director of capital improvements, and the director of housing services (see Exhibit 2).

THE RESIDENTS

GHA's 16 communities housed 2,262 families (see Exhibit 3). Most of the communities served families, although GHA designated three developments (Hall Towers, Gateway Plaza, and Stoneridge) for elderly, handicapped, and disabled residents only.

EXHIBIT 1   Greensboro Housing Authority Operating Budgets

	1992	1991	1990
Income			
Rental income	$2,360,670	$2,687,810	$3,531,840
Other income	170,940	195,470	201,990
Operating subsidy (HUD)	4,335,090	3,367,420	2,574,848
Total income	$6,866,700	$6,250,700	$6,308,676
Operating expenses			
Administration	1,396,500	1,337,070	1,292,990
Tenant services	127,110	104,700	111,560
Utilities	1,053,450	994,180	1,442,900
Maintenance	2,820,850	2,576,120	3,013,480
General	1,188,710	1,280,380	1,270,210
Total operating expenses	$6,586,620	$6,292,450	$7,131,140
Capital expenditures	$ 192,070	$ 158,250	$ 134,090
Total expenses	$6,778,690	$6,450,700	$7,265,230
Provision for operating reserve	$ 88,010	($ 200,000)	($ 956,554)
Operating reserve account			
Beginning Balance	$1,198,975	$1,398,975	$2,355,529
Ending Balance	$1,286,985	$1,198,975	$1,398,975

Source: Greensboro Housing Authority

The authority charged rent on a sliding-scale basis to make housing affordable for families who did not have sufficient income to rent in the private market. Resident families paid 30 percent of their annual adjusted income for rent. The mean gross monthly rent was $137, substantially below the private-market rate of approximately $550.

The average resident family had a $6,350 gross annual income, with 94 percent of the families earning less than $13,000 annually. About one-third of the resident families received public assistance (welfare) besides subsidized public housing. About two-thirds of the resident families had at least one wage earner. Those residents who had jobs generally earned the minimum wage.

Of the 6,500 residents, about one-third were male and two-thirds were female. Fifty percent of the residents were minors (less than 17 years old), and 15 percent were elderly (over 61 years old). Of the 2,262 families, 55 percent were one-parent, female-head-of-household families. Exhibits 4, 5, and 6 provide additional information about the families living in GHA's communities.

OTHER HOUSING PROGRAMS

The Greensboro city government and other organizations had become increasingly concerned with the need for low-income housing. Recently approved bond issues provided

EXHIBIT 2: Greensboro Housing Authority Organization Chart

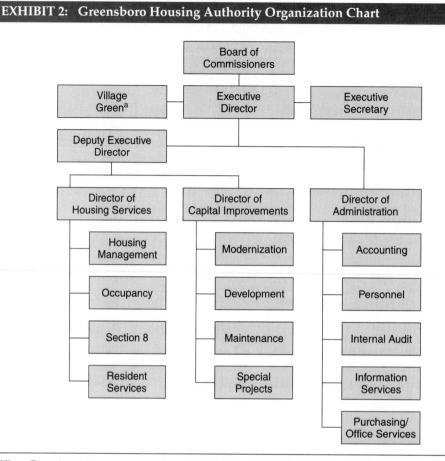

[a]Village Green is a retirement community owned and operated by GHA, but it is not federally subsidized. This complex, with its own staff and budget, is operated separately from GHA's public-housing communities.
Source: Greensboro Housing Authority

housing opportunities for families whose incomes were too high to qualify for public housing assistance but too low to qualify for private-sector mortgages. These bond issues supported programs that provided affordable housing through the renovation of existing substandard, dilapidated facilities; provided funds to help first-time buyers with down payments and initial mortgage payments; provided housing counseling to aid first-time home buyers; and provided building lots for nonprofit groups to construct housing. The City Housing Foundation, Habitat for Humanity, the Episcopal Housing Ministry, and a group called HOME all worked to create more affordable housing. These organizations worked closely with the GHA, helping some public housing families attain home ownership.

Observers felt that the city and the housing authority were progressive and innovative in the housing field. GHA had many programs in place that did not exist in many other cities. However, these combined initiatives addressed only a small part of low-income families' housing needs. According to Greensboro's Five-Year Affordable Housing Plan, the city needed 12,000 low-cost rental units to serve the 12,000 families earning

EXHIBIT 3   Greensboro Housing Authority Communities

Community	Number of Residents	Number of Units	Percentage of Minority Residents
Large complexes			
Morningside Homes	964	380	99
Smith Homes	837	430	96
Ray Warren Homes	651	236	99
Hampton Homes	884	275	97
Claremont Courts	755	250	97
Elderly complexes			
Hall Towers	159	156	21
Gateway Plaza	226	221	46
Stoneridge	55	50	14
Scattered sites			
Hickory Trail	377	127	82
Baylor Court	64	11	88
Woodberry Run	120	39	88
Applewood	113	50	73
Pear Leaf	132	50	85
Lakespring	137	60	81
Silver Briar	108	50	75
Laurel Oaks		50	—
Totals	5,582	2,435	83

Source: Greensboro Housing Authority

EXHIBIT 4: GHA Household Sizes

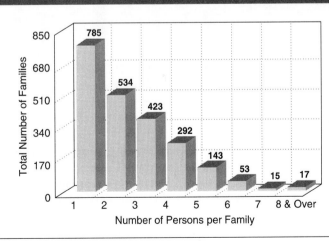

Note: In 1992, there were 2,262 families in GHA's communities.
Source: Greensboro Housing Authority

EXHIBIT 5: Length of Residence and Public Assistance Status of Public
Housing Residents

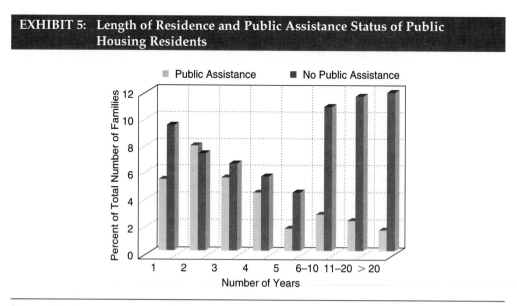

Source: Greensboro Housing Authority

EXHIBIT 6: Age and Sex of Head of Household of Public Housing Residents

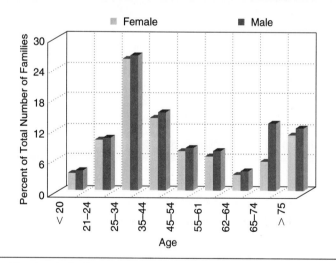

Source: Greensboro Housing Authority

less than $10,000 annually. The total existing supply of such units (including public housing) was 6,725 units, leaving an unmet need for 5,275 low-cost rental units. The GHA had a current waiting list of 1,882 unduplicated families for its public housing and Section 8 (another government-assisted program) units.

SUPPORT SERVICES FOR RESIDENTS

Over the years, many public and private agencies provided traditional support services to Greensboro's public housing families, including counseling, health care, tutoring, and a variety of other services. In addition, the GHA developed several new and award-winning programs to provide support services. Some of its most recent awards included: Youth Sports and Cultural Program Award (for achievements in the development of children's programs); the Public Housing Agency Performance Award (for recognition of the excellence of GHA's Police Neighborhood Resource Centers program), awarded by the HUD's Region IV; and First Place for the "Master Kids" Program and Second Place for the PNRC program, both awarded by the Southeast Regional Council of the National Association of Housing and Redevelopment Officials.

Police Neighborhood Resource Centers

In the late 1980s, most of Greensboro's drug trafficking had occurred in the four largest public housing communities (Smith Homes, Morningside Homes, Ray Warren Homes, and Claremont Courts). These older public housing complexes, with their large number of units and high population density, provided a convenient place for drug dealers to operate and elude arrest. Most of the residents, who were not drug users or participants in drug-related activities, were horrified that their communities had become the sites for these activities.

In response to the residents' concerns, the authority, working closely with the police, initiated the PNRC program. The Greensboro Police Department permanently assigned two police officers to patrol each of the four communities on foot. This program helped eradicate much of the illegal drug activity; and, in addition, it helped to establish an improved relationship between the residents and the police. In particular, the police provided good role models for the children.

Furthermore, the PNRC's combined on-site law enforcement activities and drug prevention and education services produced a comprehensive drug elimination program. A variety of organizations, both public and private, provided the wide range of services and resources necessary to support this comprehensive approach to drug elimination (see Exhibit 7). GHA also obtained HUD funding to support both a drug prevention coordinator and a youth activities coordinator. These individuals helped to recruit volunteers and coordinate the activities of the many agencies that provided services through the PNRC offices.

Youth Services

Many of GHA's programs targeted the young people who lived in its communities. GHA had initiated the Salvation Army Boys' and Girls' clubs. The Salvation Army provided personnel to plan and supervise these on-site youth activity clubs that furnished educational, leadership, recreational, drug prevention, and enrichment programs for young people between the ages of 6 and 18.

Frank Cuthbertson, the chairman of GHA's board of commissioners, established the Southeast Council on Crime and Delinquency. This agency provided educational and cultural enrichment activities for at-risk young people.

The Master Kids Program, an academic incentive program started by the drug prevention coordinator, rewarded and recognized students who had achieved "Master Kid" status by improving their schoolwork.

Resident Councils and Resident Services

Each public housing community established a resident council that included all persons 17 years of age or older living in the particular community. Each council elected officers,

EXHIBIT 7   Support Services for Residents: Selected Participating Community Agencies and Organizations

Drug education and prevention
Substance Abuse Services of Guilford, Inc.
Guilford County Area Mental Health,
Mental Retardation, and Substance
Abuse Services
Southeast Greensboro Council on Crime
and Delinquency
The National Association for the
Advancement of Colored People
National Black Child Development Institute
Planned Parenthood of the Triad, Inc.
The Greensboro Pulpit Forum
Juvenile Services Division of the Courts

Family and other support services
Guilford County Department of Social
Services
Guilford County Department of
Public Health
The Salvation Army
Greensboro Urban Ministry Clinic
Greensboro City Schools
United Services for Older Adults, Inc.

Economic and educational opportunities
Employment Security Commission
Guilford County Private Industry Council
Job Corps
Guilford Technical Community College
Guilford County Community Action
Program, Inc.

Youth services
Salvation Army Boys' and Girls' Clubs
Agricultural Extension Service
City of Greensboro Parks and Recreation
Department
The Boy Scouts of America
The Girl Scouts of America
North Carolina A&T State University
National Conference of Christians and Jews
Achievements Unlimited Basketball School

Facilitators
Greensboro Agency Transportation Express, Inc.
Greensboro Jaycees
Greensboro Junior League

Source: Greensboro Housing Authority.

including a president who met monthly with the executive director and the administrative staff to maintain a good working relationship between the GHA staff and residents. Resident councils sponsored educational, social, and recreational programs for their communities and worked closely with the PNRCs.

GHA's Resident Services Unit provided technical assistance for the resident councils and coordinated resident group activities. GHA's Resident Services staff helped residents deal with health problems, family matters, and financial matters. This staff also worked closely with local service agencies that were available to offer help.

Resident Management

Many resident councils in the public housing communities had entered into formal agreements with GHA to maintain their communities' grounds and manage their PNRC offices. GHA provided these residents with management training. It had helped one resident council to obtain a Resident Management Grant from HUD, to be used to develop the council's ability to take on additional management responsibilities.

In addition, GHA was developing a self-sufficiency program that would help public housing residents to obtain the services and skills needed to make the transition into the private housing market. GHA also started a small-business program to identify and support residents who wanted to start their own small businesses.

IMAGE PROBLEMS AND MISCONCEPTIONS

During the next several weeks, Jerry Lawson continued to read the letter-to-the-editor exchanges between the GHA development's supporters and opponents. Most were penned by opponents of the new community:

> As taxpayers, we feel we should have a say in the way our money is being spent; why was a public hearing denied?

> Why doesn't the government give us statistics on these nice public housing units, showing average number of arrests made, domestic disputes reported, drugs and thefts, compared to other communities?

> After HUD builds this project, will they (or anyone) pay us the true value of our property as it was before the valuation decrease due to the location of this complex on Hilltop Road?

> What will be the next undesirable surprise for our neighborhood? Public transportation? Shopping centers?

> To characterize legitimate concerns, such as property values, security, and use of tax dollars as racist is ridiculous.

In late September, Jerry had lunch with some business associates, Joe Phillips and Paul Conners, who both worked in advertising. He shared his frustrations over the public's poor image of public housing.

"I know that you have been following the controversy over the proposed location for the new GHA community and have seen the same letters to the editor that I have," Jerry began. "I asked you to lunch because I need your advice. The public's general perceptions of public housing are all wrapped up in negative stereotypes about race, crime, and bureaucracy. We need to change all that."

STEREOTYPES AND PREJUDICES

Minorities comprised 83 percent of all public housing residents, and in the five largest and best-known communities, roughly 98 percent of the residents were minorities. Thus, those members of the general population who held racist attitudes and stereotypes were likely to have a negative opinion of GHA's public housing communities.

Low-income status in itself carried a negative stereotype. Many people believed that all residents were lazy and on welfare, allowing "the system" to keep them. In reality, public housing residents paid rent, and about 65 percent of these families had at least one employed family member. However, with the average family income of only $6,350, these residents represented the city's "working poor."

CRIME AND MEDIA COVERAGE

The public also associated public housing with high crime rates. Drug dealing, murder, and violent crimes did occur in these communities. The older, more densely populated sites were once popular havens for drug sales. However, the Greensboro Police

Department's Division of Crime Analysis reported that the per capita rate of violent crimes against persons and property (the crime index) was *lower* for the GHA communities than for the city as a whole. For example, in 1990, only one of the 21 murders in Greensboro occurred in a public housing community.

The newspaper and television media unintentionally encouraged the connection between public housing communities and crime. When someone committed a crime near a GHA community, the media identified the location as "in or around Morningside Homes" or "near Smith Homes." In contrast, the media identified the locations of crimes committed in more affluent neighborhoods by street name rather than by a community name. As a result, the names of public housing communities became strongly associated with criminal activity. Unfortunately, the "good" side of public housing (the Salvation Army Boys' and Girls' clubs, the Master Kids program, etc.) remained largely unreported by the media. Thus, there was little positive information to counterbalance the negative.

AWARENESS AND REPUTATION

The public often used the terms "projects" and "tenants" to refer to public housing and its residents. GHA wanted to eliminate these terms because of their negative connotations. Unfortunately, the media continued to use these terms partly out of habit and partly because the residents themselves used them. These terms perpetuated images of dilapidated "slums," and did nothing to dispel negative attitudes toward the people who lived in public housing. Ironically, many people were unaware of the smaller, more modern scattered-site public housing communities, even though these communities made up half of GHA's housing stock. Just recently, Elaine had been talking with the mayor about a particular 50-unit complex, and even he had not realized that this community was part of public housing. On the other hand, due to extensive media coverage of the older, larger communities in southeast Greensboro, most people associated public housing only with those complexes.

Thus, public housing residents carried the stigma of living "in the projects" no matter what type of community they lived in. For the children, it was an embarrassment. In school, students and even teachers referred to individuals as "Johnny from Morningside Homes," for example.

Organizational Image

Public housing in Greensboro also suffered from public housing's nationwide reputation. Some major cities had poorly administered or unethically operated housing authorities. These abuses and negative images spilled over both to GHA's residents and to its administration. Some new city residents probably brought negative views of public housing from experiences in other cities.

Those few community leaders who were familiar with GHA's operations held it in high regard as an effectively managed organization. However, most people did not understand GHA's organizational or operational structure, nor did they completely understand the relationship between GHA and the public housing communities.

As the lunch continued, Jerry discussed how these image problems and misconceptions affected the residents.

"If people have decent housing, they have a better opportunity to become contributors to the community and society," Jerry observed. "Living in public housing is not the cause of the residents' problems but instead a result of being poor, unskilled, insufficiently educated, or unemployable. People in these situations seek public housing.

"Probably 90 to 95 percent of the residents are good, decent people who were trying to do the right things and to raise their children. It frustrates me to think that less than 5 percent of the residents shape the community's view of public housing and its residents. As a result, I believe many residents do not have pride in where they live because they do not think the community has pride in them.

"As I've told you before," Jerry continued, "before I became involved, I had many of the same misconceptions. I've noticed that others who become directly involved change their opinions also. Take the police officers who started the PNRC program, for example. Some police officers sympathized with them for having to pull 'awful duty.' In reality, we found just the opposite result. Many residents practically 'adopted' the officers, and the officers became both supportive of and complimentary about many residents. In the process, the residents developed a much better opinion of the police."

IS MARKETING IN GHA's FUTURE?

"I realize that GHA has more than just an image problem," Jerry added as the group finished lunch. "We've got to continue to build new projects, although I expect the budget situation will make federal funding for new projects difficult to obtain. We also need to continue to renovate our existing units."

"I saw in Saturday's paper that the Guilford County commissioners had voted to delete its $84,000 contribution to the authority from its '93–'94 budget," Joe Phillips interjected.

"Yes," Jerry responded, "that's one reason I wanted to have lunch with you two. The commissioners took that action in response to citizens' outcries about the new community. But the commissioners' action just hurts the people we are trying to help. We use that money to renovate existing housing units. Their action just points out that we need to deal with our marketing problem."

"Well, you certainly have a marketing problem!" Paul Conners exclaimed. "It seems to me that it is more than just a public relations or a public image problem."

"That's exactly my point," Jerry answered. "We need to look at the authority from a marketing perspective, not just focus on promotion."

"But do you think marketing is appropriate for public agencies?" Joe Phillips asked. "Many people don't feel that governments or public agencies should be involved in marketing."

"Yes, you do hear statements like that occasionally," Jerry noted. "There may even be members of our board who feel that way. That just makes it more important that we educate them about the need for marketing in its broadest sense."

"Do you have any money to support a marketing effort?" Paul asked.

"Not really," Jerry responded. "We've never had a marketing budget. We don't even have a brochure! We are not going to have much money to support marketing efforts. So, I need to be creative and see what we can do that will not cost much money.

"I know a marketing professor at the university. I think I'll give him a call and see if I can set up a meeting with him and Elaine and me. Perhaps he will have some ideas to get us started. Meanwhile, if you two have any ideas, I'd surely appreciate them."

Later that afternoon, Jerry telephoned Elaine to tell her of his lunch meeting and his idea about meeting with the professor. Elaine liked the idea, and Jerry agreed to set up the meeting.

After the conversation, Elaine sat in her office and thought about recent events. She, too, had been thinking about GHA's image and its marketing problems. She wondered exactly which image was the most important: the housing authority's, the residents', or the idea of public housing. It seemed that the Greensboro Housing Authority needed to improve its image, but the real benefactors she hoped would be the residents, especially the children. There needed to be a way to raise their self-esteem and make them less ashamed of their living conditions. Some adults would remain in public housing. However, the children needed to see a future with more possibilities.

Elaine grabbed a notepad and jotted down several key groups in the city that already affected or could affect GHA's and public housing's image, including the media, local government, public and social service agencies, business and civic groups, volunteer and charitable organizations, schools and universities, and the public housing residents themselves. She decided that she needed to do some thinking about the issues that Jerry Lawson had raised before their meeting.

Elaine reached across her desk and picked up a copy of a letter to the editor from an area property owner and read again the key paragraphs:

> For too long, those of us with means and education have built communities outside the inner city and have left those in poverty with very little resources to rise above their situation. My work has taken me into many public housing projects and other poverty areas in Greensboro and I have leaned that, like us. most residents do not want to live near drug dealers or live in substandard housing.
>
> I believe with a little bit of community involvement from the successful people contained within Adams Farm, Oaks West, and the Hilltop Road area, this public housing project will not be an area that attracts drug dealers, it will not raise crime, and it will not lower property values.
>
> Just imagine what could happen if we became friends and neighbors with this housing community. It may become instead an area where people recapture a dream, learn valuable skills from their neighbors, and become partners in building a better community.

As Elaine picked up her pad to make more notes, she thought, "We need more people who feel like that."

Not far from GHA's administration building, Mary Wilson stood at the kitchen window of her Ray Warren Homes apartment. She watched her son Kevin walk down the street on his way home from school. "That silly kid's late getting home again," she thought to herself. Although she needed him to arrive home on time to watch her two younger children so she could go to work, she couldn't get too angry with him. He had made some really good friends at school this year. However, every day he got off the bus three blocks before his designated bus stop, so the other kids wouldn't know where he lived.

Sidethrusters, Inc.

Raymond M. Kinnunen, John A. Seeger, and Robert L. Goldberg

SIDETHRUSTERS, INC. (A)

> I wanted to do something on my own. I wasn't sure what that was or how to do it. I had a little money put away so I started talking to people about a business to buy or become part owner of.

> I saw a lot of crappy businesses. Then the president of the South Shore Chamber of Commerce said, "I know an inventor who has a neat new product. You might want to meet him."

Michael Bardlow described how he got into the business of producing and installing auxiliary motors for pleasure boats. His company, Sidethrusters, Inc., produced and installed devices (often called "bow thrusters") that helped large pleasure craft maneuver safely while approaching or leaving the dock.

Excited by his meeting with the inventor, Bardlow began investigating the prospects for starting a business. He called the Boston Coast Guard Center and learned that data were available:

> I got a list of every registered vessel longer than 40 feet in the United States, not just in Boston. There were a ton of them, many more than I'd thought. I lose track of the zeros—it was 30,000.

> To get technical expertise, I called every major boat builder in the country, and every naval architect I could find the name of. They were clearly in camps, which was not surprising. Nearly all the sail people were interested; they said, "Go for it." Power boat people often said they didn't need the product, because their big boats had twin engines and were naturally maneuverable. And that's true, certainly, if you have a professional crew.

> So opinion was mixed, but I said, "All right. I'm going for it." I called a friend, a lawyer who's done this before, and we drafted an offering circular. He told me the rules, and we touched all the bases—product description, markets, competition, management, technical, financial. I was ready to go out and sell the idea.

This case was prepared by Professors Raymond M. Kinnunen and Robert L. Goldberg of Northeastern University, and Professor John A. Seeger of Bentley College, as a basis for class discussion. It is not intended to illustrate either effective or ineffective handling of an administrative situation.

During the 3 months after meeting the inventor, Michael Bardlow drafted a business plan and raised $200,000 initial capital. The plan projected $357,000 total revenues for the first year, with after-tax profits of $36,000. The total new boat market was estimated at approximately 17,000 vessels that might qualify for the product. After 3 years, the plan projected annual sales of more than $2 million, with after-tax profits exceeding $350,000. (Exhibits 1 and 2 show the 3-year projected financial statements taken from Bardlow's plan.)

THE PRODUCT

The side thruster was a motor-driven propeller mounted in a tunnel that ran sideways through the hull of a boat—usually at the bow. The propeller could apply a sideways force on the hull, below the waterline, either to the right or to the left. The idea itself was not new; for decades, bow thrusters had been standard equipment on large craft such as ferryboats and tugs, which had to maneuver in constrained spaces. The application to small boats had not been practical until the inventor, Al Carella, adapted a hydraulic motor for the purpose. Michael Bardlow described the need for his product:

> Say you've got a man 55 or 60 years old, coming into the town pilings at Edgartown with his wife. He's got a new $400,000 boat and he's petrified. To him, this is like parking a truck at twenty miles per hour without brakes. Unless there's somebody on the dock, he goes back out and comes in again until there's somebody there he can yell to, "Catch us as we're coming in." This man is not a lifelong sailor, and he needs help.

Bardlow, in his patent and trademark applications and literature, had named the product the "side thruster," to draw attention to the advantages of having total side-motion power. He conceived the product as appropriate for both bow and stern installation,

---

EXHIBIT 1   Pro Forma Year-End Balance Sheet

	Year 1	Year 2	Year 3
Assets			
Cash, Including Short-Term Investments	$232,060	$463,604	$856,010
Inventory	27,000	72,000	81,000
Patent	5,000	5,000	5,000
Total Assets	$264,060	$540,604	$942,010
Liabilities and Capital			
Accrued Expenses	$ 22,580	$ 87,046	$127,341
Capital Stock, 1,000 Shares Outstanding	1,000	1,000	1,000
Capital Surplus	199,550	199,550	199,550
Retained Earnings	40,930	253,008	614,119
Total Liabilities and Capital	$264,060	$540,604	$942,010

Source: Company financial records.

especially for longer pleasure craft and most assuredly for commercial fishing vessels, to provide the ultimate in safety and maneuverability. In vessels of greater tonnage, the installation of the side thruster in the bow, stern, and amidships would be highly feasible and desirable, he thought.

Sidethrusters, Inc., set out to establish its line of 6-, 8-, and 10-inch side thrusters in the marketplace. The experience acquired through manufacturing, marketing, and selling these units would help the research and development of new products, Bardlow thought. The units were priced at $5,000 for the smallest unit, up to $15,000 for the largest. Additional installation costs varied depending on whether the work was done on a new boat during the manufacturing process or on an existing boat in dry dock. The business plan allowed for one trip to train each installing boat yard on the procedures to be followed.

FINANCING

Having completed his plan, Bardlow contacted a group of friends and associates who were interested in boating—doctors, lawyers, dentists, and other potential investors who might contribute start-up capital. They, in turn, called their associates and soon developed a network of potential investors.

Very quickly, $200,000 was raised from sixteen investors. Two of the investors contributed $20,000, and one invested $30,000. Bardlow retained 35 percent of the company stock, his inventor/partner had 20 percent, and the investors had 45 percent ownership in the firm.

MANAGEMENT

Michael Bardlow was a CPA and Controller of Hayden Street Research and Management Company, an investment advisory firm. He had spent 6 years with Price Waterhouse before joining Hayden Street. He owned a 25-foot sailboast and was knowledgeable about the general marine industry. He intended to continue his work at Hayden Street during the start-up and to become the full-time president when Sidethrusters reached annual sales of 120 units. The CEO of Hayden Street Research supported Bardlow's plan, although he declined to become an investor in the new firm.

Bardlow's partner, Al Carella, became the company's vice president and only full-time employee. Carella had worked on propulsion systems with the Navy and Coast Guard over the past 20 years. He was the inventor of the side thruster and assisted Bardlow in the sales effort. Carella had total responsibility for manufacturing, assembly, and shipping.

The first sale was to the Shannon Boat Company, which installed a unit in a 50-foot yacht at their Rhode Island boatyard. Bardlow recalled:

> One of the most nervous days in my life was watching a brand-new $350,000 boat sitting at the dock, with the president of Shannon next to me and my engineer standing in the cockpit saying, "OK, I'm ready." I'm saying to myself, "Please work. Please, please work." Al kicked it on.

> The bow went right away from the dock. The president said, "Wonderful. This is just what I want." The inventor is standing there smiling like a Chesire cat. And I'm trying to remain cool and calm, as if I knew all along it would work.

EXHIBIT 2   Pro Forma Income and Cash Flow Statement, Years 1–3

Month of Year 1	1	2	3	4	5
Units Sold in Year 1			2	4	6
Sales	$0	$0	$8,000	$17,000	$25,000
Less: COGS	2,317	2,317	6,117	9,917	13,717
Gross Margin	(2,317)	(2,317)	1,883	7,083	11,283
Other Expenses					
MFB Salary	867	867	867	867	867
Secretarial[a]	160	320	320	480	480
Advertising	1,000	1,000	1,000	1,000	1,000
Travel	0	0	560	1,190	3,750
Postage	200	200	200	300	300
Telephone	200	200	200	300	300
Operating Supplies	200	200	200	200	200
Accounting[a]	420	420	420	420	420
Legal	4,000	0	0	0	0
Payroll Taxes	224	224	234	245	245
Miscellaneous Expenses	1,000	1,000	1,200	1,200	1,500
R&D	5,000	0	0	0	0
Total Other Expenses	13,271	4,431	5,201	6,202	9,062
Net Income Before Taxes	(15,588)	(6,748)	(3,318)	881	2,221
State Tax[a]	$0				
Federal Tax[a]	$0				
Net Income	(15,588)	(6,758)	(3,318)	881	2,221
Cumulative					
Add Back Noncash Items	420	420	420	420	420
Net Cash Before Inventory	(15,168)	(6,328)	(2,898)	1,301	2,641
Additions to Inventory	(27,000)		(3,600)	(7,200)	(10,800)
Relief From Inventory	0		3,600	7,200	10,800
Cash Payments of Accruals					
Net Cash Monthly	(42,168)	(6,328)	(2,898)	1,301	2,641
Cumulative	$47,832	$41,504	$38,606	$39,907	$42,548

Year 2 Pro Forma Income and Cash Flow Statement

Month of Year 2	1	2	3	4	5
Units Sold in This Month	20	22	24	26	28
Sales	$82,000	$90,000	$98,000	$107,000	$115,000
Less: COGS	41,183	44,983	48,783	52,583	56,383
Gross Margin	40,817	45,017	49,217	54,417	58,617
Other Expenses					
MFB Salary	5,000	5,000	5,000	5,000	5,000
Secretarial[a]	1,000	1,000	1,000	1,000	1,000
Advertising	1,000	1,000	1,000	1,000	1,000
Travel	5,740	6,300	6,860	7,490	10,050
Postage	450	500	500	500	600

6	7	8	9	10	11	12	Totals: 87
8	8	9	10	10	14	16	
$33,000	$33,000	$36,500	$41,000	$41,000	$57,000	$66,000	$357,500
17,717	17,517	19,417	21,317	21,317	28,917	32,717	$193,104
15,483	15,483	17,083	19,683	19,683	28,083	33,283	$164,396
867	867	867	867	867	867	867	$10,404
480	480	480	480	480	480	480	$5,120
1,000	1,000	1,000	1,000	1,000	1,000	1,000	$12,000
4,810	2,310	6,055	2,870	2,870	7,490	4,620	$36,525
300	300	300	300	300	400	400	$3,500
350	400	400	400	400	600	600	$4,350
200	200	200	200	200	200	200	$2,400
420	420	420	420	420	420	420	$5,040
0	0	0	0	0	0	0	$4,000
245	245	245	245	245	245	245	$2,887
1,800	2,000	2,000	2,000	2,000	2,000	2,000	$19,700
0	0	0	0	0	0	0	$5,000
10,472	8,222	11,967	8,782	8,782	13,702	10,832	$110,926
5,011	7,261	5,116	10,901	10,901	14,381	22,451	$53,470
			1,074	1,090	1,438	2,245	$5,847
			2,147	2,180	2,876	4,490	$11,693
5,011	7,261	5,116	7,680	7,631	10,067	15,716	$35,930
420	420	420	3,641	3,690	4,734	7,155	
5,431	7,681	5,536	11,321	11,321	14,801	22,871	
(14,400)	(14,400)	(16,200)	(18,000)	(18,000)	(25,200)	(28,800)	
14,400	14,400	16,200	18,000	18,000	25,200	28,800	
5,431	7,681	5,536	11,321	11,321	14,801	22,871	
$47,979	$55,660	$61,196	$72,517	$83,838	$98,639	$121,510	

Earnings per share (1,000 shares outstanding) $35.93

6	7	8	9	10	11	12	Totals: 354
30	30	32	32	34	36	40	
$123,000	$123,000	$131,000	$131,000	$139,000	$148,000	$164,000	$1,451,000
60,183	60,183	63,983	63,983	67,783	71,583	79,183	$710,796
62,817	62,817	67,017	67,017	71,217	76,417	84,817	$740,204
5,000	5,000	5,000	5,000	5,000	5,000	5,000	$60,000
1,000	1,000	1,000	1,000	1,000	1,000	1,000	$12,000
1,000	1,000	1,000	1,000	1,000	1,000	1,000	$12,000
11,110	8,610	12,670	9,170	9,730	13,860	11,480	$113,070
600	700	700	750	800	850	900	$7,850

(Continued on next page)

Exhibit 2   *(Continued)*

Year 2 Pro Forma Income and Cash Flow Statement

Month of Year 2	1	2	3	4	5
Units Sold in This Month	20	22	24	26	28
Other Expenses					
Telephone	700	800	800	850	1,000
Operating Supplies	300	400	400	450	500
Accounting[a]	500	500	500	500	500
Legal	0	0	0	0	0
Payroll Taxes	632	632	632	632	632
Miscellaneous Expenses	2,200	2,200	2,400	2,400	2,600
Total Other Expenses	17,522	18,332	19,092	19,822	22,882
Net Income Before Taxes	23,295	26,685	30,125	34,595	35,735
State Tax[a]	2,330	2,669	3,013	3,460	3,574
Federal Tax[a]	10,483	12,008	13,556	15,568	16,081
Net Income	10,482	12,008	13,556	15,567	16,080
Cumulative		22,490	36,046	51,613	67,693
Add Back Noncash Items	13,313	15,177	17,069	19,528	20,155
Net Cash Before Inventory	23,795	27,185	30,625	35,095	36,235
Additions to Inventory	(45,000)	(39,600)	(43,200)	(46,800)	(50,400)
Relief from Inventory	36,000	39,600	43,200	46,800	50,400
Cash Payments of Accruals	(22,580)			(45,559)	
Net Cash Monthly	(7,785)	27,185	30,625	(10,464)	36,235
Cumulative	$113,725	$140,910	$171,535	$161,071	$197,306

Year 3 Pro Forma Income and Cash Flow Statement

Month of Year 3	1	2	3	4	5
Units Sold in This Month	40	40	42	44	46
Sales	$164,000	$164,000	$172,000	$180,000	$189,000
Less: COGS	81,567	81,567	85,367	89,167	92,967
Gross Margin	82,433	82,433	86,633	90,833	96,033
Other Expenses					
MFB Salary	5,417	5,417	5,417	5,417	5,417
Secretarial[a]	1,125	1,125	1,125	1,125	1,125
Advertising	1,000	1,000	1,000	1,000	1,000
Travel	11,480	11,480	12,040	12,600	15,230
Postage	1,000	1,050	1,100	1,200	1,200
Telephone	1,350	1,400	1,400	1,500	1,500
Operating Supplies	750	800	800	850	900
Accounting[a]	700	700	700	700	700
Legal	0	0	0	0	0
Payroll Taxes	837	837	837	837	837
Miscellaneous Expenses	3,000	3,100	3,200	3,200	3,300
R & D	3,000	3,000	3,000	3,000	3,000
Total Other Expenses	29,659	29,909	30,619	31,429	34,209

6	7	8	9	10	11	12	
30	30	32	32	34	36	40	Totals: 354
1,000	1,050	1,100	1,200	1,200	1,300	1,300	$12,300
600	600	600	650	700	700	700	$6,600
500	500	500	500	500	500	500	$6,000
0	0	0	0	0	0	0	0
632	632	632	632	632	632	632	$7,584
2,600	2,600	2,700	2,800	2,000	3,000	3,000	$30,500
24,042	21,692	25,902	22,702	23,562	27,842	25,512	$268,904
38,775	41,125	41,115	44,315	47,655	48,575	59,305	$471,300
3,878	4,113	4,112	4,432	4,766	4,858	5,931	$47,136
17,449	18,506	18,502	19,942	21,445	21,859	26,687	$212,086
17,448	18,506	18,501	19,941	21,444	21,858	26,687	212,078
85,141	103,647	122,148	142,089	163,533	185,391	212,078	
21,827	23,119	23,114	24,874	26,711	27,217	33,118	
39,275	41,625	41,615	44,815	48,155	49,075	59,805	
(54,000)	(90,000)	(57,600)	(57,600)	(61,200)	(64,800)	(72,000)	
54,000	54,000	57,600	57,600	61,200	64,800	72,000	
	(61,510)			(71,107)			
39,275	(55,885)	41,615	44,815	(22,952)	49,075	59,805	
$236,581	$180,696	$222,311	$267,126	$244,174	$293,249	$353,054	

Earnings per share (1,000 shares outstanding) $212.08

6	7	8	9	10	11	12	
50	50	50	50	50	50	50	Totals: 562
$205,000	$215,000	$215,000	$215,000	$215,000	$215,000	$215,000	$2,364,000
100,567	105,067	105,067	105,067	105,067	105,067	105,067	$1,161,604
104,433	109,933	109,933	109,933	109,933	109,933	109,933	$1,202,396
5,417	5,417	5,417	5,417	5,417	5,417	5,417	$65,004
1,125	1,125	1,125	1,125	1,125	1,125	1,125	$13,500
1,000	2,000	2,000	2,000	2,000	2,000	2,000	$18,000
16,850	15,050	18,550	15,050	15,050	18,550	15,050	$176,980
1,300	1,300	1,400	1,400	1,500	1,500	1,500	$15,450
1,500	1,550	1,600	1,600	1,700	1,700	1,700	$18,500
900	950	1,000	1,000	1,000	1,000	1,000	$10,950
700	700	700	700	700	700	700	$8,400
5,000	0	0	0	0	0	0	$5,000
837	837	837	837	837	837	837	$10,044
3,400	3,400	3,450	3,450	3,500	3,500	3,600	$40,100
3,000	0	0	0	0	0	0	$18,000
41,029	32,329	36,079	32,579	32,829	36,329	32,929	$399,928

(Continued on next page)

Exhibit 2 (Continued)

Year 3 Pro Forma Income and Cash Flow Statement

Month of Year 3	1	2	3	4	5
Units Sold in This Month	40	40	42	44	46
Net Income Before Taxes	52,774	52,524	56,014	59,404	61,824
State Tax[a]	5,277	5,252	5,601	5,940	6,182
Federal Tax[a]	23,749	23,636	25,207	26,732	27,821
Net Income	23,748	23,636	25,206	26,732	27,821
Cumulative		47,384	72,590	99,322	127,143
Add Back Noncash Items	29,726	29,588	31,508	33,372	34,703
Net Cash Before Inventory	53,474	53,224	56,714	60,104	62,524
Additions to Inventory	(72,000)	(72,000)	(75,600)	(79,200)	(82,800)
Relief from Inventory	72,000	72,000	75,600	79,200	82,800
Cash Payments of Accruals	(87,046)			(90,822)	
Net Cash Monthly	(33,572)	53,224	56,714	(30,718)	62,524
Cumulative	$319,482	$372,706	$429,420	$398,702	$461,226

[a]Noncash items

But we had never tested the thing. We assumed it would work but we weren't sure. I was ecstatic. Shannon makes three to five 50-foot boats per year, and they gave us a blanket order.

In the first two years of company operations, approximately 110 sailboats in excess of 50 feet were built all over the world; side thrusters were installed in 70 of those boats. Mike Bardlow recognized early on, however, that the growth he wanted called for more than just installations in new sailboats. It called for more than a part-time effort, as well. He left Hayden Street Research and decided to go to the aftermarket, retrofitting existing pleasure boats. "We decided to go after the power boat market, because the ratio of power to sail is 25 boats to one," said Bardlow. (Exhibit 3 shows approximate U.S. fleet sizes.)

An aggressive ad campaign featured quarter-page ads in two industry magazines—*Yachting* and a new publication called *Power and Motor Yacht*. "New Sidethruster maneuvers boats in tight spots!" shouted the headline, over a picture of a motor yacht swinging in to a crowded dock. "The first small thruster designed for boats 40 feet to 100 feet long!" The ads went on:

> Sidethruster's new hydraulic thruster delivers big moving power in a small package. Installed in the bow, the 6-inch model (less than half the size of a conventional thruster) can turn a 40-foot yacht nearly within its own length. A unique direct drive 7-hp motor delivers 260 pounds of thrust in the 8-inch model and 230 pounds for the 6-inch model.

> Side thrusters can be installed in one day. For more information on how to put some maneuvering power on your side, contact....

6	7	8	9	10	11	12	
50	50	50	50	50	50	50	Totals: 562
63,404	77,604	73,854	77,354	77,104	73,604	77,004	$802,468
6,340	7,760	7,385	7,735	7,710	7,360	7,700	$80,242
28,532	34,922	33,235	34,810	34,697	33,122	34,652	$361,115
28,532	34,922	33,234	34,809	34,697	33,122	34,652	$361,111
155,675	190,597	223,831	258,640	293,337	326,459	361,111	
35,572	43,382	41,320	43,245	43,107	41,182	43,052	
64,104	78,304	74,554	78,054	77,804	74,304	77,704	
(90,000)	(103,500)	(94,500)	(94,500)	(94,500)	(94,500)	(94,500)	
90,000	94,500	94,500	94,500	94,500	94,500	94,500	
	(103,647)			(127,947)			
64,104	(34,343)	74,554	78,054	(50,143)	74,304	77,704	
$525,330	$490,987	$565,541	$643,595	$593,452	$667,756	$745,460	
						Earnings per share (1,000 shares outstanding)	$361.11

THE RETROFIT MARKET

In the retrofit market, side thrusters were installed on site at the boat owner's dry dock. Two oval holes were drilled on opposing sides of the fore section of the boat below the waterline. Pressure hoses, a power takeoff unit, and a precision-machined brass pump unit were installed while the boat was in dry dock. All the materials were purchased from subcontractors; they were mostly assembled from readily available components.

To install the side thruster, management had to hire its own work crew. Michael Bardlow explained:

> No boatyard would touch it. If a boatyard cuts two big holes in the hull and the boat happens to sink instead of moving sideways, that yard is liable to the tune of $250,000 to $500,000 (whatever the price of the boat was). I had to hire my own guys. We had never drilled a hole in the side of a boat—any boat.

> The very first power boat we did was a Grand Banks 36, owned by a doctor in New York. I personally led the three-man installation crew to the customer's yard. The guy doing the installation says, "I've worked on boats all of my life, this is no problem." So we arrive and there's this gorgeous fiberglass boat waiting for us. To mark the site for the holes we ran tape from the bow along the side to locate the right height and length. Fortunately, we're doing this at 9 o'clock at night with flashlights, so no one can see us.

> We drilled one hole. It is a 6-inch unit, but a hull is shaped at an angle, so elliptically the hole comes out about 14 inches high. As my crew leader is drilling this thing I am saying, "Are you crazy? Look at the size of this thing." We

EXHIBIT 3   Approximate U.S. Fleet Sizes, 1987–1988

Category	Number	Totals
1987 new boat sales		
Inboard boats (cruisers)	13,100	
Sailboats (auxiliary-powered)		
30 feet and under	1,100	
Over 30 feet	2,900	17,100
1987 industry estimate of inboard boats owned (includes powered sailboats)		481,000
1988 registration		
Over 65 feet		
Inboard	1,855	
Outboard	1,257	3,112
40–65 feet		
Inboard	33,942	
Outboard	5,735	39,677
26–40 feet		
Inboard	245,835	
Outboard	54,921	300,756
		343,545

drilled a little bit, then a little bigger. We finished the holes at 2 o'clock in the morning.

The boat owner came down the next morning at 9 o'clock, walked around the boat, and the color drained from his face. No tunnel. Just two huge holes, one on either side of the hull, and fiberglass dust all over everything. We hadn't realized how much dust we created. The owner said, "You guys have this thing in my boat by this afternoon or tomorrow morning you're going to get sued!"

The next day they put the boat in the water. There was no leakage! It was perfectly dry and it worked. It worked really well!

Sidethrusters' installation crew flew to boatyards in Maryland, Florida, Texas, California, and Alaska to install units in owners' boats. Bardlow knew the whole company would be at risk if anything went wrong, because insurance coverage for product liability was prohibitively expensive.

The retrofit market presented a great problem because every boat was different. No one boat in the powerboat market was standard. Even the same model boats were customized for individual buyers. Sidethrusters had installation agreements for half a dozen Grand Banks 42-foot cruisers, but Grand Banks offered three different engine configurations for their boats. Bardlow explained:

We did the first one, and we died putting it in, but we put it in. We get the second order, we say to ourselves, "We've already done one of these; it should be a lay-up." So we cut all the hydraulic hoses based on our previous experience, went down to do the project and the engines were in a different location. All our hoses were cut wrong. We had to air-freight new hoses in to complete the job.

I couldn't legitimately and accurately estimate how long it would take us to install a unit. Not even once.

Bardlow believed the market potential for the side thruster was very large. During the first two years of operations they had sold more than 80 side thrusters; a number of those had been retrofits. Company revenues reached nearly $500,000, but Sidethrusters had not made a profit. Bardlow had not foreseen the travel expense for the installation crews as a factor when he put together the financial projections in his business plan. Because of the large potential market, however, he was confident the company would succeed.

Gillette and the Men's Wet-Shaving Market

Lew G. Brown and Jennifer M. Hart

San Francisco

On a spring morning in 1989, Michael Johnson dried himself and stepped from the shower in his San Francisco Marina District condominium. He moved to the sink and started to slide open his drawer in the cabinet beneath the sink. Then he remembered that he had thrown away his last Atra blade yesterday. He heard his wife, Susan, walk past the bathroom.

"Hey, Susan, did you remember to pick up some blades for me yesterday?"

"Yes, I think I put them in your drawer."

"Oh, okay, here they are." Michael saw the bottom of the blade package and pulled the drawer open.

"Oh, no! These are Trac II blades, Susan; I use an Atra."

"I'm sorry. I looked at all the packages at the drugstore, but I couldn't remember which type of razor you have. Can't you use the Trac II blades on your razor?"

"No. They don't fit."

"Well, I bought some disposable razors. Just use one of those."

"Well, where are they?"

"Look below the sink. They're in a big bag."

"I see them. Wow, 10 razors for $1.97! Must have been on sale."

"I guess so. I usually look for the best deal. Seems to me that all those razors are the same, and the drugstore usually has one brand or another on sale."

"Why don't you buy some of those shavers made for women?"

"I've tried those, but it seems that they're just like the ones made for me, only they've dyed the plastic pink or some pastel color. Why should I pay more for color?"

"Why don't you just use disposables?" Susan continued. "They are simpler to buy, and you just throw them away. And you can't beat the price."

"Well, the few times I've tried them, they didn't seem to shave as well as a regular razor. Perhaps they've improved. Do they work for you?"

"Yes, they work fine. And they sure are better than the heavy razors if you drop one on your foot while you're in the shower!"

"Never thought about that. I see your point. Well, I'll give the disposable a try."

This case was prepared by Professor Lew G. Brown of the University of North Carolina at Greensboro and Jennifer M. Hart, MBA, as a basis for class discussion. It is not intended to illustrate either effective or ineffective handling of an administrative situation. The authors express their appreciation to The Gillette Company and Prudential-Bache Securities for their cooperation in developing this case.

HISTORY OF SHAVING

Anthropologists do not know exactly when or even why men began to shave. Researchers do know that prehistoric cave drawings clearly present men who were beardless. Apparently these men shaved with clamshells or sharpened animal teeth. As society developed, primitive men learned to sharpen flint implements. Members of the early Egyptian dynasties as far back as 7,000 years ago shaved their faces and heads, probably to deny their enemies anything to grab during hand-to-hand combat. Egyptians later fashioned copper razors and, in time, bronze blades. Craftsmen formed these early razors as crescent-shaped knife blades, like hatchets or meat cleavers, or even as circular blades with a handle extending from the center. By the Iron Age, craftsmen were able to craft blades that were considerably more efficient than the early flint, copper, and bronze versions.

Before the introduction of the safety razor, men used a straight-edged, hook-type razor and found shaving a tedious, difficult, and time-consuming task. The typical man struggled through shaving twice a week at most. The shaver had to sharpen the blade (a process called stropping) before each use and had to have an expert cutler hone the blade each month. As a result, men often cut themselves while shaving; and few men had the patience and acquired the necessary skill to become good shavers. Most men in the 1800s agreed with the old Russian proverb: "It is easier to bear a child once a year than to shave every day." Only the rich could afford a daily barber shave, which also often had its disadvantages because many barbers were unclean.

Before King C. Gillette of Boston invented the safety razor in 1895, he tinkered with other inventions in pursuit of a product that, once used, would be thrown away. The customer would have to buy more, and the business would build a long-term stream of sales and profits with each new customer.

"On one particular morning when I started to shave," wrote Gillette about the dawn of his invention, "I found my razor dull, and it was not only dull but beyond the point of successful stropping. It needed honing, for which it must be taken to a barber or cutler. As I stood there with the razor in my hand, my eyes resting on it as lightly as a bird settling down on its nest, the Gillette razor was born." Gillette immediately wrote to his wife, who was visiting relatives, "I've got it; our fortune is made."

Gillette had envisioned a "permanent" razor handle onto which the shaver placed a thin, razor "blade" with two sharpened edges. The shaver would place a top over the blade and attach it to the handle so that only the sharpened edges of the blade were exposed, thus producing a "safe" shave. A man would shave with the blade until it became dull and then would simply throw the used blade away and replace it. Gillette knew his concept would revolutionize the process of shaving; however, he had no idea that his creation would permanently change men's shaving habits.

SHAVING IN THE 1980s

After the invention of the safety razor, the U.S. men's shaving industry grew slowly but surely through World War I. A period of rapid growth followed, and the industry saw many product innovations. By 1989, U.S. domestic razor and blade sales (the wet-shave market) had grown to a $770 million industry. A man could use three types of wet shavers to remove facial hair. Most men used the disposable razor—a cheap, plastic-handled razor that lasted for eight to 10 shaves on average. Permanent razors, called razor and blade systems, were also popular. These razors required new blades every 11 to 14 shaves. Customers could purchase razor handles and blade cartridges together, or they could purchase packages of blade cartridges as refills. The third category of wet shavers included injector and double-edge razors and accounted for a small share of the razor market. Between 1980 and 1988, disposable razors had risen from a 22 percent to a 41.5 percent market share of dollar sales. During the same period, cartridge systems had fallen from 50 percent to 45.8 percent, and injector and double-edge types had fallen from 28 percent to 12.7 percent. In addition, the development of the electric razor had spawned the dry-shave market, which accounted for about $250 million in sales by 1988.

Despite the popularity of disposable razors, manufacturers found that the razors were expensive to make and generated very little profit. In 1988 some industry analysts estimated that manufacturers earned three times more on a razor and blade system than on a disposable. Also, retailers preferred to sell razor systems because they took up less room on display racks and the retailers made more money on refill sales. However, retailers liked to promote disposable razors to generate traffic. As a result, U.S. retailers allocated 55 percent of their blade and razor stock to disposable razors, 40 percent to systems, and 5 percent to double-edge razors.

Electric razors also posed a threat to razor and blade systems. Unit sales of electric razors jumped from 6.2 million in 1981 to 8.8 million in 1987. Low-priced imports from the Far East drove demand for electric razors up and prices down during this period. Nonetheless, fewer than 30 percent of men used electric razors, and most of these men also used wet-shaving systems.

Industry analysts predicted that manufacturers' sales of personal care products would continue to grow. However, the slowing of the overall U.S. economy in the late 1980s meant that sales increases resulting from an expanding market would be minimal and companies would have to fight for market share to continue to increase sales.

The Gillette Company dominated the wet-shave market with a 60 percent share of worldwide razor market revenue and 61.9 percent share of the U.S. market as of 1988. Gillette also had a stake in the dry-shave business through its Braun subsidiary. The other players in the wet-shave market were Schick with 16.2 percent of market revenues, BIC with 9.3 percent, and others, including Wilkinson Sword, with the remaining 12.6 percent.

THE GILLETTE COMPANY

King Gillette took eight years to perfect his safety razor. In 1903, the first year of marketing, the American Safety Razor Company sold 51 razors and 168 blades. Gillette promoted the safety razor as a saver of both time and money. Early ads proclaimed that the razor would save $52 and 15 days shaving time each year and that the blades required no stropping or honing. During its second year, Gillette sold 90,884 razors and 123,648 blades. By its third year, razor sales were rising at a rate of 400 percent per year, and blade sales were booming at an annual rate of 1,000 percent. In that year, the company opened its first overseas branch in London.

Such success attracted much attention, and competition quickly developed. By 1906, consumers had at least a dozen safety razors from which to choose. The Gillette razor sold for $5, as did the Zinn razor made by the Gem Cutlery Company. Others, such as the Ever Ready, Gem Junior, and Enders, sold for as little as $1.

With the benefit of a 17-year patent, Gillette found himself in a very advantageous position. However, it was not until World War I that the safety razor gained wide consumer acceptance. One day in 1917, King Gillette had a visionary idea: have the government present a Gillette razor to every soldier, sailor, and marine. In this way, millions of men just entering the shaving age would adopt the self-shaving habit. By March 1918,

Gillette had booked orders from the U.S. military for 519,750 razors, more than it had sold in any single year in its history. During World War I, the government bought 4,180,000 Gillette razors as well as smaller quantities of competitive models.

Although King Gillette believed in the quality of his product, he realized that marketing, especially distribution and advertising, would be the key to success. From the beginning, Gillette set aside 25 cents per razor for advertising and by 1905 had increased the amount to 50 cents. Over the years, Gillette used cartoon ads, radio shows, musical slogans and theme songs, prizes, contests, and cross-promotions to push its products. Perhaps, however, consumers best remember Gillette for its Cavalcade of Sports programs that began in 1939 with the company's sponsorship of the World Series. Millions of men soon came to know Sharpie the Parrot and the tag line, "Look Sharp! Feel Sharp! Be Sharp!"

Became company founder King Gillette invented the first safety razor, Gillette had always been an industry innovator. In 1932, Gillette introduced the Gillette Blue Blade, which was the premier men's razor for many years. In 1938, the company introduced the Gillette Thin Blade; in 1946, it introduced the first blade dispenser that eliminated the need to unwrap individual blades; in 1959, it introduced the first silicone-coated blade, the Super Blue Blade. The success of the Super Blue Blade caused Gillette to close 1961 with a commanding 70 percent share of the overall razor and blade market and a 90 percent share of the double-edge market, the only market in which it competed.

In 1948, Gillette began to diversify into new markets through acquisition. The company purchased the Toni Company to extend its reach into the women's grooming-aid market. In 1954, the company bought Paper Mate, a leading maker of writing instruments. In 1962, Gillette acquired the Sterilon Corporation, which manufactured disposable hospital supplies. As a result of these moves, a marketing survey found that the public associated Gillette with personal grooming as much as, or more than, with blades and razors.

In 1988, the Gillette Company was a leading producer of men's and women's grooming aids. Exhibit 1 lists the company's major divisions. Exhibits 2 and 3 show the percentages and dollar volumes of net sales and profits from operations for each of the company's major business segments from 1984 to 1988. Exhibits 4 and 5 present income statements and balance sheets for 1986–1988.

Despite its diversification, Gillette continued to realize the importance of blade and razor sales to the company's overall health. Gillette had a strong foothold in the razor and blade market, and it intended to use this dominance to help it achieve the company's goal—"sustained profitable growth." To reach this goal, Gillette's mission statement indicated that the company should pursue "strong technical and marketing efforts to assure vitality in major existing product lines; selective diversification, both internally and through acquisition; the elimination of product and business areas with low growth or limited profit potential; and strict control over product costs, overhead expenses, and working capital."

Gillette introduced a number of innovative shaving systems in the 1970s and 1980s as part of its strategy to sustain growth. Gillette claimed that Trac II, the first twin-blade shaver, represented the most revolutionary shaving advance ever. The development of the twin-blade razor derived from shaving researchers' discovery that shaving causes whiskers to be briefly lifted up out of the follicle during shaving, a process called "hysteresis" by technicians. Gillette invented the twin-blade system so that the first blade would cut the whisker and the second blade would cut it again before it receded. This system produced a closer shave than a traditional one-blade system. Gillette also developed a clog-free, dual-blade cartridge for the Trac II system.

EXHIBIT 1   Gillette 1988 Product Lines by Company Division

Safety Razor	**Stationery Products**
Trac II	Paper Mate
Atra	Liquid Paper
Good News	Flair
	Waterman
	Write Bros.

Toiletries and Cosmetics	**Oral Care**
Adorn	Oral B Toothbrushes
Toni	
Right Guard	
Silkience	
Soft and Dri	**Braun Products**
Foamy	
Dry Look	Electric Razors
Dry Idea	Lady Elegance
White Rain	Clocks
Lustrasilk	Coffee Grinders and Makers
Aapri Skin Care Products	

EXHIBIT 2   Gillette's Sales and Operating Profits by Product Line (In Millions)

Product line	1988		1987		1986	
	Sales	**Profits**	**Sales**	**Profits**	**Sales**	**Profits**
Blades and razors	$1,147	$406	$1,031	$334	$ 903	$274
Toiletries and cosmetics	1,019	79	926	99	854	69
Writing instruments and office products	385	56	320	34	298	11
Braun products	824	85	703	72	657	63
Oral-B	202	18	183	7	148	8
Other	5	(0.1)	4	2	48	(1)
Totals	$3,581	$643	$3,167	$584	$2,818	$424

Source: *Gillette Company Annual Report*, 1985–1988

Because consumer test data showed a 9-to-1 preference for Trac II over panelists' current razors, Gillette raced to get the product to market. Gillette supported Trac II's 1971 introduction, which was the largest new-product introduction in shaving history, with a $10 million advertising and promotion budget. Gillette cut its advertising budgets for its other brands drastically to support Trac II. The double-edge portion of the advertising budget decreased from 47 percent in 1971 to 11 percent in 1972. Gillette reasoned that

EXHIBIT 3   Gillette's Net Sales and Profit by Business (By Percent)

Year	Blades and razors		Toiletries and cosmetics		Stationery products		Braun products		Oral B products	
	Sales	Profits	Sales	Profits	Sales	Profits	Sales	Profits	Sales	Profits
1988	32	61	28	14	11	9	23	13	6	3
1987	33	61	29	18	10	6	22	13	6	2
1986	32	64	30	16	11	3	20	15	5	2
1985	33	68	31	15	11	2	17	13	6	3
1984	34	69	30	15	12	3	17	12	3	2

Source: *Gillette Company Annual Report*, 1985–1988

EXHIBIT 4   Gillette Income Statements (In Millions Except for Per Share Data)

	1988	1987	1986
Net sales	$ 3,581.2	$ 3,166.8	$ 2,818.3
Cost of sales	1,487.4	1,342.3	1,183.8
Other expenses	1,479.8	1,301.3	1,412.0
Operating income	614.0	523.2	222.5
Other income	37.2	30.9	38.2
Earnings before interest and tax	651.2	545.1	260.7
Interest expense	138.3	112.5	85.2
Non-operating expenses	64.3	50.1	124.0
Earnings before tax	448.6	391.5	51.5
Tax	180.1	161.6	35.7
Earnings after tax	268.5	229.9	15.8
Earnings per share	2.45	2.00	.12
Average common shares outstanding, 000	109,559	115,072	127,344
Dividends paid per share	0.86	0.785	0.68
Stock price range			
High	$ 49	$ 45⅞	$ 34½
Low	$ 29⅛	$ 17⅝	$ 17⅛

Source: *Gillette Company Annual Report*, 1985–1988

growth must come at the expense of other brands. Thus, it concentrated its advertising and promotion on its newest shaving product and reduced support for its established lines.

Gillette launched Trac II during a World Series promotion and made it the most frequently advertised shaving system in America during its introductory period. Trac II users turned out to be predominantly young, college-educated men who lived in metropolitan and suburban areas and earned higher incomes. As the fastest-growing shaving product

EXHIBIT 5   Gillette Balance Sheets (In Millions)

	1988	1987	1986
Assets			
Cash	$ 156.4	$ 119.1	$ 94.8
Receivables	729.1	680.1	608.8
Inventories	653.4	594.5	603.1
Other current assets	200.8	184.5	183.0
Total current assets	1,739.7	1,578.2	1,489.7
Fixed assets, net	683.1	664.4	637.3
Other assets	445.1	448.6	412.5
TOTAL ASSETS	$2,867.9	$2,731.2	$2,539.5
Liabilities and Equity			
Current liabilities[a]	$ 965.4	$ 960.5	$ 900.7
Long-term debt	1,675.2	839.6	915.2
Other long-term liabilities	311.9	331.7	262.8
Equity[b]	$ (84.6)	$ 599.4	$ 460.8

[a]Includes current portion of long-term debt: 1988 = $9.6; 1987 = $41.0; 1986 = $7.6.
[b]Includes retained earnings: 1988 = $1,261.6; 1987 = $1,083.8; 1986 = $944.3.
Source: *Gillette Company Annual Report, 1986–1988*

on the market for five years, Trac II drove the switch to twin blades. The brand reached its peak in 1976, when consumers purchased 485 million blades and 7 million razors.

Late in 1976, Gillette, apparently in response to BIC's pending entrance into the U.S. market, launched Good News!, the first disposable razor for men sold in the United States. In 1975, BIC had introduced the first disposable shaver in Europe; and by 1976 BIC had begun to sell disposable razors in Canada. Gillette realized that BIC would move its disposable razor into the United States after its Canadian introduction, so it promptly brought out a new, blue plastic, disposable shaver with a twin-blade head. By year's end, Gillette also made Good News! available in Austria, Canada, France, Italy, Switzerland, Belgium, Greece, Germany, and Spain.

Unfortunately for Gillette, Good News! was really bad news. The disposable shaver delivered lower profit margins than razor and blade systems, and it undercut sales of other Gillette products. Good News! sold for much less than the retail price of a Trac II cartridge. Gillette marketed Good News! on price and convenience, not performance, but the company envisioned the product as a step-up item leading to its traditional high-quality shaving systems.

This contain-and-switch strategy did not succeed. Consumers liked the price and the convenience of disposable razors, and millions of Trac II razors began to gather dust in medicine chests across the country. Many Trac II users figured out that for as little as 25 cents, they could get the same cartridge mounted on a plastic handle that they had been buying for 56 cents to put on their Trac II handle. Further, disposable razors created an opening for competitors in a category that Gillette had long dominated.

Gillette felt sure, however, that disposable razors would never gain more than a 7 percent share of the market. The disposable razor market share soon soared past 10 percent, forcing Gillette into continual upward revisions of its estimates. In terms of units sold, disposable razors reached a 22 percent market share by 1980 and a 50 percent share by 1988.

BIC and Gillette's successful introduction of the disposable razor represented a watershed event in "commoditization"—the process of converting well-differentiated products into commodities. Status, quality, and perceived value had always played primary roles in marketing of personal care products. However, consumers were now showing that they would forego performance and prestige in a shaving product—about as close and personal as one can get.

In 1977, Gillette introduced a new razor and blade system at the expense of Trac II. It launched Atra with a $7 million advertising campaign and more than 50 million $2 rebate coupons. Atra (which stands for Automatic Tracking Razor Action) was the first twin-blade shaving cartridge with a pivoting head. Engineers had designed the head to follow a man's facial contours for a closer shave. Researchers began developing the product in Gillette's United Kingdom Research and Development Lab in 1970. They had established a goal of improving the high-performance standards of twin-blade shaving and specifically enhancing the Trac II effect. The company's scientists discovered that moving the hand and face was not the most effective way to achieve the best blade-face shaving angle. The razor head itself produced a better shave if it pivoted to maintain the most effective shaving angle. Marketers selected the name "Atra" after two years of extensive consumer testing.

Atra quickly achieved a 7 percent share of the blade market and about one-third of the razor market. The company introduced Atra in Europe a year later under the brand name Contour. Although Atra increased Gillette's share of the razor market, 40 percent of Trac II users switched to Atra in the first year.

In the early 1980s, Gillette introduced more new disposable razors and product enhancements. Both Swivel (launched in 1980) and Good News! Pivot (1984) were disposable razors featuring movable heads. Gillette announced Atra Plus (the first razor with the patented Lubra-smooth lubricating strip) in 1985 just as BIC began to move into the United States from Canada with the BIC shaver for sensitive skin. A few months later, Gillette ushered in MicroTrac—the first disposable razor with an ultra-slim head. Gillette priced the MicroTrac lower than any other Gillette disposable razor. The company claimed to have designed a state-of-the-art manufacturing process for MicroTrac. The process required less plastic, thus minimizing bulk and reducing manufacturing costs. Analysts claimed that Gillette was trying to bracket the market with Atra Plus (with a retail price of $3.99 to $4.95) and MicroTrac (99 cents), and protect its market share with products on both ends of the price and usage scale. Gillette also teased Wall Street with hints that, by the end of 1986, it would be introducing yet another state-of-the-art shaving system that could revolutionize the shaving business.

Despite these product innovations and introductions in the early 1980s, Gillette primarily focused its energies on its global markets and strategies. By 1985, Gillette was marketing 800 products in more than 200 countries. The company felt a need at this time to coordinate its marketing efforts first regionally and then globally.

Unfortunately for Gillette's management team, others noticed its strong international capabilities. Ronald Perelman, chairman of the Revlon Group, attempted an unfriendly takeover in November 1986. To fend off the takeover, Gillette bought back 9.2 million shares of its stock from Perelman and saddled itself with additional long-term debt to finance the stock repurchase. Gillette's payment to Perelman increased the company's debt load from $827 million to $1.1 billion and put its debt-to-equity ratio at 70 percent. Gillette and Perelman signed an agreement preventing Perelman from attempting another takeover until 1996.

In 1988, just as Gillette returned its attention to new-product development and global marketing, Coniston Partners, after obtaining 6 percent of Gillette's stock, engaged the company in a proxy battle for four seats on its 12-person board. Coniston's interest had been piqued by the Gillette-Perelman $549 million stock buyback and its payment of $9 million in expenses to Perelman. Coniston and some shareholders felt Gillette's board and management had repeatedly taken actions that prohibited its stockholders from realizing their shares' full value. When the balloting concluded, Gillette's management won by a narrow margin—52 percent to 48 percent. Coniston made $13 million in the stock buyback program that Gillette offered to all shareholders, but Coniston agreed not to make another run at Gillette until 1991. This second takeover attempt forced Gillette to increase its debt load to $2 billion and pushed its total equity negative to ($84,600,000).

More importantly, both takeover battles forced Gillette to "wake up." Gillette closed or sold its Jafra Cosmetics operations in 11 countries and jettisoned weak operations such as Misco, Inc. (a computer supplies business), and S. T. Dupont (a luxury lighter, clock, and watchmaker). The company also thinned its workforce in many divisions, such as its 15 percent staff reduction at the Paper Mate pen unit. Despite this pruning, Gillette's sales for 1988 grew 13 percent to $3.6 billion, and profits soared 17 percent to $268 million.

Despite Gillette's concentration on fending off takeover attempts, it continued to enhance its razor and blade products. In 1986, Gillette introduced the Contour Plus in its first pan-European razor launch. The company marketed Contour Plus with one identity and one strategy. In 1988, the company introduced Trac II Plus, Good News! Pivot Plus, and Daisy Plus—versions of its existing products with the Lubra-smooth lubricating strip.

SCHICK

Warner-Lambert's Schick served as the second major competitor in the wet-shaving business. Warner-Lambert, incorporated in 1920 under the name William R. Warner & Company, manufactured chemicals and pharmaceuticals. Numerous mergers and acquisitions over 70 years resulted in Warner-Lambert's involvement in developing, manufacturing, and marketing a widely diversified line of beauty, health, and well-being products. The company also became a major producer of mints and chewing gums, such as Dentyne, Sticklets, and Trident. Exhibit 6 presents a list of Warner-Lambert's products by division as of 1988.

Warner-Lambert entered the wet-shave business through a merger with Eversharp in 1970. Eversharp, a longtime competitor in the wet-shave industry, owned the Schick trademark and had owned the Paper Mate Pen Company before selling it to Gillette in 1955. Schick's razors and blades produced $180 million in revenue in 1987, or 5.2 percent of Warner-Lambert's worldwide sales. (Refer to Exhibit 7 for operating results by division and Exhibits 8 and 9 for income statement and balance sheet data.)

In 1989, Schick held approximately a 16.2 percent U.S. market share, down from its 1980 share of 23.8 percent. Schick's market share was broken down as follows: blade systems, 8.8 percent; disposable razors, 4.1 percent; and double-edged blades and injectors, 3.3 percent.

Schick's loss of market share in the 1980s occurred for two reasons. First, even though Schick pioneered the injector razor system (it controlled 80 percent of this market by 1979), it did not market a disposable razor until mid-1984—eight years after the first disposable razors appeared. Secondly, for years Warner-Lambert had been channeling Schick's cash flow to its research and development in drugs.

EXHIBIT 6   Warner-Lambert 1988 Product Lines by Company Division

Ethical Pharmaceuticals	Gums and Mints
Parke-Davis drug	Dentyne
	Sticklets
Non-prescription Products	Beemans
Benadryl	Trident
Caladryl	Freshen-up
Rolaids	Bubblicious
Sinutab	Chiclets
Listerex	Clorets
Lubraderm	Certs
Anusol	Dynamints
Tucks	Junior Mints
Halls	Sugar Daddy
Benylin	Sugar Babies
Listerine	Charleston Chew
Listermint	Rascals
Efferdent	
Effergrip	**Other Products**
	Schick razors
	Ultrex razors
	Personal touch
	Tetra Aquarium

EXHIBIT 7   Warner-Lambert's Net Sales and Operating Profit by Division (In Millions)

Division	Net Sales				Operating profit (LOSS)			
	1988	**1987**	**1986**	**1985**	**1988**	**1987**	**1986**	**1985**
Health Care								
Ethical products	1,213	1,093	964	880	420	351	246	224
Nonprescription products	1,296	1,195	1,077	992	305	256	176	177
Total health care	$2,509	$2,288	$2,041	$1,872	$ 725	$ 607	$ 422	$ 401
Gums and mints	$ 918	$ 777	$ 678	$ 626	$ 187	$ 173	$ 122	$ 138
Other products[a]	481	420	384	334	92	86	61	72
Divested businesses								(464)
R&D					(259)	(232)	(202)	(208)
Net sales and operating profit	$3,908	$3,485	$3,103	$3,200	$ 745	$ 634	$ 599	$ (61)

[a]Other products include Schick razors, which accounted for $180 million in revenue in 1987.
Source: *Warner-Lambert Company Annual Report,* 1987 and *Moody's Industrial Manual*

EXHIBIT 8 Warner-Lambert Income Statements (In Thousands)

	1988	1987	1986
Net sales	$3,908,400	$3,484,700	$3,102,918
Cost of sales	1,351,700	1,169,700	1,052,781
Other expenses	2,012,100	1,819,800	1,616,323
Operating income	544,600	495,200	433,814
Other income	61,900	58,500	69,611
Earnings before interest and tax	606,500	553,700	503,425
Interest expense	68,200	60,900	66,544
Earnings before tax	538,300	492,800	436,881
Tax	198,000	197,000	136,297
Nonrecurring item	—	—	8,400
Earnings after tax	340,000	295,800	308,984
Retained earnings	1,577,400	1,384,100	1,023,218
Earnings per share	$ 5.00	$ 4.15	$ 4.18
Average common shares outstanding, 000	68,035	71,355	73,985
Dividends paid per share	$ 2.16	$ 1.77	$ 1.59
Stock price range			
High	$ 79½	$ 87½	$ 63⅛
Low	$ 59⅞	$ 48¼	$ 45

Source: *Moody's Industrial Manual*

In 1986, the company changed its philosophy. It allocated $70 million to Schick for a three-year period and granted Schick its own sales force. In spite of Schick's loss of market share, company executives felt they had room to play catch up, especially by exploiting new technologies. In late 1988, Schick revealed that it planned to conduct "guerrilla warfare" by throwing its marketing resources and efforts into new technological advances in disposable razors. As a result, Warner-Lambert planned to allocate the bulk of its $8 million razor advertising budget to marketing its narrow-headed disposable razor, Slim Twin, which it introduced in August 1988.

Schick believed that the U.S. unit demand for disposable razors would increase to 55 percent of the market by the early 1990s from its 50 percent share in 1988. Schick executives based this belief on their feeling that men would rather pay 30 cents for a disposable razor than 75 cents for a refill blade. In 1988, Schick held an estimated 9.9 percent share of dollar sales in the disposable razor market.

Schick generated approximately 67 percent of its revenues overseas. Also, Schick earned higher profit margins on its nondomestic sales—20 percent versus its 15 percent domestic margin. Europe and Japan represented the bulk of Schick's international business, accounting for 38 percent and 52 percent, respectively, of 1988's overseas sales. Schick's European business consisted of 70 percent systems and 29 percent disposable razors, but Gillette's systems and disposable razor sales were 4.5 and 6 times larger, respectively.

EXHIBIT 9   Warner-Lambert Balance Sheets (In Thousands)

	1988	1987	1986
Assets			
Cash	$ 176,000	$ 24,100	$ 26,791
Receivables	525,200	469,900	445,743
Inventories	381,400	379,000	317,212
Other current assets	181,300	379,600	720,322
Total current assets	1,264,500	1,252,600	1,510,068
Fixed assets, net	1,053,000	959,800	819,291
Other assets	385,300	263,500	186,564
Total assets	$2,702,800	$2,475,900	$2,515,923
Liabilities and Equity			
Current liabilities[a]	$1,025,200	$ 974,300	$ 969,806
Current portion ltd.	7,100	4,200	143,259
Long-term debt	318,200	293,800	342,112
Equity	$ 998,600	$ 874,400	$ 907,322

[a]Includes current portion of long-term debt
Source: *Moody's Industrial Manual*

However, Schick dominated in Japan. Warner-Lambert held more than 60 percent of Japan's wet-shave market. Although Japan had typically been an electric shaver market (55 percent of Japanese shavers use electric razors), Schick achieved an excellent record and reputation in Japan. Both Schick and Gillette entered the Japanese market in 1962, and their vigorous competition eventually drove Japanese competitors from the industry, which by 1988 generated $190 million in sales. Gillette's attempt to crack the market flopped because it tried to sell razors using its own salespeople, a strategy that failed because Gillette did not have the distribution network available to Japanese companies. Schick, meanwhile, chose to leave the distribution to Seiko Corporation. Seiko imported razors from the United States and then sold them to wholesalers nationwide. By 1988, Schick generated roughly 40 percent of its sales and 35 percent of its profits in Japan. Disposable razors accounted for almost 80 percent of those figures.

BIC CORPORATION

The roots of the BIC Corporation, which was founded by Marcel Bich in the United States in 1958, were in France. In 1945, Bich, who had been the production manager for a French ink manufacturer, bought a factory outside Paris to produce parts for fountain pens and mechanical lead pencils. In his new business, Bich became one of the first manufacturers to purchase presses to work with plastics. With his knowledge of inks and experience with plastics and molding machines, Bich set himself up to become the largest pen manufacturer in the world. In 1949, Bich introduced his version of the modern ballpoint pen, originally invented in 1939, which he called "BIC," a shortened, easy-to-remember version of his own name. He supported the pen with memorable, effective advertising, and its sales surpassed even his own expectations.

Realizing that a mass-produced, disposable ballpoint pen had universal appeal, Bich turned his attention to the U.S. market. In 1958, he purchased the Waterman-Pen Company of Connecticut and then incorporated as Waterman-BIC Pen Corporation. The company changed its name to BIC Pen in 1971 and finally adopted the name BIC Corporation for the publicly owned corporation in 1982.

After establishing itself as the country's largest pen maker, BIC attacked another market—the disposable lighter market. When BIC introduced its lighter in 1973, the total disposable lighter market stood at only 50 million units. By 1984, BIC had become so successful at manufacturing and marketing its disposable lighters that Gillette, its primary competitor, abandoned the lighter market. Gillette sold its Cricket division to Swedish Match, Stockholm, the manufacturer of Wilkinson razors. By 1989, the disposable lighter market had grown to nearly 500 million units, and BIC lighters accounted for 60 percent of the market.

Not content to compete just in the writing and lighting markets, BIC decided to enter the U.S. shaving market in 1976. A year earlier, the company had launched the BIC Shaver in Europe and Canada. BIC's entrance into the U.S. razor market started an intense rivalry with Gillette. Admittedly, the companies were not strangers to each other—for years they had competed for market share in the pen and lighter industries. Despite the fact that razors were Gillette's primary business and an area in which the company had no intention of relinquishing market share, BIC established a niche in the U.S. disposable-razor market.

BIC, like Gillette, frequently introduced new razor products and product enhancements. In January 1985, following a successful Canadian test in 1984, BIC announced the BIC Shaver for Sensitive Skin. BIC claimed that 42 percent of the men surveyed reported that they had sensitive skin, whereas 51 percent of those who had heavy beards reported that they had sensitive skin. Thus BIC felt there was a clear need for a shaver that addressed this special shaving problem. The $10 million ad campaign for the BIC Shaver for Sensitive Skin featured John McEnroe, a highly ranked and well-known tennis professional, discussing good and bad backhands and normal and sensitive skin. BIC repositioned the original BIC white shaver as the shaver men with normal skin should use, and it promoted the new BIC Orange as the razor for sensitive skin.

BIC also tried its commodity strategy on sailboards, car-top carriers, and perfume. In 1982, BIC introduced a sailboard model at about half the price of existing products. The product generated nothing but red ink. In April 1989, the company launched BIC perfumes with $15 million in advertising support. BIC's foray into fragrances was as disappointing as its sailboard attempt. Throughout the year, Parfum BIC lost money, forcing management to concentrate its efforts on reformulating its selling them, advertising, packaging, and price points. Many retailers rejected the product, sticking BIC with expensive manufacturing facilities in Europe. BIC found that consumers' perceptions of commodities did not translate equally into every category. For example, many women cut corners elsewhere just to spend lavishly on their perfume. The last thing they wanted to see was their favorite scent being hawked to the masses.

Despite these failures, BIC Corporation was the undisputed king of the commoditizers. BIC's success with pens and razors demonstrated the upside potential of commoditization, whereas its failures with sailboards and perfumes illustrated the limitations. BIC concentrated its efforts on designing, manufacturing, and delivering the "best" quality products at the lowest possible prices. Although the company produced large quantities of disposable products (for example, more than 1 million pens a day), it claimed that each product was invested with the BIC philosophy: "maximum service, minimum price."

EXHIBIT 10 BIC Corporation's Net Sales and Income Before Taxes (In Millions)

	1988	1987	1986
Net sales			
Writing instruments	$118.5	$106.7	$ 91.7
Lighters	113.9	120.0	115.0
Shavers	51.9	47.1	49.6
Sport	10.6	16.8	11.3
Total	$294.9	$290.6	$267.6
Profit (loss) before taxes			
Writing instruments	$ 16.7	$ 17.5	$ 15.0
Lighters	22.9	28.2	28.5
Shavers	9.4	8.5	8.0
Sport	(4.7)	(3.5)	(3.6)
TOTALS	$ 44.3	$ 50.7	$ 47.9

Source: *Bic Annual Report*, 1988 and 1989

EXHIBIT 11 BIC Corporation Consolidated Income Statements (In Thousands)

	1988	1987	1986
Net sales	$294,878	$290,616	$267,624
Cost of sales	172,542	165,705	147,602
Other expenses	81,023	73,785	67,697
Operating income	41,313	51,126	52,325
Other income	4,119	1,836	7,534
Earnings before interest and tax	45,432	52,962	59,859
Interest expense	1,097	2,301	11,982
Earnings before tax	44,335	50,661	47,877
Tax	17,573	21,944	24,170
Extraordinary credit	—	—	2,486 [a]
Utilization of operating loss carryforward	2,800	—	
Earnings after tax	$ 29,562	$ 28,717	$ 26,193
Retained earnings	159,942	142,501	121,784
Earnings per share	$ 2.44	$ 2.37	$ 2.16
Average common shares outstanding, 000	12,121	12,121	12,121
Dividends paid per share	$ 0.75	$ 0.66	$ 0.48
Stock price range			
High	$ 30⅜	$ 34⅞	$ 35
Low	$ 24⅜	$ 16½	$ 23¼

[a]Gain from elimination of debt
Source: *Moody's Industrial Manual* and *BIC Annual Report*

EXHIBIT 12   Bic Corporation Balance Sheets (In Thousands)

	1988	1987	1986
Assets			
Cash	$ 5,314	$ 4,673	$ 5,047
Certificates of deposit	3,117	803	6,401
Receivables, net	43,629	41,704	32,960
Inventories	70,930	59,779	50,058
Other current assets	37,603	47,385	34,898
Deferred income taxes	7,939	6,691	5,622
Total current assets	168,532	161,035	134,986
Fixed assets, net	74,973	62,797	58,385
Total assets	$243,505	$223,832	$193,371
Liabilities and Equity			
Current liabilities[a]	55,031	54,034	45,104
Current portion long-term debt	157	247	287
Long-term debt	1,521	1,511	1,789
Equity	$181,194	$164,068	$142,848

[a]Includes current portion of long-term debt
Source: *Moody's Industrial Manual*

One of BIC's greatest assets was its retail distribution strength. The high profile the company enjoyed at supermarkets and drugstores enabled it to win locations in the aisles and display space at the checkout—the best positioning.

Even though BIC controlled only the number three spot in the wet-shaving market by 1989, it had exerted quite an influence since its razors entered the U.S. market in 1976. In 1988, BIC's razors generated $52 million in sales with a net income of $9.4 million; BIC held a 22.4 percent share of dollar sales in the disposable razor market. Exhibit 10 presents operating data by product line, and Exhibits 11 and 12 give income statement and balance sheet data.

The introduction of the disposable razor revolutionized the industry and cut into system razor profits. However, despite the low profit margins in disposable razors and the fact that the industry leader, Gillette, emphasized razor and blade systems, BIC remained bullish on the disposable razor market. In 1989, a spokesperson for BIC claimed that BIC "was going to stick to what consumers liked." The company planned to continue marketing only single-blade, disposable shavers. BIC stated that it planned to maintain its strategy of underpricing competitors, but it would also introduce improvements such as the patented metal guard in its BIC Metal Shaver. Research revealed that the BIC Metal Shaver provided some incremental, rather than substitute, sales for its shave product line. BIC executives believed that the BIC Metal Shaver would reach a 5 percent to 8 percent market share by 1990.

WILKINSON SWORD

Swedish Match Holding Incorporated's subsidiary, Wilkinson Sword, came in as the fourth player in the U.S. market. Swedish Match Holding was a wholly owned subsidiary of Swedish Match AB, Stockholm, Sweden. The parent company owned subsidiaries in

EXHIBIT 13   Swedish Match AB Income Statements (In Thousands of U.S. Dollars)

	1988	1987	1986
Net sales	$2,814,662	$2,505,047	$1,529,704
Cost of sales	N/A	N/A	N/A
Operating expenses	2,541,128	2,291,023	1,387,360
Other expenses	108,206	95,420	48,711
Earnings before interest	165,328	118,604	93,633
Interest expense	5,386	19,084	21,618
Earnings before tax	159,942	99,520	72,015
Tax	57,612	29,996	39,165
Earnings after tax	102,330	69,554	32,850
Dividends paid per share	$ 0.53	$ 0.51	$ 1.75
Stock price range			
High	$ 22.53	$ 19.65	$ 66.75
Low	$ 15.00	$ 11.06	$ 22.00

Source: *Moody's Industrial Manual*

EXHIBIT 14   Swedish Match AB Balance Sheets (In Thousands)

	1988	1987	1986
Assets			
Cash and securities	$ 159,616	$ 117,027	$ 323,993
Receivables	611,372	561,479	297,321
Inventories	421,563	415,116	258,858
Total current assets	1,192,551	1,093,622	880,172
Fixed assets, net	707,664	671,409	397,411
Other assets	161,085	132,799	93,211
Total assets	$2,061,300	$1,897,830	$1,370,794
Liabilities and Equity			
Current liabilities	$ 996,214	$ 905,778	$ 576,534
Current portion long-term debt			
Long-term debt	298,505	316,542	244,118
Equity			

Source: *Moody's Industrial Manual*

the United States that imported and sold doors, produced resilient and wood flooring, and manufactured branded razors, blades, self-sharpening scissors, and gourmet kitchen knives. (Exhibits 13 and 14 present income statement and balance sheet data on Swedish Match AB.)

A group of swordsmiths founded Wilkinson in 1772, and soldiers used Wilkinson swords at Waterloo, the charge of the Light Brigade, and in the Boer war. However, as the sword declined as a combat weapon, Wilkinson retreated to producing presentation and ceremonial swords. By 1890, Wilkinson's cutlers had begun to produce straight razors, and by 1898 it was producing safety razors similar to King Gillette's. When Gillette's blades became popular in England, Wilkinson made stroppers to resharpen used blades. Wilkinson failed in the razor market, however, and dropped out during World War II.

By 1954, Wilkinson decided to look again at the shaving market. Manufacturers used carbon steel to make most razor blades at that time, and such blades lost their serviceability rapidly due to mechanical and chemical damage. Gillette and other firms had experimented with stainless steel blades; but they had found that despite their longer-lasting nature, the blades did not sharpen well. However, some men liked the durability, and a few small companies produced stainless steel blades.

Wilkinson purchased one such small German company and put Wilkinson Sword blades on the market in 1956. Wilkinson developed a coating for the stainless blades (in the same fashion that Gillette had coated the Super Blue Blade) that masked their rough edges, allowing the blades to give a comfortable shave and to last two to five times longer than conventional blades. Wilkinson called the new blade the Super Sword-Edge. Wilkinson introduced the blades in England in 1961 and in the United States in 1962, and they became a phenomenon. Schick and American Safety Razor followed a year later with their own stainless steel blades, the Krona Plus and Personna. Gillette finally responded in late 1963 with its own stainless steel blade, and by early 1964 Gillette's blades were outselling Wilkinson, Schick, and Personna combined. Wilkinson, however, had forever changed the nature of the razor blade.

In 1988, Wilkinson Sword claimed to have a 4 percent share of the U.S. wet-shave market, and it was predicting a 6 percent share by mid-1990. Industry analysts, however, did not confirm even the 4 percent share. They projected Wilkinson's share to be closer to 1 percent. Wilkinson introduced many new products over the years, but they generally proved to be short-lived. The company never really developed its U.S. franchise.

However, in late 1988, Wilkinson boasted that it was going to challenge the wet-shave category leader by introducing Ultra-Glide, its first lubricating shaving system. Wilkinson designed Ultra-Glide to go head-to-head with Gillette's Atra Plus and Schick's Super II Plus and Ultrex Plus. Wilkinson claimed that Ultra-Glide represented a breakthrough in shaving technology because of an ingredient, hydromer, in its patented lubricating strip. According to Wilkinson, the Ultra-Grip strip left less residue on the face and provided a smoother, more comfortable shave by creating a cushion of moisture between the razor and the skin.

Wilkinson introduced Ultra-Glide in March 1989 and supported it with a $5 million advertising and promotional campaign (versus the Atra Plus $80 million multimedia investment in the United States). Wilkinson priced Ultra-Glide 5 percent to 8 percent less than Atra Plus. Wilkinson was undaunted by Gillette's heavier advertising investment, and it expected to cash in on its rival's strong marketing muscle. Wilkinson did not expect to overtake Gillette but felt its drive should help it capture a double-digit U.S. market share within two to three years.

Many were skeptical about Wilkinson's self-predicted market share growth. One industry analyst stated, "Gillette dominates this business. Some upstart won't do anything." One Gillette official claimed his company was unfazed by Wilkinson. In fact, he was quoted as saying in late 1988 that, "They [Wilkinson] don't have a business in the U.S.; they don't exist."

Nonetheless, Gillette became enraged and filed legal challenges when Wilkinson's television ads for Ultra-Glide broke in May 1989. The ads stated that Ultra-Glide's lubricating strip was six times smoother than Gillette's strip and that men preferred it to the industry leader's. All three major networks had reservations about continuing to air the comparison commercials. CBS and NBC stated that they were going to delay airing the company's ads until Wilkinson responded to questions they had about its ad claims. In an 11th-hour counterattack, Wilkinson accused Gillette of false advertising and of trying to monopolize the wet-shave market.

Gillette's South Boston Plant

Robert Squires left his workstation in the facilities engineering section of Gillette's South Boston manufacturing facility and headed for the shave test lab. He entered the lab area and walked down a narrow hall. On his right were a series of small cubicles Gillette had designed to resemble the sink area of a typical bathroom. Robert opened the door of his assigned cubicle precisely at his scheduled 10 A.M. time. He removed his dress shirt and tie, hanging them on a hook beside the sink. Sliding the mirror up as one would a window, Robert looked into the lab area. Rose McCluskey, a lab assistant, greeted him.

"Morning, Robert. See you're right on time as usual. I've got your things all ready for you." Rose reached into a recessed area on her side of the cubicle's wall and handed Robert his razor, shave cream, aftershave lotion, and a clean towel.

"Thanks, Rose. Hope you're having a good day. Anything new you've got me trying today?"

"You know I can't tell you that. It might spoil your objectivity. Here's your card." Rose handed Robert a shaving evaluation card (see Exhibit 15).

Robert Squires had been shaving at the South Boston Plant off and on for all of his 25 years with Gillette. He was one of 200 men who shaved every work day at the plant. Gillette used these shavers to compare its products' effectiveness with competitors' products. The shavers also conducted research and development (R&D) testing of new products and quality control testing for manufacturing. An additional seven to eight panels of 250 men each shaved every day in their homes around the country, primarily conducting R&D shave testing.

Like Robert, each shaver completed a shave evaluation card after every shave. Lab assistants like Rose entered data from the evaluations to allow Gillette researchers to analyze the performance of each shaving device. If a product passed R&D hurdles, it became the responsibility of the marketing research staff to conduct consumer-use testing. Such consumer testing employed 2,000 to 3,000 men who tested products in their homes.

From its research, Gillette had learned that the average man had 30,000 whiskers on his face that grew at the rate of ½ inch per month. He shaved 5.8 times a week and spent 3 to 4 minutes shaving each time. A man with a life span of 70 years would shave more than 20,000 times, spending 3,350 hours (130 days) removing 27½ feet of facial hair. Yet, despite all the time and effort involved in shaving, surveys found that if a cream were available that would eliminate facial hair and shaving, most men would not use it.

Robert finished shaving and rinsed his face and shaver. He glanced at the shaving head. A pretty good shave, he thought. The cartridge had two blades, but it seemed different. Robert marked his evaluation card and slid it across the counter to Rose.

William Mazeroski, manager of the South Boston shave test lab, walked into the lab area carrying computer printouts with the statistical analysis of last week's shave test data.

Noticing Robert, William stopped. "Morning, Robert. How was your shave?"

"Pretty good. What am I using?"

EXHIBIT 15: Gillette Shaving Evaluation Card

NUMB.	CODE	STA.	TEST#	NAME	EMP.#	DATE

IN-PLANT SHAVE TEST SCORECARD

INSTRUCTIONS: Please Check One Box in Each Column

Overall Evaluation of Shave	Freedom from Nicks and Cuts	Caution	Closeness	Smoothness	Comfort
❑ Excellent	❑ Excellent	❑ Exceptionally Safe	❑ Exceptionally Close	❑ Exceptionally Smooth	❑ Exceptionally Comfortable
❑ Very Good	❑ Very Good	❑ Unusually Safe	❑ Very Close	❑ Very Smooth	❑ Very Comfortable
❑ Good	❑ Good	❑ Average	❑ Average	❑ Average Smoothness	❑ Average Comfort
❑ Fair	❑ Fair	❑ Slight Caution Needed	❑ Fair	❑ Slight Pull	❑ Slight Irritation
❑ Poor	❑ Poor	❑ Excessive Caution Needed	❑ Poor	❑ Excessive Pull	❑ Excessive Irritation

Source: The Gillette Company

"Robert, you are always trying to get me to tell you what we're testing! We have control groups and experimental groups. I can't tell you which you are in, but I was just looking at last week's results, and I can tell you that it looks like we are making progress. We've been testing versions of a new product since 1979, and I think we're about to get it right. Of course, I don't know if we'll introduce it or even if we can make it in large quantities, but it looks good."

"Well, that's interesting. At least I know I'm involved in progress. And, if we do decide to produce a new shaver, we'll have to design and build the machines to make it ourselves because there is nowhere to go to purchase blade-making machinery. Well, I've got to get back now; see you tomorrow."

THIRTY-SEVENTH FLOOR, THE PRUDENTIAL CENTER

Paul Hankins leaned over the credenza in his 37th-floor office in Boston's Prudential Center office building and admired the beauty of the scene that spread before him. Paul felt as though he were watching an impressionistic painting in motion. Beyond the green treetops and red brick buildings of Boston's fashionable Back Bay area, the Charles River wound its way toward Boston Harbor. Paul could see the buildings on the campuses of Harvard, MIT, and Boston University scattered along both sides of the river. Soon the crew teams would be out practicing. Paul loved to watch the precision with which the well-coordinated teams propelled the boats up and down the river. If only, he thought, we could be as coordinated as those crew teams.

Paul had returned to Boston in early 1988 when Gillette created the North Atlantic Group by combining what had been the North American and the European operations.

Originally from Boston, he had attended Columbia University and earned an MBA at Dartmouth's Tuck School. He had been with Gillette for 19 years. Before 1988, he had served as marketing director for Gillette Europe from 1983–84, as the country manager for Holland from 1985–86, and finally as manager of Holland and the Scandinavian countries.

During this 1983–87 period, Paul had worked for Jim Pear, vice president of Gillette Europe, to implement a pan-European strategy. Prior to 1983, Gillette had organized and managed Europe as a classic decentralized market. To meet the perceived cultural nuances within each area, the company had treated each country as a separate market. For example, Gillette offered the same products under a variety of sub-brand names. The company sold its Good News! disposable razors under the name "Blue II" in the United Kingdom, "Parat" in Germany, "Gillette" in France and Spain, "Radi e Getta" (shave and throw) in Italy, and "Economy" in other European markets.

Jim Pear believed that in the future Gillette would have to organize across country lines, and he had developed the pan-European idea. He felt that shaving was a universal act and that Gillette's razors were a perfect archetype for a "global" product.

Gillette had launched Contour Plus, the European version of Atra Plus, in 1985–86 and had experienced greater success than the U.S. launch that took place at the same time. The pan-European strategy seemed to be both more efficient and more effective. Colman Mockler, Gillette's chairman, noticed the European success and asked Pear to come to Boston to head the new North Atlantic Group. Paul had come with him as vice president of marketing for the Shaving and Personal Care Group.

Paul turned from the window as he heard people approaching. Sarah Kale, vice president, Marketing Research; Brian Mullins, vice president of marketing, Shaving and Personal Care Group; and Scott Friedman, business director, Blades and Razors, were at his door.

"Ready for our meeting?" Scott asked.

"Sure, come on in. I was just admiring the view."

"The purpose of this meeting," Paul began, "is to begin formulating a new strategy for Gillette North Atlantic, specifically for our shaving products. I'm interested in your general thoughts and analysis. I want to begin to identify options and select a strategy to pursue. What have you found out?"

"Well, here are the market share numbers you asked me to develop," Scott observed as he handed each person copies of tables he had produced (see Exhibit 16

EXHIBIT 16 Gillette Market Share of Dollar Sales 1981–1988 (By Percent)

Product or Category	1981	1982	1983	1984	1985	1986	1987	1988
Atra blades	15.4	17.3	19.4	18.7	20.2	20.9	20.0	20.5
Trac II blades	17.5	16.4	15.2	14.6	14.1	13.5	11.8	11.4
Gillette blades	47.3	48.9	52.1	54.2	55.8	57.1	54.1	56.0
Gillette disposables	14.3	15.4	17.4	20.0	21.1	22.7	22.2	24.0
All disposables	23.0	23.2	27.0	30.6	32.7	34.9	38.5	41.1
Gillette disposables as % of all disposables	67.9	66.9	64.7	65.7	64.6	64.2	57.6	58.4
Gillette razors	50.3	52.5	54.9	58.8	62.2	67.6	64.1	61.0

Source: Prudential-Bache Securities

EXHIBIT 17: Gillette System Cartridges (Dollar Share of U.S. Blade Market)

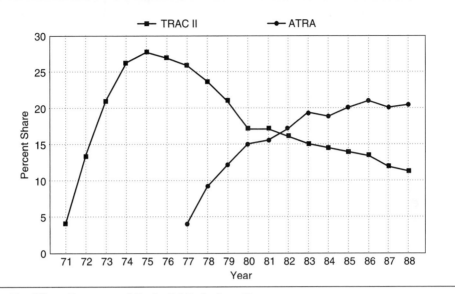

Source: The Gillette Company and Prudential-Bache Securities

and 17). Like Paul, Scott had earned an MBA from the Tuck School and had been with Gillette for 17 years.

"These are our U.S. share numbers through 1988. As you can see, Atra blades seem to have leveled off and Trac II blades are declining. Disposable razors now account for more than 41 percent of the market, in dollars, and for more than 50 percent of the market in terms of units. In fact, our projections indicate that disposable razors will approach 100 percent of the market by the mid to late 1990s, given current trends. Although we have 56 percent of the blade market and 58 percent of the disposable razor market, our share of the disposable razor market has fallen. Further, you are aware that every 1 percent switch from our system razors to our disposable razors represents a loss of $10 million on the bottom line."

"I don't think any of this should surprise us," Sarah Kale interjected. Sarah had joined Gillette after graduating from Simmons College in Boston and had been with the firm for 14 years. "If you look back over the 1980s, you'll see that we helped cause this problem."

"What do you mean by that?" asked Paul.

"Well, as market leader, we never believed that the use of disposable razors would grow as it has. We went along with the trend, but we kept prices low on our disposable razors, which made profitability worse for both us and our competition because they had to take our price into consideration in setting their prices. Then, to compensate for the impact on our profitability from the growth of the disposable razor market, we were raising the prices on our system razors. This made disposable razors even more attractive for price-sensitive users and further fueled the growth of disposable razors. This has occurred despite the fact that our market research shows that men rate system shavers significantly better than disposable razors. We find that the weight and balance contributed by the permanent handle used with the cartridge contributes to a better shave."

"Yes, but every time I tell someone that," Paul added, "they just look at me as if they wonder if I really believe that or if it is just Gillette's party line."

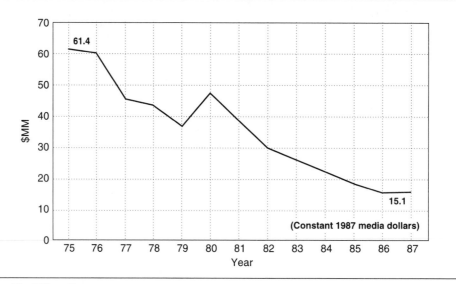

EXHIBIT 18: Blade and Razor Media Spending—United States

Source: The Gillette Company

"There's one other thing we've done," Scott added. "Look at this graph of our advertising expenditures in the U.S. over the 1980s (see Exhibit 18). In fact, in constant 1987 dollars, our advertising spending has fallen from $61 million in 1975 to about $15 million in 1987. We seem to have just spent what was left over on advertising. We are now spending about one-half of our advertising on Atra and one-half on Good News!. Tentative plans call for us to increase the share going to Good News!. Our media budget for 1988 was about $43 million. Further, we've tried three or four themes, but we haven't stuck with any one for very long. We're using the current theme, "The Essence of Shaving," for both system and disposable products. Our advertising has been about 90 percent product-based and 10 percent image-based."

"Well, Scott's right," Sarah noted, "but although share of voice is important, share of mind is what counts. Our most recent research shows a significant difference in how we are perceived by male consumers based on their age. Men over 40 still remember Gillette, despite our reduced advertising, from their youth. They remember Gillette's sponsorship of athletic events, like the Saturday baseball Game of the Week and the Cavalcade of Sports. They remember "Look Sharp! Feel Sharp! Be Sharp" and Sharpie the Parrot. They remember their fathers loaning them their Gillette razors when they started shaving. There is still a strong connection between Gillette and the male image of shaving."

"How about with younger men?" asked Brian. Brian had joined Gillette in 1975 after graduating from Washington and Lee University and earning a master's degree in administration from George Washington University.

"Younger men's views can be summed up simply—twin blade, blue, and plastic," Sarah reported.

"Just like our disposable razors!" Paul exclaimed.

"Precisely," Sarah answered. "As I say, we've done this to ourselves. We have a 'steel' man and a 'plastic' man. In fact, for males between 15 and 19, BIC is better known than Gillette with respect to shaving. Younger men in general—those under 30, these 'plastic' men—feel all shavers are the same. Older men and system users feel there is a difference."

"Yes," Paul interjected, "and I've noticed something else interesting. Look at our logos. We use the Gillette brand name as our corporate name, and the brand name is done in thin, block letters. I'm not sure it has the impact and masculine image we want. On top of that, look at these razor packages. We have become so product-focused and brand-manager driven that we've lost focus on the brand name. Our brands look tired; there's nothing special about our retail packaging and display."

"Speaking of the male image of shaving, Sarah, what does your research show about our image with women?" asked Brian.

"Well, we've always had a male focus, and women identify the Gillette name with men and shaving, even those who use our products marketed to women. You know that there are more women wet-shavers than men in the U.S. market, about 62 million versus 55 million. However, due to seasonality and lower frequency of women's shaving, the unit volume used by women is only about one-third that of the volume used by men. Women use about eight to 12 blades a year versus 25 to 30 for men. It is still very consistent for us to focus on men."

"Well, we've got plenty of problems on the marketing side, but we also have to remember that we are part of a larger corporation with its own set of problems," Brian suggested. "We're only 30 percent or so of sales, but we are 60 percent of profits. And, given the takeover battles, there is going to be increased pressure on the company to maintain and improve profitability. That pressure has always been on us, but now it will be more intense. If we want to develop some bold, new strategy, we are going to have to figure out where to get the money to finance it. I'm sure the rest of the corporation will continue to look to us to throw off cash to support diversification."

"This can get depressing," Paul muttered as he looked back at the window. "I can sense the low morale inside the company. People sense the inevitability of disposability. We see BIC as the enemy even though it is so much smaller than Gillette. We've got to come up with a new strategy. What do you think our options are, Scott?"

"Well, I think we're agreed that the 'do-nothing' option is out. If we simply continue to do business as usual, we will see the erosion of the shaving market's profitability as disposable razors take more and more share. We could accept the transition to disposable razors and begin to try to segment the disposable razor market based on performance. You might call this the 'give up' strategy. We would be admitting that disposable razors are the wave of the future. There will obviously continue to be shavers who buy based on price only, but there will also be shavers who will pay more for disposable razors with additional benefits, such as lubricating strips or movable heads. In Italy, for example, we have done a lot of image building and focused on quality. Now, Italian men seem to perceive that our disposable razors have value despite their price. In other words, we could try to protect the category's profitability by segmenting the market and offering value to those segments willing to pay for it. We would deemphasize system razors.

"Or, we could try to turn the whole thing around. We could develop a strategy to slow the growth of disposable razors and to reinvigorate the system razor market."

"How does the new razor system fit into all this?" Paul asked.

"I'm pleased that we have continued to invest in R&D despite our problems and the takeover battles," Brian answered. "Reports from R&D indicate that the new shaver is doing well in tests. But it will be expensive to take to market and to support with advertising. Further, it doesn't make any sense to launch it unless it fits in with the broader strategy. For example, if we decide to focus on disposable razors, it makes no sense to launch a new system razor and devote resources to that."

"What's the consumer testing indicating?" asked Scott.

"We're still conducting tests," Sarah answered, "but so far the results are very positive. Men rate the shave superior to both Atra or Trac II and superior to our competition. In fact, I think we'll see that consumers rate the new shaver as much as 25 percent better on average. The independently spring-mounted twin blades deliver a better shave, but you know we've never introduced a product until it was clearly superior in consumer testing on every dimension."

"Okay. Here's what I'd like to do," Paul concluded. "I'd like for each of us to devote some time to developing a broad outline of a strategy to present at our next meeting. We'll try to identify and shape a broad strategy then that we can begin to develop in detail over the next several months. Let's get together in a week, same time. Thanks for your time."

REFERENCES

Adams, Russell B., Jr. *King Gillette: The Man and His Wonderful Shaving Device.* Boston: Little, Brown, 1978.

BIC Annual Report, 1989.

Caminiti, Susan. "Gillette Gets Sharp." *Fortune,* May 8, 1989: 84.

Dewhurst, Peter. "BICH = BIC." *Made in France International,* Spring 1981: 38–41.

Dunkin, A., Baum, L., and Therrein, L. "This Takeover Artist Wants to be a Makeover Artist, Too." *Business Week,* December 1, 1986: 106, 110.

Dun's Million Dollar Directory, 1989.

Fahey, Alison, and Sloan, Pat. "Gillette: $80M to Rebuild Image." *Advertising Age,* October 31, 1988: 1, 62.

"Kiam Gets Some Help: Grey Sharpens Remington Ads." *Advertising Age,* November 13, 1989: 94.

"Wilkinson Cuts In." *Advertising Age,* November 28, 1988: 48.

Gillette Annual Corporate Reports, 1985–1988.

Hammonds, Keith. "At Gillette Disposable Is a Dirty Word." *Business Week,* May 29, 1989: 54–55.

"How Ron Perelman Scared Gillette Into Shape." *Business Week,* October 12, 1987: 40–41.

Jervey, Gay. "Gillette and BIC Spots Taking on Sensitive Subject." *Advertising Age,* March 18, 1985: 53.

"Gillette, Wilkinson Heat up Disposable Duel." *Advertising Age,* June 10, 1985: 12.

"New Blade Weapons for Gillette-BIC War." *Advertising Age,* November 5, 1984: 1, 96.

Kiam, Victor. "Remington's Marketing and Manufacturing Strategies." *Management Review,* February 1987: 43–45.

"Growth Strategies at Remington." *Journal of Business Strategy,* January/February 1989: 22–26.

Kummel, C. M., and Klompmaker, J. E. "The Gillette Company—Safety Razor Division." In D. W. Cravens and C. W. Lamb (eds.), *Strategic Marketing Cases and Applications.* Homewood, Ill.: Irwin, 1980, pp. 324–345.

McGeehan, Patrick. "Gillette Sharpens its Global Strategy." *Advertising Age,* April 25, 1988: 2, 93.

Newport, John Paul. "The Stalking of Gillette." *Fortune,* May 23, 1988: 99–101.

North American Philips Corporation Annual Report, 1987.

Pereira, Joseph. "Gillette's Next-Generation Blade To Seek New Edge in Flat Market." *The Wall Street Journal,* April 7, 1988: 34.

Shore, Andrew. "Gillette Report." Shearson Lehman Hutton, New York. (October 19, 1989).

"Gillette Company Update." New York: Prudential-Bache Securities, May 18, 1990.

Raissman, Robert. "Gillette Pitches New Throwaway." *Advertising Age,* July 9, 1984: 12.

"Razors and Blades." *Consumer Reports,* May 1989: 300–304.

Rothman, Andrea. "Gillette, in a Shift, to Emphasize Cartridge Blades Over Disposables." *The Wall Street Journal,* November 18, 1988: B6.

Sacharow, Stanley. (1982). *Symbols of Trade.* New York: Art Direction Book Company.

Sloan, Pat. "Marschalk Brains Land Braun." *Advertising Age,* March 18, 1985: 53.

"Remington Gets the Edge on Gillette." *Advertising Age,* May 16, 1988: 3, 89.

Sutor, Ruthanne. "Household Personal Care Products," *Financial World,* December 27, 1988.

The Europa World Year Book 1990, vol. II.

Trachtenberg, Jeffrey A. "Styling for the Masses." *Forbes,* March 10, 1986: 152–153.

Warner-Lambert Annual Corporate Report, 1987.

Weiss, Gary. "Razor Sharp: Gillette to Snap Back from a Dull Stretch." *Barron's,* August 25, 1986: 15, 37.

Enterprise Rent-A-Car: Selling the Dream

Lew G. Brown, Gary Armstrong, and Philip Kotler

IN THE FAST LANE

On a bright January 1997 morning, Dean Pittman, Enterprise Rent-A-Car's area rental manager for Durham/Chapel Hill, North Carolina, got out of his Dodge Intrepid at Enterprise's new office in Durham. He admired the line of clean cars and the new office with its green and white Enterprise sign. To Dean, it seemed that dreams really did come true.

A little more than six years ago, Dean had graduated with a degree in industrial relations from the University of North Carolina at Chapel Hill. When he had first scheduled a job interview with Enterprise, Dean had been skeptical. Although he did not know much about the company, he was not certain that he would like renting cars for a living or working a retail job that included washing cars. However, he had seen the potential to advance quickly, to develop strong management skills, and to learn about running a business.

Once hired, Dean had been promoted quickly to management assistant, then to branch manager at Enterprise's new office in Rocky Mount, North Carolina. A year ago, Enterprise had made him an area manager, giving him responsibility for the Durham/Chapel Hill area. He now supervised three branch offices with 22 employees, 495 cars, and annual revenues of more than $3 million. Dean felt as though he was running his own business. Enterprise gave its managers considerable autonomy and paid them based on a percentage of their branches' profits. Dean's starting salary had been in line with those of his classmates, but within three years his pay had doubled, and now it had tripled. There could not be many other companies, Dean thought, where a person his age could have so much responsibility, so much fun, and such high earnings.

COMPANY BACKGROUND

Dean's good fortune mirrored that of Enterprise itself. The company's founder, Jack Taylor, started Enterprise in 1962 with a single location and 17 cars in St. Louis, Missouri. Since then, Enterprise had grown dramatically to become the nation's largest

This case was prepared by Professors Lew G. Brown of the University of North Carolina at Greensboro, Gary Armstrong of the University of North Carolina at Chapel Hill, and Professor Philip Kotler of Northwestern University, as a basis for class discussion. It is not intended to illustrate either effective or ineffective handling of an administrative situation. The authors express their appreciation to Enterprise Rent-A-Car for its cooperation in developing this case.

rent-a-car company. In fact, Enterprise had grown at a compound annual rate of 25 percent for the past 11 years. By 1997, the company had more than 3,000 locations, 325,000 cars, $3.1 billion in sales, $5 billion in assets, and 30,000 employees.

A WINNING STRATEGY

Analysts attributed Enterprise's success to several factors. First, cars had become a more important part in people's lives. They just could not do without their cars, even for a day or two. Also, as more and more families had two adults working or were single-parent families, there was often no one else in the family who could pick people up when they had car problems. Tied in to this, the courts ruled in the 1970s that insurance companies had to offer coverage so that insured motorists could rent replacement cars if they lost the use of their cars. As a result, insurance companies began to offer rental-replacement coverage in their policies.

Beyond these environmental factors, the company's success resulted from its single-minded focus on one segment of the rent-a-car market. Instead of following Hertz, Avis, and other rent-a-car companies by setting up branches at airports to serve national travelers, Enterprise built an extensive network of neighborhood locations serving the "home-city" market—people who needed rental cars as replacements when their cars were wrecked or in the shop being repaired. Because these customers were often stranded at a body shop or repair garage and had no easy way to get to a rental office, Enterprise offered to pick them up.

However, Enterprise's first customer in the replacement market was often the referral source—the insurance agent or auto body shop employee who recommended Enterprise to the stranded customer. Few of Enterprise's customers got up in the morning thinking they would need to rent a car—but then they were involved in a wreck. Therefore, employees visited the referral sources frequently, often taking them doughnuts or pizza as a way of thanking them for their business. They also called on referral sources who were not doing business with Enterprise, as well as keeping insurance agents apprised of cars' repair status.

Auto Rental News, an industry trade publication, estimated that the replacement market was growing 10 percent to 15 percent per year (see Exhibit 1). The entire rent-a-car market, including airport rentals (the travel segment), was about $14.6 billion.

Enterprise's rental rates in the replacement market tended to be lower than rates for comparable rentals at airport-based companies—some analysts estimated up to 30 percent lower. The company usually located its offices in city areas where the rents were much lower than at airports. It also kept its cars a little longer than the typical airport-rental company. These two factors and a focus on efficient operations helped it hold rates lower.

A second segment of the home-city market that Enterprise had begun to serve was the "discretionary" or "leisure/vacation" segment. Friends or relatives might visit and need a car, or the family would decide to take a vacation and feel that the family car was really not as dependable as they would like. More and more people were renting for trips just to keep the extra miles off the family car.

Finally, Enterprise was also experiencing growth in the local corporate market. Many small businesses and some large ones had found that it was cheaper and easier for them to rent their fleets from Enterprise rather than trying to maintain their own fleets. Colleges and universities had realized that it was cheaper to rent a 15-passenger van when the soccer team traveled than to keep a van full-time for only occasional use.

EXHIBIT 1 The Replacement Car Rental Market Competitors, Revenue Estimates, and Other Market Data[1]

I. Competitor:

	1996 U.S. Revenue	% Replacement[2]	Cars in Service (U.S.)
1. Enterprise Rent-A-Car	$2.61 Billion[3]	78	315,000
2. Ford and Chrysler Systems	$490 Million	92	82,550
3. Snappy Car Rental	$100 Million	100	15,500
4. U-Save Auto Rental	$115 Million	60	13,500
5. Rent-A-Wreck	$85 Million	35	10,942
6. Premier Car Rental	$66 Million	100	9,500
7. Advantage Rent-A-Car	$76 Million	33	9,000
8. Spirit Rent-A-Car	$50 Million	100	7,500
9. Super Star Rent-A-Car	$43 Million	100	5,250
10. Many Independent Companies	$750 Million	53	—
11. Airport-Based Companies: Hertz, Avis, Budget, Dollar, National, Thrifty, Alamo[4]	$360 Million	100%	—

[1]Estimates provided by *Auto Rental News*. Data is for case discussion purposes only. Use in case does not imply certification of estimates by Enterprise.

[2]Replacement market includes insurance-replacement rentals, mechanical-repair rentals, dealer-loaner rentals, and warranty rentals.

[3]*Auto Rental News* estimate of U.S. rental revenue excluding leasing: 7% of revenue is from airport/traveler rentals and 93% is from local-market rentals. Local market includes replacement, business, and leisure rentals, with business and leisure about equal for Enterprise.

[4]Includes the portion of airport-based companies' revenue from local market operations that target the replacement market, including Hertz H.I.R.E. operations with 70 locations and Alamo with 115 locations. Hertz total fleet included 250,000 cars; Avis, 190,000; Alamo, 130,000; Budget, 126,000; National, 135,000; Dollar, 63,500; and Thrifty, 34,000.

II. Industry Average Pricing

Estimated industry average price per day for replacement rentals, not including additional insurance coverages or other rentals, such as cellular phones: Industry average daily rental is $23. Industry average rental period for replacement rentals is 12 days.

Additional insurance coverages produce about 5% of revenue, with other rental options producing about 2% of revenue. Per-day rental rates are often established through national contracts with insurance companies or automobile manufacturers' or dealers' warranty reimbursement programs.

There are approximately 150 major U.S. airport rental markets. Airport-based rental rates vary widely depending on competition. Airport rental companies also negotiate corporate rates with individual companies.

III. Overall Rent-A-Car Market

Overall 1996 U.S. market estimated at $14.62 billion, broken down as follows:

Business rentals—40%, Leisure/Discretionary rentals—33%, Replacement rentals—27%.

IV. Advertising

Advertising Age estimated that U.S. car rental companies spent $384.4 million in measured advertising in 1994, about 2.8% of revenue. It estimated that Enterprise spent $22 million in 1994, up from $13 million in 1993. Enterprise's 1994 spending compared with $47 million spent by Hertz, $31 million by Alamo, and $24 million by Avis (Sept. 27, 1995).

Source: *Auto Rental News*

Enterprise's success in the home-city market had attracted competition. Although it had the largest share of that market, a handful of major regional competitors, such as Spirit and Snappy, when combined, captured a large market share. The airport-rental companies, such as Hertz, Avis, and Alamo, got only a small portion of the home-city business. Hertz was just starting a small operation that focused on the home-city replacement market. Local "mom-and-pop" firms that often had just one office and a few cars served the remainder of the market.

Enterprise grew very quietly, depending on its referral sources and word-of-mouth promotion. It was not until 1989 that the company did its first national advertising. At that time, marketing research showed that if you showed people a list of company names and asked them to identify the rent-a-car companies, only about 20 percent knew Enterprise. The company started advertising nationally, but still kept its ads low-key. By 1997, it had more than quadrupled its annual advertising and promotion spending, using the theme: "Pick Enterprise. We'll pick you up." However, although the company's research showed that Enterprise's overall awareness was up substantially, only about one-third of those surveyed were aware of the company's pick-up service, and only about one-third were aware that it had branches nearby.

THE IMPORTANCE OF CULTURE

Although the company's strategy worked well, that strategy was driven by Jack Taylor's philosophy. Taylor believed that the employees' and the company's first job was to serve the customer. From the beginning, Taylor urged his employees to do whatever they had to do in order to make the customer happy. Sometimes it meant waiving charges. Other times, it meant stopping everything and running out to pick up a stranded customer. Employees knew that they needed to do whatever it took to make customers happy.

Further, Taylor believed that after customers came employees. He believed that to satisfy customers, a company had to have satisfied, challenged employees who worked as a team. Therefore, he set up the company so that all of Enterprise's branch employees, from assistant manager on up, earned a substantial portion of their pay based on branch profitability. In addition, the company had a profit-sharing plan for all employees. Enterprise hired primarily college graduates and promoted from within. Ninety-nine percent of its managers started as management trainees at the branch level, so they understood the customer-oriented culture. As important, they understood their local markets and the needs of customers in those markets. Thus, Enterprise was really a collection of small, independent businesses, with the corporation providing capital and logistical support.

Finally, Taylor believed that if the company took care of its customers and employees, profits would follow. Sure enough, Enterprise had consistently been profitable in an industry where many firms had suffered losses.

WHAT'S NEXT?

The question was, how could Enterprise continue to grow and prosper in the face of growing competition? The company believed it could double its revenues by 2001, but to do so it had to wrestle with a number of growth-related issues.

First, it had to continue to attract and retain college graduates. The company needed to hire more than 5,000 management trainees in 1997 alone, and that number would increase. Yet many college grads, like Dean Pittman, might know little or nothing about Enterprise and might have negative feelings about working for a rent-a-car company. How could Enterprise do a better job of recruiting college graduates?

Second, Enterprise had to examine its marketing strategy. Which markets should it target? How should it position itself in those markets? Were there new services it could offer that would make sense given its current strategy? How could it do a better job of increasing Enterprise's awareness among targeted customers? Also, how should it respond as new competitors, including the airport-based firms like Hertz, attacked the home-city market?

Perhaps the most important question was how could Enterprise continue to grow without losing its focus and without losing the corporate culture that had been so important in helping it and its employees, like Dean Pittman, realize their dreams?

Scotia Aqua Farms Limited

Robert G. Blunden and David Moffatt

In late December 1989, Gordon Malcolm, president of Scotia Aqua Farms (SAF), was reevaluating the future of the firm he had founded to commercialize and market the European oyster in North America. Although he had been through difficult times with the firm before, the situation had never seemed so bleak.

Projections indicated that SAF would lose $257,000 on sales of $158,000 for the year and that the loss would wipe out what little equity remained in the firm. The firm was out of cash and had not been able to meet its payroll that week, the last payroll before Christmas. Also, to make matters worse, SAF's development permit for an oyster hatchery and packaging facility at its oyster farm in McGrath Cove had been withdrawn because of the opposition of area residents. That facility had been an essential element of Gordon's expansion play for SAF.

Gordon knew that if SAF were to survive he needed a new strategic plan. What he did not know was whether the business could be saved; whether it was worth saving; and what strategy was appropriate. With those questions in mind he set about to assess the situation.

Scotia Aqua Farms had been started in 1981 by Gordon Malcolm to commercialize and market the European (Belon) oyster. Over the years the firm had never made money, but it had made significant technological strides. Each time Gordon thought the business was about to turn the corner and become profitable, something new happened. Exhibits 1 and 2 provide details of the firm's financial performance. The 1989 operations included three aquacultured products—oysters, mussels, and trout.

THE AQUACULTURE INDUSTRY

Although the practice of aquaculture, the controlled cultivation and harvest of aquatic plants and animals, can be dated back 12,000 years, it is still a much smaller industry than the traditional fishery. On a worldwide basis in 1984, total aquaculture production represented only about 10 percent to 12 percent of total fisheries' output. However, it had developed dramatically during the 1970s and 1980s; worldwide aquaculture production had grown from approximately 1 million tonnes (metric tons, or 1,000 kilograms) in 1967 to an estimated 11 million tonnes in 1987. It had become a major food-producing business around the world and was expected to continue increasing in importance as world

This case was prepared by Professors Robert G. Blunden and David Moffat of Dalhousie University, as a basis for class discussion. It is not intended to illustrate either effective or ineffective handling of an administrative situation.

Robert G. Blunden / David Moffatt

EXHIBIT 1   Income Statements from 1986 to 1989 (In Canadian Dollars)

	1986	1987	1988	1989 Projected
Sales	5,071	13,162	101,390	157,746[a]
Cost of sales	4,056	5,265	66,562	138,227
Gross profit (loss)	1,015	7,897	34,828	19,519
Expenses				
Salaries and Benefits	9,449	111,074	108,711	188,726
Operating	17,078	17,655	55,513	45,480
Administrative	9,938	38,029	66,627	30,822
Depreciation	1,190	2,000	5,776	11,040
Total expenses	37,655	168,758	236,627	276,068
Operating profit (loss)	(36,640)	(160,861)	(201,799)	(256,549)

[a]The 1989 projected revenue of $157,746 was expected to break down into product lines as follows: oysters $49,695; mussels $40,598; trout $34,951; and other products $32,502.
Source: Company records.

EXHIBIT 2   Balance Sheet as of December 31, 1989 (Projected) (In Canadian Dollars)

Assets

Current assets		236,824
Fixed assets	81,516	
Less accumulated depreciation	19,970	61,546
Total Assets		298,371

Liabilities and Shareholders' Equity

Current liabilities:		
Trade payables	42,095	
Long-term debt:		
Bank loan	100,000	
Federal Business Development Bank	103,500	
Nova Scotia Fisheries Loan Board	62,000	
Shareholder loans	134,151	
Total liabilities	441,746	
Preferred Shares[a]	246,000	
Capital	108,020	
Retained earnings Dec. 31, 1990	(497,395)	
Total shareholders' equity	(143,375)	
Total liabilities and shareholders' equity		298,371

[a]The equity of the company consisted of 492 preferred shares, held by 10 shareholders. Most were family or friends of the family.
Source: Company records.

142

demand for seafood expanded more rapidly than traditional supplies. In the late 1980s it was estimated that world catches in the traditional fishery would grow annually by 1 percent to 2 percent at the same time that world demand for seafood would grow annually by more than 3 percent. The gap was expected to create increased opportunities for aquaculturists; worldwide production was projected to reach 16 to 22 million tonnes by 2000.

Marine products can be cultivated in many different water conditions: from simple ponds to flowing water systems called raceways; from floating or submerged enclosed rafts and cages to entire bodies of water closed off for farming. Ideal conditions vary by species, but one consistently important requirement is an abundant supply of clean water.

Canada is ideally suited to aquaculture because of its extensive, protected coastlines and vast resources of clean water. Small-scale, government-run salmonid hatcheries first appeared in Canada in the late 1800s. In the 1950s commercial trout and oyster operations began in British Columbia and trout farms appeared in Ontario. The Canadian aquaculture industry had grown slowly and sporadically, but the 1980s had seen renewed interest and significant production increases as commercial production of other species, such as salmon and mussels, expanded. Exhibit 3 provides data on Canadian aquaculture production in 1986 by species. Exhibit 4 provides data on aquaculture production in Atlantic Canada for 1981, 1984, and 1987.

Aquaculture research programs at Canadian Government and university laboratories facilitated this growth. Private-sector operators built on that research to establish numerous operations across Canada. Foreign companies also started or expanded Canadian operations to take advantage of the ideal environment and to move closer to the United States—the fastest-growing seafood market in the world.

In Canada in 1983 aquacultured products represented less than 1 percent of total fish production but 8.3 percent of Canadian consumption. The disproportionately high share of Canadian fish consumption captured by aquacultured products was a result of Canada's position as a world leader in the traditional fishery. Canada exported about three-fourths of its traditional catch (in 1987, 73 percent of the volume and 84 percent of

---

EXHIBIT 3   Aquaculture Production in Canada, 1986

	Weight (Tonnes)	Value ($000)
Pacific salmon	397	$ 2,702
Atlantic salmon	307	3,724
Trout	2,384	16,193
Pacific oyster	3,700	3,000
American oyster	2,400	3,704
European oyster	5	60
Blue mussel	1,485	2,849
Clams	7	14
Total	10,685	$32,246

Source: Department of Fisheries and Oceans Canada as reported in *Aquaculture in Canada: Report of the Standing Committee on Fisheries and Oceans*, July 1988, p. 10.

EXHIBIT 4   Aquaculture Production in Atlantic Canada, 1981–1987

	1987		1984		1981	
	Tonnes	**$000**	**Tonnes**	**$000**	**Tonnes**	**$000**
Trout	274	$ 1,500	109	$ 414	86	$ 354
Atlantic salmon	1,334	18,734	163	1,903	28	277
Mussels	1,439	2,388	876	1,083	82	101
North American oysters	2,343	4,243	2,129	3,201	N/A	N/A
European oysters	10	27	3	20	N/A	N/A
Total	5,400	$26,892	3,280	$6,801	N/A	N/A

Source: Production and value figures for all species except oysters cultured in salt water between 1981 and 1984 are those reported by the Mariculture Committee of the International Council for the Exploration of the Seas. All 1987 figures except the ones pertaining to salmon production and the corresponding value are based on a calendar year and were made available by provincial authorities. Figures for 1987 for Atlantic salmon are the same ones reported by Saunders (1989), who conducted an exhaustive study and consulted provincial and federal authorities as well as individual producers. The latter figures are for a harvest year and exceed the unofficial calendar year figures by about 300 metric tonnes. As reported in *Cold-Water Aquaculture in Atlantic Canada*, A. D. Boghen (ed), The Canadian Institute for Research on Regional Development, Moncton, Canada, 1989, p. 15.

the value received from commercial fisheries was exported, to more than 60 countries), whereas almost 90 percent of aquaculture production was consumed domestically.

MARKET POTENTIAL

A Canadian Fisheries and Oceans report prepared in 1985 and released in 1986, "Developing Aquaculture in Canada: A Discussion Paper," assessed the market potential for Canadian aquaculture products and outlined, in detail, the problems associated with forecasting market potential for the industry. The report began with an assessment of market potential:

> It is believed that between 80 and 90 percent of Canada's output of commercial aquaculture products is consumed domestically. About 10 percent of the output is sold in the United States and these exports include: some trout (probably less than 100 tonnes per annum); small quantities of British Columbia (B. C.) and Atlantic salmon; and about 10 percent of our production of oysters.

> At this stage in our aquaculture industry's development, it appears that the sales potential is centered on the domestic market and a few other markets (U.S. and Western Europe) which have been emerging as our customers. It also seems likely that the medium term growth will be concentrated on blue mussels, Atlantic and Pacific salmon and Atlantic and Pacific oysters.

Medium-Term Potential

The report estimated medium-term growth potential as follows:

> This section of the report deals with the medium term production and sales potential for Canadian aquaculture products. The views presented are essen-

tially based on discussions with the trade since little is available in the form of "hard" data because:

1. Canadian aquaculture production is dispersed over a wide geographic area and is fragmented among numbers of small producers. No single system of data collection is in place.

2. For the most part, domestic export statistics do not treat aquaculture products as a separate item. Such products are included in the export data under "freshwater fish" or other.

3. Many aquacultured fish products are sold in very small quantities, as compared with wild fish species, so they are often not recorded separately in the trade statistics of importing countries.

Given the data limitations described above, plus the risk in trying to anticipate how the private sector will respond to market opportunities over the next 5 years, the accompanying estimates of sales potential are provided for discussion purposes on the understanding that they represent one view of the potential. (See Exhibit 5.)

The report continued with the following analysis of the market potential for each of the principal aquacultured species.

Blue Mussels. It is expected that at least half of the sales of blue mussels in 1990 may be domestic. Some work has been done toward developing the U.S. market for Canadian cultured mussels, and this export market could take 25 to 50 percent of our production in 5 years. Other large mussel-consuming markets, such as Holland, Belgium, and France, also offer potential.

Trout. The trout industry is beset by relatively high production costs, a wide dispersion of producers, and some lack of organization with regard to marketing. There is also intense competition from Idaho imports. While some of these factors will tend to limit the growth of the market for frozen domestic trout, there appears to be some potential for increases in the volume of fresh product

---

EXHIBIT 5   Medium-Term Sales Potential

Major Species	Estimated 1984 Canadian Production (Tonnes)	Estimated 1990 Potential (Tonnes)
Blue Mussels	950	2,000
Trout	1,800	2,500
Salmon		
Atlantic	300	2,000
Pacific	100	2,000
Oysters	2,800	6,000
Tuna	50	N/A
Total	6,000	14,500

Source: Company records

sales. However, there will be strong competition in the fresh trout market from some foreign producers of good-quality low-cost products.

Salmon. Atlantic and B.C. cultured salmon could become a significant product in both domestic and export (primarily U.S.) markets. Provided that the many issues related to production and competing foreign products (mainly Norwegian and U.S.) are overcome, the U.S. market could consume 50 percent of Canadian cultured salmon by 1990. Since the Canadian product will be competing with Norwegian and U.S. salmon, however, it will require effective marketing strategies in order for it to exploit these opportunities.

Oysters. The current expectation is that recent advances in oyster culturing techniques in both the Atlantic and Pacific coasts will result in more production stability than has been the case during the past decade. It is possible that our production could increase by about 50 percent over the next few years. The U.S. market could take as much as 25 percent of Canadian oyster production by 1990.

Assessment of the market prospects of cultivated European flat oysters have not been included in the estimates of sales potential. Currently, this species is being developed on a small scale in Nova Scotia and issues such as the availability of seed must be answered before this venture becomes viable on a large scale. Cultivation of this specialty product could become an interesting domestic and export market opportunity provided larger volume production becomes viable.

Barriers to Growth

The development of the aquaculture industry in Canada was far from a sure thing. Substantial barriers to growth fell into four broad categories: technical, financial, marketing, and regulatory. Although the exact nature of these factors varied to some extent from species to species and location to location, aquaculture operations in general faced serious problems.

Large-scale cultured production of seafood in Canada was a relatively young industry, and many technical problems were yet to be resolved. Aquaculturists faced numerous genetic problems, as well as disease and mortality issues. In addition, they had to develop efficient production technologies suited to the habitats used for raising each species.

Most financial problems were related to the difficulty in raising capital and securing loans. Commercial banks were hesitant to lend money to an industry they knew so little about, in which the inventory was susceptible to storm damage, disease, and widely fluctuating prices. Private investors were also wary, for similar reasons. One Nova Scotian mussel grower summed up the views of investors:

> [Aquaculture] is perceived by investors as an unknown quantity and, in this neck of the woods, investors are very conservative. If you don't have a proven track record, you're going to have to offer very good returns—and those returns just aren't available yet.

The result was that most aquaculture operations relied on government loans and were thinly capitalized by the owner with limited investor involvement.

The principal marketing problem was finding a profitable niche in the market in the face of competing wild and cultured products. Aquacultured products have several advantages over wild products. They are available fresh year-round, are of generally higher quality, and offer a more consistent product in terms of size and presentation. However, wild products are offered seasonally in much larger quantities and often at lower prices. The small, independent growers were typically unable to develop brand awareness for their products or even to guarantee continuous supply to large-volume buyers.

In order to overcome such problems, growers in some areas banded together into marketing co-ops to reach major markets while continuing to compete directly in local markets. For example, much of the mussel production in Prince Edward Island was marketed by the Atlantic Mussel Growers Corporation, which was able to offer a reliable, consistent supply to buyers of all sizes throughout North America. A similar private firm in New Brunswick managed the supply of fresh cultured salmon to markets in central Canada and the eastern United States.

Regulatory problems generally related to the influence of special interest groups, whose pressure led to stringent licensing requirements in some areas. Some traditional fishing operations opposed aquaculture development because they feared that aquaculture would damage their fisheries or interfere with navigation. Cottage owners and recreational users of coastal property opposed aquaculture operations because they saw them spoiling the beauty of nature. Environmentalists raised concerns about the possible toxic effects of fish waste buildups beneath cages of fish farms. The extent of regulatory problems varied significantly among jurisdictions. For example, the New Brunswick government had been quite supportive of the aquaculture industry, whereas the Nova Scotian government had been less so.

In Nova Scotia most aquaculture operations were small; often they were a second source of income for their owners. In 1988 there were 28 trout producers, 80 mussel producers, 18 oyster producers, 19 salmon producers, and 7 scallop producers in Nova Scotia. Production figures from 1986 to 1989 are provided in Exhibit 6.

Long-Term Prospects

The Fisheries and Oceans Canada report assessed the long-term market potential of aquacultured products as follows:

> Provided that the numerous technical, financial, and marketing issues related to aquaculture development are successfully addressed, the longer-term sales potential of the Canadian industry is promising. It is expected that the best potential for large-scale volume increases in sales will be concentrated in Atlantic and Pacific salmon, oysters, and mussels. Indications are that much of the

---

EXHIBIT 6   Aquaculture Production in Nova Scotia, 1986–1989

	1989 Estimate	1988		1987		1986
	Tonnes	Tonnes	$000	Tonnes	$000	Tonnes
Mussels	400	320	$ 485	248	$ 415	255
Oysters	132	132	207	21	46	17
Salmon	270	27	309	28	289	28
Trout	250	194	1,333	212	1,161	73
Total	1,052	673	$2,334	509	$1,911	373

Source: Nova Scotia Department of Fisheries.

growth over the next 10 years will be based on sales in the Canadian and U.S. markets. Of all our export markets, the U.S. should offer the best sales potential for the Canadian aquaculture industry largely because of the U.S. market size, its proximity, lower transportation costs than European competitors, and relatively easy market access.

COMPANY HISTORY

Gordon Malcolm, founder and president of Scotia Aqua Farms, was born in 1958 in Oakville, Ontario, to a business-oriented family of British descent. He received his early education (grades 4 to 13) from Appleby College, a private boys' school in Oakville. After graduating from Appleby in 1977, Gordon moved to Halifax to study marine biology at Dalhousie University. He focused his research and attention on bivalve molluscs and took several introductory business courses as electives.

Gordon had been active in the aquaculture industry since the early 1980s. He had been a technician at the Dalhousie Experimental Oyster Hatchery and Bivalve Genetic Research Laboratory for two years and a manager for five years. An active member of several Canadian and international aquaculture organizations, Gordon served on the board of directors of the Nova Scotia Aquaculture Association.

During SAF's formative years (1981–1985), Gordon ran Dalhousie's Experimental Oyster Hatchery, concentrating his efforts on the introduction of a new species, the European oyster, to the waters of Nova Scotia's south shore. Many believed the European oyster had the best taste, and demand for it was high. This product had never been produced in the region, and Gordon wanted to be the first to develop it successfully.

During this period, the company concentrated on developing new technologies, perfecting techniques, and gradually building up stocks. It took five years for stocks of the European Oyster to reach market size. Because the industry was generally perceived by investors and conventional lenders as highly risky, and SAF's endeavors as especially so, the company had trouble securing the capital necessary to develop large quantities of oysters. Gordon used loans from family members, government grants where possible, and even his tax returns as working capital to purchase oyster seed and hire summer students. To generate additional cash, SAF sold native North American oysters to retail seafood outlets in the nearby Halifax market.

By 1985, Gordon was ready to expand oyster operations but felt that other products were needed to finance that expansion. He began growing mussels on an experimental basis that summer for a number of reasons:

Growing techniques were similar to those used with the oysters he knew so well.

They required very little capital outlay (seed could be collected easily from wild beds and did not need to be purchased).

They reached maturity quickly (two years, compared with five or six years for oysters).

They grew very well on the Nova Scotian shores where he already possessed underutilized water leases.

In addition, Gordon felt that growing mussels was a good way to fill in slack time.

In 1986 the company put in its first crop of mussel seed, which was successfully harvested in 1988. Mussel seed had been collected and set out each year since that time.

In 1987, at the request of one of the company's investors, SAF started raising rainbow trout. Five trout cages were built in the spring of 1987 and two more were added in 1989. The cages were located on an experimental water lease in Shad Bay, Nova Scotia. (See Exhibit 7.) The cages were filled with fingerlings (trout a minimum of 6 inches long, weighing 60 to 80 grams) each spring and harvested by the following January.

Gordon's plans were to build a hatchery and packaging facility on his land at McGrath Cove. The building would be used to grow European oyster seed, to hold inventory of fresh marketable product, and to package the product for shipment. The property at McGrath Cove bordered on the company's water lease, which was ideal for growing the European oyster. The capacity of the lease was adequate for several million oysters, although more water would be required eventually. In 1985 it was evident to Gordon that he could not pursue this strategy alone; the company required more qualified staff.

PERSONNEL

Gordon felt that a well-trained and technically oriented staff was the key to success, and he steadily assembled one. In 1985, he hired Mark Millet and Bruce Rasch, each of whom held honours degrees in biology from Dalhousie University. Bruce had used the European oyster in his honours thesis experiments, and Mark had done marine research for both the Federal Department of Fisheries and Oceans and private research companies. Mark was the senior manager of operations. His task was to expand production volume and develop new techniques. Bruce was responsible for the company's shellfish grow-out activity at McGrath Cove, where the European oysters and mussels were cultured and North American oysters were finished off. In 1986, Gordon hired David Hamilton, another Dalhousie honours graduate with a bachelor of science

EXHIBIT 7: Scotia Aqua Farm Locations in Atlantic Canada

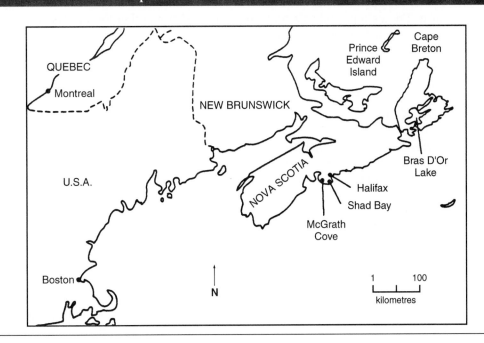

degree. David had done his thesis research on the Atlantic salmon and rainbow trout. David Hamilton was responsible for the native North American oyster culturing operations in the Bras d'Or Lakes.

Betty Connors joined the company in the same year. A New Brunswick native, Betty had studied marine biology at the University of New Brunswick from 1980 to 1983 and was a graduate of the Aquaculture Technician Training Program at Huntsman Marine Laboratory in St. Andrews, New Brunswick. She had experience setting up hatcheries and grow-out facilities, and in the pond culture of salmonids. Betty was manager of the finfish grow-out operation and ran the rainbow trout fish cage site in Shad Bay. Edward Knox, the final key staff member, was hired in 1987. He has been involved extensively in Dalhousie University's Oyster Research Program from 1982 until the end of 1986. Like most of the staff, he had an Honours bachelor's degree in science from Dalhousie University. Edward managed the company's hatchery development program at Dalhousie University in Halifax.

There was no formal hierarchy at SAF, but a strong team spirit existed among the staff. Each of the key employees was familiar with all company operations and worked wherever needed. Temporary labor supplemented the core staff as necessary.

The future looked bright for Scotia Aqua Farms in 1986. No one within the company would have predicted the problems that were to plague the company over the next four years.

PRODUCTS

SAF's product line consisted of three primary products: oysters, mussels, and rainbow trout. The company also owned a small interest in a lobster pound in St. Margaret's Bay, Nova Scotia, through which lobster was supplied to SAF's customers. The product line was broadened with items such as periwinkles, seaweed, scallops, and ocean-farmed salmon. The periwinkles and seaweed were collected on the shore of the ocean at the trout farm. The scallops and salmon were purchased from other local aquaculturists. Oysters were projected to generate 32 percent of total revenue in 1989, followed by mussels at 26 percent and trout at 22 percent. The remaining 20 percent of revenue was expected to come from other products that SAF bought and resold, primarily lobsters and scallops.

MARKETS

Historically, SAF's rather limited sales had been made to a varied group of customers through both direct and indirect channels. In the local market SAF had sold directly to supermarket chains and restaurants. In Ontario, Quebec, and the United States, sales had been made through brokers who typically charged from 2 percent to 7 percent for their services. Local and international brokers often contacted SAF seeking quality products, especially oysters.

The Atlantic Canadian Market

SAF had a significant advantage in the Halifax market because it grew European oysters, mussels, and trout and inventoried North American oysters harvested in Cape Breton, all within 30 kilometres of the metropolitan area. As a result, deliveries could be made with short lead times and freshness guaranteed. To build on this advantage, Gordon had identified several local markets for possible development—restaurants, supermarket chains, institutions, and caterers.

Local Restaurants Local restaurants sold a wide variety of seafood including trout, oysters, and mussels. Restaurants could be segmented into two categories based upon price: (1) medium-priced and (2) high-priced, specialty restaurants. Medium-priced restaurants bought mainly from wholesalers and were price-sensitive; high-priced, specialty restaurants were more concerned with product quality and were thought to be willing to pay a premium price for fresh, high-quality seafood delivered two or three times a week. Many of these outlets preferred to deal with one source for all seafood products; however, some were willing to purchase from a number of sources. SAF had been selling oysters to some local restaurants, but to develop this market significantly, it would likely have to ensure year-round supply.

Grocery Stores Supermarket chains and independent grocers were considered hard to break into because large, full-line distributors were supplying them, but the fresh-fish departments of supermarkets were thought to provide the best year-round opportunity. SAF had broken into Superstore, a local supermarket chain, but sales were sporadic and concentrated in fresh trout and lower-margin frozen trout. Sobeys, the largest supermarket chain in the Atlantic provinces, had expressed interest in purchasing trout and mussels directly from small, local producers, but oysters were only stocked seasonally and mussels were fairly slow movers at Sobeys. On the other hand, they sold a large quantity of trout.

Independent grocers were more willing to accept high-quality, competitively priced local seafood, but total volume purchased was small. Large chains had a great deal of bargaining power; hence sellers were usually price takers.

Food Service Operations Institutional food service operations used little seafood, citing high food costs, lack of seafood preparation skills, and inadequate consumer acceptance as the major reasons. Tapping this market would require substantial promotion, product development, and marketing. Potential for market growth depended largely upon the success of promotional activities. However, this market would yield high margins.

Caterers Caterers were also thought to offer potential for high-quality seafood, because 38 percent of fresh oysters sold in Canada were consumed in clubs and at private parties. Mussels were also a popular appetizer. The European oyster, with its premium quality and relative scarcity, seemed ideal for this market.

The North American and International Market

The North American market in general offered similar opportunities to those discussed previously but necessitated the use of brokers of wholesalers to reach markets beyond Atlantic Canada. The principal Canadian brokers were located in Toronto and Montreal. A number of them had approached SAF, and trial relationships were in place in some larger Canadian cities. For example, a Toronto seafood wholesaler was regularly buying European oysters, at 50 cents each, for his oyster bar.

Although the principal U.S. brokers were in Boston and New York, there were significant local distributors in most large U.S. cities. SAF had recently entered the Boston market, and trial shipments of North American oysters had been well received. The firm had also been successfully selling North American oysters to a wholesaler in Maine who distributed them primarily in the New York area.

This confirmed Gordon's view that oysters held the most sales potential beyond Atlantic Canada. Mussels could be shipped profitably but with lower margins. Trout could not compete in these markets, as it was produced in most states and provinces in North America.

U.S. oyster production had fallen in recent years (see Exhibit 8), largely because of increased water pollution along the eastern seaboard. Demand had remained high, forcing the average price paid for U.S. oyster imports up by 8.9 percent from 1986 to 1987. Prices were expected to continue to rise as U.S. supply fell.

The international market was thought to offer SAF significant opportunities if it could be developed. In particular, European buyers would probably buy all the European oysters SAF could supply if they could be delivered fresh, because European demand exceeded local supply.

One of SAF's domestic brokers had a few contacts in Europe, and of course there were other brokers, but Gordon preferred to develop permanent, long-term relationships with customers if possible. However, he was also concerned that inadequate supplies and shipping problems could jeopardize SAF's market entry if it were to attempt to develop this market before it had the capability.

OPERATIONS

Scotia Aqua Farms raised two species of oysters (the native North American oyster and the European or Belon oyster), mussels, and trout at three Nova Scotian sites. At the Narrows, near McGrath Cove, SAF raised European oysters and mussels and finished off North American oysters. At Shad Bay, about 10 kilometers away, SAF raised trout. And in the Bras d'Or Lake of Cape Breton Island, about 500 kilometres northeast of Halifax, the company raised North American oysters. The company's head office was located in Gordon Malcolm's home, near Halifax, and some research activities were conducted at Dalhousie University in Halifax. The sites are identified on the map in Exhibit 7.

EXHIBIT 8 U.S. Supply of Oysters, 1978–1987 (Meat Weight)

Year	U.S. Commercial Landings			Imports	Total U.S. Consumption
	Eastern	Pacific	Total		
1978	45,183	5,800	50,983	33,843	84,825
1979	42,325	5,756	48,081	27,131	75,212
1980	42,439	6,642	49,081	21,732	70,813
1981	44,440	5,612	50,052	25,769	75,821
1982	48,489	5,839	54,328	27,529	81,857
1983	44,729	5,431	50,160	30,775	80,935
1984	41,808	6,479	48,287	36,086	84,373
1985	36,578	7,595	44,173	45,926	90,099
1986	35,013	5,531	40,544	50,038	90,582
1987	29,957	9,850	39,807	52,085	91,892

Source: United States Department of Commerce.

Oysters

North American oysters were harvested from the company's Bras d'Or Lake lease and purchased from other oyster farmers in the same area. Grown from spat (½-inch seed oyster) collected from public beds, they took five to six years to reach market size in the Bras d'Or Lake.

Upon reaching market size, they were transferred, for a year or less, to the cooler, saltier coastal waters of the Narrows at McGrath Cove for finishing off. This additional step, although not necessary to produce a marketable product, was done to improve the taste. It was expensive. Extra handling and shipping were required, and inevitably there was some loss due to the oysters being out of the water too long, poor handling, spillage from nets and trays, and the shock of higher salinity and cooler waters. However, it also meant that SAF could supply oysters year-round, even though the Bras d'Or Lake froze over in the winter.

When buying North American oysters from others, SAF paid $50 for a box of 300 oysters. Each year SAF bought more oysters from local leaseholders. The region was able to supply several million oysters per year if well managed, but the costs of finishing them off at the Narrows were high.

Another alternative was to construct a holding and processing facility in Cape Breton. SAF estimated that such a facility would cost $875,000, but funds would be hard to secure. Some government assistance would be available because the economy in Cape Breton was depressed and construction of the facility would bring much-needed jobs to the area and provide employment for many out-of-work leaseholders.

Once harvested, North American oysters were graded by shape and size. Oysters that would sit on a flat surface without spilling after being shucked (having the top shell removed) were called "choice" oysters and were sold according to size. They ranged from cocktails (2.5 to 3 inches) to fancies (over 4.5 inches). The most common grades were the small and large choice oysters (3–3.5 inches and 3.5–4.5 inches, respectively). Oysters that would not sit evenly on a flat surface were graded "standard" or "commercial." Exhibit 9 shows the average proportion by grade from a harvest of North American oysters and the average price per oyster received in 1989.

European oysters did not grow naturally in North America, and this created both problems and opportunities for SAF. The main problem was the availability of oyster seed, which had to be hatchery-grown. Sufficient seed had always been available in the

---

EXHIBIT 9   Average Oyster Yields, 1989

Grade	% of Total Harvest	Unit Price
Standard/commercial	19	$.18
Cocktail	10	.25
Small choice	47	.30
Large choice	22	.35
Fancy	2	.40

Source: Company records

past, but the supply was not adequate to support the expanded commercial production Gordon envisaged. Thus the hatchery and processing facility planned for McGrath Cove, at a cost of about $200,000, was key to SAF's expansion plans.

On the other hand, producing European oysters offered major opportunities. There was little competition, as no one was successfully growing European oysters in North America on a large commercial scale. There were several other Nova Scotian aquaculturists, supported by the Dalhousie University project, attempting to introduce the European oyster to Nova Scotia, but SAF was in the lead and the four to five years required to grow European oysters to market size would give SAF time to develop and consolidate a market position. In addition, demand in Europe for European oysters had outstripped supply, creating a tempting market opportunity for SAF if they could deliver healthy, live oysters. In 1989 European oysters sold for an average price of 50 cents each.

Mussels

Mussels, which grow well in a variety of water temperatures and salinities, were prolific in Atlantic Canada. SAF cultivated blue mussels at the narrows location. Mussel seed was collected by suspending old fishnet or plastic mesh in the water; larval mussels settled on the mesh and metamorphosed into seed, which was transferred to mussel socks (cylindrical nylon mesh tubes suspended from buoys about 3 feet below the water's surface) when the seed reached ½ to ¾ inch long. The mussels remained attached to the mesh socks for the two years needed to reach market size (2½ to 3 inches).

When the mussels were ready to be harvested, the socks were pulled up; the mussels were pulled off in clumps and mechanically separated and cleaned. SAF did not have the necessary mussel-producing equipment, which costs approximately $25,000, so this work was done by a nearby mussel processor at $5 per bag. It required 28 pounds of ungraded mussels to fill the 25-pound nylon mesh bags in which they were sold.

SAF sold most of its mussels to a large seafood wholesaler in Halifax at $0.80 per pound. However, the number of mussel growers and the volumes being produced in Nova Scotia had increased greatly during 1989, and competition was expected to be fierce in 1990, with the large growers setting a considerably lower price for their product.

Trout

Trout operations were located at Shad Bay, just 20 kilometers south of Halifax on a small property accessed directly from the rural highway. In addition to the ocean cages, facilities included a small log cabin, a travel trailer, and a wharf. The site was serviced with electricity but did not have running water. Although the property was rented, there was little risk of losing it; in fact, SAF would probably be able to buy it.

Trout production began in early May, when trout fingerlings were purchased and placed in ocean cages (suspended fish nets, 40 feet in diameter, surrounded by floating, wooden platforms). The fish were fed herring pellets daily until October, when they reached market size (1.5 to 2.25 pounds). They were then harvested, gutted, and sold by the pound.

Prior to the fall of 1988, SAF had been selling trout off the wharf and to a grocery store chain in Halifax at $4.00 and $3.50 per pound, respectively. At that time, an algae bloom on the west coast of North America forced British Columbian producers to quickly liquidate their stocks of trout and salmon. They flooded the Atlantic Canadian market, driving prices down and precipitating an industry shakeout. As a result, SAF received an average of $2.66 per pound in 1989.

The estimated costs for each of the product lines for 1989 are detailed in Exhibit 10. At the end of 1989, inventory available for sale early in 1990 consisted of $60,000 worth of oysters and 10,000 pounds of rainbow trout. The year had been another difficult one, in part because of the effects of a hurricane that had caused severe water temperature fluctuations resulting in the loss of 30 percent to 35 percent of SAF's trout stocks and approximately 60 percent of its oyster stocks.

MUSSEL TOXIN SCARE

Just before Christmas 1987, the shellfish industry in Atlantic Canada was dealt a severe blow by a series of reports of people becoming seriously ill from Atlantic Canadian mussels. The illnesses were traced to mussels grown on the Prince Edward Island side of the Northumberland Strait, which lies between New Brunswick and Prince Edward Island. The Federal Department of Fisheries and Oceans immediately ordered an end to the sale of oysters and mussels gown anywhere in the region. In addition, the minister of Fisheries made comments implying that all shellfish in the region were unsafe, despite the fact that there had been no problems with any products other than the P.E.I. mussels. In effect, he closed down the industry, depressing the shellfish market for an entire year before public fears subsided. Even worse, the mussel toxin scare marked the beginnings of public opposition to aquaculture in Atlantic Canada, which in turn led the Nova Scotian government to reconsider its support for the industry.

Like most shellfish growers in the region, SAF's sales suffered throughout this period. That, in turn, prevented building up stocks of oysters and set back Gordon's plans for the firm. More importantly, it was public reaction to the mussel toxin scare that led to the Federal Business Development Bank's refusal to sign an agreement that would have led to the construction of the McGrath Cove hatchery and processing plant.

THE EFFECT OF PUBLIC OPPOSITION TO AQUACULTURE ON SAF

In late 1987, responsibility for aquaculture was transferred from federal to provincial jurisdiction, bringing new legislation. In Nova Scotia, the first change was a requirement to hold public hearings prior to the granting of any water leases.

EXHIBIT 10 Projected Costs by Product Line, 1989

	Oysters	Mussels	Trout
Purchases	$ 47,784	—	$34,556
Processing	223	$ 6,938	—
Equipment	3,171	1,234	850
Shipping	4,597	—	2,207
Labor	45,108	41,725	25,937
Feed	—	—	22,106
Total	$100,883	$49,897	$85,656

At this time, Scotia Aqua Farms held a two-year experimental lease for the trout site in Shad Bay, a grandfathered lease for the area known as the Narrows near McGrath Cove, and the lease in Cape Breton. The company planned to apply for another lease in Deep Cove, near McGrath Cove, where they would expand their mussel and oyster operations. SAF held informal discussions with local fishermen in December, informing them of the company's intention to put down mussel lines and to apply for a lease in Deep Cove. The fishermen indicated no concerns.

The next stage in the company's plans involved the construction of the planned oyster hatchery and packaging facility on their property at McGrath Cove. In March 1988, the company held another informal information meeting with local fishermen to ensure that it met with their approval. It was suggested that the building be constructed on the Crown land at Deep Cove because the plans involved the growing of product there anyway and it had direct highway access. Shortly after this meeting, the Blind Bay Residents Association was formed.

To get the new water lease, SAF has to hold a public hearing chaired by a government representative. At this public hearing, previously unexpressed concerns were raised. Residents were afraid of increased traffic on the local roads and unsightly buoys in the bay. They felt that their property values would be reduced and even that the expansion of aquaculture in the area would destroy a traditional way of life.

After the public hearing, the residents association launched an appeal to reverse the granting of the Regional Development Permit needed to go ahead with the construction of the facility. Their appeal was successful and the permit was revoked, citing "public opposition." Finding an alternative site would be time-consuming and difficult.

A TIME FOR DECISION

By Christmas of 1989 Gordon did not know where to turn or what to do. Much of his effort over the past year had gone into planning for the construction of the McGrath Cove hatchery and production facility and inventory expansion with the Deep Cove water lease. Losing the legal battle meant that would not now be possible. The company's financial position had deteriorated further, and Gordon was forced to reconsider his personal and corporate goals. Gordon realized that the very survival of SAF depended on the decisions he would have to make in the weeks ahead.

Anheuser-Busch Dominates in the 1990s

Thomas L. Wheelen, David B. Croll, and Moustafa H. Abdelsamad

On March 28, 1990, Patrick K. Stokes was appointed president of Anheuser-Busch, the beer subsidiary of Anheuser-Busch Companies (the holding company). He succeeded August A. Busch III, who had served as president of the subsidiary for the past three years. Mr. Busch, who maintained his position as chairman of the board, president, and chief executive officer of Anheuser-Busch Companies, said that he "will continue to participate in the management of the beer subsidiary, but will devote more time to corporate duties and working with other subsidiaries."[1] One analyst expressed his belief that Mr. Stokes' main challenge would be to reach the 50 percent market-share objective by or before the mid-1990s. The analyst went on to say, "Stokes will be under extra pressure since the achievement of this (50 percent market share) objective is a top priority of Mr. Busch."

Mr. Stokes had served as chairman and CEO of Campbell-Taggart and as chairman and president of Eagle Snacks, both food subsidiaries of Anheuser-Busch Companies. Also promoted was Michael J. Roarty, director of marketing for Anheuser-Busch, the beer subsidiary, to vice president of corporate marketing and communications for the company and chairman of Busch media group. During Roarty's 13-year tenure in the beer subsidiary, sales and market share had more than doubled—to 80.7 million barrels and 42.1 percent market share. Rather than appoint a new director of marketing, three veteran Anheuser-Busch managers shared the challenge of achieving 50 percent market share with Mr. Stokes.

COMPANY HISTORY—AN ENTREPRENEURIAL SPIRIT

In 1852, George Schneider founded the Bavarian Brewery in St. Louis, Missouri. Five years later, on the brink of bankruptcy, the brewery was sold to a competitor who renamed it Hammer and Urban. By 1860, the new company defaulted on a loan to Eberhard Anheuser. Anheuser, a successful soap manufacturer, assumed control of Hammer and Urban and four years later asked his son-in-law, Adolphus Busch, to join the brewery as a salesman. Busch, who became the driving force behind the new venture, became a

[1]"August Busch III Names Beer Successor," *Beverage World,* May 1990, p. 10.

partner in 1873, and then served as president between 1880 and 1913. In 1879, the name of the brewery was changed to Anheuser-Busch Brewing Company.

Adolphus Busch was a pioneer in the development of a new pasteurization process for beer and became the first American brewer to pasteurize beer. In 1894, he and Carl Conrad developed a new beer that was lighter in color and body. This new beer, Budweiser, gave Busch a national beer, for which he developed many marketing techniques to increase sales. By 1901, the annual sales of Anheuser-Busch had surpassed the million-barrel mark.

In 1913, August A. Busch succeeded his father as president of the company, serving as president during the Prohibition era between 1920 and 1933. He led the company in many new diversification endeavors, such as truck bodies, baker's yeast, ice cream, corn products, commercial refrigeration units, and nonalcoholic beverages. With the passage of the 21st Amendment, which repealed Prohibition, Anheuser-Busch returned to the manufacturing and distribution of beer on a national basis, and in 1934 the company went public. August A. Busch's son, Adolphus Busch III, was president of the company from 1934 until his death in 1946.

August A. (Gussie) Busch, Jr., succeeded Adolphus Busch III as president and CEO in 1946. He was elected chairman of the board in 1956. During his tenure, eight new breweries were constructed and sales increased 11-fold, from 3 million barrels in 1946 to 34 million barrels in 1974. He guided the company as it continued its conglomerate diversification strategies into real estate, family entertainment parks, transportation, the St. Louis Cardinals baseball team, and can manufacturing. Busch was serving as honorary chairman of the board of Anheuser-Busch Companies, and chairman and president of the St. Louis National Baseball Club at his death on September 29, 1989. He was 90. Before his death, Mr. Busch commented, "I've had a wonderful, competitive life filled with challenges and reward. And I'm thankful for it all. Most of all, I'm thankful for my heritage, for my family, and for my children. I'm thankful for my life with my company, Anheuser-Busch." His death marked the last of the legendary "beer barons," and the end of an era.[2]

August A. Busch III, born on June 16, 1937, was the fifth generation of the Busch brewing dynasty. He started his career hauling beechwood chips out of 31,000-gallon aging tanks. In his youth, "Little Augie" was a hell-raiser, but he changed to a conservative "workaholic" after attending the University of Arizona and the Siebel Institute of Technology, a Chicago school for brewers. He was elected president in 1974 and CEO in 1975. During his tenure, sales increased by more than two and a half times, or 264 percent, from 34 million barrels in 1974 to 89.7 million barrels in 1989. The company maintained 12 breweries having a total capacity of 85.1 million barrels, and Anheuser-Busch continued its successful conglomerate diversification efforts (Exhibit 1).

During his 15 years of managing the company, Busch transformed it from a large, loosely run company into a tightly run organization with an emphasis on the bottom line. Busch was known for his tough-mindedness and intensity, his highly competitive nature, and his attention to detail. As Mr. Dennis Long, former president of the company's brewing subsidiary, said, "There is little that goes on that he doesn't know something about." Busch, a brewmaster, was known for making unscheduled visits to the breweries at all hours of the day and night.

Mr. Busch would start his day at 5:30 A.M., then pilot his helicopter from his 1,000-acre farm in Saint Peters, Missouri, to the company's headquarters on the South Side of

---

[2]Anheuser-Busch Companies, *Annual Report 1989*, p. 1.

EXHIBIT 1   Anheuser-Busch Subsidiaries

Anheuser-Busch	Civic Center Corporation
Anheuser-Busch Investment Capital Corporation	Container Recovery Corporation
	Eagle Snacks
Anheuser-Busch International	International Label Company[a]
Busch Agricultural Resources	Manufacturers Railroad Company
Busch Creative Service Corporation	Metal Container Corporation
Busch Entertainment Corporation	Promotional Products Group
Busch Media Group	St. Louis National Baseball Club
Busch Properties	St. Louis Refrigerator Car Company
Campbell Taggart	

[a]This is a joint venture company.
Source: Anheuser-Busch Companies, Inc., *Fact Book—1989/90*, pp. 6-26.

St. Louis—a 30-mile flight. He would hold his first meeting over breakfast, which would take place at 7:00 A.M., and would rarely leave the office before 6:00 P.M. One of his final rituals before retiring at 8:30 P.M. would be to taste-test daily samples of beer that were flown in from the company's breweries. Few batches of Budweiser, or any Anheuser-Busch beer, were shipped without his personal approval. Busch was described "as a man who absolutely never wastes time." "When you have a meeting with him, it is boom, boom, boom," stated Jerry Steinman, publisher of *Beer Marketer's Insights,* an industry newsletter. Professor Amand C. Stalnaker, on the board of directors of the company, put it another way. "He's not the guy who sits back, puts his feet up on the desk, and says, 'Let's chat about this for an hour or two.' But I would call it intensity rather than abruptness."[3] Mr. Long added, "Let there be no doubt. He's at the helm and he sets the tone. For him, planning and management are one and the same; once a plan is drawn up, he tracks the follow-through to make sure that it is carried out.[4]

Encouraging openness and participation from his executives, Busch provided them with plenty of responsibility and freedom, and promoted group decision making. Henry King, former president of the United States Brewing Association, stated, "...the reason Anheuser-Busch leads the field is because it's got dynamic leadership. August Busch picks very talented people; he gives them enormous responsibilities, but he gives them the authority to execute those responsibilities, and he holds people accountable."[5]

His policy committee was a 12-member forum in which each member was expected to present an opinion on the current topic or issue and substantiate his position. Mr. Busch felt that "executives do not learn from success; they learn from their failures." What was his philosophy on success? As he stated, "The more successful that we become...the more humble we must be...because that breeds future success."[6]

---

[3]Christy Marshall, "The Czar of Beers," *Business Month,* June 1988, p. 26.

[4]"How Anheuser Brews Its Winners," *New York Times,* August 4, 1985.

[5]Larry Jabbonsky, "What Keeps A-B Hot?" *Beverage World,* September 1988, p. 22.

[6]"How Anheuser Brews Its Winners," p. 28.

Robert S. Weinberg, a brewing industry analyst and former consultant to the company, felt, "The thing that is extraordinary about A-B is their depth of management talent.... This is a very extraordinary team. They're not competing with each other; they're all working together for the common goal." However, a former employee warned, "The biggest mistake as an Anheuser executive is to wake up one morning and think you're a Busch," even though Mr. Busch spoke in endearing, almost emotional terms about the A-B family of employees.[7]

Mr. Busch's 26-year-old son, August A. Busch IV, has been learning the business over the past five years. He was the brand manager for Bud Dry. Commenting on the success of his four children, Mr. Busch said, "If they have the competency to do so, they'll be given the opportunity. You learn from the ground up. Those of us who are in this company started out scrubbing the tanks."[8] "The fact that he [August IV] is August III's son does not mean a free lunch," stated a friend of the immediate family. "It couldn't hurt, however."[9]

THE ORGANIZATION

On October 1, 1979, Anheuser-Busch Companies was formed as a new holding company. The company's new name and organization structure more clearly reflected Anheuser-Busch's mission and diversification endeavors of the past decades.

Reorganization of the Business Segments

As a result of the acquisition of Sea World in September 1989, Anheuser. Busch reorganized and redefined its principal business segments from prior years. For strategic planning purposes, the company's three business segments became (1) beer and beer-related operations, which produced and sold the company's beer products; (2) food products, which consisted of the company's food and food-related operations (Campbell-Taggart and Eagle Snacks); and (3) entertainment, which included the company's theme parks (Sea World, Cypress Gardens, Busch Gardens, Adventure Island, and Sesame Place), baseball team (St. Louis Cardinals), stadium (Busch Stadium and Civic Center), and real estate development and operations. Exhibit 2 is an outline of each of the 17 companies that comprise the three business segments.

Prior to the reorganization, the three principal business segments had been (1) beer and beer-related, (2) food products, and (3) diversified operations. The diversified operations segment included entertainment, real estate, transportation, and communications operations. In 1989, transportation and communications became part of the beer and beer-related segment.

In 1989, the beer and beer-related business segment contributed 78.1 percent of the corporation's net sales and 93.7 percent of the operating income. Financial information for each of these business segments is shown in Exhibit 3. Beer would remain the top priority, according to Mr. Busch.

Because of the company's vertical integration strategy, knowledge concerning the economics of the various industries in which Anheuser-Busch competed increased, the

[7]Jabbonsky, "What Keeps A-B Hot?" p. 22.

[8]"How Anheuser Brews Its Winners," p. 18.

[9]Jabbonsky, "What Keeps A-B Hot?" p. 22.

EXHIBIT 2 Anheuser-Busch Companies—Business Segments

Beer and Beer-Related Companies		
Company	**Year Founded**	**Activities**
Anheuser-Busch	1852	It ranked as the world's largest brewer, selling 80.7 million barrels of beer in 1989, and had been the industry leader since 1957. It distributed 14 naturally brewed products through 950 independent beer wholesalers and 10 company-owned wholesalers. Barrels sold had increased by 60.8 percent since 1980.
Busch Agricultural Resources	1962	It processed barley into malt. In 1989, it supplied 28 percent of the company's malt requirements. It grew and processed rice and had the capacity to meet 50 percent of the company's rice needs.
Container Recovery Corporation	1979	It recycled more than 350 million pounds of aluminum, or more than 9 billion cans, and 29 million pounds of glass, or 58 million bottles, in 1989.
Metal Container Corporation	1974	It operated 10 can and lid manufacturing plants. In 1989, it produced nearly 10 billion cans and 12 billion lids. This represented 40 percent of the company's container requirements. This subsidiary was rapidly expanding into the soft drink container market.
Anheuser-Busch International	1981	It was the company's international licensing and marketing subsidiary. The world beer market was 3.5 times as large as the domestic market. Sales were up 20 percent in 1989. The company exported to 40 countries and license-brewed in six countries.
Busch Media Group	1985	It was the company's in-house agency to purchase national broadcast media time and to develop and place local advertising schedules.
Anheuser-Busch Investment Capital Corp.	1984	It shared equity positions with qualified partners in A-B distributorships. It had invested in 16 wholesale dealerships.
Promotional Products Group	N/A	It was responsible for licensing, development, sales, and warehousing of the company's promotional merchandise. In 1989, more than 1,500 new promotional items were created and approximately 5,000 different items were available at any one time.
Busch Creative Services	1980	It was a full-service business and marketing communications company, selling its services to Anheuser-Busch and other Fortune 500 companies. In 1986, it acquired Innervision Productions, which produced video programming and industrial films. In 1986, it acquired Optimus, which was a post-production facility.
St. Louis Refrigerator Car Company	1878	It was one of the company's transportation subsidiaries with three facilities. It provided commercial repair, rebuilding, maintenance, and inspection of railroad cars. The rail car division had record profits in 1989.

(Continued on next page)

Exhibit 2 *(Continued)*

| Manufacturers Railway Company | 1878 | This was the other transportation subsidiary. It operated 42 miles of track in the St. Louis area, 247 insulated railroad cars used to ship beer, 48 hopper cars, and 77 boxcars. It included a fleet of 240 specially designed trailers. It also ran the warehousing for eight brewery locations. |

Food Products Companies

Company	Year Founded	Activities
Campbell Taggart	1982	It had 75 plants and approximately 20,000 employees in the U.S., Spain, and France. It was a highly diversified food products company with operations in about 35 percent of the U.S. It consisted of the following divisions: bakery operations, refrigerated products, frozen food products (Eagle Crest Foods, Inc.), and international subsidiaries—Spain and France, and other interests—which made folding cartons.
Eagle Snacks	1978	It produced and distributed a premium line of snack foods and nuts. In 1984, it began self-manufacturing virtually all of its snack products, and in 1985 it purchased Cod Potato Chip Company. It continued to move toward its goal of gaining significant market share in the snack food industry (estimated sales in excess of $10 billion).

Entertainment

Company	Year Founded	Activities
Busch Entertainment	1959	It was the company's family entertainment subsidiary. It consisted of the Dark Continent (FL), The Old Country (VA), Adventure Island (FL), and Sesame Place (PA). These parks attracted 6.2 million people. In 1989, it acquired Sea World, Cypress Gardens, and Boardwalk and Baseball. The 1989 attendance at these parks was 14 million people.
Busch Properties	1970	It was the company's real estate development subsidiary with commercial properties in Virginia, Ohio, and California. It continued to develop a planned community, Kingsmill, in Williamsburg, VA.
St. Louis National Baseball Club	1953	St. Louis Cardinals.
Civic Center Corporation	1981	It owned Busch Stadium, the Civic Center, and two and three-fourths downtown city blocks used for parking.

N/A = not applicable.

quantity and quality of supply was better assured, and both packaging and raw materials were more strongly controlled. In cultivating internally developed businesses such as Eagle Snacks, Anheuser-Busch continued its philosophy of maintaining premium quality and quantity of supply and control of both packaging and raw materials through self-manufacture. In 1985, Eagle Snacks added plant capacity through the acquisition of Cape Cod Chip Company and through plant expansion.

Company Philosophy

Anheuser-Busch's stated philosophy was "Anheuser-Busch's vision of greatness is today a reality. But the company isn't about to rest on its history of achievement. There are many new challenges to be met, and, as always, Anheuser-Busch will lead the way, because we believe that excellence is not just the act of achievement, but the process of constantly striving to achieve even more. We also believe that while a single achievement may signify luck, a history of many achievements signifies great endeavor and the promise of more to come. Anheuser-Busch has lived that philosophy. And the result speaks for itself."[10]

Diversification Activities

The company acquired Sea World for $1.1 billion from Harcourt Brace Jovanovich in 1989. The acquisition consisted of three theme parks in central Florida: Boardwalk and Baseball (closed in January 1990 because it had never been profitable), Cypress Gardens (Winter Haven), and Sea World (Orlando). Harcourt Brace Jovanovich sold the parks because it had $2.9 billion of debt that occurred as it fought a 1987 hostile takeover bid from British publisher Robert Maxwell.

In 1989, Anheuser-Busch announced its plans to build a $300 million resort and theme park in Spain near Barcelona. The park would feature five theme villages—four of these would be China, Mexico, Polynesia, and old Western United States—to be opened in 1993. The resort would be modeled after the company's Kingsmill resort near Williamsburg, Virginia, and would feature a world-class hotel and conference center, 18-hole golf course, and swimming and tennis facilities.[11]

Because they did not meet objectives, a number of subsidiaries were sold in 1988 and 1989. Master Cellars Wines, Saratoga Spring Company, and Sante Mineral Water Company of the A-B Beverage Group were sold to Evian Waters of France. Busch Industrial Products Corporation (producer of yeast products) was sold to Gist-Brocades N.V. of the Netherlands. The majority interest in Exploration Cruise Lines was sold in 1988.

In 1985, the company became an investor in its first venture capital fund: Innoven, an established fund that has been very successful over the years. Anheuser-Busch gained exposure to new business areas being developed by the small start-up companies in which Innoven invested capital.

The company extended its research and development program with Interferon Sciences, which had been developing and clinically testing both material and recombinant forms of interferon, an antiviral agent found in the human body.

---

[10]Anheuser-Busch Companies, Inc., *Fact Book 1989/90*, p. 3.

[11]"Busch Plans Theme Park in Spain," *Tampa Tribune*, May 25, 1989, pp. 1D, 8D: Anheuser-Busch, *Annual Report 1990*, p. 31.

EXHIBIT 3 Financial Information for Business Segments (In Millions)

1989	Beer and Beer-Related[a]		Food Products	
Net Sales	7,405.7	78.1%	$1,803.0	19.0%
Operating Income	1,244.7	93.7	56.9	4.3
Depreciation and Amortization Expense	298.7	72.8	87.2	21.3
Capital Expenditures	846.6	78.6	120.2	11.2
Identifiable Assets	5,902.9	68.0	1,295.6	14.9
Corporate Assets				
Total Assets				
1988				
Net Sales	$6,902.0	77.3%	$1,680.9 $	18.8%
Operating Income	1,168.2	92.4	55.0	4.4
Depreciation and Amortization Expense	252.9	70.4	70.7	19.7
Capital Expenditures	785.4	82.6	100.9	10.6
Identifiable Assets	5,102.4	76.5	1,229.7	18.4
Corporate Assets				
Total Assets				
1987				
Net Sales	$6,375.8	76.4%	$1,627.2	19.5%
Operating Income	1,090.2	94.9	54.4	4.8
Depreciation and Amortization Expense	215.4	67.3	70.4	22.0
Capital Expenditures	630.4	74.9	149.1	17.7
Identifiable Assets	4,580.5	74.7	1,230.1	20.0
Corporate Assets				
Total Assets				
1986				
Net Sales	$5,892.0	76.0%	$1,552.7	20.0%
Operating Income	945.2	92.9	56.6	5.6
Depreciation and Amortization Expense	192.3	68.4	60.5	21.5
Capital Expenditures	544.8	68.5	100.9	20.6
Identifiable Assets	4,083.2	74.2	1,114.1	20.2
Corporate Assets				
Total Assets				
1985				
Net Sales	$5,412.6	77.3%	$1,416.4	20.2%
Operating Income	797.0	95.8	28.5	3.4
Depreciation and Amortization Expense	161.7	68.5	53.2	22.5
Capital Expenditures		76.7	103.7	17.3
Identifiable Assets				20.2
Corporate Assets				
Total Assets				

[a]In 1989, Communication and Transportation were included in this segment. It was part of Diversified Operations in previous years.
[b]In 1989, Entertainment became a principal business segment. It was part of Diversified Operations in previous years.
[c]Before 1989, Diversified Operations was a business segment. Notes a and b show how it was eliminated.
Source: Anheuser-Busch *Annual Report 1989, 1988, and 1985*, pp. 58–59; p. 46; and p. 50.

Entertainment		Diversified Operations[c]		Eliminations		Consolidated
$ 286.3	3.0%			(13.7)	(0.1)%	$9,481.3
27.1	2.0				0.0	1,328.7
24.4	5.9				0.0	410.3
109.9	10.2				0.0	1,076.7
1,493.4	17.1				0.0	8,691.9
						343.8
						$9,025.7
		$361.8	4.18%	($20.6)	(0.2)%	$8,924.1
		40.9	3.2		0.9	1,264.1
		35.4	9.9		0.0	359.0
		64.2	6.8		0.0	950.5
		340.0	5.1		0.0	6,673.0
						436.8
						$7,109.8
		$366.1	4.3%	($19.4)	(0.2)%	$8,349.7
		4.0	0.3		0.0	1,148.6
		34.3	10.7		0.0	320.1
		62.3	7.4		0.0	841.8
		325.0	5.3		0.0	6,135.6
						412.3
						$6,547.9
		$ 32.4	4.2%	($21.0)	(0.2)%	$7,754.3
		15.6	1.5		0.0	1,018.0
		28.4	10.1		0.0	281.2
		87.1	10.9		0.0	796.2
		307.0	5.6		0.0	5,504.9
						393.2
						$5,898.1
		$189.6	2.7%	($13.9)	(0.2)%	$7,000.3
		6.8	0.8		0.0	823.3
		21.2	9.0		0.0	236.1
		36.1	6.0		0.0	601.0
		174.6	3.8		0.0	4,626.1
						495.3
						$5,121.4

"Along with quality, Anheuser-Busch is committed to growth and innovation. That commitment has seen the company through rough times—two World Wars, Prohibition, and the Great Depression. Although hundreds of breweries succumbed to difficult times like these and closed their doors, Anheuser-Busch survived and grew. During these trying periods, the company devised innovative ways to use its resources, its people, and its expertise. But in good times as well as bad, the company has always realized that while you have to do the best you can in the present, you must always keep your eyes turned toward the future."[12]

In planning for the future, Anheuser-Busch would continue its long-term commitment to diversification. These efforts were to be maintained as long as they were consistent with meeting the company's objectives.

THE PRODUCT

Beer uniquely fits contemporary lifestyles. The five hallmarks of beer as a consumer beverage are convenience, moderation, health, value, and thirst-quenching properties. Each member of the Anheuser-Busch family of 14 beers was positioned to take advantage of this lifestyle. Exhibit 4 shows the target market for each of the company's beers.

Domestic consumption of alcoholic beverages was declining by about 2 percent annually.[13] Exhibit 5 provides information on the consumption of beer by segments

---

[12]Fact Book 1989/90, p. 3.

[13]"Beverage Industry," *Value Line*, November 23, 1990, p. 1533.

EXHIBIT 4   Anheuser-Busch Beers

Beer	Class	Target Market
Budweiser	Premium	Any demographic or ethnic group and any region of the country
Bud Light	Light	Young to middle-age males
Bud Dry	Premium dry	New taste
Michelob	Superpremium	Contemporary adults
Michelob Light	Light	Young, active, upscale drinker with high-quality lifestyle
Michelob Dry	Dry	Yuppies
Busch	Popular	Consumers who prefer lighter-tasting beer at a value
Busch Light	Light	Popular-priced light beer
Natural Light	Light	Beverage to go with good food
LA	Low alcohol	Health-conscious consumers (ceased production May 1990)
O'Doul's	Nonalcoholic	Great-tasting beer without alcohol
King Cobra	Malt liquor	Contemporary male adults, aged 21–34
Carlsberg	Lager	Import market
Elephant Malt Liquor	Malt liquor	Consumers who enjoy imported beer

(popular, premium, superpremium, light, low-alcohol, imported, malt liquor, and ale), and growth rates by segments and per capita consumption of beer, wine, distilled spirits, and coolers. The only projected growth segments for beer appeared to be light beer and imported beers; all other beer segments had a projected negative growth factor. Some of the reasons for the decline in alcohol consumption were the rising health consciousness among consumers and the focused attention on the dangers of drinking and driving. Also, the Census Bureau indicated a drop in the 20- to 39-year-old age group (see Exhibit 6).

The perennial beer drinkers' preferences can and do change. Dry beer and nonalcoholic beer appeared to be successful in the test markets, but their true staying power remained unknown. For example, LA beer was dropped from the Anheuser-Busch line in 1990 because it lost its positioning when the company introduced O'Doul's brand of nonalcoholic beer.

Anheuser-Busch had 13 breweries located in 10 states, with an annual capacity of 91 million barrels of beer (see Exhibit 7). The 13th brewery at Centerville, Georgia, became operational in 1992 at a cost of approximately $300 million; its annual capacity was 6 million barrels. The expansion by Anheuser-Busch was the opposite of other brewers, which had been consolidating capacity. Mr. Busch saw "...expansion as necessary for 'market penetration and growth,' never blinking from Anheuser-Busch's projected 50-share by the mid-1990s."[14]

In order to meet the increasing demand for its beer, Anheuser-Busch developed an extensive expansion and modernization program. A 3.6-million barrel expansion at the Newark brewery was completed in 1990, and the capacity at the Tampa brewery was to be expanded by 800,000 barrels to 2.7 million. Mini-expansions were occurring at six other plants, and, when completed, would add approximately 2.5 million barrels of capacity.

Mr. Busch, talking about the cost of the ingredients (barley, rice, corn, hops, and others) to make beers, said, "We pay premium to the market because we demand the highest quality ingredients that money can buy. We have the highest cost of ingredients of anybody in the brewing industry. I can prove it to you. We must make sure that we are the lowest-cost producer."[15] Mr. Busch went on to say, "Quality comes first." Mr. Busch's statements tied directly into the primary reason the company gives for Anheuser-Busch's outstanding record of achievement: "Quality—first and most importantly, Anheuser-Busch believes in quality. Quality is never sacrificed for economic reasons—or for any other reason. The company is firmly convinced that its belief in and strict adherence to quality is the fundamental, irreplaceable ingredient in its successful performance for more than 100 years. That quality is there for everybody to see, to taste, to experience, and to enjoy. 'Somebody still cares about quality' is more than a corporate slogan at Anheuser-Busch. It's a way of life."[16]

PROMOTION

Anheuser-Busch, probably the largest sponsor of sporting events, racing vehicles, and broadcasts, had its beers affiliated with sports for years (see Exhibit 8). In 1989, the company spent $32 million on advertising during the Olympic games.

---

[14]Jabbonsky, "What Keeps A-B Hot?" p. 28.

[15]Ibid.

[16]*Fact Book 1989/90*, p. 3.

EXHIBIT 5   Apparent Beer Consumption by Segment (Barrels in Millions)

	1970		1975		1980		1985	
	Barrels	Share	Barrels	Share	Barrels	Share	Barrels	Share
Popular	71.6	58.3%	65.4	43.5%	30.0	16.9%	33.3	18.2%
Premium	46.1	37.5	71.6	47.6	102.3	57.5	86.1	47.1
Superpremium	1.1	0.9	5.0	3.3	11.5	6.5	8.8	4.8
Light	—	—	2.8	1.9	22.1	12.4	39.4	21.6
Low Alcohol	—	—	—	—	—	—	0.4	0.2
Imported	0.9	0.7	1.7	1.1	4.6	2.6	7.9	4.3
Malt Liquor	3.1	2.5	3.8	2.5	5.5	3.1	5.5	3.0
Ale	—	—	—	—	1.9	1.1	1.3	0.7
Total	122.8	100.0%	150.3	100.0%	177.9	100.0%	182.7	100.0%

	1990		1995		2000	
	Barrels	Share	Barrels	Share	Barrels	Share
Popular	30.5	16.5%	28.0	15.4%	26.0	14.4%
Premium	81.5	44.0	75.7	41.6	72.5	40.2
Superpremium	7.0	3.8	6.9	3.8	6.8	3.8
Light	49.0	26.4	52.0	28.6	54.0	30.0
Low Alcohol	0.1	0.1	0.1	0.1	0.1	0.1
Imported	11.0	5.9	13.5	7.4	16.0	8.9
Malt Liquor	5.2	2.8	4.7	2.6	4.2	2.3
Ale	1.0	0.5	0.9	0.5	0.7	0.4
Total	185.3	100.0%	181.8	100.0%	180.3	100.0%

Source: *Impact Data Bank,* 1988 ed. Table 4–E, p. 30; Table 4–6, p. 31; Table 8–A, p. 75.

Average Annual Compound Growth Rate

Segment	1970–75	1975–80	1980–85	1985–90	1990–95	1995–2000
Popular	−1.8%	−14.4%	2.1%	−1.7%	−1.7%	−1.5%
Premium	9.2	7.4	−3.4	−1.1	−1.5	−0.9
Superpremium	35.4	18.1	−5.2	−4.5	−0.3	−0.3
Light	—	51.2	12.3	4.5	1.2	0.8
Low Alcohol	—	—	+	−24.2	—	—
Imported	13.5	22.2	11.6	6.8	4.2	3.5
Malt Liquor	4.2	7.7	—	−1.1	−2.0	−2.2
Ale	N/A	N/A	−7.3	−5.1	−2.1	−4.9
Total	4.1%	3.4%	0.5%	0.3%	−0.4%	−0.2%

N/A = Not Available
Source: *Impact DataBank,* 1988 Ed., Table 8B, p. 76.

Per Capita Consumption (Gallons per Adult)

	Year	
Category	1989E	2000E
Wine	2.54	2.12
Distilled Spirits	2.15	1.63
Beers	33.79	29.37
Coolers	0.62	0.37
Total Alcoholic Beverages	39.10	33.48

Source: *Market Watch,* April 1990, p. 24.

EXHIBIT 6　U.S. Population Projections[a]

	1990	1995	2000	2005	2010	2015	2020	2025
All Ages[a]	250,410,000	260,138,000	268,266,000	275,604,000	282,575,000	288,997,000	294,364,000	298,252,000
Under 5 years	18,408,000	17,799,000	16,898,000	16,611,000	16,899,000	17,213,000	17,095,000	16,664,000
5 to 9 years	18,378,000	18,759,000	18,126,000	17,228,000	16,940,000	17,225,000	17,542,000	17,428,000
10 to 14 years	17,284,000	18,847,000	19,208,000	18,575,000	17,670,000	17,380,000	17,674,000	18,000,000
15 to 19 years	17,418,000	17,567,000	19,112,000	19,477,000	18,839,000	17,930,000	17,642,100	17,940,000
20 to 24 years	18,698,000	17,482,000	17,600,000	19,109,000	19,453,000	18,818,000	17,931,000	17,657,000
25 to 29 years	21,511,000	18,966,000	17,736,000	17,822,000	19,310,000	19,642,000	19,020,000	18,144,100
30 to 34 years	22,414,000	21,996,000	19,413,000	18,175,000	18,262,000	19,750,000	20,080,000	19,457,000
35 to 39 years	20,220,000	22,244,000	21,820,000	19,274,000	18,041,000	18,115,000	19,576,000	19,906,000
40 to 44 years	17,677,000	20,092,000	22,091,000	21,678,000	19,161,000	17,931,000	18,015,000	19,463,000
45 to 49 years	13,947,000	17,489,000	19,885,000	21,892,000	21,482,000	18,980,000	17,769,000	17,855,000
50 to 54 years	11,540,000	13,808,000	17,338,000	19,736,000	21,725,000	21,328,000	18,866,000	17,679,000
55 to 59 years	10,623,000	11,229,000	13,459,000	16,917,000	19,259,000	21,195,000	20,811,000	18,422,000
60 to 64 years	10,741,000	10,096,000	10,699,000	12,846,000	16,171,000	18,420,000	20,276,000	19,925,000
65 to 69 years	10,251,000	10,056,000	9,491,000	10,106,000	12,163,000	15,319,000	17,467,000	19,257,000
70 to 74 years	8,122,000	8,874,000	8,752,000	8,304,000	8,876,000	10,705,000	13,506,000	15,420,000
75 to 79 years	6,105,000	6,607,000	7,282,000	7,246,000	6,913,000	7,419,000	8,981,000	11,378,000
80 to 84 years	3,828,000	4,315,000	4,735,000	5,287,000	5,295,000	5,068,000	5,462,000	6,647,000
85 to 89 years	2,065,000	2,433,000	2,803,000	3,141,000	3,554,000	3,587,000	3,459,000	3,769,000
90 to 94 years	873,000	1,074,000	1,302,000	1,539,000	1,759,000	2,017,000	2,061,000	2,014,000
95 to 99 years	260,000	330,000	417,000	520,000	631,000	738,000	864,000	903,000
100 years and over	56,000	76,000	100,000	131,000	171,000	217,000	266,000	325,000
Median age in years	33.0	34.7	36.4	37.8	39.0	39.5	40.2	41.0
Mean age in years	35.4	36.2	37.1	38.1	39.1	39.9	40.7	41.5

[a]Includes armed forces overseas.
Source: U.S. Department of Commerce, Bureau of the Census, Population Series, p. 14.

EXHIBIT 7　U.S. Production Facilities

Brewery	Year Opened	Capacity (In Millions of Barrels)
St. Louis	1880	12.6
Newark	1951	5.8
Los Angeles	1954	12.1
Tampa	1959	1.9
Houston	1966	9.7
Columbus	1968	6.4
Jacksonville	1969	6.7
Merrimack	1970	3.1
Williamsburg	1972	9.0
Fairfield	1976	3.7
Baldwinsville	1982	8.2
Fort Collins	1988	5.9
Total in 1990		85.1
Centerville	1992	6.0
Total in 1992		91.0

EXHIBIT 8   Anheuser-Busch Companies, Sports Affiliation and Sponsorships

Budweiser		**Bud Light**	
Horse Racing	Irish Derby	Powerboat Racing	Powerboat Racing Team
	Breeders' Cup	Bowling	ABC Masters
	Budweiser International	Triathlons	Ironman World
Hydroplane Racing	Miss Budweiser		Championship
CART/Indy Car	Truesports Indy Car		U.S. Triathlon Series
Drag Racing	King Funny Car		
NASCAR	Junior Johnson Ford	**Busch**	
CART/NASCAR	Budweiser International	NASCAR	Official Beer of NASCAR
	Race of Champions		Busch Pole Award
Olympics	Corporate Sponsor		Busch Clash
PGA Golf	Anheuser-Busch Golf	Pool	British Pool League
	Classic		
Boxing	Golden Gloves	**Michelob**	
PBA Bowling	Budweiser Hall of Fame	Skiing	Team Michelob
Soccer	Major Indoor Soccer	Golf	Golf Advisory Staff
	League		
	U.S. Soccer Federation		
	World Cup		
	U.S. National Team		
Shooting	Shooting Exhibitions by		
	Willis Corbett		
Surfing	Pro Surfing Tour		

Source: Anheuser-Busch Companies, Inc., *Fact Book 1989/90*, p. 61.

The alcoholic beverage industry spent a total of $1,318,900,000 on advertising in 1988. The advertising mix by medium and by alcoholic beverage industry segment (beer, distilled spirits, wine, and coolers) is shown in Exhibit 9. The brewers spent nearly $900 million on advertising, or 68.3 percent of the total industry expenditures. The number one advertising medium for brewers continued to be television; magazines remained as the primary advertising medium for distilled spirits marketers.

Total media spending by the brewers for 1988 was more than double the level for 1980. The per-case expenditure for beer had more than doubled during the same period, from 18 cents to 37 cents. Anheuser-Busch's advertising expenditures increased by 8 percent to $385 million, or 61.6 percent of the company's total for promotion. The company's total for 1988 increased 3.2 percent over 1987. Anheuser-Busch's advertising expenditures were 42.8 percent of total brewers' expenditures. Adolph Coors increased its advertising outlays by 30.7 percent to $126 million. Miller Brewing cut its media expenditures by $12.8 million, or 6.3 percent, from $202 million to $189 million, or 21 percent of the total industry expenditures. G. Heileman Brewing (Bond Corporation) increased its expenditures by 41 percent to $42 million. Sam Frank, vice president of marketing for Heileman, said, "The way you try to build a regional brand is with regional affiliations to prevent more share erosion by national brands. You have to play

EXHIBIT 9   Alcoholic Beverage Advertising Expenditures by Medium[a] (In Millions)

Medium	Beer	Distilled Spirits	Wine	Coolers	Total
Television	$679.7	$ 0.5	$64.2	$75.3	$ 819.7
Radio	144.8	1.0	11.6	3.9	161.3
Total Broadcast	824.5	1.5	75.8	79.2	981.0
Magazines	18.0	179.6	13.2	0.9	211.7
Outdoor	22.5	34.1	0.6	0.9	58.1
Newspapers	33.5	17.9	4.7	1.7	57,8
Newspaper Supplements	0.8	7.4	1.7	0.2	10.1
Total Print and Outdoor	74.8	239.0	20.3	3.7	337.8
	$899.3	$240.5	$96.2	$82.9	$1,318.9

[a]Columns may not add up because of rounding.
Source: *Impact DataBank*, Vol. 19, August 15 and September 15, 1989, p. 4.

on the big boy's turf, so to speak, if you want to prove to consumers that you're as good as national brands. You've got to advertise heavily."[17] G. Heileman sales declined by 10.4 percent despite the substantial increase in the marketing budget.

Charles Fruit, vice president of corporate media for Anheuser-Busch, said, "Our competitors continue to focus the majority of their television advertising in sports sponsorships and I would think that would continue to be a competitive area." In 1988, Anheuser-Busch allocated $11 million to introduce Michelob Dry on a national basis, while decreasing Michelob Light's expenditures from $33 million to $18 million. Mr. Fruit commented, "With the emergence of Michelob Dry, the whole Michelob family is registering positive trends again. Our regular Michelob brand had experienced the same softness. Dry invigorated the entire family."[18]

Anheuser-Busch Promotional Products Group had approximately 10,000 different items available at any one time. This included such items as caps, glassware, mugs, clothing, and key chains, all bearing the A & B eagle, Clydesdale, or beer-brand logos. Each year more than 1,500 new promotional items were created and authorized.

Anheuser-Busch acted as the Rolling Stones' primary U.S. sponsor for their 1989 27-city tour. A 30-second TV spot, "Honky Tonk Woman," featured the concert with a Bud bottle showing up every now and then.

In 1990, Anheuser-Busch announced its "market-share strategy," which was to pull millions of advertising dollars out of radio and television to spend more on "grassroots" events and point-of-purchase promotions. This new strategy was announced to combat the price discounting in the industry (see Exhibit 10). According to Robert

---

[17]"Total Media Spending Drops 3.9% in '88 as Brewers Increase Outlays to $900 Million," *Impact*, Vol. 19, Nos. 16, 17, August 15 and September 1, 1989, p. 4.

[18]Ibid., pp. 3–4.

EXHIBIT 10   Anheuser-Busch Advertising Expenditures, 1989 and 1990

Media	1989	1990
Network Television	$181,467	$129,009
Spot Television	94,835	91,646
Syndicated Television	10,753	13,703
Cable Television	26,300	26,788
Network Radio	7,707	983
Spot Radio	42,073	21,147
Magazines	8,834	7,767
Newspapers	9,537	3,989
Newspaper Magazines	399	243
Outdoor	6,148	6,058
Total Measured Media	388,055	301,331
Total Unmeasured	203,400	157,900
Total	$591,455	$459,231

Source: *Advertising Age,* September 25, 1991, p. 4.

Weinberg, beer analyst, "Relative to competition, Anheuser-Busch was probably overadvertising.[19]

PRICING

The brewers were in the midst of a prolonged beer price war. During 1989, both Coors, the nation's fourth-largest brewery, and Miller, number two, had been aggressively promoting and discounting their prices in order to boost volume for several of their key products. In November, Anheuser-Busch joined the price war. Prices for Budweiser, the number one selling brand of beer, were discounted.

Value Line expected the price war "to lead to yet another industry shakeout. The playing field has narrowed considerably in recent years, but we think yet more changes are in the offing." They went on to say, "The most important questions are not who will be the winner and loser, but how long the price war will last and just what exactly do the victors win?" *Value Line* expected prices to continue on a downward trend and thought that the industry players recognized that there were significant long-term benefits at stake. One share point was approximately equal to 1 million barrels of beer.[20]

Most economists saw continuing recession at least through the first quarters of 1992. Historically, beer demand tended to hold up well during periods of downturns or recessions, but combined with the excise tax and inflation, brewers could experience a downturn as well. Anheuser-Busch's pricing strategy varied somewhat by market. Actually, by offering 14 different types of beer, there was a product to satisfy each price point.

---

[19]Richard Gibson, "Bud Puts Stress on Promotions, Trims TV Ads," *Wall Street Journal,* February 21, 1990, p. B–5.

[20]"Beverage Industry," *Value Line,* November 1989, p. 1528.

DISTRIBUTION CHANNELS

The company distributed its beer in the United States and the Caribbean through a network of 10 company-owned wholesale operations, employing approximately 1,600 people, and about 950 independently owned wholesale companies (see Exhibit 11). The independent wholesalers employed approximately 30,000 people. Canadian and European distribution was achieved through special arrangements with foreign brewing companies.

The Anheuser-Busch Investment Capital Corporation, a subsidiary company, was formed in 1984 to share equity positions with qualified partners in Anheuser-Busch distributorships. This subsidiary provided operating general partners to function as independent wholesalers while increasing their equity and building toward total ownership. Anheuser-Busch Investment Capital Corporation played a key role in strengthening the brewer-wholesaler team.

When Mr. Busch was asked if "strong brewers and beer products make strong wholesalers or strong wholesalers make strong brewers," Busch laid the "chicken-or-egg theory" to rest, noting succinctly, "It takes both." Henry King, former president of the United States Brewing Association, said, "I've been with August when we've been driving along and he's spotted an A-B distributor's truck." Recalled King, "He pulled up behind it and spoke into his little cassette to dictate a memo to his secretary to send a letter of compliment to the wholesaler because his truck was beautifully cleaned and

EXHIBIT 11:   Distribution Map

★ Company-Owned Wholesale Operations

• Breweries

Note: Numbers in each state represent the number of independently owned wholaleships

everything. Had that truck been dirty, there would have been a letter reprimanding him as well."[21]

Busch counted on the wholesalers as "one of our most important assets, who provide critical service to retailers. Personal service is key…they are the frontline merchandisers for the entire system and…indispensable to the system." "Together with our wholesalers," Busch stated, "we share a commitment to provide the consumer with the highest quality, best tasting, and freshest beer products through the three-tier system, in which the brewer, wholesaler, and retailer each play an important role." He went on to say, "Strong products, suppliers, wholesalers, and service equal retailer profitability. Quality to the consumer and product presentation equal sales success."[22]

THE EXTERNAL ENVIRONMENT

Competition

In 1970, the top five brewers in the United States comprised 33.3 percent of sales. In 1990, this had increased to 89.3 percent share of sales. During this same time period, Anheuser-Busch's market share increased from 18.1 percent to 43.4 percent. Miller Brewing, Stroh's Brewery, G. Heileman, and Adolph Coors increased their market share as well. Exhibit 12 illustrates the market shares of the leading brewers in the United States.

The big market share shift in the decade of the 1980s was accomplished by Anheuser-Busch, as Miller Brewing remained at approximately the same level. A major

---

[21]Jabbonsky, "What Keeps A-B Hot?" p. 28.
[22]Ibid.

EXHIBIT 12   Sales of Leading U.S. Brewers (In Thousands of Barrels)

	1970		1980		1985		1990	
	Volume	Market Share	Volume	Market Share	Volume	Market Share	Volume	Market Share
Anheuser-Busch	22,202	18.1%	50,160	28.2%	68,000	37.1%	86,400	43.4%
Miller Brewing	5,150	4.2	37,300	21.0	37,100	20.3	43,550	21.9
Adolph Coors Company	7,277	5.9	13,779	7.7	14,738	8.1	19,250	9.7
Stroh Brewery	3,276	2.7	6,161	3.5	23,400	12.8	16,200	8.1
G. Heileman Brewing	3,000	2.4	13,270	7.4	16,200	8.8	12,250	6.2
Top 5 Total	40,905	33.3	120,670	67.8	159,438	87.1	177,650	89.3
Other Domestic	80,995	68.0	52,830	29.6	15,662	8.6	12,246	6.2
Total Domestic	121,900	99.3	173,500	97.4	175,100	95.7	189,896	95.5
Imports	900	0.7	4,600	2.8	7,900	4.3	9,000	4.5
Grand Total	122,800	100.0%	177,900	100.0%	183,000	100.0%	198,896	100.0%

Source: *Impact*, Vol. 19, Nos. 16 & 17, August 15 and September 1, 1990, p. 3, *Wall Street Journal*, January 15, 1991, p. B-1.

part of Stroh Brewery's growth occurred with the acquisition of Joseph Schlitz Brewing Company in 1982, and F&M Schaefer in 1981.

The Market Share Leader   Anheuser-Busch set a corporate objective of 50 percent market share by the mid-1990s. In 1990, the company's market share was 43.4 percent, compared with 37.1 percent share in 1985, and 28.2 percent a decade before.

The Market Share Challenger   Miller Brewing was Anheuser-Busch's prime competitor from the time Philip Morris Company acquired Miller in 1970. Its market share in 1970 was 4.2 percent (5.1 million barrels), ranking it as seventh in the industry. The company experienced rapid growth in the 1970s due to the successful introduction of "Lite" beer. Although growth had been rapid during the 1970s, market share remained relatively flat through the 1980s. Offering eight different brands, Miller ranked second in the industry. Anheuser-Busch countered Miller with two separate strategies. First, the company increased its advertising budgets, taking on Miller in head-to-head competition. Second, Anheuser-Busch developed a strategy of flanking each of Miller's products in every beer category with two Anheuser-Busch beer products (e.g., premium beers— Budweiser and Busch flanked Miller High Life).

In December 1989, Miller Brewing introduced a new nonalcoholic beer called Sharp's. At about the same time, Anheuser-Busch delivered its planned O'Doul's brand. The two new brands challenged the industry leader in nonalcoholic beers, Kingsbury, brewed by G. Heileman Brewing, and a host of imported brands such as Cardinal Brewery's Moussy, Binding Brauerei's Clausthaler, and Guinness' Kaliber. Nonalcoholic beer represented less than one-half of 1 percent of domestic beer consumption, but it was growing at a 6 percent to 15 percent rate yearly.[23] Supposedly, Miller Brewing did not fully test market Sharp's in order to beat Anheuser-Busch into the marketplace.

Stroh Brewery   In 1981, the Stroh Brewery purchased F&M Schaefer and closed its Detroit brewery (7.2-million-barrel capacity). On April 27, 1982, the Joseph Schlitz Brewing Company was merged into Stroh Brewery, resulting in Stroh becoming the third-largest brewer. The company shipped 16.2 million barrels of beer in 1990, representing an 8.1 percent market share, which was a decline from its peak of 12.8 percent share in 1985.

Adolph Coors Company   The fourth-largest brewer, Adolph Coors Company. had an 11.8 percent volume increase in sales in 1990. This increase was the largest of any of the major brewers in the United States. It was enough to move Coors from fifth place to fourth in market share.

In September 1989, Coors proposed the acquisition of Stroh Brewing Company for $425 million. The acquisition was opposed in the federal courts by S&P Company, a privately held company that owned Falstaff, Pabst, Pearl, and General Brewing Companies. S&P Company alleged that the merger would violate the antitrust laws. In addition, G. Heileman Brewing was considering antitrust action against Coors as a purchaser. (Heileman also had considered making a bid for parts of the Stroh Company.) The merger had to be approved by the U.S. Department of Justice. Peter H. Coors, president of Coors Brewery, had commented on why his company was interested in purchasing Stroh's, "You can't survive long-term with a nine percent market share." The transaction was supposed to close in early 1990, but Coors eventually withdrew its offer.[24]

---

[23]"This Safe Suds Is For You," *Newsweek,* March 5, 1990, p. 42.

[24]"Insights," *Impact,* Vol. 19, No. 20, October 15, 1989, p. 12, "Coors May Take a Gulp of a Rival Brew," *Business Week,* October 21, 1989, p. 70.

G. Heileman Brewing   The United States' fifth-largest brewer, Heileman had been very effective in competing against Anheuser-Busch in regional markets. It successfully developed and implemented a strategy of acquiring struggling local brewers at low cost. After acquiring the new brewery, Heileman reintroduced its brands with an aggressive marketing plan. Anheuser-Busch countered with a strategy focused on heavy price competition from its Busch brand. Although G. Heileman halted its planned expansion into the Southwest market, the company's market share grew from 2.4 percent (3 million barrels) in 1970 to 8.8 percent (16.2 million barrels) in 1985. The company's earnings from the brewing industry declined by 11 percent in 1985, and it closed its small Phoenix plant (500,000 barrels).

In a hostile takeover in 1987, Bond Holding Corporation, an Australian conglomerate involved in the world beer market, acquired G. Heileman Brewing Company. Since the takeover, Heileman faced weakening sales and deteriorating finances. In 1989, Heileman suffered its third year of declining beer shipments. In Chicago, Heileman's largest market, supermarket sales of Old Style slipped to 15 percent market share from 21 percent.[25] In April 1990, Bond announced that Heileman was close to restructuring its bank loans. The banks would write off the debt and take an equity investment in the company. Heileman management had previously announced plans to sell some unneeded breweries and, possibly, some minor brands. However, market share further deteriorated in 1990 to 6.2 percent, which caused Heileman to lose its fourth place position to Coors. A continuation of the price war would cause further deterioration of the weaker beer companies.

Niche Strategies   During the 1980s, many micro-breweries and boutique-type breweries were started. These breweries had a different target market from the national firms. The target market for these breweries was the connoisseur, the moderate beer drinker who was particular and sought a certain taste. Actually, the select target market for the distinctive taste cut across the traditional demographic lines and was not limited to any one class.

International Competition   Anheuser-Busch's world market share was approximately 9.5 percent. Miller Brewing, which was in second place, had approximately 5 percent of the world market. The top two brewers were American, and the next three (Heineken NV—4 percent, Kerin Brewery Co.—3.1 percent, and Bond Corporation—3.1 percent) were European. These top five brewers had approximately 30 percent of the world market. The annual growth rate for the entire world market was 3 percent to 4 percent a year.[26] The per capita consumption of beer for the top 20 countries ranged from 38.73 gallons in West Germany to 16.03 gallons in Venezuela. The United States was ranked in 12th place with 13.99 gallons. Eight nations exceeded the 30-gallon per capita figure.[27]

Leonard Goldstein, president of Miller Brewing Company, said, "I think U.S. brewers have a long way to go in the overseas markets...we're in more than 50 countries...they are all very small situations to get our foot in the door...[it allows] us [to] see what innovation is around the world."[28]

The international market was estimated to be three and one-half to four times the size of the U.S. market. In the Far East and Europe, the consumption of alcoholic bever-

---

[25]Ira Teinowitz. "Heileman Close to Deal with Banks," *Advertising Age,* April 16, 1990, p. 66.

[26]Paul Heme, "King of Beers in Bitter Battle in Britain," *Wall Street Journal,* June 9, 1988, p. 26.

[27]*Impact Data Bank—1988 Edition,* Table 2-AA, p. 20.

[28]"Miller's Drive to Innovate," *Impact,* Vol. 20, No. 9, May 1, 1990, p. S.

ages was on the rise. All the U.S. brewers, except Coors, were largely pursuing a share of these markets. *Value Line* "believes overseas sales will play an increasing larger role in the results of brewers…with 1990 easing of economic barriers in Europe."[29] The world market for beer, including the U.S. market, was approximately 700 million barrels.

Anheuser-Busch International, the company's international licensing and marketing subsidiary, was formed in 1981 to develop and explore markets outside the United States. Budweiser was introduced into England in 1984 and four years later had eked out only a 1 percent share of the market. It was the same Bud that was sold in the United States. By contrast, Australian Foster's, made by Elder IXL, modified its brew to appeal to British tastes. Foster's had a 6 percent market share after seven years. Norman Strauss, British marketing consultant, said, "Foster got into the British later drinking culture with the humor of its ads [Paul Hogan of *Crocodile Dundee* is the Foster spokesperson] and an unerring eye for the pub lifestyle." Budweiser's first approach was to sell America without addressing British pub culture. Anheuser-Busch went through three advertising agencies in the past two years. John Dunsmore, a beer analyst, said, "The day Anheuser stops gaining share in the States' beer market, they'll go into overdrive in trying to develop their international business." He went on to say, "They could well be too late."[30]

Mr. Busch states, "As we go along, we are learning how to deal in these international markets from our partners.[31] Budweiser was licensed-brewed in seven countries and exported to more than 30 others. Additional expansions were planned. Budweiser was marketed in Japan as a superpremium beer and led in the category. Bud had great success in Japan and Korea. Anheuser-Busch's prominent partners around the world included Carlsberg, Guinness, Suntory, and Oriental Brewery.

Robert S. Weinberg, beer analyst, and consultant, said, "If you're talking about continuing to license and play the game as they are playing it…I think it is a very attractive and worthwhile game." He went on to say, "If you're talking about buying breweries and so forth, I don't think there are any great economies of scale in being an international brewing company."[32]

Social Values and Beer

Anheuser-Busch "is deeply concerned about the abuse of alcohol and the problem of driving while intoxicated. It supports the proposition that anything less than responsible consumption of alcoholic beverages is detrimental to the individual, society, and to the brewing industry."[33] The company was a leader in developing programs that supported this position.

Anheuser-Busch designed programs to meet the needs of its employees, its wholesalers, its retailers, and its customers. The programs covered the following areas: (1) consumer education programs—Know When to Say When, The Buddy System, and Pit Stop; (2) training retailer—TIPS (Training for Intervention Procedures by Servers of Alcohol), (3) designated-driver programs—Alert Cab and I'm Driving; (4) helping communities fight against alcohol abuse—Operation ALERT (Action and Leadership through Education Responsibility and Training; (5) helping employees deal with alcohol

---

[29]*Value Line,* November 23, 1990, p. 1533.

[30]*Impact Data Bank,* Table 4-AA, p. 43.

[31]Jabbonsky, "What Keeps A-B Hot?" p. 30.

[32]Ibid.

[33]*Fact Book 1989/90,* p. 33.

abuse—Employee Assistance Program; (6) company guidelines and policies—industry Advertising Code and Young Adult Marketing Guidelines; (7) underage drinking—SADD (Students against Driving Drunk); and (8) Alcohol Research Center, UCLA.

Legislation and Litigation

In recent years, Anheuser-Busch has become more active in monitoring and taking positions on issues that could have a major impact on the company. The Industry and Government Affairs Division expanded in order to identify and respond to such issues with specific programs.

Trademark Protection   A lawsuit, filed by G. Heileman Brewing and joined by Miller Brewing Company, against Anheuser-Busch's use of "LA" (low alcohol) as a brand name, was won by Anheuser-Busch with its claim that LA was a trademark and not a generic term. However, a short time later the company dropped LA from the product line when its O'Doul's brand was introduced.

Exclusive Distribution   The Malt Beverage Interbrand Competition Act of 1985 dealt with exclusive wholesale distribution rights for distributors within their territories. Indiana was the only state to forbid exclusive distribution contracts, and 27 states required the contracts.

In 1977, a Supreme Court decision ruled such exclusive contracts could be legal if the contracts did not hamper competition, but that a decision would be made on a case-by-case basis. Distributors and brewers said that this court decision created lawsuits by inviting competitors, both wholesalers and retailers, to challenge the competitor's exclusive distribution contracts.

A new bill, which was cleared by the Senate Judiciary Committee, would preserve the right to sue for antitrust violations. The 140-member U.S. Brewers Association and the 2,000-member National Beer Wholesaler Association lobbied for the bill, because they felt it would clarify the existing antitrust law. Opponents to the bill, including the Federal Trade Commission, Senator Strom Thurmond, Senator Howard Metzenbaum, and numerous consumer groups, felt that exempting the beer industry from the antitrust laws would increase prices and reduce competition. In fact, the New York attorney general filed a class action lawsuit against Miller, Stroh, Heileman, and Anheuser-Busch claiming that their exclusive agreements with distributors caused price increases and decreased competition.

Kickbacks   Dennis P. Long, president of Anheuser-Busch, resigned in March 1988 when Joseph E. Martino, vice president of sales, and Michael A. Orloff, vice president for wholesaling, left the company after an internal investigation of kickbacks at Anheuser-Busch. Martino and Orloff were found guilty by a federal grand jury of fraud, conspiracy, and filing false tax returns. Mr. Long "was not accused of any wrongdoing, but stepped down because of what transpired under his nose."[34] "With Mr. Long's departure, Mr. Busch became president of Anheuser-Busch and kept this position until he appointed Mr. Stokes as president.

Minimum Drinking Age   The National Minimum Drinking Age Act of 1984 granted the federal government the authority to withhold federal highway funds from states that

---

[34]Jabbonsky, "What Keeps A-B Hot?" p. 26.

failed to raise their legal drinking age to 21 by 1986. Currently, all 50 states have mandated a 21-year-old minimum drinking age.

Anheuser-Busch and Minorities In 1983, the Reverend Jesse Jackson's campaign PUSH was directed against Anheuser-Busch Companies. PUSH accused the company of discriminating against blacks and encouraged minorities to boycott Anheuser-Busch's products. Using the battle cry "Bud Is a Dud," Jackson claimed the company did not do business with enough minorities, did not hire and promote black employees, did not patronize black-oriented community organizations, and did not have enough black wholesalers in the distribution system. Eventually, Wayman Smith, vice president of corporate affairs, was able to make the Reverend Jackson aware of the company's minority hiring and promotion practices, its support to minorities throughout the country, and the role of minority suppliers.

Excise Tax In 1988, Anheuser-Busch paid $781 million in state and federal excise taxes. The company "believes that excise taxes discriminate against both the industries involved and consumers."[35]

Warning Labels Congress passed legislation that went into effect in November 1989 requiring a warning statement to appear on all alcoholic beverage containers. The two-part statement read: "Government Warning: (1) According to the Surgeon General, women should not drink alcoholic beverages during pregnancy because of the risks of child defects. (2) Consumption of alcoholic beverages impairs your ability to operate machinery and may cause serious health problems." The legislation required this two-part statement and restricted state governments from requiring any additional statements.

Advertising and Marketing Restrictions There were proposals to ban beer and wine advertising from radio and television. In addition, some groups were calling for restriction of the brewing industry's ability to advertise or promote beer and wine at sporting events. Anheuser-Busch "strongly opposes such restrictions."[36]

Concentration and Possible Antitrust Review A knowledgeable beer market analyst had wondered if the Department of Justice would take or propose antitrust action as Anheuser-Busch's market share approached 50 percent. This growth over the past decade from 28.2 percent in 1980 to 43.4 percent in 1990 was accomplished in a maturing industry through internal expansion. If Anheuser-Busch attempted to grow by merger to achieve 50 percent market share, the Justice Department would probably have rejected the mergers based on the Herfindahl Index. Named for Orris Herfindahl, an economist, the index is a calculation based on the premise that market leaders have even greater economic power in an industry than can be assumed by simply looking at market share. A possibility existed that one of the remaining small brewers would ask the Justice Department for protection or relief under the antitrust laws.

FINANCIAL CONDITION

In 1989 Anheuser-Busch completed the company's most successful decade in its 147-year history (see Exhibits 13 and 14). During the 1980s, net sales increased by 287.7 percent

---

[35]*Fact Book 1989/90*, p. 54.

[36]Ibid., pp. 54–59.

EXHIBIT 13 10-Year Financial Summary—Balance Sheet and Other Information
(In Millions Except Per Share and Statistical Data)

	1980	1981	1982	1983	1984
Balance Sheet Information					
Working Capital	$ 26.3	$ 41.0	$ 60.2	$ 173.1	$ 71.5
Current Ratio	1.1	1.1	1.1	1.2	1.1
Plant and Equipment, Net	1,947.4	1,324.5	3,579.8	3,269.8	3,579.5
Long-Term Debt	743.8	862.2	1,029.9	1,003.1	879.5
Total Debt to Total Debt Plus Equity (%)	43.4	42.5	36.8[a]	32.8[a]	28.2[a]
Deferred Income Taxes	261.6	357.7	455.2	574.3	757.9
Shareholders' Equity	1,031.4	1,206.8	1,526.6	1,766.5	1,951.0
Return on Shareholders' Equity (%)	17.8	19.3	19.9[a]	18.0[a]	18.2[a]
Book Value per Share	3.81	4.43	5.27	6.09	6.91
Total Assets	2,449.7	2,938.1	3,965.2	4,386.8	4,592.5
Other Information					
Capital Expenditures	$ 590.0	$ 441.5	$ 380.9	$ 441.3	$ 532.3
Depreciation and Amortization	99.4	110.0	136.9	191.3	207.9
Total Payroll Cost	594.1	695.5	864.0	1,361.7	1,438.6
Effective Tax Rate (%)	35.7	33.2	40.0	43.7	43.5
Price/Earnings Ratio	7.3	8.9	11.0	9.6	9.8
Percentage of Pretax Profit on Gross Sales (%)	7.1	7.3	9.1	9.2	9.6
Market Price Range of Common Stock					
High	5¼	7⅜	11⅞	12⅞	12⅜
Low	3½	4½	6½	9¾	8⅞

	1985	1986	1987	1988	1989
Balance Sheet Information					
Working Capital	$ 116.0	$ (3.7)	$ 75.8	$ 15.2	$ (25.7)
Current Ratio	1.1	1.0	1.1	1.0	1.0
Plant and Equipment, Net	4,494.9	4,994.8	4,994.8	5,467.7	6,671.3
Long-Term Debt	904.7	1,164.0	1,422.6	1,615.3	3,307.3
Total Debt to Total Debt Plus Equity (%)	26.9[a]	31.6	33.0	34.2	52.4
Deferred Income Taxes	964.7	1.094.0	1,164.3	1,212.5	1,315.9
Shareholders' Equity	2,173.0	2,313.7	2,892.2	3,102.9	3,099.9
Return on Shareholders' Equity (%)	18.9[a]	20.5[a]	22.4	23.9	24.7
Book Value per Share	7.84	8.61	9.87	10.95	10.95
Total Assets	5,192.9	5,898.1	6,547.9	7,109.8	9,025.7
Other Information					
Capital Expenditures	$ 611.3	$ 796.2	$ 841.8	$ 950.5	$ 1,076.7
Depreciation and Amortization	240.0	281.2	320.1	359.0	410.3
Total Payroll Cost	1,559.1	1,640.9	1,790.5	1,818.2	1,954.2
Effective Tax Rate (%)	43.4	45.3	42.2	38.3	37.5
Price/Earnings Ratio	14.9	15.5	16.4	12.9	14.4
Percentage of Pretax Profit on Gross Sales (%)	10.1	11.2	11.7	12.0	11.9
Market Price Range of Common Stock					
High	22⅞	28⅝	39¾	34⅛	45⅞
Low	8⅞	20	26⅜	29⅛	30⅝

Note: All per share information reflects the September 12, 1986, two-for-one stock split and the June 14, 1985, three-for-one stock split. All amounts reflect the acquisition of Campbell-Taggart, as of November 2, 1982, and the acquisitions of Sea World as of December 1, 1989. Financial information prior to 1988 has been restated to reflect the adoption in 1988 of Financial Accounting Standards No. 94, Consolidation of Majority-Owned Subsidiaries.

[a]This percentage has been calculated by including convertible redeemable preferred stock as part of equity because it was convertible into common stock and was trading primarily on its equity characteristics.

Source: *Annual Report 1989*, pp. 62–63.

EXHIBIT 14   Consolidated Balance Sheet (In Millions)

	December 31 1988	December 31 1989
Current Assets		
Cash and Marketable Securities	$ 63.9	$ 36.4
Accounts and Notes Receivable, Less Allowance for Doubtful Accounts of $4.2 in 1989 and $4.1 in 1988	463.1	527.8
Inventories		
Raw Materials and Supplies	344.6	314.6
Work in Process	84.7	99.0
Finished Goods	82.9	118.1
Total Inventories	512.2	531.7
Other Current Assets	155.1	181.0
Total Current Assets	1,194.3	1,276.9
Investments and Other Assets		
Investments In and Advances to Affiliated Companies	82.3	87.4
Investment Properties	34.9	141.1
Deferred Charges and Other Non-current Assets	225.7	312.2
Excess of Cost Over Net Assets of Acquired Businesses,	104.9	536.8
Net	447.8	1,077.5
Plant and Equipment		
Land	126.6	289.6
Buildings	1,085.1	2,683.1
Machinery and Equipment	4,715.0	5,504.2
Construction in Progress	716.3	711.0
	7,643.0	9,187.9
Accumulated Depreciation	(2,175.3)	(2,516.6)
	5,467.7	6,671.3
Total Assets	$ 7,109.8	$ 9,025.7
Liabilities and Shareholders Equity		
Current Liabilities		
Current Portion of Long-Term Debt	$ 0	$ 104.0
Accounts Payable	568.7	608.0
Accrued Salaries, Wages, and Benefits	229.4	212.0
Accrued Interest Payable	49.5	60.2
Due to Customers for Returnable Containers	40.7	42.2
Accrued Taxes, Other Than Income Taxes	60.1	65.4
Estimated Income Taxes	75.2	40.0
Other Current Liabilities	155.5	170.8
Total Current Liabilities	1,179.1	1,302.6
Long-Term Debt	1,615.3	3,307.3
Deferred Income Taxes	1,212.5	1,315.9
Common Stock and Other Shareholders' Equity		
Common Stock, $1.00 Par Value, Authorized 400 Shares	331.0	333.9
Capital in Excess of Par Value	428.5	507.2
Retained Earnings	3,444.9	3,985.9
Foreign Currency Translation Adjustment	10.9	9.7
	4.215.3	4,836.7
Treasury Stock, at Cost	(1,112.4)	(1,236.8)
Employee Stock Ownership Plan Shares	0	(500.0)
	3,102.9	3,099.9
Total Liabilities and Shareholders' Equity	$ 7,109.8	$ 9,025.7

Source: *Anheuser-Busch Annual Report 1989*, pp. 44–45.

EXHIBIT 15 Financial Summary—Operations

	1975	1980	1981
Barrels Sold	35.2	50.2	54.5
Sales	$1,036.7	$3,822.4	$4,435.9
Federal and State Excise Taxes	391.7	527.0	562.4
Net Sales	1,645.0	3,295.4	3,873.5
Cost of Products and Services	1,343.8	2,553.9	3,001.9
Gross Profit	301.2	741.5	871.6
Marketing, Distribution, and Administrative Expenses	126.1	428.6	518.6
Operating Income	175.1	312.9	353.0
Interest Expense	(22.6)	(75.6)	(90.7)
Interest Capitalized	0	41.7	64.1
Interest Income	10.9	2.4	6.2
Other Income (Expense), Net	1.9	(9.9)	(7.3)
Income Before Income Taxes	165.3	271.5	325.3
Income Taxes	80.6	99.7	107.9
Net Income	84.7	171.8	217.4
Per Share—Primary Income Before Cumulative Effect of Change in Accounting Method	.63	.64	.80
Cumulative Effect of Change in Accounting Method	—	—	—
Net Income	.63	.64	.80
Per Share—Fully Diluted	.63	.64	.77
Cash Dividends Paid			
Common Stock	22.8	44.8	51.2
Per Share	.2133	.165	.188
Average Number of Common Shares	135.3	271.2	272.4

	1982	1983	1984
Barrels Sold	59.1	60.5	64.0
Sales	$5,251.2	$6,714.7	$7,218.8
Federal and State Excise Taxes	609.1	624.3	657.0
Net Sales	4,642.1	6,090.4	6,561.8
Cost of Products and Services	3,384.3	4,161.0	4,464.6
Gross Profit	1,257.8	1,929.4	2,097.2
Marketing, Distribution, and Administrative Expenses	758.8	1,226.4	1,338.5
Operating Income	499.0	703.0	758.7
Interest Expense	(93.2)	(115.4)	(106.0)
Interest Capitalized	41.2	32.9	46.8
Interest Income	17.0	12.5	22.8
Other Income (Expense), Net	(5.8)	(14.8)	(29.6)
Income Before Income Taxes	478.6	618.2	692.7
Income Taxes	191.3	270.2	301.2
Net Income	287.3	348.0	391.5
Per Share—Primary Income Before Cumulative Effect of Change in Accounting Method	1.00	1.08	1.23
Cumulative Effect of Change in Accounting Method	—	—	—
Net Income	1.00	1.08	1.23
Per Share—Fully Diluted	.98	1.08	1.23
Cash Dividends Paid			
Common Stock	65.8	78.3	89.7
Per Share	.23	.27	.3133
Average Number of Common Shares	288.6	321.0	317.4

(Continued on next page)

Exhibit 15 *(Continued)*

	1985	1986	1987
Barrels Sold	68.0	72.3	76.1
Sales	$7,756.7	$ 8,473.8	$9,110.4
Federal and State Excise Taxes	683.0	724.5	760.7
Net Sales	7,073.7	7,754.3	8,349.7
Cost of Products and Services	4,729.8	5,026.5	5,374.3
Gross Profit	2,343.9	2,727.8	2,975.4
Marketing, Distribution, and Administrative Expenses	1,498.2	1,709.8	1,826.8
Operating Income	845.7	1,018.0	1,148.6
Interest Expense	(96.5)	(99.9)	(127.5)
Interest Capitalized	37.2	33.2	40.3
Interest Income	21.8	9.6	12.8
Other Income (Expense), Net	(23.3)	(13.6)	(9.9)
Income Before Income Taxes	784.4	947.3	1,064.3
Income Taxes	340.7	429.3	449.6
Net Income	443.7	518.0	614.7
Per Share—Primary Income Before Cumulative Effect of Change in Accounting Method	1.42	1.69	2.04
Cumulative Effect of Change in Accounting Method	—	—	—
Net Income	1.42	1.69	2.04
Per Share—Fully Diluted	1.42	1.69	2.04
Cash Dividends Paid			
Common Stock	102.7	120.2	148.4
Per Share	.3667	.44	.54
Average Number of Common Shares	312.6	306.6	301.5

	1988	1989
Barrels Sold	78.5	80.7
Sales	$9,705.1	$10,283.6
Federal and State Excise Taxes	781.0	802.3
Net Sales	8,924.1	9,481.3
Cost of Products and Services	5,825.5	6,275.8
Gross Profit	3,098.6	3,205.5
Marketing, Distribution, and Administrative Expenses	1,834.5	1,876.8
Operating Income	1,264.1	1,328.7
Interest Expense	(141.6)	(117.9)
Interest Capitalized	44.2	51.5
Interest Income	9.8	12.6
Other Income (Expense), Net	(16.4)	11.8
Income Before Income Taxes	1,160.1	1,226.7
Income Taxes	444.2	459.5
Net Income	715.9	767.2
Per Share—Primary Income Before Cumulative Effect of Change in Accounting Method	2.45	2.68
Cumulative Effect of Change in Accounting Method	—	—
Net Income	2.45	2.68
Per Share—Fully Diluted	2.45	2.68
Cash Dividends Paid		
Common Stock	188.6	226.2
Per Share	.66	.80
Average Number of Common Shares	92.2	286.2

($3,295,400,000 to $9,481,300,000); net income rose by 346.6 percent ($171,800,000 to $767,200,000); gross profits increased 332.3 percent ($741,500,800 to $3,205,500,000); and the total assets of the company increased 268.4 percent ($2,449,700,000 to $9,025,700,000). The company paid a stock dividend for 57 consecutive years (see Exhibit 15).

During 1989, the company established an employee stock ownership plan (ESOP) for its salaried and hourly employees. The plan borrowed $500 million to buy approximately 11.3 million shares of common stock from the company. The ESOP and other stock ownership plans would eventually lead to approximately 10 percent ownership by the company's employees.[37]

On November 26, 1989, Anheuser-Busch Companies registered more than 8 million shares of common stock with the Securities and Exchange Commission, which may be sold periodically by the heirs of August Busch, Jr., who died in September 1989. This secondary share offering represented about 8.4 percent of the company's outstanding common stock. Before Mr. Busch's death, about 23 percent of the company was closely controlled—12 percent by Mr. Busch and 11 percent by Centerre Trust Company of St. Louis, and 1 percent by other directors.[38]

Over the next five years, the capital expenditures were expected to exceed $4.4 billion. The company was not opposed to long-term financing for some of its capital programs, but cash flow from operations would be the principal source of funds to support these programs. For short-term capital requirements, the company had access to a maximum of $500 million from a bank credit-line agreement. In 1992, the company had an AA bond rating. In 1989, the company's long-term debt almost doubled, from $1,615,300,000 in 1988 to $3,307,300,000 in 1989. (The acquisition of Sea World was for $1.1 billion.)

The beer and beer-related segment had sales of $7,405,700,000 (78.1 percent) and operating income of $1,244,700 (93.7 percent) in 1989. The food products segment had sales of $1,803,000,000 (19 percent) and operating income of $56,900,000 (4.3 percent), and the entertainment segment had sales of $286,300,000 (3 percent) and operating income of $27,100,000 (2 percent). The combined sales and operating income for the two nonbeer segments totaled 22 percent of sales and 6.3 percent of operating income. A former Anheuser-Busch executive would attribute the performance of the nonbeer segments to the fact that they were managed by "beer guys." He said, "They continue to use 'beer guys' on the diversifications. It's a big mistake."[39]

---

[37]"Directors Approve ESOP, Employees Could Own 10%," *Wall Street Journal,* April 27, 1989, p. C-17; "Heirs' Shares." *St. Petersburg Times,* November 27, 1989, B-1.

[38]"Anheuser-Busch," *Value Line,* August 25, 1989, p. 1531.

[39]Marshall, "The Czar of Beer," p. 30.

American Greetings Faces New Challenges in the 1990s

Daniel C. Kopp and Lois Shufeldt

As CEO Morry Weiss looked at the corporate rose logo of the world's largest publicly owned manufacturer of greeting cards and related social-expression merchandise, American Greetings (AG), he reflected upon the 1980s. In 1981, he had announced the formulation of a corporate growth objective to achieve $1 billion in annual sales by 1985, which would represent a 60 percent increase over 1982 sales of $623.6 million.

It was 1986 before AG reached that goal with sales of $1.035 billion. The profit margin, however, was 5.75 percent, the lowest in five years and down from its high of 8.09 percent in 1984. In its fiscal year ending February 28, 1990, AG reported sales of $1,286 billion with a profit margin of 5.51 percent. Weiss looked at the 10-year sales, net income and selling, distribution, and marketing costs summary prepared by his corporate staff (Exhibit 1). He realized that AG's increase in sales had come at a high cost, with an escalated and intensified battle for market share dominance among the three industry leaders, Hallmark, Gibson, and AG. In the final analysis, market shares had not really changed that much among the big three. Each was determined to defend its respective market share, and the nature of the greeting card industry changed dramatically. Previously, the two leading firms, Hallmark and AG, peacefully coexisted by having mutually exclusive niches. Hallmark offered higher-priced, quality cards in department stores and card shops, and AG offered inexpensive cards in mass-merchandise outlets. However, AG's growth strategy to attack the industry leader and its niche, followed by Gibson's growth strategy and Hallmark's defensive moves, changed the industry. AG was now engaged in defending its competitive position.

HISTORY OF AMERICAN GREETINGS

The story of American Greetings is one of an American dream of a Polish immigrant who came to the land of promise and opportunity to seek his fortune. Jacob Sapirstein was born in 1884 in Wasosz, Poland, and because of the Russian-Japanese war of 1904, was sent by his widowed mother, along with his seven brothers and one sister, to live in America.

This case was prepared by Professors Daniel C. Kopp and Lois Shufeldt, as a basis for class discussion. It is not intended to illustrate either effective or ineffective handling of an administrative situation.

EXHIBIT 1: Consolidated Statements of Financial Position, 1981–1990

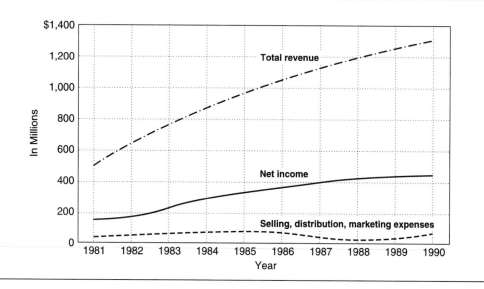

Jacob, also known as J. S., began his one-man business buying postcards made in Germany from wholesalers and selling them to candy, novelty, and drug stores in Cleveland in 1906. From a horse-drawn card wagon, the small venture steadily flourished.

J. S. and his wife, Jennie, also a Polish immigrant, had three sons and a daughter: all three sons became active in their father's business. At the age of nine, Irving, the oldest, kept the family business afloat while J. S. was recovering from the flu during the epidemic of 1918. The business had outgrown the family living room and was moved to a garage at this time.

J. S. had a basic philosophy of service to the retailer and a quality product for the consumer. He developed the first wire rack as well as a rotating floor stand to make more-attractive, convenient displays. In the 1930s the Sapirstein Card Company began to print its own cards to ensure the quality of its product. The name of the company was changed to American Greetings Publishers to reflect the national stature and functioning of the company. Its first published line of cards under the American Greetings name, the Forget Me Not line, went on sale in 1939 for a nickel. One card, which remains the company's all-time best-seller, was designed by Irving.

The company saw great expansion throughout the 1940s, as loved ones found the need to communicate with World War II soldiers. The most significant effect of this was the widespread use of greeting cards by the soldiers. In the past, cards had been primarily a product utilized by women; thus, the expansion to the male market was a significant breakthrough for the card industry.

The 1950s marked the first public offering of stock, and the name change to American Greetings Corporation. Ground was broken for a new world headquarters, which led the way for expansion to world markets. The company made connections with several foreign markets and acquired a Canadian plant.

In 1960, J. S. stepped down at the age of 76. His son Irving succeeded him as president. Under Irving's leadership and with the assistance of his brothers, Morris and Harry Stone (all three brothers had changed their names from Sapirstein, meaning sapphire, to Stone in 1940 for business reasons), the company continued to expand into gift wrapping, party goods, calendars, stationery, candles, ceramics, and perhaps, most importantly, the creation of licensed characters.

Expansion into these related items somewhat diminished AG's recession-proof profits. Greeting card sales typically increase during recessions as people refrain from gift buying and instead remember others with a less-expensive card. The supplemental items now constituted one-third of the company's sales, not enough to seriously jeopardize AG during down economies, yet greatly augmenting the company's sales during good economic times.

AG's world expansion became a major pursuit throughout the 1960s and 1970s. Morry Weiss, a grandson-in-law of J. S., became the new president of AG in 1978. Irving continued as chairman of the board of directors.

THE GREETING CARD INDUSTRY

According to GM News, in 1988 Americans exchanged more than 7.1 billion cards—around 29 per person, which was down from the highest per capita card consumption of 30 per person in 1985.[1] With the average retail price per card of $1.10, that made "social expression" nearly an $8 billion business. According to the Greeting Card Association, card buyers sent the following:

Holiday	Units Sold (In Millions)	Percent
Christmas	2,200	30.99
Valentine's Day	850	11.97
Easter	180	2.54
Mother's Day	140	1.97
Father's Day	85	1.20
Graduation	80	1.13
Thanksgiving	40	0.56
Halloween	25	0.35
St. Patrick's Day	16	—
Grandparent's Day	10	—
Chanukah	9	—
Other Seasons	5	—

Half of the total greeting cards purchased in 1988 were seasonal cards. The remainder were in the category of everyday cards. People living in the northeast and the north central parts of the country bought more cards than average, and Southerners 30 percent fewer. People who bought the majority of them tended to be between 35 and 54 years of age, came from large families, lived in their own homes in the suburbs, and had an average household income of $30,000.

Women purchased more than 90 percent of all greeting cards. Many women enjoyed browsing and shopping for cards and tended to purchase cards only if they were appropriate—when the cards' verses and designs combined to convey the sentiments they wished to express. However, because an increasing number of women were working, they were shopping less frequently or buying less impulse merchandise.

---

[1]"Greeting Cards Departments...Mass Retail Outlets," GM News, October 1989, p. 10.

Everyday cards, especially nonoccasion cards or alternative cards, were on the increase. According to *Forbes* and *American Demographics*, the alternative card market was the fastest-growing segment at 25 percent a year, and the card industry as a whole grew 5 percent a year.[2] Alternative cards were not geared to any holiday, but could be inspirational, satirical, or ethnic in nature. This segment was directed toward the estimated 76 million baby boomers. Changes in society—demographic and social—were fueling the growth of alternative cards. These changes included increases in the numbers of blended families, single-parent households, working women, divorces and remarriages, and population segments that traditionally included the heaviest greeting card users—35- to 65-year-olds. Formerly, it was the focus strategy of the many small card makers who had 70 percent of the alternative card market. However, the big three captured 87 percent of this segment.

Most industry analysts considered the greeting card industry to be in or near the maturity stage. According to Prudential-Bache, the industry unit growth rate was 2 percent to 4 percent from 1946 to 1985. The greeting card industry was comprised of 500 to 900 firms, which ranged from three major corporations to many small family organizations. The industry was dominated by Hallmark, American Greetings, and Gibson. The estimated market shares were:

Company	1977	1985	1989
Hallmark	50%	42%	40–42%
AG	24	33	32–33
Gibson	5	9	8–10

(Estimates vary according to the source.)

During the 1980s the big three engaged in market share battles through intense price, product, promotion, and place competitions. The primary price competition (through discounts to retailers) was during the period 1985–1987, although it continued at a lesser rate. According to Value Line, the end result was a reduction of profits with little change in market shares.

Generally, there was a soft retailing environment. Overall slowdown in retail traffic resulted in reduced sales. The retailing industry was overstored and promotion oriented, which could result in retailers asking greeting card suppliers for lower prices and assist them in keeping their margins from shrinking. Retailers were losing their loyalty to manufacturers that supplied a full line of products—cards, gift wrap, and other items, and were looking instead for the lowest-cost supplier of each, according to Kidder, Peabody & Company.[3] Retailer concessions made to gain accounts were difficult to remove; retailers were reluctant to give them up. Competition in the industry was expected to intensify, especially in the areas of price, sales promotion, distribution, and selling.

Market niches were also attacked. According to the *Insider's Chronicle*, the biggest battlefields were the gift and specially card shops, which once were the exclusive domain of Hallmark and alternative cards.[4] A 1989 comparison of the three firms revealed the following:

---

[2]"Flounder," *Forbes*, April 25, 1988, p. 352; "Funny Valentines," *American Demographics*, February 1989, p. 7.

[3]E. Gray Glass III, Research Reports on American Greetings and Greeting Card Industry, Kidder, Peabody & Company, May 16, 1986; May 20, 1986; December 11, 1986; and January 20, 1987.

[4]"American Greetings," *Insider's Chronicle*, February 8, 1988, p. 3.

Firm	Sales (In Billions)	Net Income (In Millions)	Number of Employees	Number of Products	Number of Outlets
Hallmark	$2.0	N/A	28,000	20,300	37,000
AG	$1.3	$44.2	29,000	20,000	90,000
Gibson	$0.4	$35.0	7,900	N/A	50,000

N/A = not available

OBJECTIVES

When asked about AG's 1989 performance, Morry Weiss replied, "Our goal was to improve competitiveness and enhance future earnings prospects in order to maximize shareholder value. AG refocused its worldwide business operating strategies. While we have not reached the upper levels of that goal, substantial progress was made in 1989. We are reducing seasonal product returns, accounts receivable, and inventories. These are indicators of how well a business is being operated, and the results show that our people have made substantial progress. We are committed to making even further improvement in these areas."[5]

Weiss further explained, "Sales in 1989 increased despite the loss of revenue caused by the divestiture during the year of the company's AmToy and Plymouth divisions and several foreign subsidiaries…net income was affected by restructuring costs which included the cost of relocating Carlton Cards/US to Cleveland, Ohio: consolidating certain manufacturing operations; and selling, consolidating or downsizing several unprofitable businesses." His assessment of AG's 1990 performance was: "It was the kind of year you have to feel good about. Our performance demonstrated our ability to produce outstanding earnings, even in a year when the revenue gain was modest. To accomplish this required enormous effort in every department. It required a diligent watch over expenses while increasing productivity."[6]

Morry Weiss also commented about AG's growth: "We are building a more synergistic relationship between our core business and our subsidiary operations in order to increase our value to our retailers. Our goal is to be a full-service provider to our retailer accounts. The more we represent a single source for a variety of consumer products, the more important a resource we become."[7]

To reach this aim of providing retailers not only greeting cards, but complementary products, AG made the following acquisitions:

COMPANY	PRODUCTS
Acme Frame Products	Picture Frames
Wilhold Hair Care Products	Hair Care Products
Plus Mark	Promotional Christmas Products
A. G. Industries	Greeting Card Cabinets/Displays

---

[5]American Greetings *Annual Report*, 1989, p. 3.

[6]*Annual Report*, 1990, p. 2.

[7]*Annual Report*, 1989, p. 3.

MARKETING STRATEGIES

Product

AG produced a wide product line, including greeting cards, gift wrap, party goods, toys, and gift items. Greeting cards accounted for 65 percent of the company's 1990 fiscal sales. The breakdown of sales by major product categories follows:

Category	1980	1984	1986	1990
Everyday Greeting Cards	34%	36%	37%	41%
Holiday Greeting Cards	27	27	29	24
Gift Wrap and Party Goods	21	21	18	17
Consumer Products (Toys, etc.)	9	7	7	9
Stationery	9	9	9	9

Source: AG's annual reports.

The essence of AG's product strategy was identifying consumer needs, creating responses that sold, and pretesting to determine the winners. AG believed in identifying consumer needs and responding to them with creative products. Research was a key ingredient. More than 12,000 North American households were surveyed annually to obtain information about every greeting card purchased and received. AG utilized focus group sessions, simulated shopping surveys, and shopping mall interviews. Especially important was ongoing lifestyle research to identify changing tastes and consumer needs for product development.

Research efforts resulted in new products. Couples, an everyday card line that answered the trend back to more sincere romantic relationships, and Kid Zone, which responded to the need for more effective communication with children, were introduced during fiscal 1990. Holly Hobbie designs, popular in the 1960s, were reintroduced when research indicated a trend toward more traditional values.

Morry Weiss commented on the Couples line: "We've proven our ability to meet the challenge of the marketplace. Couples takes its place alongside a pantheon of our major greeting card innovations."[8]

AG had one of the largest creative staffs in the world with more than 550 artists, stylists, writers, designers, photographers, and planners who were guided by the latest research data available from computer analysis, consumer testing, and information from AG's sales and merchandising departments. Careful monitoring of societal changes, fashion and color trends, and consumer preferences provided further guidance to product development. They created more than 20,000 new greeting card designs each year. AG adhered to uncompromising quality—in papers, inks, and printing procedures.

AG also engaged in retail pretesting to determine which product ideas had the greatest chance of sales. This was extremely important because of the competitiveness of the market and retailers' needs for fast turnover. A network of retail test stores was used. New cards were rated based upon actual sales performance, and those with the best sales ratings were distributed worldwide.

---

[8]"Flounder," p. 352.

AG was trying to take advantage of the alternative card segment. In 1992, alternative cards commanded 20 percent of the everyday greeting card market, and the double-digit annual growth rate was expected to continue. Carlton Cards was AG's speciality card subsidiary and recently moved from Dallas to AG's Cleveland headquarters. Carlton was to concentrate on "swiftly developing products unique to the more avant-garde tastes of the specialty store consumer."

AG pioneered licensing and was an industry leader in character licensing. Their strategy was to maximize the potential of their creative and marketing expertise. The following identifies some of AG's character licenses:

Character	Year
Holly Hobbie	1968/1989
Ziggy	1971
Strawberry Shortcake	1980
Care Bears	1983
Herself the Elf	1983
Popples	1983

Strawberry Shortcake was one of the most popular licensed characters. According to *Forbes*, however, all of AG licensed characters have not been successful.[9] One flop, Herself the Elf, was perceived by retailers as being too much like Strawberry Shortcake; it also missed the Christmas season because of production problems. Another failure was Get Along Gang, which tried to appeal to both little girls and boys. Another licensing creation, Popples, added a new dimension to a field crowded with look-alikes. Popples literally "popped out" from a plush ball to a lovable, furry, playmate, a plush toy that folded into its own pouch. Popples enabled children to make its arms, legs, and fluffy tail appear and disappear at will. AG's licensing income was:

Year	Income (In millions)
1984	$17.5
1985	$20.9
1986	$17.6
1987	$17.0
1988	$16.5
1989	$13.3
1990	$11.8

Source: AG's annual reports.

Distribution

AG distributed its products in 90,000 retail outlets in 50 countries throughout the world and in 12 languages. AG's major channels of distribution, in order of importance, included drug stores, mass merchandisers, supermarkets, stationery, gift shops, combo

---

[9]American Greetings *Form 10-K*, 1989, 1.

stores (stores combining food, general merchandise, and drug items), variety stores, military post exchanges, and department stores.[10]

AG's primary channels of distribution (which included supermarkets, chain drug stores, and mass retail merchandisers) experienced growth due to demographic and life-style changes. The increase of working women changed the location for many card purchases. In 1992, 55 percent of all everyday greeting cards were purchased in convenient locations.

AG's five largest customers accounted for about 17.4 percent of net sales. These customers included mass merchandisers, major drug stores, and military exchanges.

AG had 26 regional and 58 district sales offices in the United States, Canada, United Kingdom, France, and Mexico.

Promotion

Service was a key value to AG's marketing effort, as reflected in the following statement by Morry Weiss: "One of our cornerstone values is service to the customer. Although we are a leader in marketing innovation, we earned our reputation for superior customer service by clinging to old-fashioned ideas. We get to know our customers—and their customers—and learn how their businesses operate."[11]

The services that AG provided its retailers were based upon three key ingredients: knowledgeable sales force, in-store service personnel, and quick response to needs. AG offered the following:

- Largest full-time sales force in the industry, which was composed of highly trained experts.
- National sales force of 12,000 part-time in-store merchandising representatives who visited mass retail stores to restock goods, realign products, set up new displays and point-of-purchase materials, generate reorders, and process returns.
- A computerized network that allowed AG to more quickly and consistently ship complete and accurate orders to retailers.[12]

According to Weiss, "AG is focusing on building a strong partnership with retailers and consumers. We will expand distribution of our products in the global marketplace. We will 'partner' with retail accounts by making greeting card departments more profitable. And we will improve our response to consumers' needs for appropriate products and attractive, easy to shop departments."[13]

AG tried to achieve more sales and profits by making the space allocated by retailers more productive. This was accomplished by sophisticated merchandising that made greeting card displays more "consumer friendly." Women purchased approximately 90 percent of all greeting cards, so AG redesigned greeting card cabinets to respond to the fact that women spent less time in stores than previously. Redesigned greeting card cabinets displayed 40 percent more cards in the same amount of space. Point-of-purchase signs and new caption locators ("Mother," "Stepdaughter," and so forth) helped customers in a hurry find the right card.

---

[10]*Annual Report*, 1990, p. 2.

[11]Ibid.

[12]Ibid.

[13]Ibid., p. 5.

Themes were becoming more important in merchandising. These were used for particular seasons or occasions that projected a strong message to consumers and evoked an immediate awareness of the occasion. Related to this was a new concept called "occasion merchandising," which grouped various products for everyday occasions, such as cards, gift wrap, candles, invitations, party goods, and so on.

AG tried to design its marketing programs to increase customer traffic and profitability of the greeting card department. Realizing the need for retailers to differentiate themselves and their products, AG attempted to work on an individual basis to customize the greeting card department for each retailer. This was accomplished via market research and technology. This was especially important to large chains that had to contend with regional differences. Greeting card departments could be customized to reflect a specific area's demographics. If, for example, the demographic profile was comprised of a large number of elderly or "Yuppies," specific products would be featured to target that segment.

In 1982, AG became recognized nationwide, first through television commercials and then through a new corporate identity program. The updated corporate rose logo was featured prominently at retail outlets. The logo became a standard and highly recognizable feature on all product packaging, store signage, point-of-purchase displays, and even the truck fleet. The year-round advertising campaign in 1982 included the promotion of the major card-sending holidays and nonseasonal occasions during daytime and prime-time programming.

The aim of AG's national consumer advertising and public relations programs was to remind people to send cards, because one of AG's chief competitors was consumer forgetfulness. AG was the only company in the industry to sponsor national consumer retail promotions. These consumer-directed programs served to establish brand identity and generate retail store traffic.

A summary of AG's selling, distribution, and marketing expenses as a percentage of sales follows:

Year	Percent
1981	28.2
1982	28.7
1983	29.2
1984	29.3
1985	29.0
1986	29.9
1987	31.6
1988	33.4
1989	32.6
1990	32.9

PRODUCTION STRATEGIES

AG had 34 plants and facilities in the United States, Canada, the United Kingdom, France, and Mexico. This was down from 49 plants and facilities in 1986. The company owned approximately 4.8 million square feet and leased 11.3 million square feet of plant, warehouse, store, and office space. It met its space needs in the United States through long-term leases of properties constructed and financed by community development corporations and municipalities.

AG had taken steps from 1987 to 1990 to decrease production costs. It tried to improve its production efficiency by cutting costs and reducing work-in-process inventories. AG also invested heavily in automated production equipment to cut labor costs in 1988. AG benefited from lower costs for raw materials and fewer product returns because of better inventory control. AG's material, labor, and other production costs are as follows:

Year	Percent of Sales
1981	44.7
1982	44.3
1983	41.3
1984	40.5
1985	39.9
1986	40.2
1987	42.3
1988	45.1
1989	42.8
1990	41.5

PERSONNEL STRATEGIES

In 1989, American Greetings employed more than 15,000 full-time and 14,000 part-time people in the United States, Canada, Mexico, and Europe. This equated to approximately 20,500 full-time employees.

When asked about AG employees, Morry Weiss commented: "But perhaps our greatest strength is the men and women who create, manufacture, distribute, sell, and support our products. They are committed to knowing our customers, meeting their needs with quality products and providing service before and after the sale."[14]

AG had a noncontributing profit-sharing plan for most of its U.S. employees, as well as a retirement income guarantee plan. It also had several pension plans covering certain employees in foreign countries.

FINANCE STRATEGIES

Exhibits 2, 3, and 4 contain relevant financial information for American Greetings. The financial condition of AG has fluctuated over the years. In the early to mid-1980s, AG profit margins increased from 5.42 percent in 1981 to its high of 8.09 percent in 1984. However, AG's financial performance in the mid- to late 1980s was disappointing, with the profit margin falling to 2.84 percent in 1988 and a return on investment of 2.90 percent. In 1990, AG's profit margin had risen to 5.51 percent with a return on investment of 6.33 percent.

---

[14]Ibid., p. 1.

EXHIBIT 2   Consolidated Statements of Financial Position (In Thousands)

	1986	1987	1988	1989	1990
Assets					
Current Assets					
Cash and Equivalents	$ 26,853	$ 17,225	$ 36,534	$ 94,292	$ 122,669
Trade Accounts Receivable, Less Allowances for Sales Returns and Doubtful Accounts	240,471	284,135	278,559	242,582	254,285
Inventories					
Raw Material	59,343	56,057	56,122	48,478	51,075
Work in Process	60,179	69,668	61,406	51,625	42,139
Finished Products	181,237	202,412	245,801	197,618	208,918
	300,759	328,137	363,329	297,721	302,132
Less LIFO Reserve	76,552	75,392	77,274	83,017	85,226
	224,207	252,745	286,055	214,704	216,906
Display Material and Factory Supplies	26,826	29,770	30,299	25,192	25,408
Total Inventories	251,033	282,515	316,354	239,896	242,314
Deferred Income Taxes	36,669	26,593	39,935	49,542	51,315
Prepaid Expenses and Other	6,228	9,679	8,672	11,020	10,362
Total Current Assets	561,254	620,147	680,054	637,332	680,945
Other Assets	47,085	89,488	95,752	92,285	107,788
Property, Plant, and Equipment					
Land	7,523	7,956	7,548	6,741	6,229
Buildings	165,241	183,481	223,491	216,545	215,458
Equipment and Fixtures	222,718	269,644	319,353	340,233	354,979
	395,482	461,081	550,392	563,249	576,666
Less Accumulated Depreciation and Amortization	130,519	148,097	175,917	205,246	224,383
Property, Plant, and Equipment—Net	264,963	312,984	374,475	358,003	352,283
Total Assets	$873,302	$1,022,619	$1,150,281	$1,087,620	$1,141,016
Liabilities and Shareholders' Equity					
Current Liabilities					
Notes Payable to Banks	$ 15,921	$ 25,092	$ 13,956	$ 17,201	$ 36,254
Accounts Payable	66,685	69,175	98,270	79,591	75,146
Payrolls and Payroll Taxes	28,675	31,230	33,759	38,839	10,878
Retirement Plans	11,697	10,966	4,148	8,573	10,878
State and Local Taxes	2,763	3,056	—	—	—
Dividends Payable	5,317	5,343	5,338	5,311	5,281
Income Taxes	18,988	—	13,782	6,693	6,430
Sales Returns	23,889	29,964	28,273	24,543	21,182
Current Maturities of Long-Term Debt	4,786	10,894	54,150	3,740	—
Total Current Liabilities	178,721	185,720	251,676	184,491	200,756
Long-Term Debt	147,592	235,005	273,492	246,732	235,497
Deferred Income Taxes	64,025	77,451	86,426	91,409	100,159
Shareholders' Equity					
Common Shares—Par Value $1:					
Class A	29,203	29,552	29,628	29,692	29,946
Class B	2,982	2,588	2,528	2,497	2,063
Capital in Excess of Par Value	94,744	102,718	104,209	105,245	110,234
Shares Held in Treasury	(1,689)	(15,409)	(14,199)	(14,767)	(26,692)
Cumulative Translation Adjustment	(16,801)	(11,604)	(7,564)	(4,790)	(8,186)
Retained Earnings	374,525	416,598	424,085	447,111	497,239
Total Shareholders' Equity	482,964	524,443	538,687	564,988	604,604
Total Liabilities and Shareholders' Equity	$873,302	$1,022,619	$1,150,281	$1,087,620	$1,141,016

Source: American Greetings

EXHIBIT 3   **Consolidated Statements of Income, Years Ending February 28 or 29 (In Thousands Except Per Share Data)**

	1986	1987	1988	1989	1990
Net Sales	$1,012,451	$1,102,532	$1,174,817	$1,252,793	$1,286,853
Other Income	23,200	23,463	24,155	22,566	22,131
Total Revenue	1,035,651	1,125,995	1,198,972	1,275,359	1,308,984
Cost and Expenses					
Material, Labor, and Other Production Costs	416,322	476,725	540,143	546,214	543,602
Selling, Distribution, and Marketing	308,745	355,363	400,033	415,597	431,254
Administration and General	131,928	125,407	135,224	148,095	149,771
Depreciation and Amortization	23,471	29,059	34,191	39,527	40,251
Interest	19,125	24,875	32,787	33,479	27,691
Restructuring Charge	—	12,371	—	23,591	—
	899,591	1,023,800	1,142,378	1,206,503	1,192,569
Income Before Income Taxes	136,060	102,195	56,594	68,856	116,415
Income Taxes	61,635	38,834	23,203	24,582	44,238
Net Income	$ 74,425	$ 63,361	$ 33,391	$ 44,274	$ 72,177
Net Income per Share	$2.32	$1.97	$1.04	$1.38	$2.25

Source: American Greetings

Irving Stone commented about AG's 1990 performance: "Fiscal 1990 revenues were a record $1.31 billion. This marks the 84th consecutive year that revenues have increased since the Company's founding in 1906. And…revenue was driven by higher sales of everyday greeting cards, our low-cost high margin core products. Fourth quarter sales were particularly strong. We expect to continue reporting good sales results." He continued, "The market value of our common stock rose 47 percent, from $21.25 on February 28, 1989, to $31.25 at the fiscal year close on February 28, 1990. This compares favorably to 27 percent increases for both the Dow Jones Industrial Average and the Standard and Poor's 500 Stock Index. Total returns to stockholders—share price appreciation plus dividends—was 50 percent in fiscal 1990."[15]

AG's stock price ranged from a low of 9½ in 1981 to a high of 37⅛ in 1990.

MANAGEMENT

AG was organized via a divisional profit center basis. Each division had its own budget committee, although an executive management committee, comprised of five senior executives, approved the strategic plans for all the divisions. Strategic plans were estab-

---

[15]Ibid.

EXHIBIT 4 Selected Financial Data, Years Ending February 28 or 29 (In Thousands Except Per Share Data)

	1986	1987	1988	1989	1990
Summary of Operations					
Total Revenue	$ 1,035,651	$ 1,125,995	$ 1,198,972	$ 1,275,359	$ 1,308,984
Materials, Labor, and Other Products	420,747	476,725	540,143	546,214	543,602
Depreciation and Amortization	23,471	20,059	34,191	39,527	40,251
Interest Expense	19,125	24,875	32,787	33,479	27,691
Net Income	$ 74,425	$ 63,361	$ 33,391	$ 44,274	$ 72,177
Net Income per Share	$2.32	$1.97	$1.04	$1.38	$2.25
Cash Dividends per Share	.62	.66	.66	.66	.66
Fiscal Year End Market Price per Share	$35.62	$28.75	$17.63	$21.25	$31.25
Average Number Shares Outstanding	32,059,851	32,212,556	32,068,752	32,146,971	32,029,533
Financial Position					
Accounts Receivable	$ 240,471	$ 284,135	$ 278,559	$ 242,582	$ 254,285
Inventories	251,033	282,515	316,354	239,896	243,314
Working Capital	382,533	434,427	428,378	452,841	480,189
Total Assets	873,302	1,022,619	1,150,281	1,087,620	1,141,016
Capital Additions	61,799	68,740	96,682	41,938	42,869
Long-Term Debt	147,592	235,005	273,492	246,732	235,497
Shareholders' Equity	482,964	524,443	538,687	564,988	604,604
Shareholders' Equity per Share	$15.01	$16.32	$16.75	$17.55	$18.89
Net Return Average Shareholders' Equity	16.5%	12.7%	6.3%	8.0%	12.3%
Pretax Return on Total Revenue	13.1%	9.1%	4.7%	5.4%	8.9%
Summary of Operations					
Total Revenue	$ 498,272	$ 623,604	$ 742,683	$ 839,914	$ 945,658
Materials, Labor, and Other Products	225,356	278,866	313,769	344,313	382,205
Depreciation and Amortization	10,863	12,752	13,890	15,507	18,799
Interest Expense	13,548	21,647	24,086	16,135	15,556
Net Income	$ 26,515	$ 32,843	$ 44,582	$ 59,658	$ 74,365
Net Income per Share	$.97	$1.20	$1.54	$1.91	$2.35
Cash Dividends per Share	.26	.27	.31	.40	.54
Fiscal Year End Market Price per Share	$5.50	$9.63	$18.69	$23.69	$33.06
Average Number Shares Outstanding	27,314,594	27,352,342	28,967,092	31,240,455	31,629,418
Financial Position					
Accounts Receivable	$ 114,051	$ 131,996	$ 148,018	$ 146,896	$ 173,637
Inventories	133,836	159,623	177,459	180,019	214,449
Working Capital	167,772	215,412	241,724	275,685	330,409
Total Assets	433,204	491,854	580,675	685,894	747,897
Capital Assets	22,768	26,720	33,967	46,418	43,575
Long-Term Debt	113,486	148,895	111,066	119,941	112,876
Shareholders' Equity	205,550	227,784	316,368	365,496	425,748
Shareholder Equity per Share	$7.52	$8.31	$10.18	$11.62	$13.35
Net Return Average Shareholders' Equity	13.7%	15.4%	17.1%	17.8%	19.2%
Pretax Return on Total Revenue	9.9%	9.2%	11.0%	13.0%	14.4%

lished in 1-, 3-, 10-, and 20-year time frames. Corporate AG maintained strict budgetary and accounting controls.

The basic domestic greeting card business was placed under the U.S. Greeting Card Division. Domestic and international subsidiary operations, including the licensing division, were a second unit, with corporate management a third. AG decentralized its structure in 1983.

U.S. Greeting Card Division This division encompassed the core business of greeting cards and related products, including manufacturing, sales, merchandising, research, and administrative services. It produced and distributed greeting cards and related products domestically. The same products were distributed throughout the world by international subsidiaries and licensees.

Domestic and International Subsidiaries AG's domestic and international subsidiary operations included the following:

Domestic

Acme Frame Products

A. G. Industries

Plus Mark

Summit Corporation/Summit Collection

Those Characters from Cleveland

Wilhold Hair Care Products

International

Carlton Cards—Canada

Carlton Cards—England

Carlton Cards—France

Felicitaciones Nacionales S. A. de C. V.—Mexico

Rust Craft Canada

There were six domestic operations in 1990 versus seven in 1986. Firms divested included Amtoy, Drawing Board Greeting Cards, and Tower Products. The number of international operations in 1990 was five versus 13 in 1986. Among the international operations consolidated were one in Canada, four in Continental Europe, one in Monaco, and four in the United Kingdom.

AG's domestic and international sales follow:

SALES RECAP

Year	Domestic	Gross Profit Margin	Foreign	Gross Profit Margin	U.S. Percent	International Percent
1990	$1,088,438	11.86	$220,546	6.79	83.15	16.85
1989	1,039,464	7.75	235,895	9.22	81.50	18.50
1988	996,628	7.79	202,344	5.80	83.12	16.88
1987	940,565	13.28	185,430	1.19	83.53	16.47
1986	874,255	15.38	161,396	12.82	84.42	15.58
1985	799,805	16.51	145,853	13.18	84.58	15.42

(Continued on next page)

SALES RECAP (Continued)

Year	Domestic	Gross Profit Margin	Foreign	Gross Profit Margin	U.S. Percent	International Percent
1984	717,057	15.18	122,857	13.61	85.37	15.63
1983	631,143	14.29	111,549	13.94	85.00	15.00
1982	523,467	12.54	100,137	13.61	85.40	14.60
1981	440,516	12.27	57,756	14.87	88.41	11.59

Source: AG annual reports.

FUTURE OF AG

When asked about the future of AG, Morry Weiss responded, "We are poised for perhaps the most successful period in our history. We are prepared to strengthen our core business and improve our position in the greeting card industry; to provide a greater return to our shareholders; and to afford our employees even greater opportunities for growth and career advancement. The strategies we will employ to achieve our goals for the new year and beyond are clear. We have well defined corporate strengths which we will target to build even stronger partnerships with retailers and consumers.[16]

Irving Stone's view of the future included the following: "We are optimistic about the future. We are confident that we can achieve even more exciting results…in the future. We face the future confident that our commitment to help people build and maintain relationships will produce even more innovative products like Couples."[17]

U.S. Industrial Outlook expected industry sales to grow 3 percent to 4 percent annually through 1992. Moderate growth was predicted due to forecasted moderate growth in the gross national product, real disposable personal income, and personal consumption expenditures. For continued growth and profitability, U.S. Industrial Outlook recommended diversification into related product lines, institution of more cost-cutting strategies, monitoring of demand for current lines, divesting of unprofitable lines, and better matching of demand with supply to avoid after-holiday returns.[18]

The unit growth rate for the greeting card industry from 1987 to 2015 was estimated to be between 1 percent and 3 percent. Exhibit 5 provides the forecast according to Prudential-Bache Securities. The slowing of unit growth was primarily due to the postwar baby boomers, who had already entered their high card-consumption years. With the declining birthrate of the 1970s and 1980s, consumption of cards was expected to decline.[19]

However, greeting card officials optimistically projected that the rate of consumption would increase moderately from the current per-capita rate of 29 cards to 44 cards by 2015. Greeting card sources also reported that consumers were upgrading their purchases to higher-priced cards, thus generating more profits per sale. The aging population, those over 55, also tended to send more cards than did younger persons.

---

[16]*Annual Report*, 1989, p. 3.

[17]*U.S. Industrial Outlook*, Department of Commerce, 1988, pp. 29–16, 29–17.

[18]"Greeting Cards Industry Update," Prudential-Bache Securities, December 30, 1988; August 9, 1989, and September 27, 1989.

[19]Ibid.

EXHIBIT 5: The Greeting Card Industry—Consumption Forecast

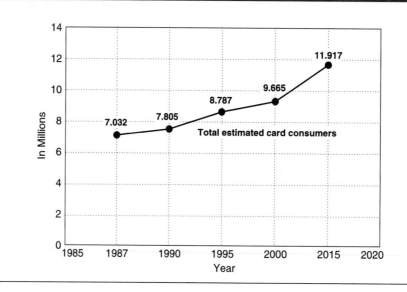

Prudential-Bache's expectation for the future of the greeting card industry included the following:

Price competition would remain a concern because of the maturity of the industry and the limited number of large players.

At least 5 percent to 10 percent of the industry's current sales were to retail outlets that the industry leaders would never serve due to the small size of these outlets, which made them too expensive to reach.

The greeting card industry was an area ripe for potential acquisition.

AG was and would continue to experience increased competition in its promotional gift-wrap area.

The big three could be challenged by any small, well-run company.

It would be unlikely that the big three with combined market shares of 80 percent to 85 percent would continue to expand to "own the market." The dynamic competitive nature of the industry would prohibit this.

There was not much room for the big three to grow by capturing more of the remaining market they were not reaching.[20]

As CEO Morry Weiss thought about the future, he wondered what changes AG should make in its competitive strategies.

---

[20]Ibid.

Shades of Black

Lester A. Neidell

Alex Corbbrey cleared space on his desk to study the initial fiscal year financial results for Shades of Black. Alex founded the company to produce greeting cards and social expression items for black consumers in the United States. In 1987, operating as an unincorporated sole proprietorship, sales of 15,239 cards ($9,640) were achieved. In 1988, the first year of incorporation, 28,188 cards were sold, and revenues reached $42,396 for all product lines.

Alex had high expectations for his product line and was somewhat disappointed in the 1988 results. The Shades of Black retail store was located in the Greenwood shopping area, a renovated and attractive, predominantly black business district adjacent to the Tulsa, Oklahoma, downtown business zone. Although he personally, and Shades of Black as a business, had received good publicity in the local media, it just did not seem that the black population of Tulsa was large enough to support the retail store he envisioned. In particular, Alex contrasted the limited and somewhat depressed black community in Tulsa with the vibrant one he had recently visited in Atlanta, Georgia. This visit to Atlanta made him wonder if perhaps a location other than Tulsa would better fit with Shades of Black's needs. But his first concern was development of a product line strategy for his young company.

THE PRODUCT/MARKET DILEMMA

It was unseasonably warm in Tulsa for a February. Alex had to force himself to study the "financials" (see Exhibit 1); his mind was brimming with ways to expand the business. He and his small staff had discussed four options for the 1989 to 1991 period.

Option 1: Expand Retail Coverage The greeting cards produced by Shades of Black were sold only in a limited number of black-owned shops in a few scattered cities in the United States. Chain drug and discount stores and supermarkets combined had the greatest market share and were also the most rapidly growing retail outlets in the United States for greeting cards. None of these retailers was carrying any Shades of Black product. Sales expansion could be achieved by expanding market coverage in the U.S. retail market.

Option 2: Military Market A possible untapped market was the U.S. military. An estimated 594,000 black Americans served in the armed forces. Many were away

EXHIBIT 1 Shades of Black Financial Statements

	Year Ending December 31,				Year Ending December 31,	
	1987	1988			1987	1988
Income Statements				**Balance Sheets**		
Sales	$ 9,640	$ 42,396[a]		**Assets**		
Cost of Goods Sold	8,337	20,224		Current Assets		
Gross Margin	1,303	22,172		Cash	305	145
Expenses				Accounts Receivable	1,797	7,956
Rent and Utilities	4,258	5,696		Accounts Receivable—Employees	0	14,029
Travel	2,682	4,863		Inventory	3,883	17,060
Advertising	1,590	204		Total Current Assets	5,985	39,190
Auto Expenses	209	277		Fixed Assets		
Taxes and License	2,155	20		Equipment	20,149	16,751
Maintenance	701	109		Furniture and Fixtures	0	3,477
Meetings	191	348		Leasehold Improvements	0	754
Professional Services	6,324	2,000		Less: Accumulated Depreciation	(1,440)	(4,045)
Office	655	1,235		Total Fixed Assets	18,709	16,937
Interest	426	2,232		Other Assets		
Freight and Postage	546	0		Deposits	610	660
Dues and Subscriptions	150	101		Total Other Assets	610	660
Depreciation	1,440	2,606		**Total Assets**	$ 25,304	$ 56,787
Insurance	306	692				
Donations	0	115		**Liabilities and Owner Equity**		
Trade Shows	0	4,790		Liabilities		
Wages	0	50		Accounts Payable	8,327	11,156
Telephone	0	2,453		Sales Tax Payable	0	572
Miscellaneous	421	294		Notes Payable	16,190	0
Total Expenses	$ 22,054	$ 28,085		Note Payable—TEDC	0	14,000
Net Income (Loss)	$ (20,751)	$ (5,913)		Note Payable—Phippe	0	10,000
				Note Payable—Alex	0	4,692
				Note Payable—Jackson	0	1,000
				Total Liabilities	24,517	41,420
				Equity		
				Owner's Draws	−5,043	0
				Equity	24,543	0
				Capital Stock	0	4,686
				Paid-In Capital	0	16,595
				Current Earnings	(18,713)	(5,914)
				Total Equity	787	15,367
				Total Liabilities and Equity	$ 25,304	$ 56,787

[a]Distribution of sales by product category:

Cards: Distributors	68.9%	Art	3.3%
Cards: Retail	7.1%	Clothing	20.8%

from family and friends for extended periods, which would seem to auger well for a company whose principal products were designed to communicate with loved ones.

Option 3: Black Colleges Another market segment contained primarily black colleges and universities. More than 100 predominantly black colleges and universities enrolled more than 173,000 students. Both campus bookstores and alumni could be reached. For example, it would be possible to "customize" greeting cards for alumni associations to use as fund-raisers. One such "package" was being designed for Morehouse College, in Atlanta, Georgia.

Option 4: Funeral Homes Finally, the product line could be expanded even further in order to reach black-owned, or black community-serviced, funeral homes. A mailing list of 12,348 black-owned funeral homes was available. It did not include those funeral parlors that serviced the black community but were not black owned.

Alex knew he had to act quickly. The Christmas season, during which approximately 31 percent of all greeting cards were sold, had a design lead time of four to six months. Any market expansion would also require some new designs, although degree and type would vary according to which of the four markets he directed his company's efforts. Furthermore, there was increasing interest on the part of both major and minor competitors in segmenting the greeting card industry. At the moment, no strong national competition existed for black-oriented greeting cards, but a flurry of recent news articles about the segment seemed to indicate that this would not be true for very much longer.

THE GREETING CARD INDUSTRY IN THE UNITED STATES

Written greeting messages originated in ancient Egypt, after the discovery of papyrus and the development of hieroglyphics and inks. "Standardized" greetings probably stem from the time of Christ and the pen of Paul. Paul began his letters with "Grace to you and peace." During the Dark Ages of Europe, when chivalry reigned, letters and messages of good cheer were widely exchanged. Thoughts were conveyed not only by written expression but by symbols, such as a handkerchief or knot of ribbon. These more durable message forms were hurled over the walls of besieged castles or through windows to gain entrance.[1] Today, retail greeting card stores in the United States sell messages as well as more-permanent remembrances.

Greeting cards are more than pretty designs, pictures, or messages of greeting. They mirror the expressions and personalities of their senders. About 7 billion greeting cards of all types were purchased in the United States in 1988, with retail sales exceeding $9 billion. Industry data at the manufacturers' level for the period 1984 to 1988 are contained in Exhibit 2. Real growth was expected to be approximately 3 percent to 4 percent through 1992, but it might increase dramatically as baby boomers aged. Market studies had shown that the heavy purchaser of greeting cards and related products and services were women ages 35 to 54. Retail prices of greeting cards ranged from 36 cents to $7.50. The high price was for a sophisticated "musical" card; more typically, adult consumers paid between $1.00 and $1.25 per card purchase.

Greeting card sales had been highly seasonal. About 31 percent of all cards were sold in the Christmas season; Valentine's Day cards added 12 percent of sales. Other seasonal "holidays" (Easter, Mother's Day, Halloween, and so on) each contributed less

---

[1] Earnest D. Chase, *The Romance of Greeting Cards* (Cambridge: University Press of Cambridge, 1956).

EXHIBIT 2   Greeting Card Publishing Industry Data (In Millions)

	1984	1985	1986	1987	1988
Value of All Products and Services Sold by the Greeting Card Publishing Industry	$2,394	$2,588	$2,793	$3,022	$3,294
Value of Above in 1982 Dollars	2,276	2,843	2,532	2,596	2,674
Value of Products Sold by the Greeting Card Publishing Industry	1,679	1,809	1,948	2,112	2,306
Value of Imports	14	15	19	23	27

Source: U.S. Department of Commerce, Bureau of the Census, Bureau of Economic Analysis.

---

than 3 percent. Nonseasonal sales were primarily birthday cards, with almost a 23 percent market share. The distribution of 1987 sales by card category is shown in Exhibit 3.

Nonoccasion or "alternative" cards were becoming more popular.[2] These products often had blank interiors to allow the sender to write personal sentiments. Hallmark Cards, the overall market share leader, recently had developed a product line targeted for parents to send to their children simply to express caring. Hallmark's advertisements for these particular alternative cards depicted children discovering the cards in their lunch boxes and textbooks. This approach by Hallmark also bypassed one of the problems the industry had encountered. Postal rate increases negatively impacted the sales of cards. Although actual cross-elasticity indices were not available, increases in postage had in the past most affected Christmas and other holiday cards. Alternative card sales, however, seemed to have been least affected by postage changes.

Although the possibility of more rapid sales growth existed as baby boomers aged, the general consensus was that the greeting card industry was mature. Historically, major competitors created demand by capitalizing on "self-promoted" holidays, such as Bosses Day, Secretary's Day, and Grandparents' Day.

For these occasions, the suppliers, led by Hallmark, created designs and promotions as if everyone knew of the holiday, which were typically joint creations of the florists, the greeting card industry, and organizations such as the National Secretary's Association. However, the public seemed to have become satiated with these "events."

General consensus in the industry was that the cards themselves were the best promotional vehicle and that advertising tended to stimulate industrywide sales rather than promote brand loyalty. Nevertheless, Hallmark and American Greetings each spent about $60 million annually on advertising.

The Black or Afro-American Segment

As competition increased and market growth slowed, product strategies of the "majors" began to emphasize segmentation. Social expression merchandise targeted at

---

[2]The term "alternative card" has had varied meanings in the greeting card industry. Originally this phrase was applied to cards that were not supplied by the three major competitors. These cards were often of an innovative design, although aimed at the standard seasons. When these nonstandard designs proved popular with consumers, Hallmark and the other national producers began to produce alternative designs for the standard seasons. Today, nontraditional seasonal cards are commonplace, with the result that the term "alternative" seems to be used principally as a synonym for nonoccasion cards.

EXHIBIT 3   Greeting Card Sales by Card Category 1987

	Percent
Seasonal Sales	
Christmas	31.5
Valentine's Day	12.2
Easter	2.6
Mother's Day	2.1
Father's Day	1.3
Graduation	1.2
All Other Seasonal	1.8
(In decreasing sales order):	
Thanksgiving, Halloween, St. Patrick's Day, Jewish New Year, Hanukkah, New Year's, Grandparent's Day, Sweetest Day, Secretary's Day, National Boss' Day, Mother-in-Law Day, April Fool's Day	
Nonseasonal Sales	
Birthday	22.9
Alternative and/or Nonoccasion	24.3
(Not in sales order):	
Birth, Wedding, Sympathy, Retirement, Congratulations, New Home, Friendship, Love	

Source: Greeting Card Association, Washington, D.C.

minorities was offered to those traditional outlets that had minority bases from which to draw. A black American, or other minority, had had a difficult time choosing a greeting card, or other social expression merchandise, suitable to his or her particular culture. The black population of the United States numbered about 12 percent of the total, and 2080 was expected to account for almost one in five Americans. In 1986, blacks spent about $360 million for greeting cards. By 1988, Afro-Americans' expenditures on greeting cards and other social awareness merchandise approached $600 million.

In 1986, 64 percent of the black population was under the age of 35, and 27 percent of all blacks were under 15 years of age. Thus, a large number of blacks would shortly enter the prime card-buying years of 35 to 54. In general, black buying patterns differed somewhat from those of white Americans. Blacks tended to be more brand loyal, and often prefered to patronize black-owned businesses. Blacks tended to make less than whites in comparable jobs and have lower savings rates than whites. However, there were a growing number of "Buppies" (black urban professionals). Career patterns of Buppies mirrored those of Yuppies, with increased mobility and greater need to communicate with family and friends left behind.

Industry Competition

Exhibit 4 illustrates greeting card market shares. Three competitors, Hallmark Cards, American Greeting Cards, and Gibson Greetings, controlled 87 percent of the market. As many as 500 publishers vied for the remainder.

EXHIBIT 4   Competitive Market Shares, 1987

| Hallmark | 40% | Gibson | 12% |
| American Greetings | 35 | All Others | 13 |

Hallmark Cards   Privately owned, Hallmark distributed its products principally through 22,000 specialty retail outlets, most of which were privately owned. Hallmark also used selected department stores for distribution. Hallmark was a fully integrated producer and was reputed to have the most efficient production facilities. Hallmark's advantages were its size and financial strength, its efficient distribution system, its quality image and "recognition" factor, and its licensed characters—Shirt tale line, Rose Petal Place, Huge Bunch, and Rainbow Bright.

Hallmark's unique distribution could be a potential weakness. Recent studies showed that mass merchandisers and chain food and drug stores accounted for about 53 percent of retail greeting card sales. This trend was expected to continue, given the societal changes of single-parent families, dual-career families, and the popularity of one-stop shopping. Another potential weakness was the inability to produce in-house an authentic ethnic greeting card, although the company obviously had the financial resources to acquire this capability.

Hallmark's principal approach to serving the ethnic market segments was via a "minority vendor resource list," provided to their stores. These were vendors who had met certain minimum quality standards. Shades of Black submitted several designs to Hallmark for evaluation. Hallmark's reaction so far had been that Shades of Black's designs had a nice style; several had been picked for a test market that had not yet been completed. Two concerns were expressed by Hallmark. First, Hallmark was hesitant to include Shades of Black on the vendor list because of the uncertainty about Shades of Black's ability to service any quantity of orders. Second, although acknowledging that Shades of Black's designs were of high quality for a company of its size, they were not yet at a level that Hallmark set for products included on their vendor lists.

American Greeting Cards   American Greetings was the world's largest publicly owned manufacturer of greeting cards and social-expression merchandise. Since 1975, American Greetings was an aggressive competitor, with a marketing strategy designed to outflank Hallmark. Their primary weapon was inexpensive cards distributed through mass merchandise outlets. American Greetings cards were carried by more than 90,000 retailers worldwide. Thirty-five percent of their sales were through drug stores and, in decreasing order of importance, mass merchandisers, supermarkets, stationery and gift shops, military post exchanges, and department stores. American Greetings initiated the practice of developing licensed characters. Its characters included Holly Hobbie, Ziggy, Strawberry Shortcake, and Care Bears.

Gibson Greetings   Gibson was the fastest growing of the three major competitors, although quite obviously the base was much smaller. Their principal distribution channels were (in decreasing order of importance) mass merchandisers, drug stores, and supermarkets. Gibson was very aggressive in licensing characters. The company had exclusive rights to the Walt Disney characters and licensed Garfield,[3] the Sesame Street characters, and the Looney Tunes and D.C. Comics comic book creations. Gibson moved aggressively into the ethnic market with licensing arrangements. One result was a line of cards directed toward the black market. Licensed from Cousin Mattie's Daddy's Sister's People in Oakland, California, "Cousin Mattie's" cards featured "soft sculpture characters" of black folksy people set in humorous domestic scenes of yester-year. Begun in 1984, Cousin Mattie's was distributed in about 350 retail outlets prior to its agreement with Gibson. Gibson was expected to distribute Cousin Mattie cards in more than 1,200 of its regular outlets.

Other Competitors   An important competitor in the black segment was L'Image Graphics of Culver City, California. This six-year-old, privately held company's investors included Sidney Poitier, and Don Clark and Berry Gordy of Motown Records. As of July 1988, L'Image cards were carried in 1,500 retail outlets in the United States, Canada, Puerto Rico, and England. About 50 sales representatives carried its line in the United States. L'Image had more than 225 designs, generally of a "fantasy-oriented" contemporary image. Originally sold in exclusive, top-of-the-line department stores, which had a clientele that was over 90 percent white, L'Image created "cross-over" designs by using tan (rather than white or black) characters. This middle-of-the-road approach created a company whose sales doubled each of the past four years.

More than 20 black-owned and operated greeting card companies were reputed to exist in the United States. These were all small, regional in scope, and lacked financial and production resources to be major players in the market for black customers.

SHADES OF BLACK HISTORY

In late 1986, Alex Corbbrey sketched a black Santa Claus and one other greeting card that he had printed and then sent to a few friends. Soon afterward, inquiries were received concerning the possibility of purchasing these cards. During the first Christmas season in operation, more than 4,000 cards were sold. Alex Corbbrey had a varied and rich background, as his artist's vita (Exhibit 5) illustrates. Shades of Black was located in Tulsa, Oklahoma, with a small retail store and headquarters (total 718 square feet) in one building, and a moderate amount of warehouse space in another facility. In addition to the founder, Shades of Black employed two full-time and one part-time person. Important professional and managerial input was provided by the board of directors, including legal and accounting help.

MARKETING

Product

All designs produced were the inspiration of the founder, although several were "farmed out" to contract artists for completion after initial sketches were developed. In 1988, five contract artists were working on new designs. Shades of Black produced 27

---

[3]Beginning January 1989, Hallmark became the Garfield licensee. Major in-store promotions were planned around the Garfield character.

EXHIBIT 5   About Alex Corbbrey

Mr. Alex A. Corbbrey, founder of Shades of Black, took his formal training in art at Oklahoma State University at Stillwater and Chinourd Art Institute in Los Angeles, California.

Upon completing his academic training, Mr. Corbbrey, seeking employment as an illustrator with I. Magnin's, an exclusive department store in the Los Angles area, found himself instead working as a buyer trainee in retail. Having had virtually no college experience in marketing, Mr. Corbbrey returned to college, studying retail marketing, accounting, statistics, and business law.

During his five years with I. Magnin's, three years as assistant buyer and two years as buyer for the southern district, which included seven stores throughout southern California, Mr. Corbbrey decided to apply his marketing experience to the business of art.

Realism, expressed through such media as oils, watercolors, acrylics, pastels, and pen and inks, was the focus of his creative interest during this period. His work drew wide attention from many people in the entertainment industry, some of whom had become his personal customers at I. Magnin. During the years 1966 to 1968, he exhibited in private showings throughout southern California. In 1973, Mr. Corbbrey was commissioned to do several portraits of prominent citizens in the Los Angeles area, including Mayor Thomas Bradley.

After much success in the more traditional media, Mr. Corbbrey became fascinated with the possibilities of engraving. He experimented with many different types of materials, finally narrowing his efforts to wood and plexiglass. The detail expressed in his wood and drypoint engravings attracted the attention of collectors across the United States. One of his limited edition prints entitled "Call to Arms" hangs in the White House. He had displayed his work in such respected galleries as Jim Settle's Art Galleries in southern California and Scottsdale, Arizona; Variations of Palm Springs, L'Academie, Southern Cost Village, Costa Mesa, California; Old House Gallery, Orange, California; and several other galleries throughout the greater Southwest.

Since returning to Tulsa, Oklahoma, in 1978, Mr. Corbbrey has added to his fine list of credits such galleries as Fields Art Gallery, The Art Market, Up Against the Wall Graphics, and Accessory Street Gallery, Houston, Texas. His wildlife studies won a first place Blue Ribbon in the 1978 Ducks Unlimited Art Show in Tulsa. However, his study of the late Mrs. Freddie Martin Rudisill on display at the Rudisill North Regional Library is one of his proudest achievements. An 8' × 10' sculpting by Mr. Corbbrey is also prominently displayed at Westview Medical Clinic of Tulsa, Oklahoma.

With such an impressive list of collectors as Dick Van Dyke, actor and producer; H. B. "Toby" Haliciki, director, producer, and star of "Gone in Sixty Seconds"; Greg Morris of *Mission Impossible* and *Vegas* fame; and Stevie Wonder, Diana Ross, and Nancy Laviska of Motown Recording Industries, Tulsa is proud to call Alex A. Corbbrey a native son.

copyrighted designs, equally divided between seasonal and alternative cards. One of its bestselling cards celebrated "Kwanza," an African harvest festival that occurs near the Christmas season. Kwanza card sales were concentrated on the East Coast; the celebration was largely unknown in many other U.S. cities with large black populations.

Production was provided by four different printers in Oklahoma and Kansas. Only fine linen paper was used, and the print quality was excellent. As an artist, Alex Corbbrey prided himself on the quality of product produced by Shades of Black.

Other items sold by Shades of Black in 1988 included original art work, framed copies of the cards, and apparel.

Distribution

Shades of Black used independent distributors to service its markets. Distributorships were originally sold by Alex at the fall 1987 National Black Caucus, held in Washington, D.C. Despite having a display of only seven designs, three distributorships were sold at that time. Distributorships cost $125, which included up to $75 of product. Through fiscal 1988, 35 distributorships were sold. A list of distributors and their sales activity is shown in Exhibit 6. Distributorships were no longer being offered as Shades of Black reevaluated its distribution policies. However, all current distributorship agreements would be honored.

Price

In 1988, the trade discount given by Shades of Black to its distributors was two-thirds (66.7 percent). Thus, for a $1.25 retail card, Shades of Black received 42 cents. Product was shipped UPS, cash on delivery. Sales to nonprofit organizations were conducted at a 50 percent discount from suggested retail price. The package of cards and stationery for Morehouse College was to be sold for $4.20, and carried a "list price" of $20. The package price to funeral homes was $13.95 per unit. All prices to organizations were FOB Tulsa (the organization paid shipping). Shipments under 70 pounds went UPS unless the customer specified otherwise. Orders exceeding the UPS weight limit were shipped by truck.

In 1988, Shades of Black's average manufacturing cost of an existing black and white card was 7 cents. Economies of scale were important in the industry. Hallmark probably produced the typical $1.25 retail card for 3 cents. New designs were expensive. For Shades of Black, an initial production run of 5,000 units for a new design would cost 35 cents per unit, which included all initial setup costs.

Promotion

Other than attendance at several trade shows, Shades of Black generated little in the way of paid promotional activities. Publicity was received in Tulsa and Oklahoma newspapers, and Sylvia Porter planned a feature in a forthcoming issue of her national publication, *Personal Finance.*

PRODUCT/MARKET EXPANSION OPPORTUNITIES

Enhanced Distribution

Primary targets were food and drug chains in the more heavily populated black cities and states. Contacts were made with the Food Lion chain (North and South Carolina and Virginia), Tom Thumb stores, Homeland supermarkets (Oklahoma), Giant Food Stores, Kroger, and Peoples' Drug Stores. As an example of requirements for these outlets, Food Lion required a one-time "slotting fee" of $240 per card rack, which would initially be stocked with 1,008 cards—84 seasonal and alternative designs. Smaller end aisle and counter display racks were possibilities. Production costs for the racks ranged from $20 to $300 apiece; slotting fees for end aisle and counter displays were negotiable. Based on talks with chain drug and supermarket executives, Alex believed that Shades of Black could have access to 325 stores by the 1989 Christmas season. The number of supermarkets and drugstores carrying Shades of Black cards would then be expected to

EXHIBIT 6   Unit Sales by Distributor

Name	Location	Date Registered	Sales 1987	Sales 1988
Ace	Missouri City, TX	11/87	$ 580	$ 1,480
Allen	Shawnee, OK	11/88	—	170
Atloms	Ferndale, MI	11/87	1,980	0
Burk	Broken Arrow, OK	02/88	—	430
Cassett	Somerset, NJ	09/88	—	0
Colbert	College Park, GA	10/87	970	0
Copeland	Hyattsville, MD	09/87	4,435	9,530
Curry	Tulsa, OK	12/87	0	525
Davis	Birmingham, AL	12/87	0	0
Evans	Tulsa, OK	02/88	—	320
Exciting Cards	Ft. Lauderdale, FL	10/87	500	0
Floral Crest	Omaha, NE	11/88	—	170
Ford	Tulsa, OK	11/87	1,800	200[a]
Francis	Jacksonville, FL	11/88	—	0
GSD Distributors	Cushing, OK	03/87	600	0
Hall	Morene Valley, CA	09/88	—	1,422[a]
Harriott	Huntsville, SC	08/87	300	0
Holman	Tulsa, OK	12/87	60	0
J & L Enterprise	Tulsa, OK	03/88	0	0[b]
Johnson, A.	E. Elmhurst, NY	12/87	664	2,470
Johnson, E.	Tulsa, OK	02/88	—	0
Joshua Enterprise	Nashville, TN	09/88	—	750[a]
LaCour	Tulsa, OK	03/87	260	0
Marshall	Austin, TX	09/87	300	0
Martin	Philadelphia, PA	09/88	—	4,960[a]
Mayo	Chicago, IL	10/87	360	0
Morans	Houston, TX	10/88	—	480[a]
Perkins	Baton Rouge, LA	10/87	300	0
RLWD Distributors	Dallas, TX	10/88	—	370
SB Marketing	Tulsa, OK	09/88	—	774
Simmons	Severna Park, MD	10/87	1,570	980
Smith	Chicago, IL	10/88	—	750
Unique Collect	Wheaton, IL	11/88	—	112[a]
Washington	Cushing, OK	11/87	560	1,115
Weathers	Kansas City, MO	10/88	—	1,180
Total Units Sold			$15,239	$28,188

[a]Purchased apparel
[b]Purchased letterhead

double in 1990, and to increase another 10 percent in the third year of this market expansion strategy.

The Military Market

Black men and women comprised more than 27 percent of the armed forces. Distribution by service is shown in Exhibit 7. Although blacks accounted for 12 percent of the U.S. population, only 8.8 percent of the American college population was black, and the number of black high school graduates continuing on to college was actually decreasing. Thus, black enlistment in the military was expected to continue to be high. If black military personnel would purchase cards at the national "average" rate of approximately 35 cards per year, military sales would exceed 40 million units. The Army and Air Force Exchange Service (AAFES) operated nearly 6,000 retail facilities on military installations worldwide, with annual sales in 1986 exceeding $6.2 billion. AAFES bought goods and services from about 40,000 U.S. producers, 88 percent of which were classified as small businesses. Card racks available in AAFES facilities were identical to those in the U.S. chain stores; however, no slotting fees were charged. The three-year goal was to obtain distribution in 10 percent of the AAFES outlets.

Black Colleges

One hundred twenty-nine predominantly black colleges existed in the United States, with total enrollment approaching 175,000 students. A list of the 17 largest is contained in Exhibit 8. In 1988, Shades of Black had a contract with Morehouse College in Atlanta for its cards and was preparing a special "packet" for that school. Negotiations were under way for a similar display and material with Spelman College in Atlanta. Several other predominantly black colleges were located in Atlanta; the black college and university population was about 17,000 in the city.

The Shades of Black product program for Morehouse was to develop a packet of cards and stationery displaying the college seal, a sketch of a campus landmark or of a famous alumni, or a collage of unique school features. These items would be marketed not only to current students, but perhaps more importantly, would be targeted at graduates and for use by the alumni association, which could use the packets for fund-raising. Similar materials could be developed for other predominantly black colleges. The sales goal was to place materials in 25 percent of these outlets by Spring 1990, and to achieve 75 percent penetration by the third year. In terms of the special college packets, designs would be prepared for a minimum order of 100 units.

EXHIBIT 7 Blacks in the Armed Forces, 1987

Branch of Service	Total Active Duty	Number of Blacks
Army	781,000	305,698
Air Force	608,000	132,388
Navy	581,000	104,804
Marines	199,000	51,876

Source: *Statistical Abstract of the United States*, 1987

EXHIBIT 8   Largest Predominantly Black Colleges and Universities

School	Location	Enrollment
University of D.C.	Washington, D.C.	14,107
Howard University	Washington, D.C.	11,650
Southern University & A&M College	Baton Rouge, LA	9,177
Tennessee State University	Nashville, TN	8,556
Norfolk State University	Norfolk, VA	7,400
Jackson State University	Jackson, MS	6,900
North Carolina A&T State University	Greensboro, NC	5,200
North Carolina Central University	Durham, NC	5,000
Grambling State University	Grambling, LA	4,775
Alabama State University	Montgomery, AL	4,044
Fort Valley State College	Ft. Valley, GA	3,970
Tuskegee Institute	Tuskegee, AL	3,768
Hampton Institute	Hampton, VA	3,200
Virginia State University	Petersburg, VA	3,000
Spelman College	Atlanta, GA	3,000
Morehouse College	Atlanta, GA	3,000
University of Arkansas	Pine Bluff, AR	3,000

The Funeral Home Program

As mentioned previously black-owned funeral homes existed in the United States. In 1988, there were no stationery-type products specifically tailored to the grieving black family. Shades of Black intended to fill this need by marketing via a direct mail campaign a package of products that the funeral homes would then resell to their customers. This package would contain a registration book, acknowledgment cards, things to remember booklets, and so on.

Initial informal reaction from the funeral home trade was very encouraging. Letters of endorsement were received from the National Funeral Directors and Morticians Associations and from the State Embalmers and Funeral Directors of Oklahoma. Sales projections were to achieve distribution of 10 percent in this market by the end of the year, with a minimum order of 25 units per customer.

ADDITIONAL CONCERNS

Alex realized that these somewhat grandiose ambitions were dependent on raising additional capital. He received a $16,300 development loan from the Tulsa Economic Development Authority, and a private investor added $10,000. One of his pressing problems was to prepare a business plan that would be submitted to venture capitalists. Another problem he continually wrestled with was the hiring of competent people. It seemed that he personally was required to handle every problem whether it was in design, production, or sales. Finally, another matter that began to assume prominence was the possibility of moving the company headquarters to Atlanta. Retail sales in Tulsa had been much less than expected. On his visits to Atlanta he was very impressed with the vitality of

EXHIBIT 9 Metropolitan Areas with the Largest Number of Black-Owned Businesses

Area	Number of Businesses
Los Angeles/Long Beach	23,520
New York	20,242
Washington	18,805
Chicago	13,660
Houston	12,206
San Francisco	9,388
Detroit	8,731
Philadelphia	8,581
Dallas	7,825
Atlanta	7,077

Source: *Statistical Abstract of the United States*, 1988.

Atlanta's black community and with the large number of black entrepreneurs, who were rare in Oklahoma. Alex had recently obtained a list of those areas in the United States with the largest number of black-owned businesses (Exhibit 9).

However, the most immediate matter was to determine in what market segments his young company could most profitably compete.

Supportive Homecare: Positioning for the 1990s

Jeffrey W. Totten and Linda E. Swayne

The early 1980s was not the best time to start a new business. The economic climate was dismal, with the country going through a severe recession and interest rates hovering above 15 percent. Oshkosh, Wisconsin, was no different from the rest of the nation. Yet, in 1983, two people decided that it was a good time to start a business in the home health care industry.

Terri Hansen had worked for Upjohn Healthcare for 18 months as director of nurses. She thought that there was a definite need for home care in the Oshkosh area and that the time was right to start the business. Her part-time partner, John Westphal, was employed full-time in the insurance business.

THE HOME HEALTH CARE INDUSTRY

Home health care provided health care and social services in the patient's home rather than in a medical facility. Home health care was less expensive (see Exhibit 1 for home health care costs compared to institutional costs) and was considered to be less disruptive to patients.

Expenditures for home health care exceeded $9 billion in 1989. Although it was a small portion of the total $223.7 billion spent on health care, the amount and proportion for home care were expected to increase because of the growing number of people aged 65 and older, the generally lower cost of home care, support by insurers, and Medicare endorsement of home care as an alternative to institutionalization.

By 1990, the home health care market was divided into three basic services: home health care services, home medical equipment, and home infusion therapy. In 1989, home health services accounted for 68 percent, home medical equipment 20 percent, and home infusion therapy 12 percent of this $16 billion industry.[1] The demand situation for home health care providers was relatively flat, home medical equipment declined slightly, and infusion therapy increased.

This case was prepared by Professors Jeffrey W. Totten and Linda E. Swayne, as a basis for class discussion. It is not intended to illustrate either effective or ineffective handling of an administrative situation.

[1]Sandy Lutz, "Hospitals Reassess Home-Care Ventures." *Modern Healthcare*, Vol. 20, No. 37 (September 17, 1990), p. 26.

EXHIBIT 1   Comparison of Various Home Health Care Costs with Institutional Costs

Average Cost per Day for Relatively Intensive Treatment	
Home Care	$25–200 per day
Hospital	$300–500 per day
Average Cost of Care for a Ventilator-Dependent Patient	
Home Care	$21,192 per year
Hospital	$270,830 per year
Average Cost of Care for an AIDS Patient	
Home Care	$94 per day
Hospital	$773 per day
Average Cost for a Quadriplegic Patient with a Spinal Cord Injury	
Home Care	$13,931 per month
Hospital	$23,862 per month
Average Cost of Care for Infant Born with Breathing and Feeding Problems	
Home Care	$20,200 per month
Hospital	$60,970 per month
Average Cost for Routine Skilled Nursing	
Home Care	$750 per month
Hospital	$2,000 per month

Source: Robin Richman, "High-Tech Home Care: What's in It for Hospitals?" *Health Care Strategic Management,* Vol. 8, No. 3 (March 1990), p. 21.

Home health care services were expected to grow to be $14.2 billion by the mid-1900s.[2] Medical equipment, because of changes in Medicare reimbursement, was a loss rather than a profit center for many in this saturated market. Home infusion therapies, such as intravenous (IV) antibiotic therapy and chemotherapy, allowed patients the flexibility of being treated at home instead of in the hospital. Because of cost-containment pressures and the changes in the composition of the patient population, home health care shifted from custodial to acute care. Thus, the home infusion therapy segment was predicted to grow and be more profitable than home health services (custodial care) or home medical equipment. Another growing home service was in the area of rehabilitation care. Because of advances in medical technology, many patients survived severe trauma. Home care could be a viable option.[3]

In June 1988, there were about 11,000 home health care agencies, an increase over the 10,848 operating in 1987. About 50 percent were Medicare certified and about 25 percent were hospital based.[4] Since the implementation of the prospective payment sys-

[2]Robin Richman, "High-Tech Home Care: What's in It for Hospitals?" *Health Care Strategic Management,* Vol. 8, No. 3 (March 1990), p. 19.

[3]Mary Wagner, "Despite Gains in Home Infusion Therapy, Home Care-Revenue Growth Remains Flat." *Modern Healthcare,* Vol. 20, No. 20 (May 21, 1990), p. 96.

[4]"Health Services." *U.S. Industrial Outlook 1990.* U.S. Department of Commerce, January 1990, p. 49–5.

tem (PPS) in 1983, hospital-based home care agencies more than doubled in number, from 700 in 1983 to more than 2,000 in 1989.[5] Hospitals actively sought additional revenues as third-party payer policies and practices resulted in shorter hospital stays. Home care seemed to offer an opportunity to add services, to remain visible in the community, and to obtain a competitive advantage. Many hospitals provided referrals (98.4 percent of patients were referred by a hospital to a home health care agency), so they had a decided advantage in developing home care services. They were motivated to enter the market because it helped to reduce a patient's hospital stay but still provided care for the patient. However, according to a study by SMG Marketing Group reported in the *Marion Long Term Care Digest, Home Health Care Edition for 1989*, long-term patients chose proprietary agencies over hospital-based home care (Exhibit 2).

As home care shifted from custodial to acute care, hospitals increased their diversification efforts into home infusion therapy, Medicare-certified home health agencies, hospices, home medical-equipment companies, and private-duty nursing/supplemental staffing agencies. Home infusion gained favor over Medicare-certified home health agencies because agencies that relied on people as inventory were more difficult to operate.[6] Hospital-based home health care agencies experienced turnover rates of 18.7 percent for registered nurses and 47.8 percent for occupational therapists in 1989.

Hospitals entered into the home infusion therapy business in various ways. In the past many hospitals developed arrangements with existing providers. They accomplished these arrangements through informal efforts, affiliations, contract services, fee-for-services, or joint ventures. For example, one hospital entered the home infusion therapy market through a joint venture with the local visiting nurses association

---

[5]Lutz, "Hospitals Reassess Home-Care Ventures," p. 23.

[6]Richman, "High-Tech Home Care," p. 1.

EXHIBIT 2   Home Health Care Choice

Type of Patient	Government	Hospital	Proprietary	Not-for-Profit Visiting Nurses Association	Average
Male	35.9%	39.0%	36.9%	35.2%	36.8%
Female	64.1	61.0	63.1	64.8	63.2
Adult	24.0	23.3	25.9	24.0	24.5
Pediatric	4.7	3.6	5.1	5.0	4.6
Senior Citizen	71.3	73.1	69.0	70.9	70.9
Patient <30 days	27.5	35.0	27.0	33.5	30.3
Patient >30 days	72.5	65.0	73.0	66.5	69.7
1 Visit/Week	44.5	36.6	18.2	24.9	29.8
2–3 Visits/Week	39.3	51.3	47.3	50.7	47.1
3+ Visits/Week	16.2	12.1	34.5	24.4	23.1
24-Hour Care Required	7.0	7.9	15.8	10.4	12.3

Source: "Planning Indicators," *Health Care Strategic Management*, Vol. 8, No. 4 (April 1990), p. 23.

(VNA). It was mutually beneficial for both parties because they expanded services without either having to invest full start-up costs.

Senior citizens represented 73.1 percent of the patients receiving IV therapies. AIDS patients were another growing segment of the patient mix that could benefit from home infusion therapy. There were 78,312 reported cases of AIDS in the United States in 1988. An estimated 1.5 million were infected by the HIV virus.[7]

Reimbursement for home infusion therapy was generally at a satisfactory level. Most private insurance carriers and health maintenance organizations provided sufficient reimbursement. Medicare covered some infusion therapies, but not all the available types. Case managers became common for in-home infusion therapy patients. Case managers were expected to scrutinize health care costs, bringing more checks and balances to the home infusion industry.[8]

Utilization of home health care agencies increased each year from 1980 to 1987 (Exhibit 3). Because home health care had been growing at a rate of 20 percent a year, the "dip" in 1987 was unusual, especially because there was an increasing proportion of people over 65. In 1987, the over-65 population accounted for 30 percent of total medical expenditures.[9]

It appeared that the lessening of demand for home health care in 1987 may have been caused by a misunderstanding by the Health and Human Services Department concerning the number of days a week an eligible home care patient could receive care under full-time and part-time services. The misunderstanding was resolved by litigation in favor of the beneficiary (see *Duggan v. Bowen*, USDC(DC), No.87-0383), August 1, 1988).[10] Home care usage increased slightly in 1988.

Some for-profit home health care agencies started offering bonuses to hospital discharge planners as a method to increase business. Similar to the frequent-flyer pro-

---

[7]"Health Services." p. 49–5.

[8]"Providers Eye Entry of Case Managers in Home Infusion." *Modern Healthcare*, Vol. 20, No. 37 (September 17, 1990), p. 30.

[9]Richman, "High-Tech Health Care." p. 19.

[10]"Health Services," p. 49–4.

EXHIBIT 3 Trends in Home Health Care Utilization

Year	Visits	Patients Served
1980	16,322	726
1981	22,688	948
1982	30,628	1,154
1983	36,898	1,318
1984	40,440	1,498
1985	39,462	1,549
1986	38,022	1,571
1987	35,676	1,295
1988	36,598	1,305

Source: "Health Services," *U.S. Industrial Outlook 1990*, U.S. Department of Commerce, January 1990, p. 49–5.

grams implemented by airlines, the agencies provided free service to hospitals that referred private paying patients. Olsten Health Care Services returned to each participating institution (350 were enrolled) 10 percent of reimbursed service hours generated from a given institution's private pay referrals. The more hours referred, the more hours of free care accumulated. The institutions used the free hours for indigent patients. "What we're doing is giving something back to the community," commented Sal Morici, marketing manager in Olsten's health care division.[11] Not all hospitals were enthusiastic about the program. Public scrutiny of referrals (especially Medicare referrals) made some hospitals reluctant to participate. Others were pleased to be able to offer the free home care to patients so that they could be discharged earlier.

HOME HEALTH CARE IN OSHKOSH

In 1983, before Terri Hansen started Supportive HealthCare, only Upjohn Health Care provided 24-hour home health care for the Oshkosh area. The Visiting Nurses Association and the Winnebago County nurses provided part-time, intermittent home care. Several hospitals in the Fox River Valley, including Mercy Medical Center (236 beds in Oshkosh), Theda Clark Regional Hospital (356 beds in Neenah), St. Elizabeth's Hospital (280 beds in Appleton), Appleton Medical Center (220 beds in Appleton), Kaukauna Community Hospital (52 beds in Kaukauna), and St. Agnes (62 beds in Fond Du Lac), provided acute (in-patient) care.

Oshkosh, a small urban community located on the western shore of Lake Winnebago in Winnebago County, Wisconsin, had a population of approximately 54,000 people (Exhibit 4). The city, located on a major state highway, about 90 minutes from Madison, the state capital, had a strong Polish, German, and Scandinavian heritage, and was tied economically to the paper industry that is concentrated along the Fox River Valley. The city was also home for Oshkosh Truck (heavy-duty vehicles), Leach (garbage trucks), Oshkosh B'Gosh (well-known children's clothing), the Experimental Aircraft Association, the University of Wisconsin-Oshkosh, Miles Kimball (catalog merchandise), Georgia Pacific (paper), and Mercury Marine (boat motors).

GETTING STARTED

Ms. Hansen started very small. "I did not want a lot of overhead, so I started the business in my home. I wanted to make sufficient income for myself and for my workers." She did not expect to generate any cash for at least six months. In fact, she had to borrow money from the bank to pay her own salary. Because she could afford so little help, she handled the nursing management, typing, telephone answering, and marketing herself. In the beginning, the company was a two-person office operation, with three part-timers providing care in the field.

Before she could actually get started, she had to apply for a license from the state. A lengthy proposal had to be written and submitted to the Wisconsin Department of Health and Social Services to show need for the service. Letters from physicians and social agencies indicating support for the idea had to be included. Three-year projections of operations were required to show that the business could be maintained for at least that period of time. The certificate of need was granted in January 1983. Supportive HomeCare

---

[11]Sandy Lutz, "Home-Care Agencies Offer Bonuses for Business." *Modern Healthcare*, August 20, 1990, pp. 73–74.

EXHIBIT 4:   Map of Oshkosh and the Surrounding Counites

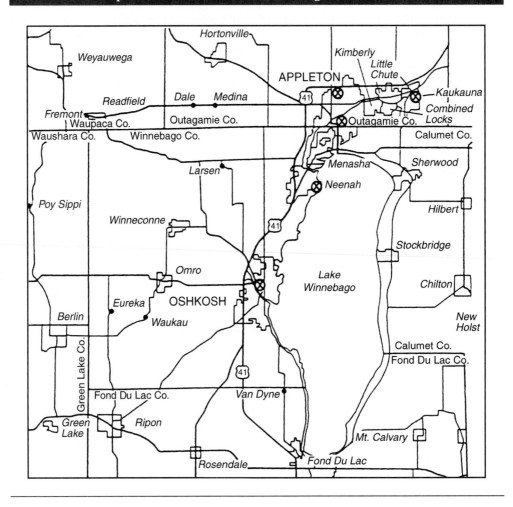

became a privately owned, independent, state-licensed home care agency. It took the company until April to get certification for third-party billing by Medicare and Medicaid. During these four months, the company could only accept private-pay patients.

Ms. Hansen spent the first months talking about the company to agencies, churches, and doctors without generating any business. Finally in March, the company cared for its first patient, quickly followed by five more. "For that first year, I was on call twenty-four hours a day, seven days a week," remembered Ms. Hansen. The company grew to two full-time and two part-time office personnel and 30 employees in the field by the end of its first year of operation.

TARGET MARKET

Ms. Hansen targeted her services toward hospital discharge planners, doctors, county nurses, county social agencies, and the Visiting Nurses Association. According to Terri Hansen, "We wanted to find a niche in the market where the company could fit in without rocking the boat, yet still provide a needed service. My goal was to provide a service with a positive image, one that works *with* other competitors, to be collaborative rather than competing against them." The population target was Winnebago County, where Ms. Hansen had her strongest contacts and greatest credibility as a health care professional. Potential consumers of home care included individuals recuperating from accidents and outpatient surgery, handicapped and disabled individuals, single and working parents, and private-duty individualized care for loved ones who were gravely ill. Exhibit 5 lists the client bases for 1989.

CHOOSING HOME HEALTH CARE

In general, if the person who would be utilizing the home health care service were currently in the hospital, he or she would typically use the Yellow Pages to find the service providers and would rely on the advice of physicians, family, friends, and "significant others" in choosing a home health care agency. Outside the hospital, prospective clients relied on their adult children and significant others for advice. The final decision was usually made by the client, the family, or close friends.

Supportive HomeCare found that clients or referral sources who made service inquiries were at one of four possible stages in their decision making: gathering information, semi-interested, desired home care services, or decided against using Supportive HomeCare. The personnel answering the telephone tried to respond promptly to all inquiries, assessing the level of decision making and determining what the client's needs were.

Fees for home health care varied considerably based on the type of care required as well as the company providing the care. Supportive HomeCare was competitively priced for the services offered (see Exhibit 6).

SERVICE GROWTH

Growth, measured in terms of hours of service provided, quadrupled every quarter during 1983 and 1984. By June 1984, Supportive HomeCare employed 40 people, including office personnel, nurses, and nurses' aides. Growth compelled the company to move out of Ms. Hansen's home. A vacant house on Mr. Vernon Street (two blocks east of Oshkosh's main street) became available, and the company moved during the summer of 1985.

Although Ms. Hansen had no formal business training, she developed and managed a very successful company. Her concern was that the health care industry was changing rapidly. There were more competitors entering the market, and the VNA was the acknowledged market leader in Winnebago County. In addition, she was concerned about the rumors warning that changes in private insurance and Medicaid would make home care less financially beneficial for patients.

Ms. Hansen decided to open an office in Appleton in January 1986. Outagamie was the largest of the three counties (Outagamie, Winnebago, and Calumet) that comprised the Appleton/Fox cities metropolitan statistical area (see Exhibit 7 for population statistics). She found that the Oshkosh market was a lot easier to break into than the Appleton market. The two major reasons for this more-difficult entry appeared to be the fact that she did not live in Appleton (though she had some connections there that have helped the company) and the strong visiting nurses programs in the area. The

EXHIBIT 5 Supportive HomeCare Client Base

	1986	1989
Primary Diagnosis of Clients Serviced		
Cardiovascular	29	53
Cancer	19	17
Arthritis	18	25
Cerebral Vascular Accident	17	24
Diabetes	11	21
Respiratory	10	22
Cerebral Palsy	7	5
Fractures	7	21
Paralysis	6	12
Mental Illness	2	13
Senile Dementia	1	19
Mental Retardation	1	8
Other Conditions	46	69
Total Clients	174	309
Referral Sources for Admissions		
Hospitals	27	36
Social Services	20	28
Supportive HomeCare Employees	6	12
Newspaper	6	10
Client/Former Client	5	26
Nursing Homes	5	2
Yellow Pages	5	4
Home Health Agency	3	19
Presentation	1	4
Other and Continuing Patients	11	168
Total Referrals	89	309
Number of Clients Discharged		
To Nursing Homes	13	33
By Death	29	26
To Self-Care	23	78
To Family	2	6
Other	20	32
Hospitalized	0	57
Total	87	232
Number of Clients Admitted by Age		
17 and Under		19
18–54		23
55–64		40
65–74		150
75–84		70
85–94		7
Total		309
Client Totals		
Number of Clients Carried Over from 1988		140
Number of New Admissions in 1989		169
Total Clients Served in 1989		309

Source: SHC State Annual Report, 1986 and 1989 (provided August 20, 1990).

EXHIBIT 6   Home Health Care Rate Comparisons

Type of Helper	Supportive HomeCare	Lakeshore Home Care	Mercy VNA[a]
Registered Nurse	$75/visit—$35 add. hr.	N/A	$79/2 hr. visit—$27 add. hr.
Licensed Practical Nurse	$55/2 hr. visit—$27 add. hr.	N/A	N/A
Home Health Aide	$36/2 hr. visit —$16.45 add. hr.	$12/hr. (1 hr. minimum)	$37/2-hr. visit—$18 add. hr.
Personal Care Worker/ Homemaker Companion	$11.50/hr.	$9.50/hr. (1 hr. minimum)	N/A
Live-in Companion	N/A	$110/24 hrs.[e]	N/A
Other			
Home Care Attendant	$16.45/hr.	N/A	N/A
Medical Social Worker	N/A	$100/2-hr. visit	$100/2-hr. visit
Speech Pathologist	N/A	N/A	$75/2-hr. visit
Occupational Therapy	N/A	N/A	$75/2-hr. visit
Physical Therapy	N/A	N/A	$75/2-hr. visit

Type of Helper	Preferred Health Care[b]	Upjohn Home Care	Neenah-Menasha NA
Registered Nurse	$80 ($70)/2-hr. visit[c]	$32 ($27)/hr.[d]	$77/2-hr. visit— 29 add. hr.
Licensed Practical Nurse	$70/2-hr. visit— $22 add. hr.	$25 ($22)/hr.[d]	$77/2-hr. visit— $25 add. hr.
Home Health Aide	$41/2-hr. visit— $16.44 add. hr.	$18/hr.	$46/2-hr. visit— $16 add. hr.
Personal Care Worker/ Homemaker Companion	$21/2-hr. visit— $9 add. hr.	$11.05/hr.	$9.75/hr. (2-hr. minimum)—$45/ overnight (8–10 hrs.)
Live-in Companion	$100/day	N/A	$110/day
Other			
Home Care Attendant	N/A	$8/hr.	N/A
Medical Social Worker	N/A	N/A	$95/visit
Speech Pathologist	N/A	N/A	$77/visit
Occupational Therapy	N/A	N/A	$77/visit
Physical Therapy	N/A	N/A	$77/visit

[a]Sliding fee available.
[b]Fees for private pay only.
[c]Higher fees for specialized RN (e.g., pediatrics).
[d]Higher fees for "hi-tech" RNs, LPNs.
[e]State sees this as a babysitter, not personal care; switch to nurses' aide live-in at $154/24 hrs.
N/A = not available
Source: Telephone interviews, October 4, 1990; Neenah-Menasha VNA Rate Sheet, October 8, 1990;
Supportive HomeCare Rate Sheet, October 8, 1990.

EXHIBIT 7 Population Statistics for the Appleton/Fox Metropolitan Statistical Area

	1980	1989
Calumet County	30,867	34,729
Appleton	5,484	N/A
Outagamie County	128,730	139,769
Appleton	53,424	65,314
Winnebago County	131,772	140,781
Menasha	14,728	15,077
Neenah	22,432	24,180
Oshkosh	49,740	53,534
Town of Menasha	12,307	14,178

N/A = not available
Source: Official population estimates for 1986, Madison: Demographic Services Center, Wisconsin Department of Administration, November 1986: Demographic Services Centers, Wisconsin Department of Administration, November 1989: Oshkosh, Wisconsin Community Profile, Wisconsin Public Service Corporation (Courtesy of Oshkosh Chamber of Commerce), October 8, 1990.

Appleton Visiting Nurses Association was well entrenched in that market, plus the Neenah-Menasha VNA was strong. Neenah and Menasha lay between Oshkosh and Appleton and were relatively closed communities (supportive of home-grown, lived-here-all-our-lives businesses).

The company continued strong growth through 1986 although not at the rapid pace of 1983 and 1984. By January 1987, Supportive HomeCare employed 30 full-time personnel in the office and 49 full-time and 150 part-time personnel in the field. It became evident that the company had to move again. Ms. Hansen investigated several options and chose a site on a corner of Main Street in Oshkosh. Supportive HomeCare wanted to stress being visible to potential customers. "The new office has 5,500 square feet of space and includes a computer department, billing and payroll, nursing department, marketing, personnel, financial services, and general administration." The location's high visibility did bring in additional growth in terms of walk-in business, which the company had never had before. Ms. Hansen anticipated that the new location would adequately serve the company for the next five years. At the end of December 1989, the staff was somewhat smaller, reflecting the difficulty of recruiting employees. The office staff included 20 full-time and three part-time employees. In the field, there were 13 full-time and 121 part-time employees.

ENTREPRENEURIAL STYLE

Terri Hansen was an entrepreneur who learned how to manage an "overnight success." She developed a team concept in managing the company. She was grooming her team, which was comprised of the nurse manager, the personnel director, the financial director, and the marketing manager. Her partner, John Westphal, served as director of computer services until she bought his share of the partnership in late July 1987. Exhibit 8 is Ms. Hansen's organization chart. Her team was very strong, especially because of the

EXHIBIT 8: Table of Organization, Supportive HomeCare

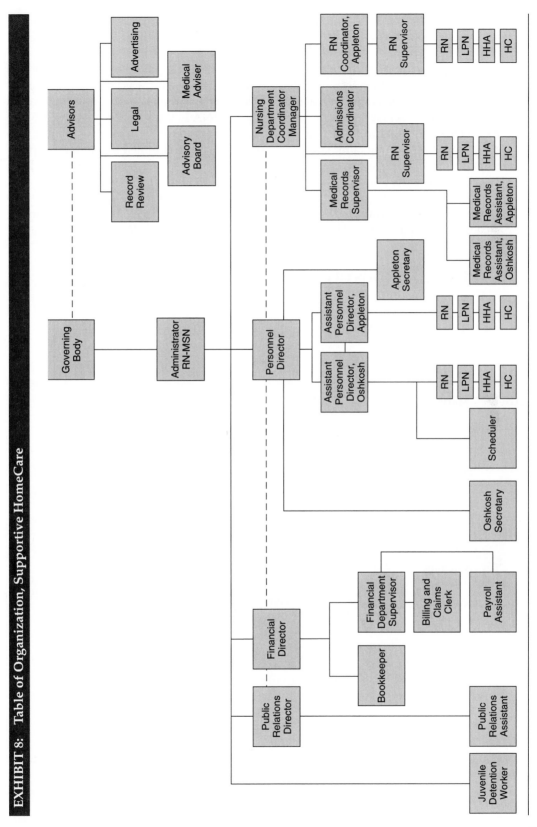

different backgrounds of the members. Decisions were made as a team: Ms. Hansen seldom overrode them, but she would if she thought something else was best for the company.

Her nurses and office staff were involved in marketing. Each office employee was given certain marketing assignments to complete. The team was working on a companywide plan to keep Supportive HomeCare in the community's mind. Ms. Hansen acknowledged the market leadership of the local VNA in the area outside Oshkosh (see Exhibit 9 for market position). "We are aiming at being number two in the market outside Oshkosh—a strong number two at that." Ms. Hansen summed up her style of management: "I believe in a strong management philosophy—I was never taught that; I just use common sense."

Ms. Hansen recognized the value of good community relations and was very active in the community. She took advantage of opportunities to speak to clubs in the area whenever possible and held an open house at Supportive HomeCare's offices.

A DIFFERENT INDUSTRY

The changes in the environment continued. More competitors entered the market and many private insurance companies decided to drop coverage of home health care pro-

EXHIBIT 9   Market Positions for the Major Home Care Providers in the Oshkosh Area

Position	1987	1990
Oshkosh		
1	Supportive HomeCare	Supportive HomeCare
2	Mercy VNA	Mercy VNA
3	Upjohn	Upjohn
4	County Nurses	Lakeshore
5	Preferred Health	County Nurses
Appleton		
1	Appleton VNA	Appleton VNA
2	Supportive HomeCare	Supportive HomeCare
3	Upjohn	Upjohn
4	Preferred Health	Preferred Health
5	St. Elizabeth's	Lakeshore
Neenah/Menasha		
1	Neenah-Menasha VNA	Neenah-Menasha
2	Supportive HomeCare	Supportive HomeCare
3	Upjohn	Upjohn
4	Preferred Health	Preferred Health
5		Lakeshore

Source: Observations of Terri Hansen, August 1990.

grams. This really hurt the funding outlook for home care in general, and Supportive HomeCare was not immune to the problem. Within a span of 10 months, from September 1986 to July 1987, as shown in Exhibit 10, the funding mix changed for Supportive HomeCare, reflecting the problems created by insurance companies' modifications in the coverage granted for home care.

In addition, Medicaid made changes that had a major impact on Supportive HomeCare. Similar to many others, the company had come to depend on third-party funding, but it appeared that third-party payments would continue to diminish. Ms. Hansen attempted to contract with other businesses, such as the city of Oshkosh, Georgia Pacific, or Mercury Marine, in order to move away from the dependency of third-party payments. She had contracts with the Appleton and Neenah-Menasha VNAs to provide extended care for hospice patients and with nearly all nursing homes in the Fox River Valley to provide staffing when needed.

Supportive HomeCare provided a variety of services, including registered nurses, licensed practical nurses, home health aides/nurses' aides, homemaker-companions, night service, insurance counseling, private duty, institutional staffing, and home care attendants.

Two new programs were introduced in 1987 when the use of home health care appeared to be declining. Personnel Resource Network (PRN) had two divisions: Home Management and Staffing. PRN Home Management was considered to be a burgeoning area primarily because of the increasing number of two-income families. Services offered included routine and extensive cleaning, laundry and ironing, grocery shopping and errands, meal preparation, and help with entertaining. Ms. Hansen admitted that she had not invested the money necessary to market this service. "It is a needed service, but health care is what we do best." PRN Staffing was successful because it provided temporary staff for hospitals, nursing homes, and other health care providers.

"LifeStyle Connection (LSC) was a concept before its time," according to Ms. Hansen. "In five years, companies will be forced to provide this type of service to keep health insurance costs down." LSC provided custom services, including health assess-

---

EXHIBIT 10 Funding Mix

Sources	September 1986	1987–88	1988–89	1989–90
Private Pay	17%	39.80%	30.99%	22.33%
Medicaid	33	27.28	33.37	43.68
Private Insurance	40	13.85	11.00	10.10
Medicare	3	0.88	2.75	3.71
County Funds	7	7.70	10.11	13.80
Personnel Resource Network[a]		7.54	7.48	3.21
Lifestyle Connections[a]		0.23	0.81	0.66
Other	0	2.65	3.49	2.51

[a]New programs started in 1987.
Source: Supportive HomeCare company records.

ment screenings, behavior-modification classes, fitness assessments, lifestyle assessments, and informational miniseminars. Only a few companies used the services of LSC.

SUPPORTIVE HOMECARE GOALS AND PHILOSOPHY

Ms. Hansen outlined the goals for Supportive HomeCare:

- To provide quality nursing and support services
- To be a quality agency by providing superior services at a competitive cost: monitoring agency expansion to meet the needs of the community; functioning within local, state, and federal guidelines; and monitoring and evaluating agency operations continuously
- To hire and retain qualified employees
- To increase community and consumer awareness via marketing and community relations
- To achieve maximum reimbursement from third-party players

Supportive HomeCare's unique selling proposition and philosophy are provided in Exhibit 11.

Staffing

"Staffing is our biggest problem," stated Ms. Hansen. "The nursing and other medical personnel shortage is real and it's everywhere. But we are not only competing with other health care organizations to get good people but with restaurants, factories, and so forth. Home health care has a problem with retaining people, too. It is difficult to predict or ensure working hours, the individual is isolated on the job because there are no other staff to talk to, the hours are often inconvenient, and travel—sometimes longer distances than I'd like—is often required."

Compounding the shortage of workers, the government instituted tougher regulations for training home health care "aides." However, a new category of health care providers was added that fit the old job description for "home health aid." A "personal care worker" could be paid about half of the wage given to a care giver ($9.00 per hour compared to $15.10 per hour).

Supportive HomeCare attempted to market itself to potential employees to entice them to come to work and developed retention strategies to keep the individuals once they were hired. On July 1, 1990, Supportive HomeCare instituted a number of changes for the field staff, including increased employee benefits, higher wages to be more in line with competition, increased personal contact by Terri and the office staff, and development of a "retention budget." Employees were rewarded with small gifts for beyond-the-call-of-duty service, flowers were sent for special occasions, and gift certificates were given for a holiday remembrance. Ms. Hansen met with the Personnel Department twice a month to actively work on problem solving for staffing. "We have the patients. We just don't have the staff," Terri lamented. She continued. "We stress the flexible hours we offer for part-time—and some full-time—staff. We are a compassionate employer. We know and understand the needs of working women. And we are a company that anyone can be proud to work for because we provide quality care and we have the reputation for providing quality care."

EXHIBIT 11   Supportive HomeCare Positioning

UNIQUE SELLING PROPOSITION

Supportive HomeCare provides skilled nursing, personal care, and homemaker/companion services up to twenty-four hours a day, seven days a week to clients in their homes. Initial contact, assessment of service needs, and exploration of payment options are at no charge to the client. Quality services are offered at a competitive price.

Supportive HomeCare maintains a reputation for being the quality service that truly cares about people and considers meeting its clients' needs as the number one goal. The agency acts as a client advocate. The staff have professional expertise in dealing with third-party payment sources and continually remain abreast of issues dealing with home care.

Supportive HomeCare maintains strict supervision policies, agency rules and regulations, service, and employment standards. Employees are thoroughly screened, trained, oriented, and inserviced on an ongoing basis.

Supportive HomeCare prides itself on case management. It maintains close communication with the client, family, physician, and significant others involved. The agency strives to develop a cooperative working relationship with other community agencies and facilities.

PHILOSOPHY OF THE AGENCY

It is the philosophy of the agency to provide quality and dependable nursing care, therapies, and homemaker/companion services, thus enabling individuals to remain as independent as possible in the least-restrictive environment. Services will be provided by employees who are qualified, experienced, and empathetic to the needs of home care clients. All aspects of the agency will be monitored to provide efficient and cost-effective quality care.

Supportive HomeCare will promote cooperative working relationships with other home health providers and community resources to attain a comprehensive level of care.

Source: Supportive HomeCare brochure.

WHAT LIES AHEAD?

There were some challenges ahead for Ms. Hansen and her company. She predicted, "In the next six months, the home care industry will see a shakeout and some home care agencies will go out of business. Relying on third-party funding and problems in billing departments with uncollected payments are two key reasons home care agencies will go under or be sold." Competition was more intense and would be a factor. "Our competitors control discharges from the hospitals—Mercy Visiting Nurses for Mercy Hospital and the Appleton Medical Center and St. Elizabeth's Hospital. It's tough to compete."

The environment changed. There was a shortage of qualified nurses not just in Oshkosh and Appleton, but all over the country. The federal, state, and local governments instituted tougher regulations for training and certifying home health aides. There were minimal increases in third-party reimbursements from Medicaid, Medicare, and county funds. Private insurance paid very few claims, and Ms. Hansen saw no turnaround in the future. Although there was an increased need for home care as the population aged, there was insufficient staff that was affordable. "People just can't afford personal home care. It is a real balancing act when the environment is hostile, there is a shortage of all health care providers, and demand exceeds supply."

According to Ms. Hansen, "Supportive HomeCare had its best year ever in 1989–90, but it was definitely the most stressful. I'd like to stop the world and get off—just for a few hours—and figure out exactly what I should do with Supportive HomeCare!"

Lowe's Companies: Battling Home Depot

Lew G. Brown and Jerredith Shearin

GOING SHOPPING

Joanne Miles had been telling her husband, Bud, for months that they needed to improve their Greensboro, North Carolina, home by turning their screen porch into a sunroom. Joanne had scoured home decor magazines and clipped articles on how to design and build sunrooms. Finally, Bud had consented to take on the project.

Bud fancied himself as a very good handyman. He was skilled at the typical do-it-yourself projects like plumbing, painting, wallpapering, and even fixing sheetrock. Bud realized that Joanne's porch project would take all his skill. However, he figured that with some good advice and a home equity loan, he would be able to complete the project himself.

Bud made a list of materials and prepared to go to a home-improvement store to get advice and prices. He invited Joanne to go with him and to pick out the color of the terra cotta floor tile. As they prepared to leave, Joanne asked, "By the way, which store are we going to? Both Lowe's and Home Depot are located right together there on Wendover Road."

"I hadn't really thought about it. Do you have any preference?" Bud answered.

"Not really. From what I've seen, both stores seem to have pretty good selections and prices. And both offer lots of advice. Let's just get in the car and see how the spirit moves us."

THE HOME-IMPROVEMENT BATTLEFIELD

Bud and Joanne are just one more target in the increasingly competitive battle for the do-it-yourself (DIY) home-improvement market. Lowe's, Home Depot, Builder's Square, and other building supply/home improvement chains, independent retailers affiliated with wholesaler groups like Ace Hardware and True Value, and individual hardware stores—all are trying to attract DIY "baby boomers" like Bud and Joanne.

This case was prepared by Professor Lew G. Brown and Undergraduate Research Assistant Jerredith Shearin of University of North Carolina at Greensboro, as a basis for class discussion. It is not intended to illustrate either effective or ineffective handling of an administrative situation. The authors express their appreciation to Lowe's Companies for its cooperation in developing this case.

The Home Improvement Research Institute, a trade association, and Management Horizons, a consulting firm, estimated that the DIY home owner and building-contractor repair and remodel (R&R) markets would grow from $126 billion in 1994 to an estimated $163 billion by 1999, a compound annual growth rate of 4.9 percent. The DIY portion of the market alone would grow from $70 billion to $113 billion during that period, a 5.5 percent growth rate. Analysts speculated that this market was recession-proof because consumers tended to see their homes as their primary assets and, therefore, protected their value.

The typical DIYer was a married, male home owner, aged 25 to 54 with a high school education or some college and an annual income of $20,000 to $40,000. However, the Home Improvement Research Institute suggested that there were additional ways to segment the market (see Exhibit 1).

HOME DEPOT

Home Depot helped stimulate the DIY market's rapid growth. Prior to Home Depot's founding in 1978, father-and-son lumber yards and a few specialty distributors who sold primarily to contractors and tradespeople dominated the hardware market. Home

---

EXHIBIT 1   Home Improvement Market Segments

Hard-Core DIYer (15.9%) Will try anything without expert help. Saving money is important. Serves as source of information for others. Youngest group, mainly male. Gets advice from friends and relatives most often, but also from retailers. Tends to shop at only one store.

Frugal Hobbyist (15.6%) Shops for best price and watches ads. Seeks advice from magazines and books, especially home-improvement magazines. Works in yard and on outside of home. 50/50 male/female. Lowest income group. Shops at different stores. Most price sensitive.

Type-A Gardner (16.9%) Wants the best yard. Convenience, not price important. Typically older male. Depends on retail store clerks. Most likely to buy from one store. Least price sensitive.

Help Me (18.1%) Takes little time or pleasure in home improvement projects. Most likely to let professional install. Installation service and retailer advice important. Typically older female. Likely to shop at different stores, but relatively less price sensitive.

Minimal Maintenance (14.7%) Does minimal home improvement. Takes no pride in home's appearance. Depends on friends and relatives for advice. Typically young male.

Style Trendsetter (19%) Likes to have unique decor, but gets little pleasure from DIY. Only interested in increasing home's value. Uses professional help and wants installation services. Depends on friends and relatives for advice. Lower dependence on retailers. Relatively price sensitive. Typically young female. Highest income group.

Source: Home Improvement Research Institute

Depot opened the market to average consumers, allowing them to buy all the pieces for a home-improvement project at one store.

Home Depot has become the world's largest home-improvement retailer and one of the 20 largest retailers in the United States. As of 1997, it operated about 530 stores in the United States and 29 stores in Canada; and it had announced plans for its first international store in Santiago, Chile. The company planned to have 1,100 stores by 2000. Of the 724 stores operated by the six largest home-improvement retailers in the top 50 U.S. markets, 390 were Home Depot Stores, compared with 96 for Builder's Square, 79 for Hechingers, 20 for Eagle, 78 for Lowe's, and 61 for HomeBase. Analysts estimated that Home Depot's 1997 sales would top $24 billion, with an estimated net income of $1.2 billion.

The average Home Depot store had approximately 103,000 square feet of indoor selling space and an additional 20,000 to 28,000 square feet of outside garden center space, including houseplant enclosures. The typical store carries 40,000 to 50,000 SKUs (stock keeping units, i.e., individual items) and offered installation services for many products. The company had approximately 122,000 employees, whom it called associates, and prided itself on the high level of customer service its associates offered. Analysts gave Home Depot high marks for its operational execution.

Home Depot targeted DIYers primarily, although home-improvement contractors and other professionals were becoming increasingly important customers. In order to sustain its growth, Home Depot planned to target what it called the PRO segments. By doing so, it could expand its defined market from about $140 billion (DIY and Repair and Remodel) to about $360 billion as a result of including the property maintenance, heavy construction, building and general contracting, trade, and flooring sectors. In early 1997, Home Depot purchased Maintenance Warehouse/America Corporation, a direct mail catalog company that targeted repair and remodeling pros. It also installed separate checkout areas for these professionals and added special products. Analysts estimated that professionals already accounted for about 30 percent of Home Depot's sales. The company also was reducing the number of SKUs it carried in order to focus on the best-selling items. Some analysts believed that Home Depot did not want to be seen as the "home solution" by offering a full range of goods and services to the home owner. Rather, it wanted to concentrate on home-improvement products for both the home owner and professional.

LOWE'S

In contrast to Home Depot, Lowe's had been in business since 1946, when the son of a dry-goods dealer founded the company in North Wilkesboro, North Carolina. The company grew by selling lumber, tools, and hardware to contractors in the rural South. In the 1980s, however, Lowe's began to cater to the retail consumer in an attempt to offset the ups and downs caused by swings in housing starts. The company added luxury housewares and fixed up its storefronts to attract women customers and to shift away from its contractor-oriented format. Chief Executive Officer Robert Tillman notes that men want to go into a store, get the item they want at a good price, and get out. Women, he says, want a shopping experience and a welcoming atmosphere.

Lowe's shift in emphasis was reasonably successful, but its business really took off in 1989. Lowe's observed Home Depot's success with its "superstore" format and decided to try its own version, a 45,000-square-foot center with 2,000 more items than its smaller stores. Lowe's stores at that time ranged from 8,000 to 25,000 square feet. Sales skyrocketed, and Lowe's began gradually to increase the size of its new stores. By 1995, the smallest store Lowe's opened had 85,000 square feet; and its largest stores, "the big boxes," had 115,000 square feet and more than 40,000 SKUs.

Although Lowe's and Home Depot's product selections were similar, Lowe's sold washers and dryers, televisions, microwaves, refrigerators, stereos, and VCRs, whereas most Home Depot stores did not carry these items.

As it developed bigger stores, Lowe's also significantly lowered its prices and moved to an "everyday-low-price" strategy. Also, like Home Depot, Lowes offered a low-price guarantee. A group of Prudential analysts priced the same basket of goods at a Lowe's and a Home Depot in Greensboro and found that Home Depot's total price was $2,006.54 versus Lowe's total price of $2,005.89.

EXHIBIT 2   Comparative Financial and Operating Statistics[a]

	Fiscal 1992	Fiscal 1993	Fiscal 1994	Fiscal 1995	Fiscal 1996
Lowe's					
Net Sales (000)	$3,846,418	$4,538,001	$ 6,110,521	$ 7,075,442	$ 8,600,241
Net Earnings (000)	$ 84,720	$ 131,786	$ 223,560	$ 226,027	$ 292,150
Total Assets (000)	$1,608,877	$2,201,648	$ 3,105,992	$ 3,556,386	$ 4,434,954
Number of Stores	303	311	336	365	402
Total Square Footage (000)	9,975	14,174	18,604	23,945	30,381
Number of Employees	21,269	28,843	37,555	44,546	53,492
Average Customer Purchase	$ 47.80	$ 48.83	$ 49.74	$ 48.15	$ 48.81
Asset Turnover	2.39	2.06	1.97	1.99	1.94
Sales per Store (000)	$ 12,694	$ $14,592	$ 18,186	$ 19,385	$ 21,394
Sales per Employee	$ 180,446	$ 157,335	$ 162,709	$ 158,835	$ 160,776
Sales per Square foot	$ 386	$ 320	$ 328	$ 295	$ 283
Square Feet per Employee	469	491	495	538	568
Gross Margin %	23.42%	23.83%	24.75%	24.92%	25.86%
Home Depot					
Net Sales (000)	$7,148,436	$9,238,763	$12,476,697	$15,470,358	$19,535,503
Net Earnings (000)	$ 362,863	$ 457,401	$ 604,501	$ 731,523	$ 937,739
Total Assets (000)	$3,931,790	$4,700,889	$ 5,778,041	$ 7,354,033	$ 9,341,710
Number of Stores	214	264	340	423	512
Total Square Footage (000)	20,897	26,383	35,133	44,356	53,926
Number of Employees	38,900	50,600	67,300	80,800	98,100
Average Customer Purchase	$ 37.72	$ 39.13	$ 41.29	$ 41.78	$ 42.09
Asset Turnover	1.82	1.97	2.16	2.10	2.09
Sales per Store (000)	$ 33,404	$ 34,995	$ 36,696	$ 36,573	$ 38,155
Sales per Employee	$ 183,764	$ 182,584	$ 185,389	$ 191,465	$ 199,139
Sales per Square foot	$ 342	$ 350	$ 355	$ 349	$ 362
Square Feet per Employee	537	521	522	549	550
Gross Margin %	27.55%	27.64%	27.94%	27.70%	27.82%

[a]Numbers in thousands where noted
Source: Casewriter's calculations

EXHIBIT 3   Lowe's Companies, Consolidated Statement of Current Earnings

	Fiscal 1992	Fiscal 1993	Fiscal 1994	Fiscal 1995	Fiscal 1996
Current Earnings					
Net Sales	$3,846,418	$4,538,001	$ 6,110,521	$7,075,442	$ 8,600,241
Cost of Sales	2,945,753	3,456,717	4,697,977	5,312,195	6,376,482
Gross Margin	900,665	1,081,284	1,512,544	1,763,247	2,223,759
Expenses					
Selling, General, & Administrative	642,799	717,028	941,079	1,127,333	1,395,523
Store Opening Costs	10,983	29,251	40,727	49,626	59,159
Depreciation	69,820	80,530	109,647	150,011	198,115
Employee Retirement Plans	35,572	37,873	49,687	46,130	68,289
Interest	15,599	18,278	27,873	38,040	49,067
Total Expenses	774,773	882,960	1,169,013	1,411,140	1,770,153
Pre-Tax Earnings	125,892	198,324	343,531	352,107	453,606
Income Tax Provision	41,172	66,538	119,971	126,080	161,456
Net Earnings	$ 84,720	$ 131,786	$ 223,560	$ 226,027	$ 292,150
Shares Outstanding					
Weighted Average	146,152	147,398	154,926	160,453	167,678
Stock Price					
High	14³⁄₈	31	41³⁄₈	34⁷⁄₈	36¼
Low	8	13⁵⁄₁₆	27³⁄₄	26	28⁵⁄₈
Square Footage (Thousands)	9,975	14,174	18,604	23,945	30,381
Employees	21,269	28,843	37,555	44,546	53,492
Assets					
Current Assets					
Cash and Cash Equivalents	$ 48,949	$ 73,253	$ 150,319	$ 63,868	$ 40,387
Short-Term Investments	5,900	35,215	118,155	107,429	30,103
Accounts Receivable	53,288	48,500	109,214	113,483	117,562
Merchandise Inventory	594,195	853,707	1,132,282	1,267,077	1,605,880
Deferred Income Taxes	8,512	12,300	18,129	19,168	19,852
Other Current Assets	34,710	60,932	29,069	32,659	37,682
Total Current Assets	745,554	1,083,907	15,571,689	1,603,684	1,851,466
Property, Less Accumulated Depreciation	787,197	1,020,234	1,397,713	1,858,274	2,494,396
Long-Term Investments	23,270	40,408	83,459	41,059	35,615
Other Assets	52,856	57,099	67,652	53,369	53,477
Total Assets	1,608,877	2,201,648	3,105,992	3,556,386	4,434,954
Liabilities and Shareholders' Equity					
Current Liabilities					
Short-Term Notes Payable	$ 3,193	$ 2,281	$ 1,903	$ 16,617	$ 80,905
Current Maturities of Long-Term Debt	21,721	49,547	26,913	14,127	22,566
Accounts Payable	330,584	467,278	675,436	655,399	914,167
Employee Retirement Plans	32,038	34,422	43,950	44,924	60,770
Accrued Salaries and Wages	39,472	45,883	63,356	67,370	71,662
Other Current Liabilities	72,626	81,765	134,334	151,494	198,461
Total Current Liabilities	499,634	681,176	945,892	949,931	1,348,531
Long-Term Debt, Excluding Current Maturities	313,562	592,333	681,184	866,183	767,338
Deferred Income Taxes	16,517	26,165	49,211	83,557	101,609
Accrued Store Restructuring Costs	45,944	28,305	9,815	—	—
Total Liabilities	875,657	1,327,979	1,686,102	1,899,671	2,217,478
Shareholders' Equity					
Retained Earnings	489,003	596,764	792,891	988,447	1,245,888
Total Shareholders' Equity	733,220	873,669	1,419,890	1,656,715	2,217,476
Total Liabilities and Shareholders' Equity	1,608,877	2,201,648	3,105,992	3,556,386	4,434,954

Source: Lowe's Company Annual Reports.

EXHIBIT 4 Home Depot, Inc., Consolidated Income Account (Dollars in Thousands)

	Fiscal 1992	Fiscal 1993	Fiscal 1994	Fiscal 1995	Fiscal 1996
Net Sales	**$7,148,436**	**$9,238,763**	**$12,476,697**	**$15,470,358**	**$ 19,535,503**
Cost of Merchandise Sold	5,179,368	6,685,384	8,991,204	11,184,772	14,101,423
Gross Profit	**1,969,068**	**2,553,379**	**3,485,493**	**4,285,586**	**5,434,080**
Selling & Store Operating	1,245,608	1,624,920	2,216,540	2,783,926	3,529,800
Preopening	26,959	36,816	51,307	52,342	54,709
General & Administrative	147,080	184,954	230,456	269,464	324,292
Total Operating Expenses	**1,419,647**	**1,846,690**	**2,498,303**	**3,105,732**	**3,908,801**
Operating Income	**549,421**	**706,689**	**987,190**	**1,179,854**	**1,525,279**
Interest Income	67,562	60,896	28,510	19,597	25,577
Interest Expense	(41,010)	(30,714)	(35,949)	(4,148)	(16,087)
Interest, Net	26,552	30,182	(7,439)	15,449	9,490
Earnings Before Income Taxes	575,973	736,871	979,751	1,195,303	1,534,769
Income Taxes	213,110	279,470	375,250	463,780	597,030
Net Income	**$ 362,863**	**$ 457,401**	**$ 604,501**	**$ 731,523**	**$ 937,739**
Average Common Shares (000)	44,989	453,037	475,947	477,977	487,752
Stock Price:					
High	68⅝	50⅞	41⅞	44⅞	59½
Low	39⅝	35	36 4/8	36⅝	42½
Total Square Feet (000)	20,897	26,383	35,133	44,356	53,926
Total Employees	38,900	50,600	67,300	80,800	98,100
Assets					
Cash and Cash Equivalents	$ 121,744	$ 99,997	$ 1,154	$ 53,269	$ 146,006
Short-Term Investments	292,451	330,976	56,712	54,756	412,430
Accounts Receivable, Net	177,501	198,431	272,225	325,384	388,416
Merchandise Inventories	939,824	1,293,477	1,749,312	2,180,318	2,708,283
Other Current Assets	30,452	43,720	53,560	58,242	54,238
Total Current Assets	**1,561,973**	**1,966,601**	**2,132,963**	**2,671,969**	**3,709,373**
Property & Equipment (at cost)	1,791,776	2,618,428	3,747,268	4,968,895	6,149,816
Less Accumulated Depreciation & Amortization	183,792	247,524	350,031	507,871	712,770
Net Property & Equipment	1,607,984	2,370,904	3,397,237	4,461,024	5,437,046
Long-Term Investments	694,276	281,623	98,022	25,436	8,480
Notes Receivable	—	35,470	32,528	54,715	39,518
Other Assets	67,557	46,291	117,291	53,651	60,753
Total Assets	**$3,931,790**	**$4,700,889**	**$ 5,778,041**	**$ 7,354,033**	**$ 9,341,710**
Liabilities					
Accounts Payable	$420,318	$521,246	$681,291	$824,808	$1,089,736
Accrued Expenses	127,133	167,489	192,151	198,208	249,356
Sales Tax Payable	46,320	57,590	101,011	113,066	129,284
Other Accrued Expenses	135,478	183,933	208,377	242,859	322,503
Income Tax Payable	23,868	40,303	8,717	35,214	48,728
Current Portion of LTD	1,828	2,077	22,692	2,327	2,519
Total Current Liabilities	**754,945**	**972,638**	**1,214,239**	**1,416,482**	**1,842,126**
Total Long-Term Debt (excluding current installment)	843,672	874,048	983,369	720,080	1,246,593
Other Long-Term Liabilities	12,968	12,276	67,953	115,917	134,034
Deferred Income Taxes	16,124	27,827	19,258	37,225	66,020
Total Liabilities	**1,627,709**	**1,886,789**	**2,284,819**	**2,289,704**	**3,288,773**
Retained Earnings	993,517	1,400,575	1,937,284	2,579,059	3,406,592
Total Stock Equity	**2,304,081**	**2,814,100**	**3,442,223**	**4,987,766**	**5,955,186**
Total Liabilities & Stock Equity	**$3,931,790**	**$4,700,889**	**$ 5,778,041**	**$ 7,354,033**	**$ 9,341,710**

Note: Some items on the Balance Sheet have been omitted to save space.
Source: Home Depot Annual Reports.

Many analysts attribute Lowe's success to its ability to lock up small, rural markets. Through 1995, 60 percent of Lowe's new-store activity was in its existing markets. In 1996, however, the company changed its strategy and announced that about 80 percent of its expansion would be in new markets, especially in major cities like Atlanta (Home Depot's headquarters) and Dallas. Lowe's intended to open 60 or more stores per year, increasing its total of 460 stores in late 1997 to 800 by 2001. Prudential Securities estimated that Lowe's 1997 sales would top $10 billion and produce net income of $351 million. Lowe's had about 60,200 employees.

Tillman noted that 50 percent of DIY sales took place in the top 25 urban cities, and Lowe's operated in only one of those cities. More importantly, much of its expansion would be in markets already served by Home Depot. By the end of 1997, about 119 of Home Depot's stores (19 percent) were competing directly with 106 of Lowe's stores (24 percent). Tillman speculated that by 2002, every U.S. market with 50,000 households would have both a Lowe's and a Home Depot. Analysts estimate that the United States will support about 2,000 "big box" stores; and by 2002, Lowe's and Home Depot combined should have that many.

Lowe's continued to see the DIY and contractor segments as its target markets, although contractor sales, including builders of new homes and contractors who perform repair and remodel jobs for homeowners, accounted for less than 20 percent of its sales, down from 35 percent in just five years. Lowe's operated 25 "contractor yards" to target that market.

Tillman indicated that Lowe's competitive strategy would capitalize on three societal trends. He noted that women have an increasing role in purchasing decisions, and many of them actually do the home-improvement work. Yet, he added, "Most of the industry's stores, staffing, advertising, and merchandising are targeted to and managed by men." Tillman also argued that baby boomers wanted less hassle, one-stop shopping, and someone they could trust to help with home-improvement projects. Finally, he noted that Generation X consumers did not waste time shopping and were into convenience, trust, and technology.

Maybe so, but America's Research Group polled 800 consumers on the subject of large home-improvement centers. The company found that the chief complaints were long checkout lines, too big and too confusing stores, time wasted getting into and out of the stores and parking lots, failure to follow through on advertised items, and lack of qualified help. (See Exhibit 2 for comparative statistics and Exhibits 3 and 4 for financial information on Lowe's and Home Depot.)

BACK WITH JOANNE AND BUD

Bud turned left off Wendover Road. The huge Home Depot store loomed just a hundred yards to the right. Down the hill stood an equally large Lowe's.

"Well, what's your choice?" Bud asked Joanne.

"Let's try Lowe's. I mean, after all, if we don't like what we see, we'll just drive back to Home Depot."

SOURCES

Nicole Harris, "Home Depot: Beyond Do-It-Yourselfers," *Business Week,* June 30, 1997;
James M. Cory, "Mass Retail or Class Retail," *Home Improvement Market,* July 1997, p. 10;

Ken Clark, "Survival of the Biggest: Lowe's CEO: Giants Rule the Roost in Home Improvement Retailing," *HFN The Weekly Newspaper for the Home,* August 18, 1997, p. 1;

W. Hood, "Lowe's Companies—Company Report," Prudential Securities, August 20, 1997; A. Rubinson, "Home Depot—Company Report," Painewebber, Inc., August 25, 1997;

Chris Roush, "Home Depot is Top Home Improvement Retailer, But Lowe's Hopes to Gain," *KnightRidder/Tribune Business News,* August 26, 1997, p. 826B0953.

Kodak Versus Fuji:
A Case of Japanese-American
Strategic Interaction

H. Donald Hopkins

"I wonder how Fuji will react," mused Frank Harris, analyst for Morris Stinson Brokers and a specialist on Kodak stock. He was referring to the planned introduction of Kodak's Photo CD, which came out in March 1992. Kodak's Photo CD was a system of electronic photography that allowed prints to be stored on a compact disk, later to be shown on a television or a computer.

For several years, Fuji and Kodak had been very sensitive to each other's competitive moves, and particularly since Fuji started to gain headway in the United States with its bright green boxes of film. Harris noted, "After the 'Battle of the Blimps' anything is possible between these two firms."

MILESTONES IN THE KODAK-FUJI RIVALRY

When Fuji began selling film in the United States, Kodak did not take the competitor seriously. Kodak felt Fuji's film colors were unrealistically bright. However, Fuji gained significant market share, reaping 10 percent of the U.S. market by 1990. The two most fascinating episodes of rivalry between these arch competitors could be labeled the "Battle of the MBAs" and the "Battle of the Blimps."

Battle of the MBAs

The University of Rochester is located in Kodak's hometown of Rochester, New York. The university received a significant portion of its endowment from George Eastman, Kodak's founder, before he committed suicide. In the 1980s and early 1990s, Kodak pledged $5 million to the university, the majority of which was targeted for the William E. Simon School of Business. In addition, Kodak sent scores of employees to the Simon School's MBA program.

To the shock and dismay of Kodak, Tsuneo Sakai was accepted in the Simon School's MBA program for the September 1987 semester. It happened that Mr. Sakai was an employee of the Fuji Photo Film Company. His position was that of planner of new imaging products.

It was later reported that Kodak officials persuaded the university to rescind its acceptance of Mr. Sakai. Instead, the university arranged for him to attend the Massachusetts Institute of Technology's business school. Apparently, Kodak feared that confidential information might be conveyed to him during classroom discussions. The university, on the other hand, feared that Kodak would withdraw "a significant number of students" from the MBA program if Mr. Sakai did attend.

Reacting to criticism of this decision, the university decided to readmit Mr. Sakai. Kodak's chairman at the time, Colby Chandler, commented, "Our actions are seen by some as an infringement upon academic integrity, which was certainly not our intent."[1]

A final chapter in this academic war happened in 1988 when Fuji announced a scholarship at the Rochester Institute of Technology (RIT) for photography students. Kodak is a large contributor to RIT, having given between $4 million and $8 million over the past 10 years. The Fuji scholarship was to be devoted solely to photography and thus would be the first of its kind at the school. A Fuji spokeswoman said they picked RIT "because of its reputation, not because it was in Rochester [home of Kodak]."

Battle of the Blimps

In the 1980s, a strange air war occurred in the skies over Tokyo. Two large blimps, one bright green, the other yellow, fought for air supremacy. This battleground was a new theater for an undeclared war pitting the two largest film companies against each other.

Kodak, after observing the green Fuji blimp keeping watch over sporting events in the United States and Europe, decided to imitate it and use that same tactic in Japan. What ensued could be characterized as blimp "dogfights." Kodak apparently escalated the rivalry by flying their yellow blimp in sight of Fuji's Tokyo headquarters. Fuji executives were amazed to be able to look out the window and observe their arch rival's name overhead.

Several months later, in November, the Fuji and Kodak blimps had a "dogfight" over nearby sporting events. Fuji was sponsoring a baseball series between American and Japanese all-stars, and Kodak was sponsoring a judo tournament a short distance away. The manager of Fuji's advertising department, Hidenobu Miyata, complained that the Kodak blimp was perilously near Fuji's blimp. He claimed that the yellow aircraft refused to comply with requests to retreat. Mr. Miyata said, "I think they were being a little too aggressive not to back off. We felt like Kodak was up for a fight."[2]

Kodak, on the other hand, accused Fuji of intentionally scheduling its blimp's flight over the baseball series to compete with Kodak's blimp. Toshio Nakano, manager of public relations for Kodak Japan, said, "So why did they wait until now? I don't call it a gentleman's act. It's nasty. It seems to me this is a hit-and-run operation on their part."[3]

Still later, in January 1987, Kodak tweaked Fuji's nose further by sending out its customary Japanese New Year's greeting cards showing the Kodak blimp with Mt. Fuji in the background. The blimp battle apparently had its opening salvo when Fuji outbid Kodak and spent $7 million to become the official film of the 1984 Los Angeles Olym-

---

[1]"Fuji Employee Is Accepted as University Shifts Stance," *Wall Street Journal*, September 14, 1987, p. 16.

[2]Karl Schoenberger, "In Skies over Tokyo, Kodak and Fuji Fight Battle of the Blimps," *Wall Street Journal*, December 30, 1986, p. A1.

[3]Ibid.

pics. The Fuji blimp was flown over the Olympic grounds. Kodak responded by buying immense periods of commercial time on the network that carried the games.

"If you watched the Olympics on American TV, you never saw the Fuji blimp," said William Reyea, a securities analyst in Tokyo. "It was part of the contract when they bought 102 ads."[4] A Kodak spokesman denied this. Kodak was the official film for the 1988 Olympics in Seoul and stationed its blimp overhead.

Me-Too Tactics

Regardless of the origin of the Battle of the Blimps, the Fuji surprise at the 1984 Olympics led Kodak from complacency to obsession. Fuji increased its market share in the United States from 2 percent to 10 percent in photographic film and paper. Much of that increase had not come at the expense of Kodak, but from weaker firms, such as 3M and Agfa-Gavaert, which Fuji specifically targeted to avoid making Kodak feel threatened.

Kodak kept a constant eye on Fuji's moves and countermoves. Researchers in Rochester painstakingly analyzed Fuji films to understand their attributes. "It's me-too technology," said one researcher with apparent disdain. "We do what Fuji does. We're obsessed with Fuji."[5]

Supersaturated colors were one attribute of Fuji film for years. Kodak thought the colors were unrealistically bright. However, to their dismay they found that customers liked Fuji's film. In 1986, Kodak introduced its VR-G film series that offered colors just as bright.

Battle of the Throwaways

Kodak and Fuji announced at almost the same time, during February 1987, plans to introduce throwaway cameras in the United States later that year. Kodak, however, beat Fuji to the punch when it announced its camera one day before Fuji had scheduled a news conference for the same purpose. Kodak's camera was called the "Fling," whereas Fuji's was called the "Fujicolor Quick Snap." For both versions, the camera was sent in its entirety to a photofinisher, instead of just the film.

Kodak apparently learned the importance of timing at the hand of Fuji. In a previous episode of one-upmanship or "being quicker on the draw" in 1983, Fuji stole Kodak's thunder by introducing a new series of films immediately before Kodak did likewise.

Thrust and Parry

After Fuji's thrust into the United States, Kodak decided in 1984 to make a strategic parry into the $1.5 billion Japanese market for film and paper. Actually, Kodak had been in Japan for many years, but the company just had never given it much attention. From 1984 to 1990, Kodak spent an estimated $500 million on the Japanese photographic film and papers markets. The company created a new subsidiary for Japan and increased employment from 12 to 4,500. Yet some argued that Kodak was too late in emphasizing the Japanese market.

In Japan, Kodak had to contend with Fuji's entrenched position and dominant technical prowess. Fuji matched Kodak on quality and surpassed it in highspeed color

---

[4]Ibid., p. A12.

[5]Leslie Helm and Barbara Buell, "Kodak Fights Fuji with 'Me-Too' Tactics," *Business Week,* February 23, 1987, p. 138.

films. In addition, Fuji had a dominant position in major Japanese film processing labs, where it controlled about 250 labs to Kodak's fewer than 150 in 1985. These labs are the main end-users of photographic paper.

Kodak's drive into Japan was partly an attempt to keep up with Japanese R&D activities by developing joint ventures with Japanese partners, as well as with its own R&D center and technical assistance center for helping customers. For example, Kodak bought 10 percent of a 35-mm Japanese camera maker, and its Verbatim floppy disk subsidiary operated a joint venture with Mitsubishi Chemical Industries.

A second element of Kodak's strategy in Japan was to try to gain greater control over the distribution of its own products. Kodak purchased Kusuda Business Machines, a company that had been marketing Kodak's micrographic and business imaging systems in Japan. Film sales in Japan were handled by a Japanese firm, Nagase & Co. In 1986, Kodak increased its control over distribution and marketing by forming a new joint venture company called Kodak-Nagase.

Kodak was successful in getting space in the 30,000 to 60,000 camera stores that sell most of Japan's film. However, it was unsuccessful in getting into the mom-and-pop stores that can afford to carry only one brand of film. That one brand was usually in a green box.

The Japanese rail network (which had thousands of small kiosks that typically carry only Fuji film) was especially hard for Kodak to crack. To get into these kiosks, Kodak would have to work with up to four agents including the kiosk operator, real estate agent, and wholesaler. Usually, regardless of Kodak's pitch, Fuji was given a chance to match or beat the offer.

One of Kodak's new products introduced in Japan to combat Fuji's lead in film processing and paper sales was the minilab. These were targeted to chip away at Fuji's 100-plus advantage in large labs. Fuji fought back by offering bigger enlargement sizes than the minilabs. Recently Fuji introduced its own minilabs.

The only two times Kodak was able to directly take shelf space away from Fuji was when they had products that were unmatched by their arch rival. These products were the waterproof disposable camera and panoramic disposable camera. Kodak apparently had the technology for the panoramic camera for years but did not see a market for it. Kodak-Japan pushed the product, because the Japanese are known to take a lot of pictures of large groups. William Jack, vice president of Kodak-Japan, noted, "When the Japanese have golf outings, they often want everyone lined up for a group picture, and getting everyone in with a conventional camera is quite difficult."[6] The waterproof disposable was a hit with Japanese youth who love to snorkel. The disposable cameras have been the central thrust of Kodak's youth-oriented advertising in Japan.

On the promotional front, besides the battle of the blimps, Kodak beat Fuji in the "battle of the neon signs." Its victory came with the construction of a gigantic yellow sign that took years to finish. It is located at the Japanese equivalent of Times Square. In terms of price, Kodak was more willing to cut prices in Japan than in the United States, where it generally sold at a premium.

Kodak claimed its market share had gone up in the amateur color film market in Japan. According to *Japan Economic Journal (JEJ)*, however, Kodak had 10 percent of the color film market in 1989 versus 13 percent in 1987. *JEJ* also reported that Fuji had gone

[6]Clare Ansberry and Masayoshi Kanabayashi, "Kodak Bid to Sell More Color Film to Japanese Remains Out of Focus," *Wall Street Journal*, December 7, 1990, p. B7.

from 71 percent to 73 percent and Konica from 16 percent to 17 percent during the same period. However, Kodak's sales of all products in Japan increased 600 percent, to about $1.3 billion during the same period.

THE U.S. PHOTOGRAPHIC MARKET

Overall market growth in the United States was sluggish and was expected to remain slow for the foreseeable future. Information about the industry is hard to obtain because it is so concentrated. Growth rates are provided in Exhibit 1.

Slow growth rates and significant overcapacity put pressure on prices. Fuji added film production lines to its large paper factory in Tilburg, the Netherlands, and built its first manufacturing plant in the United States in South Carolina in 1990 (although this plant initially was scheduled to produce sensitized plates for offset printing, not film or paper, it was expected to add these if Fuji's sales in the United States warranted expansion). Fuji was not the first Japanese photographic firm to build a plant in the United States. Konica built a U.S. manufacturing plant for photographic paper in Greensboro, North Carolina, in 1988. In addition, Polaroid increased the competition for shelf space with its entry in 1989 into conventional photography with a film called "One-Film." This film was designed to be an all-purpose film that would eliminate the need for consumers to choose among the vast array of film types available. Although it was well received by large U.S. retail chains, neither Kodak nor Fuji has responded.

Other film competitors in the United States include Fotomat (Konishiroko), 3M's Scotch brand, Agfa-Gevaert AG of West Germany, and several private label brands. GAF withdrew several years ago due to declining margins. Kodak held about 80 percent of the film market and Fuji about 10 percent.

KODAK: THE GREAT YELLOW FATHER

Kodak was described as large, lumbering, elephantine, and bureaucratic. For its traditionally paternalistic employment practices, it was sometimes referred to as the "Great Yellow Father." Kodak, along with Xerox, dominated the upstate New York town of Rochester, where its headquarters and plants spread over a 3,000-acre area.

George Eastman, Kodak's founder, sold his first camera in 1883. Kodak was the first fully integrated photographic company in the world. Its motto was, "You press the button and we do the rest." Although Kodak's share of the film market was about 80 percent in

EXHIBIT 1 Profile of the Photography Industry (In Millions)

	1984	1985	1986	1987	1988
Still Camera Sales (Units)	17.0	17.8	16.4	18.7	17.8
Film Sales (Rolls)	610	667	694	781	811
Photofinishing in Dollars	$3,500	$3,700	$4,000	$4,400	$4,800

Source: *Wall Street Journal*, December 7, 1990, p. B-7.

1990, its share of film processing was only about 15 percent because of a 1954 U.S. Justice Department consent decree that required the company to unbundle the sale of film and film development. Previously, when a customer bought Kodak film the price of development was part of the price of the film. When a roll of film was completed it would be sent by the customer to a Kodak processing lab at no extra cost. After the 1954 consent decree, independent processing labs developed rapidly to account for 85 percent of film processing. However, if the paper, processing equipment, and chemicals that Kodak sold to independent developers were included, Kodak's share was close to 50 percent.

Kodak's control of the industry as a whole grew from its leadership in film technology. Of all its photographic products, film was its premier profit maker. It was only recently that a broad scope competitor such as Fuji had been able to challenge it in this area. Previously, Kodak had almost total mastery of the photographic industry and kept ahead of every other competitor in virtually every dimension of photography. In part it was due to the tied-in nature of film and processing prior to the 1954 consent decree that eliminated the motivation of other companies to pursue innovations in color film technology.

After the consent decree, other film manufacturers had more incentive but still had trouble making inroads, as Kodak was an aggressive competitor. It would hold new innovations in reserve until a competitor would come to the market with a product it had spent vast sums to develop. Kodak would then introduce what it had been saving in reserve and wipe out the competitor's product and sunk investment. For example, in the early 1960s a joint venture between DuPont and Bell & Howell to develop a color film research program totally failed. In every instance where the partnership was able to improve its film, Kodak's film would miraculously incorporate the same improvements. In 1961, when the venture decided to introduce a new film based on tens of millions of dollars in research, Kodak retaliated with Kodachrome II, a far better quality film. The joint venture film was withdrawn before it reached the market.

For some time, competitors tried to compete with Kodak by charging lower prices. However, this tactic largely failed because consumers seemed unwilling to accept film that might be a lower quality. Fuji was able to overcome this perception somewhat by stressing a quality brand image charging slightly lower prices. Other competitors were mostly niche players that focused on a small group of consumers who wished to avoid supersaturated colors, a very high resolution, or the nonexotic image of Kodak. Polaroid's niche was instant photography, and Fotomat's niche was speedy film processing.

Systems Approach

Kodak's emphasis in the photographic market utilized a "systems approach" beginning with the highly successful Instamatic camera to the disc camera. A system was a unique film format packaged in a cartridge or magazine compatible with only cameras designed specifically for that film format.

Some of these Kodak systems were major successes. The Instamatic sold 10 million cameras in the first 26 months after its introduction in 1963. In 1972, Kodak introduced a smaller version of the Instamatic called the Pocket Instamatic. It has been estimated that by 1975 Kodak sold 60 million Instamatics, whereas competitors sold just 10 million clones. The company reinforced its dominance in the industry by surprising competitors with radical changes in camera design and film requirements. Others were required, often on short notice, to invest heavily in complex production equipment to remain competitive. For this reason Kodak rarely announced product developments ahead of time. They preferred to surprise their competitors and retain a monopoly on a new system until competitors caught up. Apparently, this was the concern when the Fuji employee was accepted at the University of Rochester.

To deflect criticism and possible antitrust action, Kodak began licensing its systems. Realistically, however, the main motive for licensing was that it increased the number of cameras that could use Kodak's highly profitable films.

Not all of Kodak's systems have been successful. Kodak's disc camera, introduced in 1982, was a disappointment. The graininess of the photographs it produce apparently left consumers dissatisfied. The disc camera sold poorly in Europe and Japan, where photographers were used to the high resolution of 35-mm photos. It seemed unlikely that the disc system would provide the 8- to 10-year life cycle of healthy sales that other products, such as the Instamatic, had. It was unlikely that Kodak would recover its development costs, estimated at $300 million. In fact, Kodak announced in 1988 it was suspending production of the disc camera.

Kodak's run at the camcorder video market was also a disappointment. In 1984, Kodak teamed up with Matsushita Electric Industrial Company to market its 8-mm video camera. It was billed as the "world's finest commercial 8-mm camcorder." It was lighter and more compact than camcorders already on the market but required narrower tape. Thus, it was considered a pioneering effort. However, the product ultimately failed; some analysts blamed outdated camera designs supplied by Matsushita.

Then there was Kodak's instant camera system, announced on April 20, 1976. Kodak explained that its camera would go on sale in Canada in May and in the United States in July. Kodak's system was billed as "completely new" compared with Polaroid's offering. It required many more components to manufacture than Polaroid's cameras. Polaroid filed a patent infringement suit at 4:59 P.M. on April 26, 1976. Polaroid ultimately prevailed in this suit, and Kodak was required to pay a large fine ($873.2 million) and withdraw from the instant photography business. They were also required to give the purchasers of the Kodak instant camera a refund, as film would no longer be available.

Prior to the judgment, however, Kodak had been disappointed with the instant photography sales. It was a much smaller market than management anticipated. What happened to possibly be a replacement for conventional photography turned out to be a novelty or niche product.

Kodak's intention was to be the "world's best in both conventional and electronic imaging.... We now have in place the strategic architecture for managing the alliance of chemical-based and electronic imaging, technology centers for development of core product platforms, and an international organization providing a fully global reach."[7] Kodak was in four business segments—photography, copiers, drugs, and chemicals. The size of each segment can be assessed in Exhibit 2. International sales in 1990 were 46 percent of total sales. In an independent survey that ranked the best-known brands, Kodak ranked fifth in the United States, Japan, and Europe, and fourth overall.

Kodak's strengths were described in its 1990 *Annual Report* as follows: "Organic chemistry, imaging, and color form the basis of the company's leadership in photography. These technologies have led to new initiatives in other fields of endeavor such as pharmaceuticals. As diverse as Kodak may appear on the surface, each of its businesses is a natural outgrowth of these core strengths."[8]

---

[7]Kodak *Annual Report*, 1990, pp. 3, 10.

[8]Ibid., p. 4.

EXHIBIT 2   Industry Statistics for SIC code 3861[a]—Photographic Equipment and Supplies

Year/Source	Number of Firms	Value Added	Materials	Shipments
1988/ASM	N/A	14,223.2	6,638.0	20,545.8
1987/Census	719	12,908.0	6,233.5	19,240.5
1986/ASM	N/A	12,335.9	6,110.5	18,580.4
1985/ASM	N/A	12,257.4	5,890.1	18,114.4
1984/ASM	N/A	12,960.9	5,682.4	18,701.9
1983/ASM	N/A	11,654.7	5,887.0	17,366.3
1982/Census	723	10,859.5	5,859.7	17,037.5
1981/ASM	N/A	11,199.2	5,902.3	16,927.3
1980/ASM	N/A	9,930.8	6,199.8	15,867.0
1979/ASM	N/A	8,812.6	4,698.5	13,410.2
1978/ASM	N/A	7,837.8	3,747.5	11,535.9
1977/Census	700	6,728.8	3,236.0	9,933.2
1976/ASM	N/A	6,077.4	2,914.7	8,844.5
1975/ASM	N/A	5,177.0	2,443.4	7,627.0
1974/ASM	N/A	5,075.0	2,565.5	7,493.4
1973/ASM	N/A	4,735.6	1,821.3	6,435.0
1972/Census	554	4,087.9	1,487.9	5,623.9

Legend

ASM	=	*Annual Survey of Manufacturers*
Census	=	*Census of Manufacturers*
Number of Firms	=	number of firms operating during year
N/A	=	Not Available
Value Added	=	shipments minus material and payroll in millions of dollars
Materials	=	cost of materials consumed in millions of dollars
Shipments	=	total value of shipments in millions of dollars

[a]Figures on SIC industry 3861—photographic equipment and supplies—are given in Exhibit 2. This category is defined and described as follows by the Department of Commerce:

This industry is made up of establishments primarily engaged in manufacturing: (1) photographic apparatus, equipment, parts, attachments, and accessories, such as still and motion projection apparatus; photocopy and microfilm equipment; blueprinting and diazotype (white printing) apparatus and equipment; and other photographic equipment; and (2) sensitized film, paper, cloth and plates, and prepared photographic chemicals for use therein...

Establishments in virtually all industries ship secondary products as well as products primary to the industry to which they are classified and have some miscellaneous receipts, such as resales and contract receipts. Industry 3861 shipped $15.0 billion of photographic equipment and supplies products considered primary to the industry [in 1987], $1.2 billion of secondary products, and had $3.0 billion of miscellaneous receipts, resales, and contract work. Thus, the ratio of primary products to the total of both secondary and primary products shipped by establishments in the industry was 93 percent (specialization ratio).

One recent initiative was the new plant built by Eastman Chemical Company in Kingsport, Tennessee, which would supply 100 percent of the company's need for acetic anhydride, a petroleum-based chemical that is a primary ingredient for the base material for photographic film.

Partly because of the problems previously discussed, profits at Kodak started sagging in the early 1980s. Financial data are provided in Exhibit 3. As a result, Kodak tried

EXHIBIT 3   Kodak Financials (In Millions of Dollars)

	1986	1987	1988	1989	1990
Income Statement Data					
Sales	$ 11,550	$ 13,305	$ 17,034	$ 18,398	$ 18,908
Earnings	724	2,078	2,812	1,591	2,844
Earnings Before Income Taxes	598	1,984	2,236	925	1,257
Net Earnings	374	1,178	1,397	529	703
Return on Sales	3.2%	8.9%	8.2%	2.9%	3.7%
Balance Sheet Data					
Current Assets	$ 5,857	$ 6,791	$ 8,684	$ 8,591	$ 8,608
Properties at Cost	12,919	13,789	15,667	16,774	17,648
Accumulated Depreciation	6,643	7,126	7,654	8,146	8,670
Total Assets	12,994	14,698	22,964	23,652	24,125
Current Liabilities	3,811	4,140	5,850	6,573	7,163
Long-Term Borrowings	981	2,382	7,779	7,376	6,989
Shareholders' Equity	6,388	6,013	6,780	6,642	6,737
Supplemental Information					
Sales—Imaging	$ 8,352	$ 6,206	$ 6,642	$ 6,998	$ 7,128
Information		3,494	3,937	4,200	4,140
Chemicals	2,378	2,635	3,123	3,522	3,588
Health	1,056	1,206	3,597	4,009	4,349
R&D Expenditures	$ 1,059	$ 992	$ 1,147	$ 1,253	$ 1,329
Employees in United States	83,600	81,800	87,900	82,850	80,350
Employees Worldwide	121,450	124,400	145,300	137,750	134,450

Notes: 1990 earnings before income taxes reflect $888 million for litigation judgment, which reduced net earnings by
   $564 million.
   1989 earnings reflect restructuring costs of $875 million, which reduced net earnings by $549 million.
Source: Kodak *Annual Report*, 1990.

to cut costs and increase productivity. Employment was reduced to 121,500 in 1986 from about 146,500 in 1983. This happened despite Kodak's virtually guaranteed lifetime employment policies that led to its being called the Great Yellow Father. Kodak profit margins had declined from 15.7 percent in 1972 to 10.7 percent in 1982. Some of this was the result of Japanese price competition; however, the advent of video and Kodak's own failure in video contributed to the decline.

Walter Fallon retired as chairman in June 1983. He was heralded as the man who made the elephant dance, but of the four major product lines introduced while Fallon was calling the shots, only the copier business has done well. Ektaprint copiers have done well at the top of the copier market, where Xerox is dominant. These high-speed, volume copiers typically sold for $75,000 to $125,000. The company's Ektaplus 7016 copier/printer was the only small-volume copier manufactured in the United States. Fallon's failures included the Kodamatic Instant camera, the disc camera, and the Ektachem 400, a blood analysis machine that proved to be unreliable.

Fallon was reported to have pounded his desk when he heard that Fuji had won sponsorship of the 1984 Olympics. Later, to become more cost competitive, he centralized some manufacturing in Rochester just as the strong dollar wiped out the resulting productivity gains.

Fallon was succeeded by Colby Chandler, who initiated corporatewide strategic planning. In addition, he created a marketing intelligence group and gave the marketing area a stronger voice in what had traditionally been a technically dominated company.

Kodak moved into electronics in a big way. To help in this effort, it acquired a small California company called Spin Physics in 1972. Spin specialized in recording heads for high-density data storage.

In 1982, Kodak was surprised when Sony introduced its Mavica camera, a "filmless" video still camera that displayed pictures immediately on TV. However, the pictures produced were fuzzy because of the small number of pixels (280,000 versus 4 million in the Instamatic), and it was a failure. However, Kodak was shocked by the prospect of photos that could be displayed on a screen and printed out on hard copies followed by erasing and reusing the tape. This led Kodak to do what it almost never does. The next October, Kodak demonstrated a product in development—a video display unit permitting film negatives to appear in color on TV. The film had to be developed and could not be erased. This was an inferior product to Sony's but in effect said to others: Think twice before marketing filmless still photography products.

With its move into electronics, Kodak was competing in areas where it was not the leader, did not have the technical advantage, and did not have cost leadership. Also, in some of these areas it bumped heads with arch rival Fuji. Fuji sold copiers, videotapes, and computer floppy disks. Kodak, through its Verbatim floppy disk subsidiary, competed against Fuji. In fact, in 1988 Kodak lodged an unfair trading claim against Fuji and others with the International Trade Commission. Kodak claimed that Fuji, Sony, and Hitachi charged 40 percent to 60 percent less for floppy disks in the United States than they did in Japan.

Kodak moved into a totally different area when it acquired the Sterling Drug Company for $5.1 billion in 1988. Previously the company had established its own drug R&D lab in Philadelphia; however, prior to the acquisition no products had been readied for the market. The potential fit between chemical-based drug research and film research seemed to be one argument for the move. Yet this large acquisition had the danger of diverting too much attention and too many resources away from photography.

Sterling's best-selling product was Omnipaque. According to Kodak, it was the number one pharmaceutical product purchased by hospitals in the United States. The product allowed for the contrasting of body organs and blood vessels for X-rays and CAT scanning. Sterling had joined with a French company, Sanofi, in a joint venture to improve its global reach. Also, Sterling broke ground in 1990 for an new $300 million R&D center in Upper Providence Township, Pennsylvania, that employed 1,200.

In the past Kodak had problems accepting non-Kodak corporate cultures. According to Al Edwards, a former vice president of Atex (a manufacturer of electronic publishing systems acquired by Kodak in 1981), "The people at Kodak are hard working but bureaucratic. They do not understand the competitive nature of computer technology. You sometimes have to react to the marketplace on a weekly basis. At Kodak, if you came up with an idea, it would be five years before you saw the product."[9] Of course, Kodak also was the company that passed up an invention called xerography, which was then developed by a small Rochester company called Haloid (now Xerox).

---

[9]Thomas Moore, "Embattled Kodak Enters the Electronic Age," *Fortune*, August 22, 1983, p. 128.

Gerald Zornow, Kodak chairman from 1972 to 1976, did not believe that outsiders could adjust to the Kodak culture. "They tried some people from the outside before and it never worked out," he said. "Kodak is like an old family that grows up together, and it is tough for outsiders to fit in."[10]

A critical concern affecting the development of electronic products, such as the photo CD, was the ability of glacial, slow, elephantine, stodgy, stuffy, conservative Kodak in cold, gray, unhip Rochester to attract "notoriously disloyal electronic cowboys who thrive best in Silicon Valley."[11] Kodak had trouble holding onto managers with a background in electronics.

Kay Whitmore, who was promoted to chairman on June 1, 1990, was enthusiastic about the prospects for Kodak's Photo CD. Photo CD was a product developed in reaction to Sony's Mavica (Canon, Toshiba, and Fuji came out with a similar product, though Toshiba and Fuji used a "memory card" rather than a floppy disk). Kodak's initial response was, "Holy cow, let's circle the wagons," noted William Fowbie, vice president and general manager for consumer imaging projects. The second reaction was Photo CD. To avoid the bureaucracy of Kodak, Photo CD functions as an independent business. With Photo CD, introduced in March 1992, photographers snapped pictures using *film* as they always have, but when the film was sent to the lab they would have the option of storing their photos on CD. Viewing what was on the CD would require a TV and a special player made by NV Philips. Photographers could then enlarge or crop their photos and return edited photos to the lab to obtain prints.

In uncharacteristic style, Kodak announced Photo CD long before its actual introduction date. The early announcement was intended to give warning to any firms developing electronic photographic products. That warning was, in effect, that Kodak, which frequently sets the standard in photographic products, was developing an electronic camera with high resolution that used film. The fact that this product used film, although the first venture into electronic photography, Sony's Mavica, did not, was obviously important to Kodak, the king of film. But the early announcement also had another effect. It gave Fuji, another company sensitive to filmless substitutes, plenty of warning.

Many analysts expressed concern about Kodak's obsession with Fuji: "Kodak is so focused on Fuji it may ignore other important current or potential rivals." New competition from Japanese consumer electronics firms and Polaroid might be a concern in the future.

FUJI PHOTO FILM COMPANY: A PROFILE

Fuji was moving in the same direction as Kodak by emphasizing electronics. It was aware that electronic, filmless photography was potentially the next era in photography. Fuji learned that where Kodak goes, it must follow. However, sometimes, when it knew where Kodak was headed, it moved faster and beat them to the punch.

In 1967, Fuji spent millions of dollars designing a new 8-mm home movie system. Fuji was set to announce its new system when Kodak "knocked them out of the water." Kodak released its Super 8, a camera with a larger film format that could not use Fuji film. Fuji junked its product.

---

[10]Ibid.

[11]Ibid.

It was at this point that Fuji decided it would be a follower to Kodak's lead. A prime consideration in its move into the United States was to avoid gaining the attention or retaliation of Kodak. Instead, it wanted to focus on taking market share away from weaker competitors such as 3M.

Fuji knew it had a problem in the United States. Kodak was too entrenched to be beat in the way the Japanese later beat U.S. firms in TVs, stereos, radios, and autos. But similar to many other Japanese companies, Fuji could subsidize the attack on the U.S. market through its dominance of the Japanese market. The latest estimate showed Fuji to have 73 percent market share in Japan. Fuji decided to target a 15 percent share in the United States, but the company made a critical miscalculation. Kodak not only noticed Fuji, they became obsessed with Fuji.

The elevation of Minoru Ohnishi over many more senior managers marked the beginning of the reign of the youngest president in the history of Fuji. With his promotion the company sought new avenues of growth given the highly saturated, slow-growth Japanese photographic market. Ohnishi moved Fuji into the United States in 1964. Under his leadership the conservative company began to move faster in the marketplace. For example, Fuji was first to market a film compatible with Kodak's disc system. Fuji engineers produced it in just eight months.

Fuji, founded in 1936, was in a variety of businesses including cameras, medical equipment, copiers, bicycles, and videotape. Film was its main business, however; 50.5 percent of its sales came from film in 1990, 10.2 percent from magnetic products (video-tape, audio tape, memory tape, and floppy disks), and 39.4 percent from commercial products (printing, medical, office, and motion picture equipment and supplies). Overseas sales represented 38.3 percent of net sales in 1990. Part of Fuji's overseas strategy is what it called "globalization through localization," which meant to compete globally but produce locally.

Despite the various battles in the aerial and academic arenas, Fuji never went looking for a fight. "Fuji is gun-shy; they've found they can live happily under the Kodak umbrella," said analyst Reginald Duquesnoy of Merrill Lynch. "Both Fuji and Kodak [traditionally] make fat margins, and they're not in the business of destroying that profitability."[12]

The goal of 15 percent in the United States was, according to Ohnishi, a long-term goal to be reached in a gradual, nonthreatening way. This gun-shyness was because almost every time the challenger (Fuji) attacked the leader, the challenger had its nose bloodied. One example occurred in 1977—Fuji reduced the price of its print paper to undercut Kodak. Kodak matched it on price and then mounted an aggressive marketing program. As another example, in 1983, Fuji brought out a new high-resolution film in two speeds. Kodak introduced a similar product without missing a beat, but one-upped Fuji by offering a high-resolution film in four speeds.

Fuji pursued a growth strategy with two elements: product diversificaiton and increased emphasis on foreign sales. By 1991, the company had gained a 50 percent share of the photographic market in Asia and 15 percent in Europe. On a worldwide basis, Fuji had about a 15 percent market share. Diversification for Fuji mostly meant a search for niche products in electronics. Ohnishi said that he will "only enter areas where Fuji can modify and improve on products [and] develop hybrids that combine electronics and photography. We want a small part of the large pies."[13]

---

[12]Johnathon Greenberg, "If Everyone Else Makes Videotape, Why Doesn't Kodak?" *Forbes,* November 22, 1982, p. 56.

[13]"Fuji Photo: Sharpening Its Image in the U.S. as It Develops New Products," *Business Week,* October 24, 1983, pp. 88, 92.

Fuji was recognized for its expertise and quality in the "imaging industry." For example, in a joint venture with Xerox it had about 40 percent of the copier market in Japan as of 1981.

Fuji was a heavy spender on R&D, which resulted in many new products. These products included office and medical equipment, semiconductors, and home computers, all areas that were growing faster than the photographic market. Fuji had a highly flexible workforce. Its employees were able to move between plants making different products as demand required. It operated one of the lowest-cost videotape plants in the world in Odawara, Japan. Its first videotape plant in the United States started production in 1991. Companywide, Fuji's sales per employee almost doubled to $157,000 per worker from 1978 to 1982. Fuji, with traditional profit margins around 10 percent, was one of the most profitable firms in Japan. Fuji's financial statements are given in Exhibit 4.

When it started in the United States in 1964, Fuji began as a private label film supplier. In 1972, it began selling under its own name but was marketed as a promotional item free with the purchase of Japanese cameras.

In 1978, given the highly saturated photographic market in Japan, Fuji decided to be a little more aggressive in the United States. It expanded distribution beyond camera stores and emphasized food stores, drug stores, and discount stores.

EXHIBIT 4 Fuji Photo Film Company Financial (In Millions of U.S. Dollars)

	1986	1987	1988	1989	1990
Income Statement Data					
Net sales: Domestic	$2,905.0	$3,633.4	$4,459.1	$4,416.2	$ 4,528.5
Overseas	1,602.5	2,002.2	2,379.3	2,312.3	2,815.7
Total	4,507.5	5,635.6	6,838.4	6,728.5	7,344.3
Cost of Sales	2,530.7	3,067.8	3,740.0	3,577.5	3,862.6
Operating Expenses					
Selling, General, and Administrative	937.7	1,232.0	1,531.2	1,615.1	1,845.8
R&D	263.3	346.8	429.4	411.5	410.6
Interest and Dividend Income	121.1	144.4	176.0	198.5	268.4
Interest Expense	58.0	63.6	75.7	89.4	136.9
Earnings Before Interest and Taxes	803.1	1,030.9	1,219.9	1,212.7	1,351.2
Net Income	$ 369.3	$ 497.8	$ 640.0	$ 603.6	$ 622.6
Balance Sheet Data					
Total Assets	$5,631.9	$7,234.0	$9,140.1	$9,683.7	$10,547.8
Long-Term Debt	205.2	192.9	357.4	503.1	691.5
Total Liabilities	2,328.4	2,872.5	3,529.2	3,749.7	4,244.2
Shareholders' Equity	$3,303.5	$4,361.5	$5,610.9	$5,934.0	$ 6,303.7
Supplemental Information					
Number of Employees	17,180	17,703	18,195	19,677	21,946
Exchange Rate (yen/dollar)	168	145	128	138	145

Source: Fuji Photo Film, Co. *Annual Report*, 1990.

Fuji tried to change its image by going after the professional market. It introduced a line of professional films and advertised to this market in photo trade books. The professional market is about as large as the amateur market, because professionals are "heavy users"—shooting perhaps 30 to 50 rolls per assignment.

Despite the desire for growth, Fuji emphasized the desire to avoid threatening Kodak. It targeted weaker firms such as 3M, Europe's Agfa-Gevaert, and Japan's Konishiroko. "We are a piquant but small Japanese pepper," says President Ohnishi. "If I were Kodak, I wouldn't worry about us at all."[14]

APPENDIX 1   THE PHOTOGRAPHIC INDUSTRY

About 17.8 million cameras were sold to U.S. dealers in 1988 (latest available), down 4.8 percent from the year before. Demand continued to be strong for lens-shutter 35-mm cameras, which accounted for more than half of industry dollar volume. Gains for lens-shutter cameras have come largely at the expense of higher-end 35-mm single-lens reflex (SLRs) and lower and disc cameras. Unit sales of the sophisticated and expensive SLRs fell about 6 percent in 1988, to approximately 1.5 million, accounting for only 8.4 percent of industry unit volume, versus 14.7 percent of that volume four years earlier. However, SLRs represented 23.6 percent of the dollar value of industry camera sales in 1988, reflecting their higher price. The rate of decline in SLR unit sales slowed in 1988, after a 16 percent drop in 1987.

The market share, in units, of disc cameras plunged to just 5.6 percent in 1988 from 27.1 percent in 1984, when 1.0 million of the pocket-size cameras were sold to dealers. Due to their lower price, these cameras accounted for only 1.9 percent of the dollar value of cameras sold. Weak prospects for disc cameras were indicated by Eastman Kodak's announcement in early 1988 that it was suspending production of this type of camera.

Sales of instant cameras have also been fading. In 1988, according to PMA (Photo Marketing Association International), about 2.1 million instant cameras were sold to U.S. dealers, down from 2.7 million the year before. Instant cameras represented 11.8 percent of industry unit volume and 7.8 percent of dollar value. As recently as 1983, about 4 million instant cameras were sold, at a time when Eastman Kodak and Polaroid were both in the market. Eastman Kodak withdrew from this segment in early 1986 following a court ruling that the company had infringed upon Polaroid patents.

Meanwhile, cartridge cameras sales totaled about 5.6 million units, down about 7 percent from the year before. Cartridge cameras accounted for 31 percent of industry unit volume, but only about 4.8 percent of dollar volume.

According to PMA, 811 million rolls of film were purchased in the United States during 1988, up about 4 percent from the year before. Film for 35-mm

---

[14]Lee Smith, "The Little Pepper That's Got Kodak Hot," *Fortune*, August 22, 1983, p. 122.

cameras was the most popular format (61 percent), followed by cartridge (16 percent), instant (11 percent), and disc (11 percent). Not surprising, 35-mm film also provided the bulk of the industry's processing volume, accounting for 75 percent of the 15.43 billion conventional exposures processed in 1988. In comparison, prior to the fast sales of "point and shoot" cameras, 35-mm film represented just 34 percent of processing volume in 1980 and 12.5 percent in 1975, according to PMA. Cartridge film represented 15 percent of processing volume in 1987 followed by disc film at 7 percent. PMA estimated that color print developing accounted for 93 percent of the 15.4 billion conventional exposures processed in 1988, followed by slide (4.5 percent) and black and white print developing (2.6 percent). (Note: Some of PMA's numbers may be only for the amateur photography market, excluding professional activity.)

Stand-alone mini-labs accounted for an estimated 28.9 percent of the retail dollars spent on photoprocessing in 1988, down slightly from 1987's 29.4 percent. Another 22.6 percent of photoprocessing sales were made through drugstores, followed by discounter/mass merchandisers (15.4 percent), camera stores (13.5 percent), and a variety of others (19.6 percent), according to PMA.

Source: Standard & Poor's Industry Surveys, March 15, 1990, p. 49.

Ito-Yokado Company

M. Edgar Barrett and Christopher D. Buehler

In mid-March 1991, Masanori Takahashi, a senior strategy analyst for Ito-Yokado Company, was preparing to depart for Dallas, Texas. Once there, he would be leading a team of Japanese and American managers responsible for establishing transitional and long-term strategies for the Southland Corporation. After nearly an entire year of intense bargaining and negotiation with Southland and its creditors, Ito-Yokado acquired Southland on March 5, 1991.

Takahashi began working with Ito-Yokado in 1972 as an assistant manager of one of the company's superstores. He had advanced to the position of regional manager by 1979. In early 1981, Ito-Yokado's Operation Reform Project was conceived and Takahashi was asked to be a member of the team leading the project.

During the first few months on the team, Takahashi quickly understood certain crucial aspects of the new project, most notably the use of point-of-sale (POS) systems. Implementation of the project advanced most rapidly in Ito-Yokado's 7-Eleven Japan subsidiary, so he also had become familiar with the operating environment of convenience stores in Japan.

As Takahashi left his Tokyo office, he could not help but feel both excitement and apprehension regarding his new position. He had gained confidence while involved with the successful Operation Reform Project at Ito-Yokado's superstores and 7-Eleven Japan convenience stores, but this experience might or might not prove to be useful in respect to Southland.

COMPANY BACKGROUND

Ito-Yokado's founder, Masatoshi Ito, was born in 1924 and graduated from a commercial high school in Yokohama. He worked briefly at Mitsubishi Heavy Industries before joining Japan's war effort in 1944. After World War II, he worked with his mother and elder brother at the family's 66-square-foot clothing store in Tokyo.[1] The store was incorporated as Kabushiki Kaisha Yokado in 1958. By 1960, Ito was in sole control of the family business. During that same year he made his first visit to the United States.

In 1960, Ito visited National Cash Register (NCR) in Dayton, Ohio.[2] While in the United States, Ito was introduced to terms such as "supermarkets" and "chain stores"

This case was prepared by Professors M. Edgar Barrett and Christopher D. Buehler of American Graduate School of International Business, as a basis for class discussion. It is not intended to illustrate either effective or ineffective handling of an administrative situation.

[1]Andrew Tanzer, "A Form of Flattery," *Forbes,* June 2, 1986.

[2]Jim Mitchell, "Southland Suitor Ito Learned from the Best," *Dallas Morning News,* April 1, 1990.

by NCR, which was interested in selling cash registers to Japanese retailers. In Japan, retailing was dominated by mom-and-pop stores and a handful of venerable department stores, with few types of retail outlets in between. At this time, Ito began to see the possible role of mass merchandisers in a society becoming "mass-oriented."

Ito soon opened a small chain of superstores in the Tokyo area. These stores carried a large selection of household goods, food, and clothing of generally lesser quality and lower price than either the mom-and-pop or department stores.[3] By 1965, Ito had opened eight superstores. In the same year, the name of the chain was changed to Ito-Yokado.

The Growth of Ito-Yokado as a Superstore

Ito's concept for the superstores was centered on having the rough equivalent of several types of retail stores contained within one multistory superstore. The initial stores were located near population centers and railroad stations in the Tokyo areas.[4] Often, several stores were located in close proximity in order to achieve "regional dominance."[5] The results were high name recognition, reduced distribution costs, and the effective squeezing out of competition.

Ito soon realized that social changes in Japan could create new opportunities for his retailing ideas. Younger and more mobile Japanese appeared to be less willing to spend a great deal of time shopping at numerous mom-and-pop stores. Also, the Japanese society was experiencing increased suburbanization. Ito decided to locate stores in suburban prefectures. There were 47 prefectures (provinces) in Japan.

One reason for locating stores in suburban areas was the lower cost of real estate. This allowed Ito-Yokado to open larger stores with more parking spaces than competitors located in congested urban areas. Ito continued to use a strategy of "regional dominance" with these new openings, most of which were concentrated in the greater Kanto district, which consists of the Tokyo metropolitan area and surrounding cities. By the early 1970s, Ito-Yokado stores were opening at the rate of four or five per year. By the late 1970s, nine or 10 new stores were opened annually.[6] In early 1987, 101 of 127 Ito-Yokado superstores were located in the greater Kanto district.

Ito also adopted a strategy of leasing some properties for new stores. As of the mid-1980s, more than 87 percent of Ito-Yokado's aggregate sales floor space, 10 of the company's 11 distribution centers, and the company headquarters in Tokyo were all leased.[7] Often, property prices were astronomical, or the owners of well-located sites would not part with their property for any price.

Constraints on Growth

The initial success of Ito-Yokado and the other superstores soon resulted in retaliatory action by a powerful competitor: the mom-and-pop store owners. These small retailers were said to "pull the strings of Liberal Democratic Party politicians at the local level."[8]

---

[3]Ito was not the first to open this type of retail outlet. Isao Nakauchi opened the first Daiei superstore in the Osaka area a few years before the first Ito-Yokado store was opened. In 1990, Daiei was Japan's largest retailer in terms of gross sales.

[4]Mitchell, "Southland Suitor."

[5]Hiroshi Uchida, *First Boston/CSFB Report on Ito-Yokado, Ltd.*, April 20, 1988, p. 7.

[6]Ibid., p. 6.

[7]Ibid., p. 7.

[8]Tanzer, "A Form of Flattery."

The action initiated by the small retailers resulted in the 1974 Large Store Restriction Act, which was subsequently strengthened in 1979. The original act restricted the opening of stores with sales areas of more than 1,500 square meters (16,500 square feet). In addition, the act restricted the hours of operation of new and existing large stores. A series of changes in 1979 added restrictions on stores with sales areas greater than 500 square meters (5,500 square feet). A Commerce Coordination Committee was established in each area in order to set policy regarding large-store openings and hours of operation. The committees were effectively controlled by the small retailers. By the early 1980s, Ito-Yokado was opening only four or five new stores annually.[9]

Factors other than the Large Store Restriction Act adversely affected Ito-Yokado. Japanese consumers' real disposable income decreased by a little more than 1 percent during 1980–1981.[10] Japan experienced a general economic downturn in the early 1980s, as did the rest of the world, again serving to limit consumer purchasing power. Net income for Ito-Yokado—which had grown almost 30 percent per year between 1976 and 1981—grew by 9.7 percent in 1982 and by 0.9 percent in 1983.[11] The legal restrictions imposed on large stores, when combined with the economic downturn, led to both lower current earnings and a projection of reduced rates of growth in future earnings.

Ito-Vokado as a Parent Company

During the early 1970s, Ito began pursuing new retailing interests. In 1972, he approached Dallas-based Southland Corporation in an attempt to secure a license to operate 7-Eleven stores in Japan. He was rebuffed.[12] He made a similar attempt in 1973 with the aid of a Japanese trading company, C. Itoh and Company, and was successful in obtaining the license. Concurrently, Ito was pursuing another U.S. firm, Denny's Restaurants, in an attempt to obtain rights for opening Denny's Restaurants in Japan. Both subsidiaries, Denny's Japan and 7-Eleven Japan (originally called York Seven but renamed 7-Eleven Japan in 1978), were established in 1973. The first 7-Eleven and the initial Denny's in Japan were both opened in 1974. Stock for each of the two majority-owned subsidiaries was traded independently on the Tokyo Stock Exchange. Both subsidiaries became profitable around 1977.[13]

ITO-YOKADO IN THE 1980s

The Ito-Yokado group consisted of three business segments: Superstores and other Retail Operations, Restaurant Operations, and Convenience Store Operations. The Convenience Store Operations segment was made up of 7-Eleven Japan. The Restaurant Operations segment consisted of Denny's and Famil Restaurants. Ito-Yokado superstores, Daikuma discount stores, two supermarket chains (York Mart and York-Benimaru), Robinson's Department Stores, and Oshman's Sporting Goods Store made up the Superstores and other Retail Operations segment. Ito-Yokado's financial statements are shown in Exhibits 1 through 3.

---

[9]Uchida, *First Boston*, pp. 7–8.

[10]Ibid.

[11]Ibid., p. 8.

[12]Mitchell, "Southland Suitor."

[13]Uchida, *First Boston*, p. 8.

EXHIBIT 1 Ito-Yokado Company, Ltd., Consolidated Balance Sheet (In Millions of Yen)

	As of February 28				
	1986	1987	1988	1989	1990
Assets					
Cash	¥ 26,188	¥ 25,596	¥ 32,527	¥ 31,566	¥ 32,529
Time Deposits	32,708	64,894	55,631	125,809	163,524
Marketable Securities	33,882	33,635	75,924	63,938	60,905
Notes and Accounts Receivable	16,570	16,582	19,042	26,949	24,195
Inventories	48,813	48,163	49,372	56,519	56,168
Other Current Assets	13,014	13,951	13,655	15,156	17,892
Total Current Assets	171,175	202,821	246,151	319,937	355,213
Investments and Advertisement	18,097	21,642	24,352	25,589	33,779
Gross Property and Equipment	465,049	505,450	544,752	600,815	663,263
Less Accumulated Depreciation	160,409	183,185	207,561	237,079	262,958
Net Property and Equipment	304,640	322,265	337,191	363,736	400,305
Leasehold Deposits	81,500	88,386	93,358	98,639	114,678
Total Assets	¥575,394	¥635,114	¥701,052	¥807,901	¥903,975
Liabilities and Owners' Equity					
Short Term	¥ 23,577	¥ 22,425	¥ 17,815	¥ 20,090	¥ 20,140
Debt Due	13,450	8,396	5,689	3,964	6,815
Accounts and Notes Payable	105,790	103,519	119,982	135,516	153,551
Accrued Liability	40,892	45,217	53,654	61,077	65,941
Other Current Liability	12,777	13,523	17,297	20,458	25,404
Total Current Liabilities	196,486	193,080	214,437	241,305	271,851
Long-Term Debt	86,802	109,563	99,961	93,720	85,265
Accrued Sev. Indemnity	1,201	1,248	1,319	1,227	1,297
Deferred Income Taxes	1,912	2,036	969	0	2,150
Minority Interests	45,011	51,974	60,619	83,102	95,920
Owners' Equity					
Common Stock	17,364	18,184	22,462	28,913	33,328
Capital Surplus	78,202	82,070	88,139	95,817	100,230
Other Capital	9,292	9,292	9,292	16,210	16,210
Legal Reserve	4,029	4,837	5,715	6,741	7,858
Retained Earnings	135,307	163,042	198,351	241,078	290,078
Owners' Equity	244,194	277,425	304,725	388,759	447,704
Less Treasury Stock	(212)	(212)	(1,423)	(212)	(212)
Net Owners' Equity	¥575,394	277,213	303,302	388,547	447,492
Total Liabilities and Owners' Equity	¥243,982	¥635,114	¥701,052	¥807,901	¥903,975

Source: *Moody's Industrial Manual*, 1990, Vol. 1.

EXHIBIT 2   Ito-Yokado Company, Ltd., Consolidated Income Statement (In Millions of Yen)

	As of February 28				
	1986	**1987**	**1988**	**1989**	**1990**
Net Sales	¥1,201,347	¥1,281,203	¥1,371,960	¥1,524,947	¥1,664,390
Cost of Goods Sold	829,077	875,343	923,771	1,025,839	1,113.659
Gross Margin	372,270	405,860	448,189	499,108	550,731
Depreciation and Amortization	27,328	31,106	32,064	33,777	37,695
Selling, General, and Administrative Expense	252,355	271,204	294,208	324,295	354,321
Operating Income	92,587	103,550	121,917	141,036	158,715
Interest Income	6,585	5,827	7,173	8,662	12,838
Interest Expense	6,982	5,962	4,755	3,400	3,751
Foreign Currency Gains	2,089	488	74	—	—
Income Before Taxes	92,279	103,903	124,409	146,298	167,802
Income Taxes					
Current	5,449	61,005	72,191	84,930	91,561
Deferred	1,153	106	(1,400)	(2,498)	3,183
Total Income Taxes	55,605	61,111	70,791	82,432	94,744
Minority Interests	7,471	8,862	11,058	13,338	15,777
Equity in Affiliated Earnings	618	829	951	1,058	984
Net Income	¥ 31,824	¥ 34,759	¥ 43,511	¥ 51,586	¥ 58,465
Opening Retained Earnings	¥ 109,717	¥ 135,307	¥ 163,042	¥ 198,351	¥ 241,078
Cash Dividends	5,570	6,216	7,324	7,833	8,348
Transfer to Legal Reserves	664	808	878	1,026	1,117
Closing Retained Earnings	¥ 135,307	¥ 163,042	¥ 198,351	¥ 241,078	¥ 290,078
Per Common Share					
Net Income	¥ 81.44	¥ 88.05	¥ 108.40	¥ 127.35	¥ 143.71
Cash Dividends	¥ 15.70	¥ 18.18	¥ 19.55	¥ 20.00	¥ 23.00
Average Number of Shares	396,798	400,449	406,554	408,037	408,770

Source: *Moody's Industrial Manual,* 1990, Vol. 1.

SUPERSTORES AND OTHER RETAIL OPERATIONS

York Mart and York-Benimaru

York Mart was a wholly owned subsidiary established in 1975. In 1990, it operated 40 supermarkets located primarily in the Tokyo area.[14] These stores sold mainly fresh foods and packaged goods, and competition was high in this geographic and retail area. Ito-Yokado's Operation Reform Program was implemented by York Mart in 1986 as a means to boost efficiency and profits. By 1990 sales were increasing at 6 percent per year.[15]

---

[14]Ibid., p. 8; and *Moody's Industrial Manual,* 1990, vol. 1, p. 1275.
[15]Ibid.

EXHIBIT 3 Ito-Yokado Company, Ltd., Statement of Cash Flows (In Millions of Yen)

	As of February 28			
	1987	1988	1989	1990
Cash Flow from Operations				
Net Income	¥ 34,759	¥ 43,511	¥ 51,586	¥ 58,465
Adjustments				
Depreciation and Amortization	31,106	32,064	33,777	37,695
Minority Interest	8,862	11,058	13,338	15,577
Undistributed Earnings of Affiliates	(603)	(719)	(811)	(732)
Deferred Income Tax and Other	985	1,328	1,641	5,677
Increase in Accounts and Notes Receivable, Less Allowance	(12)	(2,140)	(10,675)	58
Decrease (Increase) in Inventory	650	(1,196)	(6,049)	740
Decrease (Increase) in Prepaid Expenses	(2,194)	734	(1,109)	(8,875)
Increase in Accounts and Notes Payable and Accrued Liability	2,054	24,740	22,296	22,388
Increase in Other Liability	718	3,744	2,945	4,815
Net Cash Provided by Operations	¥ 76,325	¥112,854	¥106,939	¥135,808
Cash Flow from Investing				
Increase in Property and Equipment	¥ (50,832)	¥ (50,075)	¥ (55,802)	¥ (72,927)
Increase in Investments and Advertising	(3,492)	(3,260)	(1,706)	(6,339)
Proceeds from Disposal of Property and Equipment	1,460	731	1,991	1,442
Other	(6,206)	(5,629)	(5,878)	(13,888)
Net Cash Used by Investing	¥ (58,620)	¥ (58,233)	¥ (61,395)	¥ (91,742)
Cash Flow from Financing				
Issue of Long-Term Debt	¥ 37,859	¥ 7,692	¥ 9,755	¥ 10,135
Repayment of Long-Term Debt	(15,331)	(9,321)	(6,472)	(7,112)
Proceeds from Issuance of Common Stock by Subs	0	0	18,554	0
Dividends Paid	(6,216)	(7,324)	(7,833)	(8,834)
Other	(2,670)	(5,711)	(2,317)	(3,096)
Net Cash Provided by Financing	¥ 13,642	¥ (14,664)	¥ 11,687	¥ (8,421)
Net Change in Cash Equivalent	¥ 31,347	¥ 39,957	¥ 57,231	¥ 35,645
Cash Equivalent at Start of Year	92,778	124,125	164,082	221,313
Cash Equivalent at End of Year	¥124,125	¥164,082	¥221,313	¥256,958

Source: *Moody's Industrial Manual, 1990 and 1989*, Vol. 1.

York-Benimaru was a 29-percent-owned affiliate of Ito-Yokado, and was an independently managed regional supermarket chain. York-Benimaru operated 51 stores as of 1988. The stores were located in the Fukushima prefecture of Koriyama-city in northern Japan.[16] Like York Mart, York-Benimaru operated with a higher profit margin than

---

[16]Ibid.

the supermarket industry as a whole. York-Benimaru's earnings growth rate of 13 percent per year was expected to last into the 1990s, and Ito-Yokado's share of this profit was the major contribution to the "equity in earnings of affiliates" portion of Ito-Yokado's income statement (see Exhibit 2).[17]

Daikuma

Daikuma discount stores were consolidated into the Ito-Yokado group in 1986, when Ito-Yokado's ownership of Daikuma increased from 47.6 percent to 79.5 percent.[18] In 1990, Daikuma was one of the largest discount store chains in Japan with 14 stores. Although Daikuma was popular among young Japanese consumers, the discount stores attracted the critical attention of competing small retailers. Because the discount stores were regulated by the Large Store Regulation Act, intensive effort was required to open new stores. Despite these circumstances, and increasing competition, Daikuma opened two discount stores in 1989.[19]

Robinson's Department Stores

In 1984, the Robinson's Japan Company was established to open Robinson's Department Stores in Japan. The Robinson's name was used under the terms of a license granted by the U.S. store of the same name. The Japanese company was wholly owned by Ito-Yokado, and the first Robinson's Department Store in Japan was opened in November 1985 in Kasukabe City of Saitama Prefecture.[20] This was a residential community north of Tokyo and was a rapidly growing area. Although an Ito-Yokado superstore was located nearby, Ito-Yokado's management believed that a niche existed for a slightly more upscale retail store. Ito-Yokado had "shattered traditional wisdom by opening up a department store in the suburbs, not in the center of Tokyo."[21] The location was expected to serve a population area of more than 600,000 residents and to offer a broad selection of consumer goods at prices higher than superstores yet lower than the downtown Tokyo department stores.

Many of the strategies employed by Ito-Yokado in opening its Robinson's Department Store followed similar strategies employed in its superstores. The land was leased (in a suburb). Instead of purchasing goods on a consignment basis as most other department stores did, Robinson's managers were made responsible for the outright purchase of goods from suppliers. This allowed Robinson's to purchase goods at a significantly reduced price. Robinson's reported its first profit in fiscal 1989, approximately four years after opening.[22] In contrast, most Japanese department stores operate approximately 10 years before reporting a profit.[23] The single Robinson's location grossed about ¥28 billion (US$220 million) in fiscal 1989.[24] The second Robinson's Department Store opened in late 1990 in Utsunomiya, about 100 kilometers (60 miles) north of Tokyo.

---

[17]Ibid.

[18]Ibid.

[19]*Moody's Industrial Manual*, p. 1275.

[20]Uchida, *First Boston*, p. 10.

[21]Ibid.

[22]*Moody's Industrial Manual*, p. 1275.

[23]Uchida, *First Boston*, p. 10.

[24]*Moody's Industrial Manual*, p. 1275.

Oshman's Sporting Goods

Ito-Yokado licensed the Oshman's Sporting Goods name from the Houston, Texas, parent company in 1985. That year, two stores were opened. One of the stores was located inside the original Robinson's Department Store.

RESTAURANT OPERATIONS

Famil

The Famil Restaurant chain was started in 1979 as an in-store restaurant to serve customers at Ito-Yokado superstores. It had, however, expanded to 251 locations by 1988.[25] The Famil chain did not record its first positive earnings until 1986. In Famil's attempts to expand operations, the company had emphasized its catering business.[26] By 1990, the in-store operations (those located in Ito-Yokado superstores) accounted for 45 percent of Famil's sales, the catering business accounted for 32 percent of sales, and freestanding stores accounted for 23 percent of sales.[27]

Denny's Japan

Ito-Yokado opened the initial Denny's (Japan) Restaurant in 1974 with a license from Denny's of La Mirada, California. Ito-Yokado tailored the U.S. family restaurant to the Japanese market, and Denny's Japan became profitable around 1977. By 1981, 100 Denny's Japan restaurants had been established,[28] and in 1990 there were 320 such restaurants operated by Ito-Yokado.[29] In 1990, Ito-Yokado controlled 51 percent of Denny's Japan stock. In the early 1980s. Ito-Yokado decided that Denny's Japan should purchase all rights to the Denny's name in Japan. The purchase was made in 1984, and royalty payments to the U.S. parent were thereby discontinued.[30]

In fiscal year 1990 (March 1989 to February 1990), Denny's Japan reported a net annual sales increase of 10.9 percent, as compared with the 4.9 percent Japanese restaurant industry sales increase for the same period[31] Exhibits 4 and 5 contain financial statements for Denny's Japan. In 1988, Denny's Japan began using an electronic order-entry system, which allowed managers of individual restaurants to quickly order food supplies based on trends in their own restaurants. It also allowed for the periodic updating of menus to reflect new food items.

CONVENIENCE STORE OPERATIONS

7-Eleven Japan

Since the opening of the first 7-Eleven store in 1974, the chain had grown to more than 4,300 stores located in virtually all parts of Japan by February 1990.[32] At that time, about

---

[25]Uchida, *First Boston*, p. 12.

[26]Ibid.

[27]*Moody's Industrial Manual*, p. 1275.

[28]Ibid.

[29]Yumiko Ono, "Japanese Chain Stores Prosper by Milking American Concepts," *Asian Wall Street Journal*, April 2, 1990.

[30]Ibid.

[31]*Moody's Industrial Manual*, pp. 1275–1276.

[32]James Sterngold, "New Japanese Lesson: Running a 7–11." *New York Times,* May 9, 1991, p. C1.

EXHIBIT 4   Denny's Japan Company, Ltd., Consolidated Balance Sheet (In Millions of Yen)

	As of February 28		
	1988	1989	1990
Assets			
Cash	¥ 1,436	¥ 1,686	¥ 1,516
Time Deposits	4,430	4,930	13,340
Marketable Securities	104	0	14
Notes and Accounts Receivable	76	87	111
Inventories	562	569	617
Prepaid Expenses	529	610	758
Short-Term Loans	4,527	6,241	5
Short-Term Leasehold Deposits	267	286	300
Other Current Assets	414	233	341
Total Current Assets	12,345	14,643	17,092
Investments and Advances	2,452	2,133	2,273
Gross Property and Equipment	18,894	21,291	23,739
Less: Accumulated Depreciation	9,108	10,397	11,937
Net Property and Equipment	9,786	10,894	11,802
Fixed Leasehold Deposits	5,177	5,334	5,496
Deferred Charges Other Assets	4,449	3,940	3,380
Total Assets	¥34,209	¥36,944	¥40,043
Liabilities and Owners' Equity			
Accounts Payable	¥ 3,728	¥ 3,865	¥ 3,932
Accrued Expenses	1,560	1,743	1,837
Income Tax	2,009	2,210	2,140
Consumption Tax Withheld	328	0	653
Other Current Liabilities	0	383	299
Total Current Liabilities	7,625	8,201	8,861
Common Stock	7,125	7,125	7,125
Additional Paid-In Capital	9,533	9,785	9,785
Legal Reserves	233	286	345
Closing Retained Earnings	9,724	11,547	13,927
Owners' Equity	26,584	28,743	31,182
Total Liabilities and Owners' Equity	¥34,209	¥36,944	¥40,043

Source: *Moody's International Manual*, 1989, 1990, Vol. 1.

300 new stores were being opened annually.[33] Ito-Yokado owned approximately 50.3 percent of 7-Eleven Japan in 1990.

Originally, young urban workers represented the primary customer base. As 7-Eleven penetrated the Japanese market, however, almost everyone became a potential customer. In Tokyo, for example, utility bills could be paid at the chain's stores.[34]

---

[33]Ono, "Japanese Chain Stores Prosper."
[34]Ibid.

EXHIBIT 5 Denny's Japan Company, Ltd., Consolidated Income Statement (In Millions of Yen)

	As of February 28		
	1988	**1989**	**1990**
Net Sales	¥58,241	¥64,604	¥70,454
Interest Income	317	434	650
Other Revenue, Net	223	236	290
Total Revenue	58,781	65,274	71,394
Cost of Sales	20,196	22,233	23,952
Gross Margin	38,585	43,041	47,442
Selling, Administrative, and General Expenses	32,444	35,990	40,177
Interest Expense	19	9	17
Loss on Sale of Property	73	153	119
Income Before Taxes	6,049	6,889	7,129
Income Taxes	3,521	3,894	4,074
Net Income	¥ 2,528	¥ 2,995	¥ 3,055
Opening Retained Earnings	¥ 7,755	¥ 9,152	¥ 1,547
Cash Dividends	508	535	588
Transfers to Legal Reserves	51	53	59
Closing Retained Earnings	¥ 9,724	¥11,559	¥13,955
Earnings per Share (Based on 26,741,000 Weighted Average Shares)	¥ 94.50	¥112.40	¥114.20

Source: *Moody's International Manual*, 1989, 1990, Vol. 1. The data are presented here as shown in Moody's. Some minor math errors exist.

The 7-Eleven stores were small enough, with an average of only 1,000 square feet, to effectively avoid regulation under the Large Store Regulation Act. This allowed 7-Eleven to compete with the mom-and-pop retailers on the basis of longer hours of operation and lower prices. Faced with this competition, many of the small retailers joined the ranks of 7-Eleven. By converting small retailers to 7-Eleven stores, Ito-Yokado was able to expand rapidly and blanket the country.[35]

7-Eleven Japan pursued a strategy of franchising stores instead of owning them. The franchise commission for 7-Eleven stores was approximately 45 percent of the gross profit of the store (the commission was 43 percent for 24-hour stores). Ito-Yokado provided most of the ancillary functions for each store (e.g., administration, accounting, advertising, and 80 percent of utility costs). In 1987, 92 percent of all 7-Eleven stores in Japan were franchised,[36] and by 1990, only 2 percent of the 7-Elevens were corporate-owned.[37]

Within the Ito-Yokado group, 7-Eleven contributed 6.8 percent of revenues in 1990. With this relatively small portion of overall corporate revenues, however, 7-

---

[35]Tanzer, "A Form of Flattery."

[36]Uchida, *First Boston*, p. 13.

[37]*Moody's Industrial Manual*, p. 1276.

EXHIBIT 6　7-Eleven Japan Consolidated Balance Sheet (In Millions of Yen)

	As of February 28		
	1988	1989	1990
Assets			
Cash	¥ 11,868	¥ 15,739	¥ 14,373
Time Deposits	23,440	31,090	65,510
Short-Term Loans	26,169	52,228	29,136
Notes and Accounts Receivable	2,343	2,517	2,582
Inventory	247	285	222
Prepaid Expenses	223	285	124
Less: Allowance for Other Debts	1,990	320	180
Other Current Assets	351	651	369
Total Current Assets	66,631	102,315	112,136
Investments and Advances	3,534	3,382	9,355
Gross Property and Equipment	94,703	108,319	123,871
Less: Accumulated Depreciation	25,665	30,316	35,010
Net Property and Equipment	69,038	78,003	88,861
Fixed Leasehold Deposits	4,351	6,501	7,725
Other Assets	1,460	2,213	8,248
Total Assets	¥145,014	¥192,417	¥226,325
Liabilities and Owners' Equity			
Accounts Payable	¥ 40,498	¥ 46,678	¥ 52,912
Accrued Expenses	1,427	1,487	1,738
Advances	685	778	718
Income Taxes	14,818	17,341	20,068
Other Current Liabilities	867	552	3,289
Total Current Liabilities	58,295	66,836	78,725
Long-Term Debt	1,612	1,781	1,933
Common Stock	5,902	17,145	17,145
Additional Paid-In Capital	13,073	24,619	24,589
Legal Reserves	1,142	1,491	1,919
Retained Earnings	65,233	80,545	101,984
Owners' Equity	85,107	123,800	145,667
Total Liabilities and Owners' Equity	¥145,014	¥192,417	¥226,325

Source: *Moods's International Manual*, 1989, 1990, Vol. 1.

Eleven Japan contributed more than 35 percent of the group's profit. Under its licensing agreement, 7-Eleven Japan paid royalties of 0.6 percent of gross sales to the Southland Corporation. In 1989 and 1990, 7-Eleven Japan paid royalties of about $4.1 million and $4.7 million, respectively. The financial statements for 7-Eleven Japan for the years 1986 to 1990 are shown in Exhibits 6 and 7.

EXHIBIT 7   7-Eleven Japan Consolidated Income Statement (In Millions of Yen)

	As of February 28		
	1988	**1989**	**1990**
Revenue	¥96,236	¥102,314	¥118,490
Cost of Goods Sold	13,484	8,702	9,249
Gross Margin	82,752	93,612	109,241
Selling, Administrative, and General Expenses	39,672	42,491	49,185
Loss on Sale of Property	232	(66)	(230)
Income Before Taxes	42,848	51,187	59,826
Tax Expenses	23,911	28,882	33,599
Net Income	¥18,937	¥ 22,305	¥ 26,227
Opening Retained Earnings	¥49,646	¥ 62,139	¥ 80,545
Dividends	3,054	3,495	4,280
Transfers to Legal Reserves	306	350	428
Officers' Bonus	0	54	80
Closing Retained Earnings	¥65,223	¥ 80,545	¥101,984
Earnings per Share (Based on 179,569,000 Weighted Average Shares)	¥ 129.1	¥ 126.7	¥ 146.1

Note: "Cost of Goods Sold" represents primarily the cost of merchandise sold in the 152 company-owned stores.
Source: *Moody's International Manual*, 1989, 1990, Vol. 1.

OPERATION REFORM PROJECT

Ito-Yokado implemented the Operation Reform Project in late 1981 in a retail industry environment punctuated by reduced consumer spending and decreasing margins. The goals of the project were to increase efficiency and boost profitability by increasing the inventory turn while avoiding empty store shelves. The plan was originally implemented in the Ito-Yokado Superstores and the 7-Eleven Japan convenience stores.

The implementation of the project involved a coordinated effort of catering to rapidly changing consumer preferences while, simultaneously, monitoring merchandise flow more closely. This coordination was accomplished by making individual store managers more responsible for such decisions as what merchandise was to be stocked on store shelves, thus allowing managers to tailor merchandise selection in their individual stores to local preferences. Top Ito-Yokado regional managers held weekly meetings with store managers to monitor the implementation of the project. As late as 1988, these meetings were still held on a weekly basis.[38]

In order to avoid depletion of store stocks, Ito-Yokado established an on-line ordering system with vendors. In 1982, the ordering system reached only 400 vendors. By 1988, however, the system linked Ito-Yokado with 1,860 vendors.[39]

---

[38]Hiroaki Komatsu, *Nomura Securities Report on Ito-Yokado Co., Ltd.*, June 7, 1988, p. 4.
[39]Ibid.

Point-of-Sale System[40]

As implementation of the Operation Reform Project began, Ito-Yokado paid increased attention to the importance of obtaining information regarding the flow of merchandise through individual stores. The tool chosen to accomplish this task was the point-of-sale system. POS system usage was increasing in the United States in the early 1980s, but the systems were used primarily to increase productivity at the cash register.[41] In contrast, Ito-Yokado used similar systems as a part of the project by monitoring specific merchandise flow. As of the late 1980s, many retailers in the United States had begun utilizing POS in similar capacities, and some had begun to use POS to track the purchases of individual consumers.[42]

The first use of POS systems in Japan came in 1982, when 7-Eleven Japan began installing them in its stores. By 1986, every 7-Eleven store in Japan was equipped with such a system.[43] The systems available were sophisticated enough to monitor the entire stock of merchandise in a typical convenience store having about 3,000 items.[44] The systems could monitor the flow of every item of merchandise through the purchase, inventory, sale, and restocking stages.

In late 1984, Ito-Yokado decided to install POS systems in the superstores. The sophistication of those systems installed in convenience stores, however, was not adequate to handle the merchandise flow of a superstore, which could stock up to 500,000 items.[45] New POS systems were developed in a coordinated effort by Ito-Yokado, Nippon Electric, and Nomura Computer Services.

The installation of POS systems in the existing superstores was completed in November 1985, with more than 8,000 POS registers installed in 121 stores.[46] With 138 stores in 1990, Ito-Yokado had an estimated 9,000 POS registers in the superstores alone. In 1986, after the systems had been installed in all superstores and 7-Elevens, Ito-Yokado accounted for about 70 percent of the POS systems in use in Japan.[47] As of 1988,

---

[40]POS systems are computer-based merchandise control systems. They can provide a variety of functions such as inventory monitoring, price identification and registering, and—in some circumstances—merchandise ordering.

The implementation of POS systems became a reality in the early 1970s, when IBM announced the creation of a merchandise system which later became the Universal Product Code (UPC). In 1974, Marsh Supermarkets became the first retail store to utilize UPC-based POS systems. Also in 1974, the European Article Number (EAN) system, which is virtually a superset of the UPC, was introduced in Europe. The EAN system was adopted by 12 European nations in 1977. In 1978, Japan joined the EAN association (EANA). By 1989, 40 countries were members of the EANA.

The Japanese domestic market utilizes the same bar-code system used in the United States and Europe for product marking under the EAN guidelines for product marking. The Japanese coding system for consumer goods is called Japanese Article Numbering (JAN). A similar system for product marking used by wholesalers and distributors in Japan is the value-added network (VAN). The first product utilizing the JAN code was introduced in Japan in 1978.

Source: Ryosuke Assano, "Networks Raise Efficiency," *Business Japan,* October 1989, pp. 45–52; Radack et al., Automation in the Market-Place, March 1978; "Pointing Out Differences in Point-of-Sale," *Chain Store Age Executive,* October 1990, pp. 16B—17B.

[41]Tanzer, "A Form of Flattery."

[42]For an example of one such application, see Blake Ives et al., *The Tom Thumb Promise Club,* Edwin L. Cox School of Business, Southern Methodist University, 1989.

[43]Hiroaki Komatsu, *Nomura Securities Report on Seven-Eleven Japan,* March 15, 1988, p. 4.

[44]Uchida, *First Boston,* p. 13.

[45]Ibid.

[46]*Moody's Industrial Manual,* p. 1275.

[47]Tanzer, "A Form of Flattery."

7-Eleven Japan was the only major convenience store chain in Japan to have installed POS systems.[48] By August 31, 1989, Japan had 119,137 POS scanner-equipped registers in 42,880 stores, making it the country with the most POS systems in use.[49]

The POS systems used by 7-Eleven Japan and Ito-Yokado superstores were upgraded in 1986 to add a new dimension to Ito-Yokado's Operation Reform Project.[50] The upgraded systems allowed for bidirectional communication with the company headquarters. This feature essentially allowed information to flow not only from individual stores to a central location, but also from the central location back to individual stores. By linking the central system to other computer systems, more information than just sales of retail items could be transmitted. This capability allowed Ito-Yokado to increase the efficiency of deliveries by centralizing some orders. By increasing the total size of orders, Ito-Yokado increased its bargaining position with distributors. One result of this bargaining strength was more frequent deliveries of smaller volume. From 1987 to 1988, deliveries increased from one to three per week for stores in many regions of Japan, notably the Tokyo, Hokkaido, and Kyushu areas.

Using the POS systems, 7-Eleven began to offer customers door-to-door parcel delivery in conjunction with Nippon Express. In addition, some POS terminals were being used to issue prepaid telephone credit cards.[51] Since October 1987, Tokyo-area customers had been able to pay their electric bills at 7-Eleven; since March 1988, they had also been able to pay their gas bills.[52] Women traditionally manage household finances in Japan, so these services were designed to attract more women customers to the convenience stores.

Results

For the Ito-Yokado superstores alone, average days of inventory decreased from 25.8 in 1982 to 17.3 in 1987. By 1990, it was estimated to be 13 days.[53] The effect on operating margins and net income for the entire Ito-Yokado corporation was equally dramatic. In 1982, the company's operating margin stood at 5.1 percent. It had increased to 8.1 percent by 1987. By 1990, the operating margin had climbed to 10.5 percent. Net income for the corporation increased from ¥14,662 million in 1982 to ¥34,649 million in 1987, and ¥58,465 million in 1990.[54]

7-Eleven Japan recorded similar increases in operating margins and net income during the same period. In 1982, 7-Eleven Japan's operating margin was 20.7 percent. It had increased to 34.6 percent by 1987. Net income from the 7-Eleven operations increased from ¥7,837 million in 1982 to ¥33,000 million in 1987.[55]

As of 1990, the Ito-Yokado corporation was the second largest retailer in Japan, with ¥1,664,390 million of annual gross sales. The leading retailer was Daiei, with ¥2,114,909 million of revenues. Ito-Yokado was, however, the most profitable retailer in

---

[48]Komatsu, *Nomura Securities Report*, p. 4.

[49]*Business Japan*, October 1989, p. 51.

[50]Komatsu, *Nomura Securities Report*, p. 5.

[51]Ibid.

[52]Ibid.

[53]Uchida, *First Boston*, pp. 12, 22; and *Moody's Industrial Manual*, p. 1276.

[54]Ibid.

[55]Ibid.

Japan, with net income of ¥58,465 million. In comparison, Daiei recorded net income of only ¥9,457 million for 1990. Financial statements for Daiei are shown as Exhibits 8 and 9.

THE SOUTHLAND CORPORATION[56]

The Southland Corporation began in Dallas, Texas, in 1927 when Claude S. Dawley consolidated several small Texas ice companies into the Southland Ice Company. This new company was under the direction of 26-year-old Joe C. Thompson, Sr. Under Thompson's guidance, Southland began to use its retail outlets (curb service docks) to sell products in addition to ice, such as watermelon, milk, bread, eggs, and cigarettes. With the addition of these products, the concept of the convenience store was born.

During the Great Depression and the 1940s, Southland's convenience store business added several more products, including gasoline, frozen foods, beauty products, fresh fruit and vegetables, and picnic supplies. Because the store opened at 7AM and remained open till 11PM, the store name 7-Eleven was adopted during this time.

The 1950s were a period of substantial growth in terms of the number of stores and of 7-Eleven's geographical coverage. The first stores located outside of Texas were opened in Florida in 1954. During the same year, 7-Eleven's operating profit surpassed the $1 million mark for the first time. By 1959, the entire 7-Eleven empire constituted 425 stores in Texas, Louisiana, Florida, and several other East Coast states.

John Thompson became president of Southland when his father, Jodie Thompson, died in 1961. During the 1960s, a population migration toward the suburbs and changing lifestyles presented Southland with new growth opportunities. John Thompson lead Southland on the path of expansion, and more than 3,000 stores were opened in the decade. The product line of 7-Eleven also grew during this time to include prepared foods, rental items, and some self-service gasoline pumps.

The 1970s were also a period of achievement for Southland. In 1971, the $1 billion sales mark was surpassed. Southland stock began trading on the New York Stock Exchange in 1972, and the 5,000th store was opened in 1974. It was at this time that Masatoshi Ito approached Southland with the prospect of franchising 7-Eleven stores in Japan.

During the 1970s and early 1980s, Southland's activities became more diversified. In 1986, the company had four operating groups: the Stores Group, the Dairies Group, the Special Operations Group, and the Gasoline Supply Division.

The Stores Group represented the largest of the operating groups in terms of sales through the 1980s. The Stores Group was responsible for the operating and franchising of convenience stores. At the end of 1985, there were 7,519 7-Eleven stores in most of the United States and five provinces of Canada. This group was also responsible for 84 Gristede's and Charles & Company food stores. 38 Super-7 outlets, and 7-Eleven stores operated under area licensees in the United States, Canada, and several Pacific Rim countries, including Japan.

The Dairies Group was one of the nation's largest dairy processors in 1986 and served primarily the Stores Group, although aggressive marketing in the 1980s targeted service to institutional dairy needs. This group operated in all of the United States and parts of Canada. The Special Operations Group consisted of Chief Auto Parts (acquired

---

[56]A more detailed history of Southland can be found in cases written by M. Edgar Barrett, of the American Graduate School of International Business: *The Southland Corporation (A)*, 1983, and *The Southland Corporation (B)*, 1990.

EXHIBIT 8   Daiei, Inc. Consolidated Balance Sheet (In Millions of Yen)

	As of February 28		
	1988	**1989**	**1990**
Assets			
Cash	¥ 60,409	¥ 61,096	¥ 55,529
Time Deposits	89,090	61,866	85,713
Marketable Securities	18,919	18,762	20,022
Net Receivables	100,214	98,449	103,455
Inventories	95,924	90,203	108,241
Prepaid Expenses and Deferred Income Tax	7,784	11,149	15,338
Total Current Assets	372,340	341,525	388,298
Gross Property and Equipment	284,007	358,443	410,870
Less Accumulated Depreciation	108,540	120,955	141,172
Net Property and Equipment	175,467	237,488	269,698
Lease Depreciation and Loans to Lessors	231,996	245,139	266,474
Investment and Long-Term Receivables	118,009	170,676	164,853
Other Assets	13,689	16,540	21,306
Total Assets	¥911,501	¥1,011,368	¥1,110,629
Liabilities and Owners' Equity			
Short-Term Borrowings	¥256,539	¥ 338,188	¥ 350,274
Debt Due	51,488	47,816	34,667
Notes and Accounts Payable	176,450	186,390	221,815
Accruals	18,370	18,274	21,256
Income Taxes	7,872	7,284	8,445
Total Current Liabilities	510,719	597,952	636,457
Long-Term Debt	199,616	187,625	216,763
Lease Deposits	52,656	56,750	60,489
Estimated Retirement and Term Allowance	10,002	9,437	9,789
Reserve for Investment Losses	35,903	35,293	37,151
Deferred Income	7,423	7,343	7,425
Other Liabilities	1,636	4,604	7,314
Translation Adjustment	2,179	1,979	1,754
Minority Interests	663	692	2,794
Common Stock (¥50)	18,144	25,649	33,783
Additional Paid-In Capital	82,748	92,426	100,664
Legal Reserves	3,875	4,481	5,108
Deficit	(14,063)	(12,863)	(8,862)
Owners' Equity	90,704	109,693	130,693
Total Liabilities and Owners' Equity	¥911,501	¥1,011,368	¥1,110,629

Source: *Moody's International Manual,* 1990 and 1989, Vol. 1.

EXHIBIT 9   Daiei, Inc. Consolidated Income Statement (In Millions of Yen Except Earnings Per Share)

	As of February 28		
	1988	**1989**	**1990**
Net Sales	¥1,718,886	¥ 1,880,825	¥ 2,114,909
Real Estate Revenue	0	21,235	22,790
Other Revenue	45,588	37,623	55,171
Total Operating Revenue	1,764,474	1,939,683	2,192,870
Cost of Goods Sold	1,327,618	1,460,007	1,626,850
Gross Margin	436,856	479,676	566,020
Selling, General, and Administrative Expenses	392,914	432,269	510,469
Operating Income	43,942	47,407	55,551
Net Interest Expenditures	16,942	19,115	21,312
Other Expenses	1,760	1,283	3,401
Income Before Taxes	25,240	27,009	30,838
Income Tax	13,405	14,868	17,101
Minority Interests	50	32	730
Equity Losses	7,204	4,229	3,504
Translation Adjustment	211	134	(46)
Net Income	¥ 4,792	¥ 8,104	¥ 9,457
Opening Retained Earnings	¥ (13,929)	¥ (14,063)	¥ (12,863)
Decrease Due to Merger of Chain Store Operations	0	0	1,497
Cash Dividends	5,083	6,059	6,269
Transfer to Legal Reserves	73	606	627
Bonuses	114	141	143
Translation Adjustment	(344)	8	(86)
Closing Retained Earnings	¥ (14,063)	¥ (12.863)	¥ (8,862)
Earnings per Share	¥ 14.27	¥ 21.67	¥ 24.72
Shares Outstanding	N/A	369,871,000	382,499,000

Source: *Moody's International Manual*, 1990 and 1989, Vol. 1.

in 1979); Pate Foods (a snack food company): Reddy Ice (the world's largest ice company); and Tidel Systems (a manufacturer of cash dispensing units and other retailer equipment). The Gasoline Supply Division was formed in 1981 to serve the gasoline requirements of the more than 2,800 7-Eleven stores handling gasoline. This division's history was punctuated by the 1983 acquisition of Cities Service Refining, Marketing, and Transportation businesses (CITGO) from Occidental Petroleum.

Southland's Recent Activities[57]

Southland's dramatic growth and diversification during the 1970s and early 1980s resulted in 7-Eleven having a dominant position in the convenience store industry.

---

[57]Barrett, *The Southland Corporation (B)*, offers more detailed information.

Despite this position, circumstances since the mid-1980s had greatly eroded 7-Eleven and Southland's strengths.

The oil price collapse of early 1986 was the sharpest drop of crude oil prices in history. The instability of crude oil and wholesale refined products, coupled with CITGO's inventory methods and various write-downs, resulted in only modest income for a previously very profitable company. The volatility of CITGO's financial position greatly affected Southland's earnings. Southland's equity interest in CITGO contributed to a $52 million loss for the entire corporation in 1986. In order to reduce the impact of an unstable crude oil market and the accompanying volatility of CITGO's earnings, Southland entered into a joint venture with Petroleos de Venezuela (PDVSA) in late 1986.

The joint venture with PDVSA had several components. Southland sold a half-interest in CITGO to a subsidiary of PDVSA for $290 million. In addition, PDVSA agreed to both supply CITGO with a minimum of 130,000 barrels of crude oil per day and provide its share of CITGO's working capital requirements.

A takeover attempt of Southland occurred in April 1987. Canadian financier Samuel Belzberg approached the Southland board of directors with an offer of $65 per share of common stock. Unwilling to relinquish control of Southland, the Thompson family tendered $77 per share for two-thirds of the outstanding shares in July 1987. The other third of the shares would be purchased at $61 per share (plus $16 per share of new preferred shares) by the would-be private Southland Corporation.

Financing for this acquisition came from $2 billion in loans from a group of banks and a $600 million bridge loan from Goldman, Sachs and Salomon Brothers. An additional $1.5 billion was generated by the issue of subordinated debentures (junk bonds) in November 1987. This occurred after the stock and junk bond markets crashed in October 1987. Southland's investment bankers had to sell the bonds at a blended rate of almost 17 percent, instead of the anticipated rate of 14.67 percent. The Thompson family emerged from the buyout owning 71 percent of Southland at a total cost of $4.9 billion.

Paying the High Costs of a Leveraged Buyout

After Southland had been taken private through the leveraged buyout (LBO), significant changes occurred in both Southland and 7-Eleven operations. Southland was restructured, with the elimination of two levels of middle managers. During this time, Southland began selling more 7-Eleven stores than it opened in the United States and Canada. Due to the increased number of licensees opening stores overseas, however, the total number of stores worldwide continued to increase. 7-Eleven Japan was primarily responsible for this increase, with the opening of 340 stores in 1988 and 349 stores in 1989. Southland also divested itself of many large assets in the 1988 to 1990 period (see Exhibit 10). Significant in this group of divestments were the entire Dairy Group, more than 100 7-Eleven stores in the continental United States, Southland's remaining interest in CITGO (sold to PDVSA), and 7-Eleven Hawaii, (purchased by 7-Eleven Japan).

In November 1989, 7-Eleven Japan purchased 58 stores and additional properties from Southland. These properties and stores, which were located in Hawaii, were exchanged for $75 million in cash. The 58 convenience stores were organized as 7-Eleven Hawaii, which was established as a subsidiary of 7-Eleven Japan.

As of December 31, 1990, Southland operated 6,455 7-Eleven convenience stores in the United States and Canada, 187 High's Dairy Stores, and 63 Quick Mart and Super-7 Stores. Southland owned 1,802 properties on which 7-Eleven stores were located. Another 4,643 7-Eleven stores in the United States and Canada were leased. In addition

EXHIBIT 10 Asset Divestitures of Southland, 1988–1990

Date Announced	Asset	Buyer	Amount
January 1988	Tidel Systems	D. H. Monnick Corp.	Undisclosed
February 1988	Chief Auto Parts	Management & Shearson Lehman	$130 million
March 1988	Movie Quik	Cevax U.S. Corp.	$51 million
March 1988	Reddy Ice	Reddy Ice	$23 million
April 1988	402 Properties including 270 Houston-area 7-Elevens	National Convenience Stores	$67 million plus $13 million for related inventories
April 1988	473 7-Eleven stores in 10 states	Circle-K	$147 million
April 1988	Southland Dairy Group	Morningstar Foods	$242.5 million
July 1988	Snack Food Division	Undisclosed	$15 million
November 1988	79 San Antonio-area 7-Elevens	National Convenience Stores	Undisclosed
July 1989	184 7-Elevens in 3 states	Ashland Oil et al.	Undisclosed
October 1989	50% of CITGO	Petroleos de Venezuela S.A. (PDVSA)	$661.5 million
November 1989	58 7-Elevens in Hawaii, plus other properties	7-Eleven Japan	$75 million
April 1990	56 Memphis-area 7-Elevens	Undisclosed	$12.9 million
August 1990	28 7-Elevens in Florida, plus other properties	Undisclosed	$7.5 million
December 1990	Cityplace in Dallas	Oak Creek Partners	$24 million

Source: *Dallas Morning News,* November 15, 1989, p. D-1; *Dallas Morning News,* October 10, 1988, p. D-1; *Automotive News,* February 8, 1988, p. 108; *Wall Street Journal,* February 19, 1988; *Wall Street Journal,* January 28, 1988; *Wall Street Journal,* March 4, 1988; *New York Times,* March 4, 1988; Southland Corporation, 1990 Form 10-K.

the company possessed 234 store properties held for sale, of which 109 were unimproved. 77 were closed stores, and 48 were excess properties adjoining store locations.[58]

Three of Southland's four food-processing facilities were owned (the other was leased). The company owned six properties in the United States on which distribution centers were located. Five of the six distribution centers were company owned. Until December 1990 the company had also owned its corporate headquarters (called Cityplace) located near downtown Dallas.[59] Financial statements for Southland Corporation are shown in Exhibits 11 and 12.

THE PROPOSED PURCHASE OF SOUTHLAND BY ITO-YOKADO

The divestments of 1988, 1989, and 1990 constituted attempts by Southland to generate sufficient cash to service the massive debt incurred from the LBO of 1987. By early 1990, however, it was apparent that the cash generated from these divestments and Southland's

---

[58]*Southland Corporation 1990 Form 10-K,* pp. 21–23.
[59]Ibid.

EXHIBIT 11   Southland Corporation Consolidated Balance Sheet (In Thousands of Dollars)

	As of December 31			
	1988	**1989**	**1990**	**1990[a]**
Assets				
Cash and Short-Term Inventory	$ 21,783	$ 8,045	$ 108,294	$ 351,678
Accounts and Notes Receivable	208,686	188,251	161,778	161,778
Inventories	428,098	276,112	301,756	301,756
Deposits and Prepaid Expenditures	25,929	25,483	64,075	44,889
Investment in Citgo	—	469,687		
Total Current Assets	684,496	958,578	635,903	860,101
Property, Plant, and Equipment	2,632,060	2,620,137	2,504,090	2,504,090
Less Depreciation	416,822	624,807	788,589	788,589
Net Property, Plant, and Equipment	2,215,238	1,995,330	1,715,501	1,715,501
Investment in Citgo	440,777	—	—	—
Excess Acquisition Costs	986,356	—	—	—
Other Assets	534,644	484,847	447,638	397,349
Total Assets	$4,861,511	$ 3,438,755	$ 2,799,042	$ 2,972,951
Liabilities and Owners' Equity				
Debt Due	$ 527,174	$ 692,508	$ 3,522,647	$ 647,512
Accounts Payable	692,596	723,694	647,512	9,145
Income Taxes Payable	377	139	9,145	171,729
Total Current Liabilities	1,220,147	1,416,341	4,298,119	828,386
Deferred Credits	96,359	115,334	142,315	142,315
Long-Term Debt	3,787,578	3,457,015	182,536	3,118,797
Redeemable Preferred Stock	118,850	139,740	148,496	—
Redeemable Common Stock				
Purchase Warrants	26,136	26,136	26,136	26,136
Common Stock	2,050	2,050	2,050	41
Additional Paid-In Capital	18,318	18,318	20,364	594,146
Deficit	(407,927)	(1,736,179)	(2,018,926)	(1,736,870)
Total Owners' Equity	(387,559)	(1,715,811)	(1,998,560)	(1,142,683)
Total Liabilities and Owners' Equity	$4,861,511	$ 3,438,755	$ 2,799,042	$ 2,972,951

[a]This depicts the balance sheet for Southland on December 31, 1990, as if the later buyout by Ito-Yokado had been completed.
Source: Southland Corporation 1990 and 1989 Forms 10-K.

operations was not sufficient to cover its interest expense. Some experts estimated that Southland's cash shortfalls would reach $89 million in 1990 and more than $270 million in 1991.[60] Southland's long-term debt still totaled about $3.7 billion, and interest expense alone in the first three quarters of 1989 was almost $430 million.[61] In March of 1990, Southland announced that it was seeking "rescue" by Ito-Yokado.[62]

[60]Linda Sandler, "Southland's Junk Bonds Face Trouble," *Wall Street Journal,* September 7, 1989.
[61]Richard Alm, "Southland Seeks Rescue by Japanese Firm," *Dallas Morning News* , March 23, 1990.
[62]Ibid.

EXHIBIT 12 Southland Corporation Consolidated Income Statement (In Thousands of Dollars)

	As of December 31		
	1988	1989	1990
Net Sales	$7,950,284	$ 8,274,921	$ 8,347,681
Other Income	40,213	76,962	62,375
Total Revenues	7,990,497	8,351,883	8,410,056
Cost of Sales	6,268,854	6,544,237	6,661,273
Gross Margin	1,721,643	1,807,646	1,748,783
Selling, Administrative Expenses	1,543,090	1,607,312	1,664,586
Loss on Assets Sold	—	—	41,000
Write-Off, Acquired Assets	—	946,974	—
Interest Expense	560,268	572,248	459,500
Employee Benefits, Etc.	15,416	13,372	13,653
Net Before Taxes	(397,132)	(1,332,260)	(429,956)
Income Taxes	(111,900)	(11,984)	(128,459)
Loss from Continuing Operations	(285,232)	(1,320,276)	(429,956)
Discontinued Operations			
Equity, CITGO	69,001	70,480	—
Loss, Equity Disposition	—	1,070	—
Loss Before Extraordinary Charges	(216,231)	(1,250,866)	(301,497)
Extraordinary Charges	—	(56,047)	52,040
Effect of Account Change of Medical Benefits	(27,163)	—	(27,163)
Net Income	$ (216,231)	$(1,306,913)	$ (276,620)
Opening Retained Earnings	$ (166,998)	$ (407,927)	$(1,736,179)
Dividends Paid, Redeemable Preferred Stock	(20,856)	(12,634)	(1,011)
Accretion	(6,706)	(8,257)	(7,744)
Currency Translation Adjustment	2,864	(488)	(2,628)
Deficit	$ (407,927)	$(1,736,179)	$(2,018,926)
Earnings per Share Data			
Loss, Before Extraordinary Charges	$ (15.63)	$ (62.02)	$ (15.14)
Effect of Extraordinary Charges	—	(2.74)	2.54
Net Loss	$ (12.19)	$ (64.76)	$ (13.93)
Year End Common Shares (000)	205,042	205,042	205,042

Source: Southland Corporation 1990 and 1989 Form 10-K.

Proposed Acquisition of Southland by Ito-Yokado

Southland had "looked at possibilities of receiving assistance from other U.S. companies, but decided that…Ito-Yokado was the best potential partner."[63] The original proposal would have resulted in Ito-Yokado receiving 75 percent ownership of Southland for $400 million. This proportion of Southland would be split between Ito-Yokado and 7-Eleven Japan, with 7-Eleven Japan obtaining two-thirds of the 75 percent share.

The deal was contingent on Southland's ability to swap its outstanding publicly traded debt for stock and zero-coupon (non-interest-bearing) bonds. The publicly traded debt amounted to approximately $1.8 billion. There were five classes of public debt, ranging in type and interest paid. The interest rate of the bonds varied from 13.5 percent to 18 percent. Ito-Yokado's offer was also contingent on 95 percent of all bondholders of each public debt issue accepting the swap. Under this original proposal, the Thompson family would retain a 15 percent stake in Southland, and the remaining 10 percent of the company would be held by bondholders.

The original proposal had a deadline of June 14, 1990, at which time either Ito-Yokado or Southland could cancel the agreement. Neither party indicated that such action would be taken, even though Southland's bondholders balked at the swap proposal. A bigger problem was facing the two companies: a rapidly approaching interest payment due on June 15, 1990. Southland's failure to pay the $69 million payment would result in Southland having a 30-day grace period in which to compensate bondholders. At the end of the 30-day period, unpaid bondholders could try to force Southland into bankruptcy court.[64]

Revisions to the Proposed Buyout

Southland did not make its scheduled interest payment that was due on June 15, 1990. Bondholders, meanwhile, had shown little regard for the original deal struck between Ito-Yokado and Southland.

Three more revisions of the proposed debt restructuring and terms for the buyout were submitted between mid-June and mid-July 1990. In each revision, either Ito-Yokado's or the Thompson family's stake in Southland was reduced and the share of Southland stock offered to bondholders increased. With each revision came increased bondholder support, yet this support was far short of either the two-thirds majority (as required in Chapter 11 restructuring cases) or the 95 percent acceptance rate dictated by Ito-Yokado. As revisions were submitted, the expiration dates of the debt restructuring and stock purchase by Ito-Yokado were extended.

On July 16, a bondholder filed suit against Southland for failure to pay interest on June 15, because on July 15 Southland's grace period had expired.[65] By September 12, a majority of bondholders had tendered their notes.[66] This majority was still far short, however, of the 95 percent swap requirement dictated by Ito-Yokado. The deadlines were extended to September 25 for both the debt swap offer by Southland and the stock

[63]Karen Blumenthal et al., "Japanese Group Agrees to Buy Southland Corporation," *Wall Street Journal*, March 23, 1990.

[64]Karen Blumenthal, "Southland Approaches 2 Crucial Dates in Plan to Rearrange $1.8 Billion in Debt," *Wall Street Journal*, April 12, 1990.

[65]Ibid.

[66]Kevin Helliker, "Southland May Be Considering Seeking Chapter 11 Status, Thus Risking Bailout," *Wall Street Journal*, September 14, 1990.

purchase offer by Ito-Yokado.[67] As Southland was apparently headed for involuntary bankruptcy filing under Chapter 11, the proposal again seemed in jeopardy.

Acceptance of the Proposed Buyout

The deadline for Southland's debt swap offer was again extended. Bondholder approval was finally obtained in late October. Ito-Yokado's offer to buy out Southland was extended to March 15, 1991, pending court approval of the prepackaged bankruptcy deal.[68] The bankruptcy-court petition for approval of the prepackaged debt restructuring was filed on October 24, 1990.[69]

Although Southland did not have sufficient bondholder approval as dictated by Ito-Yokado, the bankruptcy court proceedings were swift. The last few bondholders who held out were placated in January when the Thompsons relinquished warrants for half of their 5 percent stake of Southland's stock.[70] On February 21, 1991, the U.S. bankruptcy court in Dallas approved the reorganization of Southland.[71] At that time, at least 93 percent of the holders of each class of debt issued by Southland had approved the reorganization.[72] On March 5, 1991, Ito-Yokado purchased 71 percent of Southland's stock for $430 million.[73] Two-thirds of this stock was purchased by 7-Eleven Japan, and the other third purchased directly by Ito-Yokado. The terms of the accepted debt-restructuring agreement between Southland and its bondholders are shown in Exhibit 13.

THE CONVENIENCE STORE INDUSTRY IN THE UNITED STATES

The convenience store industry in the United States changed dramatically during the decade of the 1980s. The number of convenience stores in the United States, the gross sales of these stores, and the gross margins all increased during this time period. The net income of convenience stores, however, decreased significantly. This outcome was largely the result of the rapid expansion of several chains of convenience stores and the increased number of convenience stores opened by oil companies.

Aggregate Measures of the Industry

The number of convenience stores grew from about 39,000 in 1982 to more than 70,000 in 1989. From 1985 to 1989, industry sales increased from $51.4 billion to $67.7 billion, an increase of 6.3 percent per year. Gross margins increased from 22.8 percent in 1985 to 26.2 percent by 1988. Despite such growth, convenience store operations experienced a decrease in net profit in the late 1980s. The total industry pretax profit peaked in 1986 at $1.4 billion, fell to $1.16 billion in 1988, and plummeted to $271 million in 1989. Some trends are shown in Exhibit 14.[74]

---

[67]Ibid.

[68]Kevin Helliker, "Southland Says Reorganization Clears Hurdle," *Wall Street Journal*, October 24, 1990.

[69]"Southland Chapter 11 Plan Needs Approval From SEC," *Wall Street Journal*, December 6, 1990.

[70]David LaGeese, "Judge Approves Southland's Reorganization," *Dallas Morning News*, February 22, 1991, p. 1D.

[71]Ibid.

[72]Ibid.

[73]"Southland Sells 70 Percent Stake, Completing Reorganization," *Wall Street Journal*, March 6, 1991, p. A2.

[74]This information is drawn largely from: National Association of Convenience Stores (NACS), *1990 State of the Convenience Store Industry*, 1990.

EXHIBIT 13 Southland Corporation Debt Restructuring Terms for $1,000 Principal Debt of Various Classes as Accepted by Bondholders on February 21, 1991

	13.5% Senior Notes	15.75% Senior Notes	16.5% Senior Notes	16.75% Notes	18% Junior Notes
Principal Retained	$450	$300	$255	$200	$95
Interest Rate of New Debt Received	12%	5%	5%	4.5%	4%
Number of Shares of Common Stock Received	86.5	40.5	35	28	11
Number of Stock Warrants Received	1	7.5	6.5	6	6

Notes:
—"Principal retained" was in the form of newly issued bonds bearing interest as shown.
—Holders of 13.5% Senior Notes also received $57 cash per $1,000 principal of old debt.
—Holders of 16.5% Notes may have received $250 of 12% Notes with no stock warrants instead of $200 of 4.5% and 6 stock warrants (per $1,000 principal of old debt). In either case the holder would have been entitled to 28 shares of common stock.
—Stock warrants gave the holder the option to purchase one share of common stock per warrant for $1.75 per share from June 5, 1991, to February 23, 1996.
Source: Southland Corporation 1990 Form 10-K.

EXHIBIT 14 Industrywide Convenience Store Performance, 1985–1989

	1985	1986	1987	1988	1989
Number of Stores	61,000	64,000	67,500	69,200	70,200
Gross Revenue (In Billions)	$51.4	$53.9	$59.6	$61.2	$67.7
Net Income (In Billions)	$ 1.39	$ 1.40	$ 1.31	$ 1.16	$ 0.27
Average Per-Store Profit Before Tax (In Thousands)	$22.8	$21.9	$19.2	$16.8	$ 3.9

Source: National Association of Convenience Stores, *1990 State of the Convenience Store Industry*.

The expansion of convenience stores in the 1980s was led by large convenience store chains and oil companies. In addition to the growth experienced by the Southland Corporation's 7-Eleven, Circle-K, a Phoenix-based convenience store chain, expanded from 1,200 stores in 1980 to 4,700 stores in 1990.

The Role of the Oil Companies

The impact of oil companies on the convenience store industry had been significant. Virtually all of the major U.S. oil companies began combining convenience store operations with gasoline stations in order to boost profits. In 1984, Exxon opened its first combination convenience store and gas station. By 1989, it had 500. Texaco operated 950

Food Marts in the same year. From 1984 to 1989, the number of convenience stores operated by oil companies increased from 16,000 to 30,000.[75]

Gasoline sold at a lower margin (about 6 percent in 1984) than nongasoline convenience store products (32 percent in the same year), so the sale of convenience store items presented an opportunity for those gas stations with good locations (i.e., street corners) to increase profits. In order to capitalize on the potential for higher profits in retailing, the major oil companies boosted their marketing expenditures. In 1979, the petroleum industry spent about $2.2 billion for their marketing efforts. By 1988, these expenditures were almost $5 billion.[76]

The convenience stores operated by oil companies were growing in both number and size. In 1986, only about 20 percent of the oil company convenience stores were 1,800 or more square feet in size (the size of about 90 percent of traditional convenience stores). By 1990, however, more than 50 percent of the oil company convenience stores were between 1,800 and 3,000 square feet in size.[77]

Merchandise Trends for Convenience Stores

Because of the intensified retailing efforts of oil companies and large convenience store chains, some trends (other than those mentioned previously) evolved. In 1985, gasoline accounted for 35.4 percent of convenience store sales. By 1989, gasoline accounted for 40 percent of sales.[78] The gross profit margin for gasoline sales had increased from 7.3 percent to 11.7 percent more than the same period.[79] Of the 61,000 convenience stores in the United States in 1985, 55 percent sold gasoline, and in 1989, 65 percent of 70,200 convenience stores sold gasoline. In 1989, 75 percent of the new convenience stores built were equipped to sell gasoline.[80]

Although gasoline sales and margins became an increasingly significant contributor to convenience store revenues, contributions of revenue from other merchandise stagnated. In 1985, merchandise (other than gasoline) sales for the convenience store industry amounted to $33.2 billion. In 1989, sales reached $40.6 billion.[81] This increase in merchandise sales, however, was offset by the large number of store openings. In 1985, the average yearly merchandise sales per store was $544,000. This number increased to only $578,000 in 1989.[82]

THE SETTING

While flying from Japan to the United States, Takahashi reflected on the success that both Ito-Yokado and 7-Eleven Japan had enjoyed over the course of many years. These

---

[75]Claudia H. Deutsch, "Rethinking the Convenience Store," *New York Times*, October 8, 1989.

[76]National Association of Convenience Stores, Challenges for the Convenience Store Industry in the 1990s: A Future Study, p. 194.

[77]Ibid., p. 198.

[78]NACS, *1990 State of the Convenience Store Industry*, p. 14.

[79]Ibid., p. 16.

[80]Ibid., pp. 25–26.

[81]Ibid., p. 14.

[82]Ibid., p. 16.

achievements were the result of long-term strategies that were carefully tailored to the Japanese market. Could these same, or similar, strategies be the foundation for making Southland financially successful again? He realized that the convenience store industry in the United States was vastly different from that of Japan. Nevertheless, he was confident that, through careful and thorough planning, the goal of making Southland profitable could be achieved.

Verbatim Challenges 3M for Market Leadership

Linda E. Swayne, Peter M. Ginter, and Chris M. Tucker

A satisfied smile appeared on Bob Falco's face as he was reading the January 19, 1992, issue of *PcWeek*. As a manager of North American branded marketing at Verbatim, he was pleased with the figures he saw in the computer publication. According to figures released by the Santa Clara Consulting Group, 3M had a 15.5 percent share of the floppy disk market, and Verbatim was right behind the market leader with a 15.2 percent share. "We *are* going to be the leader in this market," he thought to himself. "But we're more than just a floppy disk manufacturer. With our excellent tape storage products and optical disk technology, we're going to be the leader in the overall computer media market."

COMPANY HISTORY

In 1969, Information Terminals Corporation was formed in Sunnyvale, California, to manufacture computer screens (terminals). In the early days, there was virtually no competition, and profits for the company and its distributors were substantial. However, as personal computer use in business expanded rapidly, competitors entered the market and the high costs of producing screens persuaded the company managers to look to more-profitable emerging markets and products. Recognizing that the sales potential for magnetic recording materials for personal computers was much larger than that of computer screens, the company began manufacturing 8" floppy disks and changed its name to Verbatim. Research and development concentrated on digital data cassettes and floppy disks. Having the new technology for data storage available during rapid market growth, management was in a position to choose a few key distributors. They refused other potential distributors in order to enhance the profit potential for both Verbatim and its selected distributors.

Attracted by the projected $4 billion market, a number of competitors entered the floppy disk field in the late 1970s and early 1980s and threatened Verbatim's dominant position.[1] Competitors such as 3M, Maxwell, Fuji, and Sony all looked for ways to differentiate their products. In the early 1980s, Verbatim was slow to adapt to the increasingly competitive market. "For a number of years Verbatim was making a lot of money and

[1]"Malcolm Northrup Needs a Flip-flop," *Industry Week*, January 7, 1985, p. 58.

increasing its business—and that hid a lot of sins," said Falco. Several distributors began to carry the products of Verbatim's new competitors. These distributors were the very ones that Verbatim had previously refused to supply. When the marketplace continued expanding, many of these distributors in turn refused to deal with Verbatim.

Because of substantial reductions in profits, Verbatim cut 127 staff positions in November 1984 to reduce costs.[2] At the same time, the company invested more than $40 million in the development of 3.5" diskettes for personal computers under the DataLife label.[3] Leading the demand for higher disk capacities was the rapid expansion in user data bases. Software programs required more storage capacity. Generally, the easier new software programs were to use, the more sophisticated the set of instructions had to be between the software and the computer and the greater the disk capacity. Software programs were becoming available to the general consumer during this time, and the popular IBM-PC required higher-capacity disks.

The Kodak Era

In 1985, Eastman Kodak acquired Verbatim for $175 million and changed the company's marketing focus, manufacturing methods, and channels of distribution.[4] Kodak had been buying 8", 5.25", and 3.5" disks from Xidex (a competitor of Verbatim) for more than a year before the purchase, the Kodak marketed a line of accessories including computer paper, printer stands, and surge suppressors. A new philosophy came to Verbatim with the transfer of ownership to Kodak: product development was the key to increasing success. Both Kodak- and Verbatim-brand diskettes were available from Verbatim. Although Kodak-brand diskettes were a late entrant to the disk market, the high brand recognition for the Kodak name enabled the company to be a major competitor in the branded market. Mass merchandisers such as discount stores, warehouse clubs, and other retailers were particularly accepting of the Kodak name because of its recognition by consumers.

Sweeping changes occurred in 1987 with the hiring of Mark Welland as Verbatim vice president of North American marketing and sales. Welland, the former national sales and marketing manager for Maxwell, recognized that prices for floppy disks were plummeting and concentrated on repositioning the majority of Verbatim's sales from low-priced, nonlabeled disks for the original equipment manufacturer (OEM) market to premium-priced floppy disks for the branded market. Ironically, the fact that Verbatim already was a low-cost producer had allowed it to remain in business during the shakeout years in the mid-1980s. Welland wanted not only to be successful in the market, but to be first in the market with new products. Under Welland's direction, all efforts were put into branded items, especially the disks differentiated by a patented Teflon coating. The DataLifePlus brand name was superscripted by "Verbatim—A Kodak Company." The diskette line was extended with the addition of the Bonus brand for the price-sensitive market.

Mitsubishi Takes Over

In a transaction announced in March 1990 and completed in May 1990, Kodak sold Verbatim to Mitsubishi Kasei, the chemical division of the $9 billion Japanese conglomer-

---

[2]Ibid.

[3]Ibid.

[4]Sue Kapp, "Mechanic for Mending," *Business Marketing*, June 1988, p. 8.

ate. Industry experts believed the undisclosed price to be $240 million, $65 million more than Eastman Kodak paid for Verbatim in 1985.[5]

A year before acquiring Verbatim, Mitsubishi had started manufacturing 3.5" disks under its own brand, as well as other OEM diskettes in its Chesapeake, Virginia, facility. As a late entrant in the industry, Mitsubishi found it difficult to build brand awareness against 3M, Verbatim, Sony, and other well-established competitors. Therefore, Mitsubishi purchased Verbatim for its established brand name, distribution channels, and market share. Kodak agreed to allow Mitsubishi to continue using the Kodak name until May 1992, which gave Welland and Falco, who both continued with Verbatim after the sale, some time to formulate new marketing and promotional strategies.

The purchase of Verbatim by Mitsubishi offered a much-needed capital infusion that had been limited under Kodak's ownership. Mitsubishi management subscribed to the belief inherent in many Japanese companies: invest heavily in the present with an eye on long-term profitability. Mitsubishi provided more capital for Welland's ongoing advertising campaign. In contrast, Kodak had been lean in advertising dollars allotted directly to Verbatim and the DataLife brand. Instead, Kodak depended on increased sales through corporate advertising of its name, which capitalized on the fact that Kodak was the second-most-recognized name in the world (behind Coca-Cola).

THE INDUSTRY

The deluge of technology in the computer industry changed the way America did business. The introduction of the personal computer gave individual workers the power to write and edit documents, produce electronic spreadsheets, and compile large databases. Not only could businesspeople hook up to a company's mainframe, they could do it away from the office. The laptop computer meant that professionals could sit in a customer's office and work as easily as if they were sitting in their own office. Computer purchasers appeared to be interested in greater use of color and graphics, the ability to store more information on a single disk, and higher-quality printers.

In 1991, most Americans were concerned with the continuing weak economy. As a result of low consumer confidence and rising unemployment, Americans became extremely conscious of their spending behavior, especially for big-ticket items such as personal computers. PCs at the office were considered a necessity. Although office managers were cutting operating costs, computer disks were not something that could be eliminated. In part because of the economy, more people were working at home. According to Falco, "The home office is driving the business now." Sales of diskettes to this market were up substantially. On the other hand, personal computers purchased for recreational use at home were considered to be a luxury, and disk expenditures by the recreational user were expected to decrease. The costs of manufacturing data storage products, such as rewritable optical disks and 8 mm and 4 mm tape products, were expected to rise as new technologies were researched and implemented. As a result, a highly competitive industry would have to be even more concerned with differentiating its products on something other than price.

The computer media market boasted $1.8 billion in total sales during 1990, compared with $1.2 billion in 1989. Twenty-seven percent of the sales were attributed to 5.25" disks, whereas 3.5" disks made up over 30 percent of sales. Exhibit 1 outlines the

---

[5]Clifford Glickman, "After Floppies, What?" *Charlotte Observer,* January 7, 1991, p. 7D.

EXHIBIT 1 Computer Media Market Shares

Medium	Percent Share
1/2" Reel-to-Reel Tape	16
1/2" Tape Cartridges	2
8" Disks	11
5.25" Disks	27
3.5" Disks	30
Data Cartridges	14

Source: "Floppy Disks," *Purchasing,* February 22, 1990, p. 76.

market share for the various computer media. The overall growth of the 5.25" and the 3.5" segments of the media market averaged about 25 percent in the first three quarters of 1989. Sales of 5.25" diskettes did not decline as much as was forecasted but did decline about 3 percent because of the weakening demand for low-end machines for the home market. Sales of high-density (HD) 3.5" disks increased slightly, although they represented less than 20 percent of the total 3.5" units sold.[6]

According to the Santa Clara Consulting Group, worldwide sales of floppy disks in 1990 increased slightly above 1989 sales (Exhibit 2). Computer Industry Forecasts, published by the Data Analysis Group, projected 1991 sales of floppy disks to be $2.7 billion.[7]

Magnetic floppy disks were viewed as commodities, and price competition was fierce. Welland stated, "We've experienced a price erosion of about 23 percent in 1990 and about the same the year before. It was probably the purest form of open market competition—but brutal competition." Exhibit 3 provides the average price of 5.25" floppy disks from 1985 to 1990. Although the price of branded double-density (DD) 5.25" disks and generic brands fell drastically (to as low as 17 cents each), the introduction of HD 5.25" disks kept the average higher.

Interestingly, worldwide sales of computers were expected to grow by only 6.5 percent in 1991, compared with the 8.4 percent growth in 1990. Personal computer sales were forecasted to drop from 13 percent of the market to 8 percent.[8] Slow sales growth could be partially attributed to fears of recession, office budget cutting, and a slowdown in the switching from large computer systems to less-expensive desktop systems in business.[9] Price competition was expected to limit laptop and microcomputer revenues in 1991.

COMPETITION

Verbatim was faced with a number of key competitors in a highly competitive industry. Several of the competitors, such as 3M, Maxell, Sony, and BASF, had highly recognized brand names that were used on a variety of products with synergistic effects.

---

[6]"Say Good-bye to 3.5" Disk Shortage," *Purchasing,* February 20, 1990, p. 76.

[7]Computer Industry Forecast, Data Analysis Group, Georgetown, California, first quarter report, 1991.

[8]John W. Verity, "Computers Will See Lots of Downtime," *Business Week,* January 14, 1991, p. 101.

[9]David P. Brousell, "Industry Outlook—1991," *Datamation,* January 1, 1991, p. 38.

EXHIBIT 2: Sales of Disks Worldwide, All Formats

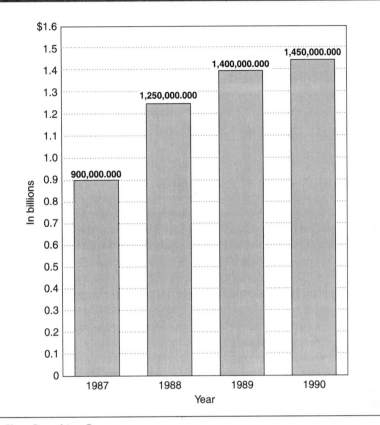

Source: Santa Clara Consulting Group

"The market for data storage products contains three segments: premium, price, and economy," according to Falco. The premium market segment included 3M, Verbatim, Sony, and Maxell brands. Fuji, BASF, and Memorex competed in the price segments, which was typically 15 percent lower in price than the premium brands. The economy segment featured value through lower prices achieved by lower manufacturing costs and included the Bonus, TDK, and Highland (3M) brands. The premium category accounted for approximately 60 percent of the market. The remaining 40 percent of the market was divided between the price segment and the economy segment.

Verbatim operated primarily in the premium market. Although the majority of its products were targeted to the upper end of the mass market, Verbatim maintained its Bonus brand diskette at the lower end of the market. "This product is offered for people who want a quality brand name and are value conscious. They don't want the cheapest thing they can find, but a brand name they recognize and trust at a moderate price point," Falco stated.

Figures from a 1990 Magnetic Industry report for 1989 activity placed Verbatim as third in market share with 8.59 percent of the industry (Exhibit 4). The category leader, 3M, had 12.14 percent market share. Maxell (Hitachi) held the second position with 10.96 percent share. Falco commented that the January 1992 figures placed Verbatim second to 3M in market share worldwide. He felt that the market was so fiercely com-

EXHIBIT 3:   Average Price for All 5.25" Floppy Disks, 1985–1990

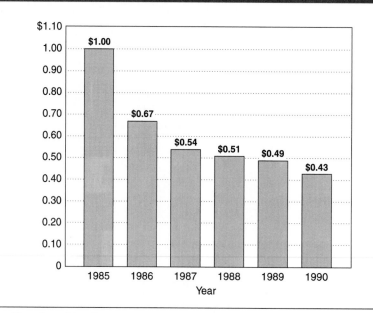

Source: Santa Clara Consulting Group

petitive that each quarter could register a different market share leader from among the top three. Companies had literally come and gone in the 1980s. Xidex, Elephant, and Syncom had all left the industry, although newcomers, primarily from Japan and Mexico, appeared occasionally.

A major factor affecting competition in the data storage industry was that the products (primarily diskettes) were relatively undifferentiated. The market was characterized by increasing technological advances by manufacturers that kept attempting to differentiate the products. Rumors were always circulating that some brands with low market share would be pulling out of the diskette market as competition heated up.

3M

Although the market share leader, 3M had only established disk production in the early 1980s and it represented only a small part of the multibillion-dollar company. 3M was a strong global competitor in all areas of marketing, manufacturing, and distribution, with worldwide visibility. In 1992, it was the only large U.S. manufacturer of diskettes that offered a complete line of media as well as many other well-known office products (Scotch tape, Post-It Notes, and so forth). The company had a strong reputation as a creative innovator of quality products. Considered the technology leader, 3M committed significant resources to R&D.

Maxell

Hitachi-Maxell was one division of Hitachi, Limited, Japan's largest electrical and electronics manufacturer. Maxell began disk production in the late 1970s. Diskettes accounted for approximately 20 percent of the company's total business. The company had a reputation for high quality, especially in audio-visual products. Although it did

EXHIBIT 4 Revenue and Unit Market Share Data for Floppy Disks

Company	Revenues (In Millions)	Percent Total Industry Revenues	Percent Total Industry Units
3M	$ 205	12.14	12.13
Hitachi/Maxell	185	10.96	9.37
Verbatim	145	8.59	8.46
Sony	117	6.93	6.22
Xidex	99	5.86	9.62
BASF	93	5.51	5.59
KAO	92	5.45	3.87
Fuji	78	4.62	4.06
TDK	67	3.97	3.92
Nashua	35	2.07	2.66
Totals	$1,116	66.10	65.90

Source: Magnetic Media Information Services Floppy Disk Industry Report, February 15, 1990.

not manufacture a full line of computer media, the company did produce diskettes and 4 mm and 8 mm tape and purchased data cartridges with its brand name on them.

Sony

Sony Corporation was a leading manufacturer of electronic and entertainment products. In the United States, Sony's business activities shifted from electronics to entertainment with the purchase of CBS Records in 1988 and Columbia in 1989. Sony and the Japanese electronics conglomerate, Matsushita, developed a 2" disk in 1988 and claimed that these would eventually be the industry standard. As of early 1992, this had not occurred.

Sony produced a full product line of computer media except for cassettes, ½" reel-to-reel tape, and ½" tape cartridges. Sony supplied many OEM customers with nonlabeled 3.5" disks and both optical drives and optical disks.

Other Competitors

Fuji and BASF entered into a joint venture to produce 3.5" disks in the late 1980s. Fuji had strength in the film market, and BASF had a strong brand image in the audio-visual market. Both competed in the lower-priced value market for computer media. KAO manufactured for the OEM market and private-label customers. The company pursued bulk and bid business based on low prices. Through 1991, KAO had little success in the branded market.

Share of Mind

All of Verbatim's top competitors were manufacturers of a broad range of products that enhanced their ability to generate high levels of awareness through corporate advertising. In 1990 and 1991, 3M and BASF both used mass-media corporate advertising for all their products, which led to high levels of awareness. In 1991, BASF began an advertising campaign that emphasized its role in technological innovation and claimed, "We don't make many of the products you buy—we make them better." In 1989, 3M spent almost three times the level of Verbatim (Exhibit 5). Such a large budget enhanced 3M's already high name recognition. 3M, in particular, received the fringe benefit of positive brand perceptions from its many other, quality products.

As indicated in Exhibit 6, there seemed to be a lack of consistency among competitors' advertising themes. Campaigns had no central focus or else they held the focus for a short period of time. Exhibit 6 summarizes the advertising campaigns of Verbatim's major competitors.

A top-of-mind awareness survey completed in 1991 by Verbatim found 3M leading, followed by Maxell, and then Verbatim (Exhibit 7). This corresponded to market-share sales figures (in Exhibit 5).

VERBATIM CORPORATION MISSION

The mission of Verbatim was to be the recognized leader of the magnetic and optical-media data storage industry by being a profitable, worldwide, quality manufacturer and marketer.

Verbatim Corporate Vision

Verbatim, on a worldwide basis, would:

- Be obsessed with customer satisfaction.
- Be known for product quality.
- Be dedicated to continuous quality improvement.
- Be a technology leader, positioned to provide new products to customers when needed.
- Give people the information and resources necessary to continuously improve quality to their customers.

EXHIBIT 5   Competitive Advertising Expenditures, 1989

Company	1989 Total Diskette Advertising Budget	Percent of Total
3M	2,705,716	40
Maxell	1,214,368	18
BASF	1,113,618	16
Verbatim	976,481	14
Sony	542,930	8
Mitsubishi	283,853	4
Totals	6,836,966	100

Source: Kodak in-house study, 1989.

EXHIBIT 6   Advertising Campaigns of Major Competitors

3M

1988–89 Theme:	"Supporting the Dream."
Ad Message:	Teamwork that provides you with technological breakthroughs, superior quality, and selection.
1990 Theme:	No consistent tag line, emphasis on reliability.
Ad Message:	"Wanted for breaking Murphy's Law" (3M diskettes): exclusive formulation and "Mark Q" manufacturing process. Secondary emphasis on convenience (preformatted diskettes).
Promotions:	11th disk free.

Maxell

1988–89 Theme:	"The Gold Standard."
Ad Message:	Maximum safety and reliability: "Ten times more reliable than conventional floppy disks, twice the durability, twice the resistance to dirt and dust."
1990 Theme:	"The Gold Standard."

BASF

1988–89 Theme:	"The Spirit of Innovation."
Ad Message:	100% error free, compatibility, data protection.
1990 Theme:	"Try it. Depend on it."
Promotions:	Cash sweepstakes.

Sony

1988–89 Theme:	"Sony, The One and Only" (corporatewide).
Ad Message:	World leader in high-density magnetic media.
1990 Theme:	No consistent tag line.
Ad Message:	Reliability.

EXHIBIT 7   Top-of-Mind Awareness for the Major Floppy Disk Competitors

Company	Percent Unaided Awareness[a]
3M	45
Maxell	24
Verbatim	23
Sony	16
BASF	7
Fuji	3

[a]Multiple responses
Source: Verbatim floppy disk tracking study, 1991.

- Be number one in revenue market share.
- Nurture partnerships with its suppliers to meet or exceed its quality goals.

Having purchased Verbatim, Mitsubishi planned to become the leader in diskette revenue market share with a continued emphasis on the most effective use of dollars for advertising, promotions, and new product introductions. CEO Nicky Hartery recently had reminded employees of the importance of being "number one" in revenue market share, as opposed to unit market share, by saying: "You can't deposit units in the bank." Verbatim directed its advertising and promotions to attain market share equal to or greater than 3M, the industry leader.

PRODUCT STRATEGY

Product Line

Verbatim manufactured and marketed a wide variety of data storage media, including magnetic storage media (floppy disks) and advanced mass storage devices (backup tapes and optical disks). Floppy disks were produced in 3.5", 5.25", and 8" sizes with varying features and were backed by Verbatim's lifetime guarantee. A new product for this market was the DataLife 3.5" extra-high-density (ED) microdisk that provided 4 megabytes of storage compared to 1 megabyte or DD and 2 megabytes for HD disks.

One segment of mass storage devices included 4 mm and 8 mm computer grade data cartridges, ¼" data cartridges, high-density streamer cassettes, digital data cassettes, and ½" reel tape. These products were used for backup and restoration of computer files and archival purposes. As hard drives expanded in size, backup media increased in importance, as it would take numerous floppy disks to back up a hard drive.

The other segment of mass storage and the newest area for Verbatim was optical disk manufacturing. Within the industry, optical disks came in three formats: ROM (read-only memory), WORM (write once, read many), and rewritable disks. "We are on the threshold of optical being a very big product," Falco stated in 1991. Verbatim was one of the first companies to offer 5.25" rewritable optical disks and the first with 3.5" rewritable optical disks.

Branded Products

Verbatim continued marketing the DataLife brand after being purchased by Kodak. Kodak wanted to use its name on disks that would be sold in mass merchant outlets because of the high recognition of the brand name. Verbatim and DataLife were better-recognized brand names in computer stores.

In the agreement with Mitsubishi, Kodak allowed Verbatim to use the Kodak name until May 1992. The transition from Kodak to Verbatim brands progressed smoothly. The Kodak brand was sold primarily by the mass merchants such as Kmart and Target, where Verbatim did not have much brand recognition. Although owned by Kodak, the box showed Verbatim in large letters with smaller letters underneath that stated, "A Kodak Company." Throughout 1991, as packages were redesigned, the Kodak brand was deleted. There was some resistance from the mass merchants to the conversion. The Verbatim product did not sell as well as the Kodak brand in the mass market, so at first, Verbatim sales reps had to convince the mass merchants to continue carrying the Data-

Life product, while advertising and promotion dollars were spent to reach the end user with information about Verbatim's brands. Sales of DataLife increased; most former purchasers of Kodak switched to Verbatim's DataLife.

During the time Kodak was being deleted from packages, there was a great deal of discussion concerning branding. Should Verbatim be the highlighted brand name with DataLife superscripted or subscripted, or should DataLife be highlighted with Verbatim superscripted or subscripted? Or should there be only one brand? If only one brand name was to be selected, should it be Verbatim or DataLife? Although "Verbatim" perfectly expressed the performance wanted from disks, it was difficult for many non-English-speaking people to pronounce. As the company supplied media storage worldwide, careful study was required to make the decision.

Product Differentiation

Magnetic Floppy Disks   In 1986, Verbatim introduced an antistatic lining for diskettes called DataHold. It discharged static electricity, protecting disks from data loss. Every disk sold by Verbatim contained this protection.

Verbatim secured a patent on its Teflon coating process, introduced in October 1987. DataLifePlus disks were protected from spills, fingerprints, and other office mishaps that might cause data loss. Many computer users were afraid of "mysterious data loss." The Teflon coating allowed the liner to wipe the disk clean inside the jacket as it was being used in the drive. Falco commented, "DataLifePlus is about 20 percent of our business. A lot of people don't worry about data loss until they have lost data." An agreement prohibited DuPont from selling Teflon to other disk manufacturers through 1991 and gave Verbatim a guaranteed, but short-lived competitive advantage in the marketplace. Although competitors could purchase Teflon from DuPont after 1991, they had to develop a process that did not infringe on the Verbatim coating patent. Apparently the competition did not judge the market to be of sufficient size to spend the R&D funds—especially when floppy disks became essentially a commodity product. As of the beginning of 1992, none of the competitors had challenged Verbatim for this segment.

Although Verbatim was the first in October 1987 to offer preformatted diskettes, 3M and others soon followed with this slightly more expensive, but more convenient product. Buyers could purchase diskettes preformatted for any number of machines from IBM and related machines, to Apple Macintosh.

In 1988, Verbatim introduced colored disk jackets for easier office organization. The new jackets tended to be more appealing to the consumer's eye. Branded under the DataLife Colors label, the colored diskettes encouraged brand loyalty by providing continuity to existing color filing systems. Other manufacturers developed their own versions of color disks after Verbatim's introduction.

In late 1990, Verbatim announced an additional enhancement for its 3.5" disks. Diskettes contained a metal shutter that was worn down by a computer's disk drive over time and could deposit potentially damaging shavings into the disk drive. Verbatim pioneered a flexible, nonmetallic DataSeal shutter that did not wear down and deposit shavings into the computer. Verbatim began shipping the product in March 1991; competitors quickly developed similar protection devices.

Magnetic Tape   In the spring of 1989, Kodak began to manufacture ½" reel-to-reel computer tape (with finish processing at Verbatim) under the DataLife brand name. However, other competitors, such as 3M, BASF, and Memorex, were already established in this mature market. The tape was a late entrant to a mature market; data processing managers were not very interested in any new brands.

Expansion into highest density tape products occurred in 1991. DataLife high capacity tape in 8 mm and 4 mm widths competed against Sony, Maxell and 3M.

Optical Disks   Although the technology had been available since 1985, it was not until August 1989 that 3M announced its entrance into the erasable (rewritable) optical disk market. Similar to popular compact disks, this product could be used repeatedly for media storage. One month after 3M, Verbatim announced that it would manufacture optical disks. This new product had required huge cash investments to develop a drastically different manufacturing process. Both Verbatim and 3M hoped that the cost of manufacturing and change in format to optical disks would prevent some competitors from entering the new market.

Unfortunately, purchases of the optical disk drives had not met expectations, thus the demand for optical disk had been disappointing as well. In early 1992, optical disk drives were too slow and expensive to replace magnetic media for most uses. Verbatim was still hoping to capitalize on the erasable optical disks. Unlike regular floppy disks, erasable optical disks were not yet considered commodities; therefore, there was little price erosion. In actuality, optical disks were not positioned to replace floppy disks. Optical disks had a huge storage capacity—128 megabytes of storage on a 3.5" disk compared to 1 or 2 megabytes for most 3.5" floppies. The 5¼" optical disks stored up to 650 megabytes. The conversion to optical disk drives had been slow because of the high cost of the hardware, but optical drive prices had started to come down. In addition, the optical disks had declined in price. There had been a problem within the industry concerning standardization and compatibility.

The legality of supplying evidence on optical disks was another issue of critical importance. When WORM technology was the only form of optical disk available, legal concerns were not a problem. However, with the development of multifunction disk drives that could use WORM *and* rewritable disks, the courts were not certain how they could be sure that evidence had not been changed. Another unknown, because the product was so new, was the "life" of an optical disk. This was particularly important for hospitals, which required a guarantee that data would "stay" on a disk for a minimum of 25 years.

International Data Corporation expected customers to buy about $100 million worth of erasable optical disks in 1991.[10] Purchasers of optical disks tend to be involved with huge data storage needs, such as libraries, government agencies, and large corporations. Some industry analysts expected optical disks to develop into an economical and popular product. Others felt that optical disks would never achieve more than a limited share of the market, and still others predicted that the 3.5" optical disk would eventually replace the floppy disk. IBM introduced new personal computers that could use 3.5" optical disks in June 1991.

Sony was expected to announce a 2.5" optical disk drive in late 1992. It would combine video, audio, and data into a process called optical imaging. The new drive would require further miniaturization of optical disks.

THE FLOPPY DISK CUSTOMER

Verbatim's products were directed at two broad categories of users, the original equipment manufacturer market and the branded market. Exhibit 8 contains a summary of

---

[10]"Say Good-bye," p. 76.

EXHIBIT 8: Verbatim Market Opportunities

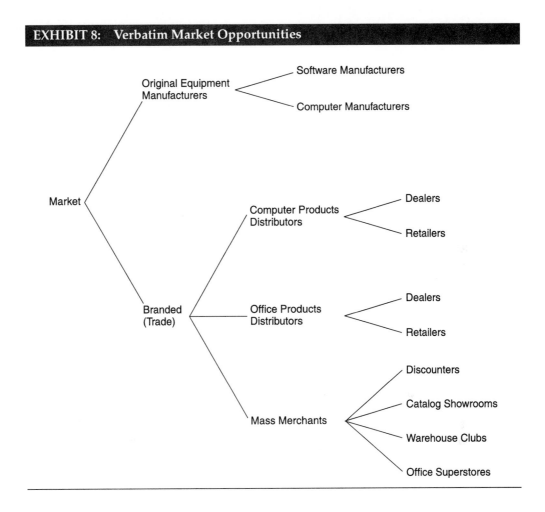

the computer media market. In the OEM market, manufacturers produced nonlabeled diskettes for companies that developed software packages or manufactured hardware that included operating system software. Lotus and Microsoft were two of Verbatim's OEM customers. Labels were added carrying the name of the purchaser rather than Verbatim's name. The branded market consisted of buyers who purchased Verbatim brands of unformatted or preformatted diskettes for personal or business use.

The OEM Market

Verbatim enjoyed a strong position in the OEM market. In fact, Verbatim was the largest nonlabeled supplier in the United States to OEMs and software publishers. The price competition in the OEM market forced Verbatim to search for economies in production and for product differentiation through quality and service. To speed delivery, Verbatim established East and West coast distribution facilities. Although price remained an important factor, Verbatim differentiated its product through quality, durability, and meeting customers' specifications. These factors carried more weight with hardware and software producers when purchasing diskettes that would bear their company's name.

Quality was an extremely important factor in the OEM market, and Verbatim's reputation for quality products anchored its strong position in this area.

The Branded Market

The branded market was very price competitive at all levels. According to Falco, "Salespeople frequently come to me and say, 'I can sell 20,000 more diskettes to this account if we lower the price by 10 cents a diskette,' and I tell them that's not the type of business we're after. We could have made $40 million more in 1990 if we could have maintained the same price levels that existed in 1989." Despite the price decline, Verbatim continued to give attention to research and development of new products in addition to its enhancement of existing products. Falco characterized the market as a "pennies industry," alluding to the fact that margins were constantly squeezed by price competition on one side and R&D, production, and new technology costs on the other.

The branded market could be divided into home users or business users, buying from Verbatim's trade customers. Falco commented, "Media Market Research profiled the end user, whether he or she is a home or office user, to be 35 years old; well educated; high income; married with children; a reader who is interested in new products, electronics, self-improvement and investments; and an active participant in individual sports activities."

Home Users   In 1992, more than 26 million Americans performed job-related work at home. By 1993, that number was predicted to reach nearly 35 million. According to LINK Resources, a research and consulting firm, there were several different categories of homeworkers. These included salaried corporate employees, self-employed workers, contract workers, and freelancers. LINK profiled the average homeworker as 39 years old, part of a dual-career family with a family income of $42,000. This was and would be an important market for Verbatim as the numbers continued to grow. The phenomenal growth of homeworkers was credited for much of the growth in sales for office equipment, including copiers, fax units, calculators, and computers. The annual investment in home-office equipment including computers, copiers, fax units, calculators, and cellular phones in 1989 was $5.3 billion, and experts predicted 1993 sales to top $8.4 billion.[11]

Business Users   The profile of users in a large business was similar to other end users, although their purchasing patterns were different. Large companies tended to have longer sales cycles, to buy in larger quantities, to buy in a highly organized fashion, and to look for value-added services. Seventy percent of large businesses purchased diskettes through a central purchasing agent, primarily for efficiency and lower costs. Instead of multiple departments within a company placing individual orders, purchasing needs were pooled and one large order for one brand was placed, generally earning significant quantity discounts.

According to a 1987 in-house study by Kodak, business users had slightly larger diskette libraries than home users. Whether business or home user, the largest acquisition of disks occurred during the first year of computer usage. Hard disk drive owners purchased more disks in the first year, but that dropped off more in the second year than that of the nonowner of a hard disk drive. Both business and home users generally owned two brands of disks.

Trade Customers   Verbatim sold branded products to various channel members (the trade) to resell to a variety of end users. The trade audience included computer dis-

---

[11]"Working at Home: Growth Is Phenomenal," *The Office,* March 1991, p. 58.

tributors, computer dealers/retailers, software dealers/retailers, national/regional wholesalers, and office megastores such as Staples, Office Depot, and OW (Office Warehouse). Mass merchants could be divided into discount chains, catalog showrooms, warehouse clubs, hypermarkets, and drugstore chains.

A shift was under way in the branded market as sales of diskettes at computer specialty stores were leveling off but increasing in superstores such as Sam's Wholesale, Pace, Office Depot, and Office America. This was attributed to growing computer literacy among end users who once felt that a specialist was needed to aid in the selection of diskettes. Verbatim shifted much of its advertisement and promotional attention to end users to correspond with this trend.

ADVERTISING AND OTHER PROMOTIONAL STRATEGIES AT VERBATIM

In 1991, Verbatim used its promotional budget to shift away from "push" advertising to the trade toward a focus on "pull" advertising to end users. Verbatim's advertising and promotion had become more dedicated to this facet of the business. Verbatim's branded advertising objectives included:

- Increasing brand name and advertising awareness levels of Verbatim above 3M,
- Establishing a preference for Verbatim,
- Establishing a specific position for Verbatim and its brands,
- Creating advertising that supported the chosen position, and
- Supporting the advertising program with sales promotions and public relations.

Verbatim used both vertical and horizontal trade publications. Full-page ads in the typical computer publications such as *Byte* and *PcWeek* were used to reach a variety of users. The vertical publications included magazines that specialized in the hospital, accounting, and legal professions. These publications targeted the corporate user and were a relatively inexpensive method of advertising. Ads would continue to be placed in trade journals. Verbatim hoped to increase advertising expenditures to match the spending of competitors, resulting in increased visibility and name recognition.

Direct mail had been used occasionally to reach some specialized markets that would have a particular interest in a new product. It was used to introduce the Verbatim tape products to data processing managers in the New York City area and to introduce the worry-free DataLifePlus disks to CEOs.

Promotions

Promotions focused on each member in the channel of distribution. Rebates in the form of a credit on future Verbatim purchases to trade customers were based on volume and growth relative to history. Occasionally "spiffs" were offered to trade customers for each unit of Verbatim sold in a selected category. (Spiffs were cash payments by trade customers to their sales reps that were reimbursed by Verbatim.) End-user promotions included on-pack or in-pack (free 11th disk, rebates, coupons, free storage box, or cleaning kit).

Public Relations

Greater emphasis was sought in the public relations arena with attempts to place stories about Verbatim in various print media that would offer a form of "free" advertising.

Case histories about the usage of Verbatim products were the best way to get placement in a publication.

Sales Force

The United States/Canada branded sales division consisted of five regional managers that each supervised up to eight sales representatives. The OEM sales group consisted of nine Verbatim sales representatives. Overall sales objectives for 1991 included increasing sales revenue by 19 percent and taking market share away from Verbatim's primary competitors. Verbatim had approximately 200 trade customers of which 35 contributed the majority of sales.

BACK TO THE BUSINESS OF CHALLENGING THE LEADER

As Bob Falco developed his plan to become the market share leader, he thought about the current situation in the industry. "In other recessions in the 1970s and 1980s, floppy disks were not really affected. But the 1991–92 recession is a white collar recession and there has been a definite slowdown in the media business—particularly in the New England area. Fortunately, sales to the home office market are doing well. That market is really carrying the business right now. We're ready for the breakthrough in optical disks, but the way the life cycle for any new technology is compressed, that will probably become a commodity market, too, and in a very short period of time."

Brøderbund Software, Inc.

Armand Gilinsky, Jr.

Our business is becoming more mainstream.
The opportunities are tremendous.
The competition will be fierce.
There will be more than one winner.

> —Bill McDonagh

Catch me if you can!

> —Carmen Sandiego

On Thursday, March 23, 1995, William M. (Bill) McDonagh, president & chief operating officer (COO) of Brøderbund Software, Inc., opened his morning newspaper to the business pages. McDonagh saw the following headlines in *The New York Times:*

The Surging Sales of CD-ROM's Sharply Raise Brøderbund Profit

Market Triples for CD-ROM's

DreamWorks and Microsoft in Multimedia Venture

McDonagh had just completed his first year as president and COO. He realized that Brøderbund had achieved recognition as a major player in what had become an intensely competitive, dynamic consumer software industry. Increasing sales of multimedia personal computers and continued demand for interactive CD-ROM titles had pushed the company's fiscal 1995 second-quarter earnings far in excess of Wall Street analysts' expectations. Brøderbund's stock had closed the previous day at $53.25, rising to an all-time high of $56.00 per share in after-hours trading. Yet McDonagh knew that many observers and analysts disagreed to what extent Brøderbund could sustain its early leadership in the industry; whether it could continue to attract the "critical mass" of managerial, financial, technical, and marketing capabilities necessary to compete; and how he, as president and COO, would be able to address and overcome any barriers to growth.

Now entering its fifteenth year of existence, Brøderbund had developed, published, marketed, and sold more than 25 million units of consumer software. In fiscal year 1994, Brøderbund posted record annual sales of $112 million and profits after tax of $11 million. International sales were static, accounting for less than 10 percent of net revenues. Brøderbund still paid no dividends.

This case was prepared by Professor Armand Gilinsky, Jr. of Sonoma State University, as a basis for class discussion. It is not intended to illustrate either effective or ineffective handling of an administrative situation.

Copyright © 1997 Case Research Journal and by Armand Gilinsky, Jr. ISBN 0-13-017167-0.

Brøderbund's executive team wondered how the growing company would manage the transition to a larger organization. McDonagh remarked,

> It's like pulling at both ends of a rope; the most creative people in the world also tend to be the least efficient. Should we follow where our creative people take us and pursue a broad path to future product development in many market segments, or take a more narrow path, concentrating our resources on a specific market niche, such as education?

To fill out its product line, Brøderbund was looking at several acquisitions and joint venture deals. Rumors that Brøderbund itself was a takeover target surfaced from time to time. Brøderbund's executive team needed to formulate a strategy that would take into consideration this apparent tug-of-war between the need to promote creativity to develop a portfolio of new products and investors' demands for greater operating efficiency to assure a continuously growing earnings stream and stock price appreciation.

COMPANY BACKGROUND

The company was founded in 1980 by Doug Carlston, its current chairman and chief executive officer (CEO), and his brother, Gary, when the personal computer software industry was still in its infancy. The brothers chose the name "Brøderbund" from "Brøder," a blend of the Swedish and Danish words for brother, and "bund," German for alliance. The name originated from Gary Carlston's travels to and employment in Sweden. Today, you can find the words "Brøder" and "Søster" on the doors to the restrooms in the corporate lobby.

In his 1986 book, *Software People,* Doug Carlston described Brøderbund's early history as follows:

> When my brother and I started Brøderbund Software in 1980, we had no idea that it would become one of the largest home computer software companies in the world. In fact, we originally entered the software business by accident. We had no business plan, no scheme to make our fortunes. We were just trying to come up with a way to pay our next month's rent.
>
> In most ways, we were unlikely candidates for the roles we assumed. Neither of us knew very much about computers, and neither of us lived anywhere near those centers of innovation where so many high-technology firms were springing up. Before we started our company, I was a lawyer, practicing my trade in rural Maine. My brother Gary had just returned from Sweden, where he had spent five years working as a coach for a women's basketball team. He was now living in Oregon, where, after a stint as field director for the March of Dimes, he became involved in an importing business that proved to be unsuccessful.
>
> What we had was computer fever—a malady we shared with all the other entrepreneurs who were forming similar companies. Of the two of us, I was the one who was more heavily stricken. Programming can be an addiction—those who get drawn into it often forget jobs, family, and friends in their absorption with these fascinating machines. My own addiction began in 1978 when I took the fateful step of entering a Radio Shack store in Waterville, Maine, in order to take a closer look at the computer that was displayed in the window. I ended up walking out with a TRS-80 Model 1 tucked underneath my arm. My life has not been the same since.
>
> Finally, in October 1979, I dissolved my law practice. I was having a lot more fun writing computer games than I was drawing up wills. The fact that I was also making

a modest but steadily increasing income from my programming efforts had something to do with my decision, but at the time it wasn't at all clear that this was a prudent career move. I had no idea whether the freelance programming business was going to continue to be financially viable, but I abandoned my law career anyway because the microcomputer software world drew me in a way that I found irresistible.

It immediately struck me—when I realized just how possible it was to make a living at my kind of programming—that I had an opportunity to lead an altogether different way of life. It took me a while to accept that I had stumbled upon such a beautiful loophole in the rules of life, but once I did I knew that my job for the immediate future was to create fantasies and translate them into computer programs. If you think that sounds a lot more like play than work, you know how I reacted to the prospect of this new career. The kind of fascinating sci-fi sagas that had occupied my spare hours—flying interstellar craft to a thousand strange planets—was now my profession as well as my avocation.

It didn't take long for my new career to change the way I lived my life. Something very different from everything I had previously planned for myself suddenly became possible, and I was still young enough to be tempted by the prospect of a romantic journey into an uncertain future. So I went along with the opportunity to become an electronic-age vagabond.

Before long, the Carlston brothers established Brøderbund in order to market Galactic Empire and Galactic Trader, computer game programs Doug had peddled at computer shows during a cross-country car trip with his dog, Benthi. By the summer of 1980, after forming an alliance with a Japanese software house, StarCraft, the company was able to market a substantial line of home entertainment products. Before the end of its third year, Brøderbund had moved from Eugene, Oregon, to California's Marin County; had grown to more than 40 employees; and was selling millions of dollars' worth of software annually. In October 1991, the company moved to headquarters in Novato, California, about an hour's drive north of San Francisco. (A list of milestones in Brøderbund's history is shown in Exhibit 1.)

Cathy Carlston, Doug and Gary's sister, joined the company in 1981. Until her departure in 1989, she served as vice president of educational market planning and was instrumental in formulating Brøderbund's marketing efforts to schools. Gary Carlston, the firm's first CEO, also left in 1989. At the time of their departure, the Carlstons felt that they had achieved financial independence and had taken the business to the point where professional managers were needed.

In 1987, Ed Auer joined the company as senior vice president, COO and director after a 23-year tenure at CBS, Inc., where he had most recently run that company's software division. Auer was appointed Brøderbund's president in 1989 and retired in 1994, remaining a member of the company's board of directors. Bill McDonagh, an accountant who had been the company's first controller and later chief financial officer, was appointed to his current position in March 1994. (Profiles of the members of the current executive team are shown in Exhibit 2.)

When asked to consider what he saw as the company's most significant early challenges, McDonagh said:

...acquiring new products, growing an organization, and building a professional management team. It's not like prospecting for gold anymore or waiting for new products to arrive over the transom; developers now come to us. All of the people who are running this company now grew up with the business. We made up the rules, learning how to

EXHIBIT 1   Milestones in Brøderbund's Evolution

1980–81	Company founded by Doug and Gary Carlston *Galactic Empire* and *Galactic Trader* introduced Cathy Carlston joins as executive VP of educational market planning
1982	*Bank Street Writer Plus,* an entry-level word processing program Company moves from Oregon to San Rafael, California Bill McDonagh hired as controller Company passes $1 million revenues, 40 employees
1984	*The New Print Shop* (developed by Pixellite Software)
1985	*Where in the World is Carmen Sandiego?* and *The New Print Shop Companion* Company passes $10 million in revenues
1986	*Where in the USA is Carmen Sandiego?*
1987	*The New Print Shop Graphics Library Sampler Edition* Ed Auer hired as senior VP and chief operating officer Focus shifts to internal product development creation of education sales and marketing organization; and expansion of production facilities Proposed initial public offering delayed by unfavorable stock market conditions Revenues—$27.0 million; Earnings—$3.0 million; R&D expenses—$2.4 million
1988	*The New Print Shop Graphics Library Party Edition* and *Where in Europe is Carmen Sandiego?* Revenues—$36.6 million; Earnings—$5.6 million; R&D expenses—$4.4 million

1989	*SimCity* (affiliated label product); *Where in Time is Carmen Sandiego?; The Playroom; The
	    New Print Shop Graphics Library School and Business Edition;* and *TypeStyler* (Mac only)
	Cathy and Gary Carlston leave company to pursue other interests; Ed Auer appointed
	    president
	Outside consultant hired to standardize staff grade levels and job descriptions
	Revenues—$36.8 million; Earnings—$3.4 million; R&D expenses—$5.5 million;
	    150 employees

1990	*SimEarth* (affiliated label product); *Where in the World is Carmen Sandiego?* (Deluxe) Sale of Nintendo products division for a loss of $1.6 million Revenues—$50.4 million; Earnings—$3.2 million; R&D expenses—$5.9 million
1991	*Kid Pix; Where in America's Past is Carmen Sandiego?; The Treehouse* *Carmen Sandiego* quiz show on PBS; licensing agreement with Western Publishing, Inc. Company moves to new facilities in Novato, California Initial public offering of 3,257,184 shares completed, raising $33 million Revenues—$55.8 million; Earnings—$7.0 million; R&D expenses—$6.8 million; 271 employees
1992	28 new products released Acquisition of PC Globe, Inc., a publisher of electronic atlases, for $1.5 million in cash Revenues—$75.0 million; Earnings—$9.6 million; R&D expenses—$10.6 million
1993	44 new products released Maxis ends distribution deal with Brøderbund; decides to handle distribution on its own Revenues—$95.6 million; Earnings—$13.6 million; R&D expenses—$13.6 million

1994	68 new products released; CD-ROM sales account for over 40% of revenues
	    (over 60% in Q4)
	Living Books joint venture partnership with Random House announced
	Fox network broadcasts animated cartoon series based on *Carmen Sandiego*
	Ed Auer retires; Bill McDonagh appointed President & COO
	Agreement to merge with Electronic Arts terminated
	Sale of common stock investment for $1.6 million in cash; two-for-one stock split
	    announced
	Revenues—$111.8 million; Earnings—$11.0 million; R&D expenses—$16.0 million;
	    438 employees

Sources: Interviews with company officials; Initial Public Offering *Prospectus;* and 1994 *Annual Report.*

EXHIBIT 2   Brøderbund's Management Team in 1995

	AGE

Douglas G. Carlston, Chairman of the Board and Chief Executive Officer   47

Carlston cofounded the company with his brother, Gary, in 1980 and served as the president and director until 1989, when he assumed his present title. His first exposure to computers came in the 1960s, when he was working as a programmer at Harvard's Aiken Computation laboratory. He graduated *magna cum laude* from Harvard and went on to study economics at Johns Hopkins School of Advanced International Studies before entering Harvard Law School, where he received his J.D. Following the commercial success of his first two games, *Galactic Empire* and *Galactic Trader,* Carlston quit the practice of law to devote his energies to programming. In addition to the inherent responsibilities of his office, he continues to devote his attention to fostering the creative process behind Brøderbund's product development.

William M. McDonagh, Director, President and Chief Operating Officer   38

McDonagh was appointed President and COO of the company in March 1994 and elected a member of the board of directors in February 1995. Now responsible for Brøderbund's day-to-day operations, overseeing development manufacturing, sales, marketing, customer service, and finance, he joined the company in 1982 as Brøderbund's first controller. He was promoted to chief financial officer in 1987 and named senior vice president in 1992. Prior to joining Brøderbund, McDonagh was an auditor with Arthur Andersen & Co. in Chicago. He graduated with a B.A. in accounting from the University of Notre Dame, holds an MBA in finance from Golden Gate University, and is a CPA.

Harry Wilker, Senior VP, Brøderbund Studios   48

Managing all aspects of Brøderbund's product development activities, Wilker is responsible for definition, design, development and publishing of all software products. He started working at Brøderbund in 1987 as manager of Technical Services, becoming the Productivity Group's executive publisher six months later. From 1990 through 1993, he was vice president of publishing and was promoted to senior vice president of the newly-formed Brøderbund Studios in 1994. Prior to joining Brøderbund, Wilker headed Sentient Software in Aspen, Colorado, which he cofounded in 1981. He received a B.S. in political science from George Washington University and a M.A. in political science from State University of New York at Buffalo.

Jan Gullett, Senior VP, Sales and Marketing   41

Gullet leads all of the sales, customer service, marketing, and brand management activities at Brøderbund. Gullet joined Brøderbund in 1995, following 18 years at Pepsico, Sara Lee Corp. and Procter & Gamble, where he progressed through marketing, sales, and general management roles. Most recently, Gullet was vice president, marketing and vice president and general manager at Pepsico's KFC division. He has a B.S. from Miami University and an MBA from Harvard.

Mason Woodbury, VP, Customer Services   42

Woodbury manages the direct marketing, customer service, and technical support divisions of the company. He is directly responsible for the evolution of the customer service department, which has grown from a staff of 20 to more than 100 employees. Woodbury joined Brøderbund in 1991 as the director of direct marketing and created relationships with on-line services, such as America On-Line, Compuserve, Ziff-Davis Interchange, and the Microsoft Network. Prior to joining Brøderbund, he was the director of product management at Businessland in San Jose, Calif. He has a B.S. in business administration and an MBA from Babson College.

Rodney D. Haden, VP, Sales   43

Haden is responsible for directing the company's sales efforts in the United States and Canada. The sales department includes internal sales coordinators, dealer-support staff, training, and a national field sales force. Haden joined Brøderbund in 1985 and was promoted to vice president in 1987. Prior to joining Brøderbund, Haden was the vice president of sales for Concentric Data Systems, Inc. Haden holds a B.A. in political science from American University in Washington. D.C.

(Continued on next page)

Exhibit 2   *(Continued)*

	AGE

Marylyn Rosenblum, VP, Education Sales and Marketing — 48

Rosenblum oversees the sales and marketing of Brøderbund products into the education channel. Since joining the company in 1992, she has instituted a number of effective new programs for the education marketplace. Prior to joining Brøderbund, Rosenblum was president of Interactive Learning Materials. Before that she was VP, optical publishing, for Grolier Electronic Publishing, where she managed all aspects of the successful introduction of The New Electronic Encyclopedia on CD-ROM. Rosenblum is a graduate of the CBS School of Management and a cochair of the Education Section Board of the Software Publishers' Association.

David Kessler, VP and Creative Director — 42

As the head of Brøderbund's in-house design department, Kessler is responsible for overseeing the graphic design of the company's packaging, advertising, catalogs, and a host of other printed materials. Several thousand projects a year flow through his department. Kessler has been with Brøderbund since 1984. Prior to joining Brøderbund, he was an account supervisor for Ketchum Communications, Inc., in San Francisco. Kessler holds a B.A. in graphic communications and advertising from San Diego State University.

M. W. Mantle, VP, Engineering, Chief Technical Officer — 45

Responsible for overseeing the internal technical development of all Brøderbund products, M. W. (Mickey) Mantle's areas of responsibility include computer art and graphics, music and sound, quality assurance, and software development. Mantle joined Brøderbund in 1991. As chief technical officer, he oversees Brøderbund's engineering staff and continues to focus on improving the product development process by standardizing development practices and adopting new technologies. Prior to joining Brøderbund, Mantle was general manager of graphics development for Pixar, which he joined shortly after it spun off from Lucasfilm in 1986. He holds a B.S. in computer science from the University of Utah and is widely known in the computer graphics community for his work.

Thomas L. Marcus, VP, Business Development, General Counsel and Secretary — 41

In addition to overall corporate legal issues, Marcus is responsible for all of Brøderbund's contract negotiations with outside software developers, affiliated labels, and licensees. He became Brøderbund's general counsel when he joined the company in 1986 and was appointed vice president in 1987. In June 1994, he was named vice president of business development to head a newly formed department created to pursue strategic partnerships. Marcus also focuses on the development of Brøderbund's international business. He holds an A.B. degree from Yale University and received his J.D. from the University of California, Berkeley, Boalt Hall.

Steven Dunphy, VP, Business Development — 39

Dunphy joined Brøderbund in December 1985 and has held six different positions at the company, including international sales manager, director of sales development and director of business development. In his current role, he is responsible for Brøderbund's international operations, affiliated labels program, OEM, and licensing functions. He has a B.A. in English from the University of California at Berkeley.

Albert Sonntag, VP, Operations — 35

Sonntag is responsible for Brøderbund's manufacturing distribution and warehousing purchasing facility management duplication, and special projects, such as the company's 1991 consolidation into new headquarters in Novato. He was hired as a production supervisor in 1983. As the company has grown, Sonntag has been charged with ever-increasing responsibility, including production manager, manufacturing division manager, and director of operation. He was appointed vice president in 1990. Sonntag earned a B.A. in marketing and production operations at Sonoma State University.

(Continued on next page)

Exhibit 2 *(Continued)*

	AGE
John Baker, VP, Product Development, Education and Entertainment	46

Now guiding the definition, design, development, and publishing of all the products within the entertainment and education product group, Baker joined Brøderbund in 1988 as chief technical officer and spent three years building up Technical Services. Prior to joining Brøderbund, Baker was a senior software engineer for Western Digital Corp. He holds a B.S. in physics and math from the University of New Orleans.

	AGE
Richard Whittaker, VP, Executive Publisher	48

Employed at Brøderbund since 1982, Whittaker has been instrumental to the success of the company's most popular software titles. His most distinguished accomplishment has been his involvement with the evolution of Brøderbund's most successful product line, *The Print Shop*, where he has managed design and development for the past 10 years. Whittaker has held eight different positions during his tenure, including marketing writer, software editor, product manager, senior product manager, senior editor, software designer, publisher and executive publisher. He graduated from the University of California, Berkeley, where he received a B.A. in psychology. He later attended UCLA, taking courses in the Masters in Fine Arts, Motion Pictures and Television Program.

Source: Brøderbund Software, Inc., internal company records.

manage people as we went along. Hiring Ed Auer in 1987 fostered our transition to a professionally run company.

Carlston and McDonagh, nevertheless, strove to retain a corporate culture that allowed plenty of room for individuality and creativity at any level. In recent years, Carlston had become more and more distant from day-to-day operations, preferring to concentrate instead on the company's long-range Internet strategy. McDonagh, on the other hand, was involved in every operational decision. McDonagh was known informally to employees as "Bill the Thrill" for his exploits on the company's softball team. New employees were introduced at monthly assemblies in a ritual known as "walking around the buoy," in which the inductee walked in a 360-degree circle to show his or her face to the veterans. Executives could still be found eating lunch with groups every day in the cafeteria. Each Friday concluded with a companywide "happy hour" that facilitated sharing ideas and socialization. Dress remained informal.

The company described its strategy in its 1994 *Annual Report*:

Brøderbund Software, Inc. offers products in multiple product categories; personal productivity, education, and entertainment. Titles are produced to run on major personal computer platforms, including Windows, Macintosh and multimedia CD-ROM machines.

The company's product strategy is to identify and develop emerging market segments and create new genres of software that achieve sustained consumer appeal and brand name recognition.

Brøderbund's distribution strength is backed by one of the largest sales forces in consumer software. The company seeks out new distribution channels such as superstores and warehouse clubs and as a result, is now selling products in over 16,000 outlets nationwide.

In the often turbulent consumer software industry, Brøderbund has succeeded because of its commitment to technology and its ability to anticipate industry trends, such as the emerging CD-ROM market. The company's products have a longstanding reputation for innovation and quality. Brøderbund has furthered its leadership role by investing in a sophisticated set of studio skills necessary to create high quality CD-ROM products.

The company has also created a new business development department to pursue strategic partnerships and corporate alliances, and to increase Brøderbund's international presence.

PRODUCT DEVELOPMENT

Brøderbund referred to its product development process as a "studio development approach," including design, prototyping, programming, computer graphic design, animation, sound, archival and video recordings, and quality assurance. Doug Carlston described this process in a March 1996 interview in *Upside* magazine:

It's an approach where you take the requisite combination of skills: product management, graphic skills, all the programming skills, and put it together in a single small team, often no more than five or six people, and they focus on a single project together. Studios...(allow) people to make the thousands of decisions that go into the creative process with a relatively tight feedback group. And frankly, we're just copying the best of what we see in other software companies. It's an approach that we adopted only a couple of years ago, at the impetus of the staff themselves.

Although the company focused on internally developed technology, it also acquired certain products and technologies from third parties. Regardless of the source of a program's original design, all programs published by Brøderbund underwent extensive editing and testing prior to release. The full production cycle for a new product typically took 12 to 14 months.

Most elements of the development process were provided by a combination of in-house and third-party resources, with the exception of quality assurance activity, which was completed solely at Brøderbund facilities. The company believed that the use of both in-house and third-party designers, artists, and programmers expanded its ability to introduce creative and innovative products. McDonagh explained:

Our mission is to be a broad developer and publisher of software for home computers. In choosing which products to develop, we use two criteria: market potential and the ability to create an advantage over someone else. We are one of the few software publishers that do both internal and external development. To develop new titles internally, there is increasing industrywide competition for the human resources to develop new products, including programmers, animators, artists, 3-D renderers, computer musicians, and so on. It is very much a creative process. Also, we have to develop "play-makers" who can bring these creative teams together. It's tough to find people with experience at this, so we generally groom people from the inside.

As far as working with third parties is concerned, we have evolved more along the lines of a book publisher, looking for complementary titles rather than those that com-

pete head-to-head with our existing offerings. For the third party developer choosing us, it's like the Beatles deciding on a record company. Third-party developers look for a software publisher who has clout in the marketplace, lets them loose to be creative, offers support and technical resources, and delivers good royalties in return. Our most important strategic assets are our reputation and our critical "eye" that enables us to envision products that are destined to become hit titles.

ORGANIZATION

"Being a small company, we don't have any formal training programs," said Patsy Murphy, the company's director of human resources. The average age of Brøderbund's employees had risen to approximately 35 years from 28 years in 1988. The company had a 14 percent employee turnover rate. "Quality of life is the reward here," said Murphy. "We may be in an aggressive, competitive industry, but we do not have a competitive atmosphere."

Brøderbund's future success depended in large part upon the continued service of its key technical and senior management personnel and upon its ability to continue to attract, motivate, and retain highly qualified employees. As of August 31, 1994, the company had 438 employees, including 154 in product development; 127 in sales, marketing, and customer service; 118 in manufacturing and shipping; and 39 in administration and finance. The company had an Employee and Consultant Stock Option Plan and a Profit Sharing and Retirement Plan. Competition for trained programmers, artists, and writers was intense, and the loss of the services of key personnel could have a material adverse effect on the company's future operations and on new product development efforts. None of the company's employees was represented by a labor union or was subject to a collective bargaining agreement. The company had never experienced a work stoppage and believed that its employee relations were good.

In early 1995, the market for consumer software was changing rapidly, requiring industry players to be nimble to respond to changing market conditions. In order to increase the agility of its rapidly growing organization, Brøderbund completed the transition from an organization structured along functional lines to a matrix of company-wide resources.

Each of the company's publishing areas contained a software engineering group to develop products internally and to convert existing programs to various hardware formats. The engineering department worked on creating more-effective development systems to permit development of software programs for several hardware platforms at once. This would enable the internal development staff to speed up the development of new products and to reduce the time to convert a product to a different hardware platform. In addition, Brøderbund engineers developed a proprietary digitized graphics system to deliver richer, more realistic images and animations.

These resources, in turn, supported small product teams—"little production houses"—each representing one of the various product families: entertainment, early learning, later learning, and productivity. The company actively encouraged lateral movement of personnel among its product teams.

Jan Gullett, Brøderbund's senior vice president of sales and marketing, echoed this view: "We are a values-driven company. People come here because they want to do good things, not necessarily make a lot of money."

SOCIAL RESPONSIBILITY

Brøderbund demonstrated its commitment to being a responsible corporate citizen in a variety of ways. In 1988, the company created the Brøderbund Foundation, a nonprofit corporation. Douglas Carlston and Bill McDonagh served on the three-member board of directors of this foundation. Each year, Brøderbund donated approximately 2 percent of its adjusted pretax profits to the foundation, which in turn made grants to qualified nonprofit organizations.

In 1994, Brøderbund became one of a growing number of software developers discovering the importance of building solutions to help parents and people with disabilities find alternatives for better living through technology. According to Karen Boylan, a member of Brøderbund's Education Marketing Group, "By learning how people with special needs use our software, we hope to find ways of building features into a product's design to enhance accessibility."

PRODUCTS AND OTHER VENTURES

By 1995 Brøderbund's best-known "evergreen" products were The Print Shop family of personal productivity products, the Carmen Sandiego family of educational products, and Myst in the entertainment category. Its products won over 250 awards. In March 1995, Brøderbund won four of 25 annual Codie Awards, the software equivalent of the motion picture industry's Oscars, handed out by the Software Publisher's Association. Brøderbund's other products included reference products, education products, and a variety of printing, graphics, and other personal productivity products. (See Exhibit 3 for a listing of Brøderbund's products by product family and Exhibit 4 for a breakdown of revenues by product type.)

Product tie-ins included a weekday children's quiz show on PBS television based on the Carmen Sandiego theme. The company also had an agreement with Western Publishing Company, Inc., to market a variety of printed materials, including children's story and activity books, puzzles, and book covers all based on the adventures of Carmen Sandiego. In February 1994, the Fox TV network began airing a new cartoon series created by DIC Animation City, Inc., based on the Carmen Sandiego software program. Although Brøderbund did not receive significant revenues from these product tie-ins, management believed that these TV series would increase the exposure of the Carmen Sandiego software and enhance brand recognition for the product family. Since its introduction to the market in April 1985, the game had sold more than four million units. With the release of new Carmen Sandiego software products on CD-ROM and also for a younger age group, management believed that it had addressed the factors that had caused the decline in revenues from this product family.

On January 1, 1994, Brøderbund and Random House, Inc., became equal partners in a joint venture called Living Books to publish the Living Books line of products. Both Brøderbund and Random House distributed Living Books through their respective distribution channels under an affiliated label agreement. In November 1994, John Girton, an analyst with Van Kasper & Co., noted, "With Living Books, Brøderbund was the first company of any size to enter the CD-ROM market, so they were pioneers. That was a significant move for them, because the CD-ROM market is going to get bigger and bigger." In the first quarter of fiscal year 1995, the Living Books venture made its initial contribution to Brøderbund's earnings in the amount of $1.7 million. Brøderbund made plans to move its Living Books division from Novato to a separate facility in San Francisco in late summer 1995.

EXHIBIT 3   Brøderbund's Product Line

Product Family	List Price	Age Group	Platform	Description
PrintShop				
The Print Shop Deluxe Print Shop Deluxe CD Ensemble	$49.95 79.95	all	DOS/Win/Mac CD-ROM	Create greeting cards, signs, banners, and other personal documents *1995 SPA Codie Award, Best Personal Creativity Program*
Carmen Sandiego				
Where in the World is Carmen Sandiego?	39.95 49.95	9 & up	DOS/Mac CD-ROM	Games designed to teach geography, history, and astronomy *1995 SPA Codie Award, Best Secondary Education Program*
Entertainment				
Myst	29.95 to	14 & up	DOS/Mac CD-ROM	Surrealistic multimedia adventure game
Prince of Persia I & II	54.95			Action-like arcade games featuring lifelike animation
Early Learning				
Kid Pix; Math Workshop; The Playroom; The Backyard; The Treehouse	39.95 to 49.95	3 to 12	DOS/Win/Mac CD-ROM	Paint and activity programs combining sounds, graphics, and special effects; *1995 SPA Codie Award*
Edutainment				
The Amazing Writing Machine	24.95 to 39.95	6 to 12	Mac CD-ROM	Creative writing illustration, and idea-generation program
Spelunx & the Caves of Mr. Seudo				Ecology, astronomy, biology, reading music, art, and fantasy
Alien Tales				Intergalactic game show teaching reading
Other Products				
3D Home Architect	59.95 to	Adult	Windows CD-ROM	Easy home design, complete with realistic 3D views
PC Globe Maps 'n' Facts	129.95			Electronic atlas
TypeStyler			Mac	Shape and style text to create special effects
Living Books				
Assorted titles	39.95 ea	3 to 10	Win CD-ROM Mac CD-ROM	Stories and poems brought to life with sound effects, original music, humor, and animation.

In addition, Brøderbund distributed and sold products written and produced by several affiliated software companies: Amtex, Books that Work, Cyan, I-Motion, Inroads Interactive, The Logic Factory, Quadrangle, Starwave, and Vicarious. Affiliated label products were generally marketed under the name of the affiliated label company, and the

EXHIBIT 4   Brøderbund Software, Inc. Fiscal 1994 Revenue Breakdown, by Product

		Change from FY 1993
Print Shop	32%	+22%
Entertainment	15	+200
Carmen Sandiego	14	(24)
Living Books	13	+200
Early Learning	10	N/A
Affiliated products	9	(45)
Other	7	N/A
Total	100%	+17%
Of which:		
CD-ROM	40%	+400%
Macintosh	30	+150

Source: Brøderbund Software, Inc. internal company records.

affiliate remained responsible for product development, marketing, and technical support. This enabled Brøderbund to leverage its investment in its sales force and add a new source of product without incurring the risks inherent in new product development. The company's agreements with its affiliated label producers provided for a specific period of time, after which these rights were subject to negotiated renewal. In the first quarter of fiscal 1995, one of the company's affiliated labels, Automap, announced it was being purchased by another company. Brøderbund's affiliated label relationship with Automap was terminated at the end of February 1995. During fiscal 1994 revenues from sales of Automap products accounted for less than three percent of net revenues. In fiscal 1995, Brøderbund signed distribution agreements with Starwave, begun by Microsoft co-founder Paul Allen, to create interactive on-line services and CD-ROM software featuring entertainers such as Clint Eastwood (The Logic Factory), the Muppets (I-Motion), and a series of pet titles, including "Multimedia Dogs" and "Multimedia Cats" (Inroads Interactive).

Management felt that new product introductions were critical to the company's future success. Doug Carlston said:

> Software has phenomenal gross margins compared to most businesses. Properly run, a software company should be kind of a cash cow. And it's enormously tolerant of mistakes. The creative process itself has a lot of built-in opportunities for mistakes. It's relatively difficult to combine the creative personalities with the numerically-oriented bean counters who often run companies when they get to a certain size. And that's a rare chemistry. Creative process also tends to suffer from just size. It's at its best when people are working with a small group of compatriots who are all very much focused on a single goal and don't have to spend an enormous amount of time justifying what they are doing up or down a corporate ladder. The best way to do it is to keep your creative units as small and cohesive as possible.

McDonagh added:

> However, blockbusters are not created every day, and there is no way of knowing whether we have or have not created a blockbuster until it takes off in the marketplace.

Therefore, new product introductions are only part of a greater challenge: to create software that people want—based on market trends—a program that can command a significant percentage of sales in the market and sustain its presence long enough to recapture its R&D costs. This is critical to any software company's success, including ours.

"Our strategic weakness is predicting what's going to be a hit, making sure that we'll have hit titles on a regular basis," said Gullett. There was also evidence of slackening growth in the consumer software market as well as evidence of emerging price competition. Competitors had begun to enter with new products priced at $19.95 in order to take market share away from an existing Brøderbund product, such as Print Shop, priced at $79.95.

PLATFORM SHIFTS

Brøderbund identified and proactively targeted upcoming market needs, beginning with the shift of its product line from the DOS to Windows platforms and from floppy disk to CD-ROM formats. Although the MS-DOS operating system had achieved by 1994 a large worldwide installed base, the number of newly shipped MS-DOS titles dropped by 10 percent during calendar 1994. Half of all those MS-DOS sales were games, with another quarter educational or personal productivity titles. With Windows integrating the business market and CD-ROM taking over the market for games, DOS was clearly at the end of its product life cycle. Replacing MS-DOS was strong consumer demand for "new" products, that is, reintroductions of older products on the newer Windows platform that could also take full advantage of CD-ROM capabilities (see Exhibit 5).

Brøderbund estimated that future demand for titles that ran on Windows and CD-ROM would continue to expand, but demand for DOS-compatible and floppy-based products would continue to decline.

As hardware platforms consolidated worldwide, Brøderbund expected to publish fewer versions of its products. In the past, Brøderbund might publish DOS, Windows, Macintosh, floppy, and CD-ROM versions of a product. However, by 1995 most of the company's new products were being released only on the Macintosh or Windows CD-ROM platforms. As a result of these platform shifts and in anticipation of potential returns of products on declining platforms, the company increased its inventory reserves for returns to $10.3 million in fiscal 1994 from $6.4 million in fiscal 1993. Future platform

EXHIBIT 5   Estimated 1994 Market Shares, by Platform

Platform	by Sales ($ Revenues)	by Shipments (# of Units Sold)
Windows	70.8%	66.8%
MS-DOS	14.3	18.9
Macintosh	13.6	11.7
Other	1.3	2.6
TOTAL	100.0%	100.0%

Source: International Data Corp., Framingham, MA

shifts and product returns in excess of the company's expectations could have a material adverse effect on operating results and financial condition.

SALES, DISTRIBUTION, AND OPERATIONS

Brøderbund sold its products to distributors and directly to software specialty retail chains, electronics chains, computer superstores, mass merchandisers, discount warehouse stores, educational dealers, schools and end-users. Brøderbund commonly participated in and provided financial assistance for its retailers' promotional efforts, such as in-store displays, catalogue advertisements, demonstration disks, and other collateral marketing materials. The company spent an estimated 0.4 percent of sales on advertising. Its largest distributor in fiscal 1994 was Ingram/MicroD, which accounted for approximately 21 percent of the company's net revenues. (See Exhibit 6 for a breakdown of Brøderbund's fiscal 1994 revenues by retail channel.)

Although the company's sales policies placed limits on product returns and product returns had not had a significant effect on Brøderbund's operating results to date, the company could be forced to accept substantial product returns to maintain its relationships with retailers and access to distribution channels.

Sales Force

Brøderbund's 33-person national sales staff operated out of eight offices situated in California (2), Georgia, Illinois, Massachusetts, Pennsylvania, Ohio, and Texas. In addition, the company had distribution arrangements in Europe, Japan, and Australia. The company opened an office in London in 1994 to serve as a hub for its sales and marketing efforts in Europe. International distribution agreements granted the exclusive right to distribute Brøderbund's products in specific geographic territories. In some cases, the distributor purchased finished goods directly from the company for resale. In other cases, the distributor developed a foreign language version and paid the company a royalty on sales of such products.

A separate 11-person education marketing and sales group focused on sales to schools. This group also produced material for teachers to tie Brøderbund learning products to current curriculum, provided suggested classroom activities for both on and off the computer, and sponsored a preview center and lending library. The company believed

---

EXHIBIT 6   Brøderbund Software, Inc. Fiscal 1994 Revenue Breakdown, by Retail Channel

Software specialty stores	21%
Electronic stores	16
Superstores	16
Warehouse stores	15
Mass merchants	10
Office stores	7
Total	100%

Source: Brøderbund Software, Inc. internal company records.

that sales to this market segment were an important element in its overall success because children were often introduced to Brøderbund's products through their schooling.

Direct Sales

Brøderbund promoted its products directly to end-users through direct mailings, catalogues, brochures, in-store demonstrations and presentations to computer user groups, advertising in computer publications, and the circulation of newsletters to specific audiences. The company maintained a substantial mailing list, comprising more than 1.6 million users of Brøderbund's products. Direct sales to end-users, free product demos, technical support, and press releases were all available from Brøderbund Software-Direct or on-line via Brøderlink, America Online, and Compuserve.

Production

Brøderbund prepared its own master software diskettes and CD-ROM discs, user manuals, and packaging. Substantially all of the company's diskette duplication was performed at the company's own facilities, using diskettes acquired in quantity from outside sources. The company used outside sources to procure and duplicate CD-ROM discs, print user manuals, and manufacture packaging and related materials. The assembly and shipment of final products, as well as the majority of floppy disk duplication that was not CD-ROM, was performed by the company at its own 93,000-square-foot facility located in Petaluma, CA. Brøderbund also supplemented the use of its own production facilities through reliance on third-party manufacturers.

As of early 1995, the company had not yet experienced any material difficulties or delays in the manufacture and assembly of its products and had experienced very low returns due to product defects. Brøderbund typically shipped product within one to two days after receipt of an order, which was customary in the computer software business. Accordingly, backlog as of any particular date was not representative of actual sales for any succeeding period. Nevertheless, management faced uncertainties in securing a supply of paper and, over the longer term, planning for increased warehouse and production line capacity.

Seasonality

Brøderbund's business was highly seasonal. Typically, net revenues, gross margins, and operating income were highest during the first fiscal quarter, ending November 30th of each year; declined in the second fiscal quarter; and were lowest in the third and fourth fiscal quarters. (See Exhibit 7 for quarterly financial information.) This seasonal pattern was due primarily to increased demand for the company's products during the calendar year-end holiday selling season. However, the company's operating results in any given quarter could be increased due to new product introductions or be adversely affected by delays in new product introductions, lack of market acceptance of new products, the introduction of competitive products, as well as a variety of other factors including changes in product mix, timing of orders placed by distributors and dealers, and the timing and extent of marketing expenditures.

INDUSTRY ANALYSIS

As of early 1995, the software market continued to be one of the fastest-growing segments of the computer industry. According to the International Data Corporation, revenues for

---

EXHIBIT 7 Brøderbund Software, Inc. Quarterly Financial Information (Unaudited)
(In Thousands, Except Per Share Data)

	Quarter Ended				
	Nov 30	**Feb 28**	**May 31**	**Aug 31**	*Year*
Fiscal Year 1995:					
Net Revenues	$53,100	$45,208			
Gross Margin					
Net Income (Loss)					
Net Income (Loss) Per Share	$ 0.57	$ 1.06			
Fiscal Year 1994:					
Net Revenues	$32,795	$25,350	$25,722	$27,907	$111,774
Gross Margin	21,280	17,111	15,433	17,361	71,185
Net Income (Loss)[a]	6,243	4,458	(4,112)	4,472	11,061
Net Income (Loss) Per Share	$ 0.31	$ 0.22	($ 0.20)	$ 0.22	$ 0.55
Fiscal Year 1993:					
Net Revenues	$32,564	$24,353	$ 16,443	$22,223	$ 95,583
Gross Margin	17,391	14,306	11,053	13,714	56,464
Net Income (Loss)	4,883	3,696	2,105	2,944	13,628
Net Income (Loss) Per Share	$ 0.25	$ 0.18	$ 0.10	$ 0.15	$ 0.68

[a]Includes one-time pre-tax charge of $11 million ($.38 per share) to terminate merger agreement with Electronic
Arts (5/94).
Sources: Brøderbund Software, Inc. 1994 *Annual Report* and 10-K statements.

---

the packaged-software market totaled nearly $78 billion in calendar 1994, $72 billion in 1993, and $64 billion in 1992. The strongest software category sales dollar gains in the first half of 1994 were from home education/reference (+144 percent) and home creativity (+103 percent). Indications were that the majority of these sales were to the home market, and that sales to this segment were expected to continue to grow exponentially. By early 1995, home "edutainment" software had become, by some estimates, a market worth nearly $1 billion, with reported growth rates as much as 128 percent.

Emerging Market Segment

Dataquest, a research firm, classified multimedia products and services into five general categories: content development tools, interactive products, simulation products, video on demand, and enhanced productivity tools. Multimedia software products were designed to combine video, animation, still pictures, voice, music, graphics, and text into a single system. Multimedia products blurred the lines between several formerly distinct products and industries: computers, software, consumer electronics, communications, publishing, and entertainment. Although industry observers predicted that the market for multimedia products (such as interactive TVs and personal communicators) was not expected to take off until the late 1990s, some products were already available by 1995. Most current multimedia products were targeted at the consumer entertainment sector, rather than at the business market. The rationale for such targeting was that consumer multimedia software applications generally ran on computers, TVs, or other entertainment devices, whereas business software applications typically ran only on computers, from personal computer workstations to mainframes.

Sales of multimedia titles increased significantly in calendar 1994. According to Dataquest, multimedia CD-ROM shipments grew from 16.5 million units in 1993 to 53.9 million units in 1994. Ninety percent of CD-ROM titles were in the game, education, and personal segments. Approximately three-quarters of the reported CD-ROM sales were for the DOS/Windows/MPC formats.

CD-ROM—based multimedia products with voice, animation, video, and sound were expected to continue to gain popularity in the entertainment and education software segment. With a continuing decline in hardware prices, more PCs were expected to turn up in homes and small businesses. Strong sales and marketing operations thus became critical to develop, maintain, and strengthen CD-ROM distribution channels. With smaller margins available to software retailers, dealers and resellers could no longer afford to advertise or to train customers in the use of products. Marketing tactics, to generate enthusiasm and end-user demand for a product, were falling to the PC software companies, who in turn were operating with smaller sales and marketing staffs and reduced budgets. With the advent of the mail-order and mass-market retail channels, distribution channels appeared to be changing. To gain shelf space, smaller software publishers began to look for partners with greater financial and marketing resources. To gain rapid entry into the high-growth consumer software marketplace, large firms sought interindustry collaborations.

STRATEGIC ALLIANCES

Alliances, particularly among large firms, came to dominate the multimedia industry for several reasons: they reduced risks, spread costs, and allowed firms to acquire expertise in the different elements of multimedia quickly. In 1994, several computer, communications, and entertainment companies joined efforts to form a consortium, called First Cities, to develop interactive multimedia for home use. Participating companies were Apple, Bellcore, Bieber-Taki Associates, Corning, Eastman Kodak, Kaleida, North American Philips, Southwestern Bell Corp., Sutter Bay Associates, Tandem, and USWest.

DreamWorks SKG, another alliance, was formed in 1995 under the joint leadership of Stephen Spielberg, Jeffrey Katzenberg (formerly head of Walt Disney pictures), and David Geffen (head of Geffen Records). In March 1995, DreamWorks announced that Paul Allen, a cofounder of Microsoft, had invested $500 million in the venture. This was soon followed by an announcement that Microsoft had signed a development agreement with DreamWorks, accompanied by an investment of an undisclosed sum.

These alliances cut across industry lines. This diversity suggested that member companies would perform different roles within the alliances. Jack McPhee, director of the Office of Computers and Business Equipment for the U.S. Department of Commerce, said, "Teaming and strategic alliances have become the order of the day; companies seek to combine their technologies and talents to address anticipated opportunities." For example, entertainment firms could provide the content of the digital media; telephone or cable companies, the ability to deliver the information; and computer hardware and software firms, the ways to use the data. Second, many alliances were international, signaling that the production of multimedia products would be global from the start.

Brøderbund's management believed that new competitors, including large software companies and other large media companies, were bound to increase their focus on the consumer software market, resulting in a proliferation of products, and increasingly fewer opportunities for small software companies to enter. "Currently, there is a proliferation of products competing for shelf space in many of our channels. In the future we expect there to be more industry consolidation as growth slows: people will start to look for partners when they feel the pinch," said McDonagh.

To remain successful, smaller vendors needed to find and exploit niche markets that were untapped by major vendors. To sell these products, smaller vendors needed to develop and maintain relationships with consumer-oriented distribution channels.

The Internet

As of early 1995, the effect of the development of the Internet on publishers, distributors, and retailers remained a major question mark. Still, many observers agreed that the potential market for publishing on the Internet, using multimedia billboards on the World Wide Web, was enormous. An estimated six million computers were linked directly to the Internet, a threefold rise from 1994, according to the Internet Society. An estimated 10,000 companies had already erected their own electronic billboards on the Web. The total number of people who could tap into the Internet from computer keyboards on any given day was estimated at 30 million worldwide. According to Forrester Research, the total market for Internet business—including services, software, and shopping—had reached an estimated $500 million. By 2000, Forrester Research estimated that business on the Internet could reach $10 billion or more. This growth was expected to mirror the exponential growth of commercial on-line services: America Online had 2.5 million customers, followed by Compuserve (a division of H&R Block) with 1.9 million, Prodigy (a joint venture of IBM and Sears) with 1.6 million, and Dephi (a subsidiary of the News Corporation) a distant fourth with 160,000 subscribers.

According to Gullett, "The World Wide Web is a substitution threat, so we have to make products that are more powerful to take advantage of new Web technology. Over 70% of our user base is on-line, 90% have modems. Yet we're less positive long-term about the Internet as a distribution vehicle for software applications than the rest of the industry."

Direct Competitors

Among Brøderbund's major direct competitors in the consumer software segment were Microsoft, Davidson & Associates, Sierra-Online, Learning Company, Maxis, MECC, and Edmark. (Exhibits 8, 9, and 10 present recent marketing and financial data on these direct competitors.) Despite the proliferation of these direct competitors, Brøderbund believed that its products competed most favorably with respect to product features and quality, reliability and ease-of-use, brand-name recognition and strength in distribution channels and, to a lesser extent, quality of support services and price.

Intellectual Property Issues

Brøderbund regarded the software that it owned or licensed as proprietary. The company relied primarily on a combination of copyrights and trademarks, trade secret laws, and employee and third-party nondisclosure agreements to protect its products. Despite these precautions, the company was mindful of the possibility that unauthorized parties might attempt to copy aspects of its products or obtain and use information that was regarded as proprietary. Such software piracy could be expected to be a persistent problem, although it was a systematic risk of trading in the software industry.

Brøderbund was a founding member of the Software Publishers' Association and supported the SPA's anti-piracy efforts to police the unauthorized use of computer soft-

---

EXHIBIT 8   Brøderbund's Direct Competitors

Company	Date Est.	Location	Industry Rank, 1994	% Sales Increase 1993–94	Best-Selling Titles
Microsoft	1975	Redmond, WA	1	28	MS-DOS, Windows, Office, Word, Excel, Home
Davidson & Associates	1982	Torrance, CA	18	50	Math Blaster, Reading Blaster, Kid Works
Sierra On-Line	N/A	Bellevue, WA	20	21	King's Quest, Leisure Suit Larry, Red Baron, Outpost
Learning Company	1980	Fremont, CA	27	36	Reader Rabbit, Interactive Reading Journey, Treasure Mathstorm
Maxis	1987	Orinda, CA	32	102	Sim City, Sim Earth, Sim Ant
MECC	N/A	Minneapolis, MN	41	18	Oregon Trail, Yukon Trail, Amazon Trail
Edmark	1970	Minneapolis, MN	N/A	66	Bailey's Book House, Millie's Math House, Sammy's Science House, Thinkin' Things Collection

Source: Software Publishers' Association *Annual Financial Survey of Members*, April, 1995.

---

ware. The company had, from time to time, received communications from third parties asserting that features or content of certain of its products might infringe on the intellectual property rights of such parties and in some instances litigation was commenced. As of early 1995, no such claims had had an adverse effect on the company's ability to develop, market, or sell its products.

TERMINATED MERGER AGREEMENTS

In late 1990, Sierra On-Line announced a planned merger with Brøderbund in a stock swap valued at $88 million, but the deal kept running into problems. Uncertainty about the economy and then the Persian Gulf War put Sierra's plans on hold. In March 1991, the two companies renewed talks and signed a letter of intent to merge. The merged entity would have been called Sierra-Brøderbund, and Brøderbund would have become a unit of Sierra. But the deal fell through again. *The Wall Street Journal* quoted Ken Williams, president of Sierra On-Line, as saying:

> There was disagreement regarding the management structure of the combined company. This was unfortunate given the underlying strength of the two companies and the dynamic company which would have evolved. Only strong companies can succeed; you need a critical mass to compete in our industry. Maturity matters in our industry, and merging with other companies is the price of being in business.

EXHIBIT 9   Sales by Top-Selling Software Publishers—Calendar Year 1994

	Dollars	Units
Games		
Sierra On-Line	$ 28,032	722,071
LucasArts	17,086	398,308
Microprose	15,459	368,136
Brøderbund	15,171	318,395
Maxis	15,130	462,997
TOTAL MARKET, GAMES	$276,772	8,742,741
Education		
Learning Company	$ 18,248	410,332
Microsoft	16,621	238,987
Brøderbund	11,758	299,016
Mindscape	9,048	193,100
Davidson	8,886	264,540
TOTAL MARKET, EDUCATION	$135,854	3,690,037
Personal Productivity		
Brøderbund	$ 15,947	311,507
Softkey	13,763	512,248
Expert Software	6,437	500,047
DeLorme	4,050	46,935
Microsoft	2,978	70,354
TOTAL MARKET, PRODUCTIVITY	$ 90,962	3,086,022
Top Selling CD Publishers		
Brøderbund	$ 22,748	416,275
Microsoft	21,930	337,330
Sierra On-Line	13,936	338,039
Virgin	8,884	187,068
LucasArts	8,577	177,002
Mindscape	7,524	190,759
Learning Company	6,950	107,620
GT Interactive	6,312	138,527
Electronic Arts	6,128	159,867
Grolier	6,042	68,097
TOTAL MARKET, CD-ROM	$243,632	5,570,949

Source: Software Publishers' Association *Annual Financial Survey of Members*, April, 1995.

The deal finally was scrapped in April 1991. The Sierra On-Line merger would have allowed early Brøderbund investors to cash out because, at the time, Sierra stock was publicly traded whereas Brøderbund's was not. Brøderbund then proceeded with an initial public offering in October of that year.

In May 1994, Brøderbund and Electronic Arts terminated an agreement to merge due to financial considerations. Brøderbund recognized a onetime pre-tax charge of $11

EXHIBIT 10   Leading Consumer Software Companies—Historical Data (Sales in $000)

	Calendar Year 12/31/94		CY 1993	CY 1992
	# Employees	Sales	Sales	Sales
Microsoft	16,379	$5,266,000	$4,109,000	$3,252,000
Brøderbund	450	132,068	95,814	86,126
Davidson & Associates	531	87,914	58,569	39,608
Sierra On-Line	650	76,500	63,354	43,269
Learning Company	206	44,761	32,873	23,852
Maxis	136	37,357	18,251	15,209
MECC	190	34,633	20,795	17,960
Edmark	115	16,807	10,118	7,368

Source: Software Publishers' Association *Annual Financial Survey of Members,* April, 1995.

million, which consisted of a $10 million payment to Electronic Arts to terminate the merger and $1 million in associated costs.

THE FUTURE

As McDonagh pondered his company's strategic direction in early April 1995, reports in the press offered seemingly contradictory futures for Brøderbund. *Business Week* published its 1995 annual roster of America's largest publicly-traded companies, ranked by market value. Brøderbund made this list for the first time, ranked at 788, with a market value of $1 billion. A sidebar article on Brøderbund went on to note: "'This little software company has a huge following because it has a very consistent track record of developing superb games,' said David T. Farina, an analyst at William Blair & Co. Farina predicted earnings would rise 95 percent, to $36.5 million by the end of fiscal 1996, on sales growth of 76 percent, to $195 million."

That same week, Jeffrey Tarter, publisher of an influential industry newsletter called *Soft•Letter,* noted that although the consumer and entertainment category was the fastest-growing category in the personal computer software industry, smaller companies should be prepared for a coming shakeout as the marketplace became increasingly dominated by a handful of powerful companies.

McDonagh responded to these analyses by saying that the challenges for the future would be how to manage changes in technology and a market that was growing faster than the company's ability to deliver new products:

> *The good news is that the consumer software industry is on the threshold of becoming a true consumer business. The drivers of this opportunity include the change from a hobbyist-oriented to a mainstream marketplace, one that will be more niche-oriented. Computer uses are changing, too, from playing back software to recording and communicating with software. The bad news is that we are not the only competitor who sees these changes. As for our future, one thing we have that the new entrants—telecommunications companies,*

media companies, film and video companies—do not have is our expertise to forecast and manage shifts in technology.

Luck had a lot to do with our early success, but we now believe that success comes from having the right people, picking the right titles, and looking at platform shifts opportunistically instead of as threats. The beauty of being in a technology-driven business is that platform shifts or discontinuities take place every three to four years, so there's plenty of opportunity out there for us to develop new products that can take advantage of new platforms.

The real question is the pace of change and what obstacles we can hurdle. Whereas today we are primarily in packaged software, we may expand our reach into communications, leveraging our distinctive competencies in ease-of-use and brand name recognition. We expect that our product portfolio will change dramatically over the next two to three years, and as a result, the company could double in size. It will be a higher stakes game: deep pockets will be important for prospective as well as defensive purposes.

Clearly, the increased technical sophistication required in new consumer software products was expected to continue to make the availability of significant financial resources a very important competitive factor. In the event that price competition were to increase substantially, competitive pressures could cause the company to reduce the prices of its products, and reduced profit margins could result. Prolonged price competition would, in turn, have a material adverse effect on the company's operating results and long-term competitive position. (See Exhibits 11, 12 and 13 for Brøderbund's financial statements and recent operating history.)

REFERENCES

Albemarle, J., "Pushing the PC limit," *Graduating Engineer,* January, 1995.
Bickford, C., "Fun and games," *MacUser,* October, 1994.
Bryant H., Myst opportunities," *Oakland Tribune,* November 20, 1994.
"The Business Week 1000," *Business Week,* March 27, 1995.
Carlston, D., *Software People,* Prentice-Hall: New York, 1986.
Caruso, D. (ed.), "The many arms of Microsoft." *Technology and Media,* 1:2, July, 1994.
Fisher, L, "Two companies in software drop merger," The *New York Times,* May 4, 1994.
Gilles, J., "Brøderbund scores at software symposium," *Mann Independent Journal,* March 16, 1995.
Leininger, L., "Disabled—not!" *MacHome Journal,* January, 1995.
Lohr, S., "Investment is a $2 billion bet on the net," The *New York Times,* May 11, 1995.
The *New York Times,* national edition, March 23, 1995.
Software Industry Report, April 15, 1991.
Southwick, K., "Doug Carlston Talks Tough," *Upside,* March, 1996.
Tarter, J., *The 1995 Soft•Letter 100,* 1:19, March 31, 1995.
U.S. Department of Commerce, U.S. Industrial Outlook 1994.
The *Wall Street Journal,* November 3, 1991.

GLOSSARY OF PC INDUSTRY TERMS

CD-ROM or Compact Disc-Read Only Memory. Similar to an audio CD or compact disk that one might play on a stereo, these 5" shiny plastic disks hold computer instructions that are "played" by the computer. A CD-ROM contains programs or information

EXHIBIT 11   Brøderbund Software, Inc. Consolidated Statements of Income for the Years Ended August 31 (In Thousands, Except Per Share Amounts)

	1994	1993	1992	1991	1990
Net Revenues	$111,774	$95,583	$ 75,085	$55,779	$50,387
Cost of Revenues	40,589	39,119	32,838	24,358	21,077
Gross Margin	71,185	56,464	42,247	31,421	29,310
Operating Expenses:					
Sales and Marketing	18,621	15,051	11,102	8,565	9,147
Research and Development	16,016	13,671	10,624	6,774	5,890
General and Administrative	7,500	7,112	6,375	5,919	5,337
Total Operating Expenses	42,137	35,834	28,101	21,258	20,374
Income from Operations	29,048	20,630	14,146	10,163	8,936
Interest and Dividend Income, Net	1,791	1,295	1,318	1,446	1,241
Terminated Merger Costs	(11,000)				
Income from Continuing Operations Before Income Taxes	19,839	21,925	15,464	11,609	10,177
Provision for Income Taxes	8,778	8,297	5,805	4,547	3,959
Income from Continuing Operations	11,061	13,628	9,659	7,062	6,218
Income (Loss) from Discontinued Operations, Net of Income Taxes					(3,061)
Net Income	$ 11,061	13,628	9,659	7,062	3,157
Per Share Data					
Income from Continuing Operations	$ .96	$ .68	$ .49	$ .38	$ .33
Net Income Per Share	$ .55	$ .68	$ .49	$ .38	$ .17
Shares Used in Computing Per Share Data	20,145	20,006	19,582	18,767	18,738

Sources: Brøderbund Software, Inc. Annual Reports and Forms 8-K.

such as encyclopedia contents coded in digital format on the side opposite the label. "Read only memory" means that users cannot change or add to the information on the disk, as opposed to the dual read-and-write capability of other electronic storage media, such as floppy disks or hard drives.

Edutainment Software. Multimedia software, including games, for educational and home use.

GUI or Graphical User Interfaces. These special instructions and devices permit users to see vivid illustrations on their computer monitors, rather than just plain numbers and letters on a blank background. Contemporary GUIs allow for very fast and dazzling graphics, including short video clips.

Information Super Highway. A high-speed information network or method of accessing vast amounts of information from remote sites, such as libraries.

Internet. A series of large computers owned by universities, government institutions, and industrial firms connected by a network of telephone and other communication

EXHIBIT 12 **Brøderbund Software, Inc. Consolidated Balance Sheets at August 31 (In Thousands, Except Per Share Amounts)**

	1994	1993	1992	1991	1990
Assets					
Current Assets:					
Cash and Cash Equivalents	$75,000	$54,316	$31,409	$29,621	$ 18,265
Accounts Receivable, Net	2,298	5,256	7,781	5,043	5,123
Income Tax Prepayments	1,156				
Inventories	2,361	3,211	4,127	2,327	1,913
Deferred Income Taxes	8,759	5,815	3,941	2,223	1,782
Other	757	378	655	360	3,854
Total Current Assets	90,331	68,976	47,913	39,574	30,937
Equipment and Improvements, Net	4,335	5,722	4,840	2,665	1,444
Other Assets	2,985	2,531	3,473	509	470
Total Assets	$97,651	$77,229	$56,226	$42,748	$ 32,851
Liabilities and Stockholders' Equity					
Current Liabilities:					
Borrowings Under Bank Line of Credit	$ —	$ —	$ —	$ 1,462	$ 1,536
Accounts Payable	5,656	4,237	2,956	1,948	1,957
Accrued Compensation	5,353	4,266	2,572	1,552	1,199
Royalties Payable	2,963	2,333	2,234	1,551	1,475
Accrued Income Taxes		1,238	461	1,551	—
Other	3,354	2,132	2,228	2,256	1,400
Total Current Liabilities	17,326	14,206	10,451	10,320	7,567
Deferred Income Taxes	—	726	1,109	—	—
Other Liabilities	146	287	496	—	—
Commitments					
Stockholders' Equity:					
Preferred Stock, $.01 Par Value: 1,000,000 Shares	—	—	—	3,417	3,236
Common Stock, $.01 Par Value					
Authorized Shares—40,000,000					
Issued and Outstanding Shares—19,624,000 in 1994, 18,998,000 in 1993	20,321	13,213	9,001	3,456	3,365
Retained Earnings	59,858	48,797	35,169	25,555	18,683
Total Stockholders' Equity	80,179	62,010	44,170	32,428	25,284
Total Liabilities and Stockholders' Equity	$97,651	$77,229	$56,226	$42,748	$ 32,851

Sources: Brøderbund Software, Inc. Initial Public Offering Prospectus and Annual Reports.

links. Access to the Internet allows users to exchange information such as electronic mail (E-mail) or computer files, and to search for information on various topics from many sources and providers. Some methods of access permit on-line interactions simultaneously with other individuals or groups, and this type of connection is sometimes called "chat."

EXHIBIT 13 Brøderbund Software, Inc. Consolidated Statements of Cash Flows for the Years Ended August 31 (In Thousands)

	1994	1993	1992	1991	1990
Operating Activities					
Net Income	$11,061	$13,628	$ 9,659	$ 7,062	$ 3,157
Adjustments to Reconcile Net Income to Net Cash Provided by (Used in) Operating Activities:					
Depreciation and Amortization	3,028	2,760	1,368	892	774
Changes in Current Assets and Liabilities					
Accounts Receivable	2,958	2,521	(2,346)	80	1,257
Inventories	850	916	(1,721)	(414)	(989)
Other Current Assets	(79)	277	(180)	1,421	(664)
Income Tax Prepayments	(1,156)				
Deferred Income Taxes	(4,325)	(2,257)	(1,155)	(441)	(132)
Accounts Payable	1,419	1,281	191	(9)	(369)
Other Current Liabilities	2,939	1,697	891	1,285	1,088
Accrued Income Taxes	(1,238)	777	(958)	1,551	(149)
Net Cash Provided by Operating Activities	15,457	21,600	5,749	11,427	3,973
Investing Activities					
Acquisition of PC Globe, Inc.			(1,500)		
Net Additions to Equipment and Improvements	(1,041)	(2,436)	(2,918)	(1,826)	(821)
Proceeds from Sale of Discontinued Operations	—	—	—	2,384	—
Other	(840)	(440)	(211)	(613)	(98)
Net Cash Used for Investing Activities	(1,881)	(2,876)	(4,629)	(55)	(919)
Financing Activities					
Reduction of Restricted Cash Deposit	—	—	1,750	—	
Inc. (Dec.) in Borrowings Under Bank Line of Credit	—	—	(1,462)	(74)	123
Exercise of Stock Options	7,108	4,183	2,130	72	480
Repurchase of Common Stock				(14)	(651)
Net Cash Provided by Financing Activities	7,108	4,183	2,418	(16)	(48)
Increase in Cash and Cash Equivalents	20,684	22,907	3,538	11,356	3,006
Cash and Cash Equivalents, Beginning of Year	54,316	31,409	27,871	16,515	13,509
Cash and Cash Equivalents, End of Year	$75,000	$54,316	$31,409	$27,871	$ 16,515
Supplemental Disclosure of Cash Flow Information					
Income Tax Payments	$11,591	$ 7,506	$ 6,455	$ 1,783	$ 6,455
Interest Payments	$ 30	$ 37	$ 64	$ 178	$ 64

Sources: Brøderbund Software, Inc. Initial Public Offering Prospectus and Annual Reports.

Multimedia. Refers to a software and hardware system that combines graphical capabilities ranging from still pictures to animation and audio capabilities such as voice and music with graphics and text. Typical media may include CD-ROM, laser disk, videotape, audio tape, and computer files such as those created by word processors, specialty graphic, photographic, and/or sound programs. Interactive multimedia provides users with an opportunity to issue commands and respond to prompts and queries from the computer, resulting in a multimedia response. An example is an encyclopedia that illustrates a bird, first perhaps by providing a written text or audio explanation, followed by a short video clip showing the bird at rest and then in flight. A game may show characters in action and allow users the choice of various paths and actions.

On-line Service. Computer users often subscribe to commercial network services that provide telephone dial-in access to and software for using the Internet or World Wide Web. Providers include Compuserve, Prodigy, America On-Line, and the Microsoft Network. Subscribers normally pay a monthly access fee and may also pay an hourly rate.

OS or Operating System. A critical piece of software, that, like the grooves in a record album, allows the computer to "play" applications. These complex programs allow other software to operate within the rules of that operating system and the computer on which it is used. Popular operating systems include IBM and Microsoft PC-OS, Microsoft Windows, Apple OS, Macintosh OS, IBM's OS/2 Warp, and UNIX.

Platform Shift. Platform shift refers to computer manufacturers and end-users migrating from using one computer operating system or format to a different operating system or format (such as from floppy disk to CD-ROM). This change in vendor or user preference may result in the user needing to upgrade, expand, or even totally change computer hardware. It also requires software developers to rewrite or modify their programs to work in different operating system environments or on different storage and retrieval formats.

RISC or Reduced Instruction Set Computing. These special integrated circuits or "chips" use advanced designs that require fewer instructions to perform the same tasks, allowing the computer to operate faster.

World Wide Web. The system that connects all the computers together on the Internet, primarily via a graphical user interface.

Baxter: Scientific Products Division the U.S. Balance Market—1987 (A)

David Rosenthal

On Tuesday morning, July 21, 1987, George Carson bantered with the cook in the cafeteria as he ordered a "short stack" of pancakes and poured himself a tall glass of orange juice, but his heart was not really in it. Carson, the president of Baxter's Scientific Products Division—Industrial Marketing, had just received what amounted to an ultimatum by one of the company's major suppliers. If his response was not satisfactory, it was likely that Scientific Products would lose the business.

The cafeteria was not particularly crowded at 7:00 A.M. and Carson was able to find an isolated seat. Chewing a mouthful of blueberry pancakes, he reflected on the problems they had been having in the scientific balance market and some possible solutions. The letter that he had received the previous day from Mettler Instrument Corporation, U.S.A. was the latest in a series of increasingly problematic issues facing Baxter in marketing scientific balances.

On the surface, the letter was a request for proposals from Mettler's distributors in the United States. It indicated that Mettler, U.S.A. intended to reduce the number of distributors handling its products. Proposals were to include commitments to Mettler regarding the number of units that would be sold, the size and organization of the sales force, and the extent of sale of competing products, among other things. Proposals were invited for semiexclusive and/or exclusive dealer arrangements.

Carson suspected that there was considerably more to the letter than what showed on the surface. Carson was thinking about Baxter's recent sales results with Mettler balances and the somewhat-strained atmosphere in recent sales meetings with Mettler, U.S.A. management. Deep in thought, Carson absently took a mouthful of scalding coffee, to his instant regret.

Gingerly sipping from his newly-acquired cup of ice water, Carson renewed his concentration on the issues relating to the Mettler letter. Mettler was unlikely to accept an exclusive dealer agreement because that would give too much power to the dealer organization. At the same time, simply reducing the number of competitors probably would not help Baxter very much. If even one other dealer continued to have access to Mettler balances, the price competition that had eroded their gross margins over the past few years would continue.

Carson glanced at his watch, glared at the offending Styrofoam coffee cup, and dutifully deposited his tray at the cleanup window. He called, "Good morning!" to the

This case was prepared by Professor David Rosenthal of Miami University as a basis for class discussion. It is not intended to illustrate either effective or ineffective handling of an administrative situation.

kitchen worker who had begun to clean the tray, and turned toward the stairs that would take him to his corner office three floors above.

"It comes down to three options," he thought to himself. "We can try to go with Mettler and hope for the best. They might be willing to go with an exclusive. Secondly, we could do an endrun and try for an exclusive with Mettler's major competitor, Sartorius. Thirdly, we could continue to develop our private-label business. Our gross margins are certainly better there!"

Carson had read the Mettler letter as soon as it had come in, the day before. He had immediately scheduled a meeting with the product managers responsible for scientific balances. The meeting was to start at 8:00 A.M., a few minutes from now. Carson hoped that Arthur Long and Julia Heldman could provide some additional insight, because they had been working on the balances market for some time.

BAXTER—COMPANY BACKGROUND

Baxter was the leading international supplier of health-care, scientific, and industrial products to hospitals and laboratories worldwide. Until 1985, when Baxter-Travenol merged with American Hospital Supply Corporation, the company had operated primarily in one industry segment. By 1987 Baxter operated in three health-care segments and one nonhealth-care segment: (1) hospital products and services, (2) medical systems and specialties, (3) alternate site products and services, and (4) industrial products. Each industry segment marketed a related group of products, systems and services. In addition, the company was organized to sell its products worldwide. Exhibit 1 presents the Baxter organization. Exhibit 2 shows Baxter's role in the channel of distribution for balances in the United States.

Consolidated sales for the company in 1987 were $6.2 billion, yielding an operating income of $692 million and placing Baxter among the "Fortune 75." Exhibit 3 presents a five-year summary of selected financial data.

Hospital Products and Services was the largest business unit of the company, with sales of $3.4 billion. The company boasted that they could supply 65 percent of a hospital's operational needs with their 120,000-item product line. The company literally sold everything from bedpans to x-ray equipment. Baxter manufactured some products and purchased other items for resale. From its very inception, the company had been a leader in inventory control and logistics management. Its philosophy had been to become "partners with hospitals" by making the supply function as efficient as possible.

EXHIBIT 1   Baxter Organization (1987)

Hospital Products & Services Business Unit $3.4 Billion	Medical Systems & Specialties Business Unit $1.5 Billion	Alternate Site Products & Services Business Unit $1.1 Billion	Scientific Products Business Unit $355 Million	
			Industrial $277 Million	Biomedical $78 Million

EXHIBIT 2:   Current Channels of Distribution—U.S. Balances (1987)

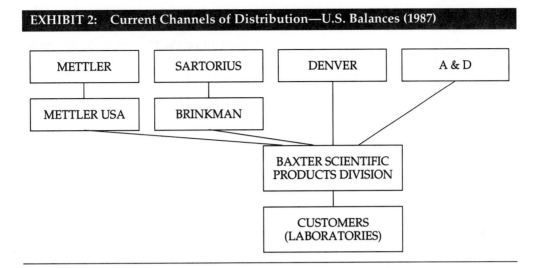

EXHIBIT 3   Five-Year Summary of Selected Financial Data

		1987	1986	1985	1984	1983
Operations	Net Sales	$6,223	$5,700	$2,446	$1,796	$1,834
(In Millions)	Operating Income	692	506	215	62	296
	Income from Cont. Operations	323	192	125	16	206
	Net Income	331	455	145	29	218
	Depreciation and Amortization	314	291	137	114	86
	Research and Development	199	203	125	109	106
Capital	Working capital	$ 881	$ 529	$1,240	$ 384	$ 461
Employed	Capital Expenditures	361	304	201	172	193
(In Millions)	Net Property, Plant, and Equipment	1,776	1,673	1,712	789	746
	Total Assets	7,638	7,258	6,994	2,001	2,127
	Net Debt	2,119	1,827	2,435	327	278
	Long-Term Obligations	1,723	1,609	2,623	206	226
	Stockholders' Equity	3,713	3,455	3,035	1,107	1,151
	Total Capitalization	5,436	5,064	5,658	1,313	1,377
Per Common Share	Average Number of Common Shares Outstanding (In Millions)	238	234	172	141	141
	Dividends Declared	.44	.40	.37	.33	.28
	Market Price—High	29.25	21.25	16.75	24.88	31.31
	Market Price—Low	16.00	15.13	12.50	11.75	20.00
	Net Book Value	11.79	10.88	9.33	7.83	8.17
Productivity Measures	Employees at Year-end	61,600	63,400	63,900	31,044	34,036

Medical Systems and Specialities focused on the technical aspects of the medical field. The company was a leading developer of diagnostic systems for disease testing in medical facilities. It also provided a variety of products used in cardiovascular medicine. Baxter also supplied hospital information systems linking medical and business departments and doctors' offices. Sales of the Medical Systems and Specialities unit were $1.5 billion in 1987. The company spent $199 million in research and development in 1987, primarily in this business segment.

The Alternate Site Products and Services business unit's focus was on filling the product and service requirements of patients being treated outside the traditional hospital environment. Baxter provided the supplies and equipment for intravenous nutrition, cancer therapy, antibiotic therapy, and dialysis therapy through a network of 150 centers. Worldwide sales were $1.1 billion in 1987.

The Scientific Products unit supplied laboratory equipment and supplies, industrial apparel, and static- and contamination-control products. The company focused on the continuing development of nonhealth-care markets. Worldwide sales in the scientific products segment were $355 million in 1987. (Exhibit 4 shows sales and growth rates of each of the four segments.)

About 21 percent of Baxter's sales were outside the United States. The company manufactured products in 23 countries and maintained sales offices in more than 100 countries. Economies of production and logistics brought about by the location of facilities worldwide, combined with the extensive breadth of Baxter's product line, gave the company a competitive advantage in the international marketplace.

Corporate management believed that the company faced two major tasks: realization of the full economic potential offered by the size and scope of the business, and positioning the firm to take advantage of the dynamic health-care field.

The size and scope of Baxter was the result of a careful consolidation of two health-care giants, Baxter-Travenol and American Hospital Supply. The two companies had been merged in 1985 to take advantage of opportunities for economic efficiencies. The two companies shared many markets and customers, but, at the same time, had few directly competing products. Health-care facilities were seeking efficiencies and cost savings of "one-stop shopping" from their suppliers, and the consolidation responded to that trend.

Health-care facilities had been aggressively seeking cost savings since 1983. Rising costs of health care and the prospect of continued increases had alarmed federal lawmakers, and in that year federal legislation was passed limiting the amounts that Medicare would pay for treatments. The law limited payments to fixed amounts for particular diagnoses or diagnostically related groups (DRGs). For example, the law would allow

EXHIBIT 4   Baxter: 1987 (Fiscal Year) Performance by Business Segment

	1987 Sales	Growth Rate	Operating Income
Hospital Products & Services	$3.4 billion	8%	$429 million
Medical Systems & Specialties	$1.5 billion	5%	$154 million
Alternate Site Products & Services	$1.1 billion	19%	$152 million
Industrial Products	$355 million	15%	$ 53 million

only a set amount for a broken arm. In the past, a hospital might keep a patient for observation, or might add treatments or therapy, charging additional amounts. Under the new law, only the fixed amount could be recouped by the hospital. Thus, profitability for medical facilities became an issue of cost containment, providing the required treatment most efficiently—with no extras.

The federal limits were often matched by similar restrictions by other insurance providers, the result of which was to create pressure to reduce operating expenses. The hospitals, in turn, applied pressure to their suppliers to reduce prices, lower costs, and improve efficiencies. Baxter management estimated that supply costs accounted for roughly 20 percent of a hospital's budget and another 20 percent was taken up by logistics and supply management. Thus, a company that could supply a large proportion of a hospital's needs would be in a position to have considerable leverage on cost containment.

The merger was not without difficulties, however. Oddly, Baxter-Travenol's sales were $1.8 billion at the time of the buyout, whereas American Hospital Supply's sales were $3.4 billion—almost double Baxter's! Baxter took on nearly $2 billion in debt in order to finance the purchase. Reorganization, the sale of several operating units, the elimination of about 6,000 jobs, and payment of staggering interest expenses followed the purchase.

A difficult part of the merger involved the differences in corporate cultures between the two companies. The Baxter side of the business was characterized as solid and stable, with its decisions being made on a slower timetable and from a centralized organization. American Hospital Supply, on the other hand, was generally decentralized and was characterized as "a bunch of hot-dog entrepreneurs going nuts."

In 1987 the company seemed to be following four basic directions. First, in the company's core business, health care, it focused on building a "partnership" with its customers. Systems for improving cost efficiencies, inventory and shipping controls, and internal policies and procedures were developed in an effort to go beyond the level of "peddling supplies." Second, the company expanded the level of expenditures on research and development. The goal of this program was to increase the ability of the company to command higher margins through proprietary products. A third effort involved increased capital expenditures. About $300 million per year was invested in improving manufacturing efficiencies through automation and improved materials handling. The fourth major thrust was to reduce the vulnerability of the company to changes in the domestic hospital business by expanding sales internationally and by increasing nonhospital sales.

BAXTER—SCIENTIFIC PRODUCTS DIVISION

The Scientific Products (S/P) Division was made up of two operating units: industrial and biomedical. S/P Industrial sold to research and development laboratories, quality control labs, and controlled-environment production areas in industry, education, and government.

S/P Industrial sales were $276.9 million in 1987, and they were forecasted to grow at an annual rate of approximately 10 percent over the next five years.

S/P Industrial divided its customer base into six segments: (1) pharmaceutical, (2) electronics, (3) biotechnical, (4) education, (5) federal, and (6) traditional laboratories. Each of the six customer segments was considered to be a separate market growing at a different rate and having different customer requirements. (Exhibit 5 shows the 1987 S/P Industrial sales by customer segment.)

EXHIBIT 5   1987 (Fiscal Year) S/P Industrial Sales by Customer Segment

Pharmaceuticals	$ 45.6 Million
Electronics	$ 47.4 Million
Biotechnical	$ 24.5 Million
Education	$ 34.6 Million
Federal	$ 3.8 Million
Traditional Labs	$121.1 Million
Total	$276.9 Million

S/P Industrial's product line included approximately 80,000 items. The company distributed the same products to all six customer segments, but in different proportions to each. (1986 sales by product line are shown in Exhibit 6.)

S/P Industrial operated out of 21 distribution centers across the United States. About 180 sales reps serviced the company's 63,000 industrial customers, focusing on large and medium-sized accounts. In late 1986, a telephone sales group was established in order to penetrate the smaller accounts and to allow the field sales reps to focus on the larger customers. Approximately 120 customer service reps were located at the distribution centers to support the sales force and to handle special customer needs. In addition to the internal support provided by Baxter, the sales force was supported by technical salespeople from the product manufacturers as well.

The sales force was organized geographically into five regions. Sales reps received extensive training in product, technical, and selling skills. Compensation took the form of commission based on profit margins achieved. The sales reps controlled the pricing for their accounts. S/P Industrial provided the reps with information on product costs, but it was up to the reps to negotiate with their customers to determine the actual prices. The commission rates varied with the level of profitability achieved, providing incentive for the sales rep to reduce prices where necessary to make a sale but to keep

EXHIBIT 6   1986 (Fiscal Year) S/P Industrial Sales by Product Type

	1986 Sales (Millions)
Supplies	$ 81.3
Equipment	52
Chemicals	43.8
Chromatography	5.6
Controlled Environments	46.7
Other	24.0
Total	$253.4

Note: Latest information available

prices high where possible. The compensation formula used by Baxter rewarded profitability. Even small increases in profit margins could, therefore, result in large increases in a sales rep's pay.

S/P Industrial utilized a product-management organization to stay abreast of market developments in each of the product lines and to maintain relations with the company's suppliers. The product managers specialized by product grouping and had the responsibility for improving sales and profitability for their products. In part, this was a function of determining which products should be included in the line and which products should be excluded. In addition, the role of the product manager involved the development of incentive programs and/or promotions for the sales force in order to publicize a particular portion of the line when an opportunity appeared.

THE S/P INDUSTRIAL MARKET

The industrial market was sensitive to real changes in the U.S. gross national product (GNP). Sales tended to outperform the GNP on both ends of the spectrum. When the GNP was showing strong growth, industrial lab sales tended to outperform that growth. When GNP was down, lab sales tended to be down even more. S/P executives explained the relationship by the willingness of industry to invest in research and development. In good times, industry tended to be willing to spend more on R&D than in difficult times.

Pharmaceutical Market

The pharmaceutical market included drug manufacturers, diagnostic and intravenous-solution manufacturers, and cosmetic companies. Generally, R&D expenditures equalled 13 percent of sales for major pharmaceutical companies. S/P's 1987 sales in the segment were $45.6 million. The total market was estimated to be $281.4 million, and growth was expected to be strong in the foreseeable future as a result of the increasing age of the U.S. population.

Electronics Market

The electronics market included manufacturers of semiconductors, circuit boards, disk drives, computer products, aerospace products, and general electronic products. Manufacturers in these industries were increasingly sensitive to production yields, and, therefore, were seeking improved quality in contamination and static-control products. The overall market size was $282.1 million, of which S/P sold $47.4 million in 1987. Electronics growth was expected to be high.

Biotechnology Market

The biotechnology market included both start-up companies such as Genetech as well as facilities supported by pharmaceutical, chemical, and food companies. Biotech was a very rapid growth market in which the technology was changing rapidly. It was expected to continue to spread into new industrial segments as new products and applications were developed. S/P 1987 sales were $24.5 million in the $194 million market.

Education Market

The education market consisted of public and private universities, junior colleges, and high schools. Limited growth was expected in this market, but the market was considered important by S/P management because product loyalty generated among students during their school years carried over into their buying habits in industry. S/P sales were $34.6 million in the $375 million market.

Federal Government

S/P Industrial sold only $3.8 million to the federal government in 1987. Government expenditures were approximately $158 million. Competition in the market was heavy, margins were tight, and difficulties in compliance with legal requirements made the segment less attractive. S/P executives believed that there was considerable opportunity in the future.

Traditional Laboratory Market

The traditional lab market was diverse and included water and environmental testing, food companies, chemical companies, quality assurance in manufacturing, medical-devices manufacturers, and many others. Traditional labs purchased a wide variety of items in all product categories. Growth in the market was closely tied to the GNP. The traditional market was the largest of the segments served, with S/P sales of $121.1 million, versus the market of $955 million.

COMPETITION

Competition in the industrial market was intense. Many of the products were supplied by manufacturers who made their lines available to multiple distributors. As a result, the competition tended to focus on pricing because the same products were available from other sources. Three distinct approaches to the market were evident among the major competitors. One approach was simply to offer to lower prices in order to protect volume. A second approach was to hold price levels by offering better, more-efficient service. The third approach was to obtain products on an exclusive basis, sometimes by self-manufacture.

The five largest competitors in the industrial market controlled nearly half of the market. The largest industrial competitor was Fisher Scientific, with 1986 industrial sales of $360 million equating to roughly 17.3 percent share of market. S/P Industrial, by comparison, had about 12.2 percent.

Although the large, national distributors accounted for nearly half of the market, small, regional distributors controlled roughly one-fourth of the market. The remaining fourth of the market was made up of manufacturer-direct sales. (The market share configuration of the industrial market is shown in Exhibit 7.)

The major distributors were not equally competitive in all of the industrial market segments. Baxter executives perceived Fisher to be the primary competitor in almost every market segment.

A recent evaluation of S/P Industrial's performance relative to competitors on a number of purchase criteria further indicated the intense level and nature of competition. Baxter was rated to be slightly behind the other distributors in the availability and use of automated-order-entry and inventory-control packages. Service levels and complete shipments were also slightly below those of competitors. Baxter prices were also marginally above the market. Baxter's major strength appeared to be the number and location of its distribution points.

EXHIBIT 7   1986 Market Share

Competitor	Market Share (%)
Fisher	17.3
S/P Industrial	12.2
VWR	12.0
CMS	3.4
Sargent	2.8
Regionals	26.8
Directs	25.5
Total	100.0

Fisher Scientific sold mainly to large customers. It had developed manufacturing capabilities in the areas of chemicals, equipment, and furniture. It had a strong national-accounts program and had established long-term relationships with many of its customers. In order to support its large customers, it had developed business-systems programs to ensure efficient order processing.

VWR Scientific tended to focus its efforts on the industrial market. It had concentrated its distribution points, maintaining a few, very large facilities in order to reduce operating costs. It had also entered into exclusive distribution agreements with some key suppliers. VWR seemed to be following a direction of focusing on frequently ordered, staple items. The high inventory turns were generated by acceptance of lower margins.

INDUSTRIAL BALANCES AND SCALES

Balances were used to accurately determine weights in the laboratory. There were two types of balances used in science and industry: mechanical balances and electronic balances.

Although it was obvious that the most important issue to a user of a balance was the accuracy of the weight displayed, other issues were important as well. Ease of use was important in terms of the ability to receive an accurate reading quickly without having to make time-consuming adjustments. Ease of reading the results also played a role.

In more sensitive balances, the issue of stability became important. Movements brought about by air currents in a room could cause the measurement to oscillate, not giving a "true" weight. Similarly, vibrations in a building brought about by machinery, or even traffic on nearby streets, could cause fluctuations in readings. In some instances, as in weighing liquids or volatile substances, or even in weighing live, moving animals, stability could prove to be a difficult problem.

Analytical balances offered a number of functions similar to those on sophisticated calculators. Weights could be manipulated mathematically, showing sums or differences, averages, etc. Readings could be communicated to other equipment, controls, or displays. Ranges could be displayed in a variety of units of measurement. Statistical calculations could be performed indicating, for example, whether the proper amount of liquid was being bottled on a production line.

Durability, need for repair, need for recalibration, ease of cleaning, and susceptibility to damage from spills, all played some role in the purchase decision. In many instances balances of a particular manufacturer were purchased simply because of the buyers' familiarity with that brand. Generally, buyers of scales and balances tended to stay with known suppliers, both for ease of using a familiar product and for risk avoidance.

The balances industry had undergone a worldwide revolution since the early 1970s. Prior to that time, balances had been primarily mechanical, or analog, in nature. The internal elements of the most sensitive balances literally rested on jewelled facets in order to provide the least resistance in the balancing process. The tooling and accuracy of construction was critical in order to provide accurate weights.

In the early 1970s, however, the development of electronic chip circuitry brought sweeping changes to the industry. As in the watch industry, the use of a microprocessor brought about vast leaps in accuracy and functionality. Further, the skills that had been so important in the manufacturing process for mechanical balances became far less important given the new technology. Manufacturing costs plummeted. Prices that had been as much as $5,000 to $7,000 per unit fell to $1,500 per unit. New producers found the entry barriers no longer insurmountable, and new competition emerged. At the same time, laboratories could now afford to purchase several balances of varying types rather than only one general-purpose balance.

In 1987, worldwide, there were only a handful of balance manufacturers who played a significant role in the market:

Mettler (Switzerland)

Sartorius (West Germany)

A & D (Japan)

Ohaus (United States)

Denver (United States)

Estimates of the 1987 U.S. industrial laboratory market for electronic balances varied considerably. Estimates ranged from $61 million to $96 million. One reason for the uncertainty over market size was the emergence of a private-label segment. Distributors who were selling private-label balances tended to be secretive about their volume for fear of harming relationships with branded manufacturers. (Estimated U.S. sales by manufacturer are presented in Exhibit 8.)

Until the mid-1980s, only Mettler, Sartorius, and Ohaus had played a significant role in the U.S. market. Their distribution channels and philosophies were similar. Both Mettler and Sartorius sold through separate import companies located on the East Coast. These import companies represented the manufacturers in the United States. Both importers maintained technical sales forces to support the distributors' sales people, and both provided service and repair functions. All three manufacturers used multiple distributors to market their products.

In the mid-1980s, pressures began to build, forcing distributor margins downward. The market had become "over distributed." Mettler products, for example, were available through more than 100 distributors. Buyers recognized that they were able to obtain the same products from many sources and, therefore, price-shopped from source to source to bring their costs down. Seeking to enhance profitability, several distributors sought out manufacturers with the capability of producing balances using the new microprocessing technology and created private-label relationships with them.

EXHIBIT 8   Laboratory Market Evaluation—Electronic Balances Only (Sales at Retail)

	$ (Millions)
Mettler	32–35
Sartorius	12–14
Ohaus	4–6
Denver	5–6
A & D	4–5
Others	4–5
Total	$61–71

Baxter had been a leader in the development of relationships with private-label suppliers. Arthur Long, the product manager responsible for balances in 1985, had conducted a series of negotiations with both A & D in Japan and with Denver Instruments in the United States. A & D was a new entrant in the international balance market and had been seeking means to establish distribution in the United States. Denver Instruments had been in the market for some time, manufacturing mechanical balances. Quality and technology issues had wracked the company, leaving little economic stability. Long-term quantity assurances from Baxter gave Denver the infusion of capital it needed to improve technology and production.

By 1987 private-label balances had captured a significant but indeterminate share of market. Fisher Scientific, among other distributors, had also begun to sell private-label along with branded lines. The private-label incursions into the market met with predictable unfavorable reactions by the branded manufacturers. Declining sales and reports of account "pirating" by their technical sales forces increased tensions between suppliers and distributors. When a laboratory inquired about buying a balance from one of the branded manufacturers, the inquiry was passed along to one of the distributors. Often the manufacturer and the distributor sent in their sales people on a joint call. The manufacturers were becoming reluctant to pass such opportunities along, believing that the distributors' sales people were trying to shift such leads to private-label products.

The motivation for such switching tactics was simple. The gross margins offered by private-label products were considerably higher than those offered by branded balances. The differences in gross margins resulted from several causes. First, overdistribution brought distributor selling prices down. Second, the private-label manufacturers lacked power in the bargaining process with distributors. Thirdly, both Mettler and Sartorius included an extra stage in their distribution channel, their import companies, Mettler U.S.A. and Brinkmann Instruments. Although these companies provided some valuable services, they also increased the prices to the distributors significantly. (Exhibit 9 shows Baxter costs and pricing for comparable products.)

By 1987, Baxter's electronic balance sales were more than one-third private label. Private-label balance profits contributed more than one-half of Baxter's total balance profits. (Sales by manufacturer and gross profits by manufacturer are shown in Exhibits 10 and 11.)

EXHIBIT 9   Examples of U.S. Pricing and Discounts, by Manufacturer

	Model	List ($)	Cost ($)	Estimated Brinkman Cost ($)
Denver	Z-210	1,695	744.00	
	Z-400	1,995	956.00	
	Z-2000DR	2,195	1,035.00	
Sartorius	H120	1,145	778.60	506
	E1220S	2,995	2,036.60	1,323
	E2000D	2,695	1,832.00	1,191
	A200S	2,595	1,764.60	1,147
A & D–S/P	B1240–1	2,295	1,123.00	

EXHIBIT 10   S/P 1987 Sales Distribution, by Manufacturer

Manufacturer	Proportion of S/P Balance Sales
Mettler	39.3%
Denver	20.8
Sartorius	18.1
A & D	14.4
Cahn	7.4
	100.0%

EXHIBIT 11   S/P 1987 Gross Profit Distribution, by Manufacturer

Manufacturer	Gross Profit
Denver	31.3%
Mettler	26.7
A & D	24.8
Sartorius	11.5
Cahn	5.7

THE MEETING: JULY 21, 1987

George Carson was seated at his desk disposing of some administrative trivia when, precisely at 8:00 A.M., Arthur Long and Julia Heldman knocked on his open door and entered his office. Both carried coffee mugs, and noting the look on Carson's face, Long inquired if he would like some. Carson declined and the ensuing explanations and sympathies took up the next few minutes.

"Okay, let's get down to business," suggested Carson. "You've had an opportunity to see a copy of the Mettler letter. I know that you haven't had the chance to study it thoroughly, but what do you think?"

Art Long shrugged his shoulders, "I think, first of all, that it is a good thing that we weren't caught completely by surprise. All of the work that we have been putting in on the balances market over the past six months at least has us up to speed. They beat us to the punch is all. Boy, were we right about the market having to change! Having this happen now...Well, thank God that we've done our homework. I can't believe that it is entirely coincidence that we already have a meeting set with Mettler in Switzerland on August 8."

"Art, what do you think that this letter means in terms of their willingness to accept our proposal?" asked Carson.

Long responded, "Well, it could really go either way. We have this big slide show proposal all set, trying to go around Mettler, U.S.A., and 'Bang!' here comes this letter out of Hightstown. I've got to believe that Mettler, U.S.A. got wind of our move to cut them out of the channel. My only question is where the letter originated. We got it from Hightstown, but they might have been told to send it by Switzerland. Either way, our proposal still makes sense. Mettler is looking for better sales in the U.S., and the only way that they are going to get them is to give better margins to the distributors. They can't do that and stay competitive in pricing without cutting out Mettler, U.S.A."

At this point, Julia Heldman entered the conversation. "I don't think that there is any question that this request for proposals came from Mettler, U.S.A. The way that this thing is worded is so far out of bounds that they just can't expect that anyone would take it seriously. Why, parts of it aren't even legal! You know as well as I do that Mettler, U.S.A. is having problems. Their volume has been off for what, the last five years? We've been hearing rumors that Switzerland has given them three years to turn a profit. They have to do something quick, and this is it!"

"It makes sense," agreed Long. "Mettler's manufacturing facility in Switzerland is fully automated, and they have spent a bundle to make it the best in the world. That is one reason that we would like to have them as a supplier. But, it costs them if the volume isn't there.... They can't leverage their costs against the big unit numbers. Our best guess is that they have been losing some share to Sartorius in Europe, and we've probably hurt them with Denver and A & D here in the U.S. Besides that, Mettler has a kind of different attitude about sales. They can almost afford to lose money on every sale.... They make it up on all of the servicing they do. So, I can see the Swiss pushing for improvement in the numbers out of Hightstown.

"But, there is a major problem here. The Swiss blame *us* for bringing Denver back from the grave and for opening the U.S. market for A & D. This is their biggest market, maybe 30 percent of their overall sales. So, they really don't like us very much. We've been having problems with Mettler, U.S.A. for several years. Our sales force probably has been trying to convert Mettler leads into A & D sales. And now, assuming that they know that we are trying to go direct to Switzerland around them, well, I think that we just got a 'drop dead' letter. They've already made up their minds."

Heldman turned to face Long, "They may have, but that just means that we'll have to change them back. We can't afford to ignore the world's leader in balances. They have what, a 40 percent share worldwide? When a lab is going to buy a new balance, the first thing that they think of is Mettler. As a salesperson you have to beat *them*, not the other way around. If we could get an exclusive with Mettler, S/P's sales and profits would go way up, not a doubt! We can show Switzerland that Hightstown hasn't been doing much of a marketing job for them. Working with the Swiss directly would clear up all of the difficulties that we have been having."

"I can't argue with what you are saying, Julia," Long responded. "But I can't believe that Mettler is going to give us an exclusive. They deal with Fisher exclusively in Canada, and they have done pretty well. Are they going to dump Fisher in the U.S.? Each of the four big distributors has its geographic- and industry-segment strengths. If they are going to go with anyone exclusively, it would probably be Fisher."

Long shifted in his chair a little uncomfortably. "I haven't brought it up before, but a couple of years ago I got a call from a headhunter. Mettler was looking for a vice president of marketing for the U.S. Anyway, the essence of the conversation was that they were looking for someone to take the company direct in the U.S.! Obviously, this guy didn't think about what he was telling me… Here I am working for the distributor, and he is telling me that Mettler is going to try to cut us out of the market. Well, anyway, they finally brought over this guy from Switzerland, and eventually he went back and took them direct *there*. They have been going that direction worldwide. I think that an agreement with them would be a three-year ticket to nowhere."

Unwilling to yield, Heldman calmly pointed out, "The bottom line is profit. The Swiss have been taking a beating on the exchange rates, and that has hurt them. That has about hit bottom. *And*, if we can eliminate the extra level in the distribution channel, we can give the Swiss much better profitability than they have been getting. It doesn't make sense that they would dump somebody who had accomplished that for them."

Carson during the debate had risen from his chair and had gone to the windows overlooking the beautifully landscaped Baxter campus. Recognizing that Heldman and Long had a considerable difference of opinion, he turned back to them and suggested that they should move on to cover some additional issues. "*If* Mettler forces an exclusive with Fisher, that would leave us with the private-label business and with Sartorius. Mettler isn't going to stand still for Fisher selling both. Where does that take your thinking?" In the ensuing silence Carson considered the "buzzed" feeling of his tongue and regretfully decided not to try a new cup of coffee quite yet.

Finally, Heldman said, "We have many of the same problems with Sartorius that we do with Mettler. They have been experiencing the same exchange-rate problems from Germany that Mettler has from Switzerland. They are almost as 'overdistributed' as Mettler. Their alignment with Brinkmann Instruments costs as much as Mettler, U.S. A. It may even be worse, because Brinkmann carries other products, too, so they don't provide the kind of service and marketing support that come out of Hightstown. In Brinkmann's case, the extra layer in the channel is costing about 36 percent. If I were Sartorius, I'd sure be taking a good look at getting rid of Brinkmann!"

Long chimed in, "That may be our big opportunity. Brinkmann hasn't been doing anything for Sartorius for some time. If Mettler goes exclusive, then what is Sartorius going to do for distribution?"

"But, Art!" Heldman protested, "Sartorius has had a relationship with Brinkmann since the end of the Second World War. Both of the businesses are family-owned, and the two family heads are personal friends. I just can't see Sartorius dropping Brinkmann. That does bring up another point, though. The inheritance laws in Germany are such that if Old Man Sartorius dies, the company might have to shut down in order to pay off the taxes!"

Long appealed to Carson, "I don't argue that, but that may be our leverage. We could develop some sort of arrangement to support Sartorius if that were to happen. As for the Brinkmann relationship, Sartorius' son is running the company now, and his ties are not as strong as his father's were. He has to see the 'writing on the wall.' He is going to lose out if he doesn't do something in the U.S. market.

"Besides, Sartorius has been gaining share worldwide. Their production facilities aren't quite as sophisticated as Mettler's, but the products that they are turning out are technically superior. They have been following a strategy of broadening their product line, specializing their balances for specific uses and industries. They have been very innovative in that way."

Heldman responded, "If we can't get Mettler, Sartorius might be an alternative, but, look at the risks. Right now Sartorius makes up about 18 percent of our sales, and about 12 percent of our profits in balances. That level of activity would have to go to 100 percent! That is a major jump! Sartorius is not as well known as Mettler, and Mettler has been outspending them on advertising as well."

Sensing another impasse, Carson decided to shift the topic again. "It seems to me that we have another option. Our private-label business is up to about 35 percent of our sales, and about 55 percent of our gross profits in balances. We have the added benefit of Denver being a domestic business. That can't help but make us look good—after all, we bailed them out. What are the possibilities of dropping both branded lines and going completely with private-label sources?"

This time it was Long who replied first, "George, I was the one who first negotiated the relationship with A & D. When I was in Japan in late 1985, it kind of hit home that they had more grasp of the technology than Denver did. As a result, they could probably take more cost out of the system than Denver could. Denver has extremely low manufacturing costs, but it seems to me that A & D has been doing some really innovative things in the way that they are making the product. I know that you weren't impressed with their plant. They are kind of a garage operation, but the way that they have figured out so that the balance parts only fit together one way makes their quality control excellent.

"The thing is that they just have more ability to do something with the technology than Denver does. They have done some really nifty things from the manufacturing standpoint. Everybody uses a cast-aluminum load cell. They made one with a precision stamping and it took two-thirds of the cost out of that part. Everybody said, 'Oh, no! You can't do that!' Well, they did it, and that is what is in their product."

Long thought for a second and then continued, "Kind of a negative and a positive at the same time.... A & D has no marketing understanding, no idea what the end user wants, the researcher. The products weigh, and weigh only, no specialty applications at all. When somebody weighs something, there's a reason behind it. A & D hasn't specialized with any direction to support that.

"The real negatives are that they have no U.S. support in terms of marketing and service. Nothing like what Mettler has. They have also been difficult to negotiate with. Not at all like the rest of the Japanese companies that we deal with. I have always had the feeling that they were not negotiating completely honestly. *That* is really different from the other Japanese companies. Maybe it is because the president has Chinese parents. Whatever it is, it is weird. We sit through their meetings and get this strange feeling. He just cuts out of the meeting, and there we are, his biggest customer. It just doesn't make sense."

Long concluded, "In my opinion, we can make A & D work and make it work very well. You may not agree with me on that, but we've taken a lot of market share with that line, we've made a lot of money with it, and it has done very well. We need to change some things. We need to do the service ourselves instead of farming it out. We would have to do the necessary marketing in order to really drive it, but I think that it would really be a winner."

Heldman added her thoughts about Denver Instruments. "Denver is a small, very adaptive company that would literally jump through hoops for us. With them we can, and have, actually designed a new product from start to shipment in 30 days. They have unbelievable response, but very little technology. They take apart a Mettler and copy it. What we have is a 'me-too' commodity product. They can't do much to develop the new and different features. They don't have an R&D center, although they do come up with some good software.

"They may have some problems with production and with making ends meet shortly. If Mettler can force an exclusive deal with Fisher, Denver could be in trouble. Fisher is their other customer. They private-label for both of us. If they lose Fisher, they are losing a chunk of business.

"We do make a lot of money with the private-label business, but the problem is that neither of our suppliers can provide us with the whole line. A & D only can give us good product in certain lines, and the same is true of Denver. We would have to deal with both in order to have even a reasonable line. That's why we have been working with both up to now. The problem is that we can't offer a consistent product throughout."

CONCLUSION

The meeting had lasted until just before noon. George Carson thanked his two product managers for their insights and called the meeting to a close. He looked out his windows again and decided that because his car had been sitting in the parking lot all morning, its temperature would not do much for his attitude. So, he headed back downstairs to the corporate cafeteria.

Along the way he reviewed the meeting. It was clear that Art Long had been leaning toward a private-label focus. Sartorius was a second choice, but Art liked the idea that he had been the major mover behind the A & D negotiations from the start. And, Carson reflected, he was right. It had been a darn good move at the time. But, was it still a darn good move?

Julia Heldman had backed Mettler as strongly as she could. She was right about a Mettler-S/P combination being a difficult team to beat. The problem was that the company had been losing share worldwide, yet it was still insisting on going direct. Given its relationship with Fisher in Canada, would it be willing to go with a different distributor in the United States? For that matter, would it be willing to drop Mettler, U.S.A.?

Carson selected broiled chicken breast and a salad, placed a glass of ice water on his tray, and decided—yes, he would have a cup of coffee after all. He again found a relatively quiet place to sit and continued to muse over the problem as he ate.

Heldman was also, apparently, not in favor of the private-label options. The money was good, but in the changing market for balances could the private-label manufacturers keep up technologically? And, for that matter, could S/P do the necessary marketing and support work? That would eat into their gross margins.

What would the other distributors do? The Mettler letter had been sent to them as well. Carson guessed that VWR would be happy to fall into line. They did not have much to lose. They liked to work for volume, so the low margins did not seem to bother them. Fisher was the likely candidate for Mettler to choose if it were going to go exclusive.

George was surprised as he looked at his watch. He had been sitting over his lunch longer than he thought. His own mandate from Baxter was to continue to grow his earnings at a 13 percent clip over the next five years. The balance decision would have an impact on that performance. Looking forward to his first sip of coffee of the day, he smiled and swallowed, only to find it was cold.

Alma Products, Inc.

John W. Mullins and Christina L. Grippi

It was a Monday morning in September in San Francisco, and Julie Brighton was in her office analyzing recent data regarding consumer buying and behavioral trends in the barbecue industry. According to the Barbecue Industry Association, consumers had spent $4.35 billion in 1992 on all barbecue-related items. This greatly excited Brighton because Alma Products, Inc., the new business venture that she had embarked upon with partner Jim Henly, intended to enter the barbecue market with its newly created charcoal starter. Once the company was realizing a profit, the plan was to gradually diversify, eventually building an entire line of barbecue-related items.

The latest demand information (see Exhibit 1) would be carefully analyzed by Brighton and Henly before they made a final pricing decision for the company's first two products, two models of a charcoal starter. It had been two months since the partners had engineered them, and although they had some idea what their competitors were charging for similar items, until now they had not had a clear picture of what the entire barbecue market looked like. It was now one week before their presentations for next spring's programs to the buyers for both Williams-Sonoma, a mail-order marketer based in San Francisco, and Builders Emporium, a chain of home centers in the Los Angeles metropolitan area. With this new industry and census data, the partners finally had as much information as they could get to make pricing decisions.

BRIGHTON AND HENLY

With an MBA from Stanford and 10 years in the retailing industry, Julie Brighton was a young businesswoman who had a restless urge for identifying and tackling new business opportunities. She had recently resigned her vice president's position with a leading retailer, where she had led the rapid growth of the chain's newest division from nine to 25 stores in just two years. Jim Henly, who had been a close friend of Brighton's since their time together in business school, worked full-time as a real estate broker and investor. He thought the two of them together could have some fun and make some money building a business around their simple but ingenious new product.

Like many entrepreneurs, Brighton welcomed the challenges that came with new business ventures, but was easily bored and disliked the bureaucracy usually associated with running older, larger companies. Hence, she hoped to build Alma Products into a

This case was prepared by Professors John W. Mullins and Christina L. Grippi of University of Denver, as a basis for class discussion. It is not intended to illustrate either effective or ineffective handling of an administrative situation.

EXHIBIT 1   Demand Data for the Barbecue Industry

Unit Sales: Barbecue Grills

Year	Charcoal	Gas	Electric	Total
1989	8,898,864	3,823,262	133,319	12,855,445
1990	8,661,621	4,002,279	190,809	12,854,709
1991	8,074,623	4,261,181	142,734	12,478,538
1992	7,946,738	4,283,387	155,895	12,386,020

Charcoal Briquette Sales—Tons

Year	Tons	% Change from Prior Year
1988	782,268	3.14
1989	745,317	(4.72)
1990	747,055	0.23
1991	752,699	0.75
1992	789,667	4.91

Selected Barbecue Industry Data

	1981	1991
% of households owning barbecue grills	79	83
% of households owning charcoal grills	73	62
% of households owning gas grills	15	54

Frequency of Barbecue Occasions

Barbecuing among Households Owning Grills, No. of Times/Year	% of Households[a]
More than 16	20
12–15	45
6–11	25
Less than 6	10

[a] According to the 1992 *Statistical Abstract of the United States,* the total number of households in the United States in 1990 was 94,312,000 and the total number of households in California was 10,381,000.
Source: Barbecue Industry Association and Alma Products, Inc.

thriving enterprise and then sell it. Brighton knew other entrepreneurs who had been quite successful at this practice. However, Brighton knew from experience that entering a market with the wrong introductory price could seriously undermine the success of any new product or business. For this reason, she planned on taking the next week to once again review all of the information related to costs, demand, target market, and the competition before determining a pricing structure for Alma's first products.

ALMA PRODUCTS, INC.

Initially, Alma Products planned to market only two products, namely, two models of the Easy Embers Charcoal Starter, ED-12 and ER-12. The ED-12, with its brightly colored label, was intended for sale through hardware stores, home centers, and discount department stores. The ER-12, packed in a sturdy reshippable cardboard box, was intended for sale through mail-order retailers such as L. L. Bean, Williams-Sonoma, and Camper's World. The charcoal starters were simply metal cylinders, approximately a foot high and tapered toward the top, with an attached wooden handle and a heat shield. Inside, a metal grate to support the charcoal was located two inches from the bottom.

Instructions for use were quite simple. Two sheets of newspaper were crumpled and stuffed underneath the grate; then the charcoal starter was set inside the barbecue. Charcoal was poured into the top and the newspaper lighted from holes along the bottom rim of the device. Once the coals were hot, they were ready to be dumped into the barbecue. The Easy Embers starter held up to 4½ pounds of charcoal briquettes, and Brighton's tests showed that it was twice as fast as using lighter fluid (10 to 12 minutes to start a typical 4-pound batch of charcoal, compared to 20 to 25 minutes for lighter fluid), which was the most prevalent method of starting barbecue charcoal. The tapered design concentrated the rising heat around each briquette, allowing an even burn and a hotter fire.

Brighton and Henly had designed the product after observing some campers light charcoal using a crude device made of a 3-pound coffee can with holes punched around the bottom and coat hanger wire.

The two of them had negotiated an arrangement with a local sheet metal fabricator, Santa Fe Engineering, Inc., to manufacture the Easy Embers in lots of 10,000 units at a cost of $3 each, which included all packaging, labor, and materials. Santa Fe was also charging a one-time tooling cost of $10,000 to make the dies with which the metal parts would be stamped. Furthermore, because Alma did not own a warehouse facility, Santa Fe agreed to ship finished products directly to Alma's customers using shipping labels and packing lists provided by Alma. The ED-12, intended for the retail market, would be shipped in a display carton of 12, and the ER-12, intended for mail-order retailers, would be shipped in cases of 12 individually boxed charcoal starters. Brighton estimated that freight charges to ship the products to Alma's customers would average $6 per case for small orders, and about $3 per case when 10 or more cases were shipped.

Another variable cost associated with the products included sales commissions to be paid to a manufacturer's representative agency retained a month ago. Davis & Davis Associates, whose other clients included well-known manufacturers of barbecue grills and other summer seasonal products, had agreed to a 10 percent commission on all sales made to retail stores and exclusive coverage of retail accounts in California. (The partners planned to obtain commitments from mail-order marketers themselves.) One of the main reasons for using the agency was cost: It would be much cheaper than hiring an internal sales force. Alma would simply pay the commission to the agency, which in turn was responsible for providing the salary, benefits, travel expenses, individual commission, and overhead expenses for each of its representatives. In addition, Davis & Davis had well-established contacts with the retail buyers in the barbecue industry, contacts that could take years for Alma to form on its own.

Fixed costs associated with running Alma were expected to be minimal. Henly, working full-time in the real estate industry, and Brighton, living off consulting income and savings from her career as a retailing executive, had both agreed to forego salaries for the first year of business. Using Brighton's home as an office for the company would save monthly rent expense, and for now, only a part-time secretary would be needed to help handle orders. Total monthly office expenses, including the phone and the secretary's salary, were expected to be around $500. Brighton thought that travel and other expenses that would be incurred in selling could be absorbed within this modest budget, at least in the first year.

TARGET MARKET

In its first year of business, Alma planned to target several national mail-order retailers, as well as retail stores located in California. Home centers, hardware stores, and mass merchandisers sold the most barbecue grills and would be the best retail distribution channels for the starters. Brighton's knowledge of retailing told her that these chains would require a 40 percent gross margin on an item like Easy Embers. Mail-order margins would probably be higher, in the area of 60 percent.

COMPETITION

In its home state of California, Alma found a few local retailers that sold a similar item, the Adamson QuickFire, for $9.95. However, this item was also new, and the manufacturer, Adamson Inc., did not appear to have established distribution with any large retail chains. Brighton and Henley looked in the stores of large chain retailers and found the QuickFire in none of them. The only stores that carried the QuickFire seemed to be small, individually owned hardware stores. A clerk in one of the small stores told Brighton that the store bought the QuickFires from "some guy from Berkeley." Brighton was able to find no telephone listing for Adamson Inc. in Berkeley or the surrounding area.

In the mail-order market, Brookstone featured a similar charcoal starter in its catalog for $16, and this product had been on the market for at least three years. Brookstone also carried this product, made by an apparently small company in St. Louis, in most of its nationwide retail stores.

Broader competition included manufacturers of electric charcoal starters, which sold for about $5.95 in most stores, and companies marketing charcoal lighter fluid. Lighter fluid still dominated the market for starting barbecue charcoal. A quart can of lighter fluid sold for about $2 in most stores, and contained enough fluid to start eight to 12 barbecue fires.

Brighton considered it a good sign that two other firms had found the charcoal starter idea a good one, and two direct competitors could hardly be regarded as market saturation. Although she knew that others could also enter the market, Brighton felt that large companies, such as those that made charcoal grills, would not bother with a market niche of this size.

THE PRICING DECISION

Brighton knew that by Friday, she needed to have price lists prepared for both models, the ED-12 for retail stores and the ER-12 for mail-order marketers. She was not yet sure whether a skimming or a penetration pricing strategy made more sense, or even whether she should employ the same strategy for both product configurations. She did know, however, that her decisions must include her intended prices to the consumer (even though she could not really control the retailers' pricing), as well as the prices she would charge the retailers and mail-order companies. Brighton and Henly had no expectations of making much money their first year in business, but they did want to be certain to at least break even on a cash basis. Henley expected that Brighton would take the lead in the pricing decision, given her retail marketing experience and her understanding of retailer and consumer needs. It was time to get started.

Southwestern Ohio Steel Company: The Consolidated Metal Stampings Decision

David W. Rosenthal

In October 1988, Dan Wilson, sales manager for Southwestern Ohio Steel (SOS), was concerned over the company's deteriorating relations with one of its larger customers, Consolidated Metal Stampings.[1] Wilson had received a telephone call from Consolidated's purchasing manager earlier in the week, who suggested that Consolidated might stop buying from SOS entirely if a proposed price increase went into effect.

Consolidated purchased roughly 30,000 tons of steel each year, 20 percent of which it bought through steel service centers, the remainder mill-direct. Consolidated contracted with suppliers on an annual basis, guaranteeing a certain tonnage at a specified price to be "released" as needed during the year. The price increase at issue was SOS's bid price for the coming year's contract.

The situation was complicated by the market supply of the grade of steel Consolidated would be buying. A shortage had existed for some time, causing many steel mills to place customers on allocation and bringing about price increases in the market from 10 percent to 20 percent in the past year. Even with the price increases, it was often difficult for users to obtain sufficient supplies. In fact, SOS's primary mill sources had established a deadline for placement of orders for the upcoming year. The deadline was today, and Wilson had not heard a definitive answer from Consolidated.

The price SOS had offered Consolidated was 10 percent over last year's prices, yet about 10 percent under the prevailing market prices. Wilson believed that the pricing was fair—but wondered what he should do. He could lower the price to Consolidated to the 1987 figure. He could lower the price but ask for concessions on shipping quantities and timing. He could simply place SOS's order for steel—without Consolidated's tonnage figured in. His recommendations had to be made quickly as they would affect the supply of steel from the mills for the coming year.

COMPANY AND INDUSTRY BACKGROUND

SOS was founded in 1945 to bridge the gap between the large order quantities required by steel mills in southwestern Ohio and the service requirements of regional businesses.

This case was prepared by Professor David Rosenthal of Miami University as a basis for class discussion. It is not intended to illustrate either effective or ineffective handling of an administrative situation.

[1]Company name disguised.

The company had grown consistently and was currently one of the largest steel service centers in the country.

Until 1985, SOS had operated as a family business, but with the retirement of the founder, the management had executed a leveraged buyout of the company.

SOS maintained three locations: Hamilton, Ohio; Middletown, Ohio; and Lawrenceburg, Tennessee. Each facility consisted of a processing center and warehousing and shipping facility. In addition to slitting and shearing machinery, and rack storage for steel coil, SOS also owned and operated a fleet of tractor-trailer trucks for the delivery of steel orders. In all, SOS employed about 400 people and shipped 285,000 tons of steel in 1987.

The role of steel service centers in the market had grown considerably over the past decade. Traditionally, steel service centers had taken large shipments of steel in the form of master coils from mills, and had, in turn, sold smaller quantities to users who did not require sufficiently large amounts to buy direct. The service centers were able to purchase sufficient quantities to receive price discounts from the mills and were able to command price premiums from the smaller buyers.

Although the traditional "bulk breaking" role continued, new functions and services had been developed. One such service was slitting the coiled steel lengthwise to meet the manufacturing needs of the users more closely. The result was to reduce the amount of scrap generated by the users. In some cases, the users who had been doing their own slitting found that the service center could do the task more efficiently and, hence, at lower cost than they could internally.

Similarly, "levelling" or "cut to length" were services that were increasingly provided by service centers. Some users found it to their advantage to have the coils unrolled and flattened, and pieces cut to specified rectangular dimensions, then stacked for use.

Quality control, metallurgical assistance in design and material specification, and inventory management had all increased the role of steel service centers in the market. The advent of "just-in-time" (JIT) inventory systems had increased demand from the service centers dramatically. For even some of the largest steel users, the instant inventory required by JIT was not available directly from the mills. As a result, service centers were increasingly used as a source of fast inventory supply.

SOS was considered by steel users to be one of the best-quality service centers in the United States. On-time delivery, quality of material provided, and price level were the normal criteria on which service centers were evaluated, and SOS was generally perceived to be among the best suppliers on each concern.

Additionally, in times of short supplies, users of steel were strongly concerned over the ability of a service center to provide continuity of supply. A supplier without metal was of no help to users. Thus, the relationship of a service center with a particular steel mill was often an important consideration in placing an ongoing order. If a service center had a strong relationship with a particular mill or mills, it could be expected to have metal available consistently. SOS was widely known to have strong ties to Armco Steel in Middletown, Ohio, thus providing it with an edge over competition in both supply and material quality.

The increasing share of market served by the steel service centers had caused some of the steel mills to begin to take steps to recapture lost sales. Some of the actions included changes in pricing structures, shipping priorities, and outright purchases of service centers by the mills. SOS, however, was the second-largest customer of Armco, and the two companies had worked closely over the years to maintain a quality relationship and even to build new business jointly.

Nationally, the relationship between mills and service centers was changing. Service centers had gained significant share of market, but the mills were beginning to strike back with pricing structures that were more favorable to end users and less favorable to service centers, generally. (See Exhibit 1.) In fact, sales by service centers were flat in 1988.

RECENT COMPANY PERFORMANCE

SOS had been experiencing a period of exceptional growth in sales, both in terms of tons and dollars and share of market. In 1985, SOS shipped approximately 215,000 tons of steel. In 1987 the level of shipments had risen to nearly 300,000 tons. Projections called for the growth to continue, reaching shipments of almost 400,000 tons in 1990. (See Exhibit 2.)

SOS's solid performance was in large part the result of management's dedication to improved information and control systems. The company boasted an advanced, custom-designed, computerized inventory control and materials management system that enabled customer inquiries about availability and status of orders to be answered instantly.

The company also had added new high-speed slitting lines and a tension levelling line that was one of the most advanced in the industry. The investment in new equipment allowed SOS to improve production efficiency and to improve the quality of output significantly. Thus, for some items that required straight cuts or square dimensions or exceptional flatness within close tolerances, SOS was the only supplier considered by some buyers. Additionally, Statistical Process Control (SPC) was increasingly being required by steel purchasers. SPC referred to a system of production controls and documentation that showed conformance with specifications on an ongoing basis. The automotive industry was particularly concerned with SPC because of its commitment to JIT, and other industries seemed to be following. SOS was an industry leader in the application of SPC in its production.

SOS's sales mix reflected the changes in demands for various types of products and the company's investments in production facilities. The value-added portions of the business, slit coil and cut-to-length were increasing in volume. (See Exhibit 3.)

EXHIBIT 1:   The "Crossover" Change in Mill Pricing Policies

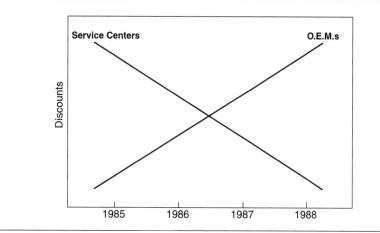

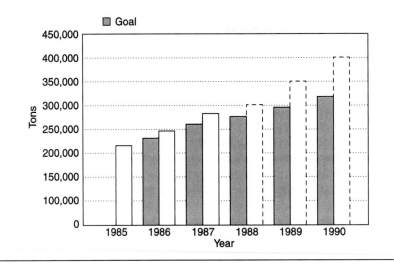

EXHIBIT 2: SOS Shipments (Tons): Actual Versus Projected

MARKETING OF SHEET AND STRIP STEEL

SOS segmented its market into (1) "inquiry" or "spot" buyers and (2) "contract" buyers. Inquiry or spot buyers bought material on an as-needed basis in order to meet changing needs. An order could consist of anything from a few thousand pounds to several truckloads. Inquiry accounts bought on an irregular basis but were not necessarily small accounts.

Inquiry accounts were often approached by SOS representatives with special offerings. As a result of mill overruns, mill errors in the chemical composition of a quantity of steel in its production, or mill-direct customers cancelling orders, SOS was often able to buy steel at less than its normal cost. When such an opportunity occurred, SOS salespeople would contact those buyers who could use that particular type of steel and

EXHIBIT 3   SOS Sales Mix by Product Type

	Typical Month			
	1986 Shipments Tons/Month	Percent of Shipments	1987 Shipments Tons/Month	Percent of Shipments
Stock	1,472	7.0	1,307	5.4
Slit Coil	13,975	66.9	17,379	72.0
Cut To Length	2,618	12.5	2,799	11.6
High-Volume Blanks	1,395	6.7	1,390	6.0
Manual Shearing	1,332	6.4	1,110	4.7
Safe Edge	95	.5	67	.3
	20,887	100.0	24,052	100.0

"inquire" about their needs. In many instances SOS could provide usable material to a buyer at significant savings over prevailing market prices.

Contract accounts tended to buy steel on the basis of a yearlong agreement for a supplier to provide material at a specified quantity and price over the length of the contract. Specific shipments of steel were "released" against the overall contract on a schedule determined in the contract negotiations. Contract accounts were often large, and the materials were used on a relatively stable basis. SOS management indicated that sales (tonnage) were split roughly 50–50 between contract and inquiry.

SOS also segmented its market according to geography. By its nature, steel engendered high transportation costs. Shipments beyond 150 to 200 miles were generally unfeasible because of the additional costs. SOS customers were typically located within this distance from the warehouses in Hamilton and Middletown, Ohio, and Lawrenceburg, Tennessee. The geographic distribution of SOS sales is shown in Exhibit 4.

SOS's top 200 customers accounted for nearly all of the company's tonnage, but no individual customer accounted for more than about 3 percent. Similarly, SOS sold to a diverse mix of customers, who used the steel for everything from automobiles to office furniture. No one industry accounted for more than 15 to 20 percent of SOS's sales. (See Exhibit 5.)

SOS maintained a sales staff consisting of both "inside" and "outside" sales personnel. The inside staff consisted of 13 salespeople. They were responsible for customer service, order placement, order facilitating, and scheduling shipping. Much of the inside salespeople's time was spent on the telephone, either answering customer questions about availability of material or status of shipments, or making price quotes. Inside salespeople were also responsible for making offering calls and entering orders or releases into the system.

It was common for buyers to develop a strong professional attachment to their assigned inside salesperson. The salesperson had access to the records of purchases made, the materials used, the prices charged, and the market availability. At a given point, a buyer could have literally hundreds of orders in process. An inside salesperson, knowing the customer's portfolio well, could provide invaluable service in tracking orders

---

EXHIBIT 4   SOS Geographic Sales Distribution

Geographic Market	1986 Percent of Sales	1987 Percent of Sales
Tri-State Market (OH, KY, IN)	64.0	64.8
Lawrenceburg Market (TN, AL, MS, GA, LA)	18.6	15.6
Eastern Market (VA, NC, WV, PA, NJ, SC, FL, MD)	7.8	9.9
North/Northwestern Market (IA, MI, IL, NE, WI)	5.3	7.4
Southwest Market (MO, AR)	3.5	2.3
Other	.8	.0
	100.0	100.0

EXHIBIT 5   SOS: Percent of Shipments by Industry

Industry	1986	1987
Appliance	12.0	15.6
Automotive Direct	3.3	4.0
Automotive Related	11.7	8.0
Construction Related	9.4	7.8
Office Furniture	7.3	7.5
Shelving	6.2	5.6
Heating and Air Conditioning	5.9	3.9
Tool Boxes	5.7	5.3
Electrical Closures	4.7	6.9
Farm Gates and Products	4.6	6.1
Health Care and Caskets	3.0	3.7
Recreational Equipment	2.8	1.7
Furniture Hardware	2.3	3.9
Small Manufactured Pdts	17.8	17.5
	100.0%	100.0%

and in offering special opportunities as they arose. Buyers often insisted on talking with only "their" inside salesperson because of their knowledge and expertise.

SOS's six outside salespeople were responsible for actually visiting the steel users' production facilities, meeting with the buyers and the production people. The outside salespeople's responsibilities included prospecting for new accounts, evaluating production items and making recommendations for the steel requirements, and examining rejected steel and making arrangements for its dispensation. The outside salespeople worked closely with the inside salespeople to first determine the needs of the users and then to service those needs accurately on a long-term basis.

SOS had recently initiated an ongoing research project to track trends in buyer needs, perceptions, and behavior. Several trends had become evident from the research. First, JIT inventory, or at least approximations of JIT, was increasingly being followed by steel users. The result of the increased attention being given to inventory levels was that lead times for suppliers such as SOS in providing materials were being shortened considerably. Safety stocks were being lowered as well. Buyers often required steel service centers to provide material with only 24 hours advance notice, although the average lead time was approximately one week.

Because lead times and safety stocks were being cut, quality control issues were becoming more important. Users simply could no longer afford to have a nonconforming shipment because they did not have the material available to continue manufacturing while the unsatisfactory material was replaced.

Secondly, there was a trend for larger, process-oriented steel users to reduce the numbers of their suppliers. The necessity of exchanging information on production scheduling, materials, and inventory needs made working with more than a very few suppliers unwieldy and inefficient. As a result, large buyers of steel had been looking for means of evaluating suppliers and limiting the number from whom they bought.

Thirdly, the trend of buying from service centers rather than direct from mills continued. The research findings indicated that the buyers simply did not perceive the mills as being able to provide sufficiently fast turnaround on orders to make them compatible with JIT systems.

THE CURRENT SITUATION

SOS had been selling steel to Consolidated Metal Stampings since 1965. Consolidated bought roughly 30,000 tons of steel each year, about 80 percent of which was bought mill-direct. The remaining 20 percent was bought through steel service centers. Over the past few years, Consolidated's steel usage had increased at the rate of about 3 percent per year.

Consolidated bought from service centers on a contractual basis, and contracts were let on a yearly basis. Typically, there were about 20 service centers who bid on the Consolidated contracts each year. For the most part, SOS had fared better than most of the other service centers on Consolidated's quotations. The reason for SOS's success was attributed to its proximity to Consolidated's manufacturing facilities, which enabled SOS to enjoy a slight freight advantage over the competitors. (SOS sales to Consolidated for the past four years are shown in Exhibit 6.)

The service-center portion of Consolidated's steel purchases was particularly attractive to the service centers, and as a result, the competition among suppliers for the contracts was termed by SOS management as "brutal." The Consolidated package offered large tonnage, relatively stable orders, and very simple quality requirements. The steel was to be used for unexposed parts, making the finish/surface requirements unimportant. The order consisted mostly of hot-rolled, pickled, and oiled (HRPO), one of the lowest grades of steel.

At the same time, the Consolidated account was not without its difficulties. Over the past few years the service requirements of the Consolidated account had become increasingly stringent. Items that had been released in truckload quantities in the past were now being released in 5,000-pound and 10,000-pound increments, thus increasing the number of transactions and shipments without increasing the weight. Because service centers sold by weight, the increased costs of shipping were eroding the profitability of the account. In addition, deliveries that had been full truckloads every third day had been changed to less-than-full truckloads delivered daily. The vendors had generally been forced to absorb these additional costs, probably about 1 percent of selling price, because of competitive pressure.

Recent market events had created a shortage of HRPO products at the mill level. Some of the large steel mills had taken furnaces offline for repair and upgrading. At the

EXHIBIT 6 SOS Sales to Consolidated Metal Stampings

	Year			
	1987	1986	1985	1984
Tons	4,200	2,500	2,500	3,000

same time, some of the mills had shifted their product offerings away from the low-priced, low-margin HRPO products. The result had been a tight supply of HRPO in the market, and many mill-direct customers had been placed on an allocation, including SOS.

Because of the shortfall in HRPO and aggressive pricing on the part of the mills, prices of HRPO on the spot market had risen steadily over the past year. Market prices now averaged $520 per ton, about 10 percent to 20 percent over last year's prices, but demand had not slackened, and inventories of HRPO were low. Users of this type of steel were able to substitute other materials, but usually of a higher quality and cost per pound. The better-grade materials were available in quantity, whereas HRPO was often difficult to locate. SOS's market intelligence indicated that the shortage conditions were not likely to change over the next year.

Consolidated's call for bids had gone out only a few weeks before, but during the past six months SOS salespeople had steadily passed on the message to Consolidated's buyers that the market was tight, and that under the allocations prevalent in the market some price increases were inevitable.

Over the past three years SOS had been holding the price of HRPO stable for Consolidated. In fact, Consolidated had not paid a single increase over that time. The current bid was $450 per ton, exactly 10 percent over last year's price, but SOS market intelligence told them that the bid price was about 10 percent *under* the prevailing market price, and slightly lower than the prices offered by other bidders. Wilson, in agreement with SOS management, believed that the offer had been more than reasonable under the circumstances and was, therefore, somewhat surprised by the harsh response of the Consolidated management. However, given some changes in the management of Consolidated, they were not totally shocked.

In 1985, Ben Ingalls was appointed president and CEO of Consolidated. Ingalls was a cost-cutting expert from the automotive industry and was well-known for his tough dealings with vendors in contract negotiations. Since his coming on board, Consolidated had removed several longstanding vendors of other products, solely for price reasons. In the view of SOS management, the 1986 and 1987 steel service center negotiations had deteriorated to a crisis atmosphere, with SOS kept in the dark until the final award was made. It became apparent over this time that Ingalls had been playing a major role in raw-materials purchase decisions.

THE TELEPHONE CALL

On November 16, 1987, Frank Shields, the purchasing manager for Consolidated, called Dan Wilson to respond to the SOS bid. Wilson had been calling Shields repeatedly during the previous week in order to find out how things stood. Armco had originally given SOS only until November 13 to place its order for the first quarter of 1988, but Wilson had asked them to postpone their deadline for one week, until he could obtain a commitment from Consolidated.

In previous conversations Wilson had learned that SOS's prices had been the lowest of the service centers who had bid, and that Shields was going to recommend that SOS receive the business at the 100 percent level. SOS had actually placed two bids, one offering a specific level of prices for a partial commitment of Consolidated's needs, and a lower level of prices for a contract covering all of Consolidated's service center needs.

Shields opened the conversation, "Dan, I'm sorry about taking so long to get back to you on this, but we've been having lots of discussions on the bids we received. I guess it is no secret that we are under some serious pressure to keep our manufacturing costs down. This tight market really has us over a barrel, so we've been exploring some options."

"That's okay, Frank," Wilson replied, mustering as much warmth to his voice as he could. The buyer for Consolidated had known about two months previously that the deadline was approaching and that SOS would need a solid answer. "What sort of options are you thinking about? Maybe we can help."

"Well, look. We just can't live with this 10 percent increase in material costs over last year. I know that you are doing your best to give us the best price you can, but it just isn't good enough. Somehow we've got to find a way to reduce the unit cost on HRPO. Is there anything that you can do for us?" Shields urged.

"Not really, Frank. Even if we have a commitment from you for 100 percent of Consolidated's service center orders, we still can't go below the price that we quoted you. You know as well as I do how tight the market is. Why, we could sell the same steel that we are offering you for a 10 percent premium over the price we quoted you. We want your business, you know that, but we have to have an answer in to our supplier by Friday," said Wilson.

"I know, and I recommended to the president, Ben Ingalls, that we accept your bid, and at the 100 percent level. We have had good service from SOS over the years, and the price was the best that we could expect to see, given the circumstances. But Ben was adamant that we couldn't absorb a 10 percent increase," said Shields.

"Frank, have him call our president. Maybe if he hears it straight from the horse's mouth instead of through us, then he'll recognize the kind of a deal we are offering. But, we just can't go any lower…Not without taking all of the profit out of it for us. And at this point we can't even go back to the supplier. They would just laugh at us if we asked for price concessions from them at this late date," Wilson noted as one of his sales people handed him a telephone memo.

"I'll ask him, but from past experience, I already know the answer. Ben Ingalls just doesn't believe in speaking with vendors, or getting to know them in any way. I do wish we could clear this mess up. God knows that we don't want a slitter in here…"

"Okay, but don't wait on this. We've only got until Friday, and our supplier won't allow us another extension," said Wilson.

"We'll get you an answer. As you know, I'm recommending that SOS be awarded 100 percent of the business at the prices you've quoted. Ten percent seems like an awful lot, but in today's crazy steel market, it really isn't that bad. Dan, just don't cut me off! I think that SOS should make sure that I'm covered."

As he ended the conversation, he wondered what Shields had meant about a slitter. It would cost Consolidated $750,000 to $1 million to install a slitting line, and at the same time, their costs would go up as a result of the space requirements of the line, the storage requirements for the steel to be cut, and the inventory that had already been cut. Additional carrying charges and scrappage would probably top off the costs of a new line, making the real cost of material as high as ever…*If* they could find the steel in the first place.

Wilson estimated that Consolidated would incur direct slitting costs of about $10 per ton, scrappage costs of $20 per ton, holding costs of $10 per ton, and allocation for space and overhead anywhere from $5 to $15 per ton. Still, at $400 per ton, the price of steel would look attractive if they bought mill-direct, and the mills were certainly doing all that they could to recapture end users' business. Frequently, these additional costs were either not considered or underestimated by users, but Shields had seemed to have a good grasp of the real cost situation.

WILSON'S OPTIONS

The telephone conversation had occurred on Monday, and as of today, Friday, neither Wilson nor SOS's president, Timothy Harson, had heard further from Consolidated. In the meantime, the mill had called several times asking for SOS's order quantities and configurations.

One option was for Wilson to reduce the prices offered to a 3 percent to 3.5 percent maximum increase. The indications were that a price reduction of this magnitude would be required in order to gain Ingall's approval. Wilson felt confident that Consolidated would accept such an offer immediately. SOS could justify such a reduction only by assuming they would underwrite the account through this difficult period, then make up profits in future years.

From a financial standpoint, Wilson wondered at the extent of the losses to SOS, and in addition, he thought that he ought to consider the profits that were being missed by not selling the same tonnage to other customers at the higher market prices. Generally speaking, a good rule of thumb for pricing was that 2,000 tons of steel sold for $1 million. Most service centers achieved a 2 percent to 4 percent profit before tax.

Wilson was concerned over the response of other customers if and when they learned of the success of Consolidated in "beating down" SOS's prices. Price protection and stability were valued by steel users, and SOS had gained considerable business over the years by dealing honestly and fairly with their customers in times of price instability.

A smaller price reduction together with concessions on delivery and transportation would provide a better financial package to SOS. By shipping full truckloads, and strict adherence to a delivery schedule, Wilson estimated that SOS could save as much as 1 percent of sales to Consolidated.

In the past Consolidated had been unwilling to fulfill its obligations on such contract covenants. Consolidated had sought bids and signed contracts for specific quantities of steel, and then had actually released as little as 35 percent to 50 percent of that amount. Shipping requirements of full truckloads had been ignored, and schedules had varied widely. Further, Wilson had no assurance that such a plan would be acceptable to Consolidated management either in terms of price or conditions, and he was running out of time to place SOS's order.

Wilson's other option was simply to place the order without Consolidated and to use the steel to supply other SOS customers who were clamoring for HRPO. Once the commitment was made to these other customers, SOS could not supply Consolidated if they turned around and wanted to buy through SOS.

Consolidated had consistently been one of SOS's largest customers, often ranking in the top 25. Wilson was proud of the increases in sales to Consolidated over the past year or two, because Consolidated had cut the number of suppliers they used down to only a handfull. SOS's quality and service levels were clearly making an impression.

Consolidated had been a regular customer of SOS for more than 25 years, and the entire SOS organization felt that some loyalty was appropriate. Market conditions shifted, but longterm customer relationships were difficult to establish and maintain. In the difficult market that currently existed, Wilson felt that cutting Consolidated off could damage relations to the extent that they might never order from SOS again. Driving customers into the arms of the competition was not consistent with SOS's growth plans, nor management philosophy. In fact, Tim Harson, the CEO of SOS had commented to Wilson on the Consolidated situation, "It has been a longstanding SOS policy not to allow a foolish short-term decision to affect a long-term relationship. Let's not start now."

Wilson believed that the pricing had been fair, but only under the prevailing market conditions. If the market were to ease, then the prices would come down, and the levels sought by Consolidated could be reasonable after all. The forecasts indicated that it would be a year before supply was plentiful, but the forecasts had been wrong before.

Wilson glared at the papers on his desk and contemplated giving Consolidated one last telephone call. Their supplier could not wait any longer, and he had put in too much time on this one issue already.

Jefferson-Pilot Corporation

Lew G. Brown and Michael J. Cook

JEFFERSON-PILOT: 1993

On February 28, 1993, Roger Soles, Jefferson-Pilot's (J-P) president, chairman of the board, and chief executive officer for the last 25 years, retired. J-P Corporation had 1992 revenues of $1.2 billion from its four business segments (individual, group, casualty and title insurance, and a communications group) and from investment income.

Soles had used a strong leadership style to guide J-P during his tenure. Decision making and management had a top-down focus, and Soles exercised a high level of control. Despite J-P's success under Soles' leadership, however, revenues had been basically flat for the last five years (1988 to 1992). Low interest rates, which affected investment earnings, and declining life insurance sales contributed to the sluggish revenues and earnings. The corporate culture also seemed resistant to change and fixed on retaining the status quo—the traditional way of doing things.

J-P's board of directors felt the company needed aggressive new leadership if the company was to be a market leader. In order to provide for a smooth transition after Soles' retirement, the board selected David A. Stonecipher to become president-elect and brought him on board in September 1992. Stonecipher had been president and CEO of Life of Georgia, an Atlanta-based insurance company. He also served as president of Southland Life Insurance Company and had recently become president of GeorgiaUS Corporation, the parent company of both Life of Georgia and Southland Life.

Stonecipher had a reputation as an aggressive, outgoing leader who was willing to change and try new things. He realized that increased sales would be the key to J-P's revenue growth and that he needed a strong management team if he was going to make the necessary changes. With that in mind, one of his first acts was to appoint Kenneth Mlekush as executive vice president of Individual Insurance. Mlekush, who had previously served as president and CEO of Southland Life, brought more than 30 years of experience to the position and specialized in marketing individual life and annuity products. Mlekush later asked Ron Ridlehuber, who had worked with him at Southland, to join J-P as senior vice president for Independent Marketing. Ridlehuber had 18 years of experience in marketing and field sales management. Stonecipher also promoted Bill Seawell from his position as an agency manager in J-P's career sales force to serve as senior vice president for Ordinary Marketing. Seawell had been with J-P since

This case was prepared by Professor Lew G. Brown and Michael J. Cook, MBA, of University of North Carolina at Greensboro, as a basis for class discussion. It is not intended to illustrate either effective or ineffective handling of an administrative situation. The authors express their appreciation to Jefferson-Pilot Corporation for its cooperation in developing this case.

1976 and had managed the Greensboro agency since 1981. During that time, the Greensboro agency had consistently been among J-P's leading agencies.

A STRATEGIC REVIEW

After assembling his management team, Stonecipher asked a major consulting firm that specialized in working with life insurance companies to conduct a strategic marketing review of the firm. Now, in early 1993, Stonecipher had assembled the new team in a conference room in the firm's corporate offices in Greensboro, North Carolina, to hear the consultant's report. He knew this report would provide a basis for the strategic decisions the group would have to make if the company were going to meet the board's and the shareholders' expectations. The managers knew that a key focus of the report and of the decisions facing them would be how J-P should structure and manage its sales force because life and annuity sales would need to grow dramatically in order to increase revenues significantly.

J-P'S SALES FORCE

J-P distributed its individual insurance products through three separate systems: career agents, independent producing general agents, and financial institutions. J-P hired career agents and provided them with extensive training, an office, and full staff support. The company paid the agents a salary subsidy during their training year and then changed them to a commission-only basis. The agents earned a commission on the premiums each policy generated. The agent earned a higher commission rate on the first-year premium and then earned a lower commission rate on renewal premiums thereafter as the policyholder renewed the policy year after year. The career agents were very loyal. In fact, the company was very selective in choosing career agents. Becoming one was difficult, and those who were successful were very proud of their position. However, growth based on a career system was slow, and the costs of maintaining the sales force were high.

In early 1993, J-P had approximately 800 career agents. They sold about 90 percent of its life insurance policies. Agents on average during 1992 wrote about 30 policies and earned about $26,000 in first-year commissions (the commissions paid on the policy's first-year premium). The first-year commission rate averaged 50 percent of the first-year's premium. The average career agent earned total income, including commissions on renewal policies, in the high $40,000 range. Bill Seawell was responsible for managing the career sales force.

At the beginning of 1993, there were approximately 1,400 independent personal producing agents (PGAs) distributing J-P's life and annuity products. Twelve salaried regional directors recruited about 15 to 20 PGAs each year, seeking agents who were already established in the insurance business. Although the independent agents did not work directly for J-P, the company provided extensive training and support. The PGAs allowed J-P to extend its marketing operations (in a limited way) beyond its core geographic distribution areas. Although there were more PGAs than career agents, many of them sold few J-P policies each year. They had contracts with J-P as well as with other insurance companies and could sell policies offered by any company they represented. First-year commission rates on policies PGAs sold were in the 80 percent to 85 percent range. These rates were higher than those for career agents because J-P did not pay any of the PGAs' expenses, as it did for career agents. Ron Ridlehuber was responsible for managing the independent sales force.

J-P also used an additional distribution channel consisting of 19 relatively small community banks and savings institutions that contracted to distribute life and annuity products. J-P designed the annuity products for these institutions and controlled pricing.

(Exhibits 1 and 2 present financial data on Jefferson-Pilot, and Appendices I and II present information on the life insurance industry and J-P.)

THE CONSULTANTS' PRESENTATION

David Stonecipher glanced around the conference room to make sure everyone was ready. "Well, gentlemen, let's begin." Aaron Sherman and Larry Richardson, who directed the project for the consulting firm, began the presentation.

"Gentlemen, I have given each of you a detailed report summarizing our findings. We wanted to meet with you today to present an overview of the key points and to answer any questions you have," Aaron Sherman said. "As you are aware, we began this process by holding a workshop with J-P's executives at which we asked them to rate issues the company faces. The number one issue they identified was the fact that your total annualized premium income has declined during the past five years while most of your major competitors' revenues have grown. Although J-P has an excellent core of field and home-office people and is in excellent financial condition, our analysis highlights areas where you need to take action.

Target and Managerial Peer Companies

"In conducting our analysis, we looked at a group of 13 companies, seven of which we call *managerial peers* and six of which we call *target companies*. The target companies are those you face on a day-to-day basis in competing for policyholders and new agents. Some of these operate using a *general agent*, that is, an independent agent who is not a company employee. The managerial peer companies are those you compete with when you sell policies or recruit agents, but all of them use a career system like J-P, with agency managers who are responsible for the agents who work out of their offices. J-P has the highest rating in terms of claims-paying ability from both A.M. Best and Standard and Poor's rating services. Only five of the 13 peer companies have similar ratings. Some of your agents see the company's financial strength as a competitive weapon, while some others question whether the company has been too conservative.

Performance Analysis

"This overhead (Exhibit 3) presents a summary of your operating performance over the 1987 to 1991 period as compared with the 13 target and managerial peer companies. As you can see, premium income and net gain before dividends have grown more slowly than the target group's average but faster than the managerial peers' average. Over this same period, the number of J-P's career-ordinary life agents has shrunk from 1,186 to 546. As a result, you have seen a decline in the percentage of your total premium income coming from life insurance. This results also from a decline in the number of policies written and in the face amount per policy. It also appears that the productivity of your agents has lagged behind competitors. You also rely heavily on the business you develop in North and South Carolina and Virginia, as this overhead indicates (Exhibit 4).

EXHIBIT 1   Consolidated Statements of Income (Dollar Amounts in Thousands Except Per Share Information)

Jefferson-Pilot Corporation and Subsidiaries

	Year Ended December 31		
	1990	**1991**	**1992**
Revenue			
Life Premiums and Other Considerations	$ 238,326	$ 230,369	$ 230,034
Accident and Health Premiums	375,872	382,624	383,552
Casualty and Title Premiums Earned	47,078	45,270	44,815
Total Premiums and Other Considerations	661,276	658,263	658,401
Net Investment Income	342,053	352,772	360,882
Realized Investment Gains	28,201	33,963	48,170
Communications Operations	127,330	125,045	129,734
Other	3,753	3,433	5,142
Total Revenue	1,162,613	1,173,476	1,202,329
Benefits and Expenses			
Death Benefits	111,444	104,131	105,013
Matured Endowments	5,223	4,455	4,576
Annuity Benefits	13,903	14,912	15,054
Disability Benefits	1,224	1,151	1,185
Surrender Benefits	59,297	47,174	38,485
Accident and Health Benefits	322,922	318,876	317,350
Casualty Benefits	34,605	36,657	30,025
Interest on Policy or Contract Funds	89,651	93,995	94,106
Supplementary Contracts with Life Contingencies	4,997	5,346	5,637
(Decrease) in Benefit Liabilities	(10,050)	(764)	(1,292)
Total Benefits	633,216	625,933	610,139
Dividends to Policyholders	16,950	16,598	16,997
Insurance Commissions	63,396	57,237	54,382
General and Administrative	125,101	124,470	128,501
Net (Deferral) of Policy Acquisition Costs	(15,745)	(12,214)	(11,536)
Insurance Taxes, Licenses and Fees	22,750	24,351	24,660
Communications Operations	95,356	92,334	93,560
Total Benefits and Expenses	941,024	928,709	916,703
Income Before Income Taxes	221,589	244,767	285,626
Income Taxes (Benefits):			
Current	68,031	77,839	88,889
Deferred	(4,079)	(8,759)	(6,501)
Total Taxes	63,952	69,080	82,388
Net Income	$ 157,637	$ 175,687	$ 203,238
Net Income Per Share of Common Stock	$ 2.94	$ 3.42	$ 3.99

Source: Jefferson-Pilot 1992 Annual Report.

EXHIBIT 2 Jefferson-Pilot Segment Information (Dollars In Thousands)

	1990	1991	1992
Revenue			
Life Insurance	$ 946,262	$ 956,426	$ 965,862
Other Insurance	55,164	53,472	53,907
Communications	127,330	125,045	129,734
Other, Net	33,857	38,533	52,826
Consolidated	$1,162,613	$1,173,476	$1,202,329
Income Before Income Taxes			
Life Insurance	$ 179,725	$ 202,349	$ 217,635
Other Insurance	6,575	919	7,820
Communications	16,902	18,023	24,262
Other, Net	18,387	23,476	35,909
Consolidated	$ 221,589	$ 244,767	$ 285,626
Identifiable Assets at December 31			
Life Insurance	$4,132,811	$4,535,398	$4,817,482
Other Insurance	136,449	147,309	158,741
Communications	111,130	102,836	99,938
Other, Net	74,518	139,677	159,676
Consolidated	$4,454,908	$4,925,220	$5,235,837
Depreciation and Amortization			
Life Insurance	$ 5,031	$ 5,741	$ 6,055
Other Insurance	155	209	194
Communications	9,980	10,013	8,425
Other, Net	324	327	172
Consolidated	$ 15,490	$ 16,290	$ 14,846

Source: Jefferson-Pilot 1992 Annual Report

Customer Analysis

"Next, we looked at your customers. This overhead (Exhibit 5) first compares J-P and the peer groups on the basis of premium per policy and average size per policy. Then, we break down your customers into male, female, and juvenile groups. As you can see, J-P has a lower premium per policy, average size policy, and premium per $1,000 coverage than do the peer companies. Like the peers, however, your typical customer is a male, under 35 years old, who is employed in a professional or executive position. Your career agents sell 91 percent of your policies, but the policies they sell are smaller in terms of size and premium than those sold by your PGAs.

"Because adult males account for a little over half of your policies and 70 percent of your premiums, we wanted to look more closely at this group. This overhead (Exhibit 6) shows the occupation, age, and income distribution for your male customers and those

EXHIBIT 3 Jefferson-Pilot's Summary of Operations 1987–1991 (Dollar Amounts in Millions)

	1987	1988	1989	1990	1991
Premiums and Annuity Considerations	$648.1	$ 718.0	$ 716.3	$ 727.2	$ 768.9
Net Investment Income	250.1	295.3	313.0	326.6	338.7
Other Income	32.0	25.8	24.1	28.0	26.8
Total Income	930.2	1,039.1	1,053.4	1,081.8	1,134.4
Total Expenses	802.3	916.8	890.0	896.9	930.6
Net Gain Before Dividends	127.9	122.3	163.4	184.9	203.8
Dividends to Policyholders	18.8	25.3	24.7	23.8	22.5
Net Gain After Dividends	$109.1	$ 97.0	$ 138.7	$ 161.1	$ 181.3

	Change from 1987–1991			Average Annual Percent Change		
	JP	Target Group Average	Managerial Peers Average	JP	Target Group Average	Managerial Peers Average
Premiums and Annuity Considerations	$ 120.8	850.9	$ 3,182.0	4.4	7.5	11.7
Net Investment Income	88.6	371.7	723.4	7.9	9.1	6.2
Total Income	204.2	796.5	3,590.1	5.1	4.7	8.6
Deductions	(128.3)	(528.9)	(3,337.8)	(3.8)	(3.5)	(8.8)
Net Gain Before Dividends	75.9	267.6	252.3	12.4	14.4	6.3

Source: Jefferson-Pilot.

of the peer companies. Although we saw earlier that your typical customer is under 35 years old, you will note that the peer companies have larger percentages of their customers in this group and that you have a higher percentage of your customers over 45 years old. This would suggest that you should have higher premiums per policy, yet your premiums per policy are lower in both the younger and older groups and overall. Our analysis indicates that your typical male customer has a median income of $37,500."

"Why do you think our premiums are typically lower than those of the peer companies?" Ken Mlekush asked.

"That's a good question, Ken," Larry Richardson responded. "Our feeling is that the lower premiums are the result of your company's concentration in the Southeast, where incomes are generally lower than in the Northeast. A number of the peer companies have a major presence in the Northeast. Also, some of your agents may not be capitalizing on the opportunities in their markets, but we believe the regional difference is the key factor."

Product Comparison

"If that answers your question, Ken, we'll move on to our discussion of your products," Aaron Sherman resumed. "Our next overhead (Exhibit 7) presents an analysis of J-P's product mix, based on first-year commissions, as compared with the peer companies.

EXHIBIT 4   Jefferson-Pilot 1991 Market Share for Selected States

	JP Share of Ordinary Life Insurance			JP's Ordinary Life Premiums (000)
	% Premium	% Issues	% In Force	
Core Southeastern States				
North Carolina	3.97%	2.86%	3.57%	$ 63,794
South Carolina	2.08	1.62	1.86	15,884
Virginia	0.94	0.54	0.88	13,017
Other Major Southern States				
Texas	0.58	0.36	0.50	19,368
Florida	0.37	0.19	0.35	10,268
Georgia	0.59	0.39	0.55	8,785
Tennessee	0.57	0.30	0.52	5,865
Louisiana	0.51	0.52	0.55	4,352
Alabama	0.36	0.07	0.28	3,108
Mississippi	0.63	0.29	0.68	2,794
Kentucky	0.33	0.35	0.31	2,181
Outside the South				
Virgin Islands	3.73	0.60	3.28	433
Puerto Rico	2.58	1.15	1.89	3,853
California	0.07	0.03	0.05	3,738
U.S. Total	0.32%	0.20%	0.29%	$175,446

Source: Jefferson-Pilot.

As the exhibit shows, J-P has been steadily selling less life insurance, down from 76 percent of first-year commissions to 63 percent, just since 1989. The other companies' life insurance shares have held relatively constant over this time. Your salespeople are selling considerably more disability income and health insurance and annuities than are the other companies."

"Why do you think our agents are selling more annuities and disability income policies?" David Stonecipher asked.

"Our experience indicates that agents find it easier to sell disability income and annuities as compared to life insurance," Aaron Sherman answered. "Consumers can understand these policies better and salespeople find them easier to explain. Thus, the salespeople go for the easy sale. What is more important to understand, however, is that it is unusual for a company with a large career sales force to stress universal life. Whole life policies provide more support for the field sales force because consumers tend to keep the policies in force longer and the renewal premiums are higher."

Sales Force Comparison

"How do our salespeople feel about the products we give them to sell?" Bill Seawell asked.

Larry Richardson responded by presenting an overhead (Exhibit 8). "This overhead summarizes our findings on that question. As you can see, relative to the norm for other companies we have surveyed, your agents were less pleased with the variety of

EXHIBIT 5   Comparison of Premiums and Average Size Per Policy

	Jefferson-Pilot	Target Group	Managerial Peers
Premium/Policy Size			
Premium Per Policy	$889	$1,211	$966
Average Size Policy	$101,470	$126,940	$91,580
Premium Per $1,000	$8.76	$9.54	$10.55

Percent of Policies (Premium Per Policy)

	Jefferson-Pilot	Target Group	Managerial Peers
Customer Demographics			
Male	51%	57%	53%
	($1,213)	($1,567)	($1,257)
Female	38	33	36
	($639)	($879)	($744)
Juvenile	11	10	11
	($233)	($255)	($303)

	Full-Time Agents	PGAs
By Whom Sold		
Percent of Policies	91%	9%
Premium of Policy	$837	$1,439
Average Size Policy	$100,920	$127,580
Premium Per $1,000	$8.29	$11.28

Source: Jefferson-Pilot.

products and were significantly less pleased with new product development. They also seemed to feel that the company is not as market driven as it should be."

"Larry, while we are on the subject of how the salespeople feel, how did we stack up relative to recruitment and retention of the sales force?" Ron Ridlehuber wondered.

"That's an important question, Ron. Our study shows that only 35 percent of J-P's new agents made it through the first year, 15 percentage points below the industry average, and only 24 percent made it through the first two years. Moreover, only 7 percent stay more than four years.

"This overhead (Exhibit 9) summarizes your situation pretty well. The first part of the overhead shows that in 1991, recruits represented 48 percent of your base sales force, as compared with 29 percent and 38 percent for the two peer groups. Further, as we've noted, your base sales force has been declining while your peers' sales groups have been stable or increasing. Likewise, your turnover rates have been consistently higher than your peers. Finally, the overhead shows that only 35 percent of your sales force has been with you more than five years as compared with 40 percent and 46 percent for the two comparison groups. And after five years, we expect agents to be in their most productive period."

"Larry, what did you determine about our agents' productivity versus the peer groups?" David Stonecipher asked.

EXHIBIT 6   Analysis of Adult Male Consumer by Occupation, Income, and Age

	Adult Males Percent of Policies (Premium Per Policy)		
Occupation	Jefferson-Pilot	Target Group	Managerial Peers
Executive	37%	36%	28%
	($1,756)	($2,003)	($1,728)
Professional	33	41	28
	($1,234)	($1,651)	($1,492)
Blue Collar	21	18	38
	($710)	($884)	($772)
Clerical	9	5	6
	($866)	($1,664)	($734)
Income			
Under $25K	26%	14%	24%
	($625)	($582)	($603)
$25K–$49.9K	45	41	51
	($841)	($811)	($956)
$50K or over	29	45	25
	($2,421)	($2,400)	($2,541)
Age			
Under 35	39%	47%	47%
	($561)	($671)	($688)
35–44	31	32	27
	($1,169)	($1,647)	($1,034)
45 or over	30	21	26
	($2,056)	($3,536)	($2,494)

Source: Jefferson-Pilot.

"We looked closely at the issue of productivity. We found that J-P agents earned on average lower first-year commissions (not including renewal commissions) in each year as compared with the peers. Your base sales force had average first-year commissions of about $22,000 versus $31,000 for the target group and almost $25,000 for the managerial peer group. When we looked at number of policies sold, we also found that your agents sold fewer individual life policies."

"Do you have any ideas as to why our productivity is lower, Larry?"

"Yes, David. Although there are many factors that affect productivity, it seems to the project team that J-P's production standards are low compared to the peers' standards. This may cause more experienced agents to place less business with J-P. They may meet their performance goals with you and then place other business with other firms in order to meet goals there.

"There is also evidence that the agents feel that the production levels are too low. As this overhead (Exhibit 10) shows, your managers believe that they help agents set high but attainable goals, yet slightly less than half of the agents feel that way. In looking at the validation requirements, the performance standards that first-year agents must meet, 69 percent of the agents believed they were modest or too low. Finally, your

EXHIBIT 7 Product Mix Trends (Percent of First-Year Commission)

	1989	1990	1991
Jefferson-Pilot			
Life	76%	70%	63%
DI/Health	9	12	12
Annuities	11	13	17
Investment Products	4	5	7
Group	0	0	0
Total[a]	100%	100%	100%
Target Group			
Life	78%	75%	75%
DI/Health	7	6	6
Annuities	4	6	7
Investment Products	5	6	8
Group	7	7	5
Total[a]	100%	100%	100%
Managerial Agency Peers			
Life	76%	78%	77%
DI/Health	5	5	5
Annuities	8	9	9
Investment Products	3	3	4
Group	7	6	4
Total[a]	100%	100%	100%

[a]All percentages are rounded numbers; columns may not total 100%.
Source: Jefferson-Pilot.

EXHIBIT 8 Sales Force's Ratings of JP's Products (Percent of Agents Agreeing)

Agents' Overall Assessment of Companies' Products	Jefferson-Pilot	Norm
I am pleased with the variety of products our company offers.	66%	78%
I am satisfied with our company's development of new products	33	65
Our company is market driven, responding to the needs of its target market with appropriate products and services.	25	66

Source: Jefferson-Pilot.

EXHIBIT 9 Sales Force Recruitment and Retention

Recruits as a Percent of Base Force

	Jefferson-Pilot		Target Group	Managerial Peers
	Rate	No. of Recruits		
1991	48%	280	29%	38%
1990	58	378	31	41
1989	34	316	30	40
1988	40	459	30	45
1987	42	501	33	41

Percent Change in Base Force

	Jefferson-Pilot[a]	Target Group	Managerial Peers
1991	–6%	–1 %	–1%
1990	–11	b	2
1989	–31	b	1
1988	–2	b	9
1987	–2	1	6

Turnover Rate

1991	36%	24%	28%
1990	44	24	28
1989	48	23	28
1988	30	23	25
1987	31	24	25

Distribution of Sales Agents by Years of Service

Years of Service

1	35%	24%	29%
2	15	14	15
3	10	9	9
4	5	7	7
5+	35	46	40

[a]The field force has declined from 1,161 to 546 full-time agents
[b]Less than ½ of –1 percent
Source: Jefferson-Pilot.

agents had considerably less activities in direct mail, telephone prospecting, etc., than did agents from the peer companies. Many salespeople don't like to perform these activities, but experience shows that the activities are a key part of building a clientele.

"Your managers and agents also seem to have different perspectives on what is required of new agents. This overhead (Exhibit 11) indicates that over 90 percent of your managers felt they give a realistic picture of an agent's career to an agent they are recruiting, yet only 32 percent of the agents felt that way. Moreover, when we asked the managers which activities they required of a new agent prior to signing a contract with

---

EXHIBIT 10   Results of Agent Survey—Production Goals

**In Our Agency, A Good Job Is Done Of Helping Agents
Set Challenging But Attainable Production Objectives**

	Percent Agreement
Agency Manager	88%
Sales Manager	73
Agent	49
Norm for FT Agent	52

**If Validation Requirements Were a Production Level Goal
Toward Which I Was Working, I Would See It As:**

	Jefferson-Pilot	Target Group	Managerial Peers
Challenging	30%	40%	48%
Modest	51	35	33
Too Low	18	23	14
Too High	1	2	5

In The Past Month, How Many:

	Jefferson-Pilot	Target Group	Managerial Peers
Prospects have you mailed to	99	231	278
Prospects have you phoned	113	211	147
Cold calls have you made	41	74	63
Appointments have you had	29	49	41
Fact-finders have you completed	22	17	17
Closing interviews have you done	17	18	18

Source: Jefferson-Pilot.

---

them, we got a very different set of responses than we got when we asked the new agents the same question. Seventy-three percent of your new hires have not been full-time life agents previously, so it is not hard to understand that they might not fully understand what being a career agent requires."

Marketing Costs

"How did we compare as far as marketing costs, Aaron?"

"Ken, our analysis indicates that your marketing costs are generally in line with the managerial peer group. As you know, because of the one-time cost of issuing a policy and the high first-year sales commission, it costs J-P about $1.65 for each $1.00 of premium income in the first year. In other words, you lose $.65 for every dollar of premium income in the first year. That's why it's so important to keep policies on the books. It takes into the second or third year before the company makes any money on the policy.

EXHIBIT 11   Results of Agent Survey—Pre-Contract

**In Our Agency, New Agents Are Given
A Realistic Picture of the Agent's Career**

	Percent Agreement
Agency Manager	100%
Sales Manager	93
Agent	32
Norm for FT Agent	39

**Managers: Which Activities Do You Typically
Require of Producers Prior to Contract?**

	Jefferson-Pilot	Target Group	Managerial Peers
Learn a sales talk	100%	63%	83%
Make joint calls	93	57	60
Market opinion surveys	93	74	78
Complete sales	81	57	53
Basic insurance knowledge	70	79	77
Become licensed	59	82	93

**Agents: Which Of The Following Activities Were You
Required To Complete Prior to Being Contracted?**

	Jefferson-Pilot	Target Group	Managerial Peers
Market opinion surveys	64	24	39
Basic insurance knowledge	51	54	51
Become licensed	49	62	66
Complete sales	47	28	27
Learn a sales talk	39	36	40
Make joint calls	30	19	18
None	8	17	12

Source: Jefferson-Pilot.

"Your $1.65 figure compares with $1.66 for the managerial group, but it is higher than the target group's average of $1.45. We think that comes from your having more smaller offices. When we controlled for office size, your costs seemed to be in line. This overhead (Exhibit 12) shows the elements of your costs as compared with the peer companies. Your costs are higher for both producer (agent) compensation and management compensation due to your competitive bonus structure and your agent financing plan. Your home office expenses are probably higher simply because you are a smaller company than some of the peers, and there are certain fixed costs you have to bear. You should be able to grow and spread those fixed costs. To help you compare your agencies' costs with the peer group's, I prepared this overhead (Exhibit 13). It shows that your agencies are on average about one-third the size of the average peer agency."

EXHIBIT 12 Components of Marketing Costs: 1991 (Per $100 of Weighted New Premiums)

	Jefferson-Pilot	Target Group	Peer Group
Producer Compensation[1]	$ 61	$ 55	$ 62
Management Compensation[2]	26	23	19
Field Expenses Paid by Company[3]	37	36	43
Field Benefits	17	17	24
Sub-Total	141	131	148
Home Office Marketing Expenses	24	14	18
Total	$165	$145	$166

[1]Includes all compensation *other than* renewal commissions; includes first-year commissions on management personal production.
[2]Includes compensation paid to agency managers and second-line supervisors.
[3]Includes all operating expenses paid by company (e.g., clerical salary, rent, postage, telephone, etc.).
Source: Jefferson-Pilot.

EXHIBIT 13 1991 Average Agency Characteristics

	Jefferson-Pilot	Peers
Manager income[a]	$100,913	$150,145
Agency First-Year Commission Revenue	$247,941	$778,431
Managers' Years of Service	9.9	6.1
Number of Agents	11.1	32.9
Number of Recruits	5.7	11.2
Number of 2nd-Line Managers	1.5	2.2
2nd-Line Manager Income	$ 23,489	$ 52,075
Number of Agencies	35	473

[a]Excludes personal production
Source: Jefferson-Pilot.

"How do our agents feel about their compensation, Larry?"

"Bill, I prepared this overhead to summarize our findings on that point (Exhibit 14). As you can see, your full-time agents are below the norm in every category for all agents in our survey. On the other hand, your managers are above the norm in each category except for how secure they feel about their income.

"David, I think that about covers the points we wanted to present at this time. We will, of course, be available to answer additional questions you have as you proceed with your planning," Larry concluded.

"Thank you, Larry and Aaron. Your work will be very helpful. We'll let you go now while we continue our discussion."

EXHIBIT 14   Attitudes Toward Compensation

Full-Time Agent Responses (Percent Agreement)

	Jefferson-Pilot	Norm
I have a secure income.	39%	46%
I have a good compensation plan.	46	58
My compensation plan is competitive.	38	49
My compensation plan is clear and understandable.	51	53
I have good fringe benefits.	51	64

Managers Responses (Percent Agreement)

	Jefferson-Pilot	Norm
I have a secure income.	33%	58%
I have a good compensation plan.	67	65
My compensation plan is competitive.	56	55
My compensation plan is clear and understandable.	66	57
I have good fringe benefits.	44	73

Source: Jefferson-Pilot.

OPTIONS

"Well, I don't know that any of the consultants' findings surprised us, but hearing them all together is certainly sobering," Stonecipher began. "We've got our work cut out for us if we are going to achieve the growth and profitability goals the board has set. It wants us to grow earnings per share by 10 percent per year and achieve above average returns on capital. Ken, what do you think our options are?"

"David, even if we choose the option of continuing to have the same kind of company we've had, that is one focused primarily on using the career agent to sell our products, we've got to make a number of changes to address the issues in the report. We seem to be in a cycle of declining performance. Fewer agents lead to less new business. This causes an expense problem. Due to that problem, we don't do the things we need to do to develop competitive products. It's a vicious cycle. Don't you agree, Bill?"

"Yes, Ken. But I think it is important for us to remember that our career-agent system is our key strength. We are known as a company because of that system. We have many long-term, loyal agents. As you know, my father worked here and was in charge of our career agents. We need to improve the quality of our recruits, train them better, and keep them with us. If we can do those things, we will grow faster and be more profitable."

"That's true, Bill," Ron Ridlehuber joined in, "but it seems to me that we need to look more closely at complementing the career system by increasing our emphasis on the independent agent. We have many independent agents now, and the report shows that they are very productive. But they have never been the focus of our system. Under a new system we would contract with existing insurance agents, allowing them to offer our products. This avoids the problem of having to hire and train new recruits, and it would allow us to expand our geographic coverage more quickly. Further, we would not have to pay the office costs and associated salaries. We could pay these independent agents on a commission-only basis. Instead of using our 12 regional directors to recruit, we could license independent marketing organizations to recruit for us, with them earning an override commission on sales their agents made."

"Ron, I know you used this kind of system at Southland, but it would be such a radical change for J-P," Bill Seawell responded. "If you increased the size of our sales force substantially by using independent agents, I'm not sure how our career force would react. I'm afraid they'd be terribly threatened. And the folks in the home office are used to working with career agents. The independents would not be loyal to the company. We would have less control over what they sell and over the quality of their work with policyholders. And can you imagine what will happen the first time one of our career agents runs into an independent agent trying to sell the same product to the same customer!"

"David, you asked about options," Ken Mlekush continued. "I guess this exchange points out that we could continue with a predominantly career-based system, move to a predominantly independent system, or have a combination of the two approaches. We're going to have to make significant changes under any of the options, and I'm sure there will be problems we'll have to address. A final growth option, of course, is to acquire other insurance companies. We certainly have the financial strength to do that, but even then we are going to have to address the issue of how we distribute, how we sell, our products to our policyholders."

"Yes, Ken, distribution is a key issue. I can see that there are many issues we need to think carefully about before we make a decision. Here's what I'd like for you to do. I'd like for each of you independently to consider our situation and develop recommendations as to how we should proceed. I'd like to meet again in two weeks to hear your presentations. I'll call you to set up a specific time once I check my calendar."

JEFFERSON-PILOT CORPORATION: APPENDIX I— THE LIFE INSURANCE INDUSTRY

Life Insurance

People buy life insurance for many reasons but mainly to provide financial protection for their families if the policyholder should die prematurely. Life insurance provides support for the insured's survivors and pays any estate obligations at the time of death; accumulates funds for retirement, emergencies, and business use; and defers or avoids income taxes. A person can use life insurance to create or add to an estate and then can protect that estate by maintaining the policy.

Historical Background

Ancient Babylonians and the early Greeks developed the concept of insurance. Under Babylonian law, a person could adopt a son, raise him, and then depend on him for support in later years, thereby providing a type of retirement insurance. The Greeks belonged to various religious sects to which they paid monthly dues. As a benefit, the sect promised a decent burial according to its rites, as well as money to pay the deceased's obligations. If members fell behind in their monthly premiums, they had to pay fines.

The Romans furthered the concepts of burial insurance and settlement of obligations. They began to place less emphasis on the religious aspects and opened membership to the general public. They created a special society for soldiers that provided death benefits and pensions for disability or old age.

However, the development of modern insurance did not begin until the early 14th century. In 1310, the first insurance company was chartered in Flanders. Life insurance first appeared in the United States in 1759, with the formation of "The Corporation for Relief of Poor and Distressed Widows and Children of Presbyterian Ministers." This company, now Covenant Life Insurance Company, is the oldest life insurance company in continued existence in the world. In 1794, the Insurance Company of North America became the first chartered general life insurance company in the United States. In 1840, the New York State Legislature enacted a law that protected a widow's life insurance proceeds from creditors' claims, strengthening a life insurance policy's protective power. In 1859, New York State established the first state government insurance department; and, in 1869, the U.S. Supreme Court upheld states' rights to regulate insurance companies. In 1911, companies introduced the first group life insurance policies for purchase by companies for their employees. In 1944, the U.S. Supreme Court held that life insurance companies were subject to federal laws because they were engaged in interstate commerce.

Classes of Life Insurance

Companies offer several different classes of life insurance. The classes differ in type of customers, policy amounts, cash values, methods of computing and collecting premiums, underwriting standards, and marketing methods.

Ordinary Life Insurance Companies usually issue life insurance in amounts of $1,000 or more with premiums payable annually, semiannually, quarterly, or monthly. The ordinary department of most life insurers is their largest department, and many insurers write only ordinary life insurance. Ordinary insurance accounts for 51 percent of life insurance in force in the United States and about 76 percent of the insurance purchased annually. Term, whole life, and universal life are all types of ordinary life insurance.

Term Insurance Term insurance is the most basic type of life insurance. Term insurance provides only temporary protection, for a specified time period, such as one, five, or 10 years, or until the insured reaches a specified age, such as sixty-five. Term insurance policies provide pure protection and do not accumulate cash values or offer any savings element. Most term insurance is both renewable and convertible. *Renewable* means that the policyholder can renew the policy for additional periods without evidence of insurability. *Convertible* means that the policyholder can exchange the policy for some type of cash value life insurance with no evidence of insurability. Term life insurance premiums increase as the policyholder ages. Purchasers use term insurance for three general situations: if their income is limited, if they have temporary needs, or if they want to guarantee future insurance availability.

Term insurance has two major limitations. First, because term insurance premiums increase with age, premiums often became unaffordable at older ages. Second, because term insurance has no cash value or savings element, it does not help the insured save money for certain purposes, such as for retirement or for their children's education.

Whole Life Insurance Whole life insurance has fixed premiums and provides lifetime protection. The most common types of whole life insurance are called ordinary life and universal life.

Ordinary life insurance has level premiums and lifetime protection to age 100. If the insured is still alive at age 100, the insurance company pays the policyowner the policy's face amount. Under an ordinary life policy, the premiums paid during the early years of the policy are higher than necessary to pay death claims, whereas the premiums paid during the later years are lower than necessary for paying death claims. Because of the higher-than-necessary early premiums, an ordinary life policy develops a legal reserve. The legal reserve becomes a liability item on the insurance company's balance sheet that formally recognizes the overpayment of premiums. The life insurer then has to accumulate assets to offset the legal reserve's liability.

Because the policyholder pays premiums that are larger than necessary, his/her policy develops a "cash value." Insurance companies use the cash value from their policies to make investments so they will be able to pay policy claims and also pay interest on the policyowners' savings. If the policyowner no longer wants the insurance, the policyowner can surrender the policy for its cash value. Although the cash surrender values are relatively low during the early years, they can accumulate to sizable amounts over time. Thus, an ordinary life policy allows the insured to provide for insurance and saving needs all in one policy.

Ordinary life policies also have disadvantages. Because ordinary life insurance is relatively expensive in the early years, some policyowners can still be underinsured. Additionally, ordinary life policies have some disadvantages as savings vehicles. Insurance companies do not have to state the rate of return on the cash value specifically when they issue the policy. Rates of return are relatively low on some policies. Finally, cash values are not legally required until the end of the third year. Thus, the amount of savings during the early years is relatively small, and the policyholder can incur a substantial loss if he/she allows the policy to lapse or if he/she surrenders the policy during the early years.

Universal Life Insurance   Universal life insurance is a relatively new, rapidly growing form of whole life insurance. Companies often sell universal life policies as investments that combine insurance protection with savings. Universal life insurance is a flexible premium deposit fund combined with monthly renewable term insurance. The policyowner pays a specified initial premium. The company credits the gross premium less expenses to the policy's initial cash value and deducts a monthly mortality charge for the pure insurance protection. The company then pays interest at a specified rate on the remaining cash value. Fundamentally, universal life insurance serves as a combination of a savings account and monthly renewable term insurance.

Universal life policies are very flexible. Policyholders can increase or decrease the premiums, skip premium payments as long as the cash value is sufficient to cover mortality costs and expenses, increase or decrease death benefits, add to the cash value at any time, and borrow money based on the cash value.

Special Purpose Policies and Riders

In addition to the basic policy types, life insurance companies offer several special policies. These policies are usually combinations of policies designed to meet specific life insurance needs. Many policies are designed as inflation-era products to help policyowners cope with the need for increasing death protection and savings as the value of the dollar declines. Many of these special policies provide coverage for more than one person, usually entire families. Others provide for payment of mortgages, etc.

Insurance companies often add supplemental agreements, called *riders*, to life insurance policies. Some riders add more life insurance, such as level, increasing, or decreasing term, to a basic whole life policy. Others deal with the waiver of premium payments in the event of disability, accidental death and dismemberment benefits, and the guaranteed right to purchase additional insurance. Some riders even increase or decrease the amount of insurance to reflect cost-of-living changes measured by the consumer price index.

Annuities

Annuities are another form of insurance that consumers can use to provide income. An annuity represents an investment that provides regular periodic payments for the owner's life or for a specified period. An annuity providing lifetime income is called a *life annuity*. A life annuity is true life insurance because it insures against outliving financial resources. Life annuities are important instruments in planning for financial security during retirement.

A consumer purchasing an annuity commits to make a specified payment each month for a specified period. Each payment adds to the annuity's cash value, and the account earns interest on that value. The owner can structure an annuity so that, at retirement, the annuity will be sufficient to make a certain monthly payment to the owner for the remainder of his/her life. Each payment has three components: interest, principle, and an insurance benefit. The interest earned declines each year as the principal is gradually liquidated through payments. Therefore, as years go by, more of the payment comes from principal and less from interest. If the owner's principal runs out before he/she dies, the payments then consist of an insurance benefit. When the owner dies, the remaining principal and accrued interest become part of his/her estate.

Life Insurance in the 1990s

Consumers purchased $1.6 trillion in life insurance in 1991, up 5.7 percent from 1990. Sales of ordinary life insurance accounted for nearly two-thirds of that amount. Purchases of whole life were 56 percent, down from 61 percent three years earlier. Universal and variable life insurance accounted for 21 percent of ordinary sales, down from a high of 40 percent in 1985.

In 1991, life insurance in force reached an all-time high, $9.98 trillion, up 6.3 percent from 1990. The average amount of life insurance per U.S. household was $102,700, some $4,300 more than in 1990. Eighty-one percent of American households owned life insurance. Approximately 70 percent of adult Americans owned some form of life insurance.

In 1991, benefit payments, excluding health insurance, reached a record $91.6 billion, up 3.6 percent. Payments to beneficiaries in 1991 totaled $25.4 billion. Companies paid about $29.6 billion to life insurance policyholders and $36.6 billion to annuity owners.

U.S. life insurance companies' assets were $1.6 trillion at year-end 1991. This was an increase of $143 billion, or 10.2 percent, from 1990 year-end. Policy loans outstanding rose slightly in 1991 and totaled $66.4 billion. They accounted for 4.3 percent of assets—the lowest proportion since 1965. Life insurance companies' largest percentage increase in investments was in stocks, up 28 percent over year-end 1990. The net rate of investment earnings before federal taxes (excluding separate accounts) continued to decline, to 9.09 percent, the lowest since 1983.

Life Insurance Purchases In 1991

Of the nearly 30 million new life insurance policies and certificates issued during 1991, 13.5 million were ordinary policies; 112,000 were industrial policies; and 16.2 million were group certificates. The average size of the ordinary policies continued to increase. In 1981, for example, the average new ordinary policy was $30,430; by 1986, the amount has increased to $55,540; in 1990, to $76,050; and in 1991 to $77,320. A sample survey of ordinary life insurance purchased by Americans in 1991 showed that 50 percent of all new policies sold were for people between the ages of 25 and 44.

In terms of the number of policies sold, term insurance accounted for 20 percent in 1991, down from 25 percent in 1987. Variable and universal policies dropped from 26 percent of sales in 1987 to 16 percent in 1991. Traditional whole life and combination sales continued to increase, to 64 percent of policies in 1991, but were still below the 69 percent share of 1982.

Life Insurance Companies' Earnings

Life insurance companies produce revenue from two main sources: premiums paid by policyholders and earnings on investments. There is a close relationship between these income elements. Part of each premium payment becomes available for investment. In calculating premiums, companies take into account the anticipated investment earnings, thereby reducing the price of life insurance.

In 1991, total income of all U.S. life companies was $411 billion, with 64.2 percent from premium receipts and 28.9 percent from investment earnings. The remaining 6.9 percent came from other sources, including payments for supplementary contracts.

Premium receipts and annuity considerations totaled $263.8 billion. Americans spent the equivalent of 4.81 percent of total disposable income in 1991 for life insurance and annuities, compared with 5.07 percent during 1990.

Life insurance accounted for about 30 percent of all premium receipts in 1991. This proportion had declined in relation to the income received from annuities. In 1971, the proportion was 56.3 percent; by 1981 the proportion had dropped to 43.8 percent.

Ordinary policy premiums accounted for $62.8 billion, or 79.2 percent of the life insurance premiums in 1991. Most ordinary premiums were renewals. Group insurance premiums amounted to $14.3 billion, or 18 percent of all life insurance premiums, whereas industrial premiums accounted for $527 million, or 0.7 percent. Annuity considerations totaled $123.6 billion in 1991, down from $129.1 billion in 1990.

U.S. life insurance companies' policy reserves totaled $1.3 trillion at the end of 1991. These reserves represented the funds set aside to meet the companies' future obligations to policyholders and their beneficiaries. State laws required each company to maintain its policy reserves at a level that would assure payment of all policy obligations. Regulators calculated the reserve amount based on actuarial tables that took into account the funds from future premium payments, interest earnings, and expected mortality experience.

Life insurance companies' total reserves at the end of 1991 included $372.1 billion for life insurance policies, $38.3 billion for health insurance policies, and $894.5 billion for annuities and supplementary contracts.

Life Insurance Company Assets

In 1991, U.S. life insurance companies' assets, including those held in separate accounts, totaled $1.55 trillion, an increase of 10.2 percent during the year, compared to an increase of 8.3 percent in the previous year. Net investments in U.S. capital markets by life insurance companies totaled $90.2 billion in 1991. Life insurance ranked second among private domestic institutional sources of funds, supplying 18.1 percent of the total funds flowing into financial markets. Companies' investments were primarily in corporate debt issues, government securities, mortgages, and preferred and common stocks.

Life Insurance Companies

In 1991, there were 2,105 U.S. life insurance companies and an estimated 50,000 life insurance agents. The number of companies reached an all-time high in 1988 but since then had been declining steadily. Most companies that discontinued operations did so by merging with other insurers or had all their outstanding business reinsured in other life insurance companies. The remaining companies terminated for various reasons, including conversion to nonlife company status.

The majority of new companies formed in recent years had remained in business. By specializing in meeting the needs of families in specific regions, many had been able to compete successfully with older and larger companies whose operations encompassed larger areas.

Trends

In the late 1970s and early 1980s, the industry had to contend with high inflation and rising interest rates. New money market funds were paying 17 percent interest compared with only 5 percent for conventional whole life policies. Consumers shifted their insurance purchases to less-expensive term insurance and invested the premiums they saved at higher rates elsewhere. Policyholders terminated their policies and took out low-rate policy loans. This aggravated insurers' liquidity problems and undermined profitability.

On the other hand, the high interest rates allowed the industry to realize higher returns on investments. As interest rates began to drop in the late 1980s, the industry once again faced financial difficulties. These problems were magnified by the real estate market's decline in the early 1990s. Many life insurance companies began increasing their real estate holdings in the early 1980s in order to improve investment returns. Unfortunately, the market slowed considerably, and commercial vacancy rates rose to the 20 percent level. Many companies were stuck holding nonperforming assets.

Analysts expected competition in the life insurance segment to increase. Aging "baby boomers" would increase the demand for products that provided retirement income and healthcare financing. Additionally, life insurance companies would have to face competition from banks, mutual funds, and other financial institutions that were able to offer products that competed with life insurance products.

JEFFERSON PILOT CORPORATION: APPENDIX II— JEFFERSON-PILOT CORPORATION

History

J-P had its origins in the Worth-Wharton Real Estate & Investment Company, which was incorporated in Greensboro in 1890. In 1905, the owners changed the name to Southern Life and Trust Company; and in 1924, the company reorganized as Pilot Life Insurance Company. A separate company, The Jefferson Standard Life Insurance Company, began operations in 1907 in Greensboro. The North Carolina business and civic leaders who founded these companies believed they could meet the needs of the region better than existing competitors. They wished to keep capital in the area to support economic development.

Both companies succeeded and rapidly extended their initial reach, eventually achieving national significance. Jefferson Standard's equity interest in Pilot dated to 1931, and, in 1945, Jefferson Standard acquired all of Pilot's stock. Both companies accelerated their expansion after World War II.

The two companies were complementary. Jefferson Standard focused on a single product line, individual ordinary life insurance, and Pilot, which began as an ordinary life company, entered the home service business in 1945, thus becoming a multiple-line company. The companies' distinctiveness lay in marketing. Jefferson Standard sold through company-owned regional agencies staffed with career agents, whereas Pilot's primary marketing channel was through independent general agencies.

With the formation in 1968 of J-P Corporation, both Jefferson Standard and Pilot became wholly-owned subsidiaries of that company. Following that, the two companies drew closer together, and, through a joint planning process, coordinated their business strategies closely. The companies jointly developed products, and each company's agents began selling the other's products. Their common interests led to the formation of subsidiaries providing services to both in investment management, data processing, pension plan sales and administration, and investor services.

As the positive aspects of the dual marketing system became evident, the owners decided to merge the two companies. On January 1, 1987, Jefferson Standard Life Insurance Company and Pilot Life Insurance Company combined to form the Jefferson-Pilot Life Insurance Corporation.

The J-P Corporation had four major business segments at year-end 1992.

Individual Insurance

This segment offered life insurance, annuities, disability income, mutual funds, and 401-Ks. The primary markets were estate planning, income protection, retirement planning, and investment. Individual insurance accounted for 68.1 percent of J-P's operating profits in 1992. More than 2,200 career agents, personal producing agents, independent brokers, and managers—along with 470 home service agents and managers, 12 individual health regional sales and service offices, and 19 financial institutions—distributed J-P's individual insurance products.

Group Insurance

This segment offered many products and services, including employee and dependent term life, mass-marketed payroll-deduction universal life, short-term and long-term disability income, dental benefits, vision benefits, accidental death and dismemberment, prescription drug benefits, and managed care. Group insurance had its primary markets in employee groups with more than 10 people, with the greatest concentration on companies with 25 to 1,000 employees. Group insurance products and services were distributed by 85 sales and service representatives, 22 regional sales and service offices, and the company's agents and independent brokers. The group insurance segment accounted for 23.3 percent of J-Ps 1992 total operating profits.

Casualty and Title Insurance

This segment offered commercial insurance lines such as workers compensation, commercial property, commercial auto, and general liability. This segment also marketed personal insurance lines such as automobile insurance, homeowners insurance, and title insurance. Six regional sales offices and 303 professional independent agents distributed the products. The segment contributed 4.1 percent of J-P's total operating profits in 1992.

Communications

This segment contained three elements: broadcasting properties, Jefferson-Pilot Sports, and J-P Data Services. J-P owned two television stations and six radio stations. Jefferson-Pilot Sports produced broadcasts of Atlantic Coast Conference and Southeastern Conference football and basketball games. J-P Data Services provided information to television and radio broadcasters, cable networks, and advertising agencies and representatives. The communications segment provided 8.3 percent of J-P's operating profits in 1992.

Investments

Although this segment did not directly produce or deliver a product or service, its objective was to invest premium income. The net investment income was $361 million in 1992, despite a low interest rate.

As of December 31, 1992, J-P had approximately 3,900 employees with revenues of $1.2 billion. The average number of outstanding shares in 1992 was 51 million, which were held by 9,881 stockholders. Besides its executive offices in Greensboro, North Carolina, it also owned facilities in Colorado, Florida, Georgia, California, and Virginia. J-P held licenses to operate in 39 states, the District of Columbia, Puerto Rico, and the Virgin Islands.

(Exhibits 1 and 2 present J-P's summary financials.)

Marketing at Replacements, Ltd.

Lew G. Brown, Tony R. Wingler,
Kristen M. Cashman, and Charles A. Kivett

A HOBBY BECOMES A BUSINESS

On September 5, 1997, a little before 1:30 P.M., a group of faculty members and an undergraduate research fellow from the University of North Carolina at Greensboro gathered outside the front entrance to Replacements, Ltd. The company's headquarters was located just off interstate highways 85 and 40 on Greensboro's eastern edge. As the group waited for everyone to arrive, a steady stream of customers entered and left the company's large, first-floor showroom.

Once everyone was present, the group entered the building, and Doug Anderson, executive vice president, escorted the visitors to the second-floor conference room. Waiting there were Ron Swanson, chief information officer; Scott Fleming, vice president of operations; and Kelly Smith, chief financial officer. (See Exhibit 1, Organizational Chart.)

A few minutes later, Bob Page, the company's president, entered the conference room. He was casually dressed, as were all the officers, wearing a dark blue knit shirt that bore the Replacements, Ltd. logo. Following closely behind Bob were his two, miniature, black and tan dachshunds, Trudy and Toby. Bob always had the two dogs with him at work, and they had free run of the executive office area. It was not unusual for them to enter and leave meetings, perhaps carrying chew-toys with them.

After introductions, Bob Page began. "I'm not comfortable making speeches, but I do like to talk about the company's history. So, I thought I would just do that as a way of helping you begin gathering information for your case.

"I was born on a small tobacco farm in Rockingham County, near the city of Reidsville. I have two brothers and a sister. We grew up working on the farm. When the time came, I went to North Carolina State University. After two years, I decided to transfer to UNC Chapel Hill, where I majored in accounting. After graduation, the Army drafted me. I got out in 1970, went to work for an accounting firm and later earned my CPA.

"After about four years, for some reason, I took a job as an auditor with the state of North Carolina. From the first day, I hated the job. I just didn't like politics and all the rules and regulations. I was very unhappy.

This case was prepared by Professors Lew G. Brown and Tony R. Wingler and Undergraduate Research Assistants Kristen M. Cashman and Charles A. Kivett, all of University of North Carolina at Greensboro, as a basis for class discussion. It is not intended to illustrate either effective or ineffective handling of an administrative situation. The authors express their appreciation to Replacements, Ltd., for its cooperation in developing this case.

EXHIBIT 1: Replacements, LTD. Organizational Chart

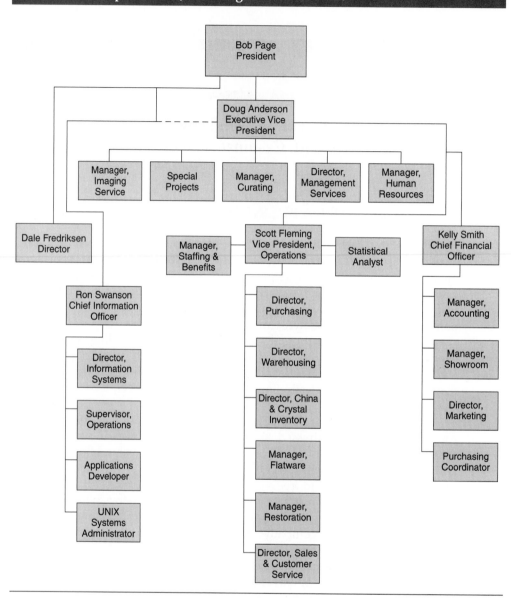

"About this time, I guess to get away from my unhappiness at work, I started going to flea markets, buying and selling things on consignment. It was not unusual for me to leave work on a Friday afternoon and drive all night in order to be at a flea market, say, in Nashville, Tennessee, the next morning.

"People learned about my hobby and began to ask me to keep an eye out for various things, especially china patterns. Perhaps they had broken a piece of their china and found that the manufacturer no longer made that pattern. Or, perhaps they had never had a full set and now wanted to complete it. When I got a request, I'd make a note on a 3-by-5 index card and put it in an old recipe box. When I was at a flea market and found a china pattern that someone needed, I'd buy it. When I got home, I'd drop them a line or give them a call.

"I was still working for the state at this time. Word of my hobby spread, and I found myself getting more and more requests. I'd come home at night and find lots of mail and phone messages. I set up a card table in my bedroom to keep up with the paperwork. I packed orders for mailing on my kitchen floor.

"By 1981, I was working late almost every night. I'd sold about $53,000 worth of china, etcetera, the previous year. I finally got up the nerve to quit my job with the state in March and to try to make a go of my hobby. My friends thought I was crazy to leave a good job with the state in order to sell used dishes, but I wanted to do something enjoyable and fun. I thought I'd be better off in the long run.

"The first thing I needed was more space, because I'd filled up my apartment. I rented about 500 to 600 square feet in a building in Greensboro. I needed some way to haul all the stuff I bought around, so I bought a used van for $3,000. Funny, I had to put up my old Toyota as collateral to buy the van. I hired a part-time college student to pack orders for me, and I did the rest. I still went on buying trips every weekend.

"By September that year, 1981, I had incorporated the business as Replacements and bought a 2,000-square-foot building that the owner financed for me. I had several part-time employees by then, and it didn't take long to run out of space, so I started looking for another location. Zoning regulations were a real problem.

"I found a place with 4,000 square feet. We filled it up in a year. This was some time in 1982. I got two more adjoining lots, and we built a 15,000-square-foot building.

"Sometime around 1986, we moved again—this time to a place with 40,000 square feet—and the company was up to 50 employees. That same year, I was nearly killed in a car wreck while on one of my trips and had to spend nearly five months in a wheelchair.

"By 1989, I realized we needed more space. This time I was going to look around to find a big enough piece of land so that we wouldn't have to move again. Moving is such a nightmare. A friend happened to see this 87-acre parcel where we are now. I bought it, and we built 105,000 square feet. It took two teams four months to move the inventory. It was 20 miles one way from the old place. Operating during that period was also a nightmare, because you were never sure where anything was. Often a piece you needed was still at the old place, and we'd have to make a special trip just to get it.

"We'd been in the building about a year when I learned that there was a plan that called for a loop road around Greensboro that would go right through our property. We asked our customers to write the state, and they did—bombarded them with letters—but the issue is still up in the air. If they build the new road, an exit ramp off the interstate will run right in front of the building and take out my two large signs. Those signs are important. We do $100,000 a month just from the highway traffic.

"In 1994, we expanded, adding 120,000 square feet this time. As you'll see when you tour the building, we're about full again, but the plan is on hold until the state decides what it is going to do with the road. I spent $680,000 building the access road into the building and then dedicated it to the state for maintenance. Biggest mistake I've made. Now the state won't allow me to undedicate it, and it creates a problem for expansion if I can't.

"Today, we have about 500 employees here and about 1,500 dealers out scouring flea markets, auctions, etcetera, looking for stuff they can buy and then sell to Replacements so we can then sell it to our customers. We publish a quarterly index that lists 95,000 patterns and what we will pay a dealer, or an individual, for any of the pieces in those patterns. We have 4 million pieces in our inventory. We also buy from manufacturers when they discontinue a pattern, and we handle current lines. We also buy silverware and flatware, collectibles, and crystal. We now get about 26,000 calls in an average week. Our sales this year will be about $60 million (see Exhibit 2). Not bad for selling used 'dishes.' And we're the largest company like this in the world. Our nearest competitor has less than $3 million in sales and 10 employees. We really don't have any competition.

"And, I'm happy. I still live in the same 1,300-square-foot house I have lived in since I bought it for $55,000 14 years ago. I drive a seven-year-old Ford Explorer. I really enjoy helping folks find and replace that piece that broke. China, crystal, and all that is so personal. We have people come in here and bring their entire set of china and crystal. They may be going into a retirement home and don't have room for it and don't have family to give it to. They ask us to find one buyer so the set won't be broken up. And we do. I take customer calls every day. This business is all about helping people out and making them happy.

"I know you folks are from the business school. We're glad you're here. We're always looking for new ideas. But, you need to understand, we don't have a business plan. We don't have a strategy. We don't have a marketing plan. We don't have budgets. We don't have much of that stuff you teach."

Replacements, Ltd., Sales by Product Type

Product Type	1995	1996	1997
China	$23,280,361	$29,180,113	$34,107,173
Crystal	2,911,824	3,594,419	4,134,168
Flatware	4,986,811	6,778,454	9,097,704
Collectibles	365,474	676,207	884,495
Showroom	1,128,235	1,665,924	1,573,174
Totals	$32,672,705	$41,895,117	$49,796,714

Source: Replacements, Ltd.

EXHIBIT 2:   Replacements, LTD. Total Sales vs. Employees

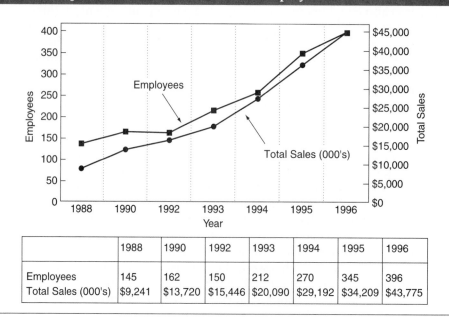

	1988	1990	1992	1993	1994	1995	1996
Employees	145	162	150	212	270	345	396
Total Sales (000's)	$9,241	$13,720	$15,446	$20,090	$29,192	$34,209	$43,775

THE TABLETOP MARKET

Bob Page had obviously identified a large, untapped market, but no one knew just how large the market for used china, crystal, and flatware was. There were no market studies or market research reports on the market.

However, information was available on the current retail "tabletop" market. *HFN Magazine* presented an analysis of the industry in its September 1997 issue. Exhibit 3 presents summary statistics from that report and information on the major manufacturers in the tabletop market. The tabletop market included dinnerware, glassware and crystal, and flatware. The dinnerware market included housewares sold by mass merchandisers (so-called "everyday" or casual dinnerware), upstairs casual (casual or everyday dinnerware with somewhat higher prices than mass market prices), and upstairs formal (including formal china). The term *upstairs* implies a higher-priced, more formal item. Crystal included stemware—crystal pieces that included a base and a stem supporting the portion that held the beverage, such as a wine glass. Flatware included sterling silver, silverplate (utensils that were plated with silver), and stainless steel pieces.

The *HFN* article noted several industry trends:

- Lifestyle stores and home superstores like Linens and Things and Bed, Bath, and Beyond were responsible for much of the industry's growth.

- There was a move to "open stock" selling, that is, allowing customers to buy individual items rather than requiring that they buy full place settings or sets of items. Some brides, for example, were requesting just dinner plates. Some consumers were mixing formal and casual tableware.

- There was a continued movement from formal to casual, as evidenced by the move to more casual dress in business settings. Color had become more important in casual china.

- Baby boomers were saving for retirement and, at the same time—to deal with stressful lifestyles—were eating out more often and spending more on leisure.

- In upstairs tabletop, upstairs casual dinnerware and crystal stemware were doing well, but analysts did not regard formal china as a growth opportunity. Noritake, the second-largest formal china manufacturer, had targeted the self-purchase customer and the "encore" bride. Although manufacturers of formal tableware were responding to the casual trend, they were not neglecting the formal.

MARKETING AT REPLACEMENTS

"As Bob Page often says, 'We'll try anything—once,'" Kelly Smith observed as he discussed Replacements' marketing strategy. Kelly served as the company's chief financial officer and also headed its marketing efforts. Kelly joined Replacements in 1995 after graduating from Wake Forest University with a degree in accounting, getting his CPA, and working with Arthur Anderson, Kayser Roth (a textile firm), and NationsBank.

"For example, in June 1994, the company decided to try advertising in *Parade Magazine*, the magazine that's inserted in Sunday newspapers all across the country. The people at *Parade* had been trying to get us to advertise. So, we advertised only in the West Coast edition, thinking there'd be consumers, especially in California, who'd be interested in our service; and advertising in one region would give us a chance to see how *Parade* worked. It so happened that the first ad followed a major California earthquake by only a couple of months. Apparently there were a lot of people who'd lost some or all of

EXHIBIT 3   The Tabletop Industry: 1996

A. Total Market

Category	Retail Dollar Volume	Percent of Total
Dinnerware	$1.659 billion	40.3
Glassware & Crystal	1.706 billion	41.4
Flatware	.753 billion	18.3
Total Market	**$4.117 billion**	**100% + 3.3% from 1995**

B. Dinnerware Analysis

Category	Retail Dollar Volume	Percent of Total
Housewares, Mass Market	$934.2 million	56.3
Upstairs Formal	431.2 million	26−2% from 1995
Upstairs Casual	293.6 million	17.7
Total Dinnerware	**$ 1.659 billion**	**100% + 2% from 1995**

C. Crystal Analysis

Category	Retail Dollar Volume	Percent of Total
Crystal Giftware	$455.7 million	68.1
Crystal Stemware	175.3 million	26.2 + 1.92% from 1995
Crystal Barware	38.1 million	5.7
Total Crystal	**$669.2 million**	**100% + 5% from 1995**

D. Flatware Analysis

Category	Retail Dollar Volume	Percent of Total
Stainless Steel	$535.9 million	72
Sterling Silver	152.0 million	20 No change from 1995
Silverplate	65.0 million	8
Total Flatware	**$752.9 million**	**100% + 5% from 1995**

MAJOR MANUFACTURERS OF UPSTAIRS TABLEWARE

1. **Lenox, Inc.** Estimated 1996 sales: $370 million. Parent: Brown-Forman, Corp. Subsidiaries: Dansk International Designs, Ltd.; Gorham, Inc.; Kirk Stieff Co.
2. **Mikasa, Inc.** Estimated 1996 sales: $372.3 million. Public company with headquarters in London.
3. **Noritake Company, Inc.** Estimated 1996 sales: $51 million. Parent: Noritake Company, Ltd. Headquarters in London.
4. **Royal China and Porcelain Companies, Inc.** Estimated 1993 sales: $30 million. Parent: Royal Worcester Spode, Ltd. Headquarters in London.
5. **Royal Doulton USA, Inc.** Estimated 1992 sales: $8.4 million. Parent: Pearson, Inc. Headquarters in London.
6. **Waterford Wedgwood PLC., Inc.** Estimated 1996 sales: $636.7 million (Wedgwood Group (china) = $378 million, Waterford Crystal = $259 million)
7. **Oneida Silversmiths Division.** Estimated 1996 sales: $270 million. Parent: Oneida, Ltd. (Oneida Ltd. 1997 sales = $376.9 million. 54% of sales from consumer tableware.)
8. **Reed and Barton Corporation.** Estimated 1995 sales: $43 million. Private company with headquarters in London.
9. **Syratech Corporation.** Estimated 1996 sales: $270.9 million. Silver, silverplated, and sterling brands marketed under Wallace, International Silver, and Westmoreland brand names. Wallace Silversmiths, Inc. 1996 sales estimated at $75 million. Corporate revenues include sale of casual furniture.
10. **Durand International.** Estimated 1994 sales: $24 million. Manufacturers lead crystal. Private subsidiary with headquarters in London.

Source: *HFN Magazine*, September 1997, pp. 5–29.

their china and crystal in the quake. The Monday morning following the Sunday ad, our telephones rang off the hook. We had over 3,000 phone calls that day, which at that time was really a huge volume of calls for one day. It was by far our record day. And for a long time that record stood.

"Just to give you an idea of how we have grown, yesterday we had—let me look at my daily call record a second—yes, we had 4,800 calls yesterday. That's a pretty normal day now.

"I know you're interested in what I think the big issues are from a marketing perspective," Smith continued. "Well, the first issue is how we can continue to find the right media to generate new leads, new customers. Historically, we've been space-ad driven. We've not done a lot of prospecting, direct mailing, or buying lists, like a lot of direct marketing companies do. What little we've done we've found to be unsuccessful if we didn't have the names of patterns associated with customer names; that is, we know what particular patterns each customer on the list owns. We've talked to bridal stores to try to get the list of clients who bought a certain pattern when we learn that a manufacturer has discontinued that particular pattern, but we really haven't had much luck with that. The big challenge is finding the right media to help us sustain our growth rate. We know it's out there; it's just a question of finding it.

"A second problem we face is having a more-defined customer contact strategy. Once we get a name on file, we tend to send them quotes several times a year. We have seasonal sales and sales on select patterns. We've some general controls on this, but in theory, we could end up sending out lots of quotes for just a little bit of inventory. We don't do any analysis of our customers' buying histories, and we rarely purge our database. We need to come up with a strategy to generate sales without spewing quotes out of our building, but, we know how important quoting is. In July 1995, we stopped quoting for a month while we converted to a new computer system and sales plummeted. We all became sensitized to how important the quoting process is to maintaining sales growth. But I was doing some estimating just last week. If you're on file with one pattern, you'll probably get four to six mailings a year from us. If you, however, had eight patterns, you might get 48 mailings a year—and they'd all come in the same old, nice-looking envelope. So we've got to figure out what we call 'smart quoting.'

TARGET MARKET

"Our target market is anyone who has china, crystal, sterling, or flatware patterns where they need to replace a broken or missing piece or just want to complete their set but the pattern is no longer produced. We also offer collectible items, like Hummel figurines, for people who like to collect those kinds of things.

"We had a study several years ago. We determined that our typical customer was between 45 and 75 years old and was generally an affluent female. I wish I could find that study, but I can't seem to put my hands on it.

PRODUCT

"I guess the first question a lot of people have is how do we get all the things we have to sell. Well, I said this is an unusual business. Unlike other retailers, we can't call up the manufacturer and say 'send us 100 suits in assorted sizes.'

"The primary source of our product is the 1,500 or so active, independent, individual suppliers who buy china, etcetera, anywhere they can find it. It might be at a flea

EXHIBIT 4   Sample Line from Page in Replacements' Supplier Index[1]

China

Pattern: Noritake	N	Pla	CS	DP	IP	SP	BB	CR	SU
Lilac Time	2483	13.5	1	11	9	1	.50	3	4

Lilac Time (con)		OV	RV	PL1	PL2	PL3	FR	CER	SO
		2	21	24	1	41	6	7	10

Lilac Time (con)		CSS	GR	BD	S/P	TP	CP	CV	DE
		17	27	23	15	45	45	49	9

Lilac Time (con)		CH	REL	MUG	BOU
		33	10	10	12

CODE KEY

Code	Description	Code	Description
PLA	Place setting, consisting of:	CER	Cereal bowl (rim or coupe)
CS	Cup and saucer	S0	Soup bowl (rim or coupe, 7"–9")
DP	Dinner plate (10" to 10¾")	CSS	Cream soup and saucer
SP	Salad plate (round, 8" to 8¾")	GR	Gravy boat with stand (1 or 2 pieces)
BB	Bread and butter (6" to 7¾")	BD	Butter dish with lid
LP	Luncheon plate (round, 9" to 9½")	S/P	Salt and pepper set
CR	Creamer	TP	Tea pot with lid (short and stout)
SU	Sugar bowl with lid	CP	Coffee pot with lid (tall and thin)
OV	Oval vegetable bowl (9"–11")	CV	Covered vegetable (oval or round)
RV	Round vegetable bowl (8"–1")	DE	DemiTasse cup and saucer
PL1	Platter One (10" to 13-7/8")	CH	Chop plate (round platter, 12"–14")
PL2	Platter Two (14" to 15-7/8")	REL	Relish (7"–10")
P13	Platter Three (16"–18")	MUG	Mug
FR	Fruit/Dessert bowl (4" to 5'3/4")	BOU	Bouillon soup & saucer

[1]Figures listed under the codes for type of piece are in dollars. For example, 13.5 listed for a place setting of Noritake Lilac Time means that Replacements will pay $13.50 for a four-piece place setting consisting of a cup and saucer, dinner plate, salad plate, and bread and butter plate.

market, an estate auction, or an antique store. The supplier can look up a particular pattern and piece in that pattern in our index to see what we'll pay for it. (See Exhibit 4.) Then the supplier can buy the piece for something less than what we will pay. The supplier makes money on the spread, just as we do when we sell the piece for more than we paid the supplier.

"That supplier then boxes up any pieces he/she may have and sends them to us. Each morning we'll get from 300 to 500 boxes delivered to us in Greensboro—about 250,000 pieces a month. It's like Christmas every day. We never know what's coming until we open the boxes.

"Once we open the box, we inspect the contents and compare them to the paperwork the supplier has completed and included with the shipment. That paperwork includes the supplier's statement as to what he/she expects us to pay. We grade the merchandise, enter it in the computer, and send it to inventory. The paperwork then goes to accounting so that we can pay the supplier. We pay the suppliers within 14 days, and sometimes sooner. Some of the suppliers just do this as a hobby. For others, it's their job. Last year we paid 61 different suppliers more than $20,000, with a few earning in the six-figure range. We want being a supplier to be a reliable and stable source of income.

"One problem is that, as in any business, about 20 percent of the suppliers produce about 80 percent of the product," Smith added. "We have a lot of inactive suppliers. We had about 3,000 suppliers two years ago. All it cost was $15 a year to be a supplier and get our index, which we publish four times a year. But it cost us $25 a year just to publish the indexes for that supplier. The index contains general information for our suppliers and lists what we will pay for every piece of china, crystal and glassware, flatware, and collectible item. The index is about two inches thick.

"So, in January 1996, we started the STAR supplier program. We raised the annual membership fee to $100. For this, the member got the indexes free, access to a special 800 number, 24-hour turnaround on quotes, electronic payment to the supplier's bank account, and a one-percent rebate on all sales to us once the supplier passed $5,000 in a year (the one percent applied to all $5,000, plus the amount above that level). That program helped a little, but we still had too many people who didn't sell anything to us.

"So we've just revised the program again. Now, you have to sell us at least $2,000 in the prior year in order to be a STAR supplier. If you sold less than $500, it will cost you $400 to be a member. We're probably down to about 1,500 suppliers now. They account for about 85 percent of our supply.

"About eight to 10 percent of our supply comes from manufacturers. When a manufacturer decides to discontinue a pattern, we will buy its inventory of that pattern. The manufacturers decided about five years ago that it was cheaper to let us handle the small orders for remnants. They'll also often sell active patterns to us as they would to any other dealer with us getting a standard discount from their recommended retail price. We have active accounts with most manufacturers now. In fact, we are Noritake's biggest customer.

"The final five to seven percent of our supply comes from individuals. People may just walk into our showroom and sell to us. Sometimes they have inherited the items and don't want them or would rather have the money. Other times, the person is going through a divorce and wants to sell the items.

"We estimate that we have about 95,000 patterns and over four million pieces in inventory. We also offer collectibles like rare figurines, collectible plates, past Christmas ornaments, etcetera. For all our products, we offer a 30-day, money-back satisfaction guarantee.

"We also have a couple of other 'products.' We offer a free pattern-identification service. We have several curators on staff who work with customers to identify patterns. Often a person doesn't know the manufacturer's or the pattern's name. They can send us a picture, tracing, or an actual piece; and our staff will conduct the research to identify the pattern and manufacturer. We also offer a flatware restoration and cleaning service and have considered offering a china repair service. We repair china now for re-sale, but we have never offered that service to our customers.

PRICE

"Bob understands supply and demand so well," Smith said. "From the very beginning he was developing his buying-pricing model so we can buy the inventory we need, not buy the inventory we don't need, and move the inventory that we have.

"Bob uses a pricing matrix that has customer groups down one axis, that is, the number of customers we have for a pattern. For example, do we have one to 10 customers or 11 to 20, and so forth. The other axis is the number of pieces we have in stock. At the intersection of each row and column is the percentage of the retail price that we're willing to pay for an item. So if we have a lot of customers for a pattern and not much inventory, we'll pay 50 percent of retail, which is the most we'll pay for anything. At the other end of the scale, if we have lots of inventory and not many customers, we'll only pay five percent of retail. Bob set these parameters up years ago. We continue to find ways to add layers of screening to make pricing more advantageous for us. We have minimum/maximum/absolute pricing we set for particular patterns that can override the matrix based on all sorts of factors. There may be a particular pattern that we really want, and we'll pay a certain price for items in that pattern regardless of what the matrix might say.

"Pricing is a continuous process. Literally every day, Bob's setting up special pricing scales for certain patterns or groups of patterns. By changing the retail prices, we automatically change the buying prices by action of the matrix. So, if we need more dinner plates in a pattern, we can raise the retail price to reflect demand. This increases the buying price. At some price point, our buyers will seek out that pattern; or, if they or others are holding that pattern, at some price they'll be willing to sell. We started getting away from the standardized pricing scales to more-customized pricing about 1½ to 2 years ago. This is Bob's biggest time-consumer and his most important job.

"Although there'll always need to be judgment in this, we need to systematize our pricing in order to reduce the amount of fine tuning or tweaking we do now.

PLACE

"In addition to selling directly to our customers by mail, we also operate a showroom here so customers can stop by and make purchases. Bob started a showroom several years ago. It was probably only about 200 square feet—pretty much of an afterthought. But more and more people keep stopping by, so the showroom had to grow. Now it takes 12,000 square feet, and we have about 100,000 people per month visiting it. We also offer guided tours every half-hour from 8:30 A.M to 8:00 P.M., seven days a week, year-round. Part of our showroom is our museum, which has over 2,000 unique pieces of china, crystal, and silver on display.

PROMOTION

"I've asked Mark Klein to join us. Mark serves as our director of marketing. He's responsible for all our communications work. He directs a graphic artist, a media placement coordinator, a manufacturer's liaison, and a senior merchandising analyst who takes care of developing and placing all our ads. He also supervises our mailing operation, which involves a manager and seven employees. Before joining us last September, Mark worked 10 years with Hecht's Department Stores as a buyer of housewares, china, and furniture, and then served as a field sales representative for a furniture company for six years. He has a degree in marketing and management from Virginia Tech.

Advertising

"Mark, perhaps you could discuss our advertising program."

"Okay, Kelly. Our advertising's obviously very important in generating leads. We track our advertising very carefully so we can determine which are the best magazines to use for advertising.

"I guess it'd be good to start by summarizing our print advertising program. I've prepared for you this table, which summarizes our print advertising program for September 1996 through August 1997 (see Exhibit 5). During this period, we advertised in 84 magazines. This table summarizes the top 14 magazines in terms of the sales dollars the advertising generated. It shows basic information on the magazine and our ad, the code our telemarketers use when they record that magazine as the source of a new customer, the return on investment (ROI) from the ad, the cost of the ad, and the number of new sales and clients it generated in the period. We calculate the ROI measure by taking 50 percent of the total sales amount (which assumes an average 50 percent gross margin on sales) and dividing that by the cost of the ad. This figure then gives us the gross margin dollars generated for each dollar of ad cost. If this number drops below 1, then we drop that magazine unless there's some other factor working.

"We also track sales for magazines in which we didn't advertise during the past 12 months. You see, once a person becomes a client and we include the client in our database, we designate the source of that client. Our operators ask the clients on their first call how they heard about Replacements. If a client says he/she saw our ad in the *New York Times Magazine*, then we put that code in the client's file. From then on, we credit all purchases that client may make to that magazine. Sometimes we may have discontinued our ads in that magazine, but we still track our sales for those customers by that magazine.

"Many of these magazines also have sections where they list the advertisers in that edition and allow readers to circle a number on a card to request information from that advertiser. This information comes to us from the magazines, and we have to enter the information manually and then mail the person a Replacements' brochure. We track these inquiries and sales from the inquiries also."

"Although it's not advertising, Mark, this might be a good time to mention how we track our other client sources," Smith interjected.

"Good point," Klein replied. "I also prepared a list of our top 16 client sources from other than publications. I took these from an overall list of about 150 such sources (see Exhibit 6). For example, if a customer calls in and says he/she was referred to us by an antique store, we would code that customer as 'AS.' The exhibit shows that in the past 12 months we had over $462,000 in sales to such customers. This table also shows the sales we credit to our lists, that is, lists of customers we've purchased over the years. You'll see on the exhibit a listing for the 'C.C.M. List' or the 'W.D.C. List.' You'll notice also the listing for 'Department Store Referral.' Many people will go to a department store if they break a piece of china or need additional pieces. If the store doesn't carry that pattern or if it's discontinued, often the store personnel will refer the customer to us. The Discovery Channel has a show called 'Start to Finish' that runs about a five-minute segment on Replacements. It's run the segment about 12 to 15 times over the past two years. Every time it runs, we get a burst of telephone calls. In fact, you can 'see' the calls move across the country as the show airs in different time zones.

"The largest total-sales-dollar item is the 'friend or relative' entry. You can see the importance of word of mouth; but, frankly, we wonder if this entry isn't just a catch-all when our operators are busy. For example, when someone calls and indicates that she

EXHIBIT 5   Advertising Analysis for Publications Advertised from 9/96 to 8/97

Publication[a]	Code	ROI	Ad Cost	Total Sales	New Clients
Better Homes & Gardens Ad-Monthly Pub-Monthly 1½" Listing ⅓ pg in 3/96	GB	$ 7.76	$ 62,295	$ 966,862	8.801
Colonial Homes Ad-Bimonthly Pub-Monthly 1/12 Pg BW	CH	$ 13.75	$ 8,444	$ 232,280	1,942
Country Living Ad-Monthly Pub-Bimonthly ⅓ Pg Masthead out May 96, 16M Classified Word Ad	CL	$ 35.40	$ 7,166	$ 507,273	4,208
Good Housekeeping Ad-Monthly Pub-Monthly 1" Listing remnant 7/96, 25M	GH	$ 7.91	$ 27,437	$ 433,917	3,735
Gourmet Ad-Monthly Pub-Monthly STF Calico blue starting in Dec 96 1/12 Page, BW	GT	$ 6.60	$ 23,099	$ 305,065	2,002
House Beautiful Ad-Monthly Pub-Monthly 1/12 Page 4-C	HB	$ 8.18	$ 41,889	$ 685,364	4,526
Martha Stewart Living Ad-Monthly Pub-Monthly Vil Holly in Dec 96 issue 1/12 Page 4-C, 10%/yr.	MS	$ 6.27	$ 30,490	$ 382,570	5,403
New Yorker Ad-Weekly Pub-Weekly 1½" weekly 1/6 thru 7/7/97	YO	$ 3.30	$ 54,137	$ 357,708	1,857
Smithsonian Ad-Monthly Pub-Monthly 2" Listing/makegood 3/97	SM	$ 5.71	$ 23,709	$ 270,819	1,605
Southern Living Ad-Monthly Pub-Monthly 39 words, Prepaid Oct—Dec 97 Prepay 3 mos. 10% discount	SL	$106.87	$ 9,567	$ 2,044,962	12,122
Sunset Ad-Monthly Pub-Monthly 4-C Test ad Oct, Nov, Dec 96, JB BW 1/12 pg 1/12 Page, 2/97 Coach Scenes	TU	$ 10.77	$ 18,117	$ 390,238	2,668
Victoria Ad-Monthly Pub-Monthly ⅓ 4-C in 3/96, 12M	VI	$ 6.94	$ 24,345	$ 337,898	5,286
Yankee Ad-Monthly Pub-Monthly	YA	$ 5.27	$ 27,417	$ 289,030	2,320
SUBTOTAL—All but Parade		$ 8.39	$ 552,346	$ 9,265,633	75,286
Parade Ad-Monthly Pub-Monthly	—	$ 2.58	$1,049,263	$ 6,246,195	89,572
TOTALS—All publications		$ 4.84	$1,601,609	$15,511,828	164,858

[a]Specific publications listed are the top 14 in terms of total sales. Subtotal and total figures include *all* publications.
Source: Replacements, Ltd.

EXHIBIT 6   Source of Clients—Non-Publications from 9/96 to 8/97

Client Source	Code	Total Sales
Antique Clubs	LZ	$ 3,380
Antique Shop	AS	$ 462,533
C.C.M. List	GP	$ 253,791
C.C. Lists	IQ	$ 290,353
Department Store Referral	DQ	$ 2,305,730
Discovery Channel—Start to Finish	DC	$ 214,899
Friend or Relative Referral	FR	$11,950,129
Jewelry Store—Referral	JS	$ 613,540
Magazine Article	MG	$ 1,456,009
Manufacturer	MF	$ 1,880,817
M.C.C. List	MK	$ 367,566
9/96 List	QS	$ 537,744
NO CODE—Mail In's Letter	NC	$ 2,452,630
Old Code—Absolute Codes	OC	$ 2,287,369
Competition Referral	OS	$ 841,373
Previous Customer—Dropped Off & Came Back	PC	$ 985,375
Signs—Front of Building & Billboard	SI	$ 1,889,706
W.D.C. List	WA	$ 1,288,942

Source: Replacements, Ltd.

saw our ad in *American Country Collectibles* magazine, the operator may not know the code for that magazine. If not, he/she must go to another screen and scroll through a list to find the code. This takes time, and our operators are very busy. We think that in such a case it is easy just to enter the code for friend or relative (FR) and save the time and trouble of looking."

"That's right," Smith noted. "Having our operators get accurate information is one of our biggest concerns. If they only realized how critical this information is to all our tracking."

"You'll also notice (on Exhibit 6) the listings for 'No Code' and 'Old Code'," Klein continued. "These categories represent customers who write a letter to place an order and technically there's no other source or the customer had an obsolete (old) code. 'Competition referral' represents customers who were referred to us by a competitor who could not meet their needs. 'Previous customer' represents customers who at some time asked us to take their names off our lists so they wouldn't get our mailings but who subsequently called to place an order. And 'Signs' represents customers who stop in our showroom because they saw one of our billboards or the signs in front of the building as they drove by.

"One of the items on that exhibit listed 'department store referrals.' We have what we call our 'Partners in Business' program. For stores that refer customers to us as a policy, we pay that store a five percent referral rebate based on the sales to clients it refers. We pay these rebates quarterly as long as the rebate is greater than $25. As you can imagine, however, this is another coding problem for our operators because we have about 130 of these partners.

"To summarize all this, I also have a table that shows the number of phone and mail inquiries, the number of inquiries from our customer lists, the number of sales transactions from those inquiries, and the conversion ratio (see Exhibit 7). The ratio is the total number of inquiries divided by the number of sales transactions. The numbers on this exhibit represent the monthly averages for each of the last six years. The category, customer list inquiries, is not broken down into mail or phone, but as you can see, the great majority of our inquiries are by phone. The monthly average for customer list inquiries has grown significantly in the last two years due to several acquisitions of customer lists. When we acquire a list we also get information on the patterns each customer on the list has. Then we send each customer a quote that lists their patterns and the items we have in those patterns and lets them know that Replacements will be their new source. These mailings generate many inquiries.

"When we speak of acquisitions here, we mean that we have acquired the company's mailing list and, in some cases, its inventory if the company is going out of business. Because of the importance of acquisitions, I also prepared this table that lists our acquisitions by year along with other information about the purchase (see Exhibit 8).

"I think Kelly mentioned earlier that we are space-ad driven. We've tried a little television and radio advertising, but they just don't seem to work very well for us. We've too much information we need to communicate, and we can't seem to do it effectively in 30 seconds or a minute. Plus, we find that people need to see sample items in the ad.

EXHIBIT 7   Average Monthly Inquiries Fiscal Years 1992–1997

	Phone Inquiries		Mail Inquiries		Subtotal Inquiries
	No.	% of Total	No.	% of Total	w/o Cust List
1992 Monthly Average	3,815	41	5,546	59	9,361
1993 Monthly Average	3,968	17	6,845	30	10,813
1994 Monthly Average	13,522	80	3,403	20	16,925
1995 Monthly Average	21,249	66	4,639	14	25,889
1996 Monthly Average	32,300	57	4,655	8	36,955
1997 Monthly Average	29,734	46	2,976	5	32,710

	Cust. List Inquiries			New Leads	
	No.	% of Total	Total Inquiries	Sales Transactions	Conversion Ratio
1992 Monthly Average			9,361	4,537	2.06
1993 Monthly Average	11,900	52	22,713	6,602	3.44
1994 Monthly Average	21	0	16,946	8,947	1.89
1995 Monthly Average	6,470	20	32,359	11,164	2.90
1996 Monthly Average	19,845	35	56,800	13,234	4.29
1997 Monthly Average	31,755	49	64,465	15,794	4.08

Source: Replacements, Ltd.

EXHIBIT 8   Replacements' Assets Acquisitions

Acquisition	Cost	What Purchased	Total Sales to 8/97	Number of Customers	Sales Per Customer
Pre 1992					
C.H.	$ 4,500	List & Inventory	$ 128,919	$ 2,727	$ 47.28
F.D.	4,000	List & Inventory	20,073	464	43.26
Il.	Free	List	61,099	5,338	11.45
M.Z.	Unk.	List & Inventory	46,979	598	78.56
V.H.	325,000	List & Inventory	651,583	15	43,439.00
1993					
Mgs.	25,000	List & Inventory	165,371	3,562	46.43
W.D.C.	14,300	List	8,904,106	123,741	71.96
C.A.	10,000	List & Inventory	124,138	3,599	34.49
1994					
Ab.	125,000	List & Inventory	272,331	6,859	39.70
Gu.	4,500	List	44,583	2,787	16.00
C.T.	65,000	List & Inventory	419,279	11,326	37.02
1995					
C.C.	10,000	List	911,620	29,261	31.15
A.S. G.	5,000	List	196,020	3,683	53.22
C.C.M.	240,000	List & Inventory	755,368	39,322	19.21
1996					
A.W.	25,000	List & Inventory	45,796	1,589	28.82
He.	1,750	List	3,442	928	3.71
C.S.	683	List	53,497	2,746	19.48
C.C.X.	5,033	List & 800#	94,207	5,570	16.91
F.G.	165	List	765	659	1.16
S.H. List	11,000	List	585,178	114,348	5.12
1997					
M.C. C.	200,000	List & Inventory	395,539	34,548	11.45
P.S.	9,000	List	42,263	4,648	9.09
W.D. S.	900,000	List & Inventory	1,450,570	82,915	17.49
P.P.	60,000	List & Inventory	35,523	1,794	19.80
TOTALS	$2,044,931		$15,408,249	$483,027	$ 31.90

Source: Replacements, Ltd.

"For example, here's a sample ad from *Parade.* You'll notice the line of plates across the bottom. One might assume that we just pick some sample plates for the ad, but we select each individual plate/pattern very carefully based on our inventory and the number of customers who might want that pattern. We'll have people call in who'll say that they recognize their pattern as being the fifth plate from the left in the ad, so our operators must have copies of the ads with pattern names noted so they can help the customers.

"Our staff does all of the creative work in developing our ads. Until 1995, we used outside companies to do this. We think we can do it just as well; and by placing the ads ourselves, we save the 15 percent fee we'd have paid an advertising agency to do that.

"Despite our focus on print ads, we're trying to get a TV ad with Visa, the credit card folks. You may remember that Visa has these ads in which it features unique or unusual businesses and notes that the establishments "don't take American Express." We think we fit Visa's criteria, and Bob has a personal goal of getting Replacements in one of those ads. We even filmed a sample ad to show Visa. We haven't had any luck yet. Visa is also developing some radio ads with the same theme, but we're not sure Replacements will work as well on radio.

"We're always looking for new home-and-shelter-type publications in which to advertise. Bob encourages us to try anything. One of the greatest things about working here is that we don't have an ad budget, so if we come up with an idea we like, we just try it. Although we don't have a budget, we spend about three to four percent of revenue on advertising. We just seem to hit that range. We could certainly spend more, but we find there is a "wear-out" factor with our advertising. For example, we only advertise once a month in *Parade*. Our ad is on the page with the 'Intelligence Report' feature, the second-most-read page in the magazine. But our space is always the same size and our ads look alike even though we change them. If we advertised every week, we'd just speed up the wear-out factor.

Personal Selling

"I've mentioned our telemarketing staff several times, so perhaps I should discuss this process in more detail," Klein continued. "We've about 70 full-time staff in this area who operate from 8 A.M. to 10 P.M. daily, year-round. When we're not open, we record messages by voice mail and return the calls the next day. About 90 percent of our sales are by telephone, with the remaining 10 percent occurring in our showroom. Our operators will handle about 26,000 calls a week. We have five T-1 lines into the building, each T-1 being 24 lines. Even though you have to add 24 lines at a time, we'll add a T-1 before we really need it because we want customers to be able to get in. It is rare that all of our lines are busy, but it has happened. People can also e-mail us at ReplaceLtd@aol.com.

"The first time a customer calls our 1–800–Replace number, he or she has typically seen one of our ads and is interested in getting a free list of patterns we carry and other basic information. Our operators try to establish rapport. Our goal in that first call is to get the customer's name and address and the names of any patterns he or she owns and a particular piece request. This is critical to us knowing how to price and how to adjust our pricing matrix. As I've noted, we also record how the customer came to call us— through an ad, a referral, or however. So our goal is to get that customer on file with as much specific information as possible. Finally, our operators are supposed to conclude the call by asking if the customer has any other china, crystal, silver, flatware, glassware, everyday stoneware, etcetera, needs that we can help them with. This is a way to educate the customer about our other offerings. So many customers think we only carry china.

"We have over 2½ million customers on file. However, one problem is that many records are so old that we are not sure if the information, such as which pieces they want, is still valid. If a customer calls in who is already on our system, the operator just punches in the customer's phone number to call up his or her information.

"So, we have a standard format that our operators follow. The typical operator will take 70 to 110 calls per day. We try to hire people with telephone experience. They need the ability to sit at a desk all day and take calls. We put them through a month's training. New employees can take monitored calls in about two weeks. They have to learn the computer screens and how to work them. They'll sit and listen as an experienced person takes calls.

"Because we can get bursts of calls from time to time, we've developed a system so that other staff members working in other functional areas are trained to handle phone calls and take orders. Even our managers, including Bob, do this. When someone calls, our automatic system answers before the first ring and delivers a prerecorded message. At the end of the message, the call goes to an operator, depending on which number the customer selects from the menu. The computer monitors incoming traffic, and whenever there are more than two calls in the queue—the queue beginning whenever the system answers a call—we have bells that ring in certain offices. For example, bells will ring in the accounting office, the mail room, and other support departments. The bells also ring in several of the managers' offices, like Kelly's and Bob's. A light in the telephone operators' room goes on so that an operator who's getting ready to go on a break, for example, knows to wait.

"That's our standard system. We also have what we call a 'Code 2.' Anyone who is involved in the system can call a 'Code 2.' They do this by announcing over the intercom that we have a 'Code 2'."

"We don't have any specific rules about when to do this," Smith noted. "For example, we've a display on our phones that tells us how many calls are in queue and what the maximum wait time is. If I notice that there are more than three calls in the queue and wait time is 20 seconds, I'll call a 'Code 2.' We do this over the intercom rather than with bells so that backup staff will hear it even if they aren't at their desks.

"As a result of this system, we can handle the peak-call periods. Our average wait time is *eight seconds.* If we do have calls that are blocked due to our lines being busy, or customers abandon a call, we have a system that captures their phone numbers, and we'll call them the next day to see if we can help them.

"We have five supervisors who monitor calls for quality-control purposes, and we produce daily reports that keep up with every detail. We know how many calls each person takes, the average talk time, and lots of other information. I noted that managers serve as 'Code 2' backups. Bob Page, for example, took 69 calls yesterday. That's high, but he enjoys taking the calls. It allows him, and all of us, to keep in touch with customers.

"We also have a similar phone system with 20 operators in our purchasing department. These folks deal with our suppliers. We have 12 people in our customer service area, handling questions, returns, or problem orders. We're considering consolidating all three groups and using the phone system to route calls to each operator based on that operator's skills and responsibilities.

"Now, once a person has called, talked to an operator, and been added to the system as a new client, we'll have their patterns on file. The next day, we send that person a quote that lists his or her patterns and the prices for the pieces that we have in stock. (see Exhibit 9). We send these letters first class because we found that bulk mail was too slow. We also can send just a brochure.

"If the person calling wants a dinner plate in a certain pattern and we don't have that pattern in stock, we ask the customer if he or she would like to be in our 'call collect first' program. This means the customer says he or she will accept a collect call if the piece he or she is looking for comes in. We'll call them before we send out letters to other customers who're looking for that same pattern or piece. This used to be an actual collect call, but we found we were spending so much time trying to complete the collect call, we just started paying for it ourselves. But by the customer saying he or she will accept a collect call, we know we have a more serious customer.

FIGURE 9: Sample Quote

REPLACEMENTS, LTD.
China, Crystal & Flatware • Discontinued & Active

1089 Knox Road, PO Box 26029. Greensboro. NC 27420
1-800-REPLACE (1-800-737-5223) • ReplaceLtd@aol.com

10/02/97R01 SHEDUCR   1952

PLEASE COMPARE THIS PATTERN NUMBER AND
OTHER DESCRIPTIVE INFORMATION WITH PIECES IN
YOUR PATTERN IF INFORMATION DOES NOT MATCH.
PLEASE ADVISE US SO WE MAY CORRECT OUR FILES.

#BWNDFCX   SHEDUCR   T010

SAHAMA SHORES DR S
SAINT PETERSBURG, FL 33705

PATTERN DUCHESS
COMPANY SHELLEY
PATTERN NUMBER 13401
DESCRIPTION RED, FLORAL BORDER
AND CENTER

THE FOLLOWING IS A LIST OF THE PIECES WE NOW HAVE AVAILABLE IN YOUR PATTERN. All pieces are subject to prior sale. For this reason, WE ENCOURAGE YOU TO ORDER BY PHONE. If ordering by mail, please fill out the quantity requested and total amount for each piece ordered in the area below, and follow the instructions found on the back of this page. Please allow 2–3 weeks for delivery.

QUANTITY AVAILABLE	PIECE DESCRIPTION	SIZE (IN INCHES)	PRICE (PER PIECE OR SET)	ENTER ORDER HERE QUANTITY ORDERED	TOTAL AMOUNT
7	CUP AND SAUCER SET (FOOTED)	2 1/2	$71.95		
3	PLATE—SALAD	8 1/8	$49.95		
8	PLATE—BREAD AND BUTTER	6	$36.95		
1	CUP ONLY—(FOOTED)	2 1/2	$67.95		
7	CREAM SOUP AND SAUCER SET		$108.95		
9	CUP AND SAUCER SET—DEMI TASSE		$62.95		
1	SAUCER ONLY—DEMI TASSE		$20.95		
8	BOWL—SOUP/RIM	8 1/4	$62.95		
2	VEGETABLE—OVAL	9 1/2	$137.00		
***	SPECIAL DISCOUNTED PIECES				***
***	Pieces below are discounted due to slight imperfection — discounts are based on the				***
***	condition of each piece and are taken off of our full retail price. They are noted				***
***	by the following symbols: #=25% discount; *=50% discount; &=75% discount. These				***
***	items have our full guarantee to have NO cracks or chips and can be returned within				***
***	30 days of receipt.				***
2	CUP AND SAUCER SET (FOOTED)	*2 1/2	$35.98		
6	PLATE—SALAD	*8 1/8	$24.98		
5	PLATE—BREAD AND BUTTER	*6	$18.48		
1	PLATTER—OVAL SERVING	*16 1/2	$147.50		
	*** Looking for pieces not shown above? ***				
	*** Ask about our Call Collect Program! ***				

IF YOU ARE RECEIVING MAILINGS PERTAINING TO PATTERN(S) THAT ARE NO LONGER OF INTEREST TO YOU, OR IF YOU ARE RECEIVING INFORMATION ON INCORRECT PATTERNS, PLEASE NOTIFY US.

SEE REVERSE SIDE FOR
TERMS AND CONDITIONS

PLEASE PROVIDE SHIPPING ADDRESS IF DIFFERENT FROM ABOVE

Name

Street Address
(No PO Box)

City   State   Zip

PAYMENT METHOD   ☐ PERSONAL CHECK (make check payable to Replacements, Ltd.)

☐ CREDIT CARD (Check One)   ☐ MASTER CARD   ☐ VISA   ☐ DISCOVER

Account #   Exp. Date   /
                        Month   Year

Cardholder Signature

SO WE MAY SERVE YOU BETTER
PLEASE PROVIDE THE FOLLOWING

Day Phone (   )

FAX (   )

SHIPPING, HANDLING & INSURANCE

CONTINENTAL USA (PER TOTAL ORDERED)

$1–$50 $7.50 $200.01–$300 $16.00
$50.01–$100 $9.50 $300.01–$400 $18.00
$100.01–$200 $13.00   over $400 $24.00

CANADA and PARCEL POST orders double above rates. International shipping rates given upon request. Duty extra.

SUBTOTAL	
NO RESIDENTS PLEASE ADD 6% SALES TAX	
SHIPPING, HANDLING & INSURANCE	
TOTAL	

off 787

Source: Replacements, Ltd.

"When we get more pieces in on a pattern than we need to satisfy our 'call collect' customers, we send out a mailing to others in the database who are looking for that pattern. These and all the other quotes we mail, with the exception of that first quote, go third class bulk with about a 10-day delivery time. We have some decision rules that determine when and if we do a wider mailing.

"Independent of these mailings are our 'sales runs.' These account for the bulk of our mailings. We group patterns into various groups to balance the size of our mailings. Based on our sales history and inventory, the computer will calculate a discount and generate sales quotes. We go through that sales cycle about five times a year, with each cycle being about three weeks and each mailing ranging from 240,000 to 375,000 letters. If we still have inventory after a sales run, we may discount the item even more the next time. One to two times a year, we go through the process of quoting everybody at full price (see Exhibit 10).

"So you can see how," Smith continued, "as I mentioned earlier, someone could get lots of mailings from us over the period of a year. This can get expensive, and we don't want to overwhelm people with quotes, so we have to work constantly on and think about our customer-contact strategy. Are there more efficient and effective ways to contact customers once we find them and get them on our system?"

(Exhibits 11 and 12 present Replacement's financial data.)

Lew G. Brown / Tony R. Wingler / Kristen M. Cashman / Charles A. Kivett

EXHIBIT 10   1997 Sales Cycle 4—Sales Run Work Process Schedule

Group	Group's Previous Sale Ends	Sale Dates	Begin Process	Greenbar to Bob	Greenbar from Bob	Start Printing	Finish Printing	Finish Mailing	Number of Customers
11&13	6/18/97	7/16–8/7	6/24	6/25	6/27	6/30	7/6	7/7	271,568
15&2	6/25/97	7/23–8/14	6/26	6/27	6/30	7/7	7/12	7/13	239,821
1&3	7/2/97	7/30–8/20	6/27	6/30	7/1	7/13	7/19	7/21	261,169
4&5	7/9/97	8/6–8/27	7/1	7/2	7/3	7/20	7/26	7/28	313,466
6&7	7/16/97	8/13–9/3	7/21	7/22	7/24	7/27	8/2	8/4	314,709
8&9	7/23/97	8/20–9/10	7/28	7/29	8/1	8/3	8/9	8/11	317,805
10&11	7/30/97	8/27–9/17	8/4	8/5	8/7	8/10	8/16	8/18	360,137
16	8/6/97	9/3–9/24	8/11	8/12	8/14	8/17	8/23	8/25	371,760
17&14	8/13/97	9/10–10/1	8/18	8/19	8/21	8/24	8/31	9/1	375,468

Group 11	Hutchenreuter Crystal—Kaysons Lenox Crystal	Group 7	Castleton Towle
Group 13	Ken Kraft China—Mauser Mfg. Co. Silver (omit Mikasa & Metlox China) International Silver (Lufberry—Zephyr)	Group 8 Group 9	Ceralene Raynaud—Englishtown Crafts Enesco China—Freeman (omit Fostoria) Fostoria
Group 15	Moncrief—Oscar de la Renta Silver		Frigast Silver—Hibbard, Spencer, Ban (omit Haviland)
Group 2	Royal Dalton Red Wing China—Royal Saxony Gorham Silver (252H—Imperial Chrysanthemum)	Group 10	International Silver (1810—Lovelace) Haviland Johnson Brothers
Group 1	Old Abbey—Rewcrest (omit Royal Doulton) Oneida (Modjeska)—Oneida (Young Love) Rosenthal	Group 12 Group 16 Group 17	Lenox China Noritake, Wallace Silver Metlox, Royal Worcester, Syracuse
Group 3	Royal Sealy—Sheffield (omit RW)		Oneida/Heirloom Silver (Abington)—
Group 4	Shafford—Warwick China (omit Syracuse) (omit Towle)	Group 14	Oneida/Heirloom Monte Carlo Mikasa
Group 5	Gorham Silver (Imperial—Zodiac) Waterford—Zylstra (omit Wedgwood China) Allan Adler Silver—Booths		Spode China
Group 6	Wedgwood Borsumy Fine China—Crown Empire (omit Castleton)		

Source: Replacements, Ltd.

EXHIBIT 11   Replacements Ltd. Income Statements 1994–1997

	Sept 94	% of Sales	Sept 95	% of Sales	Sept 96	% of Sales	Sept 97	% of Sales
GROSS SALES	$29,191,925		$34,209,290		$43,775,216		$52,150,998	
Returns and Allowances	1,327,429		1,536,585		1,880,099		2,354,284	
NET SALES	$27,864,496	100	$32,672,705	100	$41,895,117	100	$49,796,714	100
Cost of Sales	9,467,876	34	11,387,459	35	13,701,095	33	16,345,752	33
GROSS PROFIT	$18,396,620	66	$21,285,246	65	$28,194,022	67	$33,450,961	67
Salaries	1,730,479	6	2,403,150	7	2,905,275	7	2,744,300	6
Wages	3,477,359	12	4,647,444	14	5,789,083	14	7,755,830	16
Overtime	723,801	3	940,017	3	1,338,198	3	1,911,367	4
Accrued Leave	64,854	0	111,201	0	111,658	0	94,095	0
Commissions	101,989	0	225,787	1	41,791	0	51,365	0
Bonuses	96,604	0	167,976	1	202,032	0	244,339	0
Total Compensation	$ 6,195,086	22	$ 8,495,575	26	$10,388,037	25	$12,801,295	26
Unemployment Taxes	35,310	0	40,630	0	28,332	0	79,233	
FICA	452,775	2	615,470	2	794,884	2	922,148	2
(k) Employer Contribution	170,761	1	217,378	1	240,505	1	350,655	1
Workers Compensation	136,926	0	148,563	0	143,009	0	164,507	0
Group Insurance	643,607	2	949,400	3	827,184	2	1,151,450	2
401 K Admin. Expenses			8,660	0	5,171	0	3,312	0
Section 125 Admin. Expense			7,189	0	2,463	0	71,710	0
Total Benefits	$ 1,439,379	5	$ 1,987,290	6	$ 2,041.548	5	$ 2,743,015	6
Total Benefits and Compensation	7,634,465		10,482,865		12,429,585		15,544,310	
Advertising Expense	$ 1,110,577	4	$ 1,144,408	4	$ 1,732,440	4	$ 1,832,064	4
Postage/Mailing	984,218	4	1,551,568	5	2,369,697	6	2,797,134	6
Telephone	477,404	2	840,808	3	804,964	2	812,221	2
Building Rent	400,165	1	817,415	3	900,000	2	900,000	2
Credit Card Fees	498,678	2	590,588	2	785,570	2	954,801	
Depreciation	458,234	2	614,112	2	641,966	2	789,686	2
Operating Supplies	308,376	1	370,575	1	411,809	1	473,746	1
Utilities	160,891	1	231,073	1	227,696	1	255,811	1
Property Taxes	33,354	0	54,262	0	63,179	0	67,695	0
Packaging Materials	214,075	1	262,546	1	449,437	1	595,873	1
Printed Forms	408,916	1	444,797	1	488,449	1	587,632	1
Equipment Rent	8,701	0	191,204	1	342,034	1	573,204	1
Handling, Net	–2,105,453	8	–2,723,618	–8	–1,723,072	–4	–2,096,806	
Interest Expense	17,954	0	131,401	0	22,936	0	78,237	
Professional Fees							630,252	
All Other	1,615,101	6	1,968,864	6	652,204	2	595,779	1
Total Other Operating	$ 3,590,179	13	$ 5,619,610	17	$ 6,656,260	16	$ 9,847,614	20
OPERATING INCOME	7,171,976	26	5,182,771	16	9,108,177	22	8,059,035	16
Other (Income) Expense	–17,974	0	–1,629	0	33,645	0	–92,812	0
Lower of Cost or Market Adjustment[a]	–1,819,417	–7	–2,072,436	–6	–3,034,060	–7	$ 1,980,476	4
Taxes[b]								
NET INCOME	$ 5,334,585	19	3,108,706	10	6,107,762	15	6,171,371	12

[a]Adjustment to reflect changing cost of replacing inventory.
[b]Replacements is a Subchapter S Corp.; owner pays taxes.
Source: Replacements, Ltd.

EXHIBIT 12   Replacements Ltd. Balance Sheets 1994–1997

	Sept 94	Sept 95	Sept 96	Sept 97
Cash	$ –375,198	$–1,447,148	$ –104,738	$ –437,934
Accounts Receivable	211,687	55,580	296,872	366,892
Inventory, Net of Adjustment	9,412,126	10,484,204	13,123,100	18,156,111
Prepaid Expenses	589,364	785,119	798,343	1,066,523
Deposits	63,516	614,951	296,053	200,052
Total Current Assets	$ 9,901,495	$10,492,706	$14,409,630	$19,351,645
Computer Equipment and Software	1,495,687	1,441,437	1,604,709	1,785,108
Leasehold Improvements	1,139,830	1,332,881	1,717,359	1,817,643
Office Furniture and Equipment	733,000	1,125,775	980,615	835,647
Operations Equipment	801,168	895,837	871,504	916,524
Total Capital Assets	$ 4,169,685	$ 4,795,930	$ 5,174,187	$ 5,354,992
Accumulated Depreciation	2,392,598	–2,421,183	2,685,836	3,052,968
Net Capital Assets	1,777,087	2,374,747	2,488,351	2,302,024
Cash Surrender Value of Insurance	93,676	115,069	133,843	176,173
Long-Term Investments	–36,996	–39,021	–12,236	35,212
Fine Art Items	7,173	7,173	7,173	7,173
Total Other Assets	$ 63,853	$ 83,221	$ 128,780	$ 218,558
Total Assets	$11,742,435	$12,950,674	$17,026,761	$21,872,228
Credit Lines	$ 886,000	$ 973,000		$ 2,325,000
Accounts Payable, Trade	388,208	908,607	$ 1,389,684	1,450,395
Deferred Revenue	45	113,290	1,070,458	1,623,969
Accrued Compensation & Benefits	889,715	1,272,937	1,592,571	1,682,270
Other Accrued Expenses	51,455	9,625	6,539	102,180
Total Current Liabilities	2,215,423	3,277,459	4,059,252	7,183,816
Common Stock	20,000	20,000	20,000	20,000
Paid-in Capital	73,568	73,568	73,568	73,568
Retained Earnings	6,926,687	9,433,444	9,579,647	12,873,941
Distributions to Owner	–2,827,828	–2,962,503	–2,813,468	–4,450,469
Year-to-Date Net Income	5,334,585	3,108,706	6,107,762	6,171,371
Total Equity	$ 9,527,012	$ 9,673,215	$12,967,509	$14,688,411
Total Equity and Liabilities	$11,742,435	$12,950,674	$17,026,761	$21,872,228

Source: Replacements, Ltd.

Miami University:
The Redskins Name Controversy

David Rosenthal and Thomas C. Boyd

In September 1996, the Miami University Board of Trustees met to deliberate over whether the university's nickname should be changed. Since 1928 the university teams had been known as the Redskins. However, several factors had recently converged to necessitate careful consideration of a change. It was the board's responsibility to decide whether to keep the Redskins nickname or change it.

The decision was important because of the depth of emotion on both sides of the issue. The supporters of the Redskins name defended its use vehemently. This group represented many alumni and longtime friends of the school, who were also some of the university's largest contributors. As word of the pending decision spread, visible evidence of support for retaining the Redskins name appeared around the campus. Bumper stickers, T-shirts, and letters to the editor espoused phrases such as "Redskin 'til I die." Supporters of the name were angered over the board of trustees apparent willingness to even consider pressure from outside groups who, they believed, had little understanding of the traditions or significance of the Redskins name.

Those who supported changing the nickname thought that the term "Redskins" was derogatory and inappropriate for use by a university. Further, they believed that the term was racist and did not show proper respect for Native Americans. Those within the university community who supported a change also believed that the image of the university was hurt by the use of Redskins because it projected an image of the school as "out of touch," and insensitive to minorities. This latter concern was important because the school had been trying to increase its minority enrollment.

The current controversy followed an attempted compromise in 1993 by then university President Paul Risser. At that time, the university community engaged in a long and sometimes contentious debate over whether to drop the Redskins nickname. In December 1993, President Risser proposed a compromise: to allow the continued use of the Redskins name while setting the stage for gradual change. The compromise was that all teams and publications currently using the nickname could continue its official use. All other organizations and publications of the university not currently using the nickname would adopt "Miami Tribe" as the nickname of athletic teams. Following the board of trustees meeting at which the compromise measure was approved, Joseph Marcum, board chairman, said the decision allowed for change without causing deeper division between both sides. He said, "I think the term will eventually phase out, but instead of a jolt, it will be more of an evolutionary process." The Native American Miami Tribe of Oklahoma supported the compromise.

The compromise measure itself was controversial. The board of trustees vote to accept President Paul Risser's recommendation passed by a vote of 4–3 with one abstention, one absent.

Sister Jean Patrice Harrington, board chairwoman, said regarding the vote, "I think that it was the only decision that could possibly be made at this time without bringing about further division within the academic community and all the constituencies with whom Miami works."

Harold Paul, trustee from Strongsville, Ohio, voted against the proposal, and said that he thought Passer's plan would satisfy no one. "I just felt we needed to make a decision. If the connotation Redskins is offensive and those people who are offended protest, then I feel that we have to seriously consider making a change."

In the years following the compromise decision little changed. Although the university did what it could to promote the use of "Miami Tribe," few adopted the new name and Redskins continued in common usage. The Indian tribe had formally supported the use of the name and its logo since 1972 and had renewed its support in 1991 (Exhibit 1). Then, in July 1996, the Miami Tribe withdrew its support for the use of Redskins, reopening the controversy. The action by the Miami Tribe constituted a significant change in position (Exhibit 2).

BACKGROUND

Miami University was founded in 1809 and was the seventh-oldest state-assisted university in the United States. Frequently referred to as a "public ivy," Miami was known primarily for its excellent undergraduate teaching. Its emphasis on liberal education for all undergraduates was intended to encourage problem solving and critical thinking, preparing students for the ever-changing work environment. Miami's main campus, in Oxford, Ohio, had an enrollment of about 16,000 students.

Miami had recently received a significant amount of favorable publicity related to a number of national rankings. In 1995, *U.S. News and World Report* ranked Miami as the eighth-best undergraduate teaching institution in the United States. It was also named a best buy in the *Fiske Guide to Colleges* in 1996, one of only 20 public institutions listed. As a result, in 1996, 11,600 prospective freshmen applied for admission to the school.

Miami University was named for the Native American Miami Tribe that had once inhabited the rolling hills of the Ohio Valley where the school is located. Over the years, the university and tribal elders maintained a close and cordial relationship, in which university officials consistently stressed the school's desire to honor the Miami Tribe and its history. The university logo was a realistic Indian head in front of the university's block M (Exhibit 3).

Although seldom considered a national power in a major sport, Miami athletics had an interesting history. Known as the "Cradle of Coaches," Miami had been the one-time home to many top college and professional football coaches. John Pont, Woody Hayes, Bo Schembechler, Ara Parsegian, and Weeb Ewbank were among those who had coached and/or played at Miami. The school currently had a reputation as a "giant killer" who commonly created major upsets in NCAA Division 1A. For example, in 1995, the school upset the University of Arizona (a fourth seed) in the first round of the NCAA basketball tournament and then took the University of Virginia to overtime in

EXHIBIT 1 Miami University Historical Context

1809	Miami University was chartered by the Ohio Legislature and named in honor of the Miami Tribe, which gave up rights to most of its Ohio homeland in the 1795 Treaty of Greenville.
Prior to 1928	Miami's intercollegiate athletic teams were called The Miami Boys, The Big Reds, The Reds, or The Red and Whites. The university's colors of red and white had nothing to do with Indian heritage. Competing campus literary societies founded in 1825 adopted the colors, one picking red and the other white.
1928	Miami Publicity Director R. J. McGinnis coined the term "Redskins" for athletic teams; the Varsity M Club became "Tribe Miami."
1931	"Redskins" first appeared in the school yearbook in reference to athletic teams.
1940s	Student snack bar became the Redskin Reservation, also known as "The Res."
1950s	Students dressed as Indians began to appear with the marching band.
1960s	The marching band's Indian mascot gave way to Hiawabop, a student usually dressed as a Plains Indian in a war bonnet and painted face.
Late 1960s	A visit to the Miami campus by Miami Chief Forest Olds resulted in a formal relationship between the Miami Tribe of Oklahoma and the University.
1972	University President Phillip Shriver appointed a task force to examine the use of Indian symbols; the Miami Tribe passed a resolution of support for a relationship with the university.

1972 Resolution of Miami Tribe Supporting Use of Redskins by Miami University Proclamation

WHEREAS: We, the elected leaders of the 1,500 member tribe of Miami Indians, are meeting this day in solemn council in the state of Oklahoma on the lands bequeathed to the Miamis by treaty with the government of the United States for "as long as the wind shall blow." And:

WHEREAS: In the territory of what is now Ohio, Indiana, Illinois, and Michigan our ancestors once lived in peace among the forests and long waters under the hand of the Great Spirit, and:

WHEREAS: At Oxford, Ohio, where there once stood a village of the Miamis, there stands today a University bearing the name Miami and bestowing upon its young athletes the name Miami Redskins, and;

WHEREAS: It is our counsel that the name Redskins is a revered and honored name in the eyes and hearts of the people of Miami University, and that it signifies to them as to us the qualities of courage, self-discipline, respect, kindness, honesty, and love exemplified by generations of young athletes,

THEREFORE Know all peoples, that we of Miami blood are proud to have the name Miami Redskins carried with honor by the athletic representation of Miami University on the playing fields of Mid-America and in the arena of the world in International Olympic competition.

We, the Miami Redskins of Indian blood, and our namesake, the Miami University Redskins, have a mutual and cherished heritage. May it be blessed by Moneto as long as the wind shall blow.

Mid-1980s	Hiawabop was retired in favor of Chief Miami, whose regalia were provided by the tribe. Students who appeared in the role were required to learn authentic Indian dances. During this time, a liaison between the tribe and the university was established.
1984	Tom-O-Hawk, a student dressed as a comical red bird, began entertaining at athletic events.
1988	The Business Committee of the Miami Tribe of Oklahoma released a resolution reaffirming their 1972 resolution.
Spring 1993	Newly appointed President Paul Risser announced a process to study the use of the term Redskins. University Senate passed a resolution recommending the nickname be discontinued.
Nov. 1993	President Risser listened to nearly 70 individuals at a Redskin Forum on the campus. About 200 attended the meeting.
Dec. 1993	President Risser made the recommendation that all Miami University teams and publications currently using the nickname Redskins should continue to do so and that all other university-sponsored publications and organizations were to adopt the nickname Miami Tribe.
Dec. 3 1993	The Miami Tribe of Oklahoma released a letter stating in part: "The Miami Tribe supports the recommendations as set forth by President Paul Risser...We would be pleased with the use of the term 'Miami Tribe'."
Dec. 10–11	The board of trustees approved President Risser's decision to allow groups currently using Redskins to continue to do so and for all other groups to use Miami Tribe.
July 1996	The Miami Tribe of Oklahoma adopted a resolution saying it could no longer support Redskins as Miami University's athletic nickname.

EXHIBIT 2   1996 Resolution of Miami Tribe Withdrawing Support for the Use of Redskins by Miami University

---

Resolution

Whereas: The Miami Tribe of Oklahoma is a federally recognized Indian Tribe organized under the Oklahoma Indian Welfare Act of 1936, with a Constitution and By-Laws approved by the U.S. Secretary of the Interior on February, 22, 1996, and

Whereas: In the territory of what is now Ohio, Indiana, Illinois, and Michigan our ancestors once lived in peace among the forests and long waters under the hand of the Great Spirit; and

Whereas: At Oxford, Ohio, where there once stood a village of the Miamis, there stands today a University bearing the name Miami; and

Whereas: In 1972, the Miami Tribe of Oklahoma acceded to the request of Miami University to bestow upon its young student athletes the nickname Miami Redskins; and

Whereas: The bonds of friendship and shared heritage between Miami University and the Miami Tribe of Oklahoma have grown stronger over the last twenty-five years; and

Whereas: Miami University and the Miami Tribe of Oklahoma have worked together harmoniously to make sure that the nickname Miami Redskins be used to signify the qualities of courage, self-discipline, respect, kindness, honesty, and love by generations of young student athletes; and

Whereas: We realize that society changes, and that what was intended to be a tribute to both Miami University, and to the Miami Tribe of Oklahoma, is no longer perceived as positive by some members of the Miami Tribe of Oklahoma, Miami University, and society at large; and

THEREFORE, BE IT RESOLVED that the Miami Tribe of Oklahoma can no longer support the use of the nickname Redskins and suggest that the Board of Trustees of Miami University discontinue the use of Redskins or other Indian-related names, in connection with its athletic teams, effective with the end of the 1996–97 academic school year.

BE IT FURTHER RESOLVED, that the Miami Tribe of Oklahoma does not associate the athletic team nickname of Redskins with Miami's logo, exemplified by the artist's portrait of an Indian Chief. The Miami Tribe therefore urges Miami University to continue use of the respectful and dignified portrayal of the Indian Chief as its logo and as a reminder to all of the shared heritage of Miami University and the Miami Tribe of Oklahoma; and

BE IT FURTHER RESOLVED, that the Miami Tribe of Oklahoma stands ready to assist the University and to offer its counsel, as the University begins the debate on an appropriate nickname for its athletic teams; and

THEREFORE, know all peoples that we of Miami blood are proud of our relationship with our namesake, Miami University, and of our mutual and cherished heritage and that we hope to continue to strengthen this relationship for our mutual benefits. May this relationship be blessed by the Creator as long as the winds shall blow.

---

the second round. Also that year, Miami's football team was the only team to defeat eventual Big Ten champion, Northwestern University, in the regular season. Recently, however, attendance at Miami home football games had dropped to levels that potentially put its Division 1A status in question.

Despite a number of recent successes, Miami traditionally had trouble competing with larger schools in the region for fans. Miami teams were always in the shadow of the University of Notre Dame, Ohio State University and the University of Michigan,

and played in the less-competitive Mid-American conference. Thus, drawing media and fan support outside the university community was difficult. Even at the school, Miami athletic officials were constantly concerned with how to increase attendance at football and basketball games. Another factor that affected attendance was the relative isolation of the campus, which was about a one-hour drive from Cincinnati or Dayton and almost two hours from Indianapolis. The bucolic setting, usually a factor seen as an asset, was a liability when competing for fans on a fall afternoon.

At the time of the board's decision, Miami was working hard to increase interest in and support of its athletic programs. It was the consensus of the athletic administration that they needed to inject some life into the game experience for fans and improve Miami's image both regionally and nationally. Also at this time, the school's admissions office was working hard to improve minority enrollments, currently at about three percent of the student body. Minority recruiting was made harder by the image of the school as a place for upper-middle-class whites and also by the rural location.

THE MIAMI TRIBE

The Miami Tribe had its beginnings with people living on the shores of the Great Lakes, the woodlands of southern Indiana, and southwestern Ohio. At one time the tribe controlled a large inland empire. The Miamis were part of the Algonquin race. Their golden age was in the sixteenth century. During the seventeenth century, other Indian tribes began to challenge them and moved onto parts of their land. One tribe was the fierce Shawnees, who established settlements in southwestern Ohio prior to the beginning of white settlement. Eventually the Miamis were confined to an area along the Mississinewa River, a tributary to the Wabash River in Indiana.

The word "Indian" came from the same root as Hindoo, the native name of the Indus meaning "water." The Persians interpreted the word as "Hindu," the Greeks made it "Indos," and the Romans, "Indus," and it passed into the European languages. Columbus, thinking he had arrived, not in a new world, but in India, called the natives "Indios," which evolved into Indians.

The word "Miami" referred to a group of Indians who were a part of the Illinois division of the Algonquoin family. In the group were more than 80 tribes with their own names, and these all eventually associated themselves with six bands. Most who became "Miamis" called themselves "Twightwees"—meaning "cry of the crane"—others being known as "Oumamik," "people of the peninsula." According to one version of the story, these bands became so intermingled that the French converted their names to one—Miami—and by the 1740s, these bands accepted a chief of all the Miamis. The word meant "all friends" and was of European origin, not a native word.

The United States government uprooted the tribe twice in the 1800s, eventually in 1846 moving them to northeastern Oklahoma. In 1996 about 1,500 individuals with some Miami ancestry survived, the last full-blooded Miami having died about 60 years prior.

RELATED ISSUES

Historically, Miami University's official position on the use of Redskins had been that the name honored the Miami Tribe, for which the school was named, and that the nickname was used with the approval of tribal elders. Further, the nickname was symbolic of a long relationship of mutual respect between the university and the tribe. A standing commission to study the relationship between the tribe and the university, headed by the university vice president for student affairs, exemplified the importance and consideration accorded to this relationship.

In the past, when the issue arose, the school consistently took the position that as long as the Miami Tribe supported the use of Redskins that the university should not change its nickname.

In July 1996 the Miami Tribe changed its position on the use of Redskins and withdrew its support. Opponents alleged, and it was widely believed, that university officials with a personal political agenda had coerced the tribe, a charge the university vehemently denied and for which no evidence was ever produced. The tribe stated their decision was based on the changing priorities and attitudes of society.

In recent years a number of universities and teams had updated their nicknames and/or symbols, recognizing how old names could be offensive to certain parties or cultures. These changes removed ethnic references, sex biases, and images perceived to glorify war or killing. In contrast, a number of groups had chosen not to change their names or symbols. In 1991, Eastern Michigan University had changed their name from Hurons to Eagles. The school had experienced a drop in gift money in the short term, but had quickly returned to normal. (A summary of nickname and/or symbol status is presented in Exhibits 4 and 5.)

The social environment in which the Miami board of trustees was to make its decision was unsettled. Many people believed that no matter the intent, nicknames that could be perceived to reflect derogatory attitudes about sex, race, culture, or any group characteristic were unacceptable. In addition, students complained increasingly that team mascots and nicknames were not representative of the student body. However, the changes brought about by groups who opposed the use of certain names had resulted in a backlash by those who believed that tradition and honor were being sacrificed to a sense of political correctness that had gone too far.

EXHIBIT 4   Schools and Organizations That Have Changed Nicknames or Logos

Organization	Old name/logo	New name/logo	Reason
Alabama–Birmingham	Blazers—Nordic	Blazers—Dragon	Remove ethnic/gender reference
Arkansas State	Indians—Indian figure	Indians—ASU with headdress	Remove Indian figure
Lehigh University	Engineers	Mountain Hawks	Gender neutral
Stanford University	Indians	Cardinal	Remove Indian reference
Marquette University	Warriors	Golden Eagles	Remove Warlike/Gender reference
Eastern Michigan	Hurons—Indian tribe	Eagles	Remove Indian reference
St. Johns	Redmen	Red Storm	Remove Indian reference
SUNY Stony Brook	Patriots	Sea Wolves	Remove Warlike/Gender reference
Tennessee–Chattanooga	Moccasins (Indian)	Mocs (Mockingbird)	Remove Indian reference, use state bird
U. of Mississippi	Rebels—Confederate Flag	Rebels/No flag allowed	Remove civil war/racial/political reference
Bradley University	Braves—Indian	Bobcats	Remove Indian reference
Rutgers	Scarlet Knights—male knight	Scarlet Knights—gender neutral	Remove gender reference

EXHIBIT 5   Schools and Organizations That Have Not Changed Nicknames or Logos

Organization	Nickname	Logo
University of Nevada–Las Vegas	Hey Reb	Cartoon Rebel
U. of Massachusetts–Amherst	Minutemen	Minuteman
Florida State University	Seminoles	Indian Head
Washington (Football)	Redskins	Indian Head
Cleveland (Baseball)	Indians	Chief Wahoo
Kansas City (Football)	Chiefs	Arrowhead
Atlanta (Baseball)	Braves	Tomahawk

The Redskins name and images had played an important role in student life at the university for more than 60 years. For almost all alumni and current students the nickname, mascot, and images symbolized university life, pride, excellence, and tradition. The Redskins mascot was linked to student life in many ways:

At the start of every home football game, the Redskins mascot entered the football stadium on a horse at full gallop. The mascot wore authentic regalia designed by chiefs of the Miami Tribe.

The Redskins symbol, Chief Miami, performed traditional dances at many athletic events.

A group of avid student fans came to athletic events wearing red and white face paint and feathers in their hair; they were called the featherheads.

The Indian head logo appeared on the football stadium, on center court of the basketball arena, at the center of the ice arena, and at most other sports venues.

University apparel, particularly athletic apparel, made heavy use of the Indian head logo.

The student union was called the "Res" (short for reservation) by students and faculty.

The union housed a lounge with historic displays of Miami Indians, honoring the links between the university and the tribe.

A portrait of a Miami Indian by the famous artist, John Ruthven, proudly adorned the homes or offices of many alumni and faculty. The Miami Tribe had been consulted in the commissioning of this "official portrait." (Miami's Indian head logo was a stylized version of this portrait.)

A number of prominent alumni, among them Trustee William Gunlock, had come out in vehement opposition to any change. Some had also threatened to withhold donations and gifts if a change were made. According to Chris Wyrick, head of athletic fundraising, many of the people most likely to oppose the change were the biggest givers to athletics. Others opposed to the change included many current students, student-athletes, coaches, faculty, staff, and fans. Many expressed the belief that a change was simply bowing to pressures brought to bear by a small, vocal minority who were pushing a political agenda and who cared nothing for the school's traditions. "Alternative" merchandise and apparel had already appeared around campus. Bumper stickers and T-shirts bearing the motto "Redskin 'til I die!" or "Always a Redskin" were common. A letter from Lloyd O'Hara (Miami class of 1939), received by the board of trustees in early September seemed to reflect the sentiment of those who opposed the change (excerpted):

> First of all, may I suggest there is no real problem. You and I and a vast number of Miami alumni well know that the term "Redskins" as applied to Miami's athletes is one of reverence, honor, and fighting spirit—one which is entirely complimentary and in no way demeaning.
>
> I dare say that had this "problem" appeared on the agenda of Miami's Board of Trustees during the sixteen years that I served as a member thereof, our Board would have given about five or ten minutes to the subject and then voted to retain the very meaningful and appropriate Redskin appellation. We would then have moved on to important Board business...
>
> I thought it was near ludicrous when former President Paul Risser devoted the better part of a day to a public discussion of the Redskin "problem" and then recommended to your body that the Redskin name could continue in use for presently existing athletic teams, but forbidden to newly created teams. That's really some way to "ride the fence" on the "problem."
>
> ...Miami's unique heritage is one of the University's big assets. It is one of the factors that sets Miami apart from its counterparts and entitles Miami to a place on everybody's list of outstanding educational institutions in the country. Other parts of Mi-

ami's heritage which come to mind are her outstanding academic program going back to the days of the McGuffey Readers; her beautiful campus situated in a typical college town; her retention of consistent architectural design in campus buildings; her production of outstanding leaders in government, academia, business and industry; the Cradle of Coaches; the Mother of Fraternities; her successes in inter-collegiate athletics established by her athletic teams known throughout the land as the "Miami Redskins"; and last but not least, her outstanding alumni relations program which has developed a strong and loyal body.

...If you were to poll Miami's alumni body, I feel certain they would vote overwhelmingly to retain the Redskin name...The name is right—there is nothing wrong or demeaning about it...

The negligible change brought about by the compromise position adopted by the board of trustees in 1993 was evidence of the prevailing sentiment. Few groups adopted the new nickname and common usage was still overwhelmingly in favor of Redskins.

The cost of a name change was estimated to be about $100,000 for the athletic department to change uniforms and markings at venues. However, this did not consider the cost of developing new logos and trademarks, or the lost revenues from donors who chose to withhold gifts in protest of change. Miami currently had approximately 120,000 living alumni. In 1996 the university had received approximately $15.5 million in gifts. During the year roughly 68,000 alumni received solicitations for gift money from the university, and roughly one-third had responded with a gift. Miami's annual budget was approximately $250 million, with roughly $8.4 million expended on athletics. Annual gifts specifically earmarked for athletics totalled approximately $1 million and originated from about 1,700 individuals.

Another important consideration was the value of brand equity forgone by a change. At the time, Miami received more than $100,000 per year in royalty proceeds from sales of apparel and other merchandise (Exhibits 6 and 7). In addition, sales of merchandise at the Miami University Bookstore had totalled nearly $1 million during the past year, of which the school received nearly a 50 percent markup (Exhibit 8).

EXHIBIT 6   Royalties from Merchandise Sales

Year	Sales	Royalty	Commission
1987–88	$ 120,615	$ 7,840	6.5%
1988–89	$ 436,831	$ 28,394	6.5%
1989–90	$ 691,262	$ 44,932	6.5%
1990–91	$1,185,292	$ 77,044	6.5%
1991–92	$1,031,708	$ 67,061	6.5%
1992–93	$1,083,615	$ 70,435	6.5%
1993–94	$1,408,800	$ 91,572	6.5%
1994–95	$1,622,114	$115,548	7%
1995–96	$1,558,800	$109,116	7%
1996–97[a]	$ 987,357	$ 69,115	7%

[a]Partial year figures.

EXHIBIT 7   Royalties from Merchandise Sales—Quarterly Results

Year	Q1	Q2	Q3	Q4	Total
1994–95	$33,208	$35,831	$19,053	$25,456	$113,548
95–96	$38,457	$33,160	$20,605	$16,894	$109,116
96–97	$32,317	$36,798	N/A	N/A	$ 69,115

EXHIBIT 8   Miami University Bookstore (All Campuses): Apparel and Souvenir Sales ($000)

Fiscal Year	Apparel[a]	Souvenirs[b]	Total
1993	650	236	886
1994	582	261	843
1995	648	278	926
1996	659	293	952
1997	660	302	962

[a]Apparel markup: 45 percent
[b]Souvenir markup: 50 percent

CONCLUSION

"I know that this is an important issue to many members of the Miami University community. The board will give thoughtful consideration at its September meeting," said Chairwoman Harrington.

The O. Henry Hotel

Lew G. Brown and Christopher N. Prodan

WAITING FOR INSPIRATION

Dennis Quaintance leaned back in his chair, picked up his yellow pad and pen, and hoped an idea would come. It was time for him to write his portion of the summer 1998 edition of the newsletter that Quaintance-Weaver Restaurants and Hotels had begun using as a way of communicating with more than 18,000 customers and other stakeholders and friends three times a year.

Dennis and his wife, Nancy King Quaintance, had developed three very successful restaurants operating under the name Lucky 32, the name of a stock car his father once raced. Dennis had envisioned a restaurant chain that featured a jazzy decor and a menu that changed monthly and offered many choices in terms of food and prices. He would conduct extensive market research that would enable him to locate the restaurants near established, upscale neighborhoods that could provide a base of customers who would eat frequently at the restaurant. Dennis found the right spot for the first Lucky 32 in Greensboro, North Carolina, and opened it in 1989. The restaurant's success paved the way for Lucky 32s in Raleigh and Winston-Salem.

Early on, Dennis and his partner, Mike Weaver, thought they would develop a chain of restaurants over a widening geographic area—a traditional growth strategy in the restaurant industry. However, the team began to reassess the plan as it became concerned about the difficulties of coordinating monthly menu changes and controlling quality over a large geographic area. They were also concerned about the focus of the business becoming one of site selection and building construction, as opposed to managing the restaurants, which was what Dennis and Nancy enjoyed. Thus, they decided to focus their growth efforts within a 200-mile radius of Greensboro, giving them a larger presence in a smaller area. They also thought they could open different types of restaurants in the same communities.

Then, in mid-1995, a local developer called Dennis. The developer was working on a proposal to build a suite-type hotel in Greensboro for a major hotel chain. The negotiations had fallen through, and the developer wanted to know if Dennis and his partners would be interested in taking over the project and constructing a hotel. Because both he and Nancy had hotel management experience, they were able to put together a proposal that the developer liked so much that he became a partner.

This case was prepared by Professor Lew G. Brown and Undergraduate Research Asssitant Christopher A. Prodan of University of North Carolina at Greensboro, as a basis for class discussion. It is not intended to illustrate either effective or ineffective handling of an administrative situation. The authors express their appreciation to Quaintance–Weaver Restaurants and Hotels for its cooperation in developing this case.

Dennis and Nancy spent the next three years running the restaurants and planning the O. Henry Hotel, which they targeted for opening in November 1998. The planning featured the meticulous attention to detail that had characterized the couple's preparation for Lucky 32. In that effort, Dennis had rigged up his home's kitchen to mimic the setting for a table in the restaurant. This allowed the couple to experiment with and test everything from the type and level of lighting to the comfort level of the chairs and the heft of the silverware. Likewise on the hotel project, Dennis had rented a warehouse in which the team constructed a "sample room." Here they tested mirrors, lamps, beds, sheets, wallpapers, moldings, draperies, etc.—everything that would impact the customer's experience in the room.

THE NEWSLETTER

Dennis turned back to the computer screen, and the idea came to him. He had been answering more and more questions about the O. Henry as word of its development spread. Perhaps this was a good time to try to answer many of the questions he had heard. He began drafting his column:

A Personal Perspective on the O. Henry Hotel and the Green Valley Grill

I guess this venture really got started when Nancy King (my wife) and I were 15 years old. We both started our careers in the hospitality business—she with Disney in Florida, and I in Montana at the Red Lion Hotel in Missoula. Nancy went on to Cornell's hotel school, and I played various roles in several different hotels, mostly for the same company, and primarily in the West. Then, in 1978, I moved to Greensboro to open Franklin's Off Friendly (a restaurant) with Bill Sherrill. We hired Nancy during one of her Christmas breaks from Cornell, and then, well…that is how Nancy and Dennis became "Nancy and Dennis." We both stayed in the hospitality business. Nancy worked with Marriott, Guest Quarters, and with John Q. Hammons at his Embassy Suites and Holiday Inn Hotels. For the last three years, she has been with us at Quaintance-Weaver, focusing on our menus and on the O. Henry. I stayed in the business, and 10 years ago I teamed up with the greatest guy and greatest partner in the world and started Quaintance-Weaver Restaurants and Hotels.

The Community-Centered Hotel

Nancy and I have long observed a gap in the hotel business. Years ago, communities had locally owned, passionately run hotels that were "in and of" the community. These old hotels were close to where people lived and worked; and even though they served the traveling public, they also served their neighbors. They were real centers of community life and a source of pride for the city. Then came the interstate highways and commercial aviation, along with some technical advances in hotel facility design, and poof, the community-centered hotels disappeared. In their place came national, corporate-owned, brand-name hotels, situated along the highways or near the airports. These hotels don't seem to fill the place that the old hotels filled in the hearts of their neighbors. They are in the city but not "in and of" the community and neighborhoods. So, we thought, "Let's bring back the neighborhood, community-centered hotels of old. Wouldn't several North Carolina cities love to have a small, tasteful, locally owned, passionately run, boutique hotel located near where people live, yet convenient for travelers; a hotel that is "in and of" the community?" We are certain the answer is YES!

The O. Henry—"In and Of" Greensboro

We decided to begin our hotel venture in our home community, Greensboro. First we asked, "What is our community about?" Our answer is: it's about education (five colleges and universities) and culture (a rich history of writers and artists—even the North Carolina poet laureate); it's about cooperation and collaboration among industry, government, education, and society in general (I guess meaning cooperation and collaboration between neighbors for the "greater good"); it's about beauty—natural and man-made beauty; and it's about blending tradition and innovation. So, with this definition in mind, we set out to design and, of course, eventually operate our hotel, paying dutiful honor to the unique character of Greensboro.

Our "in and of" Greensboro idea goes further than the design. First the name. O. Henry, the distinguished and world-renowned short-story writer was born in Greensboro as William Sidney Porter in 1862. He authored "The Gift of the Magi," "The Last Leaf," "Of Cabbages and Kings," and "The Ransom of Red Chief," to name a few. He attended his Aunt Lina's school in Greensboro before leaving for Texas. (His aunt's schoolroom has been replicated at the Greensboro Historical Museum.) After his death in 1910, a local group decided Greensboro needed a modern hotel. So, in 1919, they built one on Bellemeade and called it the "O. Henry." With this history, we couldn't resist naming our hotel the O. Henry. "In and of" Greensboro, wouldn't you say? Additionally, our largest banquet room will be called the "Caldwell Room" for our forefather and esteemed educator, David Caldwell.

We wanted the new O. Henry to look like the original O. Henry, but the way it would look had it been built in 1998 rather than 1919 (tradition and innovation). We honored the rustication and arched windows of the first level, and the old-fashioned, double-hung windows in the guest rooms. We also turned to other Greensboro buildings for inspiration—for instance, we borrowed the design of the urns atop Aycock School. The interior will be wonderful, warm and welcoming, without being standoffish, or, as I call it "fancy-dancy." (We sometimes worry that folks think this is going to be a snobby place, but I assure you it will not. It will be nice, it will be friendly, and it will feel like a hotel that's been around for 50 years. But, it will not be stuffy. No doilies here!) We will have every modern amenity in our oversized guest rooms, including: impressive electronic data connections; an individual direct-dial phone number for each guest; two vanities; a dressing room; a shower separate from a steeping tub; a microwave; a refrigerator; a coffee maker; a full-sized desk; windows that actually open; and a complimentary breakfast, along with gardens, a courtyard, and a pavilion.

The Green Valley Grill—A Great Solution

We knew the hotel was a great idea and that people would love it, but we had a problem. In the hotel industry's evolution, it managed to give itself a "black eye" in the food and beverage quality department. The current perception is that most hotel restaurants are just "okay," and that hotel eateries are expensive, dress-up places. These are real problems and I think we've figured out a solution.

We will not have a restaurant in the O. Henry, but there will be one adjacent. The Green Valley Grill will stand proudly next to, and attached to, the O. Henry. We are determined that the Green Valley Grill will have its own, separate identity. It will be a wonderful, exciting building, with a great menu and delectable flavors. In fact, it will be like Lucky 32, only different. It will be like Lucky, in that it will feature different menus every month—menus that relate to a regional or ethnic cuisine. It will be different, because whereas Lucky's menu and decor have a distinctive American, "New World" reference, the Green Valley Grill will have a distinctive European, "Old World" reference. At Lucky's, the featured menu might offer tastes from the Pacific Northwest one month and from New England the next, but the Green Valley Grill might feature recipes from the Tuscan region of Italy one month and from the Provence region of France the next. In other words, at Lucky's it's mashed potatoes with butter, and at the Green Valley Grill, it's creamy polenta with extra virgin olive oil. (The Green Valley Grill will also handle the catering needs for the O. Henry's 5,400 square feet of banquet space and the room service for its 131 rooms.)

With the Green Valley Grill, our design concept is again a blend of tradition and innovation. Our idea was that we "discovered" an old, abandoned two-story building that was once a mill or a community store, and time had claimed everything except the shell and the roof. We fantasized that this building was designed in a Tuscan style. So, we took pictures of Tuscan-style buildings around Greensboro—like Blandwood Mansion, the old store up on Highway 150 at Lake Brandt Road, and the little pump house on Benjamin Parkway at Lake Daniel—and used them as our inspiration. Then we pretended that we truly had discovered the old building, and we restored it into a restaurant with a modern, open kitchen and a huge wood-burning oven, rotisserie and grill. The Green Valley Grill—"in and of" Greensboro as well.

Beyond Design and Name

We believe that a business won't succeed by just having a good idea. The business must decide what service it is going to provide for the community, then make providing that service its focus. We believe that success will be the natural by-product of meeting the community's needs. We have developed a five-point mission statement that is our organization's "reason for being." It is what we call "the promises we make to our guests and our staff." (When we bring new people into our company, we explain that on this team you are not subordinate to other human beings but you are subordinate to the ideas held in our mission.) We focus first to serve our guests, and second to provide rewarding employment. Then, when we do these well, we've learned that we will naturally be successful. We are proud that we operate under this idealistic premise, and I can assure you that these words are not pop culture rhetoric. They are the soul of Quaintance-Weaver Restaurants and Hotels. This community-centered approach seems simpatico with our observation that Greensboro is, to a certain extent, about cooperation and collaboration.

There you have it. That is my perspective on the O. Henry Hotel and the Green Valley Grill and our dreams for the future. It is really incredible that we have the opportunity to build and operate a dream.

THE GREENSBORO TRAVEL AND TOURISM MARKET

Tourism represented North Carolina's second-largest industry in 1996, with tourism expenditures in Guilford County (Greensboro's location) exceeding $679 million. Analysts predicted that tourism would become the state's largest industry by 2000. Private and public organizations in the county that were concerned with developing and maintaining travel and tourism felt that Greensboro was positioned to compete successfully for state, regional, and national visitors due to its unique heritage, its facilities, and its geographic location in the center of the state and in the center of the rapidly developing Piedmont Crescent that ran from Atlanta to Washington, DC. Further, as meeting groups were becoming more price sensitive, Greensboro, being a second-tier destination, stood to gain due to its generally more moderately priced facilities.

The Greensboro Area Convention and Visitors Bureau was a local, nonprofit public authority charged with soliciting and servicing all types of travelers to the area. The bureau brought together the interests of local governments, trade and civic associations, and individual suppliers of goods and services to travelers in order to increase travel to the area. The bureau was funded by a room tax—3 percent on rooms in the county and 6 percent on rooms in the city.

In its 1998–99 marketing plan, the bureau noted that it had segmented the travel and tourism market into 14 sales markets and had further segmented those segments. Using this segmentation, it had analyzed travel and tourism in the Greensboro area to determine the top 10 sub-segments generating business in the area. The top 10 were: sports, distributors, religious groups, education, business/insurance/financial groups, textile/manufacturing, civic/government, medical/health, agriculture/animal science, and technology. Each of these segments, especially the first four, were capable of generating citywide events utilizing the Greensboro Coliseum and the hotel inventory. As a result, the bureau attended numerous trade shows that catered to these groups each year. In addition, staff members made sales trips to 11 cities around the country that the bureau had identified as being strong "feeder" markets. The bureau also planned direct mail and telemarketing "blitzes" aimed at certain market segments. Exhibit 1 presents a list of publications in which the bureau would advertise during 1998–99. Exhibit 2 presents several sample advertisements.

The marketing plan noted, however, that the hotel industry, both nationally as well as in North Carolina and Greensboro, was overbuilt, with supply exceeding demand. The primary source of this oversupply was in limited-service and extended-stay hotels/motels. At the same time, more and more families were traveling and staying in high-end properties, thus limiting the availability of those facilities for use for conventions and meetings. The ability to gather and hold large blocks of rooms was crucial to attracting large meetings and conventions.

The bureau's plan noted that Greensboro had numerous strengths. It was a clean, safe city with an excellent geographic location and climate. Vehicular travel to the city was supported by excellent interstate highway access. The city had excellent convention facilities for a city its size and had generated national exposure through its hosting of many major sporting events, from the Greater Greensboro Chrysler Classic golf tournament to the NCAA eastern regional championships. The city also had a unique culture, heritage, and historical significance.

On the other hand, the bureau's plan noted weaknesses. The city lacked a strong commercial and public ground-transportation network, and air transportation to the Greensboro-Winston-Salem Airport was characterized by high fares. As noted above, it was also difficult to get hotels to make and hold block room commitments for meeting planners. Some people saw the city as being a small town with no night life or cosmopolitan appeal. The area had no high-profile attraction, and there were a limited number of available dates at the coliseum. Hotels and motels also were not concentrated either in the downtown area or around the coliseum.

THE GREENSBORO HOTEL MARKET

The Greensboro Area Convention and Visitors Bureau calculated that there were 63 hotel/motel properties that offered 7,316 sleeping rooms in the city and county area. Of these, the bureau classified 12 as full-service properties offering on-site meeting and dining facilities (3,031 rooms) and 51 as rooms-only properties (4,285 rooms). Twenty-seven

EXHIBIT 1   Greensboro Area Convention/Visitors Bureau Publications and Planned Advertising Spending 1998–99

Meetings & Conventions		Tourism (continued)	
Successful Meetings	45,000.00	Ladies Home Journal Travel	2,780.00
Meeting News	46,158.00	Travel Council of NC Travel Guides	16,708.00
Meeting Guide to South	7,972.00	SETS Canadian Vacation Guide	6,487.00
Association Management	36,505.00	SETS Vacation Guide	9,953.00
Convene	24,992.00	Preservation	2,475.00
GWSAE Directory	3,570.00	Rand McNally Road Atlas	2,600.00
Meetings & Conventions	59,959.00	Readers Digest	10,200.00
Business NC	9,360.00	Southern Living	50,668.00
Association Executives of NC	2,100.00	Southern Living Vacation Guides	—
Meeting Professionals International	10,625.00	Travel & Leisure	9,274.00
MPI Carolinas Chapter	1,500.00	Triad Guest Guide	1,800.00
Religious Conference Managers Association	8,979.00	Midwest Living	4,165.00
Association Meetings	21,983.00	TRIP Charlotte	300.00
Corporate Meetings & Incentives	8,007.00	Travel Guide	9,593.00
Black Meetings & Tourism	5,571.00	National Geographic Traveler	3,604.00
Convention South	1,805.75	American Heritage	3,540.00
Sub-Total	294,086.75	Sub-Total	153,582.00
Motorcoach		**Sports**	
Courier	6,222.00	Southern Conference	1,000.00
Travel Weekly	13,400.00	Wrangler-McDonalds	350.00
The Group Travel Leader	2,712.00	Labor Day Soccer	350.00
North Carolina Companion	3,962.00	Contingency	2,500.00
Destinations	6,171.00	Sub-Total	4,200.00
Sub-Total	32,467.00	**Directories**	
Tourism		Chamber Directory	1,800.00
AAA Tourbook—NC SC GA	5,976.00	BELLSouth Yellow Pages	210.00
AAA Road Atlas	2,600.00	800# Toll Free Directories	1,128.00
Blue Ridge Parkway file folder	300.00	Travelmaster	1,200.00
Historic Traveler	3,066.00	Business Life Triad Profile	1,500.00
Better Homes & Gardens Travel	4,913.00	Sub-Total	5,838.00
Our State	2,580.00	TOTAL	$490,173.75

Source: Greensboro Area Convention and Visitors Bureau

properties (35% of the total room inventory representing 4,719 rooms) provided some form of convention and meeting space.

Room rates in these properties ranged from $25 to $139 per night for single occupancy. Although the rooms-only properties offered published rates from $25 to $104 per night for single occupancy, the majority of properties offered rates under $45 per night. Rates in full-service properties ranged from $34 to $139 per night for single occupancy.

EXHIBIT 2: Sample Ads for Greensboro

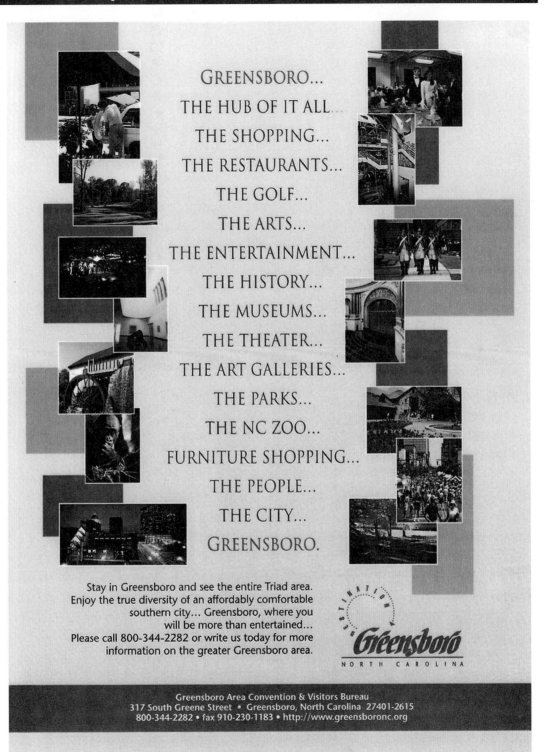

EXHIBIT 2:   Sample Ads for Greensboro (*Continued*)

Significantly, the bureau noted that the area's inventory of rooms would increase by 733 rooms during 1998 as nine properties came on line, all in the second half of the year:

Property	Number of Rooms	Location
Candlewood Hotel	122	Airport/Hwy. 68
Double Oaks B&B	3	Downtown
Drury Inn	143	Coliseum/High Pt. Road
Grandover	224	I-85/I-40 & I/85 corridor
LaQuinta	130	I-40/Hwy. 68
Lodge America	127	I-40/Wendover Ave.
Mainstay Suites	100	I-40/Wendover
O. Henry Hotel	131	Downtown
Suburban Lodge	144	I-40/Wendover

This sudden addition of properties followed a period of static room supply. A 1996 report noted that demand for rooms in the Triad area (Greensboro/Winston-Salem/High Point) had grown at about 6 percent per year since 1991 and that area occupancy rates had reached 67.1 percent, up from 59 percent in 1990. During the same period, the average room rate in the Triad had increased from $45 to $54. When taking into account both the occupancy rate and room rate increases, room revenues had grown about 8 percent per year since 1991.

A 1998 report by Horwath Hospitality Consulting/Smith Travel Research indicated that the Greensboro area occupancy rate was 63.1 percent, up 2.5 percent from the prior year. The average room rate for the area was $61 per day. April, October, and November were the months with the highest occupancy rates in the Greensboro area, with each month exceeding 70 percent. January and December were the months with lowest occupancy rates, with each month being below 50 percent.

Exhibit 3 presents a map of the Greensboro area showing the location of hotels/motels and meeting facilities. Exhibit 4 presents a detailed comparison of the full-service hotels in the area with single-occupancy rates greater than $66 per day. Exhibit 5 presents a monthly competitive survey the O. Henry staff had begun preparing.

MEETING AND CONVENTION SPACE

The area featured a wide range of meeting and convention spaces. The Greensboro Coliseum offered the largest event space, with seating for 23,500 people and arena floor space that would accommodate 20,000 square feet of displays. Adjacent to the coliseum was the Special Events Center, which included nine meeting rooms with approximately 19,000 square feet of space. The War Memorial Auditorium, also a part of the coliseum complex, offered seating for 2,400.

Following the coliseum complex were several other facilities that offered meeting space. The Holiday Inn Four Seasons/Joseph S. Koury Convention Center was the city's largest hotel with meeting facilities. In addition to its 1,014 rooms, it included more than 250,000 square feet of meeting space in 78 separate meeting areas. The Greensboro Hilton Hotel, located downtown, contained the next-largest meeting space with 22,500 square feet, including ballroom space of 6,208 square feet. Embassy Suites, located near the airport, had the third-largest amount of space with a total of 18,700 square feet, including a 9,000-square-foot ballroom. There were also many other facilities that offered unique auxiliary meeting facilities for banquets and receptions.

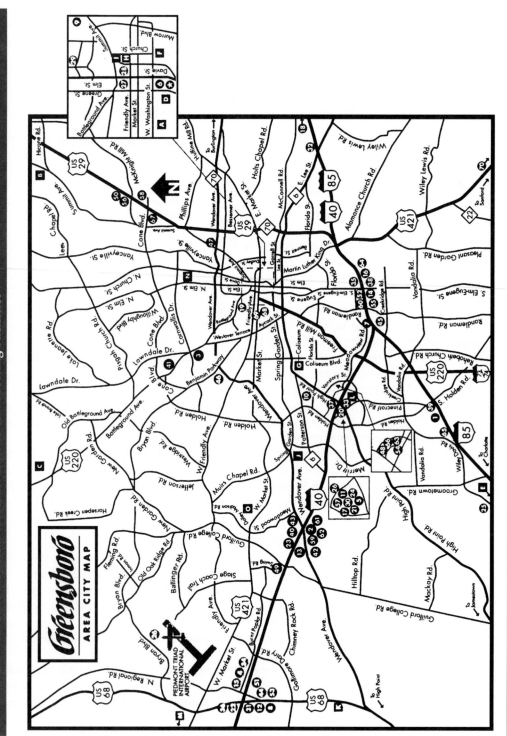

EXHIBIT 4 Full-Service Hotels in Greensboro, North Carolina, with Single-Occupancy Rate Greater than $66/Day

	Rooms	Suites	Non-Smoking Rooms	Efficiencies	Restaurant	Lounge	Golf Privileges	Pool (I= Indoor, O= Outdoor)	Whirlpool (I= In-room, O= On-site)	Pets Allowed (R= Restricted)	Handicapped-Accessible	Exercise Facility	Complimentary Meal	Meeting Rooms	Miles to Airport	Miles to Coliseum
AmeriSuites—Greensboro	126	126	96					O			•	•		•	7	4
Best Western Windsor Suites	76	76	38					O	I/O		•	•	•	•	10	1.5
Comfort Suites—Airport	113	113	66					O	I		•	•	•	•	3	8
Courtyard by Marriott	149	11	119		•	•		O	O		•	•		•	7	4
Embassy Suites Hotel	221	221	166		•	•		I	O		•	•	•	•	3	8
Grandover Resort[a]	224	40	100		•	•	•	I/O	I/O		•	•		•	17	6
Greensboro Airport Marriott	299	3	224		•	•		I/O	O	R	•	•		•	¼	7
Hilton Greensboro	281	7	195	7	•	•		I	O		•	•		•	11	3
Holiday Inn Airport	195	2	146		•	•	•	O			•	•		•	3	8
Holiday Inn Four Seasons/ Koury Conv. Center	1,014	78	756		•	•		I/O	O		•	•		•	10	1
Homewood Suites	104	104	66	100				O	O	R	•	•	•	•	3	8
O. Henry Hotel[b]	131	10			•	•		O	O		•	•	•	•	10	1
Park Lane Hotel at Four Seasons	161	3	133	1	•	•	•	O	I/O		•	•	•	•	10	1
Ramada Inn—Airport	168	2	70		•	•		I/O	I/O		•	•	•	•	3	8
Residence Inn by Marriott	128	128	64	128				O	O	R	•	•	•	•	10	1.5

[a]Opening in January 1999
[b]Opening in November 1998
Source: Greensboro Area Convention & Visitors Bureau Guide Accommodations

EXHIBIT 5 Monthly Competitive Survey—April 1998

Hotel	# Rooms Avail.	Mkt Fair Share	Occupancy Rate	Average Daily Rate	Monthly Revenue	% Mkt Share	Revenue Per Average Room/Day
Greensboro Hilton	283	13.3%	72%	$117	$ 715,197	12%	$ 84.24
Greensboro Marriott	299	14.0%	82%	$137	$ 1,007,689	17	112.34
Embassy Suites	221	10.4%	76%	$139	$ 700,393	12	105.64
HI Four Seasons	1,014	47.7%	71%	$121	$ 2,613,382	44	85.91
Park Lane Hotel	161	7.6%	81%	$105	$ 410,791	7	85.05
Marriott Courtyard	149	7.0%	84%	$115	$ 431,802	8	96.60
Total:	2,127	100.0%		$123	$ 5,879,254	100%	$ 92.14

Source: O. Henry Hotel

THE O. HENRY HOTEL

As Dennis Quaintance noted in his newsletter column, the team had designed the O. Henry as a "boutique-style" hotel with a European ambiance, gracious amenities, and an attentive staff. The hotel would feature traditional, natural materials and elaborately landscaped grounds.

The hotel was located adjacent to Friendly Center, an established and popular shopping complex, and Green Valley Office Park, a growing and successful office development. The location was convenient to downtown and the airport.

The hotel had 131 guest rooms, with 100 rooms featuring king-sized beds, 21 with double queen beds, and 10 suites. The guest rooms featured:

- 8-foot, 10-inch ceilings
- 425 square feet per guest room (as compared with about 325 square feet for budget hotels and 550 square feet for suite hotels)
- amenities including: refrigerator, microwave, coffee maker, 25-inch stereo television with remote, clock radio, sleeper sofa, a shower and a bath tub
- high-quality furnishings such as linens, lighting, dressing room, and bath furnishings
- high-tech telephones and data connections in each guest room (three phones per room with one being a speaker phone)
- complimentary breakfast for all guests
- cloister garden and outdoor catering space
- fitness room, swimming pool, video games and expanded in-room entertainment (in-room movies, etc.)
- full-service guest business center
- high-tech security and safety systems

In addition, the hotel had 5,845 square feet of public meeting space that the staff could arrange in a variety of configurations. The meeting rooms (the Hawkins-Brown Room and the Caldwell Room) were located on the lobby and terrace levels. The hotel had seven floors.

The O. Henry management team believed that, despite the opening of several hotels and the expansion of the Holiday Inn Four Seasons, it could position the O. Henry as an "upper mid-market" offering. Management believed that the convention, budget, and long-term-stay segments were becoming saturated.

Dennis Quaintance figured that the business community would generate a majority of the weekday room revenue through business meetings and training sessions. Transient-visitor room nights and people attending major area events such as the International Home Furnishings Market would enhance occupancy.

On weekends, the O. Henry planned to meet the need for full-service weddings and other special events.

FINANCIAL CONSIDERATIONS

Exhibit 6 presents a pro forma income statement for the hotel. Assumed room rates were $129 per day, single occupancy, during the week and $109 on weekends. The suites carried a rate of $359 or $449 per day. The meeting rooms rented for $100 per section,

EXHIBIT 6   O. Henry Hotel Pro Forma Income Statement

	1999	%	2000	%	2001	%	2002	%
Number of Rooms	131		131		131		131	
Rooms Available	47,815		47,946		47,815		47,815	
Rooms Occupied	34,905		35,960		36,339		36,818	
Average Room Rate	$ 114.00		$ 117.50		$ 120.00		$ 122.00	
Occupancy Rate	73%		75%		76%		77%	
Gross Revenue	$4,279,325	100.00	$4,539,704	100.00	$4,686,360	100.00	$4,830,432	100.00
Rooms Department								
Revenue	3,979,164	100.00	4,225,241	100.00	4,360,728	100.00	4,491,741	100.00
Expenses	795,833	20.00	845,048	20.00	872,146	20.00	898.348	20.00
Rooms Profit	3,183,331	80.00	3,380,193	80.00	3,488,582	80.00	3,593,393	80.00
Meeting Department								
Meeting Room Rental	150,000	100.00	157,500	100.00	165,375	100.00	175,000	100.00
Expenses	37,500	25.00	38,588	24.50	39,690	24.00	42,000	24.00
Meeting Profit	112,500	75.00	118,913	75.50	125,685	76.00	133,000	76.00
Telephone Department								
Revenue	78,536	100.00	80,909	100.00	81,764	100.00	82,839	100.00
Expenses	43,195	55.00	44,500	55.00	44,970	55.00	45,562	55.00
Telephone Profit	35,341	45.00	36,409	45.00	36,794	45.00	37,278	45.00
Other Operating Services								
Revenue	71,625	100.00	76,054	100.00	78,493	100.00	80,851	100.00
Expenses	39,036	54.50	41,450	54.50	42,386	54.00	43,660	54.00
Other Operating Profit	32,589	45.50	34,605	45.50	36,107	46.00	37,192	46.00
Comp. Service Expense	(122,167)	–2.85	(125,858)	–2.77	(127,188)	–2.71	(128,861)	–2.67
Gross Operating Profit	3,241,595	75.75	3,444,261	75.87	3,559,980	75.96	3,672,001	76.02
General And Undistributed								
Admin & General	303,832	7.10	313,240	6.90	318,672	6.80	328,469	6.80
Management Fee	171,173	4.00	181,588	4.00	187,454	4.00	193,217	4.00
Marketing	303,832	7.10	313,240	6.90	318,672	6.80	328,469	6.80
Heat, Light, & Power	136,938	3.20	145,271	3.20	149,964	3.20	154,574	3.20
Maintenance & Repairs	128,380	3.00	158,890	3.50	187,454	4.00	193,217	4.00
Total General & Undistributed	1,044,156	24.40	1,112,228	24.50	1,162,217	24.80	1,197,947	24.80
House Profit	2,197,439	51.35	2,332,033	51.37	2,397,763	51.16	2,474,054	51.22
Restaurant Revenue	225,000	5.26	225,000	4.96	231,750	4.95	231,750	4.80
Gross Operating Income	2,422,439	56.61	2,557,033	56.33	2,629,513	56.11	2,705,804	56.02
Other Capital Expenses								
Debt Service	1,005,660	23.50	1,005,660	22.15	1,005,660	21.46	1,005,660	20.82
Real Estate Taxes	200,000	4.67	204,000	4.49	208,080	4.44	208,080	4.31
Insurance	64,190	1.50	68,096	1.50	70,295	1.50	72,456	1.50

(Continued on next page)

425

Exhibit 6 *(Continued)*

	1999	%	2000	%	2001	%	2002	%
Capital Reserves	149,776	3.50	181,588	4.00	187,454	4.00	193,217	4.00
Total	1,419,626	33.17	1,459,344	32.15	1,471,490	31.40	1,479,414	30.63
Cash Flow Before								
Debt Service	2,008,473		2,103,350		2,163,683		2,232,050	
Cash Flow After								
Debt Service	$1,002,813	23.43	$1,097,690	24.18	$1,158,023	24.71	$1,226,390	25.39

Note: Exhibit has been adjusted to protect confidential information but is indicative of reality.
Source: O. Henry Hotel

with the Caldwell Room having seven sections and the Hawkins-Brown Room having four sections. The outdoor pavilion rented for $200. Management estimated that the typical variable cost per room per day was $8.50, which included $3.50 for labor (cleaning), $3.25 for coffee, utilities, and laundry, and $1.75 for room amenities (soap, shampoo, etc.). Management based the labor charge on 35 minutes per room versus about 20 minutes per room in typical hotels. The complimentary-service expense noted on the pro forma income statement represented $3.50 per guest per day for the complimentary breakfast. This was a break-even item in that the $3.50 was paid to the Green Valley Grill. The "restaurant revenue" line represented rent charged to the Green Valley Grill and was based on 10 percent of the restaurant investment ($2.25 million) or 4.5 percent of restaurant revenues, whichever was greater. The Grill was the exclusive caterer for the hotel, with the hotel receiving all banquet-room rent. The restaurant provided all room service to the hotel and retained all revenue from such service.

Exhibit 7 presents a pro forma balance sheet. The balance sheet assumed an opening on January 1, 1999. The assumed interest rate on debt was LIBOR plus 200 basis points, calculated annually.

INDEPENDENT STATUS

Dennis, Nancy, and their partners had decided not to pursue association with a nationally franchised brand-name hotel. They believed that, with the strength of the Greensboro market and the hotel's location, they would not need such a brand name. The team believed that it could launch the hotel with an aggressive marketing campaign that would result in profitable operations for both the O. Henry and the Green Valley Grill. The O. Henry could avoid franchise, marketing, and reservation fees that a franchiser would charge.

BACK TO THE DREAM

As Dennis finished his draft for the newsletter column, he tore the pages from the yellow pad, clipped them together, and carried them out to his assistant. He returned to his desk and began to examine the latest pro forma financial statements and competitive data. In addition to realizing his and Nancy's dream of opening a hotel, they also had the dream of achieving Four-Star designation for the hotel, making it the only Four-Star hotel in the area.

EXHIBIT 7   O. Henry Hotel: Balance Sheet—January 1999

Assets	
Current Assets	
Checking	$ 50,000
Short-Term Marketable Securities	200,000
Total Current Assets	250,000
Fixed Assets	
Hotel FF&E Back of House Equip.	200,000
Hotel FF&E Guest Rooms	1,500,000
Hotel FF&E Public Areas	500,000
Land—Hotel	1,000,000
Land—Restaurant	500,000
Building—Hotel	12,800,000
Building—Restaurant	1,750,000
Total Fixed Assets	18,250,000
Other Assets	
Design	250,000
Legal	100,000
MKT. & Preopening—General	250,000
MKT. & Preopening—Payroll	200,000
Systems	200,000
Total Other Assets	1,000,000
Total Assets	**19,500,000**
Liabilities & Equity	
Liabilities	—
Current Liabilities	
Accounts Payable	
Total Accounts Payable	—
Long-Term Debt	13,650,000
Long-Term Debt Total	13,650,000
Total Liabilities	13,650,000
Equity	
Owners Equity	5,830,000
Retained Earnings	15,000
Net Income	5,000
Total Equity	5,850,000
Total Liabilities & Equity	**$19,500,000**

Source: O. Henry Hotel
Note: Exhibit has been adjusted to protect confidential information but is indicative of reality.

However, Dennis knew that to achieve that dream, he and his team had to get the hotel off to a good start. As the hotel's planned opening was only a few months away, he realized that he needed to start finalizing plans for the opening and the initial marketing strategy. What was the best way to launch the hotel, and what should his marketing plan be for the first year? Dennis knew that to make it as an independent hotel in a competitive market, the O. Henry needed some good short stories to tell.

Fieldpro Manufacturing Company

Thomas H. Stevenson

Randy Autrey, president of Fieldpro Manufacturing Company (FMC), was certain that now was the time for the company to eliminate its major distributor and sell direct to dealers. After all, if the 12 percent commission he was paying to this distributor could be converted from expense to profit, his income statements would look much better. Also, with the addition of a new generation of environmentally friendly tillers and cultivators to the company's line of farm equipment, the timing was right for a change. Now if he could just convince top management in Memphis to approve the change, he could have the necessary field salespeople in place prior to the October start of the fiscal year. Randy was convinced that top management would be willing to support his decision, especially because FMC had turned in four straight years of profits. This was quite a turnaround from the three previous years of losses.

THE COMPANY

FMC was a wholly owned subsidiary of Preston Corporation. It was acquired by Preston in 1970 when poor health forced the previous owner to retire. Preston, headquartered in Memphis, was a holding company that owned 10 additional businesses that together generated revenues of about $200 million. One of these businesses, Southern Equipment, Inc. (SE), was the southeastern distributor for FMC. Preston provided financial and managerial support to each of its 11 subsidiaries, but each was relatively autonomous in its day-to-day operations. However, major changes in company operations required approval of top management at Preston.

FMC had been manufacturing farm equipment for more than 50 years. Its product line included seeders, planters, fertilizers, sprayers, and harvesters, utilized in the farming of a wide variety of crops. FMC equipment was sold throughout the southern United States and in Asia, Europe, Central America, and South America. Headquartered in rural eastern North Carolina, the company was geographically well located to serve its major markets in the Carolinas, Virginia, Georgia, and Florida. Over the years, the company had innovated many new products to meet the needs of farmers for more mechanization and less direct labor. The result was a strong reputation for quality and innovation and a product line that was broad enough to avoid having the company be whipsawed by the ups and downs of any particular agricultural commodity.

This case was prepared by Professor Thomas H. Stevenson of University of North Carolina at Charlotte, as a basis for class discussion. It is not intended to illustrate either effective or ineffective handling of an administrative situation.

Net sales last year at FMC were $14,774,000; operating income before taxes and corporate charges was $1,633,000. Five-year income statements are shown in Exhibit 1. Approximately 90 percent of sales and profits came from business in FMC's major southeastern markets. The remainder came from international operations and other sales throughout the southern United States.

FMC had no direct field sales force of its own. Instead, it relied on a network of wholesalers in the southern United States and exported directly to foreign dealers through agents located overseas. Its largest wholesaler was SEI, located in Charlotte, North Carolina. SEI and other wholesalers sold to farm equipment dealers, who sold to individual farmers. FMC did maintain an inside sales staff of five people to answer wholesalers' questions and to deal with foreign agents. The staff also handled direct calls from dealers and farmers when wholesalers were unable to answer customers' questions. Such calls were frequent, due to the wide range of products in the line and to the sheer numbers of replacement parts that were inventoried.

FMC also had a staff of four technical specialists who traveled as needed to support the field sales efforts of the wholesalers. Frequently the technical staff made service

EXHIBIT 1 Fieldpro Manufacturing Company: Comparative Income Statements (Dollar Figures in Thousands)

	Number of Years Previous				
	5	4	3	2	1
Sales					
Domestic	7,747	8,419	14,825	14,341	15,705
Foreign	158	260	458	755	827
Total Sales	7,905	8,679	15,283	15,096	16,532
Discounts	391	401	747	721	820
Returns	1,174	1,046	724	2,058	938
Net Sales	6,340	7,232	13,812	12,317	14,774
Cost of Sales					
Material	1,772	2,408	5,974	5,984	6,176
Labor	488	591	1,116	956	1,156
Manufacturing Overhead	1,306	1,353	2,157	1,967	2,888
Inventory Change	1,406	330	357	−131	−177
Transportation	77	44	38	39	61
Total Cost of Sales	5,049	4,726	9,642	8,815	10,104
Gross Margin	1,291	2,506	4,170	3,502	4,670
Operating Expenses					
Commissions	252	528	1,208	1,131	1,353
Sales Support	535	394	415	230	422
Engineering	199	152	213	188	376
Administrative	791	628	683	529	886
Total Operating	1,777	1,702	2,520	2,078	3,038
Operating Income (Loss) Before Corporate Surcharge (4% of Net Sales) and Taxes	(486)	804	1,650	1,424	1,633

visits, sometimes in farmers' fields, if that was necessary to get a piece of equipment back in service. They also accompanied wholesaler salespeople on calls if additional product expertise was required to convince new dealers to adopt the FMC line.

DISTRIBUTION

FMC relied on SEI for distribution to dealers in the Carolinas, Georgia, Florida, and Virginia. Outside of those areas, FMC sold either through wholesalers or direct to farm equipment dealers using telemarketing from its headquarters. Most of these customers had been doing business with FMC during the years when FMC had its own direct field sales force. About 10 years ago, FMC had downsized significantly in response to a protracted agricultural recession in the Southeast. In a cost-cutting move, its salespeople were either let go or were shifted to SEI. Product lines were streamlined, too. The remaining effects of the sales downturn were still evident in company losses as recently as five years ago (see Exhibit 1). However, in the past four years, sales had been higher and profits had improved dramatically as the agricultural economy rebounded.

The shift to SEI had been met with strong resistance from Autrey, who did not want to lose control of the sales force. Preston management, however, had been adamant that costs be reduced. Preston also wanted to expand the product line at SEI in order to spread travel and other costs over a larger base of sales. Rather than shift all inventory and parts to SEI from FMC, FMC maintained the inventory and shipped equipment to dealers in response to orders entered with SEI. With the exception of maintaining inventory, SEI provided all other typical distributor services for FMC, including billing, collections, customer contact, and inquiries. SEI received a 12 percent commission for doing so. FMC's remaining "full stocking" distributors (wholesalers who carried a full product line) were compensated at a rate of 15 percent, due to their additional commitment to inventory, but most larger equipment was drop-shipped to dealers. The few dealers that bought directly from FMC paid list prices.

SEI OPERATIONS

Over the years since SEI had received the FMC line, relations between Autrey and Eugene Honeycutt, SEI's president, had been cordial. Honeycutt was delighted to receive the windfall of the new line because he was interested in expanding his volume to help cover overhead; his company had also been hurt by the poor agricultural economy. Moreover, the additional agricultural lines complemented SEI's other agricultural products, such as loaders, harrowers, and plows. The agricultural product lines represented nearly 85 percent of SEI's last year's sales volume ($11.543 million) and 90 percent of last year's profits before taxes of $519,435. SEI had shown profits for eight of the past 10 years. The two years of losses were the year prior to the move of FMC's sales force to SEI and the year in which the move was completed.

The company sold agricultural equipment through approximately 800 farm equipment dealers in the Carolinas, Virginia, Georgia, and Florida. The remaining sales and profits were generated from industrial parts and equipment, mainly hydraulic hoses, jacks, lifts, and pumps, which were sold to municipalities, industrial firms, and original equipment manufacturers. SEI added the hydraulic equipment during the latter years of the farm recession to offset the declining farm revenues and the inherent seasonality of farm equipment sales (90 percent of all farm equipment was sold between March and

October in the South). Attracting hydraulic manufacturers had been difficult due to SEI's heavy emphasis on farm equipment, but over the years, trade show contacts had led to contracts with several manufacturers and the business had grown to a fairly stable 15 percent of sales. Increasing the proportion of business attained from industrial parts and equipment would be extremely difficult because competition from established distributors was strong, and other agricultural distributors were also seeking to diversify into nonagricultural lines. Nevertheless, Honeycutt was under strong pressure from top management at Preston to add more nonagricultural suppliers. Management wanted SEI to be much less dependent on agriculture. Honeycutt was getting little support on this from his sales force. Of the eight people that he employed in field sales, two sold industrial equipment full-time, two sold industrial equipment 25 percent of their time and the agricultural line the rest of the time, and four sold agricultural equipment full-time. Of the four who sold agricultural equipment full-time, two specialized in the FMC line.

In the agricultural equipment lines, SEI represented several well-known manufacturers. The largest was responsible for 25 percent of total annual billings; the next largest generated 20 percent, and FMC contributed 15 percent. The eight remaining suppliers divided the rest of the business; no one supplier generated more than 6 percent or less than 3 percent of sales revenue. The industrial line consisted of only five suppliers; the largest accounted for 55 percent of volume, and the rest divided the remaining business in approximately equal proportions.

NEW PRODUCT LINE

For the past two years, engineers at FMC had been working on a new generation of environmentally friendly tillers and cultivators. This effort had been in response to farmers' increasing desires to practice minimum tillage farming. Minimum-tillage (preparing the soil for planting by plowing or harrowing) was gaining favor because it left much of the soil undisturbed and covered with mulch. This offered protection against wind and water erosion. It also slowed water runoff and allowed greater water absorption, important benefits during the hot, and sometimes dry, southern summer months. The new line of tillers was specifically designed for this purpose and was complemented by new cultivators that would loosen the soil and reduce weeds, also with minimum ground or crop disturbance.

Autrey and his associates at FMC were quite enthusiastic about the prospects for the new equipment. The tillers and cultivators had been field-tested in Alabama (outside of SEI's territory) with very positive results. Longer-term field tests were being carried out at additional locations in Mississippi and Tennessee, and although there were no firm orders in hand, it was hoped that the farmers participating in the tests would both purchase the equipment and serve as demonstration sites for other interested buyers. Autrey and several of his engineers and technical support people had personally made the necessary field contacts through dealers in Alabama, Mississippi, and Tennessee. They had purposely avoided working through any wholesalers, because they had planned to sell the new line direct to dealers. Autrey and FMC were well known to farmers because over the years Autrey had attended farm equipment shows, dealer conferences, and county grange meetings throughout the South. Therefore, access to the market for test purposes and potential direct sales could be accomplished with minimal difficulty. Frequently, dealers and farmers called FMC to speak directly with Autrey rather than calling SEI. Some indicated that they were accustomed to dealing directly with the manufacturer, not the wholesaler. (Many competing suppliers had been slowly eliminating wholesalers and selling directly to dealers or to large corporate farms.)

FMC'S RELATIONSHIP WITH SEI

Autrey and Honeycutt had worked well together over the years. Despite Autrey's initial objections to the loss of his field sales force, he knew that the recent success of FMC was partially due to the efforts of Honeycutt and his ability to integrate the former FMC salespeople into the SEI organization. On the other hand, Honeycutt was well aware that the addition of the FMC line had provided a substantial revenue flow that offset a large portion of his fixed costs. This had allowed him to add more people and to spend time pursuing additional suppliers of industrial equipment with the aim of reducing SEI's dependence on the agricultural section. Also, because Honeycutt had little technical background in agriculture, he was more comfortable with industrial suppliers and customers.

Nevertheless, Autrey was beginning to resent SEI's increasing attention to industrial lines and Honeycutt's growing reluctance to interact with the farm equipment dealers. Contributing to Autrey's frustration was the fact that some of SEI's new inside people were unable to answer questions from customers of the FMC line. These customers were increasingly referred directly to FMC. Then, if a part or an entire piece of equipment was required, the customer had to call SEI to enter an order. Autrey and Honeycutt had discussed this, but Honeycutt felt that he was providing good service, considering the fact that SEI only received 12 percent commission from FMC, less than the 15 percent that was received from other suppliers.

Honeycutt was aware that FMC was working on the new line of tillers and cultivators; he had seen the equipment in development at FMC during visits to the plant. He knew that the line was being field-tested outside of his sales territory, but he assumed that SEI would get the equipment as soon as field tests had been successfully completed. Honeycutt thought that this would give SEI a chance to expand beyond its normal distribution area and the opportunity to grow even larger. Though he wondered how his other suppliers would react to additional competition from FMC in the tiller and cultivator markets, he needed to generate $900,000 in additional business in order to reach his sales quota for the next fiscal year, and the new environmentally sensitive line would help. After all, despite recent sales increases, agriculture in the Southeast seemed to be in a long-term decline, partially because of the steadily increasing pressure on tobacco from antismoking forces and imports, and from the shift from cotton to synthetics. Actually, Honeycutt hoped to pressure Autrey to increase his commission to 15 percent on the entire line in order to offset the costs of the additional sales effort required for its introduction.

AUTREY'S PLAN

Autrey had other ideas. After having been in the black for the past four years, he thought he could convince top management to give him back the sales force. He already had a commitment from Memphis to at least allow him to hire one salesperson to introduce the new line in states outside SEI's territory. He had made preliminary contact with a competitor's salesman in Alabama. The salesman was willing to work for FMC if financial and other details could be worked out. Also, Autrey had traveled extensively in Europe during the past six months, receiving strong assurances that farmers there would be willing to try the new equipment if field tests were positive. He had just returned from a two-week trip to Italy and Spain, where he had talked to three farmers who were willing to sign purchase agreements. Autrey knew that fielding new salespeople and expanding further internationally would be expensive and time-consuming, but he felt that the expense could be more than offset by commission savings if SEI were eliminated from the distribution system. Last year's commissions alone were $1,353,000, of which 90 percent went to SEI. Randy also felt that sales would be higher with a sales force concentrating only on FMC equipment, rather than one that had to share time with other products.

Autrey planned to ask the three former FMC salesmen who were still with SEI to return to FMC. This included the two who worked full time on the FMC line and one of the others who devoted full-time to the agricultural lines handled by SEI. Autrey felt that the time of these three people plus the new salesman from outside SEI would be at least equivalent to, or perhaps a little greater than, that now being received from the entire SEI sales force. Each would be compensated entirely on commission, as they were at SEI. Although each would have to give up commissions from sales of other agricultural products that SEI handled, Autrey felt that this would be offset by sales revenue from the new line of tillers and cultivators. Autrey knew that the total cost of commissions, fringe benefits, and overhead for the three was approximately $375,000 annually. The new person for Alabama and Mississippi would add $90,000 to costs; a new inside salesperson would add another $35,000. The field representatives would reside within their territories and operate out of their homes. The three SEI salespeople had historically operated that way; this would represent no change. Although Autrey had not approached any of the three with his proposal, he had maintained a good rapport with each since their departure from FMC. When he traveled with them to conferences or to visit dealers, they often mentioned how great things had been when they all worked together.

Autrey also planned on spending another $50,000 on one additional office employee and making other miscellaneous changes that would be necessary in order to handle the billing and other aspects of selling directly to the dealers. He knew that he would have to budget 1 percent of projected sales to cover bad debt expense (the weak farm economy meant that some dealers were unable to meet their financial obligations). SEI had absorbed these losses in the past, but Autrey thought that he could be more diligent in collecting accounts payable and in screening out bad credit risks. He thought that 1 percent was generous and hoped to eventually need less than that.

Autrey intended to discuss his idea privately with the president of Preston Corporation after the regularly scheduled April quarterly meeting. These meetings, used instead of a more-formal planning process, allowed the presidents of each of Preston's 11 subsidiaries to present their quarterly progress reports and any other information they wanted to convey. None of the companies did formal strategic planning, but top management was talking to several consultants about helping to implement a more-formal process. In the meantime, the quarterly meetings seemed to be sufficient to keep everyone informed.

THE APRIL MEETING

Autrey was looking forward to the meeting as he flew into Memphis. He enjoyed the camaraderie with his peers and liked talking about his successes at FMC. This trip he was eighth on the program, just prior to Honeycutt, who would make his report on SEI.

The afternoon was reserved for golf, as was customary during the spring meeting. Autrey's meeting with the president would come after dinner that evening, and he anticipated cooperation with his proposal to sell the new line direct, especially because he had already received approval to hire an Alabama salesperson. He was also optimistic that he could regain control of the entire sales and distribution function.

The meeting began with the usual preliminaries, after which each company president spent about 15 minutes updating the others on what was going on in his or her company. The tone of the meeting was somewhat reserved, because Preston had not had a prosperous quarter. Five of the companies were reporting losses due to competitive activities or industrywide reversals that had impacted their businesses. As Autrey spoke, his personal enthusiasm, reports of favorable progress on the new product line, and strong profit showing were met with approval from top management, especially in the face of the negative news from others. Honeycutt followed Autrey, mentioning the assistance his sales team had provided to FMC and expressing his eagerness to add the new product to his line to help support his own $900,000 growth plan for the following fiscal year. He also surprised everyone by mentioning that his second-largest agricultural equipment supplier, Ag-co, was phasing out sales to wholesalers throughout the country and would sell direct to dealers. Honeycutt was hoping to convince them to stay with SEI, but if he were unsuccessful, the new line from FMC should allow SEI to conduct business as usual without any significant downsizing.

The president of Preston expressed both surprise and anger at this probable loss of a major account and directed Honeycutt to keep him better informed about relationships with his key suppliers. He also took the opportunity to again press Honeycutt to increase his efforts to increase the nonagricultural portion of SEI's business.

Autrey was surprised by the news about Ag-co, but he well understood Ag-co's reasons for making such a move—after all, he wanted to do the same thing himself. Autrey was determined to go ahead with his plan, and he looked forward to speaking to the president later, in private. In anticipation of the meeting, Autrey began to jot down some arguments that he thought would be useful in convincing the president to allow him to regain control of the sales force. Autrey knew that as soon as Honeycutt heard of his proposal, Honeycutt would develop and present his own rationale for why the sales effort of FMC should stay under the control of SEI. Autrey wondered what Preston's management would do to resolve the looming conflict.

Johnson & Quin: The Carling[1] Printing & Graphics Decision

David W. Rosenthal and Thomas C. Boyd

It was the third week of April 1996 and the Chicago weather had begun at long last to really look as if spring might have arrived to stay. Inside the offices of Johnson & Quin, however, the "weather" was not so pleasant. After six months of negotiating, analysis, and laborious planning, the Johnson & Quin offer to purchase Carling Printing & Graphics (CPG) had been rejected out of hand. Jerry Bowling, the president and chief executive officer of CPG had been polite, but firm. The $2.2 million offer made by Johnson & Quin simply was too little money, and, for that matter, it was not even close. He had shaken hands, commented, "Maybe we can do business some other time," and had left the meeting, which had taken place a week earlier.

Dave Henkel, president and chief executive officer of Johnson & Quin was, at the least, deflated. He and his staff had put in a great many hours over the past three months, first in determining if the acquisition was a good "fit" strategically, then on the financial analysis of the various options, and finally on the feasibility of the actual implementation. In the end, Henkel believed that they had structured a deal that was well thought out, a good deal for Johnson & Quin, and the best offer they could reasonably make. At the time, he had thought that Bowling's refusal and departure had simply been a negotiating ploy to move the price upward. However, now, a week and several fruitless, temperament-gauging conversations later, he was fairly certain that the deal was dead, at least as it stood.

Henkel was rethinking his options. The $2.2 million price tag for the acquisition had not been an "easy sell" to Johnson & Quin's bank. It would be difficult to go back to it asking for approval of a higher offer—difficult but not impossible. Of course, he could wait it out and hope for a change of heart at Carling Printing & Graphics, but so far the signs indicated that they were not going to change their minds. Further, the longer things went, the more time Bowling would have to find another suitor. Ultimately, they could just walk away from the deal. There were, after all, both pros and cons for even considering the deal in the first place. To muddy the waters further, in a week Henkel and his chief financial officer were headed overseas on business, making close communication difficult, if not impossible.

This case was prepared by Professors David Rosenthal and Thomas C. Boyd of Miami University, as a basis for class discussion. It is not intended to illustrate either effective or ineffective handling of an administrative situation.

Copyright © 2000 Prentice-Hall, Inc. ISBN 0-13-017102-6.

[1]Certain names and financial data have been disguised.

437

COMPANY BACKGROUND

Johnson & Quin was established in Chicago in 1876, just five years after Mrs. O'Leary's cow kicked over the lantern that ignited the Great Chicago Fire. It was the same year that Alexander Graham Bell summoned his assistant, Watson, over the first telephone, Gen. George Armstrong Custer met his fate at the Little Big Horn, and the *Chicago Daily News* sold its first newspaper.

The company was originally called Johnson and McDonald after its principals. Nels Johnson was an enterprising Swedish immigrant who had come to Chicago as a boy. At the age of 20, he invested his life's savings of $400 (roughly a year's income at that time) into the new business, which was to produce, print, and bind blank books with ruled, lined paper for use as business journals and ledgers. Over the next 20 years Johnson changed partners five times, but in the end, in 1896, the company was named Johnson & Quin. Tom Quin added a strong talent for leadership, a gregarious nature, and a genius for public relations that complemented his partner's dedication to hard work and industry. The Johnson family continued to operate the company until 1974, when Ralph Johnson, son of the founder, stepped down as chairman of the board. At that time Robert Henkel acquired the company and became its president. His son, Dave Henkel, joined the company three years later and became president in 1988.

Products

Over the years since the production of ruled books, the company had undergone many changes in terms of product line and focus. Several themes were evident through the years and the changing markets. The company had always sought to differentiate itself in the products it produced, the service it provided, and the quality it maintained. It always considered itself to be a specialty printer and backed up its specialization with innovation and invention. The company had received a number of patents over the years in testimony to its efforts. In 1978, using advanced Xerox equipment. Johnson & Quin became one of the initial users of cut-sheet laser printing. As a result, Johnson & Quin became a pioneer in the use of this new technology and expanded into personalized direct-mail production. The company developed additional specialties over the next few years, including the ability to bring together several personalized pieces into a complex package, as well as using the first handwriting font in laser printing. The technology and skill to print magnetic characters was another strength, which opened the check-printing market to the company. In addition. the company invested heavily in computer information systems to support the printing functions. During the three years prior to the Carling Printing & Graphics decision the company had spent approximately $5 million on information systems and related expenses.

In 1996 the company was primarily involved in personalized, "upscale," specialty direct-mail production. This involved four basic steps: forms production, computer work to prepare personalization, laser personalization, and final assembly. In short, the company provided everything a client firm needed to communicate on a personalized direct-mail basis with its customers or targeted prospects.

Jeff Hellinga, director of sales, described the company's key products and markets:

> *The products and services we traditionally sell have been in the direct marketing industry. They have been heavily involved in the financial industries, although we work toward broadening that focus. Primarily, the reason that we ended up in the financial industry was the fact that by the mid-1980s we had the capability to be able to produce magnetic characters with laser printers, a key requirement for production of checks.*

When we acquired that capability, J&Q was thrust into the arena of doing financial work. Once you start a relationship, it tends to expand, and you become known as the check experts, with high-quality direct-mail production.

We found that our skills in customization made it appropriate for us to specialize further into producing convenience checks. A convenience check is part of a bank's program in marketing a credit card. When you say, 'Yes, I'll take a credit card,' the first thing the bank does is to send you a welcome package. 'Thanks for acquiring this credit card, and oh, by the way, it is going to take two weeks for your plastic to get there, but in the meantime if you need to access that, use these convenience checks.' Now there are retention programs and activation programs and several cross-sell programs that use convenience checks. If you want to send somebody a gift certificate, you are going to need cash, and if you want to access your credit line because you don't have cash available, you use a convenience check instead of writing a personal check. For us, this means personalizing a check, putting it in a marketing package, which may have brochures, and a cover letter—part of a kit. There are three or four convenience checks in this mailing along with documents explaining what the convenience check is, how to use it, and what the rate is. We really excelled in that because we took it out of that mass-production environment that was out there already to produce checks and drew it into direct marketing.

We are known as check experts. When doing checks, the printing has to be perfect. The quality and the characters have to be absolutely perfect for a check to scan in the banking system, so it starts a mindset in your organization of attention to detail, accuracy, quality, security.... Well, you can imagine if you are in a manufacturing environment and security is important, and quality is important, and attention to detail, all of your other work raises up a couple of notches because of the mentality you must have to produce this particular product.

I would say that in our industry Johnson & Quin is known as a midsized player. Most competitors are in the range of $10 million to $70 million in total sales volume. There are places that do the Ed McMahon-type mailings. That is not our bag. We handle, let's say, middle- to large-sized mailings from about 100,000 to 2 million pieces. We manage programs that are much smaller, ongoing programs, as well as many mailings over 2 million.

A breakdown of customer segments is provided in Exhibit 1.

EXHIBIT 1   Johnson & Quin: Customer Categories

Customer Type	Percent
End Users	70
Brokers & Advertising Agencies	30

Customer by Industry	Percent
Financial (Includes credit card, retail banking, mutual fund)	60
Retail	15
Other	25

Management and Philosophy

The top management team at Johnson & Quin was headed by Henkel. He joined the company in 1977 and became president and CEO in 1988. Don Danner, vice president and chief financial officer, joined the company in 1992 with a broad background in accounting and finance with companies that specialized in high-tech products. Jack Freeman, vice president of sales and chief operating officer, joined the company in June 1993 after working in the communications, computing, and credit reporting industries.

The company's mission statement read:

> As a recognized national leader providing quality services and unique business solutions, Johnson & Quin is committed to unequaled client service using superior technology and consistent development of our people, while meeting our profitability and growth objects.

The philosophy of the company is presented in Exhibit 2.

In April 1996, Johnson & Quin employed more than 200 people and had annual sales of approximately $24 million. The company operated extensively using a team environment. The management believed that good communication both internally and externally was critical to the success of the organization. The team and its functions are presented in Exhibit 3.

EXHIBIT 2 Johnson & Quin Philosophy

With our clients...
- We will consider every client as an investment in our future and will build lasting relationships.
- We will honor our commitments.
- We will listen carefully and respond thoroughly and promptly.
- We will thoroughly assess our clients' needs and provide a flow of ideas that encourages the development of a partnership.
- We will exceed expectations.
- We will continually seek to develop new markets and new products.
- We will respect the confidentiality of client information.

Among ourselves...
- We will treat each other with dignity and respect, always dealing openly and honestly with each other.
- We will encourage each staff member to develop professionally and personally by providing support and appropriate training.
- We will look for solutions instead of faults.
- We will encourage and support teamwork, while expecting outstanding contributions from each member of the team and acknowledging and using each individual's strengths.

Within our company...
- We will produce a level of profitability that allows steady company growth and provides the financial resources required to attain all our company objectives.
- We will help the company achieve increased earnings by conducting our business without waste of time, materials, or efforts.
- We will enhance the good reputation Johnson & Quin has built.
- We will seek to employ the best people.
- We will select suppliers who respect and share our corporate goals of quality, service, performance, and citizenship.
- We will deal fairly and honestly with suppliers.

Within the community...
- We will exemplify the highest values of corporate citizenship.
- We will support worthwhile charitable and community endeavors.
- We will strive to protect the environment and our natural resources.

EXHIBIT 3: Account Responsibilities

Client

- Provides job spec for estimates and schedules
- Once project is awarded, provides written authorization for production, materials purchase, DP development
- Supplies tape date and information
- Reviews and approves proofs as required

Account Executive

- Reviews all job specifications
- Draws up estimate
- Requests schedule
- Submits paperwork to production planning to initiate job
- Communicates any changes in schedules or costs as job progresses
- Communicates daily with team to monitor job progress

Production Planning

- Produce preliminary and all production schedules and updates
- Produces estimates
- Generates cost of specification changes
- Purchases materials and services to produce the job
- Authorizes and monitors outside production and services as needed
- Produces master schedules

Manager of Account Services

- All job specs are reviewed and confirmed
- Reproduction meeting with AE and ASR and client
- Assigns ASR and turns over job files
- Monitors jobs daily until mail drop
- Responsible for overseeing all ASR activities
- Reviews billing
- Represents client services teams in daily production meeting

Account Supervisor/ Account Services Representative

- Monitors all job production
- Works with each department ensuring proper specs and quality procedures are followed
- Communicates with client daily on job progress
- Communicates customer request and changes to Production areas and confirms with customer via conference report
- Provides local point if client problems occur
- Responsible for timely and appropriate escalation and communications
- Coordinates and monitors schedule with Production Planner
- Reconciles inventory
- Reviews all lettercopy and has set intran department
- Writes job tickets for production. (Print tickets, Laser/Bindery tickets, Lettershop)
- Provides programming instructions to DP
- Requests postage
- Prepares billing

Customer Relationships

Johnson & Quin described its target market as companies that currently produced laser-personalized direct mail involving complex or highly personalized packages in quantities over 50,000 pieces. It further described its best opportunities as those requiring significant data processing prior to print production, needing high quality and customer support, and looking for a strategic partner rather than price.

Hellinga described the company's target market:

> When you have a company out there and they decide to use direct mail to communicate their products or services, they use it in two respects: targeted to their client base to cross-sell or to add value to their base; or, second, to generate new business. We tend to do less of the acquisition of new clients and more of the relationship-type mailings, cross-selling of clients.

Henkel elaborated:

> And even within that, we tend to do the more-expensive and complex mailings to the more-critical customers. So, in a credit card environment, we tend to do the "gold" card mailings rather than the regular card mailings. These programs are generally more expensive to produce and have a classier look. There is more value added to the project. The mailings to the regular customers tend to be cheaper work, tend to be less expensive per thousand, less important looking, less costly. They don't use the level of quality production or quality paper. They don't make it look as nice. They don't spend as much money because they don't have as much of a justification. If the customer spends $25,000 a year on their credit card, I am going to spend more money on the effort to encourage him to spend more than I am to try to open a new account with somebody who just got into the job market and who might charge $2,500 per year. We try to work on the projects which are critical to a customer's success.

Henkel went on to describe how a customer project might begin and the role of competition and trends in buying in the market:

> The type of relationship that we have with our customers varies all over the board. Going down the top five major accounts, some have a three-bid system required, some call us up and say, "Look I'm tied up, this is what I want to do, you figure it out for me and get back to me." Some go to the extent of bringing us in with other vendors to have a round-table discussion about projects.
>
> Typically an existing account wouldn't be sitting around waiting for us to call on them; they would pick up the phone or e-mail or something and say, "We have this new project we are working on, how about giving us some help?" Typically, they contact us with an idea, and they want us to help them figure out how to do it.
>
> Quite often in the better relationships, the customer may call only us. They have the price ranges from the past, and when they call us if the price hasn't changed much, they will go with us. If they have a program that they run once a quarter, they probably won't bid that one. It would be a rare occurrence in this day and age to do that. They'll check it periodically.
>
> While we try to do as much business in an account as possible, 100 percent penetration in an account is an unusual thing. Absolutely. In our scale of things, I don't see it because the people we deal with would be nervous about not having a safety valve if we had a plant fire or something.
>
> I think that you will find that we tend to deal with larger companies that have a wide range of needs, and if you took all of their direct marketing or direct mail produc-

tion, you'd need to try to fit them all to our capabilities. Some of the large programs and some of the small projects would have to go elsewhere anyway.

"One stop shopping" means one stop shopping for that job. A big trend that we see is, 10 years ago there was much more piecemeal buying of a job, where their buyer would go out and say, "Okay, I'll get my printing here, my envelopes over here, I'll do my personalization here, and I'll go over to the letter shop separately and get it all assembled." There were four or five shops involved in doing a job. Today, for that job they'll stop at one place, maybe two. But, a big, big difference...a leaner staff tending to combine buying.

The consolidation of buying responsibilities and the reduction in the number of suppliers were parts of what appeared to be a broad trend in business. The buying function in many organizations had been focused in fewer individuals, often aided by improved automation. As a result, the buyers often needed additional services from their suppliers and tended to form deeper relationships with the suppliers who could provide the necessary support.

THE CURRENT SITUATION

The relationship with Carling Printing & Graphics, Inc.–Illinois had begun about 10 months before, when they approached Johnson & Quin asking to become a supplier. Henkel recalled the sequence of events:

In brief, they approached us to become a significant customer. George Bowling, the president, called me. I thought it was a neat idea because we had trouble getting good suppliers of preprinted forms, so I encouraged him. He worked on it for several months in various ways. Among other things, we agreed to help them with their pricing by giving them more specific feedback about where they were not competitive. We were very concerned that we were not getting competitive prices, and they kept saying, 'Well, we don't believe you.' We said that we just couldn't sell the product when we added in their desired margins and our markups. We couldn't be competitive at those prices. They had to get their prices down somehow. So we tried to work through some of the processes that would have made them more efficient...ideas like buying more at a time or giving them more lead time. We tried all kinds of things. We asked them to look at their various process efficiencies. I don't know that anybody had ever forced them to really examine some of these things.

As a result of this, they identified the categories that fit for them to be a supplier for us and we started buying some significant amounts over a very short period of time. During the second half of 1995, we were up to about $50,000 a month.

Bowling fished around at one of our earlier meetings to see if we were interested in selling our company, and I told him no, we had no interest whatsoever. And so, after building up several months of good business relationship, we had people over there and they had people over here, and we had some pretty serious discussions about what they needed to do to improve their product. They also had some quality problems that we pointed out to them. So, we were giving them a lot of good insight because we were short of good suppliers in this category. We did everything reasonable to cultivate them as a good supplier to us, having no clue whatever that selling out to us was an idea that they had.

The actual idea of selling the company was initially broached in January (1996). George called me on the phone one day, and I had no idea that it was anything other than the same trail that we had been down, and he said that he wanted to get together to talk. He totally surprised me and said, 'I was sent here with a mandate, either grow this thing or sell it. Buy another company, or.... And I can tell that you guys aren't interested in

EXHIBIT 4   Carling Printing & Graphics: Income Statement

	FY 1995	FY 1996
Total Net Sales	12,014,029	12,659,707
COGS	5,212,414	5,829,700
Labor Expense	2,660,619	2,573,397
Production Expense	2,885,906	2,812,128
Changes in Inventory	(224,254)	195,725
Total Cost of Sales	10,534,685	11,409,950
Gross Profit	1,479,344	1,249,757
Selling Expense	1,518,890	1,079,725
General Expense	1,196,568	1,052,385
Total Expense	2,715,458	2,142,112
Operating Profit (Loss)	(1,236,114)	(892,355)
Other Income (Expense)	(922,931)	(643,975)
Net Profit (Loss)	(2,159,045)	(1,536,330)

selling. I've been there; I've been through your facility. I really think that you are an ideal fit for combining because where we are strong you guys don't have it, and vice versa, and so I'd like to propose that you buy this operation.' That was on Thursday. On Saturday of that week I went over privately and confidentially to his office. This was real clear cut. He said, 'My company has told me that they really want to sell.'

Background on CPG

CPG, located in Chicago, Illinois, was one of 16 commercial printing companies owned by Carling Industries, Inc., a diversified, full-service communications company. The parent company had sales of $348.1 million in 1995, up slightly from the previous year and continuing a 10-year record of revenue growth. The parent company had been aggressive in mergers and acquisitions, and much of its growth could be attributed to this source. The company's stock was traded on the Nasdaq exchange. Henkel had some indication that the parent company was interested in selling, in part for its positive effect on their financial statements.

CPG had been struggling financially for the past several years. In each of the past four years the company had posted a loss. In the past two years, the company had lost nearly $3.7 million, although the company was forecasting an operating profit of just over $250,000 for fiscal year 1997. (Fiscal year ended January 31.) In fiscal year 1996, the company lost $1,536,330 on sales of approximately $12.7 million. Company summary and planning documents indicated that inefficient production resulting in high cost of goods sold, inability to pass along high paper costs, and, especially, insufficient volume of production were the major causes of the poor profitability. CPG income and balance sheets are presented in Exhibits 4 and 5.

Initial Impressions

Henkel described his thoughts when Bowling proposed the sale:

My immediate reaction was...very interesting. I wonder if I can afford to do it, because it is pretty big. I don't know a lot about it. I know that there have been rumors that they are ill. I know that they have an awful lot of iron. I've heard that they are sort of in a discombobulated state. Images did not pop to mind that they were just this wonderful operation, that everything is jolly. It was more, 'Gee, that is really interesting.' It is a category that we really want to have better control over. That is attractive. The company itself is not clean in the sense of it is sort of a dog in the market. Can we make it into something that fits us right? Can we digest it, because our own situation is conditioned by having an awful lot of investment for a small company and a lot of risk for a small company. Caution is a first reaction, but SERIOUS interest. 'How do we go about this? This is a new adventure for me. How can I get myself to a comfort level?'

This was 'positively shocking' news. It was good, but it was really pretty startling. For a long time we have said that we have a major competitive disadvantage in the marketplace. not having one stop shopping vis-a-vis our major competitors. Most of the companies that we compete against for the bigger business started in traditional printing and moved into laser printing personalization. We have a lot of situations where prospective customers would say, 'We really like you guys, we like the service you offer, we like the quality, we like the whole thing about Johnson & Quin, but there is the big hole in your line. You really don't offer enough of the services to make us comfortable in giving you major projects. And we really want to see, not just a buying arm where you offer to buy forms for us, but we actually want you to make them for us.'

Before the proposed acquisition surfaced, our dilemma was the cost of providing the additional products our prospects wanted. It wasn't just the cost of a press or of two presses, although certainly one would be hard enough. Two would be crazy because …how do you fill them up right away? The investment in those presses is enormous, and if you don't have a built-in customer base, the risk just then skyrockets. And on top of that, you have the factor that now you have to build up a trained work force and management has to understand the dynamics of the new business. Okay, here (CPG offer) you have all of those things built in. You have the equipment, which is older, but it's fixable. It can be brought up to date. You have a really good work force. You have some manage-

---

EXHIBIT 5   Carling Printing & Graphics: Balance Sheet

Assets	
Current Assets: Total	$ 3,405,919
Machinery & Equipment	10,587,222
(Less Depreciation)	(5,877,135)
Total Assets	$ 9,235,518
Liabilities	
Current Liabilities: Total	$ 2,673,819
Intercompany Loans	4,204,059
Shareholders' Equity	
Capital Stock—Common	$ 150,000
Additional Paid-in Capital	5,401,346
Retained Earnings—Prior	(1,657,375)
Current Earnings to Date	(1,536.331)
Total Liabilities & Net Worth	$ 9,235,518

ment to run the hands-on part of that. You have some good accounts. They have three large accounts that we have identified that we really want, that constitute the bulk of the business, and that right away creates pretty much all of the dynamics that we need.

So, the traditional old-fashioned printing is a part of the business that we have been walking away from. We have been so oriented toward the high tech, modern capabilities in computing and laser printing that we've neglected basic things of the business that fuel collective buying decisions.

We have had very little success in finding consistently strong suppliers to handle the front-end business-forms part of the business. There just aren't enough companies who have everything we want. The equipment isn't as much the problem as the attitude, the scheduling, the pricing…all those components. Often we have jobs delayed inordinately because of poor outside performance in that category. So this is a hot button for me, with a great answer for how to do it because for years I had thought about this, but I had never moved on it because it just seemed impossible.

Hellinga added his initial thoughts about the value of acquiring CPG:

One of the biggest things we would be able to do would be to produce the blank forms inhouse for the personalization that we are doing. That is a huge advantage that we can control more of that than in the past. We have always subcontracted, and when we subcontract printing, that creates certain issues. Sometimes my prices are not competitive now because I have to subcontract work outside and I have to get some margin on it after I buy it. Secondly, there are the quality issues. We have great relationships with some outside printers, but, obviously, we would prefer to control that quality ourselves, and the schedule. You want to control all of the variables around the printing. If we buy a form and it doesn't run properly, I call the vendor in and now we get into an argument: is it a good product or is it a bad product? Should they reprint it? Was it within or outside industry specifications? Is it bad forms or is it my laser personalization that is bad? You get into a lot of those discussions. That is a lot of time and money and resource that is involved. There is a lot of benefit to be able to print the forms internally. One of the most obvious ones is that I get a better competitive price. Too, a lot of clients like that you can do everything under one roof because they understand all of those variables. In fact, some clients are so emphatic about this they simply say if you can't print it internally, then they supply it. Sometimes they simply won't allow you to subcontract it, and the job goes elsewhere.

However, when Dave introduced this idea about buying CPG, my first thought was that this takes us back to hard-core production again, where I saw us evolving the other way. I saw the back end, the production of forms and such, getting smaller and smaller. The company is in the process of becoming faster, more flexible, more technologically advanced, and has fewer employees. In a lot of ways, my first thought was that this was taking us back the other way.

Other Factors

The general business outlook for the industry and for the specific direct-mail printing niche was good. Industry analysts suggested that the continuing positive economic environment, mergers in the banking arena, and ongoing advances in communications and computerization would continue to drive the direct-mail business. At the same time, senior management at J&Q noted that a number of competitors had adopted similar technology and, therefore, had eroded the company's differential advantage to a degree.

The scope of the proposed purchase was a difficult issue for the management of Johnson & Quin. From the outset they were forced to examine a variety of options whether to buy the entire business or some portion. Further, the Chicago location of CPG and the physical facilities made it nearly impossible to combine the two companies.

Don Danner noted his initial reaction:

Skeptical. I think the ability to digest it was my biggest concern. Really from three perspectives: financial, managerial, and facilities. They were in two buildings—70,000 square feet between them—and although we knew that we didn't want 100 percent of what they had, we probably only had 30,000 feet of inefficient use at the time. I was not excited about winding up with two buildings.

Henkel agreed:

The real estate issue became the first pivotal issue for us. Until we came to the point where, and this came from Kevin Cleary, our financial advisor... Kevin said after only a couple of weeks, he said, 'David, this is not going to work if you put it into two buildings. I cannot create in my mind a financial model that will make this beneficial. And I know that by the time I get the paper, it is going to be worse. So, dispense with that idea. Quit the grandiose stuff and scale it down. Offer them something for the best part of it and fit it into your operation, and then start looking at the dynamics that it creates in terms of utilization of your people, facilities, existing account relationships, and selling more to the same people. All those things start piling up on the positive side of the ledger.' He was very right about that. The two-building deal would have been horrible. It would have added tremendously to the total cost.

The situation was further complicated by the current financial condition of Johnson & Quin. (Financial statements are presented in Exhibits 6 and 7.) Henkel explained:

Financially, we are coming off of a weak year. 1995 was only a minimally profitable year for us, so we don't have the best balance sheet in the whole world. Furthermore, the first quarter (1996) just ended showed typical seasonal weakness. Cash flow has been adequate, but not great, and so, we don't have a good cash reserve. So, any time you start building a plan around, 'Well, as soon as we increase sales 10 percent, everything is going to be fine,' you are just flirting with disaster. So, where to come up with the money becomes a real serious consideration.

We also have a new banking relationship. While our traditional business has been decent, the costs associated with a large research and development project have caused the bank to express some concern. As you might expect, they aren't real excited about a new investment.

The Current Deal Structure

During the time between the initial offering of the company for sale and the proposal presented by Johnson & Quin, a great deal of analysis had been done. It had quickly been determined that the business was unlikely to be sold as a going concern. The losses had simply been too great and there did not appear to be a way out other than liquidation. Thus, the deal quickly took on the characteristics of an asset sale. J&Q's proposal was for the purchase of two of the seven presses currently being operated by CPG. The assets of CPG had been appraised, but there continued to be disagreement about the value of the equipment. The management of CPG insisted that the value of the equipment was consistent with a 1994 appraisal they had commissioned. Johnson &

EXHIBIT 6 Johnson & Quin Income Statement

	1995 Actual		1996 Estimated	
Sales	$23,840	100.0%	$29,240	100.00%
Cost of Goods Sold	17,045	71.5	20,468	70.0
Gross Profit	6,795	28.5	8,772	30.0
Expenses	6,198	26.0	7,252	24.8
Income from Operations	597	2.5	1,520	5.2
Other Expenses	142	0.6	702	2.4
Net Income	455	1.9	818	2.8

1996 Quarterly							
	10—Actual		20—Estimated		30—Estimated		40—Estimated
	(Prior to acquisition)				(Post-Acquisition)		
Sales	$5,942	100.0%	$6,298	100.0%	$8,408	100.0%	$8,592	100.0
CGS	4,272	71.9	4,427	70.3	5,811	69.1	5,958	69.3
GP	1,670	28.1	1,871	29.7	2,597	30.9	2,634	30.7
Exp.	1,622	27.3	1,663	26.4	1,995	23.7	1,972	23.0
Inc. Ops	48	0.8	208	3.3	602	7.2	662	7.7
Others	36	0.6	38	0.6	462	5.5	166	1.9
Net	12	0.2	170	2.7	140	1.7	496	5.8

Note: Certain financial data are disguised. The numerical relationships have been preserved.

Quin had also had the equipment evaluated and concluded that it was worth roughly $150,000 less. Further, estimates for the cost of removing the two presses from their current location, repair and renovation, and installation were roughly $700,000. The costs were to be amortized over a five-year term, and J&Q's banking agreements called for approximately a 9 percent interest rate.

J&Q management examined CPG's customer account lists, both for their desirability as customers and the likelihood of being able to keep them. CPG had $12.6 million in sales for fiscal year 1996, and their forecast for fiscal year 1997 proposed sales of more than $14 million. However, estimates supported by CPG indicated that sales realized by J&Q would likely be approximately $8 million for the year. J&Q consultants and management believed that only about $6 million could be realized, and even at that number it would require a considerable marketing and sales effort on the part of J&Q to develop new business. The top three accounts that they had targeted totalled roughly $3.5 million. The largest of the three accounts, representing about $2.1 million, was a previous customer of J&Q that had elected to buy from CPG. J&Q management believed that the relationship had been reinvigorated.

The J&Q management's review of the CPG accounts also revealed a number of disturbing issues. Many of the customers had been chronically late in their payments to CPG, and bad debt expenses were significant. Beyond that, much of the work was being done at very low margins. Lastly, a significant proportion of the business that was being accepted by CPG was simply work that did not fit the abilities and strengths of J&Q. As

EXHIBIT 7   Johnson & Quin Balance Sheet

	12/31/95 Actual	12/31/96 Estimated
Assets		
Current Assets		
Cash	$ 675	$ 490
Accounts Payable	3,703	4,317
Inventory	1,262	1,876
Prepaid Expenses	1,256	1,667
Total Current Assets	$ 6,896	$ 8,350
Capital Assets		
Machinery & Equipment	$ 4,172	$ 5,893
Facility	1,175	1,927
Total	5,947	7,820
Less Depreciation	(2,009)	(2,834)
Total Capital Assets	$ 3,938	$ 4,986
Total Assets	$10,834	$13,336
Liabilities and Stockholders' Equity		
Current Liabilities		
Accounts Payable	$ 2,228	$ 2,975
Bank Line of Credit	1,500	1,800
Customer Deposits	1,089	1,126
Current Portion Notes Payable	865	1,062
Total Current Liabilities	$ 5,682	$ 6,563
Long-Term Liabilities		
Capital Lease Obligations	$ 1,022	$ 807
Notes Payable	1,590	2,628
Total Long-Term Liabilities	$ 2,612	$ 3,415
Total Liabilities	$ 8,294	$ 9,978
Stockholders' Equity	$ 2,540	$ 3,358
Total Liabilities and Stockholders' Equity	$10,834	$13,336

Note: Certain financial data are disguised. The numerical relationships have been preserved.

a result of these observations, the management at J&Q believed strongly that they should limit the scope of the purchase to the equipment and the parts of the business that would benefit the company directly, and that their estimates of the sales opportunity at $6 million per year was as far as they could go. The CPG customer list and accounts-receivable aging summary are provided in Exhibit 8.

EXHIBIT 8 Carling Printing & Graphics: Customer Analysis for Fiscal Year 1996 Sorted by Profit Volume

Customer	Sales ($)	Total Cost ($)	Matls & O/S Svc ($)	Profit ($)	% Profit ($)	Value Added ($)	% Add ($)
A	807,158	651,869	448,998	155,289	19	358,160	44
B	281,955	178,622	99,926	103,333	37	182,029	65
C	120,206	74,807	37,158	45,399	38	83,048	69
D	94,584	52,139	32,814	42,445	45	61,770	65
E	585,722	543,549	296,677	47,173	7	289,045	49
F	171,963	134,103	61,764	37,859	22	110,199	64
G	112,924	76,313	68,169	36,611	32	44,755	40
H	347,164	313,781	205,831	33,383	10	141,333	41
I	174,663	145,488	71,059	29,175	17	103,603	59
J	138,645	112,693	41,959	25,952	19	96,686	70
K	299,033	273,195	134,725	25,858	9	164,308	55
L	2,144,205	2,121,117	877,240	23,088	1	1,266,965	59
M	106,092	84,723	13,059	21,368	20	93,033	88
N	648,705	627,484	195,282	21,221	3	453,423	70
0	53,577	32,639	15,878	20,938	39	37,699	70
P	63,499	48,626	26,834	14,874	23	36,666	58
Q	61,680	50,392	31,078	11,288	18	30,601	50
R	42,511	31,239	18,096	11,272	27	24,415	57
S	45,702	34,452	15,863	11,249	25	29,839	65
T	15,875	5,400	2,159	10,475	66	13,716	86
U	107,062	97,123	16,940	9,939	9	90,122	84
V	60,288	50,592	15,013	9,696	16	45,275	75
W	76,819	68,552	31,732	8,267	11	45,087	59
X	160,277	152,883	78,001	7,394	5	82,276	51
Y	44,885	38,074	16,865	6,811	15	28,020	62
Z	167,816	161,765	50,249	6,051	4	117,566	70
AA	26,697	20,804	13,423	5,893	22	13,274	50
BB	30,550	25,471	11,478	5,079	17	19,072	62
CC	12,151	7,283	3,600	4,868	40	8,552	70
DD	9,552	4,875	1,041	4,680	49	8,514	89
EE	12,762	8,486	2,896	4,276	34	9,865	77
FF	16,530	12,394	3,059	4,135	25	13,470	81
GG	34,972	31,185	16,180	3,787	11	18,792	54
HH	47,996	44,336	23,966	3,661	8	24,030	50
II	21,811	18,157	7,820	3,654	17	13,991	64
JJ	16,567	13,045	2,167	3,523	21	14,400	87
KK	18,026	14,652	9,313	3,374	19	8,713	48
LL	117,355	113,993	49,561	3,362	3	67,794	58
MM	23,125	20,068	12,510	3,057	13	10,615	46
NN	261,418	258,831	41,156	2,587	1	220,262	84
OO	37,348	34,772	19,728	2,575	7	17,620	47
PP	7,751	5,263	1,467	2,488	32	6,284	81
QQ	8,895	6,789	6,789	2,106	24	2,106	24
RR	15,344	13,626	3,012	1,718	11	12,332	80

(Continued on next page)

Exhibit 8   *(Continued)*

Customer	Sales ($)	Total Cost ($)	Matls & O/S Svc ($)	Profit ($)	% Profit ($)	Value Added ($)	% Add ($)
SS	11,722	10,091	5,103	1,631	14	6,619	56
TT	155,402	154,023	105,094	1,379	1	50,308	32
UU	56,280	55,381	30,239	899	2	26,040	46
VV	300	0	0	300	100	300	100
WW	19,085	18,926	7,509	159	1	11,576	61
XX	16,344	16,255	7,255	89	1	9,089	56
YY	0	8	8	−8	0	−8	0
ZZ	0	23	0	−23	0	0	0
AAA	0	200	20	−200	0	−20	0
BBB	10,600	10,969	9,194	−369	−3	1,406	13
CCC	9,553	9,922	4,895	−369	−4	4,659	49
DDD	26,980	27,640	15,018	−659	−2	11,963	44
EEE	5,863	6,688	1,415	−824	−14	4,449	76
FFF	8,086	8,920	6,063	−834	−10	2,023	25
GGG	6,468	7,499	3,182	−1,031	−16	3,287	51
HHH	0	1,283	1,043	−1,283	0	−1,043	0
III	0	1,312	0	−1,312	0	0	0
JJJ	14,146	15,468	6,059	−1,323	−9	8,087	57
KKK	40,033	41,796	1,507	−1,763	−4	38,525	96
LLL	14,884	17,193	8,626	−2,310	−16	6,257	42
MMM	18,435	20,759	9,015	−2,323	−13	9,420	51
NNN	31,587	34,410	11,562	−2,823	−9	20,025	63
OOO	0	3,617	350	−3,617	0	−350	0
PPP	12,259	16,016	8,844	−3,757	−31	3,415	28
QQQ	4,188	7,996	2,339	−3,808	−91	1,849	44
RRR	17,780	21,711	5,453	−3,931	−22	12,327	69
SSS	9,682	13,716	6,383	−4,034	−42	3,298	34
TTT	50,519	54,799	29,989	−4,280	−8	20,530	41
UUU	0	4,749	1,970	−4,749	0	−1,970	0
VVV	9,007	14,343	823	−5,336	−59	8,184	91
WWW	29,592	35,938	15,415	−6,346	−21	14,177	48
XXX	14,707	21,184	8,961	−6,476	−44	5,746	39
YYY	0	7,002	6,511	−7,002	0	−6,511	0
ZZZ	38,087	45,246	23,628	−7,159	−19	14,459	38
AAAA	46,972	54,913	36,339	−7,941	−17	10,634	23
BBBB	0	9,679	2,468	−9,679	0	−2,468	0
CCCC	77,062	88,233	37,403	−11,171	−14	39,659	51
DDDD	77,857	89,324	31,269	−11,467	−15	46,589	60
EEEE	0	11,503	4,632	−11,503	0	−4,632	0
FFFF	34,404	47,628	6,207	−13,223	−38	28,197	82
GGGG	125,831	139,399	65,127	−13,568	−11	60,704	48
HHHH	53,304	67,022	33,793	−13,717	−26	19,511	37
IIII	17,894	32,102	25,957	−14,208	−79	−8,063	−45
JJJJ	111,346	125,658	28,485	−14,313	−13	82,861	74
KKKK	127,114	144,189	55,069	−17,075	−13	72,044	57
LLLL	0	17,490	17,490	−17,490	0	−17,490	0
MMMM	58,308	77,355	8,147	−19,047	−33	50,161	86
NNNN	0	20,181	5,391	−20,181	0	−5,391	0

(Continued on next page)

Exhibit 8 (Continued)

Customer	Sales ($)	Total Cost ($)	Matls & O/S Svc ($)	Profit ($)	% Profit ($)	Value Added ($)	% Add ($)
OOOO	93,192	115,396	70,748	−22,204	−24	22,444	24
PPPP	0	23,599	4,606	−23,599	0	−4,606	0
QQQQ	134,334	158,248	82,546	−23,914	−18	51,788	39
RRRR	151,592	177,013	89,034	−25,421	−17	62,558	41
SSSS	1,793	28,573	12,235	−26,780	0	−10,443	−582
TTTT	430,322	482,802	215,394	−52,480	−12	214,928	50
UUUU	301,248	359,167	208,348	−57,919	−19	92,900	31
VVVV	0	61,895	61,879	−61,895	0	−61,879	0
WWWW	0	64,657	27,970	−64,657	0	−27,970	0
XXXX	20,297	98,539	98,267	−78,242	−385	−77,969	−384
YYYY	222,517	323,422	99,207	−100,905	−45	123,310	55
ZZZZ	1,202,503	1,320,854	895,647	−118,351	−10	306,856	26
AAAAA	176,529	353,147	130,277	−176,619	−100	46,252	26
BBBBB	739,871	1,078,046	481,385	−338,175	−46	258,486	35
Grand Totals	12,487,739	13,090,767	6,311,328	−598,005	N/A	6,176,412	N/A

CPG management had originally proposed that they should receive a royalty for the sales generated by the company, arguing that the relationships were a valuable asset and should be paid for by J&Q. They proposed a 3 percent royalty on their forecast of $8 million for three years. Their latest position was a $500,000 lump-sum payment at the time of the sale. The J&Q executives had agreed that the relationships were worth something, but, because their estimates of sales were, at best, $6 million per year—much of which came from new business—they were only willing to pay $400,000 and believed that they were being generous at that figure.

Henkel believed that generating significant new sales dollars would be a difficult task. First, operationally, the two major printing presses would have to be torn down, renovated, and reinstalled at the Johnson & Quin location. This would have to be done sequentially to allow some production to continue during the move. Still, the reduction in capacity would limit the company's ability to sell and complete new business. Secondly, the size of the sales force and the nature of the sales process itself dictated slow progress. J&Q's goal for the year, not including the acquisition, called for an increase of $2.4 million in sales. Having to make up additional sales on top of that figure to account for shortfalls in the CPG sales volume would put a significant burden on the sales force.

In terms of adding clients…for a successful salesperson to build a relationship with a new client, and for them to add two or three substantial relationships to their account base in a year would be good. That would be significant. Now that sounds small, but keep in mind that our average rep this year will have $3 million to $3.5 million in sales. Business forms salespeople, by comparison, sell about $700,000 to $750,000. Many of them have a lot less than that. We don't have anybody down in that range, even our new people. Now, we don't have many reps. Given the sales volume, we don't need that many.

By comparison, CPG had six salespeople who in the last year had generated a combined total of approximately $12 million from 106 accounts.

J&Q also completed a breakeven analysis based on a series of cost assumptions. The most difficult part of the cost analysis was the determination of the staffing needs for the combined enterprise. The difficulty lay in the necessity of laying off more than half of the existing CPG workforce. This was painful to both Bowling and Henkel, but their analysis indicated that the additional positions simply could not be supported financially. Of the 81 positions currently supported by CPG, only 45 would be maintained. Most of the proposed cutbacks were in areas of production that were duplicated at the two companies, or in administrative positions. Three of the six salespeople were to be retained.

> *George mentioned initially that he was very concerned that the business would be sold by St. Louis (CPG headquarters) to a company that was not interested in saving jobs. St. Louis, in a general sense, and he, in particular, felt that they had some very nice people who deserved a shot at retaining their jobs. Good workers. They produce a good product. They have a lot of good traits, and he was certainly right. That was not just a selling point. It was from the heart. He really was trying to save as many jobs as he could. That was one of the first things he mentioned to me.*

Having worked out the necessary staffing levels and the specific equipment that would be transferred, the management of Johnson & Quin were able to estimate the annual fixed costs associated with the proposed acquisition. Their most recent estimate was that the fixed expenses would be $2.7 million, although previous estimates had been as high as $3.3 million. Based on their own production history and the records from CPG, they were able to estimate a contribution margin of approximately 35 percent.

CONCLUSION

Henkel continued to contemplate his options regarding the purchase of CPG. He had invested a great deal of time and energy in the evaluation of the proposals and options since January, when the idea had been broached. He knew that he was psychologically inclined to go ahead with the deal because of his deep involvement. At the same time, he noted that part of the cost of the deal had also been the time and energy he and his executives had devoted to the project, at the expense of working on other projects and internal improvements detailed in the company's annual business plan. Those internal issues had been "put on the back burner" while the acquisition had been analyzed, but they were going to have to be addressed. To ignore them further would mean a continuing erosion of competitiveness, service, and quality relative to competition. If they were to go ahead with the deal at the inflated price asked by CPG, not only would they be paying more than they thought it was worth, but the start-up costs and managerial focus would keep the other internal issues in the background for another six months, at least. Wasn't anything ever simple?

The David J. Joseph Company: The Henderson Shredder Project

Jan Willem Bol, David W. Rosenthal, and Alison Ohl

In June 1988, the Executive Management Committee of The David J. Joseph Company (DJJ) was faced with a decision regarding building an automobile shredding facility at Henderson, Kentucky. The new shredder would provide an additional source of scrap metal for the company's customers in the Midwest and river areas, but a number of issues had yet to be resolved. The decision to be made was the culmination of a series of studies and evaluations that had taken place over the previous two years. A decision to go forward with the project would require a $3 million investment in fixed assets, plus an additional $1.5 million in working capital.

Market demand for ferrous scrap and other scrap metals had been relatively stable and even improving during the recent past. Technological changes in steelmaking had increased the usage of scrap as a basic component of finished steel. Further, new steel mills were being located in more geographically diverse areas. A strong source of scrap was critical for these "mini mills." Some of DJJ's current customers had given indications that they were planning to increase production in the region.

The economics of the shredder depended largely on the spread between the market price of the scrap metal produced and the projected average cost of raw materials incurred if the shredder were operating at efficient levels. The demand for scrap metal was strongly tied to the activity level of the economy. Although the market for scrap had been good recently, there were no guarantees that those conditions would continue.

The capital expenditures necessary to install and operate the facility and the availability of sufficient raw material for the facility to operate efficiently also played a large role in the economic feasibility of the project. Market studies suggested that scrap sources to feed the shredder could be a problem for the Henderson facility.

Environmental issues and legal constraints also concerned the committee. The operation of a shredder was, from one point of view, an activity of recycling metal from automobiles and other sources. At the same time, a shredder also produced an unusable by-product, "fluff," which was comprised of the nonmetallic materials separated from the metal in the shredding process. The shredder fluff would have to be sent to landfills. The Joseph Company had been an industry leader in its environmental standards and practices, but every new project and location brought its own problems and challenges. Environmental regulation was in a state of change, thus creating the potential for future liabilities where none currently existed.

This case was prepared by Professor Jan Willem Bol, Professor Alison Ohl, and Professor David Rosenthal of Miami University, as a basis for class discussion. It is not intended to illustrate either effective or ineffective handling of an administrative situation.

COMPANY BACKGROUND

History

In 1863, Joseph Joseph, a native of Germany, settled in Cincinnati, Ohio, and began a hide- and wool-trading operation. Subsequently, his brother Samuel joined the company, and in 1885, with the advent of growing industrialization and soaring demand for scrap metal, the Josephs turned to scrap iron trading, abandoning the hide and wool business.

The scrap iron company grew quickly and other businesses were added. After Joseph Joseph's death, his oldest son, David, then manager of the scrap trading operation, ran seven plants and branch offices in almost every major steel center in the United States. With the beginning of World War I, demand for scrap iron increased significantly, and by the end of The Great War, the Joseph Joseph and Brothers Company was one of the largest scrap metal firms in the nation, a position it again held in 1988.

In 1921, David Joseph, Sr., established the company as The David J. Joseph Company. His son became president in 1945. Consolidating its strength through the 1960s and 1970s, DJJ, in 1975, began the sale of its operations to SHV Holdings NV, a privately-held company located in Utrecht, the Netherlands. SHV had more than $2 billion in assets and operated worldwide businesses in energy, the trading of raw materials, and retail distribution of a wide variety of consumer goods. The sale was completed in 1980. By 1988, DJJ, still headquartered in Cincinnati, Ohio, employed approximately 750 people at 26 locations, including 12 ferrous-trading offices across the United States.

By the mid to late 1980s, nearly 40 percent of all the steel produced in the United States was made from purchased scrap. As a ferrous scrap broker, DJJ provided an essential link between the various sources of scrap and the steel mills and foundries that used it in the steelmaking and casting processes.

Operations

DJJ employed about 40 traders with a variety of commercial and academic backgrounds. After an initial training period, traders were assigned to a district office and immediately became responsible for arranging purchases and sales of scrap for their own clients. They often spent 30 percent to 40 percent of their time in the field, realizing that much of their business depended on information about market conditions—supply and demand—obtained from customers.

Most trades done by DJJ ranged from 50 to 5,000 tons, although some transactions exceeded 50,000 tons and dollar values of $5 million or more. Shippers of scrap often selected DJJ because of its financial strength. The practice in the industry was for brokers such as DJJ to advance a percentage of the purchase price at the time of shipment, with the balance to be paid later.

In addition to the Ferrous Department, which represented 87 percent of DJJ's business, DJJ had two other operating departments. The NonFerrous Department was involved in the sale of nonferrous scrap by-products that were generated at DJJ's processing plants, as well as in the domestic and international trading of nonferrous scrap metals. The department represented approximately 6 percent of DJJ's $500 million revenues.

The Railroad Equipment Leasing and Marketing Department represented 7 percent of DJJ's revenues. It was involved in all facets of used railroad equipment, including the purchase of equipment for scrapping at DJJ's facilities, the marketing of reusable equipment, and the owning and leasing of railroad equipment. This department was growing and was adding significantly to the company's business, in its own right, as well as enhancing some of the company's other activities through developing new markets and different transportation approaches.

An important aspect of the brokerage business was transportation. Transportation could often be a significant part of the total cost of any scrap transaction. DJJ's Transportation Department provided the company information on applicable rates for rail, truck, and barge shipments and also negotiated and monitored administration of contract freight rates and coordinated intermodal movements with transportation carriers.

To complement its brokerage business, DJJ operated 12 specialized scrap-processing and mill-service facilities. Six of these plants included automobile shredding machines, each capable of processing approximately 600 automobile bodies per day. Some of these plants, which were often located near DJJ's major customers, were also involved in scrapping retired railroad freight cars and track.

In 1985, DJJ established an International Department. This was DJJ's return to international trading of ferrous scrap after an absence of more than 40 years. DJJ was now involved in exporting U.S. scrap to overseas markets, as well as importing to the United States high-quality scrap items and other ferrous units, such as pig iron.

DJJ ventured into a number of areas of innovation. For instance, it developed the first medium-sized shredders for the purpose of upgrading the quality of automobile scrap. Also, in response to increasingly stringent environmental regulations, burning equipment was built (and patented) to facilitate the reduction of wood-lined boxcars to metal components.

Although financial information was buried in SHV's annual data, DJJ's 1988 net worth was estimated at $100 million. With operating margins between 3 percent and 4 percent, DJJ was typical of other national scrap metal brokers. DJJ dealt with several thousand suppliers, the largest of whom represented less than 2 percent to 3 percent of DJJ's total volume. However, because of regional differences, a single supplier could provide as much as 10 percent of the volume for an individual scrap yard. By contrast, the top 25 percent of its 207 customers represented approximately 90 percent of its total sales volume.

THE SCRAP BUSINESS

Sources of Scrap

"Everything made from metal eventually becomes scrap—frequently many times over," explained Joe Hirschhorn, senior vice president and member of the Executive Management Committee. "Old cars and trucks, railroad cars and tracks, and steel beams from dismantled buildings and bridges are all raw material for the scrap processor." The process of ferrous scrap recycling started with the discarding of an item made from or containing iron or steel. Scrap was also generated by many industrial companies as a by-product of manufacturing. The next activity involved collecting and processing. The activities of scrap processors included sorting and reloading material for shipment and/or using electromagnets, shears, shredders and balers to prepare material for shipment and use. After that, the scrap was melted and refined in the manufacture of new iron or steel for new products for consumer use.

Ferrous scrap could be divided into three major categories: home, prompt industrial, and obsolete. Home scrap and prompt industrial scrap were involuntary by-products of manufacturing processes. Home scrap originated in a steel mill and consisted of such items as ingot and slab ends and trimmings from the production process. Prompt industrial scrap resulted from normal machining, stamping, and fabricating operations in the production of products made from steel. Prompt industrial scrap included clippings from an auto body manufacturer and turnings from a lathe at a machine tool shop. Obsolete scrap, the third major category, was created when a product made of iron or steel had served its useful life and was discarded, such as railroad cars or automobiles.

Trend: Increasing Demand for Scrap

In spite of the general decline of the U.S. steel industry, there was a strong trend in steel-making to use more purchased scrap per ton of steel made. Purchased scrap receipts averaged slightly more than 27 tons per 100 tons of raw steel produced from 1954 to 1970. In 1984, this ratio had risen to 45 tons.

The increase in the use of purchased scrap closely tracked the growth of electric furnace steelmaking, a process that required a larger proportion of scrap as input versus traditional steelmaking processes. In 1954, only about 6 percent of U.S. steel production was in electric furnaces. In 1983, that proportion had grown to 31.5 percent and had been running just over 37 percent during 1986. Electric furnace steelmaking had become increasingly attractive for many reasons. Compared with an integrated, iron-ore-based steel plant, the modern electric furnace shop could be constructed and started up faster, required only one-sixth the capital investment per ton of capacity, used only about one-fourth the energy per ton produced, offered greater operating flexibility, and required fewer man-hours per ton of output. In 1986, only 4 percent of total raw steel production was produced by plants using open hearths, down from 91 percent in 1954. Continuous casting had risen from 7 percent of steel made in 1973 to over 60 percent in 1987. Other technologies that had been developed included the use of outside-the-furnace ladle metallurgy stations to bring the melt to precise temperature, oxy-fuel burners, and consteel scrap preheating techniques. In part, these technological changes were a reaction to increased legislation and public policy with respect to the environment.

In 1986, U.S. steel mills used 72 percent of the 38 million tons of ferrous scrap that were purchased domestically that year. Iron and steel foundries accounted for the rest. Export of ferrous scrap from the United States reached 11.9 million net tons in 1986, representing nearly 24 percent of the total market for U.S. scrap.

The conversion to continuous casting caused a sharp reduction in steel-mill home scrap generation and, therefore, in the proportion of steel made up of steel mills' own home scrap. Reduced home scrap availability and the expanding role of electric furnaces had resulted in a more than 3 percent average annual growth rate in the amount of scrap purchased per 100 tons of steel made in the United States since 1970. For each additional one point share of market increase gained by electric furnaces, it was predicted that an increase of approximately 600,000–700,000 tons in domestic purchased scrap requirements would result.

The Scrap Marketplace

"The scrap business is a demand-driven business. Scrap is bought, not sold, and is only worth what people are willing to pay for it," explained Hirschhorn. "Melting in a furnace is the only use for ferrous scrap, and, because of its heterogeneity, it is not fungible."

Mills and foundries bought scrap when they needed it. If they did not need scrap to feed their furnaces, they would not buy scrap regardless of offers made by the broker. Prices of scrap were volatile and responsive to changes in the steel industry's operating rate. Industrial plants selling scrap had to dispose of the material each month and, therefore, would accept the highest bid offered from interested buyers. Scrap dealers did not need to sell each month and could resist lower prices, sometimes choosing to hold scrap when prices were below their costs to purchase and process. Industrial scrap supply tended not to be price elastic in that higher prices did not generally expand supply. The typical price for a ton of ferrous scrap metal was $100, although this varied depending upon which of the 60 to 80 different grades of scrap metal were involved. Also, depending upon general market conditions, the price of a ton of ferrous scrap metal could fluctuate between $75 and $150.

The scrap broker's role was to connect the unorganized and complex industry, which contained several thousand dealers, tens of thousands of manufacturing plants, hundreds of mills and foundries and scores of different scrap grades, into a market. The scrap broker traded scrap iron and steel between producers and users. About 40 percent of the scrap sold by brokers and large processors was prompt industrial scrap. Brokers and processors queried steel mills and foundries before the end of each month to determine their scrap requirements for the next 30 days. Based on this information, they offered bids to companies generating prompt industrial scrap. About 20 percent of the purchased scrap tonnage originated from the 7 to 9 million cars and trucks that were scrapped in the United States each year. Five percent of the scrap purchased by U.S. scrap users originated from railroads. The remaining 35 percent of U.S. customers' scrap purchases were other obsolete iron or steel products, such as demolition material, old water pipes, manhole covers and kitchen sinks.

Discards of iron and steel products had exceeded ferrous scrap recovery each year since 1956, and the resulting additions to the inventory of ferrous scrap available for recovery had reached staggering volumes. In the United States, supply was not a constraint to increasing the recycling of ferrous scrap. Instead, level of demand, economic conditions, and the costs of processing and transportation defined the limits of the industry.

The marketplace for ferrous scrap was not national and was comprised of numerous marketing regions. There were approximately 15 distinct marketing regions for scrap in the United States, and many showed supply-demand imbalances. Interterritory shipments, grade substitutions, and increased or reduced scrap collection could bring about equilibrium. For instance, the available supply of ferrous scrap in the northeastern United States exceeded regular demand from domestic consumers in the area by such a wide margin that approximately 40 percent of all scrap exported from the United States moved from points between Baltimore and Maine.

There were approximately 3,000 U.S. scrap dealers, operating mostly on a regional basis. Overall, the industry was fragmented and highly competitive, although this varied by region. Companies such as Cozzi, Luntz, and National Material Trading operated in Chicago and Cleveland. On a national level, competitors such as Luria Bros. and Tube City ranged from 50 percent to 90 percent of DJJ's size. Most of DJJ's competitors were brokers and processors, and many, especially those operating on a regional basis, were, much like DJJ in its early days, owned and managed by families.

The slim margins and variability of demand combined with the capital intensity of the industry to make profits volatile. Thus, many companies, including DJJ, searched for ways to improve their control of scrap supplies and costs. One method was to identify an effective location to open a shredder.

THE HENDERSON SHREDDER PROJECT

In late 1986 the Statistical Department had been asked to study the Inland Waterway System to determine if there was a location that could adequately support a shredder facility of 7,000 tons per month (TPM) capacity. (See Exhibit 1 for details of the Henderson Auto Shredder.)

The study was commissioned for a variety of reasons. First, it was a response to general industry trends of increasing demand for high-quality ferrous scrap. Second, the construction of two new steel plants in the region by Nucor Steel, DJJ's largest agency account, would require additional, reliable sources of scrap. Finally, DJJ's management was concerned that competing scrap providers would build new shredder facilities if they did not act first to "dry up" the available sources of scrap in the region.

The Statistical Department's report was presented in January 1987. It focused on the question of supply of scrapped automobiles available for shredding in various locations. The report assumed that a shredder would not regularly draw cars from beyond 150 miles as a result of the cost of transportation, and that a shredder would not generally draw cars from points that were closer to competing shredders.

The report concluded:

Our analysis shows there does not appear to be any inland waterway location that could easily support such a shredder, but there are three areas—Cincinnati/ Louisville, Evansville/Paducah/Cairo, and New Orleans/Baton Rouge—that might be viable.

EXHIBIT 1   Fact Sheet: Henderson Auto Shredder

1. System connected horsepower: 4,000 HP

2. Shredder mill motor horsepower: 3,500 HP

3. Typical electrical consumption:
   - Energy   — 250,000 Kilowatt hours/month
   - Power   —   3,300 Kilowatts
   - Electrical cost   —$12,000/month

4. Production rates:
   - Input: Scrap autos and sheet iron—6,300 GT/MO
     (About one auto each 45–60 seconds)
   - Output: Shredded steel   — 5,000 GT/MO
     Nonferrous metals —   200 GT/MO
     Landfilled materials — 1,100 GT/MO

5. Shredder rotor revolves at 720 RPM, and contains 34 hammers weighing 225 pounds each.

6. Shredder mill weight: 200,000 Pounds
   Shredder mill plus foundation weight: 2,200,000 Pounds
   Shredder mill machinery occupies: 80,000 Sq. Ft.
   Auto storage area occupies: 100,000 Sq. Ft.
   Shredder mill feed chute: 20' High
   Shredder control tower: 30' High

The study used national estimates of vehicle registrations, the percentage of cars taken out of use each year, and 1984 population estimates to forecast vehicle scrappage. Each of the shredders on the Inland Waterway System was identified and its shredding capacity noted. (See Exhibit 2.) The forecast of supply was compared against the capacity of each facility. The results indicated a shortage of cars in many areas. Among several other sites, the study focused on Evansville, Indiana:

> We also looked specifically at *Evansville, Indiana,* the one area on the River System map that does not appear to be saturated with shredders. A population of roughly 2,000,000 is needed to support a 7,000 GT per month auto shredder, and the *immediate* Evansville area only has 150,000 to 200,000 people. However, based on the population in the larger Evansville-Paducah-Cairo region, this area could support 3,900 to 4,800 TPM shredding capacity. If we assume automobiles make up just 80 percent of the shredder feed, then the area could support a 4,900 to 6,000 TPM shredder. However, (there is) a shortage of cars available for shredders in St. Louis, Indianapolis, and Tennessee...which may be causing them to reach to the Evansville-Paducah-Cairo regions for supplemental tonnage.

In response to the conclusions of the initial report, it was decided that additional information was needed regarding the Evansville site. A two-page memo was forwarded in November 1987 describing the geographic location, access to transportation, distance to competing shredders, and estimates of scrap tonnage potential. The author of the memo had visited the area and had spoken to local scrap dealers and processors about their market, prices, and the other conditions. The memo concluded:

> I do not believe that we could produce much more than approximately 4,000 GT shrunk of shredded scrap per month out of the Evansville area. My figure is based on a competitive pricing structure and by not pushing more than halfway, in any direction, into a competing shredder's territory. I have factored into this number a minimal tonnage from scrap dealers within 50 miles of Evansville. It is quite possible we could push a bit harder into southwestern Indiana to Paducah, Kentucky, thereby increasing this tonnage somewhat.

Given the uncertainty and conflicting nature of some of the information, the Statistical Department was asked to summarize the findings to that time. In May 1988 they issued a report that analyzed all available data. Using the population within a drawing area of 100 miles, the report stated "assuming that no other shredders are installed in the area ...shredded production...would average approximately 4,200 to 4,700 GT/MO." Furthermore, it identified some of the advantages and disadvantages of the Evansville/ Henderson area:

Advantages

- the area is not saturated with competing shredders
- being on the river allows access to domestic river mills and to export markets
- the area's proximity to Crawfordsville provides opportunity to ship to Nucor's mill
- the area is close to major highways for easy access to surrounding major cities
- Evansville is the home of several large manufacturing plants (such as Whirlpool and ALCOA) and many smaller plants

EXHIBIT 2   Inland Waterway System: Shredding Capability, 1987

Operator	Location	GT/MO Shredding Capability
1. Pittsburh-Cleveland-Canton-Wooster		
Luria Brothers	Beaver Falls, PA	5,000
Tube City	McKeesport, PA	5,000–7,000
Luria Brothers	Cleveland, OH	15,000
Luntz Corporation	Canton, OH	10,000
Magnimet	Wooster, OH	4,000
2. Ashland		
Mansbach Metal	Ashland, KY	7,000–8,000
3. Cincinnati		
DJJ Company	Newport, KY	5,000–6,000
4. Louisville		
River City Shredding	Louisville, KY	5,000–6,000
5. Nashville		
Steiner-Liff	Nashville, TN	6,000–7,000
6. Memphis		
Mid-American	Memphis, TN	4,000–5,000
Samitized Steel Company	Memphis, TN	4,000–5,000
7. Chattanooga-Knoxville-Rockwood-Pulaski-Decatur		
Southern Foundry Supply	Chattanooga, TN	4,000–5,000
Southern Foundry Supply	Knoxville, TN	5,000
Hutcherson	Halls, TN	3,000
DJJ Company	Jackson, TN	5,500
Denbo Scrap	Pulaski, TN	4,000
Rockwood Iron & Metal	Rockwood, TN	8,000–9,000
Denbo Iron & Metal	Decatur, AL	4,500–5,000
8. Birmingham		
National Tire & Salvage	Birmingham, AL	4,000
Shredders, Inc.	Birmingham, AL	7,000
9. Pensacola		
Southern Scrap	Pensacola, FL	5,000
10. Greenville		
Friedman Iron & Metal	Greenville, MS	5,500
11. Monroe		
Monroe Scrap	Monroe, MS	3,000–5,000
12. Baton Rouge-New Orleans		
Southern Scrap Material Co.	Baton Rouge, LA	5,000
Southern Scrap Material Co.	New Orleans, LA	5,000–6,000

Operator	Location	GT/MO Shredding Capability
13. Beaumont-Houston-Victoria-Corpus Christi		
Southern Iron & Metal	Beaumont, TX	5,000–6,000
Houston Junk	Houston, TX	1,500–2,500
Houston Metal Processing	Houston, TX	5,000–6,000
Proler	Houston, TX	15,000
Rodgers Salvage	Victoria, TX	2,000
Cometals	Corpus Christi, TX	2,000–3,000
Industrial Salvage	Corpus Christi, TX	3,000
14. Little Rock		
A. Tenenbaum	N. Little Rock, AR	3,000–4,000
15. Ft. Smith-Muskogee-Sand Springs		
Yaffee Iron & Metal	Ft. Smith, AR	3,000–5,000
Yaffee Iron	Muskogee, OK	3,000–5,000
Tulsa Metal Processing	Sand Springs, OK	3,000
16. St. Louis		
St. Louis Auto Shredding	E. St. Louis, IL	10,000–12,000
Hyman-Michaels	Alton, IL	4,000
L&M Shred	St. Louis, MO	5,000
17. Kansas City		
Proler-Cohen	Kansas City, KS	12,000–15,000
K. C. Recycling	Kansas City, MO	3,000–5,000
18. Council Bluffs-Sioux City		
Alter Company	Council Bluffs, IA	5,000–6,000
Remelt	Council Bluffs, IA	500
Bernstein	Sioux City, IA	2,000–3,000
19. Waterloo-Davenport		
Alter Company	Davenport, IA	5,000–7,000
Weissman Iron & Metal	Waterloo, IA	2,000
20. St. Paul		
H. S. Kaplan	St. Paul, MN	6,000–8,000
North Star Steel	St. Paul, MN	12,000–14,000
21. Peoria		
Allied Iron & Steel	Peoria, IL	5,000–10,000
I. Bork & Son	Peoria, IL	4,000
22. Chicago		
Proler-Kaplan	Chicago, IL	12,000–15,000
Fritz Cartage	Riverdale, IL	5,000–7,000
Dudek	Lemont, IL	2,000–4,000
Pielet Bros. Iron & Metal	McCook, IL	12,000–15,000
Illinois Scrap Processing	S. Chicago, IL	10,000–15,000

Disadvantages

- DJJ may have to compete with shredders in Indianapolis, Louisville, Nashville, and St. Louis
- there are not many auto crushers in the immediate area to supply a DJJ shredder
- the area is relatively clean of abandoned autos, appliances, and sheet iron

EXTERNAL ISSUES IMPACTING THE HENDERSON DECISION

The Executive Management Committee was confronted with a number of forces that would influence the direction of the decision regarding the proposed Henderson shredder project. These forces included competitive conditions, economic considerations, the relative influence of buyers and suppliers, and the desires of DJJ's parent company, SHV.

Nucor, one of the country's leading steel producers and one of DJJ's most important customers, was planning expansion in northeastern Arkansas. The expected increase in the demand for scrap in the midwestern region was influencing the entire industry. The relationship of DJJ with Nucor was very good. DJJ was Nucor's scrap agent in the purchase of all remote (nonhome) scrap and was also used as a consultant on Nucor's raw materials site studies. Nevertheless, other suppliers were battling to gain a share of Nucor's increased demand. Competitors were pointing to the lack of a scrap yard within 50 miles of the Nucor site, suggesting that location of supplies would be very important and that DJJ could be cut out as a broker.

Further, Nucor had been discussing the need to increase the quality of its output and had been considering with DJJ and others the use of Direct Reduced Iron Pellets (DRI) and Hot Briquetted Iron (HBI) as substitutes for a portion of their required raw material. The use of these substitutes would improve the control over the chemical content of its steel output. It was clear that Nucor was concerned over the availability and quality of raw materials for its expansion, and that this concern was being communicated to DJJ by way of encouragement to develop scrap yards and supplies of DRI.

The Nucor expansion was part of a broader trend in the sense that the traditional view of scrap as an inexhaustible commodity was giving way under projections of increasing demand. An excerpt from a presentation given by Stephen W. Wulff, director of statistical services at DJJ, in June 1988, described the market conditions:

"Scrap is becoming increasingly difficult to buy in today's marketplace, and prices are many dollars a ton higher than they were just a few weeks ago. Steel mills continue to use scrap at high rates. If we look at the past 10 months' average orders for scrap placed in this country, we see that the monthly average is a record high pace, higher even than the average rate of scrap purchases in 1974. With this kind of unrelenting demand in the marketplace, the scrap supply pipelines just can't be refilled. I suspect that this summer we're going to see a replay of what happened in the scrap market early this year in February and March. Steel mills stepped back again from the market in May and June, and purchases were down about 12 percent from the first four months of this year. Part of that was in anticipation of further price erosion through the summer. But, again, they kept melting scrap at high rates. Steel mill inventories are run down and now we have transportation problems not just from the railroad industry, but also on the river system with the drought and the tie-up of barge traffic on the Ohio and Mississippi rivers. This will lead to dislocations in the market and premium prices will have to be paid for tonnages that can move in today's marketplace."

The increasing demand for scrap resulted in a change in focus in the industry. Rather than the traditional approach characterized by the industry adage, "If you control the user, the scrap will come to you," the focus was increasingly on controlling the supply. Indeed, a number of competitors to DJJ had been buying out businesses, such as scrap yards and shredders, that produced scrap. Large processors that controlled over 50,000 tons of scrap per month were all focusing on the river system, seeking shredders and feeder yards.

Similarly, the Florida market had had a significant impact on the structure of the industry. The increasing population in the state had generated more scrappable automobiles and other items, and because of its location and availability of water transportation, scrap available from Florida was expanding rapidly. The expansion attracted many of the industry competitors to build facilities. Exportation of scrap became a reality as the market continued to grow with material moving overseas as well as domestically across the Gulf of Mexico and even up the river system.

The increased demand in the market and the shift toward supply control were not the only issues facing the Executive Management Committee. In a recent meeting with the management of SHV, the president of DJJ had been told that DJJ "should be looking for growth opportunities," that they were too conservative in their investments, and that, "We haven't turned down any of your requests [for investment funds]."

Thus, there was considerable pressure to pursue a dynamic course of action in the marketplace. At the same time, the financial aspects of the Henderson shredder project were potentially a problem if the volume of automobiles was insufficient to run the facility efficiently. Further, there were environmental issues to consider.

ENVIRONMENTAL CONCERNS

Initial Approaches

As part of its investigation of Henderson as a desirable location for a shredder, DJJ's management contacted the local port authority, which was the owner of the site that DJJ had earmarked for the shredder's location.[1]

Essentially, there were two environmental issues. The first concerned DJJ's ability to control by-product disposal and cost, and the second issue concerned the obtaining of the regulatory permits. With respect to the latter, DJJ had to obtain a technical review by state authorities. Also, local community approval needed to be obtained through two public hearings, presided over by the county judge executive: one for zoning issues and one for environmental permits.

Skip Rouster, who was a regional operations manager of DJJ and reported to the vice president of operations, had been educated as a theoretical mathematician and had learned to deal with environmental regulatory authorities whenever DJJ had been confronted with environmental issues. "The first thing you have to do," said Rouster, "is to explain your business to them. Once you have done that and the authorities have obtained a general knowledge of what it is that you want, you have to demonstrate the likely impact that your business will have on the community. Only when you can show that the impact your company will have will fall within the federal, state, and local environmental regulations, will the port authority allow the project to proceed."

---

[1] The port authority was also responsible for zoning and land issues.

"In addition to the environmental issues," Rouster continued, "the company would also have to analyze and report on the impact on the community's infrastructure, the traffic patterns, local electricity, etcetera. For instance, you need specific permits for opacity (smoke) and particulate emission and how to dispose of (by-products)." Essentially, federal regulations controlled air,[2] water, and land, and compliance with these regulations was controlled at the state level. The state handled environmental permits, whereas local regulations dealt with land use and zoning issues.

The port authority's initial response to DJJ's plans was very favorable, given the anticipated positive effect the company would have on local employment and tax revenues. The facility expected to employ 20 to 25 workers and generate approximately $11,000 in monthly revenues for the port authority. In addition, the Henderson Port Authority had been trying to attract new industry to the region and was, therefore, willing to move quickly. Given that the region had been dependent on the coal industry, which also had an environmental impact on the community, the port authority was well prepared to support an industry and a company such as DJJ.

To facilitate and encourage a speedy process in Henderson, DJJ hired a local lawyer who could assist DJJ with the zoning process and who could develop a coordinated approach with the local zoning commissioner. Also, DJJ hired McCoy and McCoy Engineering, a local engineering company, to test the soil of the 7.5 acre site that it had earmarked for the shredder. Unfortunately, McCoy found three hazardous chemicals (coal tar, plasticisers, and barium), all of which exceeded allowable levels. It turned out that the soil had been contaminated by a company that made components for U.S. Army munitions and that occupied the site back in the 1940s and 1950s. Although further testing determined that ground water had not yet been contaminated, it became clear that the contaminated soil would have to be removed before the site could be used. The cost of the site cleanup would be borne by the port authority.

EPA and Landfill Issues

Shortly after beginning the investigation of a Henderson facility, DJJ also learned that the U.S. Environmental Protection Agency, through the State of Kentucky, intended to investigate the landfill used by its shredder located in Newport, Kentucky. High concentrations of hazardous materials were found at this landfill, used by DJJ for disposal of the nonusable by-product (fluff) produced by the Newport shredder. In part, the EPA's interest was driven by a number of auto shredding operations in Massachusetts that had been closed voluntarily because those companies did not send their nonmetal residues to landfills, as DJJ did. The EPA had found unsafe levels of PCBs, or polychlorinated biphenyl, and waste oils in samples it had taken.

Traditionally, auto shredders had not been regulated, but because of the possibility of generating hazardous by-products, the EPA had started to look into the problems. The EPA also believed that a different landfill used by industrial companies located adjacent to the monofill DJJ used in Newport, Kentucky, was releasing hazardous materials into the environment, causing high concentrations of hazardous materials to be found near the landfill and a nearby stream that emptied into the Ohio River near Cincinnati. DJJ

---

[2]The application for the Henderson shredder did not involve permits for air because the technology to be used was water-based. No emission of air was generated because all shredder by-product (fluff) was "caught" by a water stream. Using approximately 300,000 to 400,000 gallons per month, fluff was caught in a closed-loop water system, and the resulting sludge, after being drained, was brought to a landfill. Because the water was recycled, permits for water also were not needed.

did not believe the problems experienced at the multipurpose landfill were in any way connected to its involvement at the adjacent monofill, which it believed was later confirmed when the Kentucky state authorities approved closure of the monofill.

The finding of the possible linkage to PCB caused one landowner near the Henderson facility to oppose the project. At a preliminary local public hearing, surprising opposition to a shredder was demonstrated by some people in the community, and it appeared that many questions still needed to be answered before the community as a whole would support the port authority's enthusiasm for a DJJ application.

During the public hearing, a promotional video was shown that explained the benefits of the proposed facility and the commitment to the environment exhibited by DJJ. In the video, Skip Rouster explained: "DJJ is very environmentally responsible. There's nothing in [the shredding process] that's hazardous, and DJJ has stringent input specifications for shredders. For instance, before a car goes into one of our shredders, the battery, exhaust systems, wheel weights, gas tanks, and radiators will have to be removed. In fact, we do not buy materials that contain these items. We insist that the salvage yards, from whom we buy the cars, take those out and sell those to others."

In order to encourage and compensate salvage yard suppliers for complying with DJJ's own regulations, it generally paid them a little more for their scrap metal. Rouster added, "We firmly believe in 'GIGO' [Garbage in, Garbage out]. We want to control what goes in so that we will always be one step ahead of the environmental regulatory agencies. Environmental rules continuously change, and it is very difficult to know what is required tomorrow. Although you may try to do the best you can and be within the law, tomorrow you may find out that you are responsible for what you did yesterday and have to pay for it."

One of the recent developments Rouster was referring to involved regulations with respect to landfills. For instance, new regulations required landfill owners to install double linings to prevent leakage into ground water. These developments were particularly relevant to DJJ because its philosophy dictated that it would not open a shredder as long as it did not have a long-term landfill contract. In fact, DJJ preferred to have its own (monolithic) landfill because it would give it more control. Also, given the "cradle-to-grave" responsibility for discarded materials, regulatory agencies would eventually hold DJJ responsible, regardless of whether it owned the landfill. Because generally 20 percent of what DJJ processed through a shredder was a by-product called "fluff," which contained plastic, foam rubber, and other nonmetallic parts of shredded items, and the Henderson shredder could generate more than 1,000 tons of fluff per month, DJJ's management was eager to investigate the possibility of purchasing a landfill or securing a long-term contract with a landfill operator in the Henderson area.

An investigation into the availability of landfills showed that only one landfill, owned by Billy Gough, would meet DJJ's requirements. Gough, however, did not want to sell his site but was willing to negotiate a long-term contract with DJJ.

FINANCIAL CONSIDERATIONS

The DJJ management expected the proposed shredder facility to require approximately $3 million for the construction and purchase of the necessary fixed assets. An additional $1.5 million was needed for working capital.

The company had explored the possibility that the fixed-asset portion of the investment could be financed through the issuance of low-interest-rate Industrial Development Revenue Bonds by the Henderson Port Authority. The port authority would issue the bonds for the purpose of the construction of the facility, covered by a long-term (20 years or longer) contract with the company. Working capital would be financed internally. The expected effective cost of capital was 7.15 percent, and for the first five years only interest payments would be required.

The forecasted costs and revenues for the shredder provided for an operating income of $12 per gross ton. The planning documents anticipated a monthly volume of 5,000 to 6,000 gross tons per month. Operating costs were expected to run about $26 per gross ton, including approximately $6 landfill and transportation costs. The remaining operating costs included salaries and wages of the anticipated 20 to 25 staff members and management and were considered to be relatively fixed.

CONCLUSION

Having conducted a number of studies and evaluations over the past two years, it had become clear that the issues regarding the decision to place an automobile shredding facility in Henderson, Kentucky, were complex. After numerous meetings and discussions, the president was inclined to favorably support the decision, in part because of the encouragement from SHV to grow. Most of the members of the Executive Management Committee were also inclined to proceed because of expectations for growth. Yet, at the same time, others were troubled by the lack of supply, the environmental issues, and the uncertainty of favorable financial results.

Icon Acoustics: Bypassing Tradition

Lew G. Brown

THE DREAM

Like most entrepreneurs, Dave Fokos dreams a lot. He imagines customers eagerly phoning Icon Acoustics in Billerica, Massachusetts, to order his latest, custom-made stereo speakers. He sees sales climbing, cash flowing, and hundreds of happy workers striving to produce top-quality products that delight Icon's customers.

Like most entrepreneurs, Dave has taken a long time to develop his dream. While majoring in electrical engineering at Cornell, Dave discovered that he had a strong interest in audio engineering. Following graduation, Dave landed a job as a speaker designer with Conrad-Johnson, a high-end audio-equipment manufacturer. Within four years, Dave had designed 13 speaker models and decided to start his own company.

Dave identified a market niche that he felt other speaker firms had overlooked. The niche consisted of "audio-addicts"—people who love to listen to music and appreciate first-rate stereo equipment. These affluent, well-educated customers are genuinely obsessed with their stereo equipment. "They'd rather buy a new set of speakers than eat," Dave observes.

Dave faced one major problem—how to distribute Icon's products. He had learned from experience at Conrad-Johnson that most manufacturers distribute their equipment primarily through stereo dealers. Dave did not hold a high opinion of most such dealers; he felt that they too often played hardball with manufacturers, forcing them to accept thin margins. Furthermore, the dealers concentrated on only a handful of well-known producers who provided mass-produced models. This kept those firms that offered more-customized products from gaining access to the market. Perhaps most disturbing, Dave felt that the established dealers often sold not what was best for customers, but whatever they had in inventory that month.

Dave dreamed of offering high-end stereo loudspeakers directly to the audio-obsessed, bypassing the established dealer network. By going directly to the customers, Dave could avoid the dealer markups and offer top-quality products and service at reasonable prices.

THE PLAN

At the age of 28, Dave set out to turn his dreams into reality. Some customers who had gotten to know Dave's work became enthusiastic supporters of his dream and invested

This case was prepared by Professor Lew G. Brown, University of North Carolina at Greensboro, as a basis for class discussion. It is not intended to illustrate either effective or ineffective handling of an administrative situation. Adapted from "Sound Strategy" Inc., May, 1991, pp. 45–46. The author expresses appreciation to Dave Fokos for his cooperation in developing the case.

$189,000 in Icon. With their money and $10,000 of his own, Dave started Icon in a rented facility in an industrial park.

The Market   Approximately 335 stereo-speaker makers compete for a $3 billion annual U.S. market for audio components. About 100 of these manufacturers sell to the low- and mid-range segments of the market, which account for 90 percent of the market's unit volume and about 50 percent of its value. In addition to competing with each other, U.S. manufacturers also compete with Japanese firms that offer products at affordable prices. The remaining 235 or so manufacturers compete for the remaining 10 percent of the market's unit volume and 50 percent of the value—the high end—where Dave hopes to find his customers.

Icon's Marketing Strategy   To serve the audio-addicts segment, Dave offers only the highest-quality speakers. He has developed two models: The Lumen and the Parsec. The Lumen stands 18 inches high, weighs 26 pounds, and is designed for stand mounting. The floor-standing Parsec is 47 inches high and weighs 96 pounds. Both models feature custom-made cabinets that come in natural or black oak and American walnut. Dave can build and ship two pairs of the Lumen speakers or one pair of the Parsec speakers per day by himself. In order to have an adequate parts inventory, he had to spend $50,000 of his capital on the expensive components.

Dave set the price of the Lumen and Parsec at $795 and $1,795 per pair, respectively. He selected these prices to provide a 50 percent gross margin. He believes that traditional dealers would sell equivalent speakers at retail at twice those prices. Customers can call Icon on a toll-free 800 number to order speakers or to get advice directly from Dave. Icon pays for shipping and any return freight via Federal Express—round-trip freight for a pair of Parsecs costs $486.

Dave offers to pay for the return freight because a key part of his promotional strategy is a 30-day, in-home, no-obligation trial. In his ads, Dave calls this "The 43,200 Minute, No Pressure Audition." The trial period allows customers to listen to the speakers in their actual listening environment. In a dealer's showroom, the customer must listen in an artificial environment and often feels pressure to make a quick decision.

Dave believes that typical high-end customers may buy speakers for "nonrational" reasons: They want a quality product and good sound, but they also want an image. Thus, Dave has tried to create a unique image through the appearance of his speakers and to reflect that image in all of the company's marketing. He spent over $40,000 on distinctive stationery, business cards, a brochure, and a single display ad. He also designed a laminated label he places just above the gold-plated input jack on each speaker. The label reads: "This loudspeaker was handcrafted by [the technician's name who assembled the speaker goes here in his/her own handwriting]. Made in the United States of America by Icon Acoustics, Inc., Billerica, Mass."

To get the word out, Dave concentrates on product reviews in trade magazines and on trade shows, such as the High End Hi-Fi show in New York. Attendees at the show cast ballots to select "The Best Sound at the Show." In the balloting, among 200 brands, Icon's Parsec speakers finished fifteenth. Among the top 10 brands, the least expensive was a pair priced at $2,400, and six of the systems were priced from $8,000 to $18,000. A reviewer in an issue of *Stereophile* magazine evaluated Icon's speakers and noted: "The overall sound was robust and dynamic, with a particularly potent low end. Parts and construction quality appeared to be first rate. Definitely a company to watch."

Dave made plans to invest in a slick, four-color display ad in *Stereo Review,* the consumer magazine with the highest circulation (600,000). He also expected another favorable review in *Stereophile* magazine.

THE REALITY

Dressed in jeans and a hooded sweatshirt, Dave pauses in the middle of assembling a cardboard shipping carton, pulls up a chair, and leans against the concrete-block wall of his manufacturing area. Reflecting on his experiences during his first year in business, Dave realizes he's learned a lot in jumping all the hurdles the typical entrepreneur faces. Dave experienced quality problems with the first cabinet supplier. Then, he ran short of a key component after a mixup with a second supplier. Despite his desire to avoid debt, he had to borrow $50,000 from a bank. Prices for his cabinets and some components had risen, and product returns had been higher than expected (19 percent for the past six months). These price and cost increases put pressure on his margins, forcing Dave to raise his prices (to those quoted earlier). Despite the price increases, his margins remained below his 50 percent target.

Still, Dave feels good about his progress. The price increase does not seem to have affected demand. The few ads and word-of-mouth advertising appear to be working. Dave receives about five phone calls per day, with one in seven calls leading to a sale. Dave also feels the stress of the long hours and the low pay, however. He is not able to pay himself a high salary—just $9,500 this year.

Dave reaches over and picks up his most recent financial projections from a workbench (see Exhibit 1). He believes that this will be a breakeven year—then he'll have it made. As Dave sets the projections back on the workbench, his mind drifts to his plans to introduce two exciting new speakers—The Micron ($2,495 per pair) and the Millennium ($7,995 per pair). He also wonders if there is a foreign market for his speakers. Should he use his same direct-marketing strategy for foreign markets, or should he consider distributors? The dream continues.

EXHIBIT 1 Icon Acoustics's Pro Forma Financials ($ in Thousands)

Year	1	2	3	4	5
Pairs of Speakers Sold	224	435	802	1,256	1,830
Total Sales Revenue	$303	$654	$1,299	$2,153	$3,338
Cost of Sales					
Materials and Packaging	$130	$281	$ 561	$ 931	$1,445
Shipping	$ 43	$ 83	$ 157	$ 226	$ 322
Total Cost of Sales	$173	$364	$ 718	$1,157	$1,767
Gross Profit	$130	$290	$ 581	$ 996	$1,571
Gross Margin	43%	44%	45%	46%	47%
Expenses					
New Property and Equipment	$ 3	$ 6	$ 12	$ 15	$ 18
Marketing	$ 13	$ 66	$ 70	$ 109	$ 135
General and Administrative	$ 51	$110	$ 197	$ 308	$ 378
Loan Repayment	$ 31	$ 31	$ 0	$ 0	$ 0
Outstanding Payables	$ 30	$ 0	$ 0	$ 0	$ 0
Total Expenses	$128	$213	$ 279	$ 432	$ 531
Pretax Profit	$ 2	$ 77	$ 302	$ 564	$1,040
Pretax Margin	1%	12%	23%	26%	31%

Chemical Additives Corporation— Specialty Products Group

Lester A. Neidell and Charles Hoffheiser

Nick Williamson, general manager of the Specialty Products Group within Chemical Additives Corporation (CAC), looked out his window and sighed. It was August 1990 and the atmosphere inside his office was as unpleasant as the 100-degree-plus weather of the Ft. Smith, Arkansas, headquarters of Specialty Products Group (SPG). He swiveled back to face his management team, and said, "Okay, I've heard your arguments about positioning and pricing for R&D 601, 602, and 603. I wish there were some way to get a consensus from you guys. I'll consider our options over the weekend."

After his subordinates left his office, Nick looked at the spreadsheets and memoranda covering his desk and made a mental note that next weekend would definitely be reserved for fishing.

The marketing decisions facing Nick would have substantial impact on the future of SPG. A strategy of moving away from large-volume, commodity wax markets toward becoming a premier supplier of specialty chemical additives to niche markets was not going as smoothly as anticipated. This set of newly developed products might well be the catalyst to hasten that shift. The three new products, known by their experimental designations R&D 601, 602, and 603, were corrosion inhibitors used during the transportation and storage of liquid urea ammonium nitrate (UAN) fertilizer.

Products and Markets

These liquid fertilizers had numerous advantages over the traditional solid fertilizers principally used in U.S. agriculture: (1) excellent performance under a variety of weather conditions: (2) reduced toxicity: (3) ability to be easily blended with other nutrients, insecticides, and herbicides: and (4) milder environmental impact (but not benign—a spill or leak of undiluted UAN could still kill wildlife and vegetation).

Unfortunately, UAN liquids corroded the steel tanks, pipelines, rail cars, and barges used for transport, resulting in repair costs that could exceed $1 million per incident for the typical UAN producer. The industry had tried a variety of corrosion inhibitors (chemicals that were added in small dosages to UAN after production) to reduce the rate at which the UAN ate away the metal surface with which it came in contact. (Inhibitors did not prevent corrosion; they slowed the chemical reaction of metal dissolving into UAN.) An excellent inhibitor might increase the average life of a typical 520 million storage system from as little as three years to longer than 20 years.

Leaks and spills also created liabilities for Environmental Protection Agency (EPA) fines. If a tank failure resulted in massive environmental damage, federal lawsuits potentially could bankrupt a producer. Corrosion inhibitor suppliers might also be liable for leaks and environmental damages.

UAN fertilizer was produced in continuous-process facilities with typical minimum capacities of 10,000 tons per year. After production, UAN was stored in tanks to await shipment. Corrosion inhibitors were added just prior to storage. Upon shipment, UAN traveled through a distributor/dealer network that delivered the product to the right farmer, at the right time, and with the appropriate other agricultural chemicals added as necessary. Some larger dealers provided custom application services to apply UAN blends to fields and crops. The same distribution system also handled the solid fertilizers that UAN was slowly replacing.

The three experimental products were designed to replace SPG's earlier entries into this market, as well as to regain business previously lost to a widely used, foreign-sourced material, Corblok 105-B. Contrary tactical marketing positions were held by the sales and marketing managers. Vice President of Sales Ron White argued that, despite any performance advantages of the new SPG products, market conditions in the U.S. fertilizer industry required that the products be priced as low as possible using only the mandatory minimum corporate markup over standard cost. White had always operated under the objective that CAC/SPG plants had to be kept operating close to capacity to minimize standard costs. Price leadership and volume were, in his eyes, the key to SPG's success. Jim Walker, newly hired as director of marketing (a new position at SPG), was just as vehement in his recommendation that a value-based pricing approach, recognizing both product performance and competitive conditions, be applied to the new products. The technical director regularly reminded these two managers that the three products performed differently in different producers' UANs, and added, "You guys better start selling some of this stuff soon to pay off our investment of over four man-years of technical effort!"

CHEMICAL ADDITIVES CORPORATION

SPG was one of four divisions of the Chemical Additives Corporation, a multinational company providing solutions to production problems in oil fields, refineries, chemical plants, and other industrial applications. CAC's mission statement read as follows: "To produce and market specialty chemical products and the technical services and equipment necessary to utilize CAC's products effectively."

Its principal strategy was to develop customized equipment and chemical treatment programs to add value to customers' operations through optimization of operating efficiency or increased reliability. CAC's strengths included expertise in organic phosphate ester chemistry (the key to advanced-technology corrosion inhibitors) and in the mixing of incompatible fluids (e.g., oil and water). It considered itself to be the worldwide leader in oil industry corrosion control. It developed and patented much of the technology historically used in these applications, but over the past 10 years competitors found it increasingly easy to design products outside patent coverage, particularly as advanced computer modeling techniques were introduced into the R&D departments. Many recent advances in chemical industry technology were created by applying computer modeling to the design of new chemical species. CAC was organized into four operating groups: Oil Field Chemicals, Refinery Chemicals, Instruments, and Specialty Products. Each group maintained its own sales, marketing, and product development functions. A central research department conducted long-range, basic chemical research for all divisions.

The Oil Field Chemicals Group was the world's largest supplier of oil field production chemicals, including corrosion inhibitors and drilline aids. Because its products went "down the hole," appearance, odor, and handling characteristics, such as foaming, were not often of concern to customers. Product development was driven by the sales force's requests for customer-specific products. This division had more than 4,000 products in its line. Justification of this product line breadth was twofold: (1) no two oil deposits were identical in chemical makeup: and (2) as wells aged, increasing amounts of exotic chemicals were needed to enhance oil production.

The Refinery Chemicals Group marketed process efficiency aids for the production side of refineries. They also sold fuel additives such as fuel injector cleaners to refiners and to wholesalers of gasoline and truck diesel fuel.

The Instrument Group designed and marketed filtration and purification systems that solved a variety of water- and oil-related process problems in refineries. This equipment was often used in conjunction with CAC's chemical treatment programs. In addition, this group sold a complete line of premium-quality corrosion-monitoring instruments.

The Specialty Products Group's product line consisted of two major groups: (1) about 100 types of commodity petroleum waxes (similar but not identical to the types used in candles) that were separated from crude oil, and (2) synthetic polymers based on a chemical called propylene. Common examples of polymers are plastic food wrap film and vinyl siding for houses. SPG's synthetics, however, were not the type used in plastic film, cups, or containers. In fact, its customers often called them "synthetic waxes" because they had properties similar to commodity petroleum waxes. Williamson tried to alter this perception by extensive trade advertising and by instructing division personnel to refer to all division products as "specialty polymers." SPG's products were used in hundreds of applications, ranging from shoe polish to chewing gum to cardboard box sealing adhesives. Various SPG products had found modest use as antidust and anticaking additives for solid fertilizers, and as a result, SPG was responsible for all of CAC's business in the worldwide fertilizer industry.

Exhibit 1 contains selected CAC and divisional financial data; Exhibit 2 shows the distribution of SPG revenue and profit by end-use market.

SPG's Competitors

Each division had its own set of specialized competitors, as well as competition from various divisions of large chemical companies such as DuPont, Dow, Witco, and Shell. A key competitive characteristic of the chemical industry in the 1980s was the onset of worldwide competition. Corblok, principal competitor to SPG's UAN anticorrosion additives, was an example of this. Foreign suppliers directly impacted other SPG markets. These included Mitsui, BASF, Hoechst, and Dead Sea Works (an Israeli government-owned coal gasification plant that produced waxes as byproducts of gasoline production). Except for Dead Sea, all of these competitors were much larger than SPG (and CAC), and were reputed to be among the most-efficient chemical companies in the world. A key disadvantage SPG had compared to major chemical firms was that SPG's synthetic process required liquid polypropylene, a product form supplied by only one company. The majors often had captive supply and used much larger volumes of less-expensive gaseous polypropylene, available from many suppliers.

EXHIBIT 1   CAC Financial Data, 1985–1989 (In Thousands Except Per Share Data)

	1985	1986	1987	1988	1989
Income Statement					
Net Sales	$253,841	$297,208	$302,567	$287,931	$294,068
Cost of Goods Sold	160,268	189,498	181,531	174,919	171,769
Gross Profit	93,573	107,710	121,036	113,012	122,299
Selling Expense	33,623	41,532	49,746	53,235	56,292
R&D Expense	6,370	7,520	9,487	11,537	12,065
General Administrative Expense	10,860	12,470	14,107	14,614	15,455
Operating Profit	42,720	46,188	47,696	33,626	38,487
Investment Income	774	2,500	2,139	2,533	3,722
Interest Expense	(2,089)	(1,893)	(1,552)	(1,384)	(1,191)
Other Net	623	1,136	203	585	1,782
Earnings Before Income Tax	42,028	47,931	48,486	35,360	42,800
Income Tax	17,143	20,174	19,190	13,310	17,000
Net Earnings	$ 24,885	$ 27,757	$ 29,296	$ 22,050	$ 25,800
Balance Sheet					
Cash	$ 16,581	$ 12,478	$ 3,018	$ 37,201	$ 43,461
Accounts Receivable	45,127	61,981	55,836	51,055	56,896
Inventory	39,639	43,751	39,785	39,976	41,296
Other Current Assets	64,466	77,768	77,711	91,869	104,175
Total Current Assets	104,105	121,519	117,496	130,845	145,471
Total Assets	$175,544	$197,782	$200,318	$209,105	$221,514
Current Liabilities	$ 44,468	$ 48,579	$ 39,957	$ 39,808	$ 45,675
Long-Term Debt	12,500	11,250	10,000	8,750	7,500
Stockholders' Equity	112,999	132,989	145,159	153,042	164,148
Other Information					
Shares (000)	5,972	11,864	11,864	11,865	11,715
Dividends Per Share	$ 1.20	$ 0.76	$ 0.95	$ 1.00	$ 1.03
Revenue by Division					
Oil Field Chemicals	$158,048	$181,614	$201,378	$199,498	$211,804
Refinery Chemicals	33,069	32,524	32,117	30,342	32,499
Specialty Products	41,554	46,410	41,483	36,969	40,041
Instruments	21,170	36,660	27,589	21,122	9,724
	$153,841	$297,208	$302,567	$287,931	$294,068

SPG Marketing

Prior to 1980, SPG sold its products only through distributors. The U.S. market was served by Galaxy Wax and Schmidt Associates, both of which maintained regional warehouses. Sales to Europe, Africa, and the Middle East were the responsibility of the Leveque Group, headquartered in Brussels, Belgium. This company was also principal

EXHIBIT 2   SPG End-Use Segments in 1989

End-Use Market	Percent of Total SPG Sales	Percent of Total Pretax Profits	Stage in Product Life Cycle
Plastics	5	12	Late growth, maturity
Coatings	10	18	Late growth, maturity
Sealants	25	25	Mature
Food Additives	5	3	Mature
Laminating Wax	25	15	Decline
Others	30	27	Mostly mature

distributor of wax products manufactured by BASF and Hoechst, both headquartered in West Germany, as well as SPG products. Far East sales were the domain of a joint venture between CAC and Nissan Trading Company of Japan.

In 1979 in an attempt to capture the distributor margin for SPG, Nick Williamson hired Ron White as vice president of sales to establish a direct salesforce. By 1990, SPG had two regional managers and nine sales reps active in the United States:

Philadelphia	— East Regional Sales Office 2 sales representatives
Atlanta	— 1 sales representative
Cleveland	— 1 sales representative
Chicago	— 2 sales representatives
Ft. Smith	— 1 sales representative
Houston	— 1 sales representative
Los Angeles	— West Regional Sales Office 1 sales representative

After 11 years of direct selling, there were still situations in which SPG was beaten by wax distributors on price, delivery, and in some cases, technical service.

Annual salary and benefit costs for each sales rep averaged $80,000: the two regional managers were paid about 20 percent more. The salary/benefit figure included a company car, but not travel and other selling expenses, which averaged about 10 percent of sales revenue. Nor did these numbers include the profit bonus plan, which typically added 2 percent of sales revenue to selling costs. An annual "sales rep of the year" award, usually based on exceeding forecasted poundage figures, provided a further bonus of 5 percent of $50,000 base to one sales person. Salespeople were responsible for annual territorial sales forecasts, which provided important input to plan production runs and to order raw materials. Very little sales effort was devoted to "prospecting" because White kept a "sales efficiency" log for each representative. He calculated this as follows:

$$\frac{\text{sales calls that yielded an order}}{\text{total sales calls}} = \text{sales efficiency}$$

The UAN Corrosion Inhibitor Opportunity

In February 1985, Williamson received a memo from the general manager of the Refinery Chemical Group suggesting that certain of CAC's products might be useful in solving corrosion problems encountered by the Jackson Pipeline Company (JPL) of Ft. Smith. One of the Refinery Group's (and CAC's) largest customers, JPL was a major U.S. pipeline company, active in the transport of crude oil, gasoline, diesel and jet fuels, chemicals, and natural gas. The memo noted that, as a result of the oil bust of 1980 to 1983, JPL attempted to build its transportation volume of other products and began shipping UAN produced by JPL's wholly owned fertilizer company, Fertex Chemicals (also with its main plant in Ft. Smith). UAN was distributed throughout JPL's pipeline system, which extended to Texas, Arkansas, Oklahoma, Missouri, Kansas, Iowa, the Dakotas, Illinois, and Indiana. The maturing of the U.S. petrochemical industry further drove JPL to pursue and obtain UAN shipping business from Farm Products (Kansas City, Missouri) and Agriproducts (Sioux Falls, South Dakota). Historically UAN was shipped by (in order of increasing cost) barge, rail tank car, and tank truck. To use JPL's pipeline system, UAN producers were required to incorporate a corrosion inhibitor approved by JPL. However, unexpected corrosion problems with UAN were severely impacting profitability of the fertilizer shipping business.

This memo was timely: SPG, also, had suffered from the petrochemical industry recession. In addition, Nick was being pushed by CAC's executive committee to move away from commodity wax products into chemical specialties that could provide some protection against the price wars impacting chemical commodity markets.

Initial Entry into the Corrosion Control Market

Assuming that corrosion control was the same regardless of end-use environment, SPG, late in 1986, introduced Stealth 3660, an oil-field corrosion inhibitor, for use in transporting liquid UAN. After testing, JPL recommended 3660 to Fertex, Farm Products, and Agriproducts. Because Stealth 3660 cost 50 percent less to use than the previously approved Corblok 105-B inhibitor, all three UAN manufacturers were soon buying the product.

However, Fertex detected toxic fumes exceeding OSHA-defined lethal concentrations at the top hatch of trucks used to deliver the product from CAC's Chicago plant. In 1987, Fertex reverted to using Corblok. Unwilling to lose this market, Williamson instructed R&D to select another product from the oil-field corrosion inhibitor line. Consequently, Stealth 3662 was introduced to JPL and its three customers in mid-1987. The toxicity problem appeared to be solved, and the usage cost was the same as for 3660. By late 1987, all three fertilizer companies were buying 3662 in tank truck quantities. As mid-1988 approached, word of mouth in the fertilizer industry convinced firms such as Iowa Fertilizer, Ferticon, Nitrogen Industries, Marathon Chemical, and others to use SPG's Stealth 3662.

Both Stealth 3660 and 3662 were priced at 100 percent markup over standard cost. Tank truck (40,000-pound) quantities sold for 80 cents per pound and 55 gallon drums for 83 cents per pound, with costs of 40 cents per pound and 41.5 cents per pound, respectively. According to CAC policy, if a product was not priced at least 100 percent above cost, it was not defined as a "specialty" and did not qualify for recognition of supporting the corporate mission of becoming a specialty chemical firm. SPG's goal was to derive at least 30 percent of its gross sales revenue from specialties by 1990.

In late 1988, Fertex reported to SPG that their UAN was causing severe foaming problems when mixed with other fertilizer components such as pesticides and herbicides, a practice that was typical at the fertilizer dealer level. By spring 1989, Fertex switched back to Corblok. From the foaming incidents, SPG became aware that UAN passed through a dealer/distributor network before it was ultimately applied to fields and crops. SPG sales people typically called on fertilizer producers and not other channel members. Exhibit 3 contains the 1989 capacities of all North American UAN producers and brand of inhibitor used in mid-1988 and mid-1989.

EXHIBIT 3   UAN Corrosion Inhibitor Market 1989 Capacities (0.25 Pound/Ton Dosage)

Company[a]	City[a]	State	Country	Capacity 000 Tons	Potential SPC Volume 000 Lbs	Mid-1988 Inhib	Mid-1989 Inhib	Needs Easy Mix Product	SPG Advantage
Farm Products	Kansas City	KS	USA	250	63	3662	3662	No	—
Nitron, Inc.	St. Petersburg	FL	USA	10	3	3662	3662	Yes	—
Can-Am Corp.	Edmonton	AS	Canada	15	4	3662	3662	Yes	—
Can-Am Corp.	Lincoln	NE	USA	80	20	3662	3662	Yes	—
Agriproducts	Sioux Falls	SD	USA	238	60	3662	3662	No	—
Iowa Fertilizer	Dubuque	IA	USA	230	58	3662	Corblok	No	SVC/Cost
Marathon	Toledo	OH	USA	180	45	3662	Corblok	No	SVC/Cost
Ferticon	New Orleans	LA	USA	510	128	3662	Corblok	No	SVC/Cost
Iowa Fertilizer	Santa Fe	NM	USA	10	3	3662	Corblok	No	—
Fertex	Ft. Smith	AR	USA	1,400	350	3662	Corblok	No	SVC/Cost
Nitrogen Inds.	Spokane	WA	USA	160	40	3662	Corblok	No	SVC/Cost
Iowa Fertilizer	Miami	OK	USA	51	13	3662	RG-2064	Yes	?
Nitro Products	Pensacola	FL	USA	65	16	Ammonia	Ammonia	No	Perform.
RJS Inc	Idaho Falls	ID	USA	230	58	Ammonia	Ammonia	No	Perform.
Georgia Chemical	Savannah	GA	USA	680	170	Ammonia	Ammonia	No	Perform.
Jackson Chemical	Jackson	MS	USA	500	125	Ammonia	Ammonia	No	Perform.
Illini Fertilizer	Marietta	GA	USA	329	82	Ammonia	Ammonia	No	Perform.
NC Fertilizer	Jacksonville	NC	USA	230	58	Borax	Borax	No	SVC/Pits
RJS Inc	Fresno	CA	USA	129	32	Chromate	Chromate	No	Cost/Safe
Novatec	Windsor	MN	Canada	175	44	Corblok	Corblok	No	SVC/Cost
Eagle Industries	Bettendorf	IA	USA	175	44	Corblok	Corblok	No	SVC/Cost
RJS Inc	Winnipeg	MN	Canada	210	53	Corblok	Corblok	No	SVC/Cost
Edsel Chemical	Sacramento	CA	USA	90	23	Corblok	Corblok	No	SVC/Cost
Edsel Chemical	Portland	OR	USA	55	14	Corblok	Corblok	Yes	SVC/Cost
Edsel Chemical	Spokane	WA	USA	200	50	Corblok	Corblok	No	SVC/Cost
Comanche Powder	Tucson	AZ	USA	20	5	Corblok	Corblok	No	SVC/Cost
Illini Fertilizer	Cincinnati	OH	USA	150	38	DAP	DAP	No	SVC/Pits
Nutricorp	Council Bluffs	IA	USA	500	125	DAP	DAP	No	SVC/Pits
Ferticon	Evansville	IN	USA	80	20	DAP	DAP	No	SVC/Pits
US Industries	Cherokee	AL	USA	65	16	DAP	DAI	No	SVC/Pits
Illini Fertilizer	Dalton	GA	USA	100	25	DAP	DAP	Yes	SVC/Pits
Illini Fertilizer	LaSalle	IL	USA	300	75	DAP	DAP	No	SVC/Pits
Farm Product	Hays	KS	USA	250	63	DAP	DAP	No	SVC/Pits
Nitrotech	Kingston	ON	Canada	25	6	DAP	DAP	Yes	SVC/Pits
Cherokee Nitrogen	Enid	OK	USA	270	68	DAP	DAP	No	SVC/Pits
Nutricorp	Baton Rouge	LA	USA	1,000	250	DAP	DAP	No	SVC/Pits
Nitrogen Inds.	Lincoln	NE	USA	158	40	DAP	DAP	Yes	SVC/Pits
Canadian Nitrogen	Niagara Falls	ON	Canada	120	30	OA-5	OA-5	No	SVC/Foam
Fertilex	Stockton	CA	USA	200	50	OA-5	OA-5	No	SVC/Foam
Fertilex	Compton	CA	USA	100	25	OA-5	OA-5	No	SVC/Foam
Edsel Chemical	Burlington	IA	USA	200	50	OA-5	OA-5	No	SVC/Foam

[a]Names and locations changed to protect confidentiality.

Worried about SPG's ability to compete effectively in the LAN corrosion control market, Williamson directed Ron White to hire a sales engineer or product manager to get the UAN corrosion inhibitor program on track. In August 1989, Bob Brown joined SPG in this capacity.

Williamson also hired a director of marketing, Jim Walker, in October 1989. Walker was charged with changing the culture of SPG from a sales/manufacturing/technology-driven business to a market-driven business. SPG's 1989 organizational chart is shown in Exhibit 4. Exhibit 5 contains background information on SPG's key personnel.

Corrosion Inhibitor Technology

Corrosion is a complex chemical reaction, changing steel to useless iron oxide. Two basic types of corrosion inhibitors were available: passivities and film-formers. Passivities formed a protective "coating" by chemically reacting with the steel surfaces they were supposed to protect. Although some people believed them to be effective, evidence was mounting that corrosive materials could penetrate the coating resulting in rapid formation of deeply corroded pits. Typical repair costs for a storage tank exceeded $1 million, and there had even been one or two complete tank failures. Film-formers left a microscopic layer of inhibitor on the steel surface by incompletely dissolving in the corrosive liquid UAN. This new technology was considered by the National Association of Corrosion Engineers to be a sound alternative to designing tanks and piping with expensive, exotic steel alloys or with plastics.

All products SPG introduced to the UAN industry were of the film-forming variety. This, as well as control of solubility, was a basic and very strong technology for CAC and the source of numerous patents.

The UAN Corrosion Inhibitor Market

For most of the 1980s, the U.S. agricultural industry was depressed. By 1988, the fertilizer industry (including UAN producers) experienced a shakeout that saw a 20 percent re-

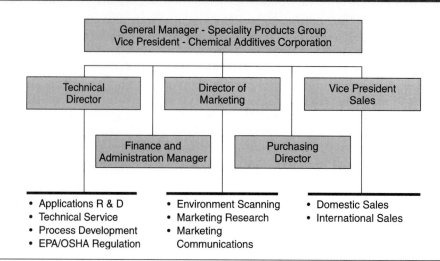

EXHIBIT 4: Organizational Chart—Specialty Products Group, Chemical Additives Corporation

EXHIBIT 5   Key SPG Personnel

Nick Williamson—Executive Vice President and General Manager

With a degree in chemical engineering, Williamson joined SPG in 1966 as a process engineer and worked his way through the production and process engineering ranks to his current position in 1982. He had no sales, marketing, or finance experience. Along the way, he completed his masters in chemical engineering and developed a process to make synthetic wax. He convinced corporate management to invest $10 million in 1975 to build a plant for these products, and it came on stream in 1976. First commercial sale of any significance occurred in 1979 to a hot-melt adhesive manufacturer, a mature industry at the time. His management philosophy is to be involved in every detail of the SPG operation.

Ron White—Vice President of Sales

A personal friend of Williamson's, he was hired in 1980. A former Air Force KC-135 tanker pilot, he had for years been a member of the leading country club in Ft. Smith, and was a 3 handicap golfer. Before his employment at SPG, he was the sole U.S. distributor of potassium permanganate, a commodity reagent widely used as a catalyst in research laboratories. His college degree was in chemistry.

Jim Walker—Director of Marketing

With a chemical engineering degree, he joined American Cyanamid in 1970 as a process engineer. He moved to sales and marketing in 1974, responsible for contract sales of sulfuric acid and alum. He became marketing manager for specialty urethane catalysts at Dow in 1978. By this time, he had earned his MBA in chemical marketing from Fairleigh Dickinson University. He was appointed director of marketing for Corn Products Corporation in 1984. He joined SPG in 1989.

Bob Brown—Sales Engineer

The newest member of the management team, Bob graduated from Carnegie Mellon University with a chemistry degree in 1978. First employed by Firestone's chemical division, he concentrated in specialty urethane adhesives sales. Three years later he became a water-management chemicals and services specialist at Western Corporation. He was a highly successful salesman, with a specific training in consultative needs, satisfaction selling, and technical service.

duction in industry capacity. One UAN plant with book assets of more than $40 million netted just $3.5 million on the auction block. Although the prospects for U.S. farmers were looking better by the end of 1988, fertilizer producers were facing stiff, low-cost foreign competition on their largest-volume solid products, sometimes losing money on every ton sold. Although the cost of ocean shipment of liquid UAN prohibited imports attacking the North American market, domestic producers, in a competitive frenzy, had cut UAN prices such that they sometimes made only $1 per ton pretax. The shakeout led many to believe that this would soon return to the more "normal" $30 per ton.

UAN liquids were produced as 28 percent and 32 percent blends in water. They had to be diluted with more water at the dealer level before being suitable for application to crops. As a rule, the more dilute the UAN, the more corrosive it was to steel. Once a corrosion inhibitor such as Corblok 105-B or Stealth 3662 was successfully added in the proper dosage at the producer's plant, corrosion control was effective through the entire distribution network.

Corrosion control was necessary once UAN entered the distribution system. A number of different products had been used over the years to reduce corrosion. Some UAN producers tried (unsuccessfully) to differentiate based on the presence of a corrosion inhibitor. Dealers and farmers were more concerned with the cost per acre of fertilized land and on-time, fast delivery, especially during the hectic schedules of spring planting and fall harvest. Processing problems, such as incompatibility with other agricultural chemicals and foaming, could not be tolerated. There was little dealer loyalty among farmers when they needed to plant or harvest.

Competitive Products

A variety of inhibitors were available in January 1989 as SPG began its program to develop a replacement for Stealth 3662 (Exhibit 6 outlines the typical products used). Except for borax, all were liquid materials.

Ammonia A toxic gas used as a fertilizer, ammonia was the cheapest source of nitrogen—the same nutrient provided by UAN. Some producers believed that corrosion could be eliminated simply by neutralizing acids from the production process by adding ammonia. It was one of the raw materials in the manufacture of LAN. During the 1970s, instances of rapid pitting corrosion led many producers to try other inhibitors. Ammonia's principal advantage was that it was virtually free.

Borax Although classified as "acceptable" by the Tennessee Valley Authority (TVA), only one manufacturer used it. Several other UAN manufacturers had found it to be unacceptable.

Sodium Chromate The fact that a material considered by the Environmental Protection Agency to be a primary pollutant was allowed in fertilizer points out the strange regulatory environment typically faced by the chemical industry. This product was an excellent corrosion inhibitor but was toxic to fish and wildlife. Only one plant used sodium chromate. It was a film-former.

Corblok A phosphate ester film-former produced in Germany by Servo, a well-respected chemical firm, Corblok was supplied to North American markets by IWC, a Dutch company, and sold through M. Joseph & Company of Philadelphia. Corblok was

---

EXHIBIT 6   Competitive Inhibitors, 1990

Product	Supplier	Type[a]	Price/Pound	Treatment Cost/Ton[b]
Ammonia	Many	P	$ 0	$ 0
Borax	Many	P	.14–17	.28–.35
Chromate	Many	F	.47	.28
Corblok	IWC	F	1.87	.47
DAP	Many	P	.082	.20–.25
OA-5	Tennessee	F	.375	.30
RG 2064	Western	F	1.90	.19–.38
Stealth 3662	SPG	F	.80	.24

[a]P = Passivating: F = Film-Former
[b]Treatment cost is per ton of UAN.

shipped to Houston via ocean freight. Storage facilities were leased at the port of Houston. Although this product did not foam, it was difficult to dissolve in UAN, but provided excellent corrosion protection. Technical service was the responsibility of a corrosion engineer based in Holland. The Leveque Group confirmed claims of many European customers for this product.

DAP Also a fertilizer (at 100 percent strength), DAP was made by several UAN producers. Tested "effective" by the TVA, Jackson Pipeline had tried it but found that it left deposits that interfered with pipeline pumps and that there was pitting corrosion beneath the deposits. Still, DAP enjoyed a 30 percent market share and was sold by direct sales reps or distributors depending on the location. The nutrient content that it imparted to LAN was negligible, but it enjoyed a psychological benefit of "providing crop nutrients."

Stealth 3662 Similar in chemistry to Corblok, Stealth 3662 was easily soluble in UAN, it was an excellent inhibitor, but as noted previously, there were some foaming problems. It was produced in Chicago and Galveston, Texas, using the same process equipment as many other CAC products.

OA-5 Tennessee Chemical produced this material in Knoxville and sold it through a direct sales force. SPG's own tests proved OA-5 to be effective, but it was extremely difficult to dissolve in LAN. Sometimes it merely floated to the surface of the LAN storage tank, even after plant operators were sure that they had mixed it properly. Several plants reported foaming problems when attempting to mix OA-5 with their UAN. This foaming was of a different type than reported for Stealth 3662. This film-former was completely different in composition from Corblok or Stealth 3662.

RG-2064 and Equivalents Although neither Consolidated nor Western had promoted any products specifically for UAN transport and storage, both were strong in organic phosphate ester chemistry, and they had applied it to water treatment applications, a market much larger than UAN. Both companies employed many more sales reps than SPG and CAC and were already selling water treatment chemicals to UAN plants for boiler, cooling, and waste water treatment applications. These operations were run by the same people who ran the UAN process equipment. These companies were attacking CAC's oil field business and achieving significant success, despite the fact that their products were more expensive to use than CAC's. Consolidated's revenue was equal to CACs, but its profit margin was 20 percent higher than CAC. Western had sales and profits double those of CAC.

Product Development

After the foaming problems with Stealth 3662, SPG began to develop product specifically designed for UAN corrosion control. In 1988, SPG's technical director estimated that four man-years of technical effort over two years were required. The typical cost per man-year was $100,000, including salary benefits, the use of all group and corporate laboratory facilities, and the cost to build corrosion test apparatus. Jim Walker believed that a one man-year marketing effort at $80,000 per year was required to adequately understand market needs and to develop literature and marketing communications programs. Additional annual marketing expenses of $5,000 would be incurred by hosting a hospitality suite at an annual meeting of the Ammonium Nitrate Producers Study Group. White was confident that his department could sell any product, given a good price; the technical director was confident in the success of the development effort. Selling could be done one of two ways: (1) 100 percent of Brown's time at $80,000 per year (salary, benefits, car), plus 2 percent of revenue for travel and entertainment costs (T&E), or (2) 5 percent of the entire sales force's (including regional managers) plus the same T&E.

Williamson considered these cost and success estimates and reviewed following data:

1. Tax rate: 33 percent
2. Corporate cost of capital: 8 percent
3. Corporate mandate for 30 percent value after tax return on investment
4. SPG requirement that new businesses generate at least $2,000,000 in sales and $800,000 gross profit within three years of market entry.

He then instructed his technical director to develop a direct replacement for Corblok.

Early in 1989, Brown arranged a trip with a Fertex sales representative to several fertilizer dealers. He obtained extensive information about how UAN was used at the dealer level—other nutrients added, mixing techniques, blending with pesticides and herbicides, and so forth. Brown was quite surprised when dealers responded to his questions about foaming. Despite using Fertex UAN containing Stealth 3662, they had not experienced this condition. Brown began to wonder if only certain blends and ingredients foamed, and if these blends were used only in certain regions of the country.

He also learned that a considerable amount of UAN "trading" occurred in the industry. For example, if Fertex had a customer in North Dakota, they would receive the sales revenue, but Agriproducts' Sioux Falls plant would actually supply the UAN. Fertex would return the favor if Agriproducts had a customer in Arkansas. Computerized accounting systems kept track of the trades, and accounts were settled quarterly.

In addition to these market factors, the technical director's staff, after running hundreds of corrosion and foaming tests with several producers' UANs, discovered three factors that influenced the interaction between UAN and steel surfaces: (1) higher temperature; (2) higher UAN velocity, especially in a pipeline environment; and (3) presence of impurities. The technical department also found that different producers' UANs, though identical in nutrient content, required different dosages of any corrosion inhibitor for effective corrosion control. Other inhibitor suppliers (including IWC/Corblok) recommended the same dosage throughout the industry. SPG's technical director suggested using an industry-wide inhibitor dosage rate of 1.5 to 2.0 pounds per ton of UAN, so that even the most drastic conditions would not cause corrosion problems.

Although the three newly developed products were similar, each had slightly different performance characteristics. R&D 601 worked well in Fertex UAN but would not function in several others. It was easier to disperse than 602, but 602 was effective in all UAN brands. Most UAN plants used high-speed pumps to move the UAN through their systems. For this reason it was believed that there would be few problems dispersing SPG's R&D 601 and 602 products into the UAN. Once dispersed, no separation occurred. R&D 603 was easiest to disperse (although not quite as easy as the existing 3662 product), but it exhibited a slight foaming tendency (not believed to be as severe as that of 3662). R&D 603 was effective in all UANs.

All three products could be delivered in tank truck (40,000-pound) quantities. Also, in response to increased state and local regulations on the disposal of empty drums, SPG planned to offer all three products in 300-gallon returnable and reusable tote tanks, each costing $1,200. The tank supplier estimated 30 to 40 round-trips could be obtained before the tanks had to be refurbished at a cost of $300 each. Exhibit 7 shows the cost structure of SPG's products.

Sales (White) and marketing (Walker) continually debated the UAN corrosion inhibitor marketing program as fall 1990 approached. The planned October 1990 rollout

EXHIBIT 7   SPG Inhibitor Costs, October 1989 (Per Pound in Tank Car Lots)

Product	Fixed	Variable	Total
Stealth 3662	$0.10	$0.30	$0.40
R&D 601	0.16	0.48	0.64
R&D 602	0.16	0.48	0.64
R&D 603	0.16	0.48	0.64

Notes:
  (1) R&D 601 for "easy to treat" UAN such as Fertex.
  (2) R&D 602 for "hard to treat" UAN such as Agriproducts.
  (3) R&D 603 for easy dispersion all UANs, but very slight foam.
  (4) Add $0.015 to variable costs for 55-gallon drums, net weight: 473 lbs (215 Kg).
  (5) Add $0.06 to variable cost for 300-gallon, returnable tote tanks: net weight 2,580 lbs (1,173 Kg).
  (6) Billing terms net 30, freight collect, FOB CAC plant.

would give SPG a "strategic window" of approximately three months as UAN producers went to high production rates to prepare for spring fertilizer consumption. Failures to obtain business by February would effectively close the window until July, when another production push would occur for fall fertilizer consumption.

DECISIONS, DECISIONS, DECISIONS

As Nick Williamson shuffled the papers on his desk, he thought about the decisions he had to make. The discussion earlier in the afternoon focused on pricing issues of the new products, but Nick realized that pricing was only one of many factors that had to be resolved. The R&D 601, 602, 603 nomenclature was the standard in-house description for developmental products. White wanted to continue to use the Stealth name to provide continuity to salespeople and customers. Walker desired a new name to convey the technological newness of these products.

White had lobbied long and hard with Williamson to price at $1.04 per pound and then to "turn my salespeople loose." Walker was just as adamant that selective pricing to different market segments was desirable. R&D had concluded that all inhibitors (UAN) were not the same in terms of corrosion control and a single dosage of one inhibitor might not be effective in all UANs under all conditions.

As he packed his briefcase, Nick knew that he had to have some decisions by Monday morning.

Thai Chempest

William A. Stoever

In January 1991, Shep Susmar, president of Agricultural Chemicals International Corporation (ACIC), had to decide whether his company should set up manufacturing with a local partner in Thailand. He had received a letter in November 1990 from Kau Ah-Wong, president of Kau Teck-Meng & Co., in Bangkok, saying that rising tariffs might make it impossible for the Kau company to continue importing one of ACIC's profitable pesticides. Mr. Kau[1] suggested that the two companies might begin a joint venture to do some of the processing in Thailand, a move that might be mutually profitable while also aiding the development of agriculture in his country. Mr. Susmar had to decide whether to enter into a joint venture, what problems might arise if they did enter it, and how to plan for and deal with such problems.

HISTORY OF ACIC

Agricultural Chemicals Corporation was founded in Rutherford, New Jersey, in 1960 by Tyrone Susmar, Shep Susmar's father. It specialized in developing and producing pesticides to meet the needs of individual purchasers. It kept in close contact with current and potential customers in order to learn about and supply their specialized needs. There was a steady demand because various insect species mutated rapidly and developed immunity to existing pesticides. Basically a niche marketer, the company had to keep seeking new products that the large, resource-rich chemical manufacturers did not yet produce commercially. In the late 1970s, Tyrone decided that the company could support a modest R&D program that went beyond the mere combining of previously known components. Agricultural Chemicals set up a small applications-oriented research laboratory to study new infestations that kept cropping up. The laboratory had a small, top-quality staff that was highly productive. It usually developed products to order for large customers, but sometimes it produced new compounds that were marketed under the company name. Some of these were innovative enough to qualify for patents. In order to protect the technology, the company established a small plant to manufacture some of these proprietary products.

Shep had started working full-time for the company in 1970 after completing a B.S. in chemical engineering. He earned an MBA part-time during the next five years while working in a variety of functions, and he took over as president in 1985.

This case was prepared by Professor William A. Stoever, as a basis for class discussion. It is not intended to illustrate either effective or ineffective handling of an administrative situation.

[1]As with many Chinese, the family name was ordinarily given first, and the two given or "first" names came last.

OVERSEAS GROWTH

By the mid-1970s, Tyrone realized that the company had to go international if it wanted to maintain a steady rate of growth. To signify his commitment, Tyrone changed the company name to Agricultural Chemicals International Corporation. The markets abroad, particularly in less-developed countries (LDCs), were smaller, less mechanized, and less accustomed to the use of chemical aids than those in North America, and the giant chemical companies did not find it worthwhile to devote a lot of effort to them. This meant that once ACIC established a market in a particular country, it could hope for several years of sales without strong international competition.

In 1978, Tyrone hired a young man named Bill Greene and gave him the title of "international manager." Greene had earned a B.S. in chemical engineering in 1970 and an MBA in 1976. He had eight years of experience in domestic and foreign sales for a large chemical manufacturer. His responsibilities in his new job were rather vaguely defined, but he seemed to have a good feeling for how to make his way.

Greene appointed area managers for Europe, the Middle East, and Asia. The Asia area manager was Mike Mingas. They were all based in New Jersey but had to spend a lot of time traveling to stay close to their areas. ACIC began seeking distributors in southern Europe, the Middle East, and Asia. The initial contacts were made rather haphazardly, sometimes from approaches by local companies seeking a foreign supplier and sometimes on the recommendations of intermediaries. Some of the distributors had worked out, but a few had proven to be politically unastute, incompetent, lazy, or plain dishonest. Some arrangements failed to live up to expectations because of government restrictions, lack of foreign exchange, disappointing sales, or loss of interest by the local partner. In at least one case, ACIC believed the local distributor had deliberately hidden revenues and had failed to deliver ACIC's share of its profits.

Greene and the area managers had to rely on the parent company for technical assistance and staff functions. The responsibilities were not formalized; they just grew up over the years. In general, the international people had been able to get what support they needed, except on the occasions when the staff and technical people's workloads were too heavy. Some of the parent company's personnel were becoming increasingly interested in the international aspect of the business; others paid little attention to the overseas operations.

In 1980 an Italian chemical company approached ACIC seeking a license to use its processes to manufacture finished products from basic raw materials purchased in Italy. The products were sold to distributors in Italy and other EC countries. ACIC received a healthy royalty, 2 percent of gross sales of the licensed products, but in exchange it gave up the right to export to the EC from its U.S. plants. ACIC received a royalty of almost $1 million in 1990.

In 1981, following a trip by Greene and Mingas to Australia, ACIC set up a processing plant, a wholly owned subsidiary, in that country. The plant contracted with local chemical companies for purchases of particular components that it blended into finished products and packed for shipment. Its operations followed the processes specified by the parent company. The venture lost money for the first four years, finally turned a profit in 1987, and paid back the original investment in 1989. It contributed almost $1 million to the parent's profit before tax in 1990, and the prospects for further growth were promising.

By the mid-1980s the Susmars and Greene recognized that ACIC would have to begin producing in more overseas markets rather than simply exporting to them. Some distributor relationships were running into trouble because of import-substitution policies and shortages of hard currencies in many LDCs. Also, ACIC foresaw heightened competition from companies in Korea, Turkey, India, and other industrializing, low-wage Third World countries. However, ACIC wanted to evaluate any given country carefully before deciding whether to make an equity investment (100 percent or joint venture), to license its technology, to serve the market by exports (where allowed), or to give up the market. They hoped to start on a small scale, with a minimum commitment of capital and management time.

A condensed version of ACIC's income statements for the past four years is presented in Exhibit 1.

DEALINGS WITH KAU & COMPANY

In 1985 Kau Ah-Wong visited the United States. Among his goals was to find something to combat a wood-boring beetle that infested both hardwood and palm trees in Thailand and other countries of Southeast Asia and that had apparently developed resistance to the available insecticides. Mr. Kau heard about ACIC through professional contacts and called on the Susmars. Figuring there was nothing to lose, ACIC appointed Kau & Company as its distributor in Thailand and agreed to supply trial quantities of a newly developed pesticide called 3,5-D. (ACIC was waiting for a decision on its application for a U.S. patent on this compound.) The trials soon demonstrated that the new insecticide was effective in controlling the beetle. Kau did not set up any formal marketing programs but his company began receiving commercial orders from the more-progressive producers who had heard about the success of the trials. Volume was small at first, but enough to whet ACIC's interest.

EXHIBIT 1 Agricultural Chemicals International Corporation: Condensed Four-Year Statement of Earnings (Dollar Figures in Millions)

	1990	1989	1988	1987
Sales and Other Revenue				
Net sales	62.2	60.5	58.7	59.8
Royalties	1.3	1.0	1.1	0.6
Total	63.5	61.5	59.8	60.4
Costs and Other Charges				
Cost of Sales	32.0	31.1	29.7	30.0
Depreciation and Amortization	8.2	8.0	7.7	7.8
Direct Labor	7.8	7.8	7.5	7.7
Selling and Administrative Expenses	6.0	6.0	5.8	5.6
Interest Expenses	3.1	2.9	3.0	2.7
Other Income Charges	1.0	0.9	0.9	1.1
Taxes	2.1	1.9	1.8	2.0
Total	60.2	58.6	56.4	56.9
Earnings for the Year	3.3	2.9	3.4	3.5

Subsequently Mingas made several trips to Bangkok to help promote the relationship. By 1989 ACIC was exporting about $1 million a year of the insecticide to Thailand, which Kau was reselling for about 50 million Thai baht. (See Exhibit 2 for baht-dollar exchange rates.) Even so, Mingas believed they had barely scratched the surface of the Thai market, and Kau had not yet promoted 3,5-D elsewhere in Southeast Asia.

MR. KAU'S LETTER

Kau Ah-Wong's letter of November 1990 came as something of a shock because it seemed to indicate that ACIC's exports to Thailand were threatened. The letter noted that the government was vigorously seeking to diversify Thailand's economy by developing manufacturing industries. It intended to restrict imports of selected products in order to promote manufacturing, and it especially favored products that promoted the country's agriculture. It intended to impose tariffs of 25 percent to 50 percent on imports of agricultural pesticides like 3,5-D, although it would allow importation of components or ingredients at low or no duties for a while, provided that Thailand's portion of the value added was increased as quickly as possible. The Ministry of Industry wanted to restrict imports of 3,5-D immediately, but the Ministry of Agriculture and Cooperatives prevailed upon them to allow imports at a reduced level for at least one more year.

In view of this new development, Mr. Kau proposed that ACIC and Kau Teck Meng & Company set up a joint venture to use ACIC's technology and know-how to start production of 3,5-D and other pesticides in Thailand. He even suggested a name:

EXHIBIT 2   Financial Statistics on Thailand

	1978	1979	1980	1981	1982	1983	1984	1985	1986	1987	1988
Millions of Baht											
Total											
Exports	83,065	108,179	133,197	153,001	159,728	146,472	175,237	193,366	233,383	299,851	403,570
Imports	108,899	146,161	188,686	216,746	196,616	236,609	245,155	251,169	241,358	334,209	513,114
Billions of Baht											
Foreign											
Debt	48.25	56.77	74.59	92.27	123.30	132.19	155.78	158.48	172.42	175.50	128.05
Millions $											
Official											
Reserves	2,557	3,129	3,026	2,727	2,652	2,556	2,689	3,003	3,776	5,212	7,112
Baht per U.S. $											
Official											
Exchange	20.39	20.43	20.63	23.00	23.00	23.00	27.15	26.65	26.13	25.07	25.24
Index 1985—100											
Consumer											
Price											
Index	59.80	65.70	78.70	88.60	93.30	96.80	97.60	100.00	101.80	104.40	108.40

Source: International Monetary Fund, International Financial Statistics.

Thai Chemical Pesticides Corporation. He offered to supply the buildings, local sales and administrative staff, and most of the working capital, and proposed that ACIC's contribution be imported equipment, technological knowledge, the necessary engineering and staff advice and support, and some of the working capital. Kau & Company wanted somewhere between 51 percent and 75 percent ownership because it was contributing the bulk of the capital, physical assets, and personnel. The new company would use ACIC's processes, which would be protected to the fullest extent possible under Thai law.

GREEN'S TRIP TO BANGKOK

Shep Susmar decided not to travel to Bangkok himself, both because of domestic business pressures and because he felt that Kau's business did not justify the investment of his time. Susmar telephoned Kau that ACIC's international manager would go in his place. When Greene arrived in early December, Kau expressed some displeasure at not seeing a counterpart of equally high rank from the American company, but he was quite gracious. He showered Greene with hospitality, including visits to some of Bangkok's notorious night spots. He also took him to call on officials at the Board of Investment, the Thai Development Bank, and in the Ministries of Industry, Agriculture and Cooperatives, and Commerce. The Board of Investment officials assured Greene that it should be no problem to get approval of a Kau-ACIC joint venture, provided of course that Thailand's rules, regulations and procedures were followed. Officials at the Development Bank seemed to be amenable to granting a long-term loan at a concessional interest rate,[2] again provided that the venture satisfied the bank's criteria. Greene had heard, however, that other ministries sometimes imposed roadblocks and that the approval process could be very corruption-prone, time-consuming, and frustrating.

After a week in Bangkok, Greene returned and reported on his findings. The Kaus were a wealthy family of Chinese origin who had been in Thailand for four or five generations. They had political connections built up partly by substantial contributions to General Prem Tinsulanonda's political party (see Appendix). Nonetheless, the Chinese were a somewhat distrusted minority in Thailand, and the government might discriminate against them or a company they were associated with. Kau Ah-Wong had made several trips abroad and was fairly fluent in English. Greene liked Kau personally and thought he was probably pretty reliable.

Kau Teck-Meng & Co. had been founded by Kau Ah-Wong's grandfather and his brothers. It was a trading company that imported and exported a variety of products. Among its imports were M.A.N. trucks, Massey-Ferguson tractors, some industrial chemicals from Monsanto Corporation that it wholesaled to local plastics manufacturers, and some Japanese industrial control devices. It sold the bulk of its turnover in Thailand but exported rice and air-conditioning equipment to other nations of the Association of Southeast Asian Nations (ASEAN)[3] and Laos, Cambodia, and Burma. It also exported palm products and hand-carved teak furniture to the United States and to the EC. Greene could not be certain, but he had the impression that sales of ACIC's insecticide constituted 4 percent or 5 percent of its gross revenues.

---

[2]The interest rate on loans from Thai commercial banks was about 8.5 percent to 9.0 percent at the time. The Development Bank was offering loans to qualified borrowers at 3 to 4 percentage points lower.

[3]The ASEAN countries consisted of Brunei, Indonesia, Malaysia, Philippines, Singapore, and Thailand. ASEAN was originally intended to be a customs union, but its members sometimes found it easier to cooperate on political matters than on economic.

Greene speculated that sales of the insecticide could increase markedly over the next five years if supplies were available; he guesstimated that sales might reach 250 million baht by 1995. He worked up a pro forma income statement, mostly based on figures from the U.S. and Italian plants and following American accounting principles (Exhibit 3). At present the Thai government was requiring only that the final production stages be completed in Thailand; these were reasonably simple processes, and the necessary equipment was not too complicated or costly. Greene was aware that the government might demand that more production be moved to Thailand in the not-too-distant future. Nonetheless, the prospects looked good enough to suggest that ACIC consider a joint venture with as large an equity share as possible. He estimated that ACIC's initial capital expenditure need not exceed $800,000, of which about $400,000 would be for imported equipment and the rest for setup costs, expatriate expenses, etc.

Exhibit 2 and the Appendix contain information Greene collected on Thailand's economy and rules and policies on foreign investment.

ACIC'S RESPONSE

Shep Susmar held a meeting of his top domestic and international executives in mid-December 1990 to discuss the Kau proposal (which they'd already begun referring to as "Thai Chempest"). He opened with these comments:

Our friend Mr. Kau seems eager to set up an alliance with us. It looks like a possibility to me, but there are some definite problem areas. Among them:

- *Would it be more cost-effective or less risky to continue exporting as long as the government allows it, unless they raise the tariffs higher than Mr. Kau seems to anticipate?*
- *Should we license our processes to Kau's organization?*
- *If we go the joint venture route, what possible problems might there be with the Thai business climate and government?*
- *What terms might Kau want, and how should we respond?*
- *What kind of incentives, guarantees, and other terms could we get from the government?*

EXHIBIT 3   Thai Chempest: Pro Forma Income Statement (In Millions of Baht)

Year of Operations	1st	2d	3d	4th	5th
Sales Revenue	50	100	150	200	250
Cost of Goods Sold	35	70	105	140	175
Administrative Costs	30	30	30	30	30
Depreciation and Amortization[a]	4	4	4	4	4
PBIT	−19	−4	11	26	41
Interest[a]	2	2	2	2	2
PBT	−21	−6	9	24	39

[a]Depreciation (straight-line) at 10% on $400,000 imported equipment and 10-million-baht buildings, etc., plus amortization of 40-million-baht loan from government Development Bank at 5% interest, repayable in 20th year.

Kau might want to be managing director or president if we went into a joint venture. We'd have to decide whether that's a good idea, or how to handle it if we decide against him. We'd also have to figure out the financing and ownership structure. We want to be careful to avoid another situation where we get ripped off, like those so-and-so's in Asiatica did to us.

If we do go ahead there, we'd need a plant manager, a chief financial officer, a chief technical officer, and maybe a sales manager to start in Bangkok. An immediate question is whether these should be Americans or Thais.

I need you to draft some plans for what to do about Kau's proposal. Be as specific as you can; don't use phrases like "This problem will have to be planned for." We need concrete suggestions, nuts-and-bolts details.

APPENDIX: POLITICAL AND ECONOMIC DATA ON THAILAND[4]

Political Structure

Thailand is a constitutional monarchy with a bicameral National Assembly. The Thai Senate includes members who are appointed and who represent constituencies ranging from labor to the military. The lower house consists of roughly 350 members who are elected for four-year terms. The prime minister is appointed by the king based on the recommendations of the National Assembly. The current king, Bhumibol Adulvadej, does not possess a great deal of legislative power but does exercise strong moral leadership.

1932–1980

The modern era is generally considered to have begun in 1932 with a coup d'etat that eliminated most true powers of the king. The absolute monarchy was replaced by a constitutional government, with the support of the king. The military has continued to exert strong influence over the government from the 1932 initial coup up to the present. The name of the country was changed from Siam to Thailand in 1939. The government's effectiveness was diminished during the country's reluctant involvement in World War II as an ally of Japan and during the wars in Vietnam, Laos, and Cambodia in the 1960s and 1970s. Between 1932 and 1980, there were 26 coups and countercoups and the adoption of 13 constitutions. There were a number of military governments mixed with several attempts at democracy.

1980–1990

General Prem Tinsulanonda took power in a coup in 1980 and held it into 1988 through a series of coalition governments. He never stood for election but was able to put down coup attempts in 1981 and 1985. His governments were noted for stability (itself something of an achievement in Thailand), rather than progressive policies. His government strove to improve the environment for foreign investment.

---

[4]The sources for the appendix material were: Business International Corporation, *Investing, Licensing and Trading Conditions Abroad*, July 1990, pp. 3–5; International Trade Administration, U.S. Department of Commerce, "Thailand." *Guide to Doing Business In the ASEAN Region*, February 1990, pp. 48–56; and current news reports.

Prem's government resigned in 1988 rather than face a no-confidence vote called by Chatichai Choonhavan's Chat Thai party. Chatichai was elected president in the subsequent elections. He formed a coalition consisting largely of the same core as Prem's coalition. There were predictions that his government would not last long, due partly to intimations that his cabinet ministers were mainly interested in feathering their own nests—corruption has long been rife in Thai governments. However, Chatichai outlasted the initial expectations. He adopted a pro-business stance that benefited his cabinet as well as foreign investors.

Currency

The Thai baht was tied to the U.S. dollar during the 1950s, but it became progressively overvalued and was eventually floated. In 1963 it was again fixed against the U.S. dollar. Up until 1978 there were a series of devaluations in the baht's gold backing in order to maintain a relatively stable correspondence to the U.S. dollar, which was gradually losing its value against gold. In 1978 the baht was detached from the dollar and its value pegged to a basket of currencies. Since then it has been somewhat more stable than the dollar (see Exhibit 2).

Foreign Investment

The government officially supports foreign investment. Multinational corporations should expect substantial delays in obtaining approvals of their investment applications, although these should be no greater than for Thai businesses. Thai governments have long been known for being weighted with bureaucracy and for their slowness in making decisions. As of 1984, U.S. investment in Thailand was estimated at $4 billion, about 30 percent of all foreign investment in the country. By 1989, however, the United States accounted for only 8 percent of incoming investment, whereas Japan accounted for more than half.

The Thai Investment Law, which was passed in 1977, includes assurances against nationalization.

Foreign Equity Ownership

Industries approved for foreign investment are regulated by the Alien Business Law of 1972, which created three separate levels of foreign ownership depending on the industry. The first level requires majority Thai shareholders for a public corporation. The second level requires majority Thai ownership for new investments but allows grandfathering of businesses that existed prior to the passing of the law. The third level allows majority foreign ownership as long as an alien business license is approved. Despite these provisions, as a practical matter, 49 percent foreign ownership has been permitted even in the most restricted industries, although recent changes may reduce allowable foreign ownership levels.

Among the restrictions relating to specific industries are the requirements for:

- 60 percent Thai equity in businesses involved in large-scale agriculture, livestock raising, and the production of fertilizers
- 100 percent Thai equity in businesses involved in agricultural-product processing and rice milling

Land Ownership

Land ownership is restricted to Thai nationals except when special allowances are granted.

Local Content Requirements

There are strict requirements for local content in the automobile and motorcycle industries, but the proportion of local content in most other industries is generally controlled by high duties on nonlocal materials.

Remittability of Funds

Firms have little difficulty in repatriating funds as long as they can establish the foreign origination of those funds. Profits may be repatriated as long as proof of tax payment is presented.

Corporate Taxes

The nominal corporate tax rate is 30 percent for companies listed on the Securities Exchange and 35 percent otherwise. Tax evasion is common among Thai companies, however, either through hiding of profits or through bribes to the tax authorities. In practice the amount of many companies' tax payments is determined by negotiations with the government.

Incentives

The Investment Promotion Act of 1977 allows certain incentives to be offered for foreign investment. Industries eligible for incentives include: agricultural products and commodities; minerals; chemicals and chemical products; general manufacturing; and others.

Because of the recent influx of foreign investment, the government is granting fewer incentives than before. It is trying to target incentives to ventures that make a strong contribution to national development. Among the criteria to be considered:

1. Location in up-country provinces
2. Efficient use of natural resources
3. Use of domestic labor and raw materials
4. Share divestiture to Thai nationals and employee share ownership
5. Advanced technology transfer
6. Mobilization of offshore funds

Incentives include but are not limited to:

- Guarantees against nationalization
- Competitive protection
- Expatriate permission
- Land ownership permission
- Tax holidays and tax loss carryforwards

The regulations establish a special category of Target Businesses, which includes those that develop natural resources or use agricultural raw materials for export manufacturing. An investment designated as a Target Business may be eligible for additional incentives such as:

- Exemption from machinery import tax
- 50 percent reduction of import duty on raw materials used in goods for local consumption

- Five-year exemption from import duties on raw materials used in export goods
- Five-year, 90 percent exemption from business tax
- 50 percent reduction in corporate income tax for five years after the tax holiday or from the first income-earning year
- Ten-year, 200 percent tax deduction for expenses for transport, electricity, and water
- Special depreciation rights for original installation

The regulations divide the country into three zones:

1. Bangkok and the five adjacent provinces
2. Ten provinces located near Bangkok, in the central region and on the eastern shore
3. The up-country provinces

The tax holidays, tariff exemptions, and other incentives are more generous for investments located in Zone 2 than for those in Zone 1, and the incentives for Zone 3 are substantially more generous than for Zone 2.

Labor

Thailand has a large supply of unskilled labor, but there is a shortage of skilled labor, particularly in newly introduced industries.

Patent Protection

Patents are governed by the Patent Act of 1979, which was adopted following strong pressure from the United States and other governments who objected to the flagrant copying in Thailand of products and processes that had been developed and patented in other countries. Patents may be registered by Thai nationals and nationals of countries that have provided reciprocal patent rights to Thai nationals. Patents are granted for 15 years from filing date with the possibility of cancellation after six years if no production is undertaken. Protection of trademarks and intellectual property has improved under this legislation, although strict enforcement still poses a problem.

Patents may be granted or recognized in Thailand only if the invention is new, involves an innovative step, and is capable of industrial application. Patents are not allowed in a variety of areas, including agricultural equipment, pharmaceuticals, food, beverages, biological species, and computer programs.

One current issue is the protection of computer software and pharmaceuticals as mandated under the Uruguay Round of the General Agreement on Tariffs and Trade in 1983. The United States is pushing for a quick resolution and is attempting to influence Thailand's decision through various international channels.

In late 1990 the U.S. government identified Thailand as a Priority Foreign Country that inadequately protects U.S. intellectual property under Section 301 of the Omnibus Trade and Competitiveness Act of 1988. As a result, the United States started investigating whether to institute or raise tariffs against selected imports from Thailand.

Southwestern Ohio Steel LP: The Matworks Decision

David Rosenthal

In late March 1994, Dan Wilson, vice president of sales for Southwestern Ohio Steel Limited Partnership (SOSLP), shook his head and laughed out loud. He had just read a letter from Matworks, an important and long-standing customer. The letter requested that SOSLP participate in sponsoring a portion of Matworks' annual sales meeting. (Letter is shown in Exhibit 1)

Wilson's first reaction was that the letter was some sort of joke. If this were a bona fide request, it would put him and SOSLP in an uncomfortable position. SOSLP generally did not spend large amounts on any type of promotional activity, and certainly not on individual customers. Undoubtedly the people at Matworks knew the limited nature of SOSLP's promotional budget. Still, Wilson resolved to consider the letter carefully, because Matworks was an important customer whose request had to be taken seriously.

SOSLP management considered the concept of partnership with customers to be very important. SOSLP customers often had long-standing relationships with the company, having worked together out of mutual respect, loyalty, and good business practice. Matworks was such a customer, dating to the very first days of SOSLP's operation in the 1940s. Whatever decision Wilson made, he did not want to upset the ongoing relationship between the two companies.

COMPANY BACKGROUND

Bill Wolf founded Southwestern Ohio Steel in 1945 to supply steel to a new General Motors Fisher Body Plant in Hamilton, Ohio. The steel service center bought sheet or coiled steel from local producers, then transported, warehoused, processed, and resold the metal to local users. The basic functions of maintaining inventory, breaking bulk (buying in large quantities and selling in smaller amounts), intermediate processing, and rapid and accurate delivery were hallmarks of the company and had led to consistent growth.

By 1994, the company had more than 500 employees, annual sales of roughly $250 million, and annual shipments of approximately 400,000 tons. SOSLP was widely considered to be one of the industry leaders in technology and service.

Several structural changes impacted the company during the 1970s and 1980s, including a leveraged buyout by its management. Subsequently, the company was sold to its leading supplier, Armco, Inc. In 1991 Armco, Inc. sold half of SOS to Armco Steel

---

EXHIBIT 1   Matworks Letter

Matworks, Inc.
1038 Industrial Blvd.
Cincinnati, OH 45201
(513) 231–2200

March 18, 1994

_____ *MATWORKS*_____

Mr. Dan Wilson
Southwestern Ohio Steel
903 Belle Avenue
Hamilton, OH 45012

Dear Mr. Wilson:

MATWORKS is planning a very special meeting October 12–16, 1994, in Hilton Head, South Carolina, at the Cottages Resort and Conference Center. It will be attended by the top achievers in our sales and service organization who have achieved the *MATWORKS* Peak Club, as well as all of the *MATWORKS* executive management staff. We are writing to offer your company a unique marketing opportunity to solidify relationships with *MATWORKS* regional vice presidents, district general managers, and sales representatives in conjunction with this event.

The meeting will mix business and pleasure as a reward for a job well done by our "Peak Performers." We are discussing the possibility of subsidizing our meeting with our larger suppliers. The events that are available for sponsorship are:

1. Carolinas Reception—This Welcome to Hilton Head reception will be held poolside at the Cottages, Wednesday evening, October 12.

- Guests receive hats and vests upon arrival
- Southeastern/Carolina decor
- Island band with strolling fiddlers
- Assorted hot and cold regional hors d'oeuvres
- Beer and wine served

Sponsorship $14,000

(Continued on next page)

Exhibit 1 *(Continued)*

March 18, 1994, Page 2

2. Evening Cruise—Thursday evening, October 13, the *MATWORKS* Peak Club cruises the waters around Hilton Head. Once frequented by galleons and pirates, the waters of Hilton Head are both beautiful and mysterious.

- Cocktails and snacks prior to dinner
- Buffet featuring New York strip steak and swordfish fillet
- Bluegrass band entertains during dinner
- After dinner, naturalists will lead wildlife viewing

Sponsorship $25,000

3. Dessert Extravaganza—Following a "Dine Around" on Hilton Head, Friday evening, October 14, guests return to the Cottages for a sumptuous dessert buffet and after-dinner cordials.

Sponsorship $6,000

4. Golf Tournament—You may choose to sponsor a golf outing on the famous Jack Nicklaus/Pete Dye Harbortown Golf Course, a regular stop on the PGA Tour. Available the afternoons of Wednesday, October 12, or Thursday, October 13.

Sponsorship $5,000

5. Grand Banquet—The premier event of the entire Peak Club program, the Grand Banquet features:

- Elegant decor—Colonial theme
- Gourmet dinner with veal, beef, or lobster entree
- Wine with dinner
- Peak Club ice sculpture
- Cordials after dinner
- Islands, a contemporary dance band

Sponsorship $30,000

We hope you will consider this exciting opportunity to involve your company with a select group of highly motivated *MATWORKS* representatives. Along with event sponsorship, we would like to talk to you about the display of your company's logo and product and your possible involvement in our business program to provide attendees with a better understanding of our valued business partnership. Linda Lewis, director of communications, will be contacting you to discuss your participation in more detail.

Joseph P. Pendleton
Vice President and General Manager

Corporation in Middletown, Ohio, and the other half to Itochu Corporation of Japan. The new company was named Southwestern Ohio Steel Limited Partnership. Neither owner company took an active role in SOSLP's functional management.

In addition to conducting its primary activities and functions, SOSLP also operated four subsidiaries:

- SOS Leveling (SOSL) provided state-of-the-art tension leveling services for those customers who required superior flatness.
- SOS Lawrenceburg was a full-service facility located in Lawrenceburg, Tennessee, to serve that region. Transporting steel was expensive; therefore, inventory and delivery services could only be maintained from nearby facilities.
- J. R. Metals (JRM) marketed secondary steel. Secondary steel was steel that did not meet its production standards or had some sort of flaw. Expertise in metallurgy, the ability to correct some of the problems, and superior knowledge of the markets and customers allowed JRM to sell secondary steel profitably.
- Clark Cincinnati, Inc. (Clark) produced metal framing wall studs. Clark employed roughly 80 people and generated sales of approximately $15 million to $20 million per year.

SOSLP sold to approximately 500 customers. The top 25 customers produced about two-thirds of the company's sales. SOSLP sold to a broad spectrum of industries, thereby limiting the company's exposure to business downturns.

One of the company's key strengths was its value-added processing. The company bought "master coils" of steel from producers. Master coils were generally 48 or 72 inches wide and weighed as much as 60,000 pounds. The company provided processing of master coils in a number of ways, such as "cut to length" (providing sheets of a certain size rather than coils), precision slitting (providing coils of a narrower width), and tension leveling (providing very flat sheets of specific sizes). Other strengths included sophisticated market forecasting that enabled the company to purchase at the best possible prices, inventory control, and efficient transportation. SOSLP maintained a fleet of 29 trucks to ensure control over transportation time and delivery schedules.

INDUSTRY BACKGROUND

The steel service center business was generally very competitive. The weight of steel made shipments of more than 200 miles cost-prohibitive, thus limiting competition to local suppliers. However, more than in any given geographical market, there were several competitors, all providing similar products, services, and prices. It was not difficult for a buyer to shop among the various suppliers in a given region. Large customers with established requirements were highly-prized targets among the steel service center competitors because their consistent orders made it possible to accurately forecast demand and, therefore, manage inventory to reduce costs. Similarly, well-established service requirements (delivery scheduling, order response time, need for consistent availability of material, dimensional tolerances, etc.) made it possible to measure and demonstrate customer satisfaction and, thus, justify higher gross margins. Customers varied in their supplier loyalty, some focusing entirely on the steel's price per pound and changing suppliers frequently, others focusing on service and overall cost of operation, and tending to be more loyal. Competition in the industry was such that an average profit margin was about 3 percent of sales.

RELATIONSHIP WITH MATWORKS

Matworks was a leading national and international producer of heavy industrial equipment. Its main production facility was located only a few miles from SOSLP, and it had become one of the company's best customers.

Wilson commented:

> *At one time, Matworks was our largest customer. The major portion of the raw materials required in manufacturing Matwork's product line is steel, and they buy almost exclusively from us. That goes back a way, too. They buy on a contractual basis. We negotiate a contract with them on a yearly basis and ship according to a schedule. They are pretty good about maintaining that schedule, and so are we.*
>
> *Over the past few years, though, they have run into trouble. Their sales have been off by quite a bit, and so they haven't been buying as much from us. The recession hit them pretty hard, and the reduction in military spending has affected them as well.*
>
> *In the 1980s, they were among our top 10 customers in sales. By 1990 they had dropped to 29th. In 1990 and 1991 they were about 40th, and last year they were about 90th. They have gone from buying about $2.4 million in 1990 to $770,000 in 1991 to $1 million in 1992 to only about $672,000 last year. It is clear that they are having some hard times.*
>
> *It isn't too difficult to service the account. They have some high expectations regarding the surface finish of the product they receive, but it really isn't anything extraordinary. They are consistent in their demands.*

DAN WILSON

Dan Wilson was the vice president of sales for SOSLP. Wilson had begun his work with the company on the processing floor where, as a student, he had worked summers. He had graduated from the business school of a well-known midwestern university in 1982 and had gone into "inside" sales (customer service and telephone sales). He had been very successful in both inside and outside sales and had risen through the sales ranks. He had been promoted to his current position only about a year ago.

In the parable about "the tortoise and the hare," Wilson would definitely be cast as the tortoise. It was not that he was slow, he accomplished a great deal. Rather, he could be characterized as steady. He was very even-tempered and appeared to be careful in his consideration of all of the issues when faced with a decision. In conversations, Wilson would often be found doing most of the listening, and when he spoke, his comments were well thought out, and most often, very insightful. At the same time, Wilson would not "pull any punches." He would give his opinion in as honest and straightforward a manner as he was able. His word was his bond, something that he had had reinforced during his tenure at SOSLP. Wilson commented:

> *Much of customer satisfaction is the management of expectations. Your service can be absolutely terrific, but if you have created the wrong expectations, your customer may still be dissatisfied. If you tell your customer, for instance, that the steel will be there by 10:00 A.M., and it arrives at 10:05, it doesn't matter that no other company in the region could have gotten it there before noon! You've failed in your promise. If you promise it by noon and get it there by 10:05, then you are a hero!*

501

The company was known for its honesty and integrity, as well. Its roots as a family-owned business and the long-term relationships with many of the customers supported an atmosphere of loyalty and open, cooperative practices. During times of short supply of steel and consequent rising prices, SOSLP had often been known to "hold the line" on prices for their customers, thus smoothing the ups and downs of the market. The management of the company tended to take a long-term view of business and relationships rather than taking advantage of situations to "make a quick buck."

THE CURRENT SITUATION

The letter that Wilson received had been a shock to him. He had always thought that the relationship with Matworks had been positive and very professional. The negotiations for contracts had been conducted fairly and had provided good value to both parties. The idea of asking for a large donation was clearly something new.

SOSLP had no formal policy regarding such an expenditure. SOSLP executives and salespeople occasionally gave a buyer a mug or some other specialty advertising piece. An occasional lunch or tickets to a Cincinnati Reds baseball game were not uncommon, but not the rule, either. The idea of giving one customer $5,000 or more simply was way out of line with normal activity.

SOSLP generally did little advertising or promotion. The sales force, both outside and inside, prided itself on maintaining good communications and relationships with its customers. What little advertising was done was nearly always in the form of direct mail. Wilson estimated that the company spent less than one one-hundredth of a percent of sales on advertising and promotion.

Wilson remarked about the letter:

You have to give them credit. It takes a lot of guts to ask for something like this. And they didn't do it halfway, either. They went 'whole hog.' It kind of makes you wonder what they are thinking.

It's kind of funny. We had a situation where we had a golf outing for some of our buyers, just to say, 'thank you.' When we finished the outing, there were hamburgers and hot dogs and drinks for everyone. I took the young SOSLP guy who organized the thing over to one side and asked him where the food came from, since it wasn't in his budget. He told me not to worry, that he had gotten the company that runs the vending machines in our plant to put up the food. I told him never, ever, ever *to do that again. I think he got the point.*

Wilson could shed no light on what would happen if SOSLP declined to participate. It was obvious from the letter that somebody at Matworks expected their big suppliers to take part in the program. Was this some wild idea that someone at Matworks had hatched to generate whatever funds they could, or did they really expect participation at the levels indicated? What were they willing to do if a supplier failed to support their activities? There was no question in Wilson's mind that some of SOSLP's competitors would jump at the chance to contribute in order to break into the account.

Wilson had never heard of Linda Lewis before this letter, but he had communicated with Joe Pendleton on a number of occasions, and the relationship between the two companies had always been good. The letter made it clear that Linda Lewis would be calling to discuss the matter further, and that SOSLP would have to have some response.

Starbucks Coffee: The Dorosin Issue

Terri Feldman Barr, David Rosenthal,
and Thomas C. Boyd

Betsy Reese, corporate customer relations manager for Starbucks Coffee, sat back in her chair, unsure of what to do next. She had just hung up the telephone with Jeremy Dorosin, a loyal and frequent Starbucks customer, who was completely dissatisfied with what he felt was the company's response to an escalating sequence of unsatisfactory encounters. Dorosin had taken his concerns up through company channels all the way to the corporate offices without resolution. He had attracted considerable national media attention over the situation in recent weeks. Reese, other company executives, and Dorosin had been working to resolve the problem for almost six weeks to no avail, and, at this point, the company representatives were perplexed and Dorosin was upset.

In April 1995, Betsy Reese had become aware that Dorosin had purchased one of Starbucks' Estro Vapore Espresso machines at the Berkeley, California, store, and that he had experienced some problems with it. Returning the machine, he was given a loaner until a replacement machine came in. He liked the loaner well enough to purchase one, an Estro 410, as a wedding gift for a friend. Dorosin's initial problem was complicated by this additional $189 purchase. He did not receive the free coffee that went with each machine purchase, and the gift machine was not in good working order.

Despite several telephone calls to various people at both the retail store and Starbucks corporate offices, Dorosin felt that the problem remained unresolved. He demanded that Starbucks send a top-of-the-line replacement machine to his friend, or he would take out an ad in the *Wall Street Journal*. Starbucks apologized for the problem, agreed to send letters of apology to both Dorosin and his friend, and to send a machine of "better" quality to Dorosin's friend, but not the $2,500 replacement that he had requested. Dorosin found Starbucks' solution unacceptable, and in the following weeks, he proceeded to take out four ads in the regional edition of the *Wall Street Journal,* asking for other people's customer service problems with Starbucks (Exhibits 1 and 2). He installed a toll-free (1-800) telephone number for people to call. He also appeared on several radio and television programs, discussing his experiences with the company. Newspapers around the country picked up the story.

In the meantime, Starbucks, confident that the company could come to some mutually agreeable solution to the problem, offered replacement machines, steaming pitchers, and coffee. Dorosin refused the offer. Starbucks sent a full refund for both machines and a letter of apology to Dorosin's friend, along with the promise of a

---

This case was prepared by Professor Terri Feldman Barr, Professors David Rosenthal and Thomas C. Boyd of Miami University, as a basis for class discussion. It is not intended to illustrate either effective or ineffective handling of an administrative situation.

replacement machine. Both the check and the letter were refused. Dorosin was demanding that Starbucks underwrite a shelter for runaway juveniles, which he would run.

Starbucks had to make a decision. How were they going to respond to this customer's demands? They had several options as Reese saw it: The company could meet Dorosin's initial demand for two top-of-the-line replacement machines, although there was some uncertainty as to whether they would be accepted; they could help to underwrite the runaway shelter that Dorosin had proposed; or they could do nothing more, assuming that they had exhausted all means of satisfying Dorosin, and consider the matter "closed."

COMPANY BACKGROUND

Starbucks Corporation purchased and roasted high-quality whole-bean coffees and sold them, along with fresh-brewed coffees and Italian-style espresso beverages, primarily through company-operated retail stores. In addition to coffee beans and beverages, the company's stores offered a wide selection of coffee-making equipment, accessories, pastries, and confections. The company's objective was to establish Starbucks as the premier specialty-coffee brand.

Starbucks was formed in November 1985 under the name Il Giornale Coffee Company. In August 1987, Il Giornale purchased the Seattle assets, which included seven retail stores, a roasting plant, and the rights to the name "Starbucks," of Starbucks Coffee Company, a corporation founded in 1971. In January 1988, Il Giornale changed its name to Starbucks Corporation.

The company grew rapidly over the next several years. Starbucks' sales for 1994 were approximately $285 million, with corresponding earnings of more than $10 mil-

lion, from almost 400 stores. The company's stock was publicly traded. An additional 200 stores were expected to be opened in 1995.

Retail Stores

Location   Starbucks stores were typically clustered in high-traffic, high-visibility locations in each market. Starbucks stores varied in size from approximately 300 to 2,200 square feet, with an average of approximately 1,200 square feet.

Product Mix   The product mix in each store varied and was dependent on the size of the store and its location. The company's mix of merchandise as a percentage of retail sales was approximately 55% coffee beverages, 21% whole-bean coffees, 14% food items, and 10% coffee-related hardware and equipment.

Coffee   All Starbucks stores offered a choice of regular or decaffeinated coffee beverages and changing "coffees of the day." Larger stores carried more than 30 varieties of whole-bean coffees; smaller stores and kiosks carried a more-limited selection of whole-bean coffees. Starbucks priced its coffees at or above the prevailing high-end coffee prices in each of its markets, reflecting the higher quality of the company's coffees and its higher level of customer service. The average customer transaction was approximately $3.01, about the price of a large espresso.

Coffee-Related Products   The larger Starbucks retail stores carried a range of coffee-related products, including high-quality coffee-making equipment. Espresso machines, coffeemakers that allowed coffee connoisseurs to brew strong espresso beans and steam milk for a frothy combination, ranged in price at the company stores from less than $75 to more than $2,000. Competition for the espresso machine market was intense, because these specialty coffeemakers could be purchased at local department stores, gourmet kitchen specialty stores, and the national discount retailers at a wide range of prices.

Starbucks stores also sold accessories bearing the Starbucks logo. Accessories included coffee mugs, coffee grinders, storage containers, coffee filters, and specialty food products. There was a two-year limited warranty on the coffee and espresso makers and coffee grinders. A copy of the Limited Warranty is found in Exhibit 3.

Customer Service   Customer service was a key ingredient to Starbucks' success. One of the five guiding principles of the company was "Develop enthusiastically satisfied customers all of the time." A statement from the 1994 annual report elaborated:

> Of all of our valued relationships, the one we enjoy with our customers is most honored. It's a relationship of trust that's renewed day by day. It's based on consistency of our coffee, our merchandise, and our service. On flexibility—each beverage is made the way you'd like. And on a promise that goes something like this: come in, you're welcome here; know that these are the world's best beans, freshly roasted; that the products on our shelves have been tested and found superb; that everyone here is truly knowledgeable—passionate!—about coffee; and that we genuinely look forward to your visits every day.

The company took customer service very seriously. Employees received 24 hours of formal classroom training at a Starbucks training center, and up to 30 hours of practical on-site training, before they worked as a "barista," the term for people who made coffee drinks. They were taught "drink-calling, drink-making and cup management" skills and terminology, along with three key "Star Skills"—Maintain or Enhance Self-Esteem, Listen and Acknowledge, and Ask for Help.

Retail Management   Starbucks' retail managers were responsible for the ongoing day-to-day running of the stores. They reported on a regular basis to district offices. The Berkeley store manager reported to the Northwest District Office in San Francisco.

Social Responsibility/Community Service

Starbucks strongly adhered to its corporate principle: "Contribute positively to our communities and our environment." To this end, each retail store chose a local charity to which coffee was donated. Additionally, each store had a "bean bank"—coffee it could donate to other community events. The goal of the company was to be an active, responsive corporate citizen. Another example of the company's commitment to the world community was its partnership with CARE, the international relief organization. Starbucks had created a variety package that it called a "CARE Sampler." Starbucks donated two dollars of every CARE Sampler that it sold, in addition to providing an ongoing, annual grant to CARE. The support helped people living in several coffee-producing countries around the world.

Starbucks was also involved in environmental issues and was "committed to making responsible environmental choices." The company recycled, reused, and examined the environmental impact of all of the products that it sold.

EXHIBIT 3: Starbucks Limited Warranty

No. 263490

Thank you for choosing this exceptional product from Starbucks Coffee Company. Your enjoyment of this purchase is a priority for us. Please read the enclosed operating instructions carefully. Should you have any questions about initial set-up, Starbucks Warranty Services can assist you by calling our toll-free number, 1-800-334-5553 between the hours of 6:00 am and 8:00 pm Monday through Friday and 8:00 am to 5:00 pm Saturday and Sunday Pacific Standard Time. To ensure your satisfaction with the quality of this product, Starbucks includes a Limited Warranty with this purchase.

We hope that this equipment from Starbucks provides you with many cups of coffee enjoyment.

Limited Warranty

This product is warranted to you by Starbucks Coffee Company for two (2) years from date of purchase against defects in workmanship and materials. During the warranty period, a defective part of product will be replaced either with a new or reconditioned part or product, depending on the availability at the time of replacement.

This warranty covers normal consumer usage and does not cover damage which occurs in shipment. Failure which results from alteration, accident, misuse, abuse, vandalism, neglect, installation, commercial use or improper maintenance is not covered under this warranty. Nor does this warranty extend to any products which have been used in violation of written instructions, or to products which have been altered or modified. This warranty does not cover damage which results from unauthorized repairs.

Warranty Service

This product has been carefully engineered for optimum performance. Do not attempt to repair this product yourself. Attempts to repair this appliance yourself may render it dangerous to use. Should the appliance malfunction, you should first call toll-free 1-800-334-5553 between the hours of 6:00 am and 8:00 pm Monday through Friday and 8:00 am to 5:00 pm Saturday and Sunday Pacific Standard Time and ask for WARRANTY SERVICES stating you are a consumer having a problem with your appliance. A customer service representative will assist you. If necessary the customer service representative will provide you with directions on receiving your replacement parts or products. All products being returned should be shipped to Starbucks Coffee Company, 18411 77th Pl. S., Kent, WA 98032, attn: Warranty Service. Under no circumstances should you attempt to open the housing and repair the appliance. Should you do this, your warranty will be voided.

Type of electrical product purchased: ❑ Espresso Machine   ❑ Drip Maker   ❑ Blade Grinder   ❑ Burr Grinder

Model Name/Number _____

Store # _____   Date of purchase _____

Over

To be filled out at time of purchase.

Name _____

Address _____

City _____ State _____ Zip Code _____

Telephone _____ Date of purchase _____

Purchased from store number _____ Was this purchased for ❑ own use? ❑ gift?
Do you own any other electrical products purchased at Starbucks? ❑ Yes ❑ No
If yes, which items? _____
_____

Type of electrical product purchased:

❑ Espresso Machine
❑ Drip Maker
❑ Blade Grinder
❑ Burr Grinder

Model Name/Number _____

Model Name/Number _____

Would you like to receive our mail order catalog?
❑ Yes ❑ No

No. 263490

SKU 115004 5/95

INDUSTRY OUTLOOK

Competition

The company's coffees and coffee products competed directly against specialty coffees sold at retail through supermarkets, specialty retailers, and a number of specialty coffee stores. The company's coffee beverages competed directly against all restaurant and beverage outlets that served coffee, as well as an increasing number of espresso stands, carts, and stores. The specialty-coffee segment was becoming increasingly competitive. Both the company's whole-bean coffees and coffee beverages competed indirectly against all other coffees on the market. The company believed that its customers chose retailers primarily on the basis of quality and convenience, and, to a lesser extent, on price.

Management believed that supermarkets, carrying a vast number of nationally-branded premium coffee products, posed the greatest competitive challenge in the whole-bean coffee market because supermarkets offered customers the convenience of not having to make a separate trip to the company's stores. In addition, the company competed for whole-bean coffee sales with numerous franchise operators and locally-owned specialty coffee stores in both the United States and Canada.

The company's primary competitors for beverage sales were restaurants, shops, and street carts. Although competition in the beverage market was fragmented at the time, a major competitor with substantially greater financial, marketing, and operating resources than the company could enter this market at any time and compete directly against Starbucks. The company also expected that competition for additional retail space would become more intense.

THE SEQUENCE OF EVENTS

Betsy Reese reviewed the sequence of events leading up to her present dilemma. Keeping in mind that Dorosin's version of the events did not match the company's version of what happened, she contemplated the options. (Note: Dorosin's story is presented in regular typeface; Starbucks' story is presented in italics.)

Sometime prior to April 1995

Jeremy Dorosin went to the Berkeley, California, Starbucks store and bought himself an Espresso maker (Vapore) for $299.

April 1995

He found it defective, returned it, and received a loaner of a less-expensive machine (which he loved), an Estro 410, which retailed for $189.00. He got his new replacement and gave the loaner back, but he asked if Starbucks planned to sell the loaners because he really liked it. An employee at the Berkeley Starbucks store replied, "No, we're sending them back."

Jeremy Dorosin returned a defective Vapore ($299) and we gave him a loaner Estro 410 ($189). Dorosin returned the loaner when his new replacement came in.

End of April 1995

Approximately two weeks after picking up his replacement, Dorosin bought a new Estro 410 model (like the loaner) as a wedding gift for a friend. It had to be ordered, as the store had none of that model number in stock.

He (Dorosin) later came back to buy a machine like the loaner as a gift for a friend, Ms. Cohen.

A Few Days Later

Dorosin came back into the store to pick up the gift machine for his friend; however, it could not be found. The store employee then found the machine in a different (and damaged) box. Dorosin expressed concern that they were giving him a loaner or a used machine, prompting him to ask the clerk to inspect it, which she did. She said it was fine. He also did not get the half-pound of free coffee that was supposed to come with each machine purchase. He took the gift machine to his friend. However, there was no instruction manual. He called the store manager and explained his dissatisfaction with his prior visit and the fact that this new machine had no manual. The store manager apologized and said to come in for the manual, the half-pound of coffee, and a free cup of coffee.

Dorosin did not get the half-pound of coffee to which he felt he was entitled when he picked up the gift 410. He called the store manager, who agreed he should have gotten the half-pound, apologized to him, and told him to come back in for the coffee.

At Some Point Shortly Thereafter

His friend for whom he purchased the Espresso machine found rust in the machine, and there were parts missing. Dorosin called the Starbucks store where he purchased the machine and was told that those parts did not exist. Dorosin returned the gift to the store where it was purchased and told his story to the store manager. The manager offered a refund, which Dorosin refused.

He was then sent to the San Francisco (district) office, where he told his story a second time. He finally ended up speaking by telephone to Bill Stein, customer service supervisor, in Seattle, to whom he told the whole story again for a third time.

In his conversation with Bill Stein, Dorosin proposed that Starbucks:

A. Replace his machine (the Vapore), which had just broken for the second time.
B. Send his friend, the bride, a letter of apology.
C. Send the bride the nicest replacement they had, then asked what the next-best machine was. Stein told him it was the $495 model. Dorosin said to replace his, send an apology, and the $495 machine to his friend, and the matter would be resolved.

May 1, 1995

Starbucks district manager (San Francisco) called Corporate Customer Service Supervisor Bill Stein (Seattle) and explained the situation the retail store had with Dorosin. Stein called Dorosin, listened to his concerns about the way he was treated in the store and the condition of the gift machine (Estro 410). Dorosin demanded that a $2,495 Starbucks' top-of-the-line machine be sent to his friend to compensate for the defective $189 gift, or he would place an ad in the Wall Street Journal. *Stein apologized for his frustration and told him the company would work with him to get either replacement machines at better quality or a refund.*

May 2, 1995

Stein called back with a counterproposal:

A. Send Dorosin a $269 machine (although he paid $299) to replace his twice-broken machine.
B. Send his friend a $269 machine for her original one, which was priced at $189.

Dorosin said that he was not happy with the company's proposal and asked Stein to reconsider his (Dorosin's) proposal. Stein called back and said that the company's proposal was the best that could be done. Dorosin was incensed.

Stein spoke to Dorosin a second time. Stein told Dorosin again that the company would replace the machines with ones of equal or better value and write a letter of apology to him and his friend, but that a $2,495 replacement machine was not a reasonable solution. Dorosin gave Stein a two-hour ultimatum: send him a $2,495 machine or he'd place an ad in the Wall Street Journal *soliciting other dissatisfied Starbucks customers. Stein expressed concern, but he could not meet Dorosin's demands and began preparations to send replacement machines, coffee and letters of apology.*

Immediately Thereafter

Dorosin called attorneys, who told him that he did not have a case. He then decided to run a local ad ($800) in the *Wall Street Journal.* Upon informing Stein about his plans, Dorosin reported that Stein said, in a condescending tone, "Gee, I'm sorry you feel this way." Dorosin said he thought Stein's implication was that Dorosin was lying. Upon the first advertisement's appearance, Dorosin received a "ton of calls." Some were from stockholders of Starbucks who were angry. He said he had received thousands of calls, from customers, competitors, and employees who felt Starbucks misrepresented themselves to the public. He said that competitors told him that Starbucks was devious and unfair.

May 5, 1995

Dorosin ran his first Wall Street Journal *ad, in the West Coast, San Francisco edition. Betsy Reese, corporate customer relations manager, talked to Dorosin, expressed Starbucks' concern for his dilemma, and once again offered to work toward a reasonable solution. Reese explained the steps that Starbucks was taking (sending machines, coffee and letters). However, Dorosin said it was too little, too late. He instead demanded that Starbucks place a full-page ad of apology, admitting that the company knowingly sold used equipment, signed by the company chairman. He further wanted the opportunity to proofread the ad contents. Otherwise, he indicated that he would place a second ad. Reese told him that further ads would not be necessary, that the company was confident that the two parties could come to a mutually-agreeable solution for his experience. Starbucks offered replacement machines for him and his friend, steaming pitchers, and free coffee—all of which were in excess of his original purchases by more than $175. Dorosin refused the offer, for the second time.*

Dorosin suggested that Starbucks take out a double full-page ad in the *Wall Street Journal* apologizing, although he insisted that this was not about money. Reese suggested that instead of taking out an ad, the company take the amount that an ad would cost and donate it to charity. Dorosin agreed.

(Note: Although Dorosin apparently believed at this point that an agreement had been made, the conflict continued further.)

May 10, 1995

Because Starbucks could not satisfy Dorosin, a decision was made to try to at least take care of his friend. Starbucks sent an apology letter to Dorosin's gift recipient, Ms. Cohen, explaining that a replacement machine was on its way as an apology gift to her.

Additionally, Starbucks sent a full refund via certified mail. Dorosin ran a second ad in the Wall Street Journal.

May 11, 1995

Stein had another conversation with Dorosin. Starbucks sent verification of the May 2, 1995, offer in writing to Dorosin via certified mail.

May 14, 1995

KGA News (the ABC affiliate in San Francisco) did a story on Dorosin.

May 18, 1995

Dorosin ran the third Wall Street Journal *ad.*

May 19, 1995

The written offer of May 11, 1995, was returned to Starbucks by Dorosin, refused. The refund check sent on May 10, 1995, to Dorosin was returned, refused.

May 23, 1995

The apology letter to Ms. Cohen was returned to Starbucks, refused by Ms. Cohen.

May 25, 1995

Dorosin ran the fourth ad in the Wall Street Journal.

May 26, 1995

Betsy Reese sent a written recap and reiterated offers to Dorosin.

May 30, 1995

A news story on the situation was reported in Contra Costa News. *Dorosin called Reese with a new demand, asking for collaboration on a juvenile runaway shelter. Reese expressed that the company did not see this as a reasonable solution, nor did Starbucks see a correlation between this demand and his original complaint.*

May 31, 1995

Dorosin called Reese to ask for a face-to-face meeting to negotiate a settlement. Reese said she would consider the request. Reese again asked for Dorosin to at least accept the refund money, which he refused.

June 1, 1995

Reese received a letter from Dorosin via fax.

June 2, 1995

KIRO radio in Seattle did a talk show with Dorosin.

June 3, 1995

KGO radio in San Francisco interviewed Dorosin and Reese.

June 4, 1995

KIRO-TV in Seattle on Morning at 7 show interviewed Dorosin and Reese.

June 13, 1995

The New York Times *reported the story.*

June 14, 1995

KFI radio interviewed Starbucks' president and Dorosin. An offer was made (by the president) to fly Dorosin up to Seattle to talk, but Dorosin refused.

June 16, 1995

Reese initiated a telephone conversation with Dorosin, during which Dorosin denied he declined the offer on KFI radio to come up to Seattle. Dorosin stated he was going to open a runaway shelter and run it himself. He wanted Starbucks to underwrite or sponsor it, but he did not want the company to have a public presence with it. Dorosin said he planned to get celebrity endorsements for the shelter and do TV telethons. Betsy Reese once again expressed that the company did not see this as a reasonable solution, nor did they see a correlation between the shelter and his original complaint. Dorosin stated that he was no longer interested in talking to the company because he wanted to negotiate the shelter and saw that Starbucks was unwilling to meet his request. Dorosin then claimed that the company had not made him an offer to replace his machines or apologized until after the second ad had run in the Wall Street Journal. *(Starbucks had apologized from the beginning and offered replacement machines on the second day.)*

REESE'S DILEMMA

Betsy considered the options available to the company. Dorosin's demands seemed excessive, but at the same time, he was very persistent and the advertisements were certainly uncomfortable. Something needed to be done to move on from this conflict.

Hoechst-Roussel Pharmaceuticals, Inc.: RU 486

Jan Willem Bol and David W. Rosenthal

INTRODUCTION

In July 1991, the management of Hoechst-Roussel Pharmaceuticals had, as yet, made no public announcement about their plans for marketing RU 486 in the United States. The product had been available for testing in very limited quantities, but the steps necessary to bring the new drug to market had not yet been taken.

RU 486 was a chemical compound that was commonly referred to as "the morning after pill" in the press. The compound had the effect of preventing a fertilized egg from attaching to the uterine wall or ensuring that a previously attached egg would detach. The pill had been thoroughly tested in several European countries with significant success.

RU 486 had become the focus of a great amount of publicity, press coverage, and industry speculation. The compound was also the center of a series of U.S. Senate hearings. Activists, both in support of and in apposition to RU 486, had sought to influence the company's course of action since the product's inception.

Pharmaceutical industry observers suggested that the company was not marketing the product aggressively in order to "maintain a low profile." It was clear that the Hoechst-Roussel management had an ongoing and very complex issue to resolve about the disposition of RU 486.

THE DRUG INDUSTRY

The drug industry consisted of three primary components: biological products, medicinals and botanicals, and pharmaceutical preparations. Pharmaceuticals were generally classified into one of two broad groups:

- Ethical pharmaceuticals—drugs available only through a physician's prescription, or
- Over-the-counter (OTC) drugs, both generic and proprietary (drugs sold without prescription).

This case was prepared by Professors Jan Willem Bol and David W. Rosenthal of Miami University, as a basis for class discussion. It is not intended to illustrate either effective or ineffective handling of an administrative situation.

The pharmaceutical industry had grown steadily since 1970, as a result of rising health care costs throughout the world and continuing product innovations from manufacturers. From 1970 to 1980, worldwide sales grew at an average of 10 percent to 12 percent, in real dollars. In the 1980s, growth was slightly lower at about 7 percent, and real growth rates were expected to decrease slightly during the early 1990s, at a projected rate of 6 percent to 8 percent. The growth rates varied considerably among countries and product categories. An estimated breakdown of 1987 worldwide sales of ethical pharmaceuticals by country or region, with projected growth rates, is shown in Exhibit 1.

Size and Composition

In the late 1980s, the industry was not particularly concentrated; the top four firms comprised slightly less than 10 percent of the market. Within specific product categories, however, there were much higher concentration levels, with the top four competitors often sharing 40 percent to 70 percent of total sales. Exhibit 2 lists 1987 pharmaceutical sales of the leading global pharmaceutical companies.

Research and Development

The overall health of the pharmaceutical industry was measured by the number of products it developed, the value of its exports, and the high level of its profits. These factors were, in turn, directly affected by the amount of dollars spent on research and development.

The U.S. drug industry spent about $6 billion on R&D in 1988, up from $5.4 billion in 1987 and $4.7 billion in 1986. As a percentage of sales, the drug industry spent more

EXHIBIT 1   Leading Pharmaceutical Markets

Country	1987 Sales U.S. millions	1990–1995 Growth Potential
United States	$23,979	Moderate
Japan	15,690	Moderate
Germany	6,527	Moderate
France	5,992	Moderate
China	4,890	Low
Italy	4,690	High
United Kingdom	3,370	Low
Canada	1,710	Moderate
South Korea	1,500	High
Spain	1,480	Moderate
India	1,400	High
Mexico	1,300	Declining
Brazil	1,180	Declining
Argentina	856	Declining
Australia	685	Moderate
Indonesia	590	Moderate
Others	33,200	High

Source: Thompson from Arthur D. Little Inc.

EXHIBIT 2   Twenty Leading Global Pharmaceutical Companies

Company	Country	1987 Sales, $US000
Merck & Co., Inc.	U.S.	$5,060,000
American Home Products Corp.	U.S.	5,020,000
Pfizer Inc.	U.S.	4,910,000
Hoechst Corp.	Germany	4,610,000
Abbot Laboratories	U.S.	4,380,000
Smithkline Beckman Corp.	U.S.	4,320,000
American Cyanamid Co.	U.S.	4,160,000
Eli Lilly & Co.	U.S.	3,640,000
Warner-Lambert Co.	U.S.	3,480,000
Schering Plough Co.	U.S.	2,690,000
Upjohn Co.	U.S.	2,520,000
Sterling Drug Inc.	U.S.	2,300,000
Squibb Corp.	U.S.	2,150,000
Schering Corp.	U.S.	1,900,000
E.R. Squibb & Sons Inc.	U.S.	1,800,000
Hoffman LaRoche Inc.	Switzerland	1,500,000
Miles Inc.	U.S.	1,450,000
Glaxo Inc.	U.S.	937,000
Rorer Group Inc.	U.S.	928,000
A.H. Robins	U.S.	855,000

Source: Estimates based on various industry sources. The figures should be regarded as approximations, due to differences in fiscal years of companies and variations in data due to different definitions of pharmaceutical sales.

on R&D than any other major industry group. In 1988 research accounted for more than 15 percent of revenues. Exhibit 3 lists R&D expenditures for some of the leading pharmaceutical companies.

The Outlook in 1991

There were a number of positive factors affecting the industry at the beginning of the 1990s. The demographic growth trend in the over-65 segment of the population presented both a larger and more-demanding market. The nature of the pharmaceutical business tended to make sales and revenues recession-resistant. High and increasing profit margins tended to attract capital to support the ambitious R&D needs of the industry.

Not all conditions were positive, however. Pharmaceutical firms had been increasingly criticized for their drug pricing policies. Critics argued that relatively low manufacturing costs should be reflected in the pricing of drugs, and that high profit levels proved their point. Generic (unbranded) drugs continued their trend of high growth, supplanting the higher-profit, proprietary segment of the market. Liability costs and the costs associated with compliance with increasingly complex and restrictive regulations continued to soar.

Drug companies in the United States were essentially free to price their products as they wished. This was contrary to the policies in many countries outside the United

EXHIBIT 3   Research and Development Expenditures (Sales in Millions of Dollars)

Company	1986		1987		1988	
	Sales	%	Sales	%	Sales	%
Abbot	$295	8	$361	8	$455	8
Bristol-Myers	311	8	342	8	394	7
Johnson & Johnson	521	7	617	8	674	7
Hoechst Group	395	10	540	10	608	10
Eli Lilly	420	13	466	13	541	13
Merck	480	12	566	11	669	11
Pfizer	336	7	401	8	473	9
Rorer Group	70	8	82	9	103	10
Schering-Plough	212	9	251	9	298	11
SmithKline	377	10	424	10	495	10
Squibb	163	9	221	10	294	11
Syntax	143	15	175	16	218	17
Upjohn	314	14	356	14	380	14
Warner-Lambert	202	7	232	7	259	7

Source: Annual reports

States, where pharmaceutical prices were strictly regulated by governmental agencies. However, as a result of the rapid increase of health care costs during the 1970s and 1980s, there was a movement toward a more-restrictive pricing environment both at the state and federal levels. In order to make their operations more-efficient and to acquire economies of scale, many companies had chosen to form alliances with other firms. A trend toward consolidation through merger and acquisition resulted.

The growth of the generic-drug segment posed a significant problem to the industry because generic products were priced much lower than proprietary products. The price of a generic drug was often as much as 50 percent lower than the price of the corresponding proprietary drug. All 50 states had laws that permitted substitution of generic drugs for proprietary drugs. As a result, the generic drug market doubled in sales from 1983 to 1987.

Pharmaceutical companies faced extensive product-liability risks associated with their products. This was especially true for "high risk" products such as vaccines and contraceptives. The cost of liability insurance to cover these adverse effects had forced many companies to coinsure or curtail their research efforts in these areas. In 1991 liability insurance coverage for the manufacture and sale of contraceptives was in most cases impossible to obtain. As a result of this "insurance crunch," the industry had become polarized. Only small companies with few assets and large corporations with the ability to self-insure tended to market contraceptives.

The pharmaceutical industry's high profit levels and "heavy" expenditures on marketing made it a frequent target for attack by political figures and consumer advocates. Critics suggested that the pharmaceutical companies priced drugs so high that only wealthy patients could afford treatment. Marketing expenditures were blamed for "overprescribing," or the tendency for physicians to rely too heavily on drugs for treatment. Marketing was also blamed for hiding from physicians information regarding side effects and contraindications in order to boost sales.

Outpatient Drug Coverage

Regulation of health care played an important role in the pharmaceutical industry. Increasingly complex regulations at the state and federal levels resulted in corresponding increases in costs of compliance. Further, the political nature of the regulatory system often resulted in uncertainty for the industry. For example, the outpatient-drug-coverage provision of the Medicare catastrophic health insurance bill was expected to have both a positive and negative impact on the U.S. market, with the overall impact uncertain. Scheduled to begin a three-year phase-in period in 1991, the plan was to cover 50 percent of Medicare beneficiaries' approved drug expenditures, after an annual deductible of $600 was met. Although the new coverage was expected to expand the overall market, it also made the industry more dependent on the federal government, whose reimbursements were increasingly affected by cost constraints. Further, policies regarding other social issues, such as race or sex discrimination, abortion, and even environmental protection, came into play for those health care facilities that dealt with Medicare recipients. The documentation necessary to show compliance with the relevant regulations was sure to result in increased costs for facilities. Pharmaceutical company managers were uncertain what effect such regulation would have on specific products.

HOECHST CELANESE

Hoechst Celanese was a wholly-owned subsidiary of Hoechst AG of Frankfurt, Germany. Hoechst AG and its affiliates constituted the Hoechst Group, one of the world's largest multinational corporations, encompassing 250 companies in 120 nations. The Hoechst companies manufactured and conducted research on chemicals, fibers, plastics, dyes, pigments, and pharmaceuticals. The United States was the largest and fastest-growing segment for the Hoechst product lines and was often the key to establishing worldwide marketing capability.

Within its Life Sciences Group, Hoechst Celanese, in affiliation with Roussel-Uclaf (a French pharmaceutical company), provided leading products to the prescription-drug markets in the United States. The division was referred to as Hoechst-Roussel Pharmaceuticals Incorporated (HRPI). Exhibit 4 lists the primary prescription drugs provided by HRPI to the U.S. health care market.

The company also marketed stool softeners and laxatives, including Doxidan and Surfak, directly to consumers, and it was developing potential drugs for many conditions, including Alzheimer's disease, cardiovascular disease, some kinds of tumors, and diabetes. HRPI had not previously invested in research into contraceptives or abortion drugs.

ROUSSEL-UCLAF

Roussel-Uclaf, founded in Paris, France, was engaged in the manufacturing and marketing of chemical products for therapeutic and industrial use, perfumes, eyeglasses, and nutritional products. In addition, Roussel was one of the world's leading diversified

---

EXHIBIT 4   Hoechst-Roussel's Prescription Drugs

Drug Name	Description
Lasix (furosemide)	A widely prescribed diuretic.
Clarofan (cefotaxime)	One of the largest selling third-generation cephalosonn antibiotics used to treat infections.
Topicort (desoximetasone)	A steroid applied to the skin.
Streptasea (streptokinase)	A product used to dissolve clots in blood vessels, e.g., in the treatment of heart attack.
Trental (pentoxifylline)	Improves arterial blood flow, and is used to treat intermittent claudication (leg pain associated with arteriosclerosis).
Diabeta (glyburide)	An oral antidiabetic agent used in the treatment of non-insulin-dependent diabetes.

Source: Hoechst AG *1998 Annual Report.*

---

pharmaceutical groups. Within its pharmaceutical group, Roussel poured its research dollars into a wide range of product categories, including antibiotics, diuretics, steroids, and laxatives.

Roussel employed 14,759 people, and its 72 subsidiaries yielded a total net income of more than $84 million in 1988. Ownership was held by two groups: the German company Hoechst AG, with 54.5 percent of common stock, and the French government with 36 percent.

In 1979, George Teutsch and Alain Belanger, chemists at Roussel-Uclaf, synthesized chemical variations on the basic steroid molecule. Some of the new chemicals blocked receptors for steroids, causing inhibition of the effects of the steroids, including the hormones involved in sexual reproduction. Because of the controversy surrounding birth control, Roussel had maintained a company policy not to develop drugs for the purpose of contraception or abortion and did not want to pursue research into the type of compounds that had been synthesized by Teutsch and Belanger. However, Dr. Etienne-Emile Baulieu, one of Roussel's research consultants, argued persuasively that such compounds represented a revolutionary breakthrough and might have many important uses other than those involved with reproductions and Roussel continued its research. The research led directly to the discovery, by Dr. Baulieu, of RU 486, and Roussel began manufacturing the drug in the early 1980s.

HISTORY

The trade name for RU 486, a synthesized steroid compound, was Mifepristone. The company referred to the product as a "contragestive," something between a contraceptive and an abortifacient, and marketed it as an alternative to surgical abortion. Like birth control, it could prevent a fertilized egg from implanting on the uterine wall and developing. It could also ensure that an implanted egg "sloughed off" or detached, making the product more like a chemical abortion. Its use was primarily intended for first-trimester pregnancies, because if it were taken up to 49 days after conception, it was 95 percent successful. In the office of the doctor or woman's health center, a woman would take a 600-milligram dose of RU 486. She would return two days later for a prostaglandin injection or pill, which would result in a vaginal blood flow two to five days later that was comparable to that of a menstrual period and that lasted approximately one week. A follow-up visit to her doctor would then determine whether the abortion was complete and make sure the bleeding had been controlled. If the fertilized egg was not completely expelled, a surgical abortion could then be performed. Researchers believed that the success rate would approach 100 percent when dosage levels were more defined. A few patients did feel slight nausea and cramps. Complications were rare, but it was recommended that the drug be taken under a physician's care because of the potential for heavy bleeding or the failure to abort.

The drug was first offered to the French market in September 1988. During the time it was on the market, 4,000 women used the drug, reporting a 95.5 percent success rate. However, during this period strong protests and proposed worldwide boycotts of Hoechst products (Roussel's German parent company), brought about the removal of RU 486 from the market and all distribution channels. Dr. Baulieu said the company's decision was "morally scandalous." At this point the French government, which owned 36 percent of Roussel-Uclaf, intervened. Two days after the pill's removal, Health Minister Claude Evin ordered RU 486 back into production and distribution in France, saying, "The drug is not just the property of Roussel-Uclaf, but of all women. I could not permit the abortion debate to deprive women of a product that represents medical progress." After that, the product had been sold only to authorized clinics. More than 100 French women took the drug each day. Thus, approximately 15 percent of all French abortions were conducted through the use of RU 486.

Because RU 486 triggered such strong emotion for and against its use, Roussel management was hesitant to make it available to the world. A Roussel researcher, Dr. Eduoard Sakiz, commented: "We just developed a compound, that's all, nothing else. To help the woman.... We are not in the middle of the abortion debate." Roussel held the patent to the compound, but it willingly supplied it for investigations around the world.

The only U.S. research on RU 486 was a joint effort of the Population Council, a nonprofit research organization in New York City, and the University of Southern California. Early results showed a 73 percent efficacy rate. Shortly after the drug became legal in France, China was able to officially license the use of the drug and by 1991 was close to manufacturing the drug itself. In 1990, Roussel management decided to market RU 486 to Great Britain, Sweden, and Holland as well.

It was generally believed that groups opposed to abortion under any circumstances had been largely responsible for keeping the drug out of the United States. Similarly, interest in research on the drug in the United States had apparently been curtailed by the intimidating tactics of the antiabortion groups. No U.S. drug maker had sought a license from Roussel. However, other compounds, similar to RU 486, were in the process of development by pharmaceutical companies both in the United States and worldwide.

No long-term risks or effects had been found to result from continuous use of the drug, nor were any problems expected from its occasional use. There was no information about how the drug might affect a fetus if the woman decided to continue her pregnancy after RU 486 failed, because the limited number of reported failures had all been followed by surgical abortions. Some studies reported that the drug seemed to suppress ovulation for three to seven months after use. One medical journal did report that use of the drug created birth defects in rabbits, but the results could not be duplicated in rats or monkeys.

RU 486's primary function was obviously that of an abortifacient. It was thought that the drug was particularly beneficial for three segments of the population. First, it would be important in the developing nations, where many women lacked access to medical facilities and the anesthetics needed for surgical abortion. Second, it would be useful among teenagers, whose use of contraceptives was erratic at best. Third, it would be useful for women who for various reasons were unable to use other methods successfully.

Secondary markets were potentially available as well because RU 486 functioned by inhibiting progesterone. The drug could, therefore, be beneficial in the treatment of Cushing's disease, in which an overactive adrenal gland releases too much of a steroid similar to progesterone. The drug could also be used to treat types of cancer that depend on progesterone for growth, such as tumors of the breast and other cancers of the reproductive system, and endometriosis (abnormal growth of uterine lining). In addition, RU 486 had potential for treatment of the nearly 80,000 women yearly who have ectopic pregnancies, a dangerous condition in which the egg develops outside the uterus.

In France, the availability of RU 486 was limited, and the product was used only under medical supervision. Because of these conditions the price was high, about $80 (U.S. dollars). Industry analysts believed that with larger markets and an increased production scale, the cost of the drug could be reduced in the United States. U.S. industry consultants believed that when drug companies identified the large profit potential associated with RU 486, U.S. interest in the drug would grow.

POLITICAL AND LEGAL ENVIRONMENT

The management of Hoechst-Roussel faced many problems with the introduction of RU 486 into the United States. The process of obtaining FDA approval was not likely to begin without the vocal support of American women who saw the drug as an important means to achieve more personal and political control over their fertility. The process of satisfying FDA requirements was likely to require considerable time and expense. Despite criticisms, the FDA had shown little inclination to reduce the time required for licensing new drugs, and the politically sensitive aspects of RU 486 were unlikely to speed the process.

Although the approval process for RU 486 could have, in theory, been significantly shortened because of the test data already generated by foreign researchers, no American company had yet petitioned the FDA to even begin the process. The standards required before the FDA would approve a new drug were (1) safety for the recommended use and (2) substantial evidence of efficacy. The clinical trials and testing occurred in three phases. Statistically, of every 20 drugs that entered clinical testing under the FDA, only one would ultimately be approved for the market. It frequently cost a pharmaceutical company up to $125 million and 15 years to move a contraceptive from the lab to approval for the market.

With RU 486, the FDA had apparently resolved to be even more restrictive than normal. Special policies and exceptions to normal FDA rules had been enacted. Under normal circumstances, the FDA allowed patients to ship certain unapproved drugs into the country if the drugs were to be used to treat life-threatening conditions. The agency refused to apply these rules to RU 486. FDA Commissioner Frank Young had written to a Congressional representative that the FDA would not permit RU 486 to be imported into the United States for personal use—for *any* reason.

The FDA did not, however, change an established rule that might permit RU 486 to be imported for the purpose of a "secondary use" such as the treatment of breast cancer. The FDA did not have jurisdiction to regulate the administration of a drug by a physician, so a doctor could theoretically prescribe RU 486, which had been presumably imported for treatment of breast cancer, for the purpose of inducing abortions. However, the potential liability for a physician who chose to prescribe RU 486 in this manner was probably sufficient to render this possibility remote.

RU 486 was not without its advocates. The National Academy of Sciences recommended that RU 486 be marketed in the United States, but also reported that for that to be possible, the FDA would have to streamline its stringent rules for the approval of new contraceptives. It also recommended that pharmaceutical companies be given federal protection from liability suits so they would be encouraged to reenter the contraceptive business.

If the federal government approved the pill, an individual state could not limit a doctor's decision to prescribe it. The fundamental tenet of the U.S. Supreme Court decision *Roe v. Wade* was that abortion in the first trimester should remain free from intrusive regulation by the state. Thus *Roe v. Wade* would permit U.S. use of RU 486 as an abortifacient to be administered under close medical supervision. The remote possibility of use of RU 486 as a monthly antifertility drug would also be well within abortion law, and it perhaps would allow RU 486 to be treated under law as a contraceptive.

Paradoxically, some observers argued that the United States was most likely to witness the appearance of RU 486 if the *Roe v. Wade* decision were overturned and abortion again became illegal. It was suggested that a black market for the pill would evolve to meet the need for illegal abortions. Dr. Sheldon Siegel of the Rockefeller Foundation stated, "If there is a serious attempt to constrain further progress and further knowledge about RU 486, then it is likely that a black market manufacturer and supply system would develop."[1] The black-market scenario posed very serious health risks for women. Many could suffer side effects, especially in the absence of medical supervision. Still more frightening was the idea that women using the pill illegally would not have access to the backup of safe surgical abortion.

THE CONTRACEPTIVE INDUSTRY

As of 1991 there were nearly 6 million unwanted pregnancies each year in the United States, and as a result, there were 1.5 million to 2 million abortions. Yearly, there were 500,000 pregnancy-related deaths, and 200,000 of those were from improperly performed abortions.[2] Up to half of these unwanted pregnancies and deaths could have been prevented if women had more birth control options. In 1991 American contraceptive research had come to a virtual halt, causing the United States to fall far behind other countries in developing new techniques. In the early 1980s, 11 companies in the United States did research in the contraceptive field, but by 1991 only two were engaged in such studies. Political opposition and the possibility of large liability suits appeared to be the most important reasons for the decline in focus on these drugs.

In 1991 several "morning after" abortifacients had been approved by the FDA for use in the United States. These drugs, based on prostaglandins, which are powerful hormones that can cause serious side effects, were distributed only to hospitals approved by the manufacturer, the Upjohn Company. The drugs were only available by prescription and under the most controlled conditions. The FDA allowed the drugs to be used only for second-trimester pregnancies. The drugs were neither advertised to the public nor promoted to physicians by company sales representatives. Likewise, samples of the

---

[1] *60 Minutes,* April 9, 1989.

[2] *Time,* 26 February 1990: 44.

drugs were not provided to the medical profession. Jessyl Bradford, spokeswoman for Upjohn, stated, "We believe that our commitment to provide a safe and effective alternative to saline and surgical procedures is a responsible one. However, we do not promote abortion. It is an individual decision, made in consultation with a physician. We make no effort to influence such decisions."[3]

The contraceptive market was relatively small; its value was about $1 billion yearly worldwide. Within this market, $700 million was accounted for by the use of oral contraceptives. There were, however, nearly 3 million women in the United States who used nonoral methods.[4] The profit margin on contraceptives was very high. To illustrate, the U.S. government, buying in bulk for shipment overseas, was able to buy a monthly supply of birth control pills for about 18 cents, whereas the average consumer paid about $12 a month. The leader in the contraceptive field was a company named Ortho, which sold contraceptive pills, diaphragms, spermicides, and other products for family planning (e.g., home pregnancy kits). Ortho was continuing to develop improved oral contraceptives that would provide better cycle control and have fewer side effects; however, as mentioned previously, the estimated cost of development of a contraceptive from the laboratory to the market was estimated at $125 million.

Although pro-life forces attributed the decline in contraceptive development in the United States to their efforts, companies and outside experts argued that the reduction was the result of three main factors: high research costs, relatively low potential profit, and the enormous risk that liability suits presented. Robert McDonough, spokesman for Upjohn Company, said, "[Upjohn] terminated its fertility research program in 1985 for two reasons. There was an adverse regulatory climate in the U.S.; it was increasingly difficult to get fertility drugs approved. And there was a litigious climate.... Litigation is terribly expensive, even if you win."[5]

In 1988, an $8.75 million judgment was passed against GD Searle in favor of a woman injured by the company's Copper-7 intrauterine device. Similarly, Dalkon Shield cases forced the AH Robbins Company into bankruptcy. In the late 1980s, AH Robbins was forced to establish a $615 million trust fund to compensate victims of IUD-caused pelvic infections and deaths. Such settlements made liability insurance for contraceptive manufacturers nearly impossible to obtain.

One of the few organizations in the United States that continued research on contraceptives was the Population Council, a nonprofit organization backed by the Rockefeller and Mellon foundations. The Population Council had been conducting U.S. studies of RU 486 on a license from the French developer. Additional support for contraceptive development was evident in proposed legislation that would provide $10 million for the "development, evaluation, and bringing to the marketplace of new improved contraceptive devices, drugs, and methods." If passed, the legislation would put the federal government into the contraceptive marketing business for the first time.

TECHNICAL ISSUES

RU 486 acts as an antiprogesterone steroid. Progesterone is a hormone that allows a fertilized embryo to be implanted on the inner wall of the uterus. Progesterone also

---

[3]"Letter to Columbia from Upjohn," 1987.

[4]*Business Week,* 1 April, 1985, p. 88.

[5]"Letter to Columbia from Upjohn," 1987.

reduces the uterus's responsiveness to certain contractile agents that may aid in the expulsion of the embryo. Additionally, progesterone helps the cervix to become firm and aids in the formation of a mucous plug that maintains the placental contents. All of these steps are necessary for an embryo to properly develop into a fetus. Without progesterone, which initiates the chain of events, an embryo cannot mature.

RU 486 masks the effects of progesterone by binding to the normal receptors of the hormone and prohibiting a proper reaction. The embryo cannot adhere to the uterine lining, so the subsequent changes do not occur and the normal process of menstruation (shedding of the uterine wall) begins.

The Population Council sponsored two studies (1987 and 1988) at the University of Southern California that examined the efficacy of RU 486. The tests were all conducted on women within 49 days of their last menstrual cycle. In the 1987 study, 100 milligrams per day for seven days was 73 percent effective, and 50 milligrams per day was 50 percent effective. In the 1988 study, one 600-milligram tablet was 90 percent effective.

The studies were conducted without prostaglandin, a compound that dramatically increases the effectiveness of RU 486. With prostaglandin, RU 486 was tested at 95.5 percent efficacy.

The general conclusions drawn from the Population Council research were that RU 486 was more effective at higher doses and that the earlier it was administered in the gestational period, the greater its efficacy.

OPPOSITION AND SUPPORT

The National Right to Life Committee of the United States played an important role in keeping RU 486 from being introduced in the United States. The group referred to RU 486 as the "death pill," claiming that a human life begins at conception and that RU 486 intervenes after conception. A former vice president of Students United for Life said in 1990:

> RU 486 is a poison just like cyanide or other poisons. Poisons are chemicals that kill human beings.... RU 486 is such a poison which kills the growing unborn human being.[6]

Antiabortionists also resisted the marketing of RU 486 because in clinical testing, women were required to agree to surgical abortions if the drug was unsuccessful. Pro-lifers also suggested that by simply taking a pill to end a pregnancy, a woman was evading the moral significance of the act. One antiabortion legislator, a Republican congressman from California, Robert Dornan, wrote a letter to his colleagues in 1986 to gain support to curtail federal funding for the testing of the pill. He stated his concerns as follows:

> The proponents of abortion want to replace the guilt suffered by women who undergo abortion with the moral uncertainty of self-deception. Imagine with the Death Pill, the taking of a pre-born life will be as easy and as trivial as taking aspirin.

Pro-life groups reacted strongly and even violently to prevent the drug's introduction into the U.S. market. The U.S. Right to Life group began its campaign by pressuring the French company that originated the pill, Roussel-Uclaf. At one point, as a result of

---

[6]Personal telephone conversation, April 1990.

the efforts and the influence of this group, which included bomb threats on Roussel executives, the company temporarily discontinued its production of RU 486. Subsequently the strategy of the group was focused on preventing the drug's introduction in the United States. The transfer of pressure to the U.S. domestic market occurred as a result of RU 486's expansion into the British and Chinese markets and the resultant fear that the United States was the next logical market for introduction.

Pro-life groups continued their letter-writing campaign to Roussel and extended the campaign to Roussel's parent company Hoechst AG. Further, they threatened to boycott Hoechst's American subsidiary Hoechst Celanese. The right-to-life campaign succeeded in getting Hoechst to place a "quarantine" on the drug, limiting its distribution to current markets.

Another strategy used by antiabortionists included putting pressure on the U.S. Congress to limit federal funding for research on the drug. Such limitations would strongly impede the Food and Drug Administration approval process. At the same time, pro-life members of Congress continued to lobby for legislation to prohibit further testing. The position of the president, and the increasingly conservative character of the Supreme Court, suggested that the introduction of RU 486 would meet stiff resistance.

In addition to the antiabortion concerns, pro-life groups and some feminist groups were concerned over the short and long-term physical dangers associated with the use of the drug. Advocates for the pill stressed that a main advantage of the drug was that it was a "safe" method of abortion compared with the probabilities of injury associated with surgical abortion. The safety claim was largely unsubstantiated, however, due to the lack of available objective test results. According to the *Yale Journal of Law and Feminism*, "The level of ignorance about the long-term effects of RU 486 makes it premature to apply the adjective 'safe.'"[7] Although Dr. Baulieu stated that studies had been performed using rabbits and immature human eggs, no direct objective evidence from these tests had been provided to substantiate his claims of safety.

There were additional concerns that the drug could harm subsequent offspring or cause malformation in unsuccessful abortions. Baulieu admitted that there had been cases in which the drug was unsuccessful in causing the abortion and the women had foregone surgical abortion. He indicated that there had been no evidence of maldevelopment. RU 486 was said to be "quickly flushed from a woman's system, making long-term effects less likely." This claim had not yet been proved through empirical evidence.

Although the efficacy of RU 486 was increased significantly when used in conjunction with a prostaglandin, the possibility of incomplete abortion remained. Such a condition was dangerous because of the potential for the tissue remaining in the uterus to cause infection. The threat to the health and life of the woman was, therefore, a reasonable concern.

The final concern that pro-lifers had about the dangers of RU 486 was that it had been proved to be ineffective on ectopic pregnancies, pregnancies that occur in the fallopian tubes or the ovary rather than in the uterus. The concern was that the number of ectopic pregnancies in the United States was on the rise and that women with ectopic pregnancies who used RU 486 and thus believed themselves no longer pregnant were in danger of dying if their fallopian tubes burst.

Gynecologists and obstetricians were mixed in their views toward the introduction of RU 486 into the United States. Pressure from doctors belonging to the World Congress of Obstetrics and Gynecology had forced the French government to require

---

[7]*Yale Journal of Law and Feminism*, 1(75) 1989: 96.

Roussel-Uclaf to resume distribution of the drug after its 1988 withdrawal. However, some doctors considered the product to be unnecessary. One prominent gynecologist and obstetrician believed that there were other chemical alternatives available and stated:

> The drug will be a fiasco for whoever decides to market it due to the stink from Right to Life groups…. We already have similar forms of chemical abortifacients that are legal and are used in the U.S. For example, Ovral is used as a 'morning after' pill. In residency…when a rape victim came into the emergency room, she was given one dose of Ovral then and another one in the morning. This makes the uterus incapable of conception which is similar to the effects of RU 486. This method is 95.5 percent effective whereas RU 486 alone [without prostaglandins] is only up to 90 percent effective. Not many people are aware that this goes on so there is not much publicity.[8]

RU 486 was not without supporters. The controversy surrounding the drug elicited the attention of many consumer and political groups. Family planning establishments such as Planned Parenthood Federation of America, the World Health Organization, and the Population Council, and feminist groups such as the Committee to Defend Reproductive Rights, Boston Women's Health Book Collective, and the National Women's Health Network, all supported the drug. During the period that Roussel had stopped production and sales of RU 486, the World Congress of Gynecology and Obstetrics had planned to ask physicians to boycott Roussel products if the company did not reverse its decision. Kelli Conlin, president of National Organization for Women in New York, called for a campaign urging U.S. pharmaceutical companies to test abortion drugs such as RU 486. She said, "Companies cannot let these (anti-abortion) groups push them around. And that group is really a minority."[9]

Right-to-life groups considered RU 486 to be a particular threat because one of their main avenues of action had been picketing abortion clinics and making the process more difficult for those people who chose to terminate their pregnancies. RU 486 could be used in a doctor's office, thus making pickets and public demonstrations less effective. Further, the drug was to be used within the first seven weeks of pregnancy, and the emotional appeal of showing developed fetuses in danger of abortion would be limited because all that would be observed would be bleeding similar to menstruation. One fear of pro-life groups was that if RU 486 became common, the very term "abortion" could become obsolete. Dr. Baulieu told the *MacNeil-Lehrer News Hour* in September 1986, that "Abortion, in my opinion, should more or less disappear as a concept, as a fact, as a word in the future…."

If RU 486 were authorized for use, it would be possible for a woman to take the pill safely and privately very soon after missing her period without ever knowing whether she was actually pregnant or not. In fact, if used monthly, there was some question whether it should actually be labelled an "abortion drug." Depending on when it was taken, RU 486 worked virtually the same way as the "pill" or an IUD. Normally, the pill prevented pregnancy by suppressing ovulation, but certain forms (containing lower doses of hormones to reduce the side effects) occasionally failed to suppress ovulation and instead prevented the fertilized ovum from implanting in the uterus. The IUD, too, worked by irritating the uterus and preventing implantation. If RU 486 were used within eight days of fertilization, it brought about the same effect.

---

[8]Personal telephone conversation, April 1990.

[9]*The New York Times*, 27 October 1988, pp. Al, B18.

One of the reasons given most often in support of RU 486 was safety. The United States had one of the highest percentages of accidental pregnancies in the industrialized world. According to the World Health Organization, "Surgical abortions [in the world] kill 200,000 women each year. Companies are retreating from research in abortion for fear of controversy, special interest pressure, and product liability questions—creating a major health care crisis."[10]

Likewise, there were increased safety problems when an abortion was postponed until later stages of pregnancy. Women facing an unwanted pregnancy often attempted to avoid the physically and emotionally painful abortion decision by ignoring it. If the abortion options were less harsh, it was thought that many women would face up to their situations more immediately and, therefore, more safely. Polls indicated that "Americans tend to oppose early abortions much less fervently and in fewer numbers than late abortions."[11]

Pro-life groups argued that conception is equivalent to fertilization, thus making RU 486 a form of chemical abortion. However, the federal courts and the American College of Obstetrics and Gynecology defined "conception" as implantation. In 1986, the Federal Appeals Court overturned an Illinois law that had used the pro-life definition in its legislation pertaining to abortion. The implantation definition was based on the fact that 40 percent to 60 percent of all fertilized ova fail to implant. Some pro-choice advocates suggested that if the pro-life argument were carried to its logical (but absurd) conclusion, women should be required to take progesterone to encourage implantation and prevent accidental death of the fertilized ova.

One of the most significant reasons for support for the introduction of RU 486 was the improvement it provided over other abortion options. With RU 486, there would be "no waiting, no walking past picket lines, no feet up in stirrups for surgery." In many cases, abortion clinics would be unnecessary. The clinics, instead, could be replaced by a few 24-hour emergency clinics that could treat any potential complications. It would make the abortion decision much more a personal matter. In some cases it would remove the psychological agony of deciding on an abortion at all. Women who took the pill just a few days after missing their period would never even know if they had been pregnant. Considering the extreme emotional trauma an abortion often caused, this was considered by supporters to be a great benefit. Finally, the cost of RU 486 would make it much more attractive than other methods. According to a *Newsweek* article, "If RU 486 is approved, Planned Parenthood plans to make it available free or 'at cost' at its family planning centers."[12]

A number of industry observers suggested that the availability of RU 486 in the U.S. market was inevitable. They argued that there were enough people who supported RU 486 for a black market to develop. Such a market was even more likely because the drug was already legal and easily available in other countries. Some radical groups even called for their members to support the illegal use of RU 486. Norma Swenson of the Boston Women's Health Book collective argued that RU 486 would save so many women from death by "botched abortions" that it would be worth it for women's groups to encourage its underground use. According to Swenson, "Using RU 486… would be a type of civil disobedience."

[10]*Business Week,* 14 November, 1988.

[11]Mishel, D. R., *American Journal of Obstetrics and Gynecology,* June, 1988, pp. 1307–1312.

[12]*Newsweek,* 29 December, 1988, p. 47

CONCLUSION

The management of Hoechst-Roussel held the legal and moral responsibility for the decision regarding introduction of RU 486 to the United States. It was clear that, regardless of its direction, the decision would have far-reaching implications for vast numbers of people—not only Hoechst-Roussel's stockholders and customers, but also U.S. society as a whole. It was also evident that the pressures being brought to bear would continue to build.

InterMark: Designing UNICEF's Oral Rehydration Program in Zambia

Ronald Stiff

The setting sun gave a pink tone to the Washington skyline across the Potomac as the jets glided over the river to National Airport in early August 1991. Allison Boyd enjoyed the view, but her thoughts were far away. For weeks she had been occupied with the children of Zambia. As a project manager for InterMark, an international consulting firm, she had been working for the past six months on UNICEF's oral rehydration program for reduction of diarrheal disease in Zambia. Her final recommendations were due in a week.

United Nations International Children's Emergency Fund (UNICEF) had contracted with InterMark to recommend how UNICEF should spend their funds in the next three years to reduce the incidence of diarrheal disease, primarily through increased use of oral rehydration salts (ORS). UNICEF had so far spent $87,000 in 1991 to donate imported ORS to the Ministry of Health for free distribution to hospitals and clinics. They were willing to spend between $87,000 and $113,000 annually for purchase of ORS or for alternative programs that would meet UNICEF program objectives:

- To substantially reduce infant and child deaths and illnesses associated with diarrheal disease
- To maximize the likelihood of sustainability after the withdrawal of UNICEF funds in three years

The assignment had been interesting and challenging. During two, month-long visits to Zambia, Allison had gathered a large amount of information. Now she was expected to provide written recommendations on increasing the effectiveness of ORS use in Zambia and to make a presentation to the UNICEF staff.

ZAMBIA

The Republic of Zambia (formerly Northern Rhodesia) attained independence from Britain in 1964. Zambia, which in 1990 had a population of 8 million, is situated on an elevated plateau in south-central Africa. A land-locked country with an area of 752,614 square kilometers (slightly larger than the state of Texas), Zambia is dependent on

This case was prepared by Professor Ronald Stiff of the University of Baltimore, as a basis for class discussion. It is not intended to illustrate either effective or ineffective handling of an administrative situation.

either its neighbors or air transport for links with the countries outside Africa. Exhibit 1 is a map of Africa; Zambia is shown in black.

For many years, the mining of copper dominated the Zambian economy, although its contribution had declined significantly in recent years. The agricultural sector received the active support of the government and international donors, but it had never lived up to expectations, and agricultural exports were declining. The per capita GNP, which stood at US$290 in 1988, gave Zambia a ranking of eighteenth poorest country worldwide, as determined by the World Bank. Per capita GNP in 1991 was expected to be as low as US$150, or 10,500 kwacha.[1] Many households earned less than K2,800 per month.

HEALTH EXPENDITURES AND STATUS

In 1986 the government spent K250 per capita for health care. Estimation of morbidity (illnesses) and mortality (deaths) levels and trends were uncertain in many developing countries, including Zambia, because of problems with the quality of measurements. The national infant mortality rate fell from around 130 deaths per 1,000 in the mid-1950s to about 115 in the early 1970s. This was still considerably higher than the infant mortality rate in the 25 highest-income countries, which was 9 per 1,000 in 1988. The proportion of children dying between birth and their fifth birthday (childhood mortality) fell

---

[1]The kwacha is the Zambian currency. In 1991, K70 equaled US$1.

EXHIBIT 1:   Zambia's Location in Southern Africa

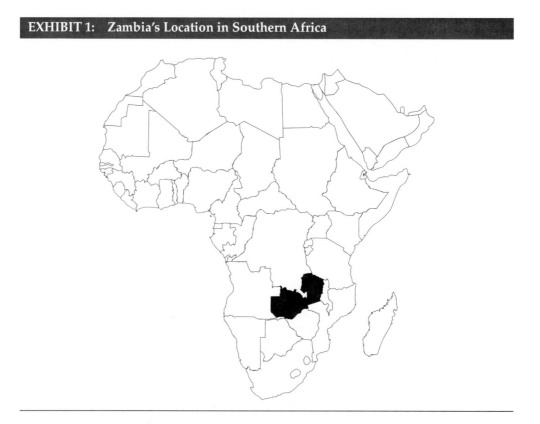

from 22 percent in the mid-1950s to 19 percent in the 1970s, where it remained through 1991. One of every five children died before reaching age 5.

These national statistics, which were within the general range of other countries in central and southern Africa, concealed regional differentials in mortality that had implications for the effective delivery of health programs. Childhood mortality estimates for the 1960s showed a clear general pattern: the highest mortality was in the rural provinces, the lowest mortality was in the two most urbanized provinces, and there was an intermediate level in Southern Province. The infant mortality rate for the 1960s ranged from 82 (Copperbelt Province) to 175 (Eastern Province), giving a national average of 121.

Boyd analyzed the most current Zambian statistical reports and grouped the Zambian provinces into three regions to evaluate geographical differences (Exhibit 2). She noted that the central provinces, along the main rail line, were far more urbanized than the provinces she grouped as northeastern and northwestern. The lower population densities and less-developed road systems in these areas made delivery of health care services challenging. Allison wondered if UNICEF had the resources to achieve widespread distribution of ORS in both rural and urban regions.

This infant mortality pattern fit well with what was known of background factors such as income levels, general economic development, nutrition, education, and fertility levels. The leading causes of mortality at Zambia's health centers in 1981 were measles (26 percent), pneumonia (14 percent), malnutrition-anemia (14 percent), malaria (10 percent), and diarrheas (10 percent). The leading causes of outpatient morbidity in children under 15 years were respiratory illnesses, malaria, diarrhea, and injuries, most of which were preventable. Diarrhea cases for children under 15 years of age at health centers in 1986, 1987, and 1988 were:

1986	805,880
1987	758,151
1988	842,142

EXHIBIT 2　Population Statistics for Zambia

	Northwest[a]	Central[b]	Northeast[c]	Total Zambia
Population	990,643	4,459,486	2,368,318	7,818,447
% of Total Population	12.8	57.0	30.2	100
Population under 5 Years of Age	200,704	903,492	479,821	1,584,017
Area km^2	252,000	232,000	268,000	752,000
Population Density/sq km	4	19	9	10
% Urban	20.8	68.4	17.7	48
Population per Physician—1988	12,926	17,380	23,449	15,544
Expected Births	49,037	220,744	117,232	387,013
% Births in Medical Units—1988	27.7	37.2	21.7	31.3

Note: All figures 1990 except as noted.
[a]Combines North-Western and Western provinces.
[b]Combines Central, Copperbelt, Lusaka, and Southern provinces.
[c]Combines Eastern, Luapula, and Northern provinces.
Sources: *Country Profile, Republic of Zambia: 1989–1990*, Central Statistical Office: Lusaka. (2) *Bulletin of Health Statistics: 1978–1988*, Ministry of Health, Health Information Unit: Lusaka. (3) *Monthly Digest of Statistics: January 1991*, Central Statistical Office: Lusaka.

Public Sector Health Services

Most patients received free medical care through Ministry of Health, missionary, military, or mining-company facilities. The medical facilities existing in 1988 are given in Exhibit 3. The total number of public health care providers in 1987 was 9,499, consisting of 500 physicians, 1,100 clinical officers, 5,250 nurses, 1,135 midwives, 531 health assistants, and 983 community health workers.

Private Sector Health Services

There were several private medical practitioners, primarily seeing patients in Zambia's capital, Lusaka. In addition, approximately 10,000 traditional healers provided services throughout the country. It was estimated that as many as 9 out of 10 patients sought help from traditional healers before coming for "scientific" treatment; some continued traditional medicine while hospitalized. The cost of the traditional healer's consultation fees could be greater than that paid to private medical doctors for the same symptoms.

THE CAUSES AND TREATMENT OF DIARRHEA

Diarrhea results from consuming contaminated food or water. The percentage of Zambian households supplied with piped water and sewage systems declined in the later half of the 1980s. In 1991, about 50 percent of the total population had access to water defined as "reasonably" safe by World Health Organization standards.

Diarrhea was one of the most critical health problems in Zambia. For children under 5 years of age, who constituted more than 18 percent of the total population, diarrhea was a leading cause of morbidity and mortality. In 1982, diarrhea accounted for up to 13.5 percent of total admissions, 19.2 percent of total outpatient visits, and 13.2 percent of total deaths in rural health centers. It was also responsible for 7.8 percent of total

---

EXHIBIT 3   Zambian Medicial Facilities in 1988

Facility	Number
Hospitals	
Government	42
Mission	29
Mines	11
Clinics: Rural	
Government	643
Mission	64
Clinics: Urban	
Government	142
Mines	75
Total	1,006

Source: *Bulletin of Health Statistics*, Ministry of Health, Health Information Unit, Republic of Zambia.

admissions, 17.3 percent of total outpatient visits, and 8.6 percent of total deaths in the hospitals.

Management of diarrhea cases involves restoring and maintaining fluids by oral rehydration and, in a few cases, intravenous therapy. The treatment regimen often includes improving or maintaining nutritional status by appropriate feeding (including breast-feeding) both during and after the diarrhea, as well as treating fevers and other complications with drugs. The most effective treatment is drinking oral rehydration salts, as recommended by the World Health Organization and UNICEF. Oral rehydration salts contain three essential salts (the formulation of ORS has some similarities to sports drinks such as Gatorade). The label text from a typical packet is shown in Exhibit 4. At the onset of diarrhea, weak tea and juice are often given to children, but a correctly prepared salt-sugar solution is better. ORS is, however, by far the most effective means of establishing rehydration. Health care educators consider it essential that parents understand that a dehydrated infant can die in less than 24 hours and know how to provide the child with the best available rehydration solution. Caregivers should be trained to recognize when a case is serious enough to require that the child be taken to a trained health care provider.

Diarrhea produces severe dehydration especially damaging to the health of infants. The typical sequence leading to diarrhea deaths, and factors to reduce diarrheal deaths at each stage, are given in Exhibit 5. In this sequence, ORS does not stop diarrhea but reduces dehydration by replacing fluids and electrolytes. Use of antidiarrheal drugs, such as kaolin, codeine, or activated charcoal, can cause severe, life-threatening

EXHIBIT 4   Label Text from 1-Liter ORS Foil Packet

**ORAL
REHYDRATION SALTS**

Each sachet Contains the equivalent of:

Sodium Chloride:	3.5 g.
Potassium Chloride:	1.5 g.
Trisodium Citrate, dihydrate:	2.9 g.
Glucose Anhydrous:	20.0 g.

DIRECTIONS
Dissolve in ONE LITER of drinking water.

To be taken orally—
Infants—over a 24 hour period
Children—over an 8 to 24 hour period,
according to age or as otherwise
directed under medical supervision.

CAUTION: DO NOT BOIL SOLUTION

MANUFACTURER

Jianas Bros., Packaging Co.
Kansas City, Missouri, U.S.A.

EXHIBIT 5   Typical Sequence Leading to Diarrhea Deaths and Factors to Reduce Mortality at Each Stage

Stage	Factors Reducing Mortality
1. Low per capita income	Better distribution of national income Increase national productivity Additional donor aid in cash and materials
2. Low-protein diet 3. Malnourishment	{ Add soya to mealy meal (corn meal) { Add Kapenta (fish) to mealy meal
4. Poor sanitation	Effective sewage system Use of latrines Proper disposal of the stools of young children Pure water Boiled water
5. Air or water infection	Increase persons immunized Breast feeding Washing hands Well-cooked foods Increase AIDS prevention programs
6. Diarrhea episode 7. Dehydration	{ IV Solutions { Manufactured oral rehydration solutions { Increased availability of health centers { Effectively trained health care professionals and parents { Home-prepared oral rehydration solutions { Home-prepared fluids
8. Diarrhea death	

reactions in young children because these drugs do not reduce dehydration. Boyd found that some pharmacists encouraged use of these drugs either because they were not educated in the use of ORS or because they wanted to sell products that were higher-priced than ORS.

Health care educators believed that ideal communications directed to parents should include this information:

- Diarrhea, any diarrhea, is a potentially serious illness for children.
- A child who has diarrhea should receive appropriate and sufficient fluids and food while diarrhea persists and should receive extra fluids and food after an episode of diarrhea for a period equal to the duration of the illness.
- The parents of a child with diarrhea should observe and monitor the child for danger signs, persistence of diarrhea, and the presence of blood in the stool.
- Children with these danger signs must be taken for appropriate medical treatment as soon as possible.

THE NEED AND DEMAND FOR ORS

Without reliable health statistics, determining the need and demand for ORS was diffi-cult. In 1988, 842,142 new cases of diarrhea in children under 15 years of age were treated at hospitals or health centers. Many cases did not receive preadmission care. Additionally, the population under age 5 was increasing at a rapid rate. In 1991, 400,000 births were expected, with as many as 100,000 to new mothers, who were unlikely to understand the proper care of sick infants because virtually no prenatal education was provided. It was estimated that there were about five episodes of diarrhea in each of the 1.6 million children under 5 years of age each year; at least one-third of these required ORS. There were at least 1 million more cases in older children and adults each year. Effective treatment required about 2 liters of ORS. Treating these cases with ORS would require 6 million 1 liter packets or the equivalent in packets of other sizes. (In Zambia, ORS was supplied as concentrated salts, requiring the user to mix with the correct quantity of water.) Only about half of this amount was available, either through free distribution at health clinics or hospitals or for sale in the marketplace.

In fact, the demand for ORS was less than the actual need for it, as a result of the following factors:

- Limited awareness of its benefits
- Shortages of the ORS supplied at no cost through hospitals and health centers by the Ministry of Health
- The distance and time involved in obtaining free ORS from these sources (It was estimated that 25 percent of the population lay outside a 12-kilometer radius of a health clinic or hospital.)
- Frequent long waiting lines for health care services
- Limited marketplace (that is, private) distribution because of cost (As with most products, demand varied with the price charged.)

The need for education of parents was extensive. Many parents with children under 15 years of age were not knowledgeable about oral rehydration therapy. Adult literacy in 1985 was reported to be 67 percent. Boyd thought that literacy was likely to be lower than reported because the average number of years in school was only 2.6.

FACTORS IMPEDING CONTROL OF DIARRHEAL DISEASE

Some factors impeding control of diarrheal disease present in the general economic and social environment applied specifically to control of the disease itself—problems with the supply of ORS and lack of mothers' knowledge of how to use it. Other constraints applied more broadly to delivery of all primary health care service but had a direct bearing on the success of the ORS program.

General Environment

Although Zambia had the most highly urbanized population in sub-Saharan Africa, about 60 percent of the population lived in rural areas, where there were few points of population concentration. Household contact between mothers and the health system were common for the 75 percent of families who lived within 12 kilometers of clinics (average of five contacts per year for children under 1 year of age); however, contact was far less likely for those who lived further away. Distribution of ORS packets was expensive, and delays were frequent in many rural areas where the means of transportation were limited.

Cash available in households for purchases of ORS, radio batteries, public transport, and even "mealy meal" (the local term for corn meal, the major food staple) was scarce. The typical high-end expenditures for traditional medical treatment were generally between K70 and K350 for a routine course of treatment. Many households had monthly incomes of K2,800 or less. This highlighted the need for education about the most cost-effective medical treatments, such as ORS for diarrhea. There was a large proportion of female-headed households in rural areas as a result of male labor migration to urban communities in search of higher wages. The approximately 25 percent of rural households headed by females were those most likely to be at the bottom of the income scale. Because these mothers needed to produce income, they were less likely to have time to seek health services, get health education, or give health care at the onset of diarrhea. Because of financial and time constraints, these households were less likely to participate in, or benefit from, a treatment program such as ORS.

Health System Constraints

The overall problems in Zambia's health care delivery system were shortages of field-level staff, shortages of supplies, inadequate support measures, and lack of appropriate supervision at all levels. Field supervision suffered from shortages of staff and inadequate provision of transportation. The large percentage of attrition found among trained community health workers and other peripheral workers was felt by Boyd to be the result of infrequent or nonexistent supervisory visits. Workers at remote rural health clinics were likely to feel isolated in any case, and total lack of contact with supervisory personnel exacerbated the problem, contributing to high employee turnover. Ideally, the supervisor's role included in-service training, checking on procedures, reinforcement, and encouragement; all vital for good performance. This support was needed for workers in isolated areas, and transportation was very important.

Drastic cuts in the Ministry of Health budget made it unlikely that the ministry would be able to buy an adequate supply of ORS because most funds would go for essential hospital supplies. It was likely that the Ministry of Health would encourage donor assistance for ORS rather than supporting an oral rehydration therapy program directly or instituting a patient fee for drugs or services. Boyd thought that UNICEF would be required to play a larger role than the Ministry of Health during the next three years.

Constraints Specific to Control of Diarrheal Disease

Boyd visited hospitals and clinics with UNICEF physicians and observed inadequacies in diagnosis and treatment of diarrhea by all categories of health workers. There was a lack of awareness of the vital importance of oral rehydration therapy in clinical management and in-home use for early prevention of dehydration. Health workers said that diarrheal disease was not strongly emphasized in their education, suggesting a need for refresher courses.

Doctors and clinical officers (physicians' assistants) often delegated the dispensing of ORS and giving parents instructions in the use of ORS to nurses. Because nurses did not have the same credibility with clients as the doctors or clinical officers, clients were less likely to accept the recommended regimen. When the role of instructing parents in treatment of diarrhea fell to pharmacists, they often failed to recommend ORS at all, sometimes because of a lack of education but often because of a desire to boost profits by selling more-expensive drugs, which were often less-effective than ORS, and could even be harmful.

ORS could be manufactured either as a premixed solution in bottles or cardboard containers or as a powdered concentrate in foil packets to be mixed with water by the consumer. Although premixed ORS had the advantages of being mixed in the correct proportions and being sterile, it was significantly more expensive—up to eight times more costly—than the packets. Thus in developing countries, packets were used far more widely than the premixed solutions.

ORS in packets required careful mixing, with the correct proportion of salts to water. Although ideally the solution was supposed to be prepared with boiled water, use of unboiled water was unlikely to cause serious problems because most patients had developed a resistance to the impurities in the local water supply. Mixtures that were too diluted were less effective than correctly prepared solutions. The most serious mixing problem was excessive concentrations of salts, which could lead to severe illness and even death in infants.

The mixing of ORS was complicated by the lack of standardized 1-liter measuring containers in most rural Zambian households. To mix one 1-liter ORS packet, caregivers often had to measure the water in two 500-milliliter cups, a size that was more commonly available. Instructions for mixing could easily be misunderstood.

When ORS was not obtainable through the health care system, and the caregivers could not afford to buy it, it was possible to prepare a homemixed solution. However, home preparation was problematic, both because of the frequent unavailability of salt, sugar, and/or mixing containers and teaspoons and the lack of consumer knowledge of oral rehydration therapy. Incorrect formulations could be harmful to children, especially infants.

Boyd found that information provided to caregivers when oral rehydration therapy was promoted often did not state that ORS is not designed to stop the diarrhea but rather to maintain hydration throughout the disease course. Diarrhea often has a self-limiting course if the child is kept hydrated and there is no serious underlying cause. If this is not explained carefully to the caregivers, those who believe that ORS should stop the diarrhea are not only likely to end the therapy when the diarrhea does not cease immediately but also may be unlikely to use ORS therapy in future diarrheal episodes.

ALTERNATIVES FOR INCREASING THE USE OF ORS

Boyd considered several interrelated alternatives for increasing the use of oral rehydration therapy using ORS. These included how best to ensure a reliable supply of ORS, what method of distribution would be effective in reaching consumers, what method of packaging should be encouraged, what training in the use of ORS should be given to health care professionals, and how to best promote ORS therapy with consumers.

Supply

The major supply of ORS was from the Swedish International Development Agency, which included 150 one-liter packets of ORS in each essential-drug kit delivered monthly to the 707 rural health clinics. As a result the supply of ORS was greater in some rural health clinics than in urban areas. There was no inventory control in place to balance out supply and demand between the rural health clinics. Consequently, there could be several months' supply at some clinics and no ORS stock at all at others. The Swedish International Development Agency was considering increasing the number of ORS packets in each kit to 200 in 1992. They were also considering supplying some stocks at the district level for reallocation to clinics on an as-needed basis, developing methods to reallocate inventories, and distributing to urban clinics. Boyd was concerned that the Swedish International Development Agency's policies of free distribution were likely to have an effect on the motivation of private manufacturers and distributors of ORS.

UNICEF remained the most likely donor for additional ORS supplies; it could agree to help the Ministry of Health by continuing to donate imported 1-liter packets. In the past year 1.2 million 1-liter packets had been donated at a total cost of $87,000—about K5 per packet. UNICEF also had the option of supporting production by subsidizing the production of ORS packets by local manufacturers. UNICEF had done that in Haiti and Indonesia, where it paid the local producers the equivalent of the imported cost of packets.

The major constraint to this type of arrangement in Zambia was the high cost of the locally produced ORS packets. The approximate cost breakdown for local manufacturing of 1-liter packets of ORS is given in Exhibit 6. Packets were produced for free distribution at health clinics and hospitals through the Ministry of Health by the government-owned company, General Pharmaceutical Ltd., and at various times for sale in the private sector by Cadbury Schweppes' Zambian operations and the Zambian firms Gamma Pharmaceuticals and Interchem. A UNICEF grant of K7 million helped supply the equipment necessary for General Pharmaceutical to 2 million packets per year. (UNICEF's grant was estimated at half the total cost of production.) General Pharmaceutical Ltd. had produced 1.4 million 1-liter packets under the brand name Madzi-a-moyi (Water for Life) in the past year, but it had halted production due to the high cost of imported raw materials and packaging.

A small amount of the General Pharmaceutical Ltd. production was sold through about 100 government-owned pharmacies for K6 to K10. Although the low range of this

---

EXHIBIT 6   Local Manufacturing Costs for a 1-Liter Package of ORS

Materials	K3.58	
Labor	.80	
Direct Costs		K4.38
Factory Overhead		1.10
Production Cost		5.48
Company Overhead		1.33
Factory Cost		6.81
Profit Margin		1.19
Manufacturing Price		8.00

Notes: Costs are based on an annual production volume of 2 million packets. Retail price is higher due to markups. Costs for smaller packets are identical, except that materials cost is less per packet.
Source: Company interviews.

price appears to be less than the manufacturer's cost, those packets had been produced in 1990, when the kwacha had not devalued to its current level. The retail price was expected to be higher if General Pharmaceutical resumed production.

Gamma Pharmaceuticals and Interchem each had the capacity to manufacture 2 million 1-liter or 250-milliliter packets per year. Neither was producing ORS in 1991. Gamma used their packaging machine to produce other products, and Interchem had not been able to use their Korean-made machine for two years due to failure of a part. Distribution of drug products was either through deliveries to sales agents in the Copperbelt and Livingstone, or to general merchandise wholesalers who came to Lusaka to purchase ORS. There was also some direct distribution to pharmacies and other outlets in Lusaka.

The manufacturer's costs and prices were expected to be approximately the same for either manufacturer. Additional production capacity was expected to cost about K14 million for each 2 million units produced per year for either 1-liter or 250-milliliter packets. However, long delays were experienced in supplying equipment to General Pharmaceutical Ltd. due to shipping delays, building construction problems, and the need to install a three-phase electrical supply. Interchem's parent company was evaluating replacing its idled machine.

Cadbury Schweppes had recently received Ministry of Health approval to market orange-flavored ORS in 250-milliliter packets using the brand name Oresa (*oral rehydration salts*). They had manufactured 500,000 packets; 40,000 had been distributed directly to chemists (drugstores) to test market acceptance, and the remainder was in inventory. The manufacturer's price was K12, with a suggested retail price of K15. Some chemists, however, charged K18. Flavored ORS was neither encouraged nor discouraged by the World Health Organization, although at one time WHO had opposed flavored ORS due to the potential for unnecessary use and its increased cost relative to unflavored ORS.

Boyd noted that 300-milliliter soft drink bottles (Coke, Fanta, Torino, etc.) were widely available in Zambia (many were distributed by Cadbury) and could be used safely for mixing 250-milliliter ORS packets if the smaller-sized packets were widely marketed. Research at the University Teaching Hospital showed that children, even at very young ages, were more willing to drink flavored ORS and, as a result, consumed more total fluids than when given unflavored ORS. Cadbury Schweppes had the capacity to produce 18 million packets a year in one shift, using capacity that was currently used to produce powdered Kia-Ora, a children's drink that was similar to Kool-Aid. These ORS packets could be either 250-milliliter flavored or 1-liter unflavored. The manufacturing cost of the unflavored packets would be about the same for Cadbury as for other local manufacturers. The per packet cost of 250-milliliter flavored ORS was slightly more than that of 1 liter of unflavored. Cadbury could also supply either flavored or unflavored ORS in bulk packages for hospitals and health clinics.

Flavored ORS had been imported in limited quantities. Small quantities of Rehidrat, from Searle, were available in lemon-lime 250-milliliter packets for K30. ORS imported for resale, however, was subject to a 100 percent import duty under import substitution laws. An additional 200,000 to 400,000 packets were supplied annually by the Red Cross, churches, and other nongovernment organizations.

Cadbury was the only firm that had the potential to produce ORS in bottles. It was expected that the cost for 250-milliliter bottles would be about the same as for soft drinks—K40 per bottle, including a K20 bottle refund. Thus a 2-liter treatment would cost the consumer considerably more than the cost of buying packets—K320 without refund and K160 if bottles were returned.

It seemed unlikely that ORS could be priced cheaply enough for its low-income target consumers without some type of subsidy. An ORS price subsidy to manufacturers or importers could create a financial burden that would be intolerable over the long run. In the short term, UNICEF might use the value of the raw materials as a subsidy or provide promotional or educational services for branded products. Another option was for industry to offer a modest price to low-income consumers and still create revenues to help pay program costs by charging a much-higher price for a different, more "modern" product aimed at higher-income consumers.

Distribution

Even given substantial donor support for free ORS distribution through clinics and hospitals, there was a need for other modes of access to ORS, as well as a need to promote home-mix solutions. The commercial sector in Zambia offered several possibilities.

As a normal business practice in Zambia, a manufacturer established the recommended consumer price for the product. Trade discounts based on the recommended consumer price were 20 percent to retailers and 20 percent to trade channel members. Boyd conducted interviews with the general managers or the marketing managers of the major organizations that expressed an interest in distributing ORS. Each had a large number of potential retail outlets, as shown below:

Firm	No. of Potential Outlets
Gamma Pharmaceutical	1,000
Interchem	1,000
Cadbury Schweppes	5,000
Lyons Brooke Bond	2,200
Colgate-Palmolive	8,000

Gamma Pharmaceutical Gamma Pharmaceutical, which started activities in 1984, manufactured pharmaceutical products for the Zambia market and for export. It sold its products to private pharmacies, government and industry health facilities, and retail outlets including supermarkets. Gamma had a fleet of six delivery trucks and one van and two sales agents. Gamma was a sound, fast-growing company with a strong production and marketing team.

Interchem Interchem manufactured a variety of pharmaceutical products. Interchem's marketing manager was interested both in distributing ORS and in resuming production. They needed to either repair their existing packaging machine or purchase a new one. It was not certain that repair parts were available from the Korean supplier. A new machine would cost K14 million.

Cadbury Schweppes Cadbury Schweppes was a major producer of soft drinks, drink syrups, and other consumer packaged goods. Cadbury distributed its products direct to their retail outlets. Cadbury was evaluating flavored ORS and deciding if they should introduce Oresa throughout Zambia. They had about 460,000 packets in inventory and could begin production of additional packets within a month.

Lyons Brooke Bond Lyons Brooke Bond, Zambia, formerly a Lever Brothers company, was an independent firm incorporated in Zambia. Lyons Brooke Bond manufactured and distributed processed food products. The managing director of the company had shown an interest in distributing ORS, although Lyons did not handle any pharmaceutical products.

Colgate-Palmolive Colgate-Palmolive, one of the largest distributors in Zambia, had five sales agents, four delivery vans, five freight trucks, and more than 10 large wholesalers. The company manufactured and distributed personal care and hygiene products.

Evaluation of Distribution Alternatives

Boyd's review of distribution capabilities in Zambia offered several options in terms of cost-effectiveness, marketing opportunities, sustainability, and possible future self-sufficiency. Although historically the bulk of ORS had been distributed at no cost by nonprofit organizations, the commercial firms in Zambia could be enlisted in the implementation of an ORS program. These firms had strong experience in marketing, sound management capabilities and financial stability and well-developed infrastructures that allowed them access to thousands of retail outlets. All were interested in participating in an ORS marketing program, both as good corporate citizens and as business people interested in making a profit.

Boyd believed that these firms had a good understanding of the marketing environment in Zambia and that their existing distribution channels could provide an effective method of distributing ORS. One or more firms might be encouraged to make a long-term financial commitment to supplying ORS. However, she felt that there were several problems in encouraging increased participation by local manufacturers and distributors. Would the market price to consumers be too high to encourage appropriate use? Was the market large enough to encourage sufficient participation of manufacturers and distributors? Would free distribution by the government and other organizations reduce the private sector's interest in entering the market? Finally, would an oversupply be created as a result of competition, which would lead to either reduced quality control or withdrawals from the markets by manufacturers and distributors?

Packaging

As stated previously, the form of packaging had significant implications for correct use of ORS. ORS could be packaged as a premixed solution in bottles or cardboard containers or as powdered salts in 1-liter or 250-milliliter foil packets.

Premixed ORS The pros of using premixed ORS were:

- Premixed ORS was sterile.
- The consumer did not have to mix the salts with water, ensuring the correct proportions.
- Less-intense consumer education was required for use.
- One firm, Cadbury, had the in-place capacity to package premixed ORS in bottles.

The cons were:

- Only one firm had the capacity to produce bottles.
- Premixed ORS was as much as eight times more expensive per treatment to the consumer than packets.
- It required more space in delivery vehicles and on store shelves.
- Use of bottles would involve the deposit and return system, because Zambia's supply of bottles was limited.
- No Zambian firm had the capacity to produce cardboard containers suitable for liquid ORS.
- Use of cardboard would create waste and litter.

Packets

Boyd believed that using only one size packet—either the 250-milliliter or the 1-liter size—would be most effective. Distributing both risked potentially dangerous confusion. Whichever size was used, distributors would have to convey simple, consistent messages to caregivers and provide effective training and education. Following are the pros and cons of each size.

250-Milliliter Packet

Pros

- 300-milliliter soft drink bottles were widely available and could be used to mix 250-milliliter packets.
- 250-milliliter tea cups were widely available.

Cons

- Half a million 1-liter packets were already in the distribution system.
- Imported ORS was generally available in 1-liter packets.
- Bottlers of soft drinks could change bottle size at any time.
- If caregivers mixed 250-milliliter packets in 1-liter containers, ORS was less effective.

1-Liter Size Packets

Pros

- Half a million 1-liter packets already existed in the supply system.
- UNICEF's imported cost was less than that of local manufacturer's price.
- In case of emergency shortages of commercial ORS, UNICEF's 1-liter packets could be purchased economically.
- 500-milliliter cups were widely available.

Cons

- The variety of cup sizes available in homes and at retail outlets was increasing, and many cups of nonstandard size were available.
- If parents mixed 1-liter packets in 300-milliliter bottles, vomiting and serious damage to the heart and nervous system could result, especially in younger children.

Boyd's task for InterMark was to develop a sustainable ORS supply system—one that could continue beyond the three-year UNICEF horizon. A key question was when local production could begin and whether local production would provide a substantial, reliable supply of acceptable quality. If production was delayed or unreliable, UNICEF or another supplier would have to fill the gap with 1-liter packets.

TRAINING OF HEALTH CARE PROFESSIONALS

Physicians, nurses, clinical officers, pharmacists, and traditional healers were collectively responsible for setting standards for medical care. If any one of these groups did not understand and have confidence in oral rehydration therapy, it would be difficult to establish oral rehydration as the standard treatment for diarrhea in Zambia.

Physicians needed training in appropriate clinical management of infants and children with diarrhea. Physicians needed to go beyond eliciting statements of symptoms as a basis for prescribing treatment for diarrhea. The treatment basis should include a patient history, an examination, and therapeutic management. Because physicians were opinion leaders, it was desirable to make special efforts at the beginning of a program to inform them about oral rehydration therapy through seminars and refresher training courses.

Diarrheal Training Units

Diarrheal training units had been effective in training health care workers in other developing countries; however, only one such unit existed in Zambia. The purpose of diarrheal training units was to develop the skills and confidence of physicians and nurses in assessing and managing diarrhea. Participants attend clinical training sessions designed to teach them how to treat simple and complicated cases and how to communicate what they have learned to caregivers and colleagues.

Experience suggested that a three- to five-day training course was needed to be effective. This approach made training expensive. Also, some professionals found it difficult to leave their responsibilities for the required period. Because diarrheal training units emphasized the clinical approach, only relatively small numbers of professionals could be trained at any time. In effective diarrheal training units, the number of participants ranged from 5 to 15. In addition, the need to have enough diarrhea cases of various types for each trainee to handle meant that some diarrheal training units could be run only during the rainy season.

The only diarrheal training unit in Zambia was a World Health Organization-funded unit at the University Teaching Hospital in Lusaka that trained doctors and nurses. Boyd felt that additional diarrheal training units could be effective, but their costs needed to be evaluated. Costs involved in training are included in Exhibit 7.

PROMOTION

Zambians owned an estimated 3 million radios. There were two state-owned broadcasting stations: Radio Mulungushi, a popular station with a primarily urban listening audience, and Radio Zambia, which was primarily rural. There were as many as 250,000 television sets and one state-operated television station, which operated from 5 p.m. to midnight weekdays, with longer hours on the weekend. There were seven major languages; therefore, it was considered critical to advertise in English plus several other languages to reach the population effectively. A media rate card is provided in Exhibit 8.

Message Content

A major challenge for ORS advertising was to persuade consumers that restoring the child's activity and preventing dehydration was a sufficient reason for using the product. Most communications and promotions efforts had chosen not to deliver "negative" messages such as "oral rehydration therapy does not stop diarrhea" or "antidiarrheals do not stop diarrhea," although both are factual. Programs chose to address these issues in other ways, such as educational seminars for physicians or working to change national drug policies.

EXHIBIT 7 Local Costs for Diarrheal Training Units

Program Component	Cost per unit, Kwacha	
Land cruiser truck (four-wheel drive)	1,200,000	
Fuel and maintenance	300,000	per year
Driver	30,000	per year
Trainers (if full-time with program)		
Physician	72,000	per year
Public health nurse	36,000	per year
Public health trainer	30,000	per year
Training materials		
For health care personnel	120	per year
For caregivers	10	per year
Jugs (1-liter)	100	per year
Measuring spoons	30	per year
Mugs (250 ml)	15	per year
Banana cups (500 ml)	35	per year
Poster—each	500	per year

Source: Interviews with health education professionals.

A second major challenge was not only to stimulate sales of the product, the traditional goal of advertising, but also to emphasize the correct use of ORS. ORS product advertising needed to include brand-specific advertising from the beginning for maximum commercial effectiveness, but generic advertising might also be appropriate within the same campaign for educational purposes.

THE SUSTAINABILITY ISSUE

Any donor program was considered sustainable when the flow of benefits from the program could be maintained or enhanced after donor funding ceased. Thus, "sustainability" with regard to use of ORS did not refer to each activity undertaken as part of a program to control diarrheal disease, but rather to the lasting impact of the program. The global smallpox eradication program, for example, had achieved the ultimate in sustainability: the target population continued to receive the health benefits resulting from the eradication of the disease. Ultimately, the goal of any diarrheal disease program was that the program result in a sustained reduction in morbidity and mortality from diarrhea.

There were various levels at which diarrheal disease program activities took place, and different actions would have shorter or longer-term impacts on diarrhea. For example, the installation of a water and sewer system would be likely to have a greater long-term impact on diarrhea morbidity and mortality than an advertising campaign promoting oral rehydration therapy. However, this was a considerably more-expensive

EXHIBIT 8   Basic Media Rates for Zambia, December 1, 1990 (Gross Rates Include 20% Sales Tax)

Television

```
TIME SLOT      RATE FOR 1 AD

PRIME TIME
        60 SEC  K12,000
        45 SEC    9,600
        30 SEC    6,000
        15 SEC    3,600
         7 SEC    3,000

A TIME
        60 SEC  K9,600
        45 SEC   6,600
        30 SEC   4,200
        15 SEC   3,000
         7 SEC   2,160

B TIME
        60 SEC  K6,000
        45 SEC   6,600
        30 SEC   3,600
        15 SEC   1,800
         7 SEC   1,200
```

TV TIME DISTRIBUTIONS

```
PRIME TIME    18:55 TO 20:00

A TIME        07:00 TO 11:00
              20:00 TO 23:00

B TIME        06:00 TO 07:00
              15:00 TO 18:55
              23:00 TO CLOSE
```

Radio

```
TIME SLOT      RATE FOR 1 AD

A TIME
        60 SEC  K1,800
        45 SEC   1,500
        30 SEC   1,200
        15 SEC     900

B TIME
        60 SEC  K1,440
        45 SEC   1,200
        30 SEC     900
        15 SEC     720

C TIME
        60 SEC  K1,080
        45 SEC     780
        30 SEC     720
        15 SEC     540
```

RADIO TIME DISTRIBUTIONS

```
A TIME           05:00 TO 08:00
                 12:00 TO 14:00
                 16:30 TO 22:00
     WEEKEND     05:00 TO 22:00

B TIME           08:00 TO 12:00
                 14:00 TO 16:30
                 22:00 TO 23:00
     WEEKEND     22:00 TO 23:00

C TIME           23:00 TO CLOSE
     WEEKEND     23:00 TO 24:00
```

Press   **One Centimeter Down by One Column Wide**

```
TIMES OF ZAMBIA                K100.80
ZAMBIA DAILY MAIL                70.87
```

Source: Zambia National Broadcasting Company Rate Card, 1991.

545

solution. Boyd knew that multiple actions were possible, but it was not possible to do everything and solve all of the problems. One important goal would be to find ways to ensure that caregivers and health workers maintained appropriate case management practices (the use of ORS being one of them) after the initial program investment had been made. More directly, efforts could be concentrated on ways to sustain the resource base for projects such as training, information systems, ORS production and distribution, or any other activities designed to reduce the incidence of diarrheal disease.

Donors wanted to invest in development efforts and then see the benefits resulting from their investment continue without the need for prolonged outside support. The developing countries themselves did not want to be dependent on donor funding over the long term. Thus donors tried to avoid paying recurrent costs, such as salaries, routine supervision, and transportation. When such costs were regularly paid by donors, the program was in danger of being dropped or critically underfunded when it reverted from donor support to the routine government budget. If the government did not have sufficient funds to match the level of donor funding, the program's organization and activities might break down to the point where they were no longer effective. This situation described what could happen to an "unsustainable program," one in which insufficient thought had been given to how the host country could support the program.

DEVELOPING UNICEF'S ORS PROGRAM

In less than a week, Boyd had to make both an oral and a written presentation to UNICEF in which she would outline InterMark's recommendations for UNICEF's role in Zambia. Among the issues she had to consider were:

- What steps should be taken to increase the supply of ORS? Should the emphasis be on increasing imports or purchasing from local manufacturers?
- How could private manufacturing and distribution of ORS be encouraged in Zambia?
- Should UNICEF subsidize local manufacturers?
- How could the distribution of ORS be made more effective?
- What were the best ways to effectively educate health care providers and parents about when ORS was necessary and in the correct use of ORS?
- Should packet size be standardized at either 250 milliliters or 1 liter, or should two sizes be distributed?
- Was there any role for premixed ORS?

Boyd realized that she could recommend a variety of activities, but not everything could be accomplished in the UNICEF budget, which was $87,000 in 1991. UNICEF was willing to spend as much $113,000 annually in the years 1992 through 1994 if they felt that their objectives were likely to be met. She suspected that there were some actions that would greatly improve the functioning of the system and had begun to think about the processes involved in the flow of ORS from supply by the manufacturer to demand and use by the consumer. She was also concerned about the flow of ORS information. Where were the leverage points? How could appropriate use be achieved on a sustainable basis?

Chateau des Charmes Wines Ltd.

Ruth Cruikshank and Kenneth F. Harling

Paul Bosc, Jr., was sitting at his desk, bathed in the sunshine of an early morning in May 1991. He was in a trailer that was overwhelmed by the concrete block building beside it—the present winery of Chateau des Charmes Wines Ltd. (CdC). The company, a boutique-type winery located in the township of Niagara-on-the-Lake, Ontario, had sales of more than $2 million the previous year.

Paul Jr. was reviewing his father's ideas for replacing the winery with a new $5 million chateau that would double the company's production capacity. Paul Jr. wondered how he would respond to his father's proposal. His father, Paul Sr., had presented it and said, "I don't think there has been a day in my career that I haven't thought about this chateau. Do you think we should move ahead with it?"

The decision would have broad implications for the future of the family business. As vice president of marketing, Paul Jr. was particularly interested in the marketing implications of his father's grand vision. He was aware that sales of all wine in Ontario had risen from $556 million in 1988 to $584 million in 1990. Unit volume, however, had fallen from the peak of 90 million litres to 80 million litres over the same period. The cause of this decline was thought to be a combination of an economic recession that started in 1989, the aging of the "baby boom" generation, and a more socially responsible, health conscious society. Nevertheless, Ontario wines were some of the few alcoholic products that recorded increasing unit sales over the period.

THE ONTARIO WINE INDUSTRY

Winemaking and Wineries

The principal steps in making wine are destemming and crushing grapes, fermenting them, extracting the fermented juice, and then bottling the wine. The breakdown of variable costs was 31 percent for labor, 29 percent for packing materials, 12 percent for grapes, and 26 percent for other items. Wineries were able to capture economies of scale. Compared with a winery making 5,000 cases, a winery making 20,000 cases a year could produce a bottle of wine for 15 percent less; a winery making 100,000 cases for 25 percent less; and a winery making 2,000,000 cases for 50 percent less.

Ontario wineries competed both among themselves and with foreign competitors. In 1991, imported wine accounted for 64 percent of all wines sold through the major channel, the Liquor Control Board of Ontario (LCBO). Imported wine held such a significant share because it was seen as higher in quality and better value for the money. This dominance was being challenged for the first time by the development of higher-quality Ontario-made wines more in line with consumer preferences. These new wines were based on recently introduced vitis vinifera grapes, premium European grape varieties. Making wines using such grapes was a relatively new business in Ontario. Although it cost more to make them than traditional wines, customers had shown they were willing to pay higher prices for these products.

In order to bolster its quality image, participants in Ontario's wine industry had formed the Vintners Quality Association (VQA) in 1989. Paul Bosc, Sr., had been one of the key leaders in bringing this voluntary association into being. VQA set up and administered an "Appellation of Origin" system similar to that of leading wine producers of France, Italy, and Germany. However, the system was not officially recognized by these procedures because it was a provincial rather than a national system. For wines carrying the VQA symbol, the following regulations applied:

1. To carry an appellation of origin bearing the word "Ontario," the wine must be made of 100 percent Ontario-grown vitis vinifera grapes, more simply referred to as vinifera grapes.

2. To be called a varietal, that is, to bear the name of a grape variety, 75 percent of the wine must be produced using the specified variety.

3. To be a blended or nonvarietal wine, the wine must be made from 100 percent Ontario-grown vinifera grapes.

4. To carry a vintage date, at least 95 percent of the wine must be from the designated year.

5. To be a designated vineyard, 100 percent of the wine must come from that vineyard.

6. To be estate bottled, the wine cannot have left the estate, and the estate must have been leased by the winery bottling the wine for at least three years.

Wines meeting these criteria and satisfying taste tests were allowed to carry the VQA symbol. Those that failed could still be listed with their original varietal label but could carry no other designation. Though only 5 percent to 10 percent of Ontario wines were expected to meet the VQA standards, those backing the system thought that the standards would improve the perceived quality of all Ontario wines. The advantage for an individual winery in having a product designated VQA was that it was likely to be listed automatically by the LCBO. In 1990–1991, approximately 600,000 litre of VQA wines were sold at an average price of $10 per bottle.

In 1990, Ontario wineries fit into three groups (Exhibit 1). The dominant group, which had been in the business for many decades, offered a broad range of lower-quality products that were sold under brand names. The other two groups were subsets of the boutique wineries. One group consisted of older, more-established boutique wineries, though they were at most a little more than a decade old. The second group included the more recent entrants. All the boutique wineries offered higher-quality wines produced using European grape varieties.

The Boscs saw the established boutiques as their principal competitors: Hillebrand Estates, Inniskillin Wines, and Pelee Island Wines (see Exhibit 2). Hillebrand

EXHIBIT 1   The Ontario Wineries in 1990

Group	Number of Wineries	Total Case Volume
Dominant	4	2,319,000
Boutique—Established	5	279,000
Boutique—New	12	26,000

Estates came into being in 1989 when Newark Winery was acquired by a German winery and then renamed. The company relied on 45 independent grape growers for its grapes. Its marketing strategy relied heavily on its 25 retail stores. An Environics survey in 1989 found that 40 percent of Ontario wine drinkers recognized the company's name. Their Niagara winery was toured by 100,000 visitors annually.

Inniskillin Wines, established in 1974, was the first winery in Ontario to sell wines made from the vinifera grapes. Three quarters of its grapes were grown by independent

EXHIBIT 2   Cases of Wine Sold Through the LCBO by Selected Competitors, 1987–1991[a]

	1987	1988	1989	1990	1991
Chateau des Charmes					
Red Wine	7,429	8,875	11,308	9,637	10,319
White Wine	22,786	22,338	21,141	23,079	22,642
Other Wine	256	19	—	11	20
Total	30,471	31,232	32,449	32,727	32,981
Hillebrand Estates					
Red Wine	4,921	5,093	7,270	6,834	7,161
White Wine	61,210	79,657	81,087	68,779	75,068
Other Wine	2,634	3,297	2,580	2,096	2,000
Total	68,765	88,047	90,937	77,709	84,229
Inniskillin Wines					
Red Wine	30,370	25,928	22,759	17,825	23,376
White Wine	54,671	57,672	60,702	50,689	62,665
Other Wine	2,355	1,948	1,650	736	500
Total	87,396	85,548	85,111	69,250	86,541
Pelee Island Wines					
Red Wine	5,675	6,792	8,582	8,618	13,614
White Wine	17,666	27,485	35,756	41,579	61,159
Other Wine	127	129	75	117	100
Total	23,468	34,406	44,413	50,314	74,873

[a]Year ending March 31: one case contains 9 litres.

growers. The owners, Donald Ziraldo and Karl Kaiser, were leading speakers for the company and well-known champions of the Ontario wine industry. The winery's marketing strategy relied heavily on media advertising and promotion. Forty-seven percent of Ontario wine drinkers recognized the Inniskillin name and associated it with mid-priced table and varietal wines. More recently, the business had built its reputation with its ice wine, a specialty product. Their Niagara winery drew 80,000 visitors annually.

Pelee Island Wines was licensed in 1983. Owned by German and Austrian investors, it grew most of its own grapes. It operated one retail outlet near Windsor on the north shore of Lake Erie; its offerings were mid-priced wines. After signing an agreement with a Californian winery, Pelee Island Wines began moving more heavily into blended wines. The company was known for the use of attractive labelling to create image and low introductory prices to penetrate the market. Twenty percent of Ontario wine drinkers recognized the company's name.

Retailing

Consumers bought wine for home consumption at stores of the government-run LCBO and at winery-owned retail stores. In 1990, the 623 LCBO stores sold $535 million and 71 million litres of wine. The 243 winery-owned retail stores sold $49 million and 9 million litres of wine. Retail prices were controlled by the LCBO and were the same at all stores. The LCBO set the price of a wine by taking the wholesale price from the winery and adding various taxes, markups, and charges. The industry projected that the structure of these marketing costs would change over the next few years (see Exhibit 3). Of particular significance was the change in the LCBO's retailing markup due to agreements under the General Agreement on Tariffs and Trade (GATT) and the Free Trade Agreement between Canada and the United States. The differences among markups on wines from different countries were narrowing (See Exhibit 4). Though retail prices were the same at

EXHIBIT 3   Retail Price Breakdown on CdC Wines, 1990[a]

	LCBO Sales	Own Stores Sales		LCBO Sales	Own Stores Sales
Varietal Wine			**Table Wine**		
Retail Price	$8.84	$8.84	Retail Price	$5.30	$5.30
GST (7%)	0.54	0.54	GST (7%)	0.32	0.32
PST (8%)	0.61	0.61	PST (8%)	0.37	0.37
Retail, Pretax Price	7.69	7.69	Retail, Pretax Price	4.61	4.61
LCBO Flat Charge	1.84		LCBO Flat Charge	1.84	
LCBO Markup at 13%	0.67		LCBO Markup at 23%	0.52	
Price to LCBO	5.18		Price to LCBO	2.25	
License Fee		0.15	License Fee		0.11
Excise Tax	1.5	0.51	Excise Tax	0.51	0.51
Price to Winery	4.67	7.03	Price to Winery	1.74	3.99

[a]Using product mix per 1990. Average weighted price for varietal and blended wines developed from Exhibit 6.

EXHIBIT 4   Projected Retail Markups on Table Wines by the LCBO in Percent, 1990–98[a]

Type	1990	1991	1992	1993	1994	1995	1996	1997	1998
100% Canadian[i]	13	27	30	37	42	49	53	60	66
Blended Canadian[b]	23	39	43	51	58	66	66	66	66
U.S.	62	62	61	62	63	64	70	75	80
European Community	75	75	73	73	73	73	73	73	73

[a]Reflects the impact of GATT and Free Trade.
[b]In this instance, "blended" means includes imported wine or juice.

LCBO and winery-owned stores, their retail margins were different. The retail markup at the winery-owned stores equalled the LCBO price less federal sales tax, excise tax, provincial sales tax, general sales tax, and a license fee of two percent of gross revenue.

All products carried by LCBO were "listed" after they passed a rigorous screening for quality and uniqueness. The first year a wine was listed, its supplier could force up to 100 LCBO stores to carry it. Store managers resented this practice because unknown wines did not sell well. To continue to be carried, the wine had to sell in sufficient volume to meet individual store quotas and an LCBO system quota. Managers were quick to drop a wine that failed to meet these quotas, so the suppliers' sales representatives worked hard to make sure their wines sold in sufficient volume. They would call on stores carrying the wine to ensure that it was shelved and properly displayed. They also carried the suppliers' promotional campaigns into LCBO stores and erected promotional displays as allowed by the LCBO.

Individual Ontario wineries ran their own retail stores, provided they held the necessary license for each store. Virtually every winery had a store (at the winery) where it sold wine to tour groups and conducted special promotions. All 263 available store licenses had been distributed among the wineries. Each store was only allowed to sell its own wine, and most operating decisions including location, pricing, promotion, and hours of operation, had to be approved by the LCBO.

Wine was also sold to consumers at restaurants and bars licensed by the Liquor Licensing Board of Ontario (LLBO) to serve poured drinks. Sales representatives from the wineries tried to convince each establishment's wine buyer to carry their wines. Often they had to educate the buyer and servers about wines. Once the licensee decided to carry a wine, all purchasing activities were handled through the local LCBO store. Wine in bottles was picked up at the store, whereas wine in kegs (sold by the glass or carafe rather than the bottle) was shipped directly from the winery to the licensee. The licensee paid 10 percent below the LCBO's retail list price, but the taxes paid on each litre of wine were the same as those paid by the retail customer. The LCBO applied its retail markup on bottles but not kegs; the winery charged the licensee directly for delivery of kegs.

A survey of restaurants in 1989 found that virtually all fine dining restaurants served Ontario wines, but only 20 percent had an Ontario wine as a house wine. Seventy percent of these restaurants had heard of the VQA designation, and 40 percent would consider adding an Ontario wine if recommended by a knowledgeable person. Family-style restaurants were less aware of VQA designation (29 percent) but more likely to have an Ontario-made wine as the house wine (41 percent).

Consumption

A 1989 survey by Environics of 1,000 randomly selected wine consumers found that only 12 percent of Ontario's wine drinkers were aware of the VQA. Seventy-five percent of them paid less than $10 per bottle when buying wine in retail stores, and two-thirds chose the brand they had tasted as a house wine in a restaurant. Other places where consumers learned about wines were wine and food shows (31 percent) and from reading articles on wine (44 percent). Only one percent belonged to wine clubs.

CHATEAU DES CHARMES

Paul Sr., the founder of CdC, was born in French Algeria in 1935 and grew up in the wine business. With a degree in oenology, the science of winemaking, from the University of Dijon in France, he returned to Algeria to manage his family's vineyard and subsequently a cooperative winery. He emigrated to Canada in 1963 after a revolution in Algeria.

He soon found employment with Chateau Gai Wines, a profitable family-owned business located in Niagara Falls, Ontario. During the next 15 years, he rose to become Chateau Gai's chief wine maker and director of research. He introduced numerous innovations at Chateau Gai, including the development of "Alpenweiss," a blended wine that became Canada's largest-selling white wine in the late 1970s. He also promoted the use of French hybrids and vinifera grapes for making wine. After the purchase of Chateau Gai by John Labatt Ltd. in 1973, Paul Sr. became increasingly frustrated with the internal politics that predominated under the new ownership. He felt that the new management was interested only in "meeting the numbers," that new workers lacked the technical knowledge necessary to produce high-quality wines, and that his own ability to innovate was being curtailed. He was frustrated because, as he later said enthusiastically, "I enjoy making good wine, and I want people to consider the wine I make the best in Ontario."

Convinced that he would be unable to pursue his dream of producing a high-quality, European-style wine at Chateau Gai, Paul Sr. decided to establish his own winery. In 1977, he joined with two partners to buy 62 acres near Niagara-on-the-Lake. That same year, 57 of those acres were planted in grapes. The next year he left Chateau Gai and founded Chateau des Charmes, building a winery on the land and processing its first grapes. In 1980, CdC sold its first wines commercially. Since then more land had been acquired by CdC and planted: in 1981, 100 acres, of which 50 were planted; and in 1987, 93 acres, of which 14 were planted. The Bosc family also purchased 50 acres on its own account in 1983 and held it outside the company. This acreage, called the Bosc Estate, had 33 acres yielding grapes in 1991.

Paul Sr. was generally pleased with the inroads his winery had made into the Ontario market over the decade. By the early 1990s, CdC estimated it was shipping 40,000 to 50,000 cases of wine annually, with each case containing 9 litres of wine. In addition, CdC was consistently profitable (see Exhibit 5 for the financial statements). The company had four separate but related operations: several vineyards, a winery, a nursery, and a research laboratory.

Operations

The Vineyards   Paul Sr.'s original vision for the winery had included growing its own grapes. "You just can't make good wine without growing your own grapes. You have to

EXHIBIT 5   Chateau des Charmes—Financial Summary for Years Ending
August 31, 1987–1990

	1987	1988	1989	1990
	(Thousands of Dollars)			
Balance Sheet				
Assets				
Current Assets				
Trade	324	205	538	317
Other	214	80	100	96
Total Current Assets	538	285	638	413
Inventory	1,096	1,572	1,487	1,532
Prepaid Expenses	243	210	209	245
Fixed Assets	1,752	1,953	1,895	1,975
Other Assets	72	159	113	100
Total Assets	3,801	4,179	4,342	4,265
Liabilities and Shareholders' Equity				
Current Liabilities				
Bank Loan	532	743	654	257
Accounts Payable	140	221	318	228
Current Portion LTD	53	53	54	55
Total Current Liabilities	725	1,017	1,026	540
Long-Term Debt	572	518	446	319
Shareholders' Equity				
Capital Stock	1,742	1,742	1,742	1,742
Retained Earnings	762	902	1,128	1,664
Total Shareholders' Equity	2,504	2,644	2,870	3,406
Total Liabs. and Shareholders' Equity	3,801	4,179	4,342	4,265
Income Statement				
Sales	2,489	1,973	2,368	2,073
Gross Profit	878	772	1,023	890
Expenses:				
Marketing Expenses	264	284	357	515
Administrative Expenses	195	215	228	230
Depreciation and Amortization	120	154	172	139
Interest	50	75	74	61
Operating Income (Loss)	249	44	192	(55)
Other Income, Tax Credits, Etc.	24	20	34	40
LESS Taxes	68	(16)	0	5
PLUS Extraordinary Items[a]	139	92	0	547
Net Income	344	140	226	537

[a]In 1990, extraordinary items include compensation paid for pipeline easements on land.

control their quality if you want to make good wine." This was an especially important consideration in 1977 because few farmers grew the vinifera grapes needed to make the kinds of wines Paul Sr. wanted. By 1990, 70 percent of the 600 to 700 tons of grapes CdC crushed came from CdC's three vineyards and the Bosc Estate. The other 30 percent came from three growers who had supplied the company for many years on the basis of verbal contracts. These growers were unlikely to expand their production of grapes in the future.

Although Paul Sr. had been careful to select only the best available land for the CdC vineyards, he was especially pleased with the 50-acre Bosc Estate because he considered it the best land in the Niagara peninsula. All the planted land and half the unplanted land had drainage installed at a cost of $5,000 an acre. Paul Sr. felt that well-drained land enabled the roots of the vines to grow deeply and extensively and that this produced healthier vines and higher-quality grapes. Paul Sr. managed the four vineyards with the help of Pierre Jean Stephane, Paul Jr.'s younger brother. The field workers were migrant workers from the Caribbean who came to Canada each year as needed. Some stayed longer and helped in the winery as well.

Agricultural practices in the vineyard were what Paul Sr. considered optimal for producing high-quality grapes in Ontario. They included both traditional and innovative techniques he had developed. He observed, "France is steeped in tradition. In Canada, we have been working to make our own tradition." Paul Sr. had helped do this by introducing many innovative cultural practices, ranging from how to prune vines in May to how to harvest the grapes in September and October. These practices had made CdC one of the first vineyards to grow vinifera grapes commercially in Ontario.

The grape harvest varied over the life of the vineyard. The first viable harvest was produced three years after the vines had been planted and was 25 percent of normal yields; in the fourth year it was 70 percent, and in the fifth year it was a full 3.5 tons of grapes per acre. Paul Sr. chose not to pursue higher yields because he felt it would mean lower-quality juice and greater risk that vines would die from severe winter weather. As the vines aged, the quality of grape juice tended to improve, but the volume declined so that after 25 to 40 years the vines might have to be replanted.

Prices paid by wineries for grapes were set through negotiations between the Ontario Grape Growers' Marketing Board and the wineries. All wineries paid the same price adjusted for the variety and quality of the grapes delivered. Paul Sr. felt that prices were approximately the same as those of grapes of equivalent quality in France.

The Winery   The present winery was a concrete block building of 13,000 square feet. It housed all production and storage activities. Maximum capacity was 60,000 to 70,000 cases of wine a year; however, actual capacity was only 45,000 cases because vintaged varietal wines had to be handled separately to maintain their identity by grape and year produced. The building also contained a retail wine store and some offices. Serious overcrowding had led to 12 surplus, stainless steel tanks being placed outside, up against a side wall of the winery; the Boscs' offices were located in a trailer parked behind it.

Paul Sr. was modest about his abilities, although he was regarded as a "vintner extraordinaire" by those who knew him. He commented,

> *Anyone can make wine! All you have to do is follow a recipe. But to make good wine every time, you have to know what you are doing. This is why winemaking is a science and an art. When I make wine, I check things daily, making corrections as necessary. Every time I make wine, the decisions are different. And I don't blend or bottle a wine until I have tasted it personally. Big wineries have problems making good wine because their management just wants to blindly follow recipes.*

The time span from crushing the grapes immediately after their harvest to shipping the wine varied. A few wines were shipped soon after crushing—Beaujolais nouveau was shipped in November and young white wines were shipped in the late spring of the next year. In general, production of higher quality vinifera wines took longer because they required aging: one to two years for white wines and two to three years for red wines. Most of the workers in the winery were migrant laborers.

Provincial government regulations controlled winemaking in Ontario. CdC had to follow strict control procedures to ensure that taxes were collected on all the wine produced from the grapes it crushed. CdC was also limited to pressing 150 gallons of juice per ton of grapes, although Paul Sr. only chose to produce 130 gallons per ton because he felt doing so produced superior-quality juice. The amount of imported juice or wine that CdC could blend with its Ontario wine was limited as well, though this limit had not constrained CdC's production in the past. Finally, the labels used on wine bottles had to be approved by the government.

Paul Sr. monitored manufacturing costs informally. He felt that the cost of manufacturing each type of wine was roughly the same. He thought the big cost difference among the wines he made was the price of the grapes, with grape costs being higher for vinifera varieties. (Bosc estimated the average cost of goods sold for varietal wine at $2.60 per bottle, whereas table wine was $1.65.) Wine could be improved by blending in low-cost, higher-quality, imported bulk wines or using unfermented grape juice. This wine, which came from various countries including Chile, Argentina, the United States, and France, was chosen based on price, availability, and quality. Only 8 percent of CdC's volume consisted of bulk wine. This was considerably less than other medium-sized Ontario wineries that were CdC's competitors.

Other Operations   Research at the company had been largely funded by the federal and provincial governments. CdC had been given grants in recognition of the technical expertise at the winery. These grants had been an important source of revenue for CdC in earlier years. Early research efforts had focused on cloning superior vines that Paul Sr. had identified in CdC's vineyards. This work was done by a scientist with a doctorate in biology that Paul Sr. had hired from the University of Waterloo. The clones the scientist produced went to CdC's nursery, where they were grown into vines. Paul Sr. considered the clonal work finished. Now he was directing the scientist's research into production practices such as reverse osmosis and carbonic maceration. The scientist was attempting to do this work in a small laboratory in the winery.

The nursery was important both to CdC and to the Ontario wine industry because it was the principal source of vines for those in Ontario who wanted to grow vinifera grapes. The Boscs were proud of their contribution to the Ontario wine industry. They were also pleased that their wines often competed with wines from other Ontario wineries, many of which were produced from grapes grown on vines from CdC's nursery. The nursery's sales represented 10 percent of CdC's sales revenue. It had always been a profitable operation and provided timely cash flow each spring.

Marketing

By 1991, the company's product line spanned the low and medium prices. This had not always been so. Initially, CdC produced lower-priced, blended table wines appealing to the mass market. Its "Cour Blanc" was, in fact, the same blend as the "Alpenweiss" blend that Paul Sr. had developed while at Chateau Gai. Starting in 1988, Paul Sr. moved to upgrade CdC's product line to higher-quality wines, typically vintaged, varietal, and estate-bottled wines. (See Exhibit 6 for the winery's recent product mix.) Paul Sr. also sought the VQA designation on all CdC's varietal wines to help validate their quality.

Paul Sr. priced all company wines so that they represented "good value" for the consumer. He priced the table wines directly against low-price foreign wines. He priced varietal wines so that the customer received higher-quality wine than similarly priced French wines. Generally speaking, higher-price point products and specialty products provided higher margins for the company. (See Exhibit 6 for prices.)

Approximately 80 percent of CdC's case volume was sold through the LCBO. CdC wines were carried regularly in 503 of the LCBO's 620 retail stores. CdC's penetration of LCBO stores was lowest in northern Ontario. The other 20 percent of company sales came from its own retail stores. CdC had only three stores in 1991, although it had licenses for six. One store was in the winery. This store sold primarily to those touring the winery, though some direct sales to licensees were also made. A second store was located in Ottawa's Minto Plaza, a large office development in downtown Ottawa; a third store served customers in Oakville's trendy Bronte Harbor. A fourth store had been closed recently because it failed to break even. The decision about opening new stores using their remaining licenses was complicated by Paul Jr.'s concern that the government might issue licenses to a broader retail base, including grocery and convenience stores. If CdC proceeded to use its open licenses, the initial cost of setting up a new store would be $50,000, and annual fixed operating costs would be $70,000. Past experience had shown that, if a store was going to be successful, it reached break-even volume within two years of opening.

The company had four sales representatives who each served a sales region (Ottawa/eastern Ontario, Toronto, the Niagara horseshoe, and Southwestern and central Ontario). The representatives called on more than 500 licensed restaurants and bars. Once a licensee was ordering CdC wine on a regular basis through the LCBO store, the representative would approach the store manager and encourage him to stock CdC wines for public sale. The sales mix in each of the four sales regions was very different, although total volume was similar. For example, in Toronto, "Chardonnay" and other varietal wines were the company's best sellers, whereas in Niagara white table wine was the best seller. Sales volume was highest in Toronto, followed by southwestern and then central Ontario. From monthly sales reports produced by the LCBO, Paul Jr. knew that 75 percent of all wine sales were in the "Golden Horseshoe," the area ringing the western end of Lake Ontario. A survey by Environics in 1989 had found that 29 percent of Ontario wine drinkers recognized the company by name.

Both Paul Sr. and Paul Jr. saw the wine business as a lifestyle business. Consequently, they "worked hard to be close to the customer." They sought to learn what the consumer wanted and to educate everyone about wine and wine appreciation. They encouraged and provided wine tastings at the winery and at other private and trade gatherings in Ontario. Paul Jr. had attended every trade show in Ontario that was attended by food and wine journalists over the past several years. At all of these events, they promoted the quality and the "sense of artistry" of CdC's wines. Paul Sr. was often personally featured in CdC's promotional literature because of the image he projected. He spoke with a French accent, looked Italian, and was the principal owner of the business—all features that consumers were thought to associate with quality wine.

The Boscs had their own perceptions of customer purchasing behavior. Paul Sr. said:

Consumers purchase wine on the basis of price, quality, sweetness, originating country, and reputation. Their selection is heavily influenced by personal recommendations and, to a lesser extent, by the reputation of the winery. A certain romance is often

EXHIBIT 6 Chateau des Charmes Ltd. Product Shipments, Year Ending August 31, 1990

Brand	Price[a]	Shipped[b]
Varietal Wines		
1989 Seyval Blanc	$ 6.25	2,000
1989 Garnay Noir (VQA)	7.85	2,500
1988 Garnay Blanc	7.65	3,000
1989 Chardonnay (VQA)	8.95	4,000
1989 Estate Chardonnay	10.35	1,500
1989 Riesling (VQA)	7.40	1,500
1987 Estate Riesling (Private Order)	10.70	370
1989 Estate Aligote (VQA, Vintaged)	9.20	1,250
1989 Estate Pinot Noir	9.10	750
1988 Pinot Noir	7.35	2,500
Champagne Brut (Private Order)	13.00	1,000
Champagne Sec	13.00	1,000
Estate Auxerrois (VQA, Vintaged)	10.45	350
Late Harvest Riesling (VQA, Vintaged, 375 ml. Bottles)	7.95	350
1988 Est Gewurztraiminer (Private Order, 375 ml. Bottles)	7.25	300
Average Weighted Price and Total Case Volume	$ 8.84	22,370
Table Wines[c]		
Sentinel Blanc. 1.5 Litre Bottles	$10.25	4,500
Sentinel Rouge, 1.5 Litre Bottles	10.90	2,500
Sentinel Blanc	5.25	4,000
Sentinel Rouge	5.45	1,000
Sentinel Blanc, 375 ml Bottles	3.10	200
Sentinel Rouge, 375 ml Bottles	3.30	200
Gamay—Caberbet	6.50	1,000
Cour Blanc, I Litre	6.90	3,000
Cour Rouge, I Litre	6.55	2,130
Average Weighted Price and Total Case Volume	$ 5.30	18,530

[a]Unless stated otherwise, prices are per 750 ml. bottle.
[b]Each case contains 9 litres of wine.
[c]Table wines are made by mixing the juice of different grape varieties, as follows:
Sentinel Blanc: Riesling, Sauvignon Blanc
Sentinel Rouge: Cabernet Sauvignon, Marechal Foch
Cour Blanc: Sauvignon Blanc, Riesling, Seyval Blanc
Cour Rouge: Cabernet Sauvignon, Marechal Foch, Garnay Noir
Source: Company records and estimates.

associated with the winery of choice. Brand loyalty is a purchase factor, with switching most common in the lower priced table wines. Wineries encourage this by changing labels and names of wines often to catch the "roving consumer." I try to do the same thing but in my own way. I bring out one or two new varietal wines each year so consumers check back regularly to see what's new.

Paul Jr. realized that CdC would need to develop greater customer awareness. One venue for further promotion was point-of-purchase promotion in LCBO stores. The LCBO rented out the right to promote in its stores for three weeks at a time. CdC would have to pay the LCBO $500 for each store used, and at least 100 stores would have to be included in the promotion. Paul Jr. was convinced that this could be effective though it would cost $30,000 for the promotional materials. What had held him back from pursuing this so far was his concern that the company simply did not have the people needed to erect all the displays in a timely fashion.

Although 75 percent of Ontario's wines were produced by the three largest wineries in the province—Brights, Andres, and Cartier—the Boscs viewed Hillebrand, Inniskillin, and Pelee Island wineries as CdC's major competitors.

Organization

CdC operated with a relatively informal organizational structure. The company had relied in the past on Paul Sr.'s judgment rather than on formal decision making. Paul Sr., as the ultimate authority, made all the crucial decisions. Two clerical staff handled the day-to-day office tasks. The lack of clear delegation of authority and responsibility had initially worked well for the company; more recently, it had caused staff to feel that "everybody was going in different directions."

Clerical staff enjoyed the authority they exercised under this arrangement but had trouble coordinating their work. Sometimes product was out of stock and orders went unfilled. Part of the reason was that CdC's inventory system did not allow for integrated control of inventories, shipping, and billing. Nor did the record system provide sales data by representative. Although he still signed every check, Paul Sr. admitted he lacked administrative expertise: "How should I know what to say to a bookkeeper?"

The formalization of CdC organization had followed Paul Jr.'s joining the company. After graduating from the University of Toronto in political science and completing business courses at Niagara University in New York State, Paul Jr. had become CdC's sole sales representative. In 1989, he had been promoted to vice president of marketing after demonstrating a high level of commitment to the business. With this move, Paul Sr. took charge of the vineyard and the winery, and Paul Jr. took charge of marketing. Paul Jr. then divided Ontario into four sales regions and hired a sales representative for each. The representatives were paid salary plus a modest bonus based on performance. The organizational structure in 1991 is characterized in Exhibit 7.

Paul Jr. felt that hiring good sales representatives was one of the biggest marketing challenges facing CdC. Paul Jr. commented:

Sales representatives don't need to be wine experts, but they certainly need to be more knowledgeable than their customers. This can be a high standard because customers range from those who want an inexpensive wine with dinner to those who want wines with specific characteristics. It can take a full year of training on the job before a new representative is productive. And only when they are trained do you know if you hired the right person. I hired four representatives in 1989 but have only been satisfied with the performance of two of them. Finding good representatives is difficult because the sales function has switched

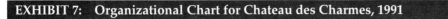

EXHIBIT 7:   Organizational Chart for Chateau des Charmes, 1991

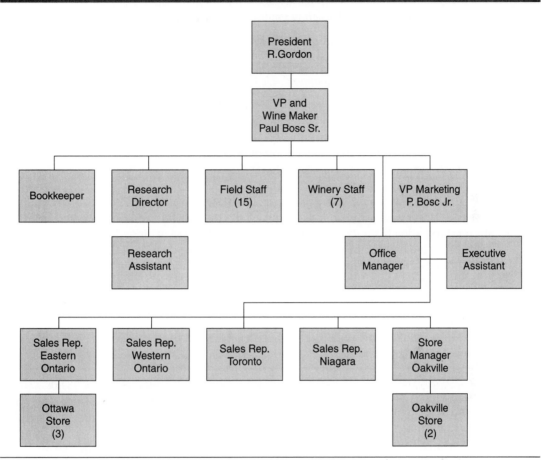

from selling based on personal relationships to selling based on knowledge and strategic marketing. You can't find the new kind of representative; you have to train your own.

Finance

Paul Sr. had strong views about the financial aspects of the business.

In this business you can't be poor. You are exposed to a lot of bad luck so you have to have a lot of equity in the business because you can't control risk. You don't want to be heavily in debt. There is nothing wrong with this. For me, having money in a business is as good as having money in the bank. Either way you have to administer your investment.

He went on to say:

Our business has been a very good investment for us. When we started, the company's book value was $1.6M and now it's $3.4M. The Estate vineyards' book value was $280,000 and now it's $600,000.

CdC had purchased land over the years because Paul Sr. saw it as a valuable and productive asset. He explained:

When you own the land your grapes come from, you also own a vineyard designation. You have to have this to be in the highest price points for wine. The French have made consumers think that each location produces a unique wine.

Paul Jr. appreciated these land acquisitions.

Dad has made the tough decisions about site selection and land acquisitions. He has bought some of the best land around. He has made the wine business easier for me and my children.

CdC and the Bosc family had benefited from the sale of easements for a gas pipeline through three of their properties in 1991. CdC itself had negotiated $2 million as compensation for the impact that installation of the pipeline had on the productivity of their vineyards—vineyards were a valuable use of land. Some of the money had already been received and more was forthcoming.

Cash flow was most difficult during the harvest season and improved through the winter as wine was shipped. CdC received payment from the LCBO six weeks after it shipped the wine from its warehouse. The company had arranged an operating line of credit from the bank to provide working capital during these periods.

In early 1991, ownership in the company was divided among Paul Bosc, Sr.; several other family members; and Rodger Gordon. Paul Bosc, Sr., and his family held 55 percent of the common stock, and Rodger Gordon, the company's lawyer and a supportive but passive investor, held the balance.

THE NEW WINERY

Under Paul Sr.'s proposal, the existing winery was to be replaced with a 35,000-square-foot chateau boasting sufficient equipment to produce 120,000 cases of wine per year. Paul Sr. was not concerned about its larger size, saying, "You do not have to be small to be good!" In fact, the proposed winery was generally thought by the industry to be optimal size for a boutique winery, maintaining quality while benefiting from economies of scale. The planned chateau would contain, in addition to production equipment, storage space for aging wines, a tasting room, a kitchen, an entertainment room, a wine store, and a research laboratory. The grounds would provide parking for 72 cars and four buses, a garden, and an experimental vineyard. The exterior of the new winery would project the image of Paul Bosc's dream, a chateau in the French tradition. Paul Sr. was eager to move ahead with the new chateau because the recession had made construction costs lower than they had been for many years.

The chateau could be built on property already owned by CdC. This property was in an area known as St. David's Bench, the warmest part of the Niagara escarpment. It sat directly across the road from the 50-acre Bosc Estate. The land was fronted by Regional Rd. 81, which had an average daily traffic flow in 1990 of 4,200 cars. It was backed by Highway 405, which was constantly busy with people going to and from the United States over the Lewiston bridge. Access would only be possible from 81, though the chateau would be highly visible from Highway 405.

Paul Jr. thought aloud about how the new chateau could contribute to the company's success.

A chateau would be good for everyone around here because it fits so well with the tourist business in the Niagara region. The tourists who come to Niagara Falls and the Shaw Festival in Niagara-on-the-Lake fit the profile of consumers of high-quality wines: middle- to upper-class tourists who enjoy fine dining and are able to afford entertainment. A chateau would give us a way of prolonging their stay in the area. It could even draw some to the area. And it could be featured in all promotion. That would help build consumer recognition and recall.

A chateau should be able to draw 90,000 to 100,000 tourists annually, compared to the 8,000 we now get. That means the store in the chateau should sell 15,000 to 20,000 cases of wine each year. We're going to have to add two or three staff to handle that volume. Also, Dad's idea of having hospitality rooms in the chateau would let us hold lots of events like food and wine seminars for opinion leaders. We can't even think of that in the current building.

The chateau would let us make plenty of essential operating changes, too. Equipment layout would allow efficient product flow, eliminating the occasional stoppages we now have. The new $250,000 bottling line that we've been considering could be installed as well. That would cut bottling costs by $1.05 a case.

The total cost for building and equipping the new chateau would be more than $5 million. Anticipated costs (production equipment included the new bottling line) were:

Land	$ 250,000
Building	4,000,000
Processing Equipment	1,100,000
Lab Equipment	70,000
Total	$5,420,000

Actual cash requirements would be less than suggested in the capital budget because the land was already owned by the company, and $840,000 of processing equipment could be transferred from the old winery. Paul Sr. planned to use the existing winery as warehouse space.

A $2.2 million forgivable loan, in effect a grant, had already been approved by the Ontario Development Corporation based on this projected capital budget. It was available under the terms of the Ontario Wine Assistance Program, a program developed to make the industry more competitive after the signing of the Canada—U.S. Free Trade Act in 1988. In order to qualify for the grant, CdC had to put up an equal amount of capital and had to have invested all funds by December 31, 1994. This meant that either the Bosc family would have to put more money into the business or a new equity partner would be required.

Paul Sr. did not anticipate any startup problems with the new winery that could not be handled. He felt that the new chateau could be built and operational in 10 to 12 months. Once in operation, marketing costs, which included the cost of tours and wine tastings, were naturally expected to rise. Increased costs would be offset by increased revenues as sales rose.

THE DECISION

Paul Jr. realized that building a chateau would be the crowning achievement of his father's career. However, his own enthusiasm for the new chateau was tempered by his reflection that management had been "running to keep up" with company growth. It was increasingly difficult to maintain internal consistency and a sense of control over day-to-day activities. This made the decision a challenging one for him.

Schweppes Raspberry Ginger Ale

Shreekant G. Joag

As Sam Johnson stood looking out from the window of his luxurious office, he wondered how he should go about evaluating the performance of his division's new product—Schweppes Raspberry Ginger Ale—during the first half of 1991, as compared with his expectations at the beginning of the year when the product was introduced to the market. Further, he wondered if, in fact, the product would take his division into the mainstream soft drink market as he had hoped.

COMPANY BACKGROUND

Cadbury Schweppes Public Limited Company was one of the largest British-owned confectionery and soft drink companies, with marketing operations in more than 100 countries around the world. In 1989, the company recorded total sales of £2,843.2 million and a before-tax profit of £251 million.[1] The company managed its beverage operations in North America through Cadbury Beverages North America (CBNA). CBNA was organized into several subdivisions, each handling products under a specific brand: namely, Schweppes, Canada Dry, Sunkist, Crush, Hires, and Mott's. Although divisions of one company, they operated independently and competed freely in the market. As a product director and an associate product manager, Sam Johnson managed the Schweppes subdivision for the whole of North America. Exhibit 1 presents the organization structure of Cadbury Schweppes Public Limited Company.

THE ADULT SOFT DRINK BUSINESS

Of the several subdivisions of CBNA, both Schweppes and Canada Dry marketed products that came under the broad category of adult soft drinks. These included beverages that were used as mixers with alcoholic beverages as well as others that were consumed as general soft drinks. Adult soft drinks consisted primarily of ginger ale; club soda; tonic water; bitter lemon; unsweetened, manufactured, and natural sparkling waters; and sweetened sparkling waters. By composition, the sweetened sparkling waters were in

[1]£1 = U.S. $1.70.

EXHIBIT 1: **Organization Structure of Cadbury Schweppes Public Limited Company**

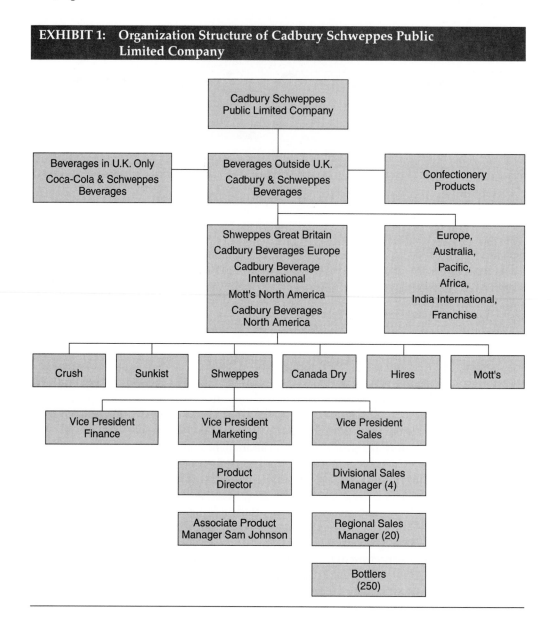

fact identical to regular soft drinks even though they were marketed as waters. Exhibit 2 presents some basic information about adult soft drinks and the alcoholic beverages with which they are mixed. There were four leading brands in the adult soft drink market: Schweppes, Canada Dry, Seagrams, and Polar. Many brands sold flavored and unflavored versions of sparkling water. Exhibit 3 presents the adult soft drinks marketed by Schweppes and major competing brands.

Although these four brands dominated the adult soft drink market, numerous small local brands together contributed a large portion of sales. Exhibit 4 presents the sales of the leading brands, collective sales of all other small brands, and total industry sales of each type of adult soft drink in 1990. In the soft drink industry, general soft drinks constituted the bulk of the market. The share of adult drinks in the total soft

EXHIBIT 2 **Basic Information About Adult Soft Drinks**

Soft Drink	Composition	Used as a Mixer With	Percent Consumed as a	
			Mixer	Soft Drink
Ginger Ale	Carbonated water, sugar syrup, ginger flavor	Bourbon, rye	5	95
Club Soda	Carbonated water, sodium carbonate (soda), common salt (sodium)	Whiskey	50	50
Tonic Water	Carbonated water, quinine, sugar	Gin, vodka, rum	85	15
Bitter Lemon	Carbonated water, quinine, sugar, lemon flavor	Gin, vodka	95	5
Unsweetened Sparkling Manufactured/Seltzer/ Seltzer Water	Purified water, carbonation	Used by itself for digestion	5	95
Natural	Carbonated water from natural springs	Used by itself for digestion	5	95
Sweetened Sparkling Waters	Soft drinks marketed as waters	Used by itself	5	95
Bottled Still Waters Manufactured	Purified natural lake or spring water	Used by itself for drinking	0	100
Natural	Lake or spring water as available in nature	Used by itself for drinking	0	100

Source: Schweppes, CBNA.

drink market had increased modestly from 6 percent in 1980 to 7 percent in 1990. Exhibit 5 presents the trends in market shares of various soft drink flavors and the leading marketers within each flavor for the period 1980 to 1990.

The soft drink industry as a whole competed with all other hot and cold beverages and liquids for a share of the consumer's stomach. In the period between 1965 and 1990, the soft drink share of the average per capita consumption of all liquids increased from 17.8 gallons to 48.0 gallons per year. The total U.S. population increased from 194 million to 250 million in the same period, resulting in the increase in total soft drink sales/consumption from 2,490 million cases per year to 7,940 per million cases per year. Exhibit 6 presents the market trend in 9 terms of per capita consumption of various liquids in the United States from 1965 to 1990. The exhibit reports all liquid consumption figures based on the assumption that the consumer, on average, consumes 182.5 gallons of liquids in a year. The exhibit also presents the U.S. population figures and actual total sales of all soft drinks for comparison.

Because of their popular image and use as mixers, adult soft drinks were primarily sold in 1-liter polyethylene (PET) bottles rather than 12-ounce cans and 2-liter PET bottles, which were popular packages for all other soft drinks. Exhibit 7 presents U.S. market trends in packaging for the industry. Exhibit 8 presents similar market trends in the diet versus regular versions.

EXHIBIT 3   Competing Brands of Adult Soft Drinks

Adult Soft Drink	Schweppes (SP)	Canada Dry (CD)	Seagrams (SG)	Polar (PR)
Ginger Ale	SP ginger ale SP diet ginger ale	CD ginger ale CD diet ginger ale	SG ginger ale SG diet ginger ale	PR ginger ale PR diet ginger ale
Club Soda	SP club soda SP sodium-free club soda	CD club soda	SG club soda	PR club soda

Tonic Water	SP tonic water,
	SP diet tonic
	  water
		CD tonic water,
		CD diet tonic
		  water
			SG tonic water,
			SG diet tonic
			  water
				PR tonic water,
				PR diet tonic
				  water

Bitter Lemon	SP bitter lemon	CD bitter lemon		
Unsweetened Sparkling Waters				

Manufactured—
  Unflavored
	SP unsweetened,
	  unflavored,
	  sparkling water
		CD unsweetened,
		  unflavored,
		  sparkling water
			SG unsweetened,
			  unflavored,
			  sparkling water
				PR unsweetened,
				  unflavored,
				  sparkling water

Manufactured—
  Flavored
	SP unsweetened,
	  flavored,
	  sparkling water
		CD unsweetened,
		  flavored,
		  sparkling water
			SG unsweetened,
			  flavored,
			  sparkling water
				PR unsweetened,
				  flavored,
				  sparkling water

Source: Schweppes, CBNA

**EXHIBIT 4   Sales and Market Shares of Major Brands of Adult Soft Drinks in 1990
(In Thousands of Cases)**

Adult Soft Drink	Schweppes	Canada Dry	Seagrams	Polar	Others	Industry Total Cases	Percent of Industry
Ginger Ale	23,820	55,580	9,600	700	69,100	158,800	2.0
Club Soda	6,350	23,820	1,400	100	90	31,760	0.4
Tonic Water	19,850	15,880	2,500	450	8,960	47,640	0.6
Sparkling Waters	1,240	—	—	—	316,360	317,600	4.0
Others	—	17,845	2,980	—	177,675	198,500	2.5
Total Adult Soft Drinks	51,260	113,125	16,480	1,250	572,185	754,300	9.5
Other CBNA Products							
Sunkist		56,000					
Diet Sunkist		3,500					
Total Soft Drinks	51,260	172,625	16,480	1,250		7,940,000	100.0

Source: Estimates based on *Beverage Industry Annual Manual 90–91*, Edgell Communications Inc., New York, N.Y., 1990; Scanner Data, Schweppes, CBNA.

EXHIBIT 5   Soft Drink Market Trends in the United States by Flavor

	1980	1985	1990
Cola	63.0%	67.5%	70.0%
Coca-Cola Company	30.0	33.0	33.0
PepsiCo	25.0	25.0	26.0
Royal Crown Company	3.0	3.0	3.0
Others	5.0	6.5	8.0
Lemon-Lime	13.0	12.2	10.0
Coca-Cola Company	4.0	4.0	5.0
Seven-Up Company	5.0	5.0	4.0
Others	4.0	3.2	1.0
Pepper	6.0	4.9	5.0
Juice Added	—	3.9	—
Root Beer	3.0	2.7	3.0
Orange	6.0	4.7	2.5
Sunkist			0.8
Others			1.7
All Other Flavors[a]	9.0	8.0	9.5
Total All Flavors Together	100.0	100.0	100.0

All Other Flavors In 1990	9.50%
Ginger Ale	2.00
Schweppes	0.30
Canada Dry	0.70
Other	1.00
Club Soda	0.40
Schweppes	0.08
Canada Dry	0.30
Other	0.02
Tonic Water	0.60
Schweppes	0.25
Canada Dry	0.20
Other	0.15
Sparkling Waters	4.00
All Remaining Flavors	2.50

[a] All figures are rounded up.
Source: Estimates based on *Beverage Industry Annual Manual 90–91,* Edgell Communications, Inc,. New York, N.Y., 1990.

EXHIBIT 6   Liquid Market Trends in the United States

	U.S. per Capita Liquids Consumption in Gallons						
	1965	**1970**	**1975**	**1980**	**1985**	**1989**	**1990**
Soft Drinks	17.8	22.7	26.3	34.2	40.8	46.6	48.0
Coffee	37.8	35.7	33.0	27.4	25.8	24.7	23.6
Beer	15.9	18.5	21.6	24.3	23.8	23.3	23.0
Milk	24.0	23.1	22.5	20.8	20.2	20.9	20.5
Tea	3.8	5.2	7.3	7.3	7.3	7.3	7.3
Bottled Water	—	—	1.2	2.7	4.5	7.1	12.0
Juices	3.8	5.2	6.7	6.8	7.0	6.8	7.0
Powdered Drinks	—	—	4.8	6.0	6.2	4.8	5.0
Wine	1.0	1.9	1.7	2.1	2.4	2.2	2.4
Distilled Spirits	1.5	1.8	2.0	2.0	1.8	1.4	1.3
Subtotal	105.6	113.5	127.1	133.6	139.8	145.2	150.0
Imported Tap Water	76.9	69.0	55.4	48.9	42.7	37.3	32.5
Total	182.5	182.5	182.5	182.5	182.5	182.5	182.5
U.S. Population (In Millions)	194.0	205.0	216.0	223.0	238.0	247.0	250.0
Soft Drink Consumption (192-oz cases in Millions)	2.490	3.090	3.780	5.180	6.500	7.710	7.940

Source: *Beverage Industry Annual Manual 90–91*, EdgeIl Communications, Inc., New York. N.Y., 1990; figures estimated by extrapolation and *Current Population Reports: Population Estimates and Projections*, U.S. Bureau of the Census, Washington, D.C., various years.

MANUFACTURING OF SCHWEPPES ADULT SOFT DRINKS

Both Schweppes and Canada Dry were primarily marketing companies. They imported the concentrate for tonic water from Great Britain. Concentrates for all other Schweppes soft drinks and most Canada Dry soft drinks were manufactured by the Dr. Pepper Company in the United States. Both Schweppes and Canada Dry sold the concentrate to

EXHIBIT 7   Soft Drink Packaging Trends in the United States— Percent of Soft Drinks Using Each

Packaging	1980	1985	1990
Cans	40.0%	40.8%	50.0%
Polyethylene (PET) Bottles	30.0	30.6	30.0
Nonrecycled Glass	14.0	13.0	12.0
Recycled Glass	16.0	15.6	8.9
Total	100.0%	100.0%	100.0%

EXHIBIT 8   Soft Drink Market Trends in the United States—Diet Versus Regular

		1980	1985	1990
Diet	M Cases	770.0	1,500.2	2,223.0
	%	15.0	23.1	28.0
Regular	M Cases	4,403.0	4,999.8	5,717.0
	%	85.0	76.9	72.0
Total	M Cases	5,180.0	6,500.0	7,940.0
	%	100.0	100.0	100.0

their separate bottlers under a licensing agreement. Each bottler was assigned a territory on an exclusive basis.

Historically, colas dominated the U.S. soft drink market (70 percent market share in 1990) and, to a much lesser extent, lemon-limes (10 percent market share in 1990). Further, the cola market was dominated by Coca-Cola or PepsiCo brands. Therefore, most major bottlers had exclusive agreements with either Coca-Cola or PepsiCo to market their colas as the primary product line.

Because of their heavy dependence on the cola giants, the bottlers were under great pressure to bottle and market the other soft drink products produced by the cola companies. Many medium-sized bottlers had exclusive agreement with the Seven-Up Company and depended on 7-UP as their principal product. The remaining bottlers were mostly small, local companies dependent on other, smaller, soft drink brands. Once the principal product line was established by an exclusive agreement, the bottlers widened their product assortment by marketing other noncompeting adult soft drinks such as ginger ale, tonic water, sodas, and bottled waters and general soft drinks such as the peppers, oranges, and root beers. Thus a typical product line of a medium to large-sized bottler would consist of one of the following three combinations:

1. Coca-Cola, Fanta, Sprite, and Schweppes or Canada Dry (but not both)
2. Pepsi Cola, Slice, Mountain Dew, and Schweppes or Canada Dry (but not both)
3. 7-Up, 7-Up Gold, a noncompeting cola, and Schweppes or Canada Dry (but not both)

Fortunately for Schweppes and Canada Dry, Coca-Cola, Pepsi, and Seven-Up did not have their own brands of adult soft drinks. Therefore, the products marketed by Schweppes and Canada Dry complemented the general soft drinks of the cola and the lemon-lime giants. This made it relatively easy for them to convince major bottlers to accept adult soft drinks as complementary to their main product lines. Thus, though rigidly defined by factors beyond their control, Schweppes and Canada Dry found the market structure to be excellent. In some territories Schweppes had exclusive agreements with Coca-Cola bottlers to market its adult soft drinks and Canada Dry had exclusive agreements with Pepsi bottlers. In some other territories, Schweppes went with Pepsi bottlers and Canada Dry went with Coca-Cola bottlers. Thus, Schweppes and Canada Dry both marketed their products through Coca-Cola as well as PepsiCo bottlers. However, in no territory did Schweppes and Canada Dry use a common bottler.

The competition between Schweppes and Canada Dry was carried out in earnest in every aspect of the business.

In addition, historically, Canada Dry had developed a network of exclusive Canada Dry bottlers. Though totally committed to Canada Dry, their strength and importance in the market as well as to Canada Dry had gradually been reduced because of their limited product line. The total volume of soft drink business handled by each bottler ranged from 500,000 cases to 50 million cases per year, with 3 million cases per year as the typical size.

DISTRIBUTION OF ADULT SOFT DRINKS

The exclusive agreements made the bottlers solely responsible for distributing the soft drinks of their principals in the assigned territories. Armed with the exclusive distributorship of a full range of products, each bottler competed with the others to market its products through the various channels available. Depending on its relative influence, each bottler obtained its share of the space in supermarkets, drug stores, retail chains, convenience stores, gas stations, vending machines, and other outlets for soft drinks.

Marketers commonly classified store space as shelf space or display space. Shelf space was the regular space allocated to a product on the shelves in the aisles. Display space was the space on the shelves located at the end of the aisles that faced outward toward the periphery of the store. Over half of all shoppers invariably circled the store to buy daily necessities such as meats, vegetables, dairy products, and bakery products that the stores positioned along the periphery. The customers entered the aisles only when they needed specific items located there. As such, the end-of-aisle displays received the maximum consumer exposure and served to remind consumers of the items they might need. Thus, the shelf space and the display space each had its unique role in generating sales. Both were very precious to retailers, bottlers, and the soft drink companies alike. Naturally, there was great competition to acquire an adequate share of the limited store space.

Once a bottler had negotiated the store space with the retailers, management had to determine how to allocate it optimally among the various soft drink brands to offer a complete assortment to consumers and to maximize sales and profits. Conventionally, the bottlers displayed the general soft drinks, adult soft drinks, and bottled waters in separate groups, though in close proximity to one another. Typically the colas and the lemon-limes accounted for most of the business of a bottler, with the adult soft drinks constituting an important but very small portion of the business. Invariably the cola and the lemon-lime companies were able to dictate their terms in deciding the allocation of the total store space available to a bottler. As such, the colas and the lemon-limes dominated all prime display space and a large portion of the shelf space as well. In comparison, adult soft drinks had to fight hard for adequate shelf space. Fortunately, the dominant position of Canada Dry and Schweppes in the adult soft drink group and the noncompeting nature of their product lines made the task of obtaining shelf space slightly less difficult. Adult soft drinks accounted for 1 percent to 15 percent of the total business of Schweppes' bottlers, with 3.3 percent as the typical proportion. Generally a store carried an average inventory of six cases of each soft drink product, which turned over 25 times in a year. The relatively low bargaining power of even large bottlers of adult soft drinks made the marketing of adult soft drinks one of the toughest and most challenging tasks. Convincing the bottlers to allocate adequate space to adult soft drink brands became the primary focus of Schweppes' marketing efforts. Johnson described the task: "Our bottlers spill more Coke or Pepsi than the ginger ale they sell. We have no illusions here. Although we make an important contribution to their profits, it is only a small contribution. They do not really depend on us. We need them far more than they need us."

SCHWEPPES GINGER ALE PRODUCT LINE

Ginger ale consists of carbonated water, sugar syrup, and ginger flavor. Both Schweppes and Canada Dry marketed their own brands of ginger ale in regular and diet varieties. A much larger quantity of ginger ale was consumed when used as a soft drink than as a mixer. Therefore, in regions where both applications were popular, the consumption as a soft drink invariably generated the bulk of the sales volume. The relative consumption of the product for these two purposes varied in different regions of the United States. In the Northeast ginger ale was equally popular as a soft drink or as a mixer. In the West, it was primarily consumed as a mixer with alcohol. Because the sales of both Schweppes and Canada Dry were heavily concentrated in the Northeast, a very large proportion of the total ginger ale marketed by the two divisions was consumed as a soft drink.

It was fair to assume that the various brands of ginger ale competed among themselves for the market segment preferring ginger ale flavor. However, in a general sense, they also competed with all other adult soft drinks as well as all general soft drinks, and even all hot and cold beverages. Canada Dry was the largest marketer of ginger ale in North America, controlling 33.5 percent of the U.S. ginger ale market. Schweppes was the second-largest marketer, with 16.6 percent share of the market. The third competitor, Seagrams, had only 3.1 percent of the market.

CONSUMER IMAGE OF GINGER ALE

Despite the predominant use of ginger ale as a soft drink, most consumers did not think of ginger ale as a soft drink. Several unaided recall tests among users and nonusers of ginger ale had shown that very few people remembered or considered ginger ale to be a general soft drink. Most people primarily considered it either as a mixer or as a soft drink for special occasions such as adult social gatherings when alcohol was being consumed. There were many possible explanations for this phenomenon.

As mentioned previously, a person tended to consume a much larger quantity of ginger ale as a soft drink compared with the quantity consumed as a mixer. Although the bulk of the ginger ale was consumed as a soft drink, only a small number of consumers were involved in generating that volume, with each person consuming a relatively large quantity. In contrast, a relatively larger number of consumers were involved in generating a relatively smaller sales volume of ginger ale as a mixer, with each person consuming a small quantity of the soft drink. Such consumption was often in an adult setting where at least some people were consuming alcohol. This further confirmed the association of ginger ale with alcohol in consumers' perceptions.

In addition, the small market share of ginger ale compared with all soft drinks suggested that a large proportion of individuals were nonusers of the product. The image of ginger ale in the minds of such consumers was based on where they saw it being consumed and what they heard about it. On both these accounts, the probability was far greater that the nonusers encountered the ginger ale as a mixer rather than as a soft drink.

The bottlers also perceived ginger ale primarily as a mixer; therefore, they distributed it mainly in 1-liter PET bottles and promoted it as a mixer. This further confirmed and perpetuated the consumer image of ginger ale as a mixer. The only exception was in the Northeast, where the product was widely available in popular soft drink packaging of 12-ounce cans and 2-liter PET bottles.

Interestingly, surveys showed that even those who consumed ginger ale as a soft drink considered it primarily a mixer. Johnson was always puzzled by this apparent contradiction in the use of the product and its image. Further, he often felt that such a distorted image prevented ginger ale from exploiting its full potential as a tasty, refreshing general-purpose soft drink for all occasions. He wondered what he could possibly do to change the image of the product and reposition it in the consumer's mind as a mainstream general soft drink.

SCHWEPPES RASPBERRY GINGER ALE

In May 1988, one of the Schweppes' leading bottlers conceived the idea of marketing raspberry-flavored ginger ale as a general soft drink for all occasions. After obtaining initial clearance to explore the concept further, Johnson spent considerable time perfecting the product ingredients and conducting laboratory and field tests. The tests indicated that the product had a unique, appealing taste, and many of those who tried it felt that it was a fascinating new soft drink. By October 1990, the product was fully developed and Schweppes had to make the final decision about its commercial introduction. Johnson realized that product development was perhaps the easiest part of the whole process. The real challenge was to analyze the feasibility of the idea and prepare a new-product proposal to convince top management to proceed with the product's introduction. Once that decision was made, Johnson would have to convince the bottlers to adopt the product and obtain their commitment to make it available in retail outlets by January 1991.

Johnson was really excited about Schweppes Raspberry Ginger Ale (SRGA). He had always felt that for some unknown reason all Schweppes adult soft drinks, and especially ginger ale, had been locked in the upscale mixer image that limited their growth potential and isolated them from the volume business of the mainstream general soft drinks. However, he was confident that the SRGA had a unique and distinct personality that was powerful enough to make a clear break from ginger ale's traditional image and present itself as a legitimate general soft drink before the bottlers as well as the ultimate consumers. He felt that this product could launch the company on a totally new course to become a major player in the soft drink industry in times to come. This was an ideal way to bridge the gap between the company's image as a marketer of mixers and its desire to be a mainstream soft drink company.

In principle, the idea of creating new flavored versions of established soft drinks was not totally new. Other leading soft drink manufacturers had introduced different-flavored soft drinks. Some of these products, such as Cherry Coke and Cherry 7-UP had achieved limited success in the market, whereas others such as 7-UP Gold had failed and had to be withdrawn. Although the moderately successful products had created small segments of loyal consumers, they had been tried and rejected by many others. These consumers might be less enthusiastic about trying such new product versions the next time. Thus, despite the support of a major bottler, the product's unique refreshing taste, and strong consumer appeal, the company feared that it might face strong consumer resistance or disinterest. Moreover, Schweppes had always taken pride in its upscale image, if not its snob appeal. The new product concept aimed at the mass market might not fit this image as well.

Another area of uncertainty was the effect SRGA would have on other Schweppes products, as well as on Canada Dry and other CBNA divisions. Johnson felt that his immediate concern was to estimate the extent to which SRGA would cannibalize Schweppes' own ginger ale business. As a conservative estimate, he felt that initially about 20 percent of all SRGA sales would come from ginger ale. The cannibalized volume of Schweppes ginger ale would peak at 2 million cases per year and level off. However, he had no idea how the new product would impact various other brands of CBNA and other competitors in the market.

Johnson realized that he would have to modify the strategy he had developed to convince his top management for them to persuade the bottlers. In turn, he would have to help the bottlers convince the retailers to adopt the product. His major thrust would have to be on the new business generated by SRGA and the increase in total profits earned by each channel member.

In order to analyze the feasibility of SRGA, Johnson had compiled all relevant information. He estimated that ginger ale sold at an average price of $10 per 192-ounce case to the ultimate consumer. SRGA would be sold at about the same price. The retailers expected a margin of 20 percent on their sales revenue. Similarly, bottlers expected a margin of 25 percent on their sales to the retailers. The cost of each case to the bottler was $1 for the ginger ale concentrate paid to Schweppes, $2 for other variable materials, and $3 for all other variable costs. In Johnson's opinion, the channel members earned similar margins on all other major competing brands. Schweppes would have to sell SRGA concentrate to the bottlers at the same price as that of ginger ale concentrate.

For Schweppes, the cost of buying the ginger ale concentrate from its supplier was 15 percent of its sales revenue. In addition, Schweppes spent 45 percent of its sales revenue for marketing expenses. The SRGA concentrate would cost Schweppes 20 percent of sales and its marketing costs would be 50 percent of sales. In addition, $990,000 would have to be spent on introductory promotions.

Johnson realized that his first task would be to analyze how consumers were likely to perceive the new product in comparison with Schweppes ginger ale. Such an analysis would help him understand what efforts he had to make to successfully position SGRA as a mainstream soft drink. On the basis of his previous experience with new products and considering the fact that SRGA was to be introduced as a mainstream soft drink, Johnson's conservative forecast of SRGA sales in the first five years was 2, 5, 8, 10, and 14 million cases. Using these figures as the basis, Johnson now had to establish SRGA's feasibility for Schweppes, its bottlers, and its retailers. He would also have to estimate the likely consumer response to the new product. He realized that he would have to prepare his new-product proposal shortly so there would be sufficient time to approach the bottlers and actually introduce the product by January 1991.

MARKET INTRODUCTION OF SCHWEPPES RASPBERRY GINGER ALE

In January 1991, Schweppes Raspberry Ginger Ale was introduced nationally in the United States with full fanfare and with $1 million spent on introductory promotions. By the end of June, the company had surpassed all sales forecasts and sold 2 million cases of SRGA. When management compared the performance of various Schweppes product lines in the first six months of 1991 with the same period of 1990, they observed that Schweppes ginger ale sales had stayed at 15.6 million cases, although all other Schweppes products had recorded an increase of 4 percent, the same as the growth rate of the soft drink industry.

In an attempt to understand what impact SRGA had made on the other brands, the company conducted a consumer survey. Using a consumer panel, the study compared actual purchases of various brands during the first six months of 1990 with the first six months of 1991. The data were analyzed to determine what percentage of total SRGA sales had been generated at the cost of various other brands. The results of the study are summarized in Exhibit 9. Johnson realized that he had only a few days to analyze the SRGA's sales performance and the results of the survey. By the following week, he would have to present his findings before CBNA's top management and recommend a future course of action.

EXHIBIT 9   Percent of SRGA Sales Sourced from Various Competing Brands

Soft Drink Types	Schweppes	Canada Dry	Other CBNA	Total CBNA	Other Competitors	Total
Colas					22	22
Lemon-Lime					10	10
Peppers					1	1
Root Beer					5	5
Orange			3	3	11	14
All Other Flavors[a]	4	23		27	21	48
Total	4	23	3	30	70	100
[a]All Other Flavors						
Ginger Ales	3	23		26	10	36
Club Soda +						
Tonic Water	1	0		1	0	1
Bottled Waters					1	1
Other					10	10

Source: Schweppes, CBNA Consumer Study, January–June 1991.

Appendix A: Analyzing Strategic Marketing Cases

W. Jack Duncan, Peter M. Ginter, and Linda E. Swayne

How does a manager learn to make strategic marketing decisions? The most obvious way, and perhaps the most valuable if you were to have the opportunity, is to work your way up the organization and observe how senior executives deal with strategic issues. Then, when the opportunity presents itself, combine what you have learned with your own marketing philosophy to do the best you can. In this ideal world, there would never be "negative consequences" for mistakes, because the fear of losing our job or looking stupid restricts our willingness to try creative or unusual solutions that might not work. We learn best from our mistakes. Unfortunately, such opportunities are not practical in most organizations.

Even if this approach were feasible, it is very risky; and business firms, hospitals, educational institutions, and other organizations trust important strategic decision making only to the most "seasoned managers." For this reason, the case method has been successfully used to give aspiring managers opportunities to make strategic decisions without "betting the organization" on the outcome. In other words, cases offer an opportunity to deal with real decisions in a low-risk environment—an opportunity to try creative and unusual solutions.

LEARNING THROUGH CASE ANALYSIS

Cases contain situations actually faced by managers documented in a way that makes them useful in training decision makers. The decisions required to solve cases represent a wide range of complexity so that no two are addressed in exactly the same manner.

CASES: REAL AND IMAGINED

Many different types of cases are used in strategic marketing texts. Sometimes the cases are invented to illustrate a specific point. Usually these appear as "Ajax Corporation" or some similar name. Other cases are real but disguised. A writer may, for example, have information from an organization such as IBM or Maytag Corporation, but the company, for some reason, has requested that the case author not use its name. The information and the situation are real. Only a few cases in this book are disguised. If a case has been disguised, there is a statement in the footnote at the bottom of the first page of the case.

Most cases describe real and undisguised, ongoing organizations dealing with today's problems and opportunities. In addition, there are less well-known cases that have been selected because of the important issues they present to prospective managers. Sometimes the issues presented are not "problems" in the negative sense of something being wrong or impending doom for the company. Often the greatest challenge facing an organization is recognizing and acting on an opportunity rather than solving a problem.

Cases that have obvious solutions upon which everyone agrees are not good aids to learning decision-making skills. Managers rarely face decisions where the solution is self-evident to everyone. This does not mean that there are no good and bad answers or solutions in case analysis. However, the evaluation of a case analysis as good, better, or best is more often based on the approach and logic employed rather than on the precise recommendation offered.

CASES AND STRATEGIC MARKETING

Cases add realism that is impossible to achieve in traditional lecture classes, a realism that comes from the essential nature of cases. We may justifiably complain that cases fail to provide all the information necessary for decision making, but the fact is that decision makers never have all the information they want or need when they face strategic decisions. Risks must be taken in case analysis just as in any other decision-making activity.

Risk Taking in Case Analysis

Decisions about the future involve uncertainty. Strategic decision making, because it is futuristic and involves judgment, is particularly risky. Decision making under conditions of uncertainty requires that we devise some means of dealing with the risks faced by managers. Cases are valuable aids in this area because they allow us to practice making decisions in low-risk environments. A poor case analysis may be embarrassing, but at least it will not result in the bankruptcy of the company. At the same time, the lessons learned by solving cases and participating in discussions will begin to build problem-solving skills.

Unfortunately, many future decision makers are not familiar with how to analyze cases. Customarily, prospective managers learn how to succeed as students by taking objective examinations, writing occasional term papers, and crunching numbers on a computer, but they seldom solve real case problems. For this reason this appendix may be helpful—not to prescribe how all cases should be solved but to offer some initial direction on how to "surface" the real issues presented in the cases.

Solving Case Problems

Solving a case is much like solving any problem. First, the issues are defined, information is gathered, and alternatives are generated, evaluated, selected, and implemented. Although the person solving the case seldom has the opportunity to implement a decision, he or she should always keep in mind that recommendations must be tempered by the limitations imposed on the organization in terms of its human and nonhuman resources. As the strengths and weaknesses of the recommendations are analyzed, lessons are learned that can be applied to future decision making.

ALTERNATIVE PERSPECTIVES: PASSION OR OBJECTIVITY

Different hypothetical roles can be assumed when analyzing cases. Some students prefer to think of themselves as the chief executive or key administrator in order to impose a perspective on the problems presented in the case. This allows us the liberty to become a passionate advocate of a particular course of action. Others like to observe the case from the detached objectivity of a consultant who has been employed by the organization to solve a problem.

Either perspective can be assumed, but we believe the first offers some unique advantages. Because there are no absolutely correct or incorrect answers to complex cases, the most important lesson to learn is why managers behave as they do, why they select one alternative over all others, and why they pursue specific strategies under the conditions presented in the case. Becoming the manager, at least mentally, helps us learn the lessons case histories have to teach. On the other hand, a consultant may be able to look at a situation more objectively. If you are having difficulty developing a solution for a particularly challenging case, try assuming a different perspective.

Looking at a case from different perspectives assists in moving beyond strategy to implementation and includes political issues within the organization, including the importance of interpersonal preferences in decision making.

Although the approach outlined here is logical, it is important to remember that each case should be approached and appreciated as a unique opportunity for problem solving. The unlimited combinations of organization, industry, and environment make every case different.

DOING YOUR HOMEWORK

Effective case analysis begins with data collection. This means carefully reading the case, rereading it, and sometimes reading it again. Rarely can we absorb enough information from the first reading of a comprehensive case to adequately solve it. Therefore, collect information and make notes about details as the case unfolds. We have found that if the case is read *several* days ahead of the due date, the student has the opportunity for "free" thinking time—when you stand in line for tickets, in traffic, in the shower, and so on. Although some people are creative under pressure, too much pressure leads to poor case analysis.

Getting Information

The information required to successfully solve a case comes in two forms. The first type of information is given as part of the case and customarily includes things such as the history of the organization. its form of organization and management, its financial condition, and its current marketing strategy. Frequently a case will include information about the industry and maybe even some problems shared by competing firms. This is the easy part because the author of the case has done the work.

A second type of information is "obtainable." This information is not given in the case or by the instructor but is available from secondary sources in the library in familiar magazines and related publications. Obtainable secondary information helps us understand the nature of the industry, the competition, and other important environmental factors *at the time of the case.* Unless your instructor indicates otherwise, you should not investigate beyond the time of the case. It is natural, once you may have discovered what the company actually did in a given situation, to think that its response was the "correct" one. Often other solutions would have been better.

If the case does not include industry information, your instructor may expect you to do some detective work before proceeding. Find out what is happening in the industry and learn enough about trends to position the problems discussed in the case in a broader industry context. The culture of the organization or the style of the chief executive officer may also constitute relevant information.

CASE ANALYSIS

In the following discussion, one method of case analysis is presented. This approach, illustrated in Exhibit 1, offers a process or way of thinking about cases rather than prescribing the only way to approach the task of case analysis. Exhibit 1 is a model or outline that may be used to direct your thinking about solving problems and developing strategic marketing plans. This general framework for thinking through problems or opportunities can be applied to a variety of organizations. We believe this approach to case analysis is useful because it is a logical method of decision making.

First, it is important that we learn about the economic, social, technological, and political environments facing the organization. We begin with economic, social, political, and technological aspects of the general environment and then progress to the specifics of the industry in which the firm competes.

EXHIBIT 1   An Outline for Case Analysis

   I. Situational Analysis
      A. External Environmental Analysis
         1. General Environmental Analysis—Economic, Social, Political, Technological
         2. Industry Analysis—Economic, Social, Political, Technological
         3. Market Analysis
      B. Internal Environmental Analysis
         1. Evaluation of the Mission
         2. Evaluation of the Objectives
         3. Evaluation of the Functional Areas
            a. Marketing
            b. Finance
            c. Production
            d. Human Resources
         4. Evaluation of Marketing Strategies
            a. Target Market
            b. Product Strategies
            c. Pricing Strategies
            d. Distribution Strategies
            e. Promotional Strategies
               (1). Advertising Strategies
               (2). Selling Strategies
               (3). Public Relations/Publicity Strategies
               (4). Sales Promotion Strategies
      C. Strengths, Weaknesses, Opportunities, and Threats (SWOT) Analysis
  II. Identification of the Problem (Opportunity)
 III. Development of Strategic Alternatives
 IV. Evaluation of the Strategic Alternatives
  V. Recommendations
 VI. Implementation
VII. Finalizing the Report

Next, we gather as many facts as we can about the environment of the organization under examination. This may be a consumer durable-goods manufacturer, hospital, retail operation, or industrial-goods marketer. We then relate the strategic capabilities of the organization to the external environment. A thorough and objective analysis of the organization's internal strengths and weaknesses is required. It is also necessary to understand the unique culture of the organization, including its mission and strategic objectives.

Next, the capabilities and interactions of the various subsystems—marketing, finance, operations, personnel—must be evaluated. These subsystems will determine, to a great extent, the likelihood that a particular strategy will be implemented. Although marketing strategy might dictate introduction of a new product line, financing may be too limited or the plant already may be operating at full capacity.

Once the situational analysis is complete, strategic alternatives can be generated as possible solutions to the problems identified in the case. This is the strategy formulation stage and is an important part of solving strategic marketing cases. The strategic direction is determined on the basis of the unique "fit" between the organization's internal strengths and weaknesses and the external opportunities and threats. Companies should attempt to take advantage of the opportunities in the environment and avoid the threats—based on organizational strengths. Organizational weaknesses may suggest areas that management needs to investigate and change, especially if a weakness is related to a threat.

The problem is identified, strategic alternatives generated, and a course of action is recommended. Finally, the effectiveness of the chosen strategic alternative must be evaluated. Because of the nature of case analysis, this aspect of strategic control is not always possible. However, at least some thought must be given to the likely outcomes resulting from different strategic choices.

SITUATION ANALYSIS—A CLOSER LOOK

The first step in case analysis is to understand the environment, the organization, the industry, and the decision makers at the time a strategic decision is needed. This is called "situation analysis" because we must understand the circumstances and the environment facing the organization if good decisions are to result from our analysis. Situation analysis is one of the most important steps in analyzing a case. The list below highlights some of the important areas that might be included in this stage of case analysis.

A. External Environmental Analysis

1. The General Environment.

What are the macroenvironmental factors that will affect the organization? What are the prevailing economic conditions affecting the nation or world? What regulatory philosophies, trends, and legislation will affect citizens and organizations within the society? What lifestyle and demographic factors are changing and how rapidly? What technological forces are likely to influence strategic decision making?

2. The Environment Within the Industry.

What is the size of the industry? Growth trends?

What is the nature of the competition? How many direct competitors are there, and is the competition increasing or decreasing? What are the relative market shares of the different competitors? Which organizations are indirect competitors?

What are the macroenvironmental factors that will affect the industry? What are the prevailing economic conditions? What regulatory philosophies, trends, and legislation will affect the industry? What lifestyle and demographic factors are changing and how rapidly? What technological forces are likely to influence strategic decision making within the industry?

3. The Market.

Who are the organization's primary customers—baby boomers, the elderly, working mothers? To what extent are the customers loyal to the organization's products and services? Is price the only major determinant in the purchasing decision? Will customers travel and otherwise be inconvenienced to obtain the organization's products and services?

How sophisticated are the organization's customers in terms of their buying habits and processes? What does this tell management about advertising and promotion?

Is the market for the organization's products geographically concentrated? Located in the top 100 ADIs (areas of dominant influence)?

Are market segments easily identified? Are different strategies for each feasible or advisable?

B. Internal Environmental Analysis

1. Mission. Does the organization have a clear sense of mission? Is there a mission statement and is it communicated to those responsible for accomplishing it? Does the organization have the human and nonhuman resources necessary to accomplish its mission?

2. Objectives. Are there well-developed and communicated long- and short-range objectives? Are they shared with those responsible for achieving them?

3. Functional Area Analysis. Are the functional areas working synergistically to achieve the organization's objectives?

Are the financial resources needed to compete available, or is the organization undercapitalized, too highly leveraged, or not leveraged enough? How do the key financial ratios of this organization compare with others in the industry and region?

Is the organization operating at capacity? Are equipment, facilities, and so forth new and up-to-date? Are the company's products labor-intensive? Is quality at a desirable level?

Are the organization's managers and employees skilled in their work? Is turnover a factor? Is there a shortage of trained personnel to fill jobs?

4. Marketing Strategies. Are the organization's marketing strategies appropriate to achieve the organization's objectives?

How sophisticated is the organization in terms of its marketing activities? How flexible are the organization's marketing policies? When was the last time management tried something new and innovative in the area of marketing? More important, perhaps, has the organization ever done any serious marketing of its services?

What about products and services? Does the organization offer a full range of products? Is the present product mix complementary, or does the organization compete with itself in some areas? Could the overall level of business be significantly increased if selected new products and services were added? Should any products or services be discontinued?

Are the company's prices acceptable to customers? Are the prices above, at, or below competition? What image is price meant to convey?

Has the appropriate channel(s) of distribution been identified and utilized? Is distribution national or regional? Is company ownership of the channel appropriate? Would intensive, selective, or exclusive distribution be most appropriate? Is location an important factor?

Has serious thought been given to a promotion strategy? What is the proper blend of the promotional elements—advertising, personal selling, publicity, and sales promotion?

If you are not comfortable with your answers to this list of questions, read the case for a second or third time.

Purpose or Mission of the Organization

Peter Drucker says that anyone who wants to "know" a business must start with understanding its purpose or mission.[1] If a mission statement is included in the case, does it serve the purpose of communicating to the public why the organization exists? Mission statements provide valuable information, but they also leave much to be inferred and even imagined. Missions are broad, general statements outlining what makes the organization unique.

A good mission should answer a series of questions. When you read the assigned case, ask if you know enough about the organization's mission to confidently speculate about the following:

1. Who are the customers? The customers may be children, older adults, women, or patients in a hospital. This group or these groups must be identified before any serious strategic analysis of the organization can be initiated.

2. What are the organization's principal services? Does the organization have unique experience and expertise in some areas of specialization?

3. Where does the organization intend to compete? Is the case about a small retail outlet that competes only in one local market, or is it a regional or national force in the delivery of consumer goods?

4. Who are the competitors? Is the case about an industrial product with a few well-known competitors, or does it operate in a market along with many other similar competitors? In other words, how much competition is actually present in the market(s) where the organization competes or intends to compete?

5. What is the preference of the organization with regard to its public image? If a large clothing manufacturer wants to be perceived in certain ways, it may have to limit its options when defining and solving strategic issues. Is it, for example, important to the leadership of the clothes manufacturer that it be regarded as a producer of designer clothing or a good value for the money?

6. What does the organization want to be like in the future? Does the information in the case indicate the organization wants to continue to operate as it

---

[1]Peter F. Drucker, *Management: Tasks, Responsibilities, and Practices* (New York: Harper & Row, 1974).

does at the present time, or does it wish to expand its markets and services offered or even change its own basic operating philosophy?[2]

If a formal mission statement is not presented in a case, it may be important to attempt to construct one based on the information provided.

Objectives: More Specific Directions

Mission statements are broad and provide general direction. Objectives should be specific and explicitly point to where the organization is expected to be at a particular time in the future. Sometimes the case will indicate what the organization plans to achieve in the next year, where it hopes to be in three years, or even its five-year objectives. As with mission statements, if the objectives are not explicitly stated, there is a need to speculate about them because they will be the standards against which the success or failure of a particular strategy will be evaluated.

When constructing or modifying organization objectives, be sure they are as measurable as possible. This is important so that decision makers can use them as a reflection of organizational priorities and as a way of determining how to set their own personal and professional priorities. Make sure that the objectives are motivational and inspirational, yet feasible and attainable. Moreover, because strategic marketing is futuristic and no one can predict the future with complete accuracy, objectives should always be adaptable to the changing conditions taking place in the organization and in the industry. Sometimes an organization will have to face a major strategic problem simply because it was unwilling to alter its objectives in light of changing conditions in the industry.

As a test of your own understanding of the organization under examination, before attacking problems, reflect on what your reading of the case told you about the mission and objectives of the organization. Are the objectives being pursued consistent with what you understand to be the mission of the organization? Are the aspirations of the organization's managers realistic in view of the competition and the organization's strengths and weaknesses?

Strategic Marketing Issues

Once the corporate mission and objectives have been reviewed, the current marketing strategies should be evaluated. A good starting point for this analysis is to consider the company's stated target market in relation to what you have discovered concerning the external environment. Proper identification of the target market is a key decision in strategic marketing. In most cases you should consider such questions as:

1. Has the market been segmented by competitors? What is the basis for segmentation? Which segments are the largest? Which have the most potential? How well are the segments being served?

2. Is the total market growing? Is the company's segment growing? Is the company's segment of the market large enough to support the product or service?

3. Are there segments that are not currently being served? Could the company successfully serve these markets?

---

[2]John Pearce II and Fred David, "Corporate Mission Statements: The Bottom Line." *Academy of Management Executive,* May, 1987, pp. 109–116.

4. Are the company's products and services matched well with the specified target market?

5. Are there any economic, social, political, regulatory, technological, or competitive changes anticipated that will change the dynamics of the industry?

In addition to these important questions, you should do a complete analysis of the marketing mix developed to meet the needs of the target market. This analysis will require you to perform a comparative analysis of industry pricing practices, promotional approaches, distribution methods, and product attributes. Because the marketing mix for direct and indirect competitors is linked with their segmentation strategies, you will gain new insights about the dynamics of the industry. If you are to develop an effective marketing strategy, you need to understand the key "players" in the industry.

Strengths, Weaknesses, Opportunities, and Threats

Once we have reviewed our situation, a better evaluation of the opportunities and threats facing the organization can be made. Moreover, we must be able to look objectively at our own organization and ask: "Given the organization's apparent strengths and weaknesses, how do we take advantage of our opportunities and avoid the dangers in the environment?" An effective way of asking these questions is with the use of SWOT (strengths, weaknesses, opportunities, and threats) analysis. Exhibit 2 presents an example of how SWOT analysis is organized.

An illustration may help you to understand how SWOT analysis relates strengths, weaknesses, opportunities and threats. Suppose in the case that you are studying, the chief executive officer of a regional restaurant chain specializing in steaks is considering expansion into a new geographic region (market development). An environmental analysis confirms that people are increasingly eating out because of more disposable income, more two-income families, and less time available for meal preparation. In addition, the analysis has revealed that the market is extremely large and well segmented.

EXHIBIT 2   Strengths, Weaknesses, Opportunities, and Threats (SWOT) Analysis

Internal Strengths
1. The ability to deliver a quality product at a reasonable price.
2. Strong consumer franchise in the southeastern region of the United States.
3. Operating at near-capacity with current menu.
4. Strong in current market niche.

Internal Weaknesses
1. Limited menu.
2. Limited geographic area.
3. Limited number of qualified restaurant managers.
4. Aging restaurants.

External Opportunities
1. Eating out is increasing in the United States.
2. Dining-out market is extremely large.

External Threats
1. Health trends in the consumption of red meat.
2. Aggressive competition.
3. Decline in the steak segment of the eating-away-from-home market.

Also, it has been determined that interest rates are at a 20-year low and expansion could be financed through debt. Research reveals that the consumption of red meat is on the decline and there is a trend toward declining market share for steak-menu restaurants. In addition, there is increasing competition in the non-red meat segment.

The CEO believes that the restaurant chain has a number of internal strengths. It has, for example, a reputation for delivering a quality product at a reasonable price. It has developed a strong image and loyalty in the southeastern region of the United States. In addition, the chain is operating at near-full capacity with their steak menu. There are few strong competitors in its niche of the market. A review of the restaurant chain's financial statements indicated that it could easily absorb additional debt financing that would be necessary for aggressive expansion.

The CEO does worry about the chain's limited menu. In addition, many of the company's restaurants are aging and will need to be remodeled in the coming years. Although management is currently strong, finding well-qualified restaurant managers is becoming increasingly difficult. The CEO also worries that, because of his current level of penetration in the southeastern market, further growth will be limited without expansion into a new geographic market.

Through the use of SWOT analysis, the CEO can systematically look at the opportunities, threats, strengths, and weaknesses and make a more informed decision.

FINDING PROBLEMS

From your very first reading, start to list the strategic marketing problems and opportunities facing the organization. When a problem is discovered, mark it for more-detailed examination. Situation analysis is designed to surface present and potential problems. Perhaps there are few, if any, apparent problems. In case analysis, problems include not only the usual idea of a "problem" but also situations in which things may be working well but improvements are possible. As noted previously, the "problem" may actually be an opportunity that can be capitalized on by the organization if it acts consciously and decisively.

When we analyze things carefully, patterns can be detected, and discrepancies between what actually is and what ought to be become more apparent. In other words, fundamental issues, not mere symptoms, begin to emerge.

Looking for Real Causes, Not Symptoms

It is important to realize that the things observed in an organization and reported in a case may not be the "real" or essential problems and opportunities. Often what we observe are the symptoms of more-serious core problems. For example, declining sales appears to be a problem in many case analyses. In reality, the problem may be poor training of the sales force, inferior product quality, distribution problems causing out of stocks, incorrect positioning, prices that are too high (or too low), and so forth. The fundamental problem, however, might be changes in the demographics of the market. Problems may have more than a single cause, so do not be overly confident when a single, simple reason is isolated. In fact, the suggestion of a simple solution should increase rather than decrease our skepticism.

Getting to core problems requires that information be carefully examined and analyzed, and quantitative tools can often help. Financial ratio analysis of the exhibits included in the case will sometimes be helpful in identifying the real problems. Appendix B illustrates how financial analysis and information can be used to identify core problems in an organization.

In arriving at the ultimate determination of core problems, case analysis should never be "paralyzed by analysis" and waste more time than is necessary on identifying problems. At the same time, premature judgments about problem areas should not be made because of the risk of missing the "real" issues.

Always review the obtainable sources of data before moving to the next step. One general guideline is that when research and analysis cease to generate surprises (when we can confidently say, "I have seen that before"), we can feel relatively, but not absolutely, sure that adequate research has been conducted and the core problems have been identified.

Identifying Important Issues

Once the problems are identified, they must be precisely stated and the selection defended. The best defense for the selection of the core problem is the data set used to guide the problem-discovery process. The reasons for selection of the problems and issues should be briefly and specifically summarized along with the supportive information upon which judgments have been based.

The problem-statement stage is not the time for solutions. Focusing on solutions at this point will reduce the impact of the problem statement. If the role of consultant has been assumed, the problem statement must be convincing, precise, and logical to the client organization or credibility will be reduced. If the role of the strategic decision maker has been selected, you must be equally convincing and precise. The strategic decision maker should be as confident as possible that the correct problems have been identified in order to pursue appropriate opportunities. After all, the manager will be the one responsible ensuring things actually happen and strategies are actually implemented.

The statement of the problem should relate only to those areas of strategy and operations where actions have a chance of producing results. The results may be either increasing gains or cutting potential losses. Long- and short-range aspects of problems should also be identified and stated. In strategic analysis the emphasis is on long-range problems rather than merely patching up emergencies and holding things together.

It is important to keep in mind that most strategic decision makers can deal with only a limited number of issues at a single time. Therefore, identify key result areas that will have the greatest positive impact on organizational performance.

Analysis

When the problems in the case are satisfactorily defined, they must be analyzed. This involves generating alternative solutions and evaluating the alternatives. This should not be done without thinking about and using the concepts that you have previously learned in marketing and other courses that you have taken.

Developing a Theoretical Perspective

One of the most serious mistakes made in case analysis is to attempt analysis inside a "theoretical vacuum." It is important that the problems be defined and opportunities be evaluated according to some consistent theoretical perspective. Do not be afraid to use the concepts and terms that you have learned from various marketing classes. At the same time, do not "load" your analysis with explanations and definitions of those concepts and terms. Your professor has taught those ideas, and fellow students are supposed to know them.

It might be that problems concerning lack of revenue growth are really problems of not responding adequately to customer needs—the lack of a marketing orientation. In the past, some organizations have tended to disregard the importance of the "strategic decision" to focus on the customer. Many revenue shortfalls could be resolved with the use of the relatively simple marketing philosophy. A proper theoretical perspective, for example, might suggest that consumers are less concerned with the location than they are with how they are treated when they arrive.

Diffusion of innovation is a concept that could be used to explain why a product in the introductory stage of the product life cycle is not increasing in sales as rapidly as the company had hoped. Suggesting that a dominant firm in an industry buy out competition to increase market share illustrates that you do not understand the forms of business competition and the constraints facing each form. Do not become so focused on the case that you forget the realities of the marketplace.

Alternative Actions and Solutions

If the job of obtaining and organizing information has been done well, the generation of alternatives will be a challenging yet attainable task. Good alternatives possess specific characteristics. They should be *practical*, or no one will seriously consider them. Alternative courses of action that are too theoretical or abstract to be understood by those who have to accomplish them are not useful. Alternatives should be *carefully stated* with a brief justification of why they are useful ways of solving at least one of the core problems in the case. Alternatives should be *specific*. Relate each alternative to the core problem it is intended to address. This is a good check on your work. If the alternatives generated do not directly address core problems, ask yourself if they are important to the case analysis or whether they should be eliminated from consideration.

Finally, alternatives should be *usable*. A usable alternative is one that can be reasonably accomplished within the constraints of the financial and human resources available to the organization. Alternatives should be ones that can be *placed into action* in a relatively short period of time. If it takes too long to implement a proposed solution, it is likely that the momentum of the recommended action will be lost. Of course, implementation should always take place in light of potential long-range effects of shorter-term decisions.

After the alternatives have been generated and listed, each one must be (1) evaluated in terms of the core problems and key result areas isolated in the prior analysis, (2) evaluated in terms of its relative advantage or disadvantage compared with other possible solutions to core problems, and (3) justified as a potentially valuable way of addressing the strategic issues found in the case.

Evaluating Alternatives

Alternatives should be evaluated according to both quantitative and qualitative criteria. Break-even analysis provides one basis for examining the impact of different courses of action. However, a good alternative course of action is more than merely the one with the lowest breakeven. A poorer quality product, offered at a low price, would achieve a low breakeven, but would it diminish the prestige of the company's other brands? What other long-term effects might occur?

Carefully think through the advantages and disadvantages of each alternative. All alternatives have disadvantages; you cannot ignore an evaluation/assessment of the risks associated with an alternative. Sometimes information in the case will provide the basis for evaluating the alternatives. The company states that it is intent on growth but refuses to borrow money. Which alternatives can offer growth at a very low cost?

Once the alternatives have been evaluated, one must be selected. At this point it is *absolutely essential* to completely understand the criteria upon which the selection is being made and the justification for the criteria. Sometimes the key to identifying the criteria is in the case itself. At other times it is necessary to look outside to what is going on in the industry. Is competition for services so fierce that capital investment decisions are likely to radically affect the organization's ability to compete? If so, should the organization intentionally postpone short-term actions to ensure sufficient resources are dedicated to modernization of facilities and the purchase of up-to-date technologies in order to improve the chances of long-range growth and development?

Making Recommendations

Making good recommendations is a critical aspect of successful case analysis. If recommendations are theoretically sound and justifiable, people will pay attention to them. If they are not, little is likely to result from all the work done to this point.

One effective method for presenting recommendations is to relate each one to organizational strengths. Or, if necessary, a recommendation can illustrate how it assists in avoiding known weaknesses. For example, if the marketing resources are limited, it will be important to avoid recommendations that rely on resources that are not available. Beware of recommending marketing research. In most instances, the decision maker does not have six months or a year that it would take to perform the research. If you see no other alternative, specify concisely the type of research you would do, what results you expect, what decision you would make based on the results expected, and your prediction about the likelihood of the results you expect. In case analysis, further research is a difficult recommendation to support.

Implementation

Once the strategic alternative(s) has been selected to recommend, implementation has to be considered. Implementation moves the decision maker from the realm of strategic marketing to marketing management. The question becomes, "How do we get all this done in the most effective and efficient way possible?"

The task of case analysis cannot require that the student implement a decision in a real firm. However, because alternatives must be "implementable," it is necessary that thought be given to how each alternative would actually be put into action. Implementation requires two important steps for each recommended alternative. First, the decision maker must decide what activities are needed to accomplish the alternative action. This involves thinking through the process and outlining all the steps that will be required. Next, the list of required activities should be carefully reviewed to determine who in the organization will be assigned the responsibility for accomplishing the different tasks.

Although implementation is not generally possible in case analysis, it is important that consideration be given to how, in a real organization, the recommendations would be accomplished. If, in the process of thinking about completing the different activities it becomes apparent that the organization does not have the resources nor the structure to accomplish the recommendations, other approaches should be proposed.

Finalizing the Report

The preparation and presentation of the case report are the end result of case analysis. The report can be either written or oral, depending on the preference of the instructor, but the goal is the same—to summarize and communicate in an effective manner what the analysis has uncovered. In view of the strategic problems and the operational condition of the organization, the *alternative* courses of action can now be generated and listed. Each of the alternatives can then be *evaluated*. When the evaluation is complete, the *recommendations* should be presented in considerable detail and particular attention given to the problem of *implementation*.

Conclusions

Case analysis is an art, and there is no one precise way of accomplishing the task. Adapt the analysis to the case problem under review. The thing to keep in mind is that case analysis is a logical process that involves (1) understanding the organization, industry, and environment; (2) clear definition of strategic problems and opportunities; (3) generation of alternative courses of action; (4) analysis, evaluation, and recommendation of the most-promising courses of action; (5) and at least some consideration of implementation.

The work of case analysis is not over until all these stages are completed. Often a formal written report or oral presentation of the recommendations is required (see Appendix C). Case analysis and presentation should always be approached and accomplished in a professional manner. Case problems provide a unique opportunity to integrate all you have learned about decision making and direct it toward specific problems and opportunities faced by real organizations. It is an exciting way to gain experience and decision-making skills. Take it seriously and develop your own systematic and defensible way of solving strategic marketing problems.

REFERENCES

Edge, Alfred G., and Denis R. Coleman. *The Guide to Case Analysis and Reporting,* 3rd ed. Honolulu: System Logic, 1986.

Ronstadt, Robert. *The Art of Case Analysis.* Dover, MA: Lord, 1980.

Appendix B: Financial Analysis for Marketing Strategists

Bennie H. Nunnally, Jr.

INTRODUCTION

Marketers cannot make decisions without considering the financial implications of those decisions. It requires capital to pursue growth opportunities, to battle for market share as a challenger against a strong market leader, to introduce new products, and to try a multitude of other alternatives that a marketing manager may consider. But does the firm have sufficient flexibility, in a financial sense, to pursue one or more alternatives? An investigation of the firm's financial condition can lead to better decision making.

Financial condition is represented by the firm's profitability, liquidity, asset management, and financing pattern. Although profitability is probably self-explanatory, the other concepts, which may be observed and analyzed from the firm's financial statements, will briefly be explained. Liquidity represents the firm's ability to pay its current liabilities (e.g., accounts payable, wages/taxes payable) out of its current assets (e.g., cash and accounts receivable). Asset management information reveals the firm's ability to make use of its cash, land and buildings, and equipment in order to increase the value of the firm. The firm's financing pattern refers to the amount of debt used by the firm to finance its assets, and how, if at all, that pattern compares to similar firms or to the firm's own operating history.

Once specific alternatives have been determined and marketing managers are assessing the costs and benefits of each alternative, break-even analysis can provide additional useful information. Break-even analysis has as its foundation those factors that affect profit: sales volume, variable costs, and fixed costs. Break-even volume is that level of sales wherein profit is zero, or revenue equals fixed plus variable (total) costs.

Financial planners, marketers, and others involved in planning are interested in the break-even concept because it highlights the sales volume of the firm's products. The level of sales affects profitability, production, purchasing, personnel, and more, and bears directly on the need for funds, either short-term or long-term.

THE BASIC FINANCIAL STATEMENTS

The financial statements issued by for-profit firms are found in their annual reports. The annual report is both an official (audited financial statement) and unofficial (management assessments and projections of a relatively nonquantitative nature) record of the company's position at that point in time. An annual report is issued by all firms whose stock is publicly traded. The financial statements found in the annual report are the balance sheet, income statement, statement of changes in financial position, and the statement of retained earnings.

To analyze financial statements it is necessary to understand the relationship among the statements. In order to understand such an interrelationship it is important to become familiar with each individual statement. A first step in becoming skillful in statement analysis is to learn the general format. If the format is familiar, it becomes much easier to learn the techniques of analysis.

For example, there is a pattern to the structure or format of the balance sheet. Simply, the balance sheet items are arranged in descending order of liquidity. Familiarity with the statements will greatly contribute to the interesting, useful, and, yes, marketable things that will be learned in this note.

Exhibits 1, 2, 3, and 4 illustrate the financial statements of the Wick Manufacturing Company. The format of each statement is typical of those released by most firms. Wick manufactures various paper and cardboard containers, and most sales are to the grocery industry.

The Income Statement

The firm's income statement, sometimes called a profit and loss statement, reflects the sales less the expenses related to making those sales for a specific period of time. Taxes are also shown on the income statement, with a final figure being net income. In Exhibit 1 the net income after tax is divided by the number of common shares outstanding to reflect the earnings as it applies to each share of outstanding common stock (earnings per share, or EPS). In addition, the amount of net income actually paid out as dividends is shown on Wick's income statement. The dividends paid are based on a predeter-

EXHIBIT 1   Wick Manufacturing Company Income Statement for Years Ended 1992 and 1993

	1992	1993
Sales	$109,848	$126,540
Cost of Goods Sold[a]	68,068	72,834
Gross Profit	41,783	53,706
Expenses (Selling, Administrative, Interest, Depreciation)	27,462	31,044
Profit before Tax	14,321	22,662
Taxes (45%)	6,444	10,198
Net Income	$ 7,877	$ 12,464
Earnings per Share (EPS)	7.88	12.46
Dividends per Share (DPS 49% of EPS)	3.86	6.11
[a] Determined as follows:		
Beginning Inventory	$ 28,663	$ 27,462
Purchases	66,864	76,953
Goods Available for Sale	95,527	104,415
Ending Inventory	27,462	31,581
Cost of Goods Sold	$ 68,065	$ 72,834

EXHIBIT 2   Wick Manufacturing Company Balance Sheet, December 31, 1992, and December 31, 1993

	1992	1993
Assets		
Cash	$ 6,925	$ 8,185
Accounts Receivable	418	481
Inventory	27,462	31,581
Total Current Assets	34,805	40,247
Property, Plant, Equipment	14,328	16,477
Accumulated Depreciation	1,194	1,374
Net Property, Plant, Equipment	13,134	15,104
Total Assets	$47,939	$55,351
Liabilities and Stockholders' Equity		
Accounts payable	4,537	5,218
Accrued Wages and Taxes	2,448	2,815
Total Current Liabilities	6,985	8,033
Long-Term Debt (12%)	5,134	5,134
Common Stock (1,000 Shares)	11,940	11,940
Paid-In Capital	5,970	5,970
Retained Earnings	17,910	24,274
Total Liabilities and Stockholders' Equity	$47,939	$55,351

EXHIBIT 3   Wick Manufacturing Company Statement of Retained Earnings

Retained Earnings Balance, December 31, 1992	$17,910
Plus Net Income, 1993	12,464
Less Dividends Paid, 1993	(6,100)
Retained Earnings Balance, December 31, 1993	$24,274

mined and relatively stable company policy but are declared by the board of directors in each dividend period.

The Balance Sheet

A balance sheet (Exhibit 2) shows the financial condition of the firm at a particular point in time. In the case of Wick Manufacturing Company, the balance sheets are provided for the end of the calendar years 1992 and 1993. The calender year and the firm's fiscal year (the accounting period that begins and ends at a particular time during the year, as determined by company management and at the end of which the annual reports are issued) may not coincide. The assets shown in Exhibit 2 represent the means of production that

EXHIBIT 4   Wick Manufacturing Company Statement of Changes in Financial Position, December 31, 1993

Sources

Profit after Tax	$12,464
Depreciation	180
Total Sources	$12,644

Uses

Dividends	$ 6,101
Fixed Assets	2,149
Net Change in Working Capital	4,394
	$12,644

Analysis of Working Capital Changes

Increase (Decrease) in Current Assets		Increase (Decrease) in Current Liabilities	
Cash	$1,260		
Accounts Receivable	63	Accounts Payable	$ 681
Inventory	4,119	Accruals	367
Total	$5,442	Total	$1,048
Increase in Current Assets		$5,442	
Increase in Current Liabilities		1,048	
Net Change in Working Capital		$4,394	

are owned by the firm. The liabilities and equity represent the claims on these assets. That section shows all current liabilities and other debt items and the owner-supplied capital such as stockholders' equity. (The sum of common stock, retained earnings, and paid-in capital, which is dollars received for common stock in excess of par value, equals stockholders' equity.) The assets must equal the liabilities plus capital of the firm.

Statement of Retained Earnings

A firm has two uses for its profit (Exhibit 3). A portion is paid to the owners (equity holders) as dividends. The remaining profit is retained in the firm, thereby becoming a part, or perhaps all, of the financing for the assets of the firm. That part retained in the firm is added to the balance sheet item "retained earnings" at the end of each accounting period. This is an important way in which the income statement and balance sheet are interrelated.

Statement of Changes in Financial Position

A company's managers, its creditors, and other individuals or organizations will at some point be interested in a firm's liquidity. Liquidity refers to the ease with which an asset can be converted to cash. This would be most important to creditors, say, if the firm were to become bankrupt. The change in financial position, as well as the current financial position, relates directly to the question of liquidity. Exhibit 4 illustrates the uses of funds by Wick Manufacturing Company and the sources of funds between 1992 and 1993. The statement of changes in financial position is often referred to as a "source and use of funds" statement because it illustrates the origin or source of money used by the firm in a given time period. The following definitions may help to clarify the nature of sources and uses of funds.

A *source of funds* is an increase in the liability or capital account or a decrease in an asset account. A *use of funds* is a decrease in a liability or capital account or an increase in an asset account. For example, in Exhibit 2, Wick Manufacturing had an increase in accounts receivable of $63 ($481—$418) between year-end 1992 and year-end 1993. That was a use of funds of $63 for that period because Wick committed $63 in additional funds for that period to an asset. By contrast, the $681 increase in accounts payable for the same period represents a source of funds for the firm because Wick's suppliers financed Wick's increased payables for that period.

The preparation of the sources and uses of funds statement begins with the selection of an interval of time, one fiscal year to the next, for example. Then the items that provided cash or require cash, for that time period, are compared. The result will be the effect of the "cash movement" upon working capital. *Working capital* is current assets and current liabilities collectively; *net working capital* is current assets minus current liabilities.

A sources and uses of funds statement also permits the maturity of the sources and uses to be compared. It is necessary, in general, that the maturity of the source (short-term, such as an increase in accounts payable) be matched with the maturity of the use (short-term, such as an increase in inventory). Such maturity matching will likely lead to improved control over the firm's working capital. That improved control will likely reduce the level or frequency of borrowed funds.

SELECTED FINANCIAL RATIOS

The analysis of financial statements involves recognizing the information conveyed by each statement and the interrelationships among the statements. In addition, the time for which the statement is analyzed should be consistent if more than one type of statement is being reviewed. The information content of the financial statements can best be illustrated in terms of financial ratio analysis.

Financial ratio analysis is a means of reviewing financial data relative to some standard. That standard may be trend (activity over time) or industry comparison or both. The ratios may be divided into five categories: (1) current ratios, (2) debt ratios, (3) asset management ratios, (4) profitability ratios, and (5) market value ratios. The financial data presented for Wick Manufacturing Company will be used to illustrate the ratios used most by marketers: the liquidity ratios, the asset management ratios, and the profit to sales ratio.

Liquidity Ratios

As noted previously, a firm's liquidity is a major concern for anyone who has dollars invested in that firm or anticipates investment in the firm. Liquidity ratios indicate whether a firm has enough cash or other liquid assets to meet its short-term obligations.

Current Ratio The current ratio is equal to current assets divided by the current liabilities. Current assets are those assets that will be converted to cash within the near future, usually a year or less. Current liabilities are those liabilities that will likely be paid within a year's time. The current assets and liabilities are liquidated as a normal part of the firm's business activities. The current ratio is a direct measure of the firm's liquidity. For Wick Manufacturing the current ratios for 1992 and 1993 are as follows:

$$\text{Current ratio} = \frac{\text{Current assets}}{\text{Current liabilities}}$$

$$\text{Current ratio}_{1992} = \frac{\$34,805}{\$6,985} = 4.98 \times$$

$$\text{Current ratio}_{1993} = \frac{\$40,247}{\$8,033} = 5.0 \times$$

An interested party can immediately draw the following information from the company's current ratio: (1) if the firm had to liquidate (pay its creditors and cease operation), it would be able to cover each dollar owed in current liabilities with approximately $5 of current assets. (2) Assuming an industry average of 4 times, then Wick is 25 percent more liquid than the average firm in the industry. Therefore, Wick's current ratio is favorable.

Quick Ratio   Again, the items on the balance sheet are arranged in descending order of liquidity—if inventory (often the least-liquid of the current assets) is not a part of the firm's liquidity then we may calculate a "quick" ratio for Wick. The quick ratio is equal to the current assets, minus inventory, divided by total current liabilities. Thus, if Wick had to liquidate quickly it could still cover its current liabilities even if inventory were not readily convertible to cash. As with the current ratio, the quick ratio (sometimes called the acid-test ratio) can be compared to an industry average or to the firm's own performance during some prior period.

$$\text{Quick ratio} = \frac{\text{Current assets} - \text{inventory}}{\text{Current liabilities}}$$

$$\text{Current ratio}_{1993} = \frac{\$40,247 - \$31,581}{\$8,033}$$

$$= 1.08 \times$$

Asset Management Ratios

The asset management ratios illustrate the firm's effectiveness (relative to an industry or trend comparison) in managing its assets. In order for a firm's performance to be at maximum, the assets should be neither too high nor too low in terms of their dollar value as shown on the balance sheet. Excessive asset levels (e.g., inventory) will generally reduce the return on total assets, and inadequate asset levels may cause missed sales opportunities.

Average Collection Period (ACP)   The ACP provides a view of the firm's management of its accounts receivable. Specifically, the ratio answers the question "How long have the receivables, on average, been outstanding?" Thus, the ratio provides an answer in number of days:

$$\text{ACP} = \frac{\text{Accounts receivable}}{\text{Average sales per day}}$$

$$\text{ACP}_{1993} = \frac{\$481}{(\$126,540/360 \text{ days})} = 1.37 \text{ days}$$

The foregoing ACP implies that Wick does virtually a "cash" business, meaning it has very little (1.37 days) lag time between the time a sale is made and the time of collection for that sale. If Wick's terms of sale are cash, then its ACP corresponds very closely to those terms. A very high number of days may indicate the firm is too liberal in its credit policies.

Inventory Utilization   The inventory utilization ratio (sometimes called stock turnover) is sales divided by inventories:

$$\text{Inventory utilization} = \frac{\text{Sales}}{\text{Inventories}}$$

$$\text{Inventory utilization}_{1993} = \frac{\$126,540}{\$31,581} = 4.01 \times$$

Again, the ratio of slightly over four times for Wick's inventory utilization may be compared to the industry average or to the company's trend data. It would be more representative of the month-by-month sales of the company's goods if the average inventory were used as the denominator in the foregoing ratio. Average inventory may be thought of as the addition of the beginning-of-the-year inventory plus the end-of-year inventory divided by 2. Other averaging techniques should be used if sales follow a seasonal pattern or a pattern that is other than evenly spread throughout the year.

Fixed Asset Utilization   Many of the funds obtained by a firm to produce continued growth in sales and earnings are invested in fixed assets. The fixed asset utilization ratio tells us in very specific, comparative terms how well the fixed assets are being used as a means of generating sales. We see those assets shown as "property, plant, and equipment" on Wick's balance sheet:

$$\text{Fixed asset utilization} = \frac{\text{Sales}}{\text{Net fixed assets}}$$

$$\text{Fixed asset utilization}_{1993} = \frac{\$126,540}{\$15,104} = 8.38 \times$$

Profitability Ratios

The firm's profitability is important to every individual or organization connected in any way to the success of that firm. In the business media we hear or read about "profits," return on equity, and other references to a company's profitability. There are several ways to measure profitability.

Profit Margin   One of the most commonly used measures is the profit margin on sales or the relationship of dollars of profit to dollars of sales:

$$\text{Profit margin on sales} = \frac{\text{Net income}}{\text{Sales}}$$

$$\text{Profit margin on sales}_{1993} = \frac{\$12,464}{\$126,540}$$

$$= 9.8\%$$

Thus, for each dollar of sales made by Wick in 1993, 9.8 cents was profit after all expenses had been paid. The dividends to the firm's owners (stockholders) are paid from the 9.8 percent of profit, and the remainder becomes a part of the balance sheet item identified as "retained earnings." Retained earnings represent the accumulation of the dollars reinvested in the business over the entire life of the firm.

Return on Assets (ROA)   This ratio measures company profitability as it relates to the total assets of the firm. It answers the question "How much profit is earned on each dollar of assets?"

$$ROA = \frac{\text{Net income}}{\text{Total assets}}$$

$$ROA_{1993} = \frac{\$12,464}{\$55,351}$$

$$= 22.5\%$$

Each dollar of assets earned Wick 22.5 cents in after-tax profit in 1993. That level of return may be assessed against an industry average or Wick's previous years.

Return on Equity (ROE)   Those who invest equity funds in the firm, the common stockholders, will obviously be interested in the profitability of their investment. If we are able to determine the profitability of assets (ROA) or of sales (profit margin), then it is also useful to compute the return on the equity portion of the firm's financing:

$$ROE = \frac{\text{Net income}}{\text{Common equity}}$$

$$ROE_{1993} = \frac{\$12,464}{\$42,184} = 29.5\%$$

From the profitability ratios, then, we may view profitability in terms of sales, assets, or equity. As before, industry and trend comparisons allow an evaluation to be made about the firm's effectiveness in any of these areas.

LIMITATIONS OF RATIO ANALYSIS

The financial ratios that have been discussed in the preceding sections provide valuable, easily interpreted information concerning a firm and the industry in which it operates. We see that much of what is illustrated by the ratios—profitability, asset management, and so on—depend upon certain reasonable similarities between the firm's financial condition and the industry in which it operates, or between the firm's present and past operating environments, or both.

If inflation were severe in the early or later years of a trend analysis, the trend comparison would be less meaningful. For example, abnormally higher inventory prices in a period may distort resulting inventory values and corresponding ratios. Another example would be more or less cash on hand based on the prevailing economic conditions or the expected economic conditions.

If the age of the assets owned by the company is less than is typical in the industry, certain ratios may also be affected. For example, if old assets, fully depreciated, are held by the industry, and the firm's assets are new, the firm's asset management ratios (e.g., fixed asset utilization) cannot be meaningfully compared to industry ratios.

Therefore, when conducting a trend or industry comparison using financial ratios, the foregoing precautions must be taken into consideration. How to take such factors into consideration and to what extent require judgment relative to each situation. Such judgment is developed by the "learning-by-doing" method, based on the techniques presented in this note.

THE BREAK-EVEN POINT

The steps involved in assessing the break-even point (*BEP*) of a firm require the following: (1) Costs must be separated into one of two categories—fixed costs or variable costs. (2) The firm's production capacity must be known. (3) Equally important is a clear knowledge of the demand level for the product.

Once the foregoing factors are well understood, work can focus upon the break-even analysis. The break-even analysis is merely a tool. It has relevance for the following functions:

a. Marketing

b. Capital acquisitions (property, plant, and equipment)

c. Production

Marketing personnel are interested in break-even analysis because it provides the very valuable information necessary for comparing break-even volume to demand. If break-even volume is 100,000 units for a product and the demand forecast is for 80,000 units, the product under most circumstances will be omitted from the firm's product line.

Much the same could be said for the capital budgeting analysts' use of break-even analysis. A combination of demand and break-even volume information will assist in the decision concerning whether new machinery or plant space should be acquired. Production personnel would use similar information as gathered by the other two functions for use in the production planning process.

The components of break-even analysis are fixed costs (*FC*), variable costs (*VC*), and selling price per unit (*SP*). The formula for determining breakeven is:

$$BEP = \frac{FC}{SP - VC}$$

Data for the Garrison Engineering Company, a maker of precision, metal stress-measuring devices, is provided in Exhibit 5 to illustrate the break-even concept.

The company developed a new metal X-ray device called product G-3. G-3 will sell for $300 per unit. The variable cost per unit to produce G-3 is $150. The company's cost accountants have, in addition to estimating variable costs, determined total fixed costs of production to be $1,200,000. What is the break-even point for G-3? That is, what number of units of the product must be produced and sold to just cover total costs?

$$BEP_{G3} = \frac{\$1,200,000}{\$300 - \$150}$$

$$= 8,000 \text{ units}$$

EXHIBIT 5   Garrison Engineering Corporation—Sales Level, Cost, and Profit

1 Units Sold	2 Variable Cost	3 Fixed Cost	4 Total Cost	5 Total Revenue	6 Profit (Loss)
0	0	$1,200,000	$1,200,000	0	$(1,200,000)
4,000	600,000	1,200,000	1,800,000	$1,200,000	(600,000)
8,000	1,200,000	1,200,000	2,400,000	2,400,000	0
12,000	$1,800,000	$1,200,000	$3,000,000	$3,600,000	$ 600,000

Eight thousand units of the G-3 device must be sold in order for the firm to break even on the product. Put differently, if 8,000 units are produced and sold, revenue will just cover total cost. Profit at 8,000 units will be zero. Exhibit 5, which illustrates costs and volume at various levels of production, further highlights the concept of the break-even point.

The information in Exhibit 5 permits an inspection of the interrelatedness of the sales and costs as they directly affect the profit or loss of the product. It may be equally useful to depict that interaction using a graphical representation as shown in Exhibit 6. The intersection of the sales revenue and total cost lines is the product's break-even point. Again, at the break-even sales level of 8,000 units of the G-3 device, total costs and total revenue are equal at $2,400,000. Profit is zero at the break-even point. As usual, the graph permits a more visual interpretation of the idea. A graph often facilitates a more immediate and clear understanding of the facts or assumptions at hand.

Break-Even Analysis and Risk

The concept of the break-even point is a risk assessment concept. Break-even analysis permits the firm's management to more clearly answer the following questions:

EXHIBIT 6:   Garrison Engineering Corporation Break-Even Chart

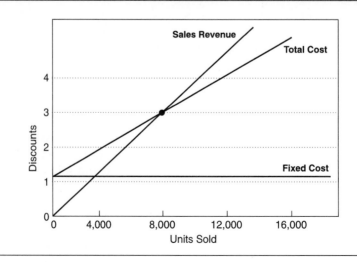

(1) What quantity of a product must be sold in order to begin to earn a profit? (2) How likely is it that such a sales level will be reached? The break-even point permits a straightforward answer to the first question.

The second question can be answered with greater assurance if the weighted average probabilistic concepts are put to use. Sources from inside or outside the firm familiar with the sales prospects of the product can provide data and information on the likely sales level. Such information can easily be transformed into a weighted average level of sales. That sales level, along with pessimistic and optimistic sales levels, is then compared to the break-even volume. A decision is then possible as to whether to proceed with production.

For example, if the most likely (weighted average) sales level is 12,000 units, as in the case of Garrison, then the firm can see that reaching the break-even sales level is likely. If the weighted average demand for the product were 8,500 units, or even 9,000 units, then the chance of reaching the *BEP* would seem less likely. Such judgments, however, depend upon the probability distribution of the sales projections.

Contribution to Fixed Costs and Profit

To return to the actual dollar values in the break-even concept, the concept of contribution margin is important. When variable costs are covered by the selling price of an item, as in the case of product G-3, for example, the difference between the variable cost per unit and the selling price per unit is called the contribution margin—the amount above the variable cost that contributes to the coverage of fixed costs and profit.

If we consider Exhibits 5 and 6, sales of 8,000 units (the break-even point) allows coverage of the fixed costs. When the sales level goes beyond the break-even point, the $150 contribution margin contributes entirely to profits. Exhibit 6 illustrates an increasing profit level (the distance between the total cost and total revenue lines) as the sales level exceeds the break-even point.

Cash Break-Even Analysis

The discussion of break-even analysis to this point has focused upon variable and fixed costs without considering the composition of these costs. Not all the fixed costs call for an outlay of cash. Consider depreciation, a common element of the firm's total fixed costs. Because depreciation is not a cash item, the break-even concept developed so far may represent an overstatement of the true break-even concept in terms of cash. If we again consider Exhibit 5, the fixed costs amount to $1,200,000. If we assume that 10 percent of the fixed costs is depreciation, then what is the break-even point on a cash basis? That is, what sales level must be achieved in order to cover the firm's cash needs? The answer would appear as follows:

$$\text{Cash break-even} = \frac{\text{Fixed costs} - \text{noncash portion}}{\text{selling price} - \text{variable cost per unit}}$$

$$= \frac{\$1,200,000 - (\$1,200,000 \times .10)}{\$300 - \$150}$$

$$= \frac{\$1,080,000}{\$150}$$

$$= 7,200 \text{ units}$$

Thus, the break-even sales level necessary to cover the cash needs of production is 7,200 units, fewer than the 8,000 units needed to break even relative to total fixed costs.

What does it mean for the firm if it operates at say, 7,500 units of production—above cash break-even but below the "total cost" break-even? The 7,500 unit operation level will sufficiently cover the firm's cash needs. The significance of the firm's operations being below total cost coverage depends upon the level of noncash charges in the total cost amount. If depreciation is greater than the total of any negative profits after tax, the firm is in no danger in the short run. Over the longer term, however, the cash benefit of the depreciation charge (i.e., depreciation is charged against revenue but is not actually paid out, thus reducing the firm's tax liability) will be offset by fixed assets that need to be replaced or expanded. Therefore, the continued health of the firm depends upon pricing policies and cost control that will ensure operations above the *BEP*. Generally, firms are concerned with the coverage of total fixed costs, because that approach conforms to reported income.

Before leaving the specific idea of break-even, it is important to note that the *BEP* formula will accommodate a desired profit level. For example, following the earlier illustration of a break-even point of 8,000 units for product G-3, suppose Garrison Engineering Company desired a 15 percent pretax profit on the item. The *BEP* formula would be adjusted as follows:

$$\text{Break-even point, with 15\% profit requirement} = \frac{FC + 15\% \text{ of } FC}{SP - VC}$$

$$= \frac{\$1,200,000(1.15)}{\$300 - \$150}$$

$$= \frac{\$1,380,000}{\$150}$$

$$= 9,200 \text{ units}$$

Thus, to generate a 15 percent pretax profit, in addition to achieving the break-even sales level, the company must achieve a sales level of 9,200 units.

The concept of a break-even level of sales is important for many decision makers in the firm. Marketing will be interested in the concept of break-even when the question of new-product introduction arises. Marketing personnel are usually the first to know what the likely demand for a product will be, based upon the general economic and industry analysis that is a part of market research. Such information will be shared and coordinated with production personnel. Also, it is often necessary that those responsible for "capital budgeting" be brought into the planning process as new depreciable assets are needed for production.

The advantages of the break-even concept are many and varied. Once the idea of breakeven is clearly understood (i.e., its components defined and measured and properly assembled), it can be used in many situations within the firm. It must be remembered, however, that it is only a tool and as such is subject to revision as the items included in the calculation change based upon the experiences of the firm. The break-even concept refers to a relationship among costs, fixed and variable, and production level. In general, added fixed costs will increase the break-even point. Beyond the break-even point, however, the sales-to-profit relationship is magnified.

Appendix C: Presenting Marketing Cases Orally

Gary F. Kohut and Carol M. Baxter

The methods for communicating information orally are similar whether you are presenting to a large or a small group, to your classroom peers, or to a business audience. Regardless of the audience or the type of presentation, effective oral presentations involve three major steps: planning, organizing, and delivering the information.

Planning the Presentation

Before you can plan your presentation effectively, you must determine the type of presentation you are making, analyze your audience, conduct your research, and consider the logistics of the speaking site.

Types of Presentations

Generally, oral presentations are divided into two broad categories: informative and persuasive. Informative presentations convey information or ideas, whereas persuasive presentations sell an idea or a product to an audience. Informative presentations include progress reports, instructions, and explanations. For example, you may need to convey the status of a new product that is being developed; you might discuss past progress, current developments, and work yet to be done. At other times, you may need to train employees on techniques for conducting telephone surveys or leading focus groups.

Many presentations in marketing are persuasive. For example, you may need to convince individuals to contribute to a charitable organization's fund drive. On other occasions, you may need to sell a promotional campaign to a client, persuade a customer to purchase a product or to frequent a particular place of business, or you may need to influence the buying decisions of your organization. In case analysis, you are attempting to persuade your audience to understand the logic of your arguments and accept your recommendations.

Types of Appeal

Three appeals are used in persuasion: the ethical, the emotional, and the logical. The **ethical appeal** addresses an individual's or an organization's credibility. It is impossible to separate the speaker's effect on an audience from the content of a message. If listeners regard the speaker highly, they will adopt a more favorable attitude toward the product or service than if they have a negative impression of the person. Consequently, a speaker must bring to the platform a strong, positive, personal style. Credibility hinges on believability; you may have a high ethical appeal with members of an audience if they perceive you to have acted with integrity in the past. If you have acted rudely, unethically, or unprofessionally toward the audience, your ethical appeal will be very low. Many characteristics such as honesty, dependability, and expertise help to develop credibility. Although it takes some time to establish credibility, it takes only an instant to lose it.

The **emotional appeal** uses the audience's motivations to change their thinking or behavior. Because emotion provokes action, speakers often seek to arouse the feelings of their listeners. The emotional appeal is characterized by the use of fear, sympathy, love, jealousy, desire for attention, or a host of other emotions to persuade the audience. To use the emotional appeal, first analyze the specific emotions to which the audience will respond. Then determine which words, pictures, or actions will best evoke the desired emotion. Once members of the audience are drawn into the persuasion by the emotional "hook," it is easy to ask them to take action to meet the need or to satisfy the emotion that was touched. Speakers should be aware, however, that attempts to arouse emotions excessively can lead to a rejection of their arguments by an audience. The emotions should not be aroused beyond believable or common-sense levels.

The **logical appeal** draws on a person's ability to think and reason. This appeal uses good reasons to show members of an audience why they should change their opinions or actions. The reasoning process and the supporting materials used to give credence to an argument comprise the elements of the logical appeal. For example, if you needed to persuade an audience to buy a compact auto, you might stress fuel efficiency, style, and dependability. Another example is in industrial advertising. Such ads show purchasing agents how products work and how they can benefit the purchasing company. Because the purchasers are not buying the product for their own use, the emotional appeal would not work as it does in consumer advertising.

Audience Analysis

You will give your presentation to a specific audience, so you need to analyze that audience carefully. Audience analysis is a method of examining the knowledge, interests, and attitudes of the people who will hear your presentation. Your analysis will help you determine how to organize your material, select supporting information, choose the appropriate wording, and select or produce appropriate visual aids.

Some considerations in analyzing your audience include the size of the group, their knowledge about the subject, their interest in the material, their predisposition toward the information, and their relationship to you. Every audience is unique. The differences among people cause every presentation to be different. Individuals have different perceptions based on personal experiences that influence their attitudes about any subject. Understanding these predispositions will prevent you from making assumptions that may offend the audience.

For example, if your audience is made up of individuals aged 60 to 70, do not *automatically* assume that they would be interested in denture adhesives, laxatives, and Big Band music. On the other hand, if your audience is made up of people aged 20 to 30, do not assume, by virtue of their age, that they would be interested in rock music, fashion, and alcoholic beverages.

We may look at individuals as members of a group and categorize them accordingly, but we should also look for those things that make each individual member unique. For example, if we know an audience appreciates details, we may include more than the usual details in our message.

The more you know about the members of an audience, the better you can predict what will appeal to them. For instance, avoid using examples that audience members cannot understand because they have not experienced them. Because experience is such an important factor in understanding an audience, you would not use the same explanations and examples with an audience who had children as with an audience made up entirely of childless people. When analyzing an audience, ask yourself, What does this group want, need, or expect from me?

Gather Information

Your effectiveness as a speaker depends on what you say about the topic you have selected. For case analysis presentations, a thorough understanding of the case is crucial. Knowing where to look is a starting point for finding the best possible information on your topic. Sometimes the information will come from your own knowledge, experience, or research. At other times you may use information collected by others such as census data, sales records, inventory records, or pricing information. Furthermore, information from electronic data bases provides current data that may enhance the quality of your presentation.

Your credibility as a speaker will be largely determined by the quality of the information you present. For example, if you are talking about recent trends, data from the 1980 census would damage your credibility. Conversely, year-to-date sales records would be beneficial to an audience that needs to establish sales goals for the forthcoming year.

Logistics of the Speaking Site

Before you can organize your presentation, you must consider some logistical concerns. First, you need to know where you will make the presentation. Will it be made in a conference room, in a traditional classroom, a large auditorium, an office, or a dining hall? The location of your presentation will determine the kind of delivery and the types of visual aids you will use as well as how you set up the room. Some guidelines for setting up the speaking site are:

1. Arrange seating so that every member of the audience can see and hear you. The horseshoe arrangement is preferred if the room and the size of the audience will allow for it.

2. Check the lighting, temperature, and noise level of the site to ensure that your audience will be comfortable. Avoid high traffic areas, such as a room next to a kitchen, that may distract your audience.

3. Check any equipment you intend to use to be sure that it can be easily viewed or heard by your audience. Remember, if anything can go wrong, it generally will. Therefore, try to anticipate any problems before they occur. For example, when using any kind of projected visual aids, you should carry an extra bulb or have alternate visual aids in case the equipment breaks down. If you are speaking at a site that you have not visited previously, you may even want to bring an extension cord and an adaptor plug, tape, push pins, or other supplies that may not be available at the site.

Organizing the Presentation

In an oral presentation, your audience may not have the opportunity to refer to written material; therefore, you must structure the information so that it is very easy to understand the first time it is heard. Every effective presentation has an introduction, body, and conclusion. We suggest that you prepare a written outline of the information you want to include in these three parts.

Introduction

People tend to remember the beginning and the end of presentations, so a strong intro-duction is necessary. An introduction should fulfill three purposes: (1) gain the audi-ence's attention, (2) establish rapport or goodwill with the audience, and (3) introduce the audience to the topic. Introductions may include the following:

1. A reference to the event or the occasion
2. A brief story that relates to the topic
3. A quotation by a recognized authority on the subject
4. A thought-provoking question that requires the audience members to partici-pate by answering the question or to get involved by raising their hands
5. A startling statement; it may or may not be a statistic
6. A personal story or reference about the topic
7. A joke

Remember, your introduction should relate to the topic and set the stage for the next part of the introduction. Once you have successfully chosen an attention-getting statement, tell the audience the *purpose* of your presentation by stating the thesis. The **thesis** is a statement that tells what you want to accomplish in the presentation. Al-though the introduction is designed to get the audience members to think about the topic, you must be sure that they understand what you intend to do with the topic. The thesis statement helps focus the entire presentation. Below are examples of thesis state-ments from two team members making a case analysis presentation to the class:

Speaker One: Our team believes that consumer tastes are changing and the steak-only-menu restaurants share of the dining out market will continue to decline.

Speaker Two: Our team proposes an alternative marketing strategy for the re-gional steak-only-menu restaurant chain that will better position it with respect to the changing tastes of the dining-out market.

The attention span of an audience varies from one occasion to the next. Therefore, keep your audience attuned to what you are saying by **previewing** the main points of your presentation. Below are two examples of previews that come after the thesis state-ments of the case analysis team members:

Speaker One: Steak-only restaurants' share of the dining out market will con-tinue to decline because (1) consumers have become more health conscious, (2) there is a decline in the consumption of red meat be-cause of concerns over cholesterol, (3) people are eating "lighter," and (4) there is an increasing number of alternative restaurants.

Speaker Two: The regional steak-only-menu restaurant chain should change its marketing strategy by redefining its target market, expanding its menu options, and engaging in a promotional campaign to inform customers of the new positioning.

Later, during the body of the presentation, you will develop in more detail each point mentioned in the preview.

Body

Various methods are available to develop the body of each of the presentations used in the examples above. Below are some common ones:

1. Use statistics or other facts
2. Cite quotations or expert testimony
3. Employ examples, real or hypothetical
4. Refer to personal experiences
5. Use comparisons, contrasts, or analogies to experiences the audience has had

Conclusion

A presentation can have an excellent introduction and body but still not be effective. Good speakers must leave a favorable impression in the minds of members of the audience. An effective conclusion can accomplish this objective. Conclusions can be developed in a number of ways:

1. Summarize your main points
2. Ask the audience to take some action such as buying your product or service or contributing to a particular cause
3. Recall the story, joke, or anecdote in the introduction and elaborate on it or draw a "lesson" from it

Now that you have structured your presentation, you must find ways to enhance it further. Visual aids are the tools to accentuate the information you want to share.

Visual Aids

Because we live in a visually oriented society, we expect to see as well as hear information. Therefore, effective speakers show as well as tell their points. Two broad categories of visual aids are available to enhance presentations. One category, **direct viewing visuals,** includes such things as real objects, models, flip charts, diagrams and drawings, photographs, and handouts. The second category, **projected visuals,** includes transparencies, slides, and videotapes.

Visual aids attract and hold attention, clarify the meaning of your points, emphasize ideas, or prove a point. Several factors must be considered in selecting the appropriate visual aid:

1. *The constraints of the topic.* Some topics will limit your choice of visual aids. For example, if you were explaining how a large robot operates, you would probably use a videotape of the robot in operation. A scaled-down model of the robot may not be as effective because the scope and movement of the machinery may be a persuasive point. Similarly, a drawing or photograph of the robot would be the least effective visual aid.
2. *The availability of the equipment.* If the speaking site does not have an overhead projector, you could not use transparencies. Similarly, if the site does not have an electrical outlet near the podium, you would not be able to use a projected visual. Always check to see what equipment is available or bring your own.
3. *The cost of the visual.* If your budget is very small, a transparency, flip chart, or a handout may be preferable to the more elaborate types of visual aids such as slides or videotapes.

4. *The difficulty of producing the visual.* If you have only two days to prepare for your presentation, it may be impossible to assemble a scale model of a home interior or process slides of a manufacturing operation.

5. *The appropriateness of the visual to the audience.* The type of audience and the nature of the presentation affect the choice of visual aids. Some charts, graphs, and diagrams may be too technical for anyone but specialists to grasp. Detailed and complicated tables and charts that require considerable time to digest should be avoided. When in doubt, keep your visuals short and simple.

6. *The appropriateness of the visual to the speaker.* Visual aids require skill for their effective presentation. A person must be able to write legibly and draw well-proportioned diagrams to use a flip chart. Projected visuals require skill in handling slides, videotape, or film. If you do not feel comfortable with a particular visual medium, do not use it.

7. *The appropriateness of the visual to the time limit.* The speaker should carefully check the time required to display and explain a visual aid to make sure the main ideas of the presentation will not be neglected. Any visual aid that needs too much explanation should be avoided. An appropriate visual aid should be simple, clear, and brief.

Once you have planned and organized the content of your presentation and prepared your visual aids, you are ready to deliver your presentation.

Delivering the Presentation

The delivery of a presentation is mainly determined by the situation, the audience, and the speaker. The formality or informality of the situation greatly affects delivery. The more formal it is, the fewer gestures and movements speakers make. They limit themselves more to their position behind the lectern and use a more emphatic speaking style. In very informal situations, speakers are free to move away from the podium.

The available equipment will also determine delivery. For instance, if the size of the audience necessitates a microphone, speakers should not move away from the microphone. They may also need to adapt themselves to various tables or other unusual speaking platforms that will hold their notes, visuals, or other forms of support.

The larger the audience, the louder speakers must talk unless there is a microphone. Likewise, eye contact is more challenging with large groups. Generally, delivery to small groups can be more informal and conversational.

Types of Delivery

There are several methods for delivering material to an audience and each has its unique advantages. The four methods of delivery are (1) impromptu, (2) manuscript, (3) memorized, and (4) extemporaneous.

Impromptu delivery requires speaking spontaneously on a topic. This type of delivery is generally inappropriate for technical or complex material because you may forget crucial information if the presentation has not been carefully planned. Impromptu delivery is often used at social occasions such as introductions at an after-dinner speaking engagement or at a professional meeting.

Manuscript delivery requires that the speaker read from a prepared text. This type of delivery is ineffective in most presentations because audiences generally prefer more eye contact (they also dislike having material read to them). However, manuscript delivery is a must in one particular situation: when a crisis has occurred. For example, if someone dies as a result of a tampered product, the media will immediately "look for the story." The spokesperson for the organization should never deliver the information in an impromptu manner. Rather, the response should be carefully prepared and read to the media because any misstatement in such a situation could result in litigation against the organization.

Memorized delivery is self-explanatory. In most cases it should be discouraged because memorized presentations usually sound "canned" rather than natural. However, this type of delivery might be appropriate in situations where the presentation will be only a few minutes long, such as a short advertisement.

Extemporaneous delivery is the preferred approach for most presentations. This type of delivery involves using notes or an outline to deliver your information. The speaker should talk in a conversational tone but refer periodically to notes to be sure that all the information is covered.

Practicing the Delivery

Preparation influences a speaker's delivery. A speaker who is well prepared and has something valuable to communicate will be more comfortable physically and vocally. If speakers are unsure of themselves and the material, they may be tempted to read word for word from their outline. Being too self-conscious or nervous can cause physical and vocal qualities and mannerisms that detract from the message. Too much concern with the ideas and too little with the audience will also hinder a speaker's delivery. Practicing aloud what you want to say will give you confidence.

Delivery is not something added to a speech but a part of it. Consider the following when delivering a presentation:

1. *Focus on the specific purpose.* Effective speakers know what they want from an audience and, therefore, should avoid such distractions as fiddling with a pen or pencil, scratching the nose, playing with hair, and jingling coins.

2. *Work toward being heard and understood.* A speaker's voice must be loud enough to be heard in the very last row. Pronunciation and articulation must be distinct.

3. *Convey enthusiasm.* An essential part of delivery is to keep the audience listening. One way of conveying enthusiasm is to vary the qualities of the voice such as volume, rate, and pitch. Movements and gestures should also be varied.

4. *Stress the main points.* Some points in a speech are more important than others. If all ideas are spoken in exactly the same way, the importance of your key points will suffer. A slower speaking rate, a pause before and after an idea, a shift in body position, an increase or decrease in volume are only a few of the many ways to emphasize points through delivery.

5. *Involve your audience.* Each member of the audience should feel that the speaker is imparting information to her/him personally. Consequently, eye contact is a critical part of effective delivery. The speaker should look at all audience members, talking to each one from time to time but to no particular person or segment of the audience for a prolonged time.

Establishing Credibility

Credibility is crucial to effective presentations. As mentioned earlier, credibility refers to the confidence an audience has in a speaker. Several factors work together to determine credibility, including the speaker's enthusiasm, expertise, and trustworthiness.

Enthusiasm is projected through tone of voice, eye contact, and energy. Obviously, the major ways speakers can display these characteristics are by believing in the subject and acting as if they enjoy conveying the information. For example. a sincere smile at the beginning of a presentation sets the tone for both the speaker and the audience.

Expertise is conveyed through the accuracy of your information, the amount of experience you have had with the subject, and the confidence with which you speak. Make sure you check your facts before you communicate them to the audience.

Trustworthiness refers to whether the speaker is perceived as biased. Consistency in conveying information over a period of time is important to establishing trust with an audience.

Controlling Speech Anxiety

One factor that detracts from credibility is excessive nervousness. Most speakers are nervous, but they have learned techniques for handling the condition so that there are few outward signs of anxiety. Several techniques are recommended for managing speech anxiety:

1. Avoid taking medications that will dry your mouth and produce more anxiety
2. Practice deep breathing exercises just before speaking to reduce your anxiety
3. Reduce tension by squeezing your hand into a fist and releasing it, tensing your leg muscles and releasing them, or stretching your facial muscles with exaggerated expressions

Using Your Visuals Effectively

Although visual aids enhance presentations, poor use of them can actually hurt your credibility. Some guidelines for using visual aids are as follows:

1. Avoid turning your back on the audience while you look at a visual aid; talk to the audience, not to the visual aid.
2. Show the visual aid only when you are using it; otherwise, the audience may be distracted from what you are saying. For example, if you are using transparencies, cover everything except the information you are talking about at the moment.
3. Refrain from removing the visual before the audience members have had an opportunity to look at the information for themselves. Also, avoid talking about something on a visual aid after you have put it aside.
4. Organize the visuals in the order in which you will use them so you will appear prepared and confident when using them.

Managing Nonverbal Communication

Nonverbal communication enhances or detracts from the credibility you have worked to establish. Several dimensions of nonverbal communication include (1) **kinesics,** the way people use their bodies to communicate; (2) **proxemics,** the way people use space to communicate; and (3) **paralanguage,** the way people use their voice to enhance the verbal message.

When making presentations, two of the most important types of kinesic behavior are gestures and eye contact. Speakers are rarely credible when they stand rigidly behind a podium, grasp it as if it were a crutch, and seldom glance from their notes to look at the audience. Similarly, poor posture, hands in pockets, and playing with objects such as chalk or pointers lessen a speaker's impact.

Speakers who recognize that "space communicates" will use it wisely. For example, if an audience is very small, it may be better to sit at the head of the group rather than standing to deliver your information. Also, if you are conveying unfavorable information, it may be better to stand close to the audience as if to appear sincere and understanding.

Aspects of the voice that affect credibility include volume, rate, pitch, tone, and voice quality. The "sound" of the voice (voice quality) such as raspiness or a nasal whine evokes images in the mind of listeners; however, it is very difficult to change the voice quality you have. On the other hand, tone, pitch, rate, and volume are easily controlled. For example, a person who has a monotone can make the voice *seem* less monotonous by saying some words softly and others quite loudly. Even though the speaker's tone has not changed, the audience perceives that the tone is varied. Pitch is often associated with nervousness. Speakers should start speaking at the lowest pitch they can achieve, because a lower pitch is generally viewed as more credible in our culture.

Handling Questions from the Audience

Some speaking situations require that the speaker give the audience an opportunity to ask questions. At other times, the speaker may simply want to involve the audience by following a presentation with a question-and-answer session. Whether or not you use this procedure depends on the occasion, the audience, and the amount of time available. You can use this procedure to reinforce key points and gain acceptance of your ideas. Any question-and-answer period should be well organized and brief. To make the most of the available time, follow these guidelines:

1. Ask for questions in a positive way. For instance, you could say, "Who has the first question?" If no one asks a question, you may say, "You may be wondering..." or "I am often asked..." After supplying an answer to the question you have asked, you may ask, "Are there any other questions?

2. Look at the entire audience when answering a question. You are addressing everyone, not just the person asking the question.

3. Keep your answers concise and to the point; do not give another speech. You risk losing the audience's attention as well as discouraging further questions.

4. Cut off a rambling questioner politely. If the person starts to make a speech without getting to the question, wait until he or she takes a breath and then interrupt with, "Thanks for your comment. Next question." Then look to the other side of the room.

5. Remain in control of the situation. Establish a time limit for questions and answers and announce it to the audience before the questions begin. Anticipate the types of questions your audience may ask and think how you will answer. Never lose your temper as you respond to someone who is trying to make you look bad. You may respond with something like, "I respect your opinion even though I don't agree with it." Then restate your response to the issue.

Your presentation does not end when you finish your speech, so your credibility can be enhanced or lost in the question-and-answer period. Prepare intelligently and establish strategies for handling difficult situations.

Closing Comments

Developing the skills needed to present your point of view in a convincing manner is essential to reaching your personal and career goals. Presenting information orally is a challenging task. However, if you follow the guidelines we have suggested, your presentation will be rewarding to both you and your audience.